AF608064

GEOMETRY OF THE PASSIONS

Fear, Hope, Happiness: Philosophy and Political Use

THE LORENZO DA PONTE ITALIAN LIBRARY

GEOMETRY OF THE PASSIONS

Fear, Hope, Happiness: Philosophy and Political Use

Remo Bodei

TRANSLATED BY GIANPIERO W. DOEBLER

UNIVERSITY OF TORONTO PRESS
Toronto Buffalo London

Toronto Buffalo London
utorontopress.com

ISBN 978-1-4875-0336-9

The Lorenzo Da Ponte Italian Library

First published as *Geometria delle passioni* in January 1994
by Giangiacomo Feltrinelli Editore, Milan, Italy

Library and Archives Canada Cataloguing in Publication

Bodei, Remo, 1938–
[Geometria delle passioni. English]
Geometry of the passions : fear, hope, happiness : philosophy and political use /
Remo Bodei ; translated by Gianpiero W. Doebler.

(Lorenzo da Ponte Italian library)
Translation of: Geometria delle passioni.
Includes bibliographical references and index.
ISBN 978-1-4875-0336-9 (cloth)

1. Emotions. I. Title. III. Title: Geometria delle passioni.
English V. Series: Lorenzo da Ponte Italian library.

B815.B6413 2018 128'.37 C2018-901340-0

This volume is published with the assistance of the Franklin D. Murphy Chair
in Italian Renaissance Studies at the University of California, Los Angeles.

University of Toronto Press acknowledges the financial assistance to its publishing program
of the Canada Council for the Arts and the Ontario Arts Council,
an agency of the Government of Ontario.

Funded by the Government of Canada
Financé par le gouvernement du Canada
Canada

Contents

Introduction to the English Translation of *Geometry of the Passions*

Looking back at this book, twenty-seven years after the first Italian edition and twenty-four after the fourth revised one (*Geometria delle passioni: Paura, speranza, felicità: Filosofia e uso politico*, Milan, Feltrinelli, 1991 and 1994), twenty-three years after two Spanish translations (*Geometría de las pasiones: Miedo, esperanza, felicidad: Filosofía y uso político*, Mexico, D.F., Fundo de cultura económica, 1995; *Una geometría de las pasiones: Miedo, esperanza y felicidad: filosofía y uso político*, Barcelona, Muchnik Editores, 1995), and twenty-one years after the French (*Géométrie des passions: Peur, espoir, bonheur: De la philosophie à l'usage politique*, Paris, Presses Universitaires de France, 1997), I do not seem to have found sufficient reason to diverge from its original formulation. For this reason, I have not modified the structure or rhythm of the discussion, which seem to me to still hold up to the wear and tear of time. Of course, the bibliography is not updated (in this translation, therefore, I have sacrificed many of the notes present in the Italian edition), but it is worth the trouble to note that this book anticipated the rage for studies on emotional intelligence or sad passions.

The years that have passed may weigh little or much. They weigh little, because philosophical works aspire to be independent of their temporal conditionings. They weigh a lot if one thinks about how these decades have been so rich in unexpected events as to have literally changed the world in which we were used to living and, therefore, our way of posing questions about it as well. In their essential nucleus, the problems discussed here should not be touched by the passage of time, and yet the tools of meaning we use to interpret things undergo endless distortions, fractures, and movements. Philosophy explores, redesigns, and illustrates the drift and the fault lines of those symbolic continents on which our common thought and feeling rests. The mental and emotional maps are transformed, like languages, in a generally slow and inexorable way, but only at a certain point are "catastrophic" discontinuities produced or felt that oblige us to think again about how much has happened. Ideas undergo a transformation, molecular or sudden, owing to the very distance from which one looks at the problems and at the change in the frames that surround them. They have the tendency to ferment on their own, and every investigation is therefore destined to remain incomplete. One puts an end to them because, at a certain point, one has reached a saturation phase with respect to the assembled materials and reasoning. Subsequently, however, new and relevant conceptual ramifications are inevitably discovered; there emerges, sometimes by chance, other important literature on the subjects previously addressed; and one reconsiders observations made by friends or reviewers.

Is there consequently a need to rewrite books and constantly adapt them to the changing situations and moods of the public? It would be a useless effort to follow current events *ad infinitum* or to believe that everything must be connected back to them. One could certainly assert that philosophies do not express eternal truths, that they are at once outdated and current, within and outside of time. The tradition of bipartition, formulated by Benedetto Croce, between "what is alive" and "what is dead" in a given work or philosophy therefore loses value. If one abandons the idea that the philosophies of the past are useful to current events, what is living and what is dead changes with every theoretical season. What is current today is already outdated tomorrow (and vice versa). Thus, even the beautiful Crocian simile expressed in *La storia come pensiero e come azione* (*History as Thought and Action*) appears reductive – i.e., that history must revive the petrified and sclerotic past "almost in the way one speaks of certain images of Christs and Madonnas, which, wounded by the words and actions of some blasphemer and sinner, issue red blood."[1] Bringing everything back to the present, conceiving all of history as "contemporary history," means, in fact, cannibalizing the past – subordinating, in an exclusive way, its inexhaustible reserve of meaning to the transient interests of the present. It must be added that human passions and desires transform themselves in a much slower way than ideas, and they thus preserve a greater consistency and duration (which facilitates their analysis) and that, at the time I wrote *Geometry of the Passions*, much less had been written on the French Revolution and the Jacobins (it was then close to the Bicentennial of 1989).

1 B. Croce, *La storia come pensiero e come azione* [1938] (Bari, 1973), 19.

On the other hand, if what Schopenhauer asserts is true – that every one of us does nothing else for all our lives than develop a single idea – every book contains within it the premises for further developments. As the Latin proverb says, *habent sua fata libelli*: books have their destiny; they are witnesses to a particular era. Precisely because a book contains the basis of later, distinctive developments that bear the imprint of the person who wrote it, every work is not only inherently incomplete, but it is also historically conditioned, an aspect from which one must not pull away.

I have, however, changed the perspectives of this book – elaborating, developing, and changing its contents and aims, explicit or implicit – thanks to two other volumes that, along with this one, represent a sort of triptych: *Ordo amoris: Conflitte terreni e felicità celeste* (Bologna, Il Mulino, 1991) and *Destini personali: L'età della colonizzazione delle coscienze* (Milan, Feltrinelli, 2002). In my intentions, each of them should have made up part of the constellation of theoretical interests that still guide me and that focus on the genesis of Western individuality from the point of view of the formation of identity, the articulation of the passions, the succession of conflicts, the intensification of expectations of change, and the temptations of flight from the world towards the recesses of inwardness or towards the sphere of the religious dimension. I conducted an expanded reflection on the passions, and specifically on one of those most discussed since ancient Greece, in *Ira: La passione furente* (Bologna, Il Mulino, 2011).

In *Geometry of the Passions*, these subjects were addressed by placing in relief the paradoxical conflict-collaboration between passions and reason and by extending the theoretical and historical investigation across the arc of time that runs from the ancients (and relative to the moderns, from Descartes, Hobbes, and Spinoza) to the French Jacobins. In *Destini personali: L'età della colonizzazione delle coscienze*, on the other hand, I examined the problem of the birth of modern individuality starting from two different sources. One is represented by Locke, who emphasizes the value of the individual, laying down the foundations of the theory of human rights and political liberalism; the other is represented by Schopenhauer, for whom individuality is simply appearance, while what truly counts is the anonymous will to live that dwells within us and renders our *I* nothing other than "a voice that resounds in a hollow sphere of glass."[2] Thus, what seems most ours, the consciousness of being of an *I* or a subject, is in reality something foreign. In this work, however, I reconstruct the

2 A. Schopenhauer, *W* §54; Ital. trans., 319.

antagonistic confluence of these two lines to the present through a series of figures that have in common the abdication of the subject and the loss of its unity, of its supremacy. In chronological terms, I did so, in particular, by considering the imprint left by some exponents of French culture of the last decades of the nineteenth century and by Nietzsche, which replace the "pyramidal" Goethian model.

In fact, the so-called French *médeciens-philosophes* of the late nineteenth century (Ribot, Janet, and Binet) affirm the idea that the *I* is plural; it is composed – like coral colonies – of an original multiplicity of *I*s, which subordinate themselves to a "hegemonic *I*" that in turn, in a "democratic" way, becomes either a sort of president or "coalition" government or, in an "autocratic" way, a sort of Louis XIV, a *Moi Soleil*. When the coordinating or hegemonic function of the *I* is no longer capable of withstanding new challenges, welcoming into itself new increases in complexity, the personality (which, generally speaking, is already insufficiently coherent and lacks that unity, simplicity, and identity that philosophical and religious tradition attributes to the soul, now examined according to categories that are "scientific" and no longer theological or metaphysical) splits into independent entities. The will does not succeed, then, in maintaining its identity, torn as it is by the plurality of conflicting desires over which it has no power. The hegemonic *I* is then forced to renounce its mandate or to abdicate. With the government fallen and the throne overturned, the federation of souls and the absolutist state of the psyche dissolve. As soon as the hegemonic *I* is weakened, the *I*s that were previously abandoned or excluded return, strengthened from their exile, and they restore a type of partial power. It can be noted that these *I*s are not aliens or strangers but, rather, old acquaintances who were repudiated and too often known (even if consciously or unconsciously ignored) and who, up to that point, had been able to express themselves through either dreams or *rêveries*.

Subsequently, and for most of the twentieth century – until Lacan or Lévi-Strauss – the *I* was denied unity and continuity, and instead there was assigned to each "dividual" an original and discreet plurality of poles of consciousness. One thinks of Nietzsche, for whom the *I* is "a plurality of personal forces, of which sometimes one, sometimes the other, comes to the fore as *ego*, and they look at others as a subject looks at an outside world rich in influences and determinations. The subject is now in one point, now in another."[3] Formulating the same idea in other ways, he

3 F.W. Nietzsche, *Kritische Studienausgabe* 9: 211.

asserts that consciousness is formed by a "multiplicity of drives,"[4] just as the body is formed by "a plurality with one sense, a war and a peace, a flock and a shepherd."[5] Or, again, the *I* is "a social structure composed of many 'souls' [*Gesellschaftsbau vieler Seelen*],"[6] a unity and a plurality, that excite each other in their interaction.

Ordo amoris poses the problem of love in Augustine and in ancient Christian culture as the capacity of structuring forms of individuality open to change through a remodulation of the passions. Love dissolves the knots that block the will; it heals the conflicts and removes the weight of the past, permitting each person to reformulate and restart their own love from the beginning. The previous state, which in its irreversibility continues to oppress and make us unhappy, no longer blocks faith in the possibility of repeated beginnings. In conformity with the good story, in which "the old is destroyed" and "everything becomes new," the old figure of destiny appears defeated.

Love opens not only towards the future, but also towards the past: the evil committed is endured, the sufferings inflicted and received find their redemption. Reconciling each one with the existence that it has passed through prevents events from petrifying in rancour or remorse. It prevents the will from dividing itself between exacerbated attachment to the memory of old errors or wrongs and the hard-won acceptance of peace with oneself or of forgiveness, which, etymologically, is a strengthened gift, one that is extreme and made by others. Love certainly does not retroactively annul the event, nor even forget it. Judging it to be incomplete, love reopens its processes, re-examines its acts, and modifies its judgments. The healing strength of love – making fluid the viscous, congealed, or hardened past and reconverting it into fresh, available energy – condones guilt and pains that might have seemed inexpiable. Thus, at least temporarily, life begins again: its tears are rewoven, its hostility unvenomed, its worry calmed.

Inventive and disciplined, open and hierarchical, the *ordo amoris,* in an Augustinian sense, is the result of human freedom and obedience to a divine commandment. Illuminating the way of men through the worries of this world ("squeezed in the press" by the millstone of hunger, war, and death), it guides them towards the beatitude of Paradise. The non-illusory existence of this goal may already be carried out on earth thanks

4 Nietzsche, *Kritische Studienausgabe* 11: 650.
5 Nietzsche, *Also sprach Zarathustra* [1883], part 1.4.
6 Nietzsche, *Jenseits von Gut und Böse* [1886], §19; Engl. trans. *Beyond Good and Evil,* trans. H. Zimmern (New York, 1954).

to the irrepressible attraction towards a happiness that is unconditional and without end. In fact, all of us have always aspired to it – paradoxically, even without knowing. Remembered and forgotten to the point of not even remembering having forgotten, it refers back to the presence of a "beauty so old and so new," so far and so near, as to often be understood too late. In fact, sinking into ourselves, we manage to glimpse, through the wrapping of opacity that surrounds us, the enigmatic and inextricable knot of light that pushes the consciousness of every person to God, time to eternity, the body to the spirit, immanence to transcendence, and Exodus to the Kingdom. In fact, God constitutes the most intimate nucleus of the *I*, more internal to myself than I am with respect to my most hidden life. Although not coinciding with me, God is, therefore, more me than I am.

But how can love become an order, in the double sense of a free disposition of the heart and the obedient response to an external commandment? How will it be capable of conserving its spiritual flame, its inventive and nonviolent power, if it is required to comply with the substantial rigidity of an invitation to the imperative of someone – however inclined to mercy and to amnesty for crimes – who does not hide the threat of horrible penalties in the case of rejection? Further, how will it reconcile the realization of the new and the possible with respect for an order already given and willed by God since the creation of the world, even if that was then distorted, with regard to man, by the original sin? And finally, at least for our modern feelings, doesn't love constitute the highest form of spontaneity, the "transgressive" passion *par excellence* that bends neither to the predictability of order as routine nor to its authoritarian imposition? Does it not, perhaps, in order to exclude the suspicion that it might become an opportunistic fiction, safeguard its nature as an unforeseeable, surplus, and free gift?

Ira: La passione furente (Rage: The Furious Passion) analyses the different manifestations of rage in time and space; its relationship with political and religious power; its natural and cultural origins; its presentation, at the level of reality and the imagination, on the basis of opposing pairs made up of men and divinity, men and women, and men and animals; its decline into forms of historical life and into theoretical reflections that involve the identity and role of individuals and communities. Since antiquity, in fact, there has been imputed to it the temporary loss of the most precious of goods: the light of reason and the capacity for self-control. In its inflamed manifestations, it has been considered a form of blindness or temporary madness that undermines lucidity of the mind and freedom of decision. Those who are victims of it appear "outside of themselves," subjugated to another, to a tyrannical interior father who deprives them of the ability to understand and desire.

This is born generally from an unmerited offence one believes one has received, from a burning wound inflicted culpably by others on our own self-respect and our (sometimes exaggerated) self-esteem. More precisely, it stems from the conviction of having been betrayed, insulted, tricked, manipulated, scorned, humiliated, neglected, deprived of due respect, or treated in an unjust or inappropriate way. It arises from the disconsolate or irritating observation of the inadequacy of our behaviour in particular circumstances, from the bitter regret for having wasted opportunities or even life itself. Above all, it depends on ruminating and on impotent recrimination for not having reversed the course of time in order to rectify our conduct, *a posteriori*, and remedy errors committed.

This passion is an ambivalent indicator of both the level of vulnerability of one's *I* and, simultaneously, its desire for assertiveness. It sometimes even represents an excess of legitimate defence of personal psychic and physical space and the system of principles and beliefs with which the individual or group identifies. It seems to be associated with the need to preserve, reactively, one's own public image (actually or presumably threatened by the offence) and the need to restore the self-esteem that one believes to have been wounded. It basically concerns the reaffirmation of one's own role, dignity, or authoritativeness in interpersonal or political relationships.

Rage makes up part of the sad passions Spinoza speaks of in his *Ethics* that – along with hate, envy, or avarice – suppress our will to live or "power of existing." They make us suffer, but they also contain (and Spinoza does not take this into account) an intrinsic compensation, a portion – even if not prevalent – of bitter pleasure, of the satisfaction of getting back, often enjoyed at the level of fantasy. In rage, this compensation is represented from the perspective of a reprisal or revenge that the imagination foresees in a more or less violent way; in hate, by looking forward to the destruction of one's own enemies; in envy, by joy in the misfortune of others; and in avarice, by the enjoyment of contemplating money saved as repayment for the sacrifice of not spending it.

In Western culture, the image of rage is twofold. On one side, it is considered a noble passion of rebellion against offences and injustices, the desire to punish the person believed to have insulted one. On the other, it represents a feared loss of autonomy and judgment. Tradition is divided, therefore, into two branches that have lasted more than two millennia: one that accepts rightful anger but condemns irascibility, the other that rejects every type of anger and asks that one abstain from it completely.

In the triptych that makes up *Geometry of the Passions, Ordo amoris,* and *Destini personali,* as well as in the volume on rage, I tried to elaborate theoretical and ethical models to understand the near and distant bases of the formation of our identity. In all of these cases, I never separated the historical dimension from the theoretical. I wanted to construct what I call crystals of historicity, conceptual formations that are the result of the depositing and structuring over time of events and ideas that undoubtedly change, but according to specific formal and "figural" modes. Thanks to this new Introduction, I hope to have contributed to a better understanding of *Geometry of the Passions.*

Remo Bodei

GEOMETRY OF THE PASSIONS

Fear, Hope, Happiness: Philosophy and Political Use

Introduction

I

1. The passions have long been condemned as creators of disturbance or temporary loss of reason. An evident sign of a power extraneous to man's best side, they would control him, distorting his clear vision of things and diverting his spontaneous propensity towards goodness. When disturbed, the mirror-like water of the mind would become cloudy and rippled, ceasing to reflect reality and impeding the will from discerning alternatives to the inclinations of the moment.

Obeying the imperious call of impulses, surrendering to the tortuous flattery of desires, would mean abandoning one's defenceless self to unpredictable and contradictory states of the heart, renouncing freedom, awareness, and self-control in favour of an interior master more demanding than any external one.

Confronted with the multiple strategies that have been formulated for eradicating, moderating, or domesticating the passions (and, in parallel, for attaining control over oneself, making one's intelligence consistent, one's will constant, and one's character robust), it nonetheless seems valid to ask ourselves if the opposition between reason and the passions is capable of taking into account some of the phenomena to which it refers and whether it is right, in general, to sacrifice one's own "passions" in the name of ideals that could be the vehicle of unmotivated unhappiness.

When, at the end of this book, the completed journey can be observed from a distance – revealing its direction more clearly – it will be possible to note, by means of internal lines, how "reason" and "passions" can constitute part of theoretically and culturally conditioned constellations of meaning (*senso*), even if they are now familiar to us and difficult to replace. In other words, "reason" and "passions" are pre-judged terms, and we must become accustomed to considering them as correlated – and non-obvious – notions defined with respect to each other (by contrast or difference) only within determined conceptual horizons and specific evaluative parameters – all of them, however, subordinate to the nature of the movements and mental maps at the beginning.

At their base, we find the assumption that the passions represent "alterations" of an otherwise neutral state and that they do not disturb the heart or the customary composition of the "humours" in each individual's character. In this way, we confuse what is, if anything, the historical result of efforts that tend towards the impartiality and tranquility of the soul with a natural condition. Nevertheless, nothing prevents us from thinking of the "passions" (emotions, feelings, desires) as states that are not added externally to a wholly indifferent consciousness, clouding and confusing it, but are constituents of the tonality of every psychic mode of being and even every cognitive orientation. Therefore, why not conceive of them (like music, which combines the most rigorous mathematical precision with the most powerful emotional charge) as forms of communication that are tonally "accentuated," as mimed languages or expressive acts that simultaneously elaborate or transmit messages that are vectorially oriented, modulated, articulated, and gradable in direction and intensity?

The passions prepare, preserve, memorize, rework, and exhibit "reactive meanings" more directly attributed to people, things, and events by subjects who carry them out within specific contexts, whose forms and metamorphoses they highlight. They let it be seen in reality as "reason" itself – presented *a posteriori* as temporarily swept away or seduced – that establishes the objective and range of their actions, identifying the objects onto which they spill, measuring the point at which to arrest the impulse, dosing out the virulence of dissipative attitudes.

Some important consequences might result from the possible confirmation of such a hypothesis. In particular, it could damage the idea of an energy that is deeply opaque and uncultured, one that is to be subjugated and disciplined. In this way, passion may seem like a shadow of reason itself, as a construct of sense and as an attitude already closely fitted with an intelligence and culture of its own, the fruit of elaborations over millennia. In turn, reason – "dispassioned," selective, and partial – may prove to abet the very passions that it claims to be fighting. We would thus discover the inadequacy of the concept of passion as mere blindness. It would render its demonization and the consequent appeal to its exorcism (and symmetrically, its exaltation as the mirror opposite of reason) less plausible. The recurring, austere figures of reason as "charioteer," "shepherd," tamer, and educator of the passions (of body and soul, of spirit and flesh) would thus become unfocused and partially unreliable.

To presume energies that are wild and groping in the dark ("passions"), energies that should be directed and kept in check by an illuminated, ordering need ("reason"), often means foreshadowing a contentious pretext for repressing or channeling them. Declaring their dangerousness and inability to guide themselves, denying them an intrinsic orientation and wisdom, we automatically legitimize the lawfulness of delegating external interventions of censorship or corrective safeguards to either inflexible imperial power or the persuasive paternalistic severity of "reason."

If we really wish to remain in the conceptual environment of a duality between reason and passions – leaving for later the formulation of a new lexicon and syntax of their relations – we must at least abandon the image of this relationship as an arena for the clash between logic and absence of logic (between order and disorder, transparency and obscurity, law and will, monolithic unity of "reason" – which is just the name for a family of different strategies – and plurality of the passions). If necessary, we could interpret this relationship as a conflict between two complementary logics that operate according to the pattern of "neither with you nor without you." Bound by antagonistic solidarity, they would operate according to ordering structures that are functionally differentiated and incongruent, justifiable (each at its respective level) in reference to its own principles. From their opposition to the principles of reason come the areas of opacity of intelligence, and bends and fluctuations of will, as well as the feeling of ineluctable passivity, unintentional action, and involuntary impotence that seem to define "passion." Knowing the passions would be nothing other than analysing reason itself "against the grain," illuminating it with its own presumed shadow.

2. Despite all this, however, the passions cannot be reduced to just conflict or mere passivity. They tinge the world with vibrant, subjective colours; they accompany the unfolding of events; they shake experience from inertia and monotony, making existence full-bodied despite its discomforts and pains. Would it be worth the trouble to live if we did not feel any passion – if stubborn, invisible strings did not bind us to how much they lie "at heart" (to put it another way) and whose loss we fear? Would not total apathy, lack of feelings and resentments, incapacity to rejoice or become sad (or be "full" of love, rage, or desire), and disappearance of passivity (understood as that virtual and welcoming space for the presentation of the other) be tantamount, perhaps, to death?

The discovery of the passions' positivity is fairly recent. It has taken place largely in contemporary times, in a period subsequent to the one explicitly examined in the present volume. And although Kant would continue to consider them a "cancer of reason," Descartes and Spinoza had in the meantime already justified their role, economists had exalted their civilizing function, and the Romantics would shortly proclaim their inalienability. Beginning with the end of the eighteenth century, there arrived – reversing earlier worries – a fear of their irreversible weakening or virtual disappearance. Systematically reported from at least the times of Stendhal and de Tocqueville, however, was the eclipse of great and noble passions owing to the dominance of egotistical calculation, individual vanity, and, particularly, increased security of life. Progressively assuming the task of protecting the individual in critical moments of existence (birth, childhood, old age, illness) and assuming the burden of justly indemnifying it in the face of offences endured – or prohibiting all involvement in escalations of private revenge – the state would arrogate to itself, in some way, the legitimate monopoly of some of the strongest and most exclusive passions. The absence of passions, and not passion itself, now becomes the true sin.

The expansion of rationalization would "dry up" the source of emotions, bridling the tendency towards a "bigger heart" and dissipating those energies with which life renews itself. There would begin an era of mediocrity (even politically), of progressive closure of the individual within himself, of a reduction in the intensity and range of human relationships emotionally invested with feeling and engaging merit. The rarefaction of generous impulses and heroic tendencies would correspond with a flourishing of "petty passions," weak desires, and, frequently, the triumph of the crazy and the vulgar.

Independently of its author's intentions, one fable effectively expresses such a presumed condition:

> A group of porcupines, on a cold winter day, huddled close together to protect themselves, with reciprocal warmth, from freezing. Soon enough, however, they felt each other's quills; the pain forced them to separate from each other once again. Then, when the need to warm themselves brought them together again, the other misfortune recurred; such that they were tossed back and forth between two kinds of suffering until they found a moderate reciprocal distance that represented the best position for them.[1]

1 A. Schopenhauer, *Parerga und Paralipomena,* 2, ch. 30, §6, in *Zürcher Ausgabe: Werke in zehn Bänden* (Zürich, 1977), vol. 10, 708.

Incapable of avoiding the quills (or frightened by the idea that their possible relinquishment would make them more vulnerable), men would be pushed towards the "borderland between solitude and community" noted by Kafka.[2] And so they would endlessly accept poor compromises between painful distance and prickly promiscuity. Caught between warmth and freezing, they would content themselves with tepid relationships with others and with themselves. The result of this parallelogram of attractive and repulsive forces would be a tolerable or banal happiness.

3. It continues to be repeated today that the contemporary world is characterized precisely by the blunting of desire, reciprocal indifference, and mass individualism that would mark the passage from the *homo hierarchicus* of societies of caste and order to the *homo aequalis* that asserted itself in eastern civilizations.[3] Rejecting direct contact and complete detachment from others, such a "doctrine of the mean" would have led to emotional withering and the disappearance of solidarity. The need to be participants in collective events having failed, the sense of belonging to the community would dry up. Reason, having become a calculator or "instrumental," would thus distance itself from passions and feelings that had become narcotized.

In the second book of *Democracy in America* (1840), de Tocqueville was among the first to diagnose such symptoms. His thesis is that the United States represents only the harbinger of a form of life destined to propagate itself throughout the entire planet, the mirror in which Europe could already stare at its own future. He connects the new regime of passions and desires to a permanent dissatisfaction that seeks to placate itself by means of an obsessive search for "material goods." This follows the acquisitive impulse that had often been condemned, from Plato forward, as typical of the shallowest part of the soul and the most vile strata of the community.

In a Europe marked by the existence of insurmountable social barriers, however, generalized "passion" for well-being was not yet felt in all its virulence. The aristocrats and the rich enjoyed such well-being as if it were simply their right. The poor continued to perceive it as an objective so far beyond their own reach that daring to imagine it was difficult. The

2 Franz Kafka, "Dieses Grenzland zwischen Einsamkeit und Gemeinschaft ..." [29 October 1921] in *Tagebücher: Textband* (Frankfurt, 1990), s. 871.

3 See G. Lipovetski, *L'ère du vide: Essais sur l'individualisme contemporain* (Paris, 1963), and L. Dumont, *Essai sur l'individualisme, une perspective anthropologique sur l'idéologie de la modernité* (Paris, 1983). On the positions of Dumont, see A. Renaud, *L'ère de l'individu* (Paris, 1989), 69–112.

enormous inequality of the hierarchical ladder inhibits, at the lowest steps, vigorous aspirations towards equality and change of the conditions of existence. Desire gets stuck in the mind easily or projects itself endlessly in the expectation of celestial happiness as recompense for suffering and deprivations endured.

On the other hand, in the young American democracy, the unstoppable pursuit of equality joins emulation of, and intolerance for, the distinctions of grade, the race towards success, and the hypertrophy of acquisitive desire – a passion that risks suffocating every other. But far from leading to happiness, such exclusive yearning appears to de Tocqueville to be veined with subtle sadness. In their "honest materialism," Americans would think more about the goods they do not yet have and the brevity of the time in which to use them than about their actual enjoyment.

In the hope of calming this "strange restlessness" and better guaranteeing the pursuit of happiness, they would thus rely on a sweet tyranny that (at the cost of manipulating desires and maintaining citizens in a perpetual state of political minority) would allow everyone to place themselves in a social universe where each person believes he is – like the sun – at the centre of a multiple Ptolemaic system:

> The first thing that strikes the observation is an innumerable multitude of men, all equal and alike, incessantly endeavoring to procure the petty and paltry pleasures with which they glut their lives. Each of them, living apart, is as a stranger to the fate of all the rest; his children and his private friends constitute to him the whole of mankind. As for the rest of his fellow citizens, he is close to them, but he does not see them; he touches them, but he does not feel them; he exists only in himself and for himself alone.[4]

Politically "tormented by two conflicting passions," caught between "the need to be guided and the desire to remain free," Americans do not manage to make up their minds between dependency and self-rule. The reciprocal isolation resolves itself in considerable paralysis of will and (once again) in emotional tepidness, while the uncertain satisfaction of the need for security is reduced by considerable apathy and the rejection of autonomous thought:

4 See A. de Tocqueville, *De la démocratie en Amérique,* in *Oeuvres complètes,* ed. I.-P. Mayer (Paris, 1951), bk. 1, vol. 2; Engl. trans. *Democracy in America* (New York, 1840, rpt., 1945), vol. 2, ch. 6, 318.

> Above this race of men stands an immense and tutelary power, which takes upon itself alone to secure their gratifications and to watch over their fate. That power is absolute, minute, regular, provident, and mild. It would be like the authority of a parent if, like that authority, its object was to prepare men for manhood; but it seeks, on the contrary to keep them in perpetual childhood: it is well content that the people should rejoice, provided they think of nothing but rejoicing. For their happiness such a government willingly labors, but it chooses to be the sole agent and only arbiter of that happiness; it provides for their security, foresees and supplies their necessities, facilitates their pleasures, manages their principal concerns, directs their industry, regulates the descent of property, and subdivides their inheritances: what remains, but to spare them all the care of thinking and all the trouble of living?[5]

Subsequent scenarios revealed themselves to be much more varied than de Tocqueville, with his acute and nearly prophetic forecasts, was able to predict. Similarly, some ideological presuppositions – previously invisible because they were mixed in his analyses and narrations – broke away from them over time and became clear. But de Tocqueville's ideas nonetheless constitute precious testimony. They represent the evidence of a widespread and durable dissatisfaction with the tendency (considered unstoppable in contemporary democracies) that simultaneously pushes individuals towards an increment of acquisitive desire and towards a complementary drying up of passions judged worthy of being carried out.

II

1. That this "acquisitive push" would progressively assume strength – to the point of acclimating itself in a flourishing way among inhabitants of many areas of the world to arrive at current levels – is a fact plainly seen by everyone. But beyond frequent moralistic judgments and the hasty taking of positions, for the most part it does not seem that the phenomenon has been given (from this perspective) the attention that it deserves. In particular, it turns out that study of its impact on the statics and dynamics of passions and desires is lacking. Further, we know very little about the architecture of the interior hierarchies of the "soul"

5 Ibid.

and of their transformations. Little more is known about their external behaviours, which are more easily noticeable.

A few events, presented here didactically, will illustrate what is meant and will suggest ideas for other possible avenues of research that may extend the paths taken here along dotted lines. For example, one might consider the disturbing (if, at first, subjectively little-noticed) effects that were felt in the daily life of an economy oriented towards consumption. Two familiar images that have become typical of the urban landscape are enough to evoke them: department stores and shop windows. In 1852, seven years before de Tocqueville's death, Aristide Bourcicault opened a store in Paris called Bon Marché that presented a revolutionary novelty. He accumulated there a colossal quantity of merchandise, sold at relatively low unitary prices (so as to generate earnings, particularly on quantity). The system of fixed retail prices was introduced, eliminating bargaining and ensuring equal treatment for everyone. He established the practice of returning products purchased in exchange for other merchandise or for cash. Finally, he allowed and encouraged free access by potential clients to the place of business, without imposing any obligation for purchase.[6] In this way, temptations spread and multiplied in space and time, while the opportunity to make purchases concentrated itself. The department stores "democratized luxury,"[7] exposing customers to the seduction of induced supplementary needs and triggering within them mental chain reactions. In these stores and in the *passages* associated with them, "clients felt themselves to be part of the crowd," and entered into communication in an anonymous way with the objects of their desires (there even existed in Paris a *Passage du désir*!).[8]

Exactly half a century later, this power of fascination was extended also to passersby, involving those who had no intent or need to enter into a commercial exercise. Specifically, in 1902, the Frenchman Foucault discovered a method for producing plates of glass of large dimension (resolving a series of problems caused by the fragility of the material in relation to its weight, by poor strength in the event of temperature

---

6 See H. Pasdermadjian, *The Department Store: Its Origins, Evolution and Economics* (London, 1954), 3–4; R. Sennett, *The Fall of the Public Man* (New York, 1974), 141 et seq.; M.B. Miller, *The Bon Marché: Bourgeois Culture and the Department Store, 1869–1920* (Princeton, 1981).

7 This is the idea of Zola in *Notes de travail sur les grands magasins* (in addition to the novel *Au bonheur des dames*); see also Pasdermadjian, *The Department Store*, 125.

8 See W. Benjamin, "Passagen, magasins de nouveautès, calicots," in *Das Passagenwerk*, in *Gesammelte Shriften* (Frankfurt, 1983), vol. 5, 1, 98 et seq.

fluctuation, and by persistent cloudiness). And so, wide shop windows were born, the displayers of merchandise separated from their hypothetical purchasers only by an invisible – though very real – barrier.[9] The "dark object of desire" literally became transparent, and being visible and (seemingly) at one's fingertips simultaneously trivialized and intensified every acquisitive desire, which encompassed not only goods but, more generally, life itself.

2. In the past, this had not been the case. For millennia, morals and customs taught people, above all, to moderate desires. *Pleonexia*, the insatiable yearning for possession, represented the mortal sin of classical ethics. The technique employed to reject it consisted of lowering the threshold of an individual's pretensions rather than raising the threshold of his expectations, according to a precept concisely expressed by a Stoic philosopher: "Questioned in order to learn how one could become rich, Cleante responded: 'if one is poor in desires.'"[10]

In our cultures, it has not been long since this attitude has been limited and partly removed, profoundly modifying the conduct of billions of people and transforming them almost into "mutants" with respect to the habits and value systems of the past. With the virtual end of the scarcity of some fundamental resources (for a substantial number of people), and with the aspiration of those people previously excluded from pursuing similar advantages, desires that were previously repressed, sublimated, or denigrated were partly freed from their previous constraints, rendering the demands of self-control less apparent and binding. The extensive consumption of visible and invisible goods (always the prerogative of narrow *élites*) and their relative abundance at generally reasonable costs modified the position and orientation of desires and expanded the range of possibilities, even on the level of the imaginary.[11]

9 Cf. J. Fourastié, *The Causes of Wealth* (Glencoe, IL, 1959), 107, and D. Bell, *Cultural Contradictions of Capitalism* (New York, 1976), 86.

10 Stobaeus, *Florilegium*, 95, 28.

11 The emphasis placed on acquisition and consumption cannot, however, be explained exclusively on the basis of economic utility. Without considering the fact that there is a searching for consumption of experiences, happiness, sexual relations, etc., things become part of a new system of communication, symbols that exchange information on the social role and on the combinatory art of individual tastes, factors of distinction, of economic and cultural status within a uniformity that inevitably tends to recreate itself, stimulating, in turn, the birth of new distinctions (beyond the classical analyses of Simmel on fashion, see M. Douglas and B. Isherwood, *The World of Goods: Towards and Anthropology of Consumption* [London, 1979]). Regarding the search for cultural distinction through objects of art and prestige, often called *kitsch*, see

Material and spiritual indigence had thrown the overwhelming majority of people (particularly those less protected from the storms of existence) at the mercy of the most tumultuous or icy passions, of the most exalted hopes or the darkest resignation. Political economy, aimed at the "wealth of nations" and at the satisfaction of ever more urgent needs, continued beyond the Pillars of Hercules of ancient *pleonexia.* It thus implicitly moved the boundaries of limitation or self-limitation of desires, causing radical changes in their organization, since it did not aim simply at satisfying them, but multiplying them.[12]

Parallel to the rise of political economy, passions began to distinguish themselves more clearly from interests.[13] In this way they came to be divided – sometimes implicitly – into the "calm" passions, as Hume called them (or "cold" or quiet, pervious to rationality and compatible with an ordered structure – in short, interests) and the "agitated" or "hot" ones (i.e., normally unruly, boiling, rebellious to reason and will, or even delicate but vague, changeable, or inconsistent).

Political economy is also defined thanks to this neat division that would run through the corpus of the passions. In fact, it is based upon an "as if": on the hypothesis that men, in pursuing the maximization of their own interests, will always behave in an egotistically rational way, thereby making the course of their conduct predictable, in principle. Next to two final elements of intrinsic intelligibility – the inelastic nature of needs[14] and the homeostatic mechanisms of the marketplace[15] – is the choosing

---

M. Thompson, *Rubbish Theory* (Oxford, 1979). This is why, with respect to goods for purchase and consumption, there is at play a complex "strategy of desire" aimed largely at gratification that is either immediate or not much deferred (see E. Dichter, *The Strategy of Desire* [New York, 1960]). It is interesting to observe the confluence of two etymologies in the origin of the word "consumption": from *cum sumere* ("take with," "use entirely") and *cumsummare* ("total," "bring to completion"); see R. Williams, "Consumer," in *Key Words: A Vocabulary of Culture and Society* (Oxford, 1976, 68–70).

12 A powerful rhetoric is now notoriously at work through commercial advertising, shaping desires and establishing the rituals of consumption, blurring in the imagination the limits between reality and daydreams.

13 See, for some aspects, the points laid out by A.O. Hirschman, *The Passions and the Interests: Political Arguments for Capitalism before Its Triumph* (Princeton, 1977).

14 On needs as demands that are "objective," not plastic, unavoidable, and that require rigorously prioritary choices, see G. Thomson, *Needs* (London, 1987).

15 The regulation of the marketplace occurred in the eighteenth century, from Cantillon to Smith, through a theoretical model that took into account feedback loops, the automatisms of retroactivity. For example, if there are too many hat-makers in a city or on a street with respect to demand, some will be forced to close. If, on the other hand, there are too few, others will set up shop. See O. Mayr, "Adam Smith and the Concept of the Feedback System," *Technology and Culture* 12 (1971), 1–22.

of sides in favour of calm or cold passions in order to allow the political economy of the eighteenth century to assume the status of a science.

Symmetrically, even morals are based on an "as if," in circumstances much more improbable than the first. That is, men may behave among themselves according to criteria dictated by feelings of benevolence and altruism, which are unfortunately not susceptible to generalization to an extent that renders them an object of rigorous science, as is the case with selfishness in political economy.[16]

The other half of the passions – the "hot" or "agitated" ones – emptied of any characteristic of rationality, is thus rejected (not only in political economy, but by different developments in ethics and customs) in the weak gravitational field of emotion or of "irrationality" in general. However, this half assumes sentimental or murky traits without containing intelligent passions capable of understanding them. The fatal consequence is that the agitated passions are now rendered even more blind, mute, or pale. They are reduced to pure movements of the heart – that is, to emotion – walled within the private sphere of intimacy or called upon to support widespread stereotypes, like that of the woman (whose internal habitat is identified in the "hot" world of affectivity that is poor in reason, in contrast with the universe of masculine logic, which constitutes its mirror opposite) or of the *crowd* (which would be dominated alternately by incandescent passions of hope and excitement or frozen sentiments of fear and resignation, but always by fluctuating states of the heart).[17]

---

16 Although such a division between calm and agitated (or cold and hot) passions may be consolidated with the triumph of political economy as science, it would however be wrong to attribute it directly to Adam Smith, reducing his position to that of a defender of selfishness in the economic field and of sympathy or benevolence in the field of morals (that is, contrasting *The Wealth of Nations* with *The Theory of Moral Sentiments*). We forget that love itself, self-love, is at the base of egoism as much as it is of sympathy, and that interests are in reality a concentration of passions. Cf. J-P. Dupuy, "L'individu libéral, cet inconnu: d'Adam Smith à Friedrich Hayek," in *Individu et justice sociale: Autour de John Rawls* (Paris, 1988), 98–9. Moreover, for Hume himself, the opposition between selfish and benevolent passions does not stand at all. "A man is no more interested when he seeks his own glory than when the happiness of his friend is the object of his wishes; nor is he any more disinterested when he sacrifices his ease and quiet to the public good than when he labours for the gratification of avarice or ambition" (*An Enquiry Concerning Human Understanding*, in *Philosophical Works* [London, 1875; rpt., Aalen, 1964], vol. 4, 11).

17 Today the tendency timidly reoccurs to also attribute to the "emotions" (being composed of belief, evaluation, and feeling) a side that is indirectly cognitive. See R. de Sousa, *The Rationality of Emotion* (Cambridge, MA, 1987); P. Greenspan, *Emotion and Reason: An Enquiry into Emotional Justification* (New York, 1988).

Order, then, seems to rule only the calm or cold passions adopted by political economy or calculating reason, while the other passions appear to grow savage and wild (although it would be better to say "insufficiently tended," because there is no culture of the passions to which they might be subjected, no "education of feelings" even remotely equal to the "civilization of reason").

The phenomena noted under the label of *Sturm und Drang*, of "Romanticism," "philosophies of life," or "irrationalism" can also be read as forms of overcompensation in the face of the formation of a bloc of alliances among cold or selfish passions and reason, which has exasperated and rendered wild the passions abandoned by rationality.

3. It could be said that both the cold passions and the hot, the instantaneous and explosive ones (like rage) and those that are stubborn and long-lasting (like rancour) today may be ceding ever greater space to desires – that is, to the waiting passions bent on goods or imagined future satisfactions. This is how extraordinary, incalculable, fleeting, and indeterminate projections of desire assert and propagate themselves: as fantasies of individual fulfilment, no longer held back by sufficiently solid external levees or by resolute exertions of self-control; as expectations no longer anchored to ideals of limits (reflecting cosmic order or commandments established by God's will); as plans no longer focused on the explicit search for a presumed ultimate end or "supreme good."

More than asymptotic (en route to nearing their objective, without ever being able to reach it), these desires are unplaceable; they stand in a "somewhere else" that is never fully identifiable except at the cost of destroying the pleasures of waiting. They aim not so much at satisfaction of impulses or specific needs per se as they do at indistinct aspirations to happiness raised by any sort of opportunity or pretext (happiness, the unprogrammable or indefinite fulfilment of desires, in this case seems to be complementary to distress, as fear without an object). Highly unpredictable, evanescent, and "opportunistic," no longer circumscribing the sudden burst of emotion or the duration of passions that have metamorphosed into character traits, they insert themselves by definition into the perspective of the future.

Desire – multiplied, diversified, and branching out – thus preserves its classical nature of yearning to see who (or what) is not yet in our presence.[18] As it then depends on a constituent absence of the object, on a

18 Cf. Cic., *Tusc.* IV, 12: *libido eius, qui nondum adsit, videndi,* and cf. IV, 14.

void or ghost, it generally defers to the size of upgradable hopes, whose realization is conditioned by objective factors, by "filters" (physical, economical, juridical, or psychological) that restrict the field of possibilities and expectations.[19] Thus, desire inserts itself into the folds of an elastic temporal agenda, articulated according to deadlines that are not strictly binding. On the contrary: the more the future is considered available and the more the mobility of social processes increases, the less desires become susceptible to repressive control or to the shrewdness of the "reason" that tried to force the more static passions into obedience and that is now played by means of skilful "bypass" systems that go around the negligible controls. This situation currently makes more difficult the understanding and control of the hypertrophy of desires. No adequate theoretical solution has been proposed for it, nor has an effective "police force" been organized.[20]

Although the passions have a character either of relative fixedness or of a sticky attachment to their object, such desires present themselves as essentially restless and incapable of crystallizing. Released from the tight control of reason and will, closer to daydreaming than to calculation and considered decision, they are also more exposed to illusions and delusions that do not, however, impede the incessant sprouting of trunks that are necessarily damaged or cut down (even if the number of expectations might produce effects of inflation or mental anesthesia that exhaust individuals' tempers and generate a second-order desire – essentially, the desire to feel desires). The wall of Platonic separation between the rational and the arational parts of the soul has collapsed, producing a short circuit between rationality and desire. In fact, it is this latter – reversing the hierarchy of the winged amphora – that now uses two grey horses, so to speak.

We pass from the relatively calculable and predictable logic of interests, or from the techniques for repressive chaining of the passions, to the massive advancement of uncertain but very powerful desires. Concomitantly

19 Cf. J. Elster, *Nuts and Bolts for the Social Sciences* (Cambridge, 1989), 13–21. Desires and possibilities seem to condition themselves reciprocally, such that there corresponds, to expansion of the "opportunity set," a widening of the compass calipers of desire and vice versa.

20 This, incidentally is one of the reasons why politics is always operating less in terms of rational organization of interests or of repression and manipulation of the passions and ever more in terms of constant and updatable reshaping or remodelling of the incommensurability of desires and of their objects (and this in the register of both the real and of the imaginary).

with the wearing down of inhibiting mechanisms, or with the slowing or delay of desires, even work (understood in the Hegelian sense of "appetite held in check") tends by countermeasure to lose its previous ethical and social centrality. From a key value that attributes dignity to *homo faber* and legitimacy to criteria of resource allocation, it returns to being, for many, an instrument of torture (according to the etymology that some have suggested for *travail*, particularly *tripalium* – and if it's not true, it's a good story).

Anchored in the continuous renegotiation between partly amorphous desires, choices whose costs and benefits can be measured, and rationally arguable plans for life, a "submerged moral philosophy" tends to partner with and partially replace the remaining official ethics, while still clinging to relatively rigid rules. Desires, already dependent on the uncertainty of the future, assume a physiognomy that is even more uncertain due to the acceleration endured over historical time, which introduces faster rhythms in the changing of their contours and the reformulation of their objectives (which in some cases can become more modest). The frequent resorting to "narcissistic" motivations – understanding the expression in the sense of the proven incapacity to adequately distinguish between the projections of one's desires and the "reality" in which they are reflected – adds a final element of uncertainty to the operation.

And if tradition previously proposed variants of a model of compact individuality, whole and in full relief, in recent decades there seems to have prevailed an ideal of the individual loosened from the imperative of consistency, free to take on only "non-binding commitments" or perhaps to pursue them with the *arrière-pensé* of not respecting them.[21] This individual was as unconstrained as necessary in his desires, versatile in repairing his identity, and cautious in his affiliations, but ultimately free from external "ties."

The reduction of social insecurity – when it actually exists – certainly damages the *pathos* felt in the face of iron-like and direct political control of the passions and similarly rigid ethical self-control. A monolithic and strongly centripetal *I* would seem now to take the place of a mental system that disassembles it into modules to be recombined, that undramatizes its scissions and reduces its incongruities (while increasing "tolerance" and complicity in the face of the desires' stimulus). Can we

21 For these non-binding commitments, see N. and G. O'Neill, *Open Marriage: A New Life Style for Couples* (New York, 1972), and R. Nozick, *Philosophical Explanations* (Cambridge, MA, 1981).

presume that – in the presence of changed circumstances – even these attitudes would change?

III

1. No ethics, however, is capable of circumscribing, measuring, and cataloging desires *more geometrico*, as once happened with the other passions, either according to a panoply of tactics of confinement within an inflexible *cordon sanitaire* drawn by reason and will or according to plans for man's emancipation by means of their collective liberation. The two extremes (on the one hand, reason or will repressively dominating passions and desires and, on the other, the latter's rebellion and insubordination) reveal a mirror-like systemic connivance and substantial impracticability. Even in this first sense, the "geometry of the passions" failed, its oxymoronic binding partly loosened.

This book reconstructs – in a more distant chronological zone, organically and analytically – the theoretical and historical bases of the topics I have sketched to this point in a necessarily allusive fashion. Thanks to a thick weaving of textual and problematic references, it now presents a broad, detailed, and consistent concatenation of thoughts and data.

Although choosing to pursue expository rigour and not erasing the tracks of the completed path of research (so that others may eventually follow, verify, and correct it), this volume does not, however, possess a scholarly structure, nor does it simply tell a story.[22] Its purpose is to explain problems, trace a plausible line of interpretation, and elaborate some solutions relative to the charter of passions and desires and their treatment in the ethical and political spheres.

---

22 Following Descartes, who professed to have begun to think from an absolute *da capo*, Walter Benjamin wanted to compose a work formed entirely by quotations. More modestly – according to Bacon's model of the "bees" that elaborate and give flavour to what they have patiently gathered, in contrast with the "ants" who limit themselves to accumulating the material of others and with the "spiders," who self-sufficiently secrete from their mouths their own ideas – the author of this book would be content with knowing how to properly use the tools of argumentation that is dense and not watered down, capable of weaving together theory and history, logical clarity and philological precision, constructive time and genealogical time: all of this with the awareness of the difficulty of the undertaking, of the fact that wise "ants" and "spiders" also exist and a reader who is not interested in following the "optional masochism" of the back-and-forth of text and footnotes is capable of finding on his own the "fast lane" of the text through a more comfortable (but perhaps less interesting) passage through the volume.

In its conceptual structure, it is conceived in "geometrical" terms: in the form of an ellipse sketched from time to time along pairs of "foci" (or points of irradiation and condensation of problems). Fear and hope, in their complementary tension, make up its deepest internal generating nuclei. From them – also in the framework of a sort of archaeology of passions and virtues, whose results are contextually translated into philosophical demands – begins the analysis of principal families of strategies put into action with respect to the passions, both to free oneself from them and to use them with the purpose of better serving the "multitudes." That journey concludes with another polarization, two other "foci" that emit a different type of heat: reason, in its coalition with the cold passions, and another element, of which we will speak later, because the halo of misleading meanings surrounding it could, at the moment, give rise to unnecessary misunderstandings.

Hope and fear allow privileged access to fundamental philosophical and political problems. Fed by the need to exorcise the dangers of the present and the uncertainty of the future, they are simultaneously unstable and impetuous, deaf to the dictates of reason and the commands of will, but sensitive to threats and promises. Therefore, they seem like an obstacle to those who propose reaching full mastery of oneself, while they offer the most effective tool of domination to those who govern others. (Their role, however, ends up being contradictory at the level of civil and religious institutions. Although favouring the creation and maintenance of despotic and theocratic regimes that generally support the passivity and resignation of their subjects and followers, they are, however, capable of triggering waves of panic, terror, fanaticism, and collective ferment that backfire against the established powers.)

Glorified by Christian and utopian thought, hope is framed here in a perspective that, considering merely the reverse side of fear, proposes an ethics released from both fear and hope, one that is not subject to the repressive or paternalistic domination of will and reason, but not laxly abandoned to the random accumulation of desires that, if they reach critical mass, implode or end up weakening the heart and that, in any case, do not possess the absolute plasticity or easy reformulation sometimes attributed to them in an "affluent" society.[23]

23 See Christopher Lasch, *The Culture of Narcissism: American Life in the Age of Diminishing Expectations* (New York, 1979), and Lasch, *The Minimal Self: Survival in Troubled Times* (New York, 1984).

2. The ellipse's first focus of concentration – towards which the opening discussion gravitates in centripetal fashion – is represented by the thought of Spinoza. This is read at first according to a viewpoint that favours the "metaphysical" dimension of politics as government of the passions. It then lingers on its most specific theoretical part, examining the progressive *transitio* from the passions to the "feelings" ("passions" deprived of their element of passivity, made intelligible and intelligent by means of their adequate understanding and their non-repressive treatment) to the point of reaching the key idea of "intellectual love."

In the framework of criticism symmetrical to that of his contemporaries, Spinoza fights on two fronts. On one side, he opposes the supporters of monarchical absolutism and the *raison d'état*, including Hobbes, who placed the society of men under the sign of reason born under the fear of death that does not cut the umbilical cord that ties it to its origin, and the politicians of cunning, dissimulation, and violence, who take human nature to be immutably wicked and hold the masses to be passionate by nature – superstitious and destined always to be governed by the methods of the "fox" and of the "lion." On the other side, Spinoza argues against the apostles of earthly hope and the preachers of celestial bliss – that is, against those who imagine men different than they are, who outline perfect, utopian societies where reason and liberty reign supreme over the passions (without seeking refuge, disillusioned, in melancholy solitude or in bitter disappointment in the face of the empire of vices).

Spinoza resolves the seemingly insoluble dilemma of considering and treating men either as they actually are (with their unreformability and wicked inclinations, against which only force and trickery can be applied) or as they should ideally be (purified of the passions thanks to mere moral commitment or respect for religious obligations). If their existence were made less precarious, less exposed to the unpredictable whims of "fortune," their reason would spontaneously grow stronger, and their respect for laws would increase proportionately. Offering greater collective security, democracy encourages the development of rationality in its citizens' conduct, whereas regimes founded on fear and hope decrease the rate of rationality and self-control and increase that of superstition, the virulence of passions, and the overheating of the imagination's passive side. The masses are not, then, condemned by principle to an eternal state of theological-political servitude maintained and organized by the church and by the state.

The relative failure of all of these repressive morals or utopian sublimations of the passions depends, among other things, on their inadmissible requirement of abnormal struggle for renunciation and self-control that ends up fraying the individual's "power to exist." Ethics cannot be based ascetically on the systematic demolition, permanent humiliation, or repeated deviation of all of the passions to the heaven of the idea. Since desire (or *cupiditas*) constitutes, in a Spinozan sense, the essence of man, reason is not its crowning achievement but only an intermediate state between the passions and intellectual love, the one that is most "golden" and "calm." It represents the fulcrum of the lever that elevates the passions to the level of feelings, but that nonetheless remains marked by insufficient power and limited satisfaction, although not by the discontentment to which Aristotle referred when he observed that in the heart not yet completely inclined towards good, dissatisfaction remains when reason both complies with desire and when it suffers from it.[24]

The subordination of the passions to rigid, rationally human rules and to threatening divine commandments presents multiple theoretical and practical disadvantages. The goal of dominating the passions is that of internalizing social and cultural imperatives so as to arm, immunize, and mithridatize the individual (centralizing the individual's *I* and actively committing his energies) in the face of real, destabilizing powers that present themselves to him as strangers, but that have always lived within him – in fact, they *are* him. Moreover, when these passions meet those of other men, they possess a hypothetically explosive chemism for the social order. But the obligations imposed by morals and tradition (institutionally rendered acceptable by "servomechanisms" such as compromise, pain, and forgiveness) enter into conflict with other demands and values, so that the passions are often banned and forced to hide in the clandestineness of the conscience, generating feelings of guilt, rancour, discomfort, and discontentment.

3. Spinoza comes from a similar logic, showing how, within these ethical dimensions, happiness may be attained only rarely. In fact, there the passions are felt as if they were enemies to be subdued or wiped out, to be cajoled or weakened by means of exhausting civil wars of the will, lacerations, stratagems, subterfuges, and surrenders of intelligence, hard physical and spiritual exercises, punishments, or promises – never as something to understand.

Among the perverse effects of these theories or techniques founded on exorbitant demands for control and self-control are apathy and

24 Cf. Arist., *Eth. Eud.* II, 8, 1224b.

aridness of feelings, mental barrenness, impoverishment of experience, and ritual respect for the rules and sanctification of customs. Or, on the other hand, there is the tragic antinomy of the divide between "reason" and the "heart," obsessive attraction to death or suffering, dogmatic trusting of extra-human powers or undisputed terrestrial authorities. In essence: stupidity, affliction, inconsistency, resignation, lowering of the sense of responsibility, and regression into the zone of amorphousness that extends beyond the law, into the private reserve of an incommunicable emotionality or the public sphere of obedience to precepts and obligations unaccompanied by any sort of acceptable explanation.

Spinoza does not at all expect individuals to sacrifice themselves and their passions, either in the name of the state or in the name of God. He supports the pursuit of *utilitas*, the tendency towards far-seeing rather than farsighted self-preservation that becomes stronger with joy, sociability, and "intellectual love" of God (or of all the special beings of nature). Against every self-punishing renunciation, he pushes towards a possible happiness within the confines of understood necessity, in the context of a universe whose inevitable power stands over and dominates it but to which we must not bend, supine, because we are also part of it.

Understanding the passions, instead of stubbornly opposing or repressing them, means preliminarily accepting their presence and the inability to remove them, with a sort of humble attitude that, paradoxically, gives the rational faculties a greater strength that exalts them and constitutes the prerequisite for eliminating the passions' perverse effects. Without condemning or praising them, it is necessary to formulate an adequate idea of them, to discover their pathways, their blockages, their points of stagnation or variation – understanding why they do not flow towards an outlet broad enough to contain their range and force, so as to emerge in superior satisfaction and disperse their destructive and self-destructive character across a broader surface. This means finding a more agile intellectual order within which to place them, a logic that is more in our power, precisely in order not to have to endure their inflexible "external" order, their crushing logic (that particularly dominates in situations of danger and uncertainty). Understanding is the equivalent of dampening the contradictory variations attributed to the passions – those that astound and alarm reason – that produce opposing and disturbed states of the heart (fear and hope, sadness and joy, hate and love) in rapid succession. Therefore, acquiring a greater awareness of the passions and their transfiguration into feelings implies that we not content ourselves with being transported by *fluctuationes* or *perturbationes animi* produced by winds that press the individual from every side or that we not let ourselves be guided by unreflexive automatic reactions.[25] Spinoza understood that the two-part opposition, direct and frontal, between reason and the passions is generally destined to exhaust the individual's energies and to paralyse and permanently tear at his acts of will – that is, to the triumph of impotent, opposing desires.

In effect, only two main roads open in the great philosophies to those who wish to loosen the knots of will. The first consists of unblocking the forces of the passions and desires previously repressed, immobilized, and unutilized – increasing their intensity in light of a parallel growth of "joy" and of the individual's power to exist (this is the strategy followed by Spinoza himself and, in certain respects, by Descartes). The second is in trusting an entity that may simultaneously be both inside and outside an individual – that is, a power capable of mediating from within both singularity and the universal. (This is the strategy followed by Augustine when he tries to "tune" human will to that of God, "more inward than my most inward part" [*interior intimo meo*],[26] or by Kant when he attributes to reason and its manifestation in man the form of moral law – that is, a commandment that demands unconditional obedience, the nature of a majestic and sublime power capable of respecting the autonomy of the individual just as it commands and transcends it.) In both the first and second cases, it is necessary to defuse the immediate and binary conflict between passions and reason, moving the level of the conflict, and introducing indirect strategies or a third element to take over, one that is common to the first two, with the double role of arbiter and partial cause of the dispute.

Spinoza represents the bridge between an ethics stretched between self-control and the political manipulation of the passions and one that leaves the field open to the immeasurability of desire. He thus contributes to knocking down the double wall that traditionally divides, on one side, the passions from reason and, on the other, the restlessness of the masses from the "serenity" of the wise.

In fact, the need to set a brake on the passions has pushed society to forge, in a millennium-long process with few variants, the figure of an individual who – in the real and the imaginary of our culture and others – constitutes the touchstone between values and virtues. More than a hero

---

25 In modern language, it could be said that one does not find satisfaction living – as often happens – by engaging the "autopilot." (For the expression, see R. Nozick *The Examined Life: Philosophical Meditations* [New York, 1989], p. 11.)

26 St Augustine, *Confessions*, III, 6.11.

of knowledge as an end in itself, he is often a champion of the "good life," an example of steadfastness, lucidity, and courage. Capable of challenging fate, he makes himself invulnerable to its guile and its enticements. He thus protects his own consistency and integrity, victoriously resisting the otherwise intolerable pressure of his own passions and the will of others. He remains irreducibly (but intelligently) faithful to his own decisions, because he knows they are founded on deducible reasons and well-considered motives. Unlike the multitudes who live in an atmosphere of fear and endure the fascination of hope, he is free from such perturbations of the heart. His passions are disciplined, flexible, or submissive; those of the masses are rebellious, stubborn, and indomitable.

IV

1. The ellipse's second focus of concentration is given, in chronological terms, by the theoretical practices of French Jacobinism, through the use (completely backwards relative to Spinoza) of fear and hope, which now, from the revolutionary vantage point of emancipation, are no longer seen as enemies but as auxiliaries of reason. They are not yet seen as instruments for subjugating the masses but as spurs of the autonomy of individuals and peoples. The paradoxical Jacobin "despotism of liberty" – as a vehicle of political and moral progress – institutionalizes these two passions (strengthening the hope or fear) and redistributes the roles of others in an attempt to rationalize them according to universal principles and make them become, over time, drivers of both spontaneous behaviours and reflections. With Jacobinism (which, however brief and fulminant its trajectory might have been, can be considered here almost as an archetype of modern political movements of radical emancipation), power changes into terror, clarified by a reason that is armed and supported by a collective will that is concentrated in the hands of a few men. Simultaneously, revolutionary hope transforms into a secular faith in the regeneration of future humanity and into religious faith that establishes, by decree, the existence of the Supreme Being and the immortality of the soul. An otherworldly guarantee thus rewards the citizen's "virtue," remunerating his sacrifice to the general interest. The semi-spontaneous "great fear" in the summer of 1789 and the "great hope" that cut through all phases of the revolution were translated into political and religious forms at the same time. Unlike Spinoza, who derives politics from the essence of man insofar as it is *cupiditas* (of which the passions are an irremovable expression), the Jacobins want to compress and shape this essence across politics and "virtue."

The heroic Jacobin fury was born in the face of the fragility and impotence of goodness to materialize, which raised organized terror to a therapeutic instrument of "regeneration." The "altars of fear" were erected beside those of "reason" and those of hope. Fear and hope in the afterlife were secularized, producing, for the considerable poor masses, both condensed expectations of the fulfilment of the ancient "dream of a thing," and intensification of horror in the face of the world's then-present state of the world – true hell on earth.

From that point, the gaze would begin to turn – on a grand scale and on the part of the countless masses – to the map of the future, the place where hopes are realized through politics. The experience and awareness of hundreds of millions of men and women would be substantially modified by politics in the arc of the most recent eight generations, emphasizing the idea of man no longer as a creature, but as a historical "creator" of himself.[27]

The revolution professed to call back to life existences that were disheartened and oppressed. It made the appeal, calling on everyone to emerge from passivity and trying to break up forever the mechanisms that had produced it. The revolution intended to contrast what de Tocqueville pointed to as the unavoidable destiny of modern egalitarian democracy, which strips its citizens "of all common passions, mutual necessities, need of a common understanding, opportunity for combined action: it ripens them, so to speak, in private life."[28] The Jacobins' struggle was that of moving the problem of will and the passions from the private and individual sphere to the public and collective one. It was no longer asked – positively – what pushes the individual to prefer this rather than that, or which passion impedes him from being fully free and rational. Rather, it was asked – negatively – which impediments might rein in the rationality of choices and might favour the triggering of the passions and selfishness. The revolution intended to create the "new man" not so much through the endogenous or exogenous element of the passions, but through eliminating the conditioning and the obstacles that induce socially harmful inequalities, the impotence or overbearing nature of acting, illusions, and conflicts.

27 For the rise of this political figure, see T. Schabert, *Der Mensch als Schöpfer: Formen und Phasen revolutionären Denkens in Franckreich 1762–1794* (Munich, 1971), 13–15.

28 A. de Tocqueville, *L'Ancien Régime et la Révolution*, in *Oeuvres complètes*, bk. 2, translated as *The Old Regime and the Revolution* (New York, 1856), viii.

2. Looking back at events, it is impossible not see the extent to which the twentieth century (particularly its first half) was characterized by the flowering of great collective hopes and the diffusion of indescribable fears. There was a desire to put into practice plans of social engineering and imposed morals in an attempt to "scientifically" produce the "new order" and the "new man." Entire populations and parts of the planet were engaged in that tragic and exhilarating undertaking that should have been brought to completion through a just and inevitable violence intended as a temporary means rather than as an end in itself (through this, modern democracies and even the rights of man received a baptism of blood). We must not forget, even viewing it indirectly (reflected in the mirror of history), the horrifying head of Medusa, under whose sign the achievements and failures of the present grew. Only this way can we avoid a static and fetishistic concept of the democratic "rules of the game" – those norms that simply must be respected and applied (which is, however, necessary) and not, instead (and indissolubly), a temporary arrival point that must be defended and must not be given up, establishing other formal rules for their own later, non-guaranteed development. Today, these hopes seem for the most part to have collapsed and have been rapidly replaced by other expectations. After the fall of the "god who failed," and the discredit that struck the great projects of collective transformation, there dominates – not without psychologically and politically plausible reasons – a hyper-realistic reason under the sign of a "principle of responsibility" and a "heuristics of fear" that should replace the "principle of hope." That is, the question is no longer how to reach the "supreme good," but how we might avoid the supreme danger of life's destruction within the thin layer of the biosphere.[29]

Shifting the political Acheron, we seek to show how, during the years of the French Revolution, the modern knots of reason-violence and reason-passions might have formed and how the task of loosening those links, without any Thermidor of oblivion, may have become theoretically and practically urgent.

3. The reasons for this approach (itself "elliptical") will be clarified in the construction and the arc of the discussion.

Spinoza and the Jacobins, respectively, stand at the beginning and end of criticism of the absolutist state, but they are at the antipodes of the

---

29 See H. Jonas, *Das Prinzip Verantwortung* (Frankfurt, 1979); Ital. trans. *Il principio responsabilità* (Torino, 1989), 34 et seq.

evaluation of the *moi soleil*,[30] both as a subject of sovereignty and as a morally responsible individual or citizen. For the Dutch philosopher, every man, as a "desirous animal," can realize himself through the maximum expansion of his own *utilitas*, which does not isolate him from society, but neither does it lead him to make fulfilment of his own *vis existendi* correspond with it or to consider the state as the incarnation of reason. The problem that bothers Spinoza – one that had already struck Étienne de la Boétie and that, at the height of the French Revolution, would amaze Jacques Necker *comme une idée presque mystique*[31] – hinges on why the majority of men might accept sacrificing their lives, their goods, and the goods of others (going against their own most obvious interests) to unilaterally benefit other individuals for whom they often make the final sacrifice – namely, monarchs who follow their passions (ambition, avidity, or thirst for glory) or the authority from which they generally receive more harm than benefit. Spinoza's response consists of saying that until some individual or group accumulates enough power to impose themselves on others, every outrage over such sacrifices is in vain. The only remedy to such a situation consists of forming a coalition of citizens to reach, together, a common power that can impede every excessive imbalance among its components.

In fact, in their brief experiment, the Jacobins – who implicitly would have accepted this solution – follow a diametrically opposite path. Instead of eliminating fear and hope from the individual and collective horizon, they consolidate it. Instead of transforming the passions, they divide them (both fighting the cold and calm ones tied to "selfishness" and indifference, and praising the hot, torrid, or "icy" ones tied to friendship, brotherhood, and love for country and humanity, or to hate and terror). Instead of making a "meditation on life," like Spinoza, they return to a "meditation on death," reproducing, in tragic circumstances, the classical nexus between death and reason. Instead of seeking security and happiness in the individual's arc of existence, they differentiate them and project them in an ideal of the stable bliss of generations to come (buttressing this ideal in the present by means of a new "theological-political" tyranny and by making the moral effort tolerable through praise of frugality and self-limiting one's needs and desires). Virtue ends up being a duty and not the sign of an achieved satisfaction.

30 For the expression, see A.J. Krailsheimer, *Studies in Self-Interest: From Descartes to La Bruyère* (Oxford, 1962), 7.

31 J. Necker, *Du pouvoir exécutif dans les Grand États* (Paris, 1792), 20 et seq.

The characteristics of fear and hope vary as a function of the role attributed to reason and its traditional representative, the wise man. In Spinoza, this figure, although distancing himself from isolation and apathy, did not participate directly in politics, nor did he judge the premeditated use of the passions as an instrument suited to consolidation of rationality and the democratic regime. With the Jacobin model, philosophical wisdom merges with the passions. It becomes ideology, as the marriage between reason and passions, between philosophy and common sense, between political heads and the masses. In its attempt to influence nascent public opinion, the distinction between truth and opinion, between reason and desire, diminishes almost to the point of disappearing. From the figure of wisdom, we pass to what I would like to call the modern *homo ideologicus*, who uses or believes he is using the passions as a last resort with the benefit of reason, orienting – according to "rational myths" full of conscious illusions and serially constructed hopes – the same population that had previously been guided by "passionate myths." The wise Spinoza (who had rejected fear and hope) is now transformed into a politician-agitator-philosopher, into an "intellectual" who works on their behalf on reason and society – with the purpose, however, of extending to the entire social corpus the freedom and happiness that Spinoza assigned to the *sapiens*.

Spinoza and the Jacobins stand at the beginning of two opposing perspectives of democracy. The Dutch philosopher based recognition of the right of individuals to political self-determination on real power that, from time to time, is collectively followed by the political body. The French revolutionaries based it on universal principles of human emancipation that establish a plan and marching orders to be practised across long and difficult times and that presuppose either a rigid mould or the individual's adaptation to the "general will." On the one hand, this requires a virtue that reshapes itself from moment to moment through an affirmation of itself and of its own *utilitas* and the development of a rationality that is not disturbed by the passions or by intensification of joy. On the other, it requires an ethics that presumes, at least at first (through reprising ancient models of republican virtue), abnegation of the individual, sacrifice of the present, and deferral of happiness. Rejecting every propensity to asceticism and the renunciation of oneself, Spinoza shows the way for a democracy that is not exclusively "formal" – that is, for an individuality that does not infer its rights only from universal principles or laws (which, however indispensable, could come into conflict with each other) but rather, from the level that one's own "power of existing" has reached in relation to, and in political coalition with, one's fellow creatures.

V

1. After examination of the problems' two points of concentration, there follows the examination of the foci of irradiation. This means, on one hand, that a conceptual and historical sequence must be constructed backwards, one that throws a "glancing light" on the basis of Spinoza's thought and on the convictions of the Jacobins. On the other, it means the questions thus raised are projected forward and compared critically (mostly in an implicit way) with some significant positions of contemporary ethics.

The ellipse's first focus of irradiation consists of examining the ways of treating the passions in the development of ethical strategies. Confronted with the normal failure of reason or will in an attempt to get a handle on the passions through commands or obligations, some theories come to be considered insufficient – or practicable only at an individual and social cost that is very high or with benefits that are very low. These are ethics based on discipline and the rigid norms of universal nature, those that try to dominate the uncertainty of the passions through the calculation or local evaluation of relationships of strength and of concrete situations; the more tolerant line of "temperament" and of "paternal" education of the passions; and the search for compensation in the future and in the afterlife for renunciation of the needs and temptations of the present and of this world.

Theoretically and historically, Spinoza's position is placed in relation to his most explicit polemical objectives: the inflexible ethical rigour of the Stoics and the most nuanced positions of the Neostoics (broad space is reserved for both, particularly with regard to analysis of the figures of Seneca and Justus Lipsius and the treatment of subjects such as constancy and steadfastness in the face of pain, torture, and death and for the tragic conflict between individual conscience and political-religious power). Spinoza's position is also placed in relation to Cartesian revenge, in the environment of a medicine of the body and soul, of the primacy of will over the passions that would "generally be important" and would "dispose the soul to desire the things that nature tells us are useful": training itself to control the passions and learning the "good use" for them. "Even the weakest souls" – although conditioned by prenatal passions developed at the fetal level (joy, sadness, love, hate) – would be capable of guiding their own existence.[32]

32 See Descartes, *Les passions de l'âme,* in *Œuvres,* ed. C. Adam and P. Tannery (Paris, 1897–1913), new presentation (Paris, 1964), art. 52.

However, also discussed (in themselves and in their virtual impact on Spinoza's philosophy) are the ethics of Platonic origin that pursue "temperance" or measuring of the passions; those of Aristotelian origin based on virtues, the golden mean, and the educability of the passions; and, finally (taking seriously the uncertainty of reasons for acting), those that bifurcate. These latter split, on one hand, in the direction of the Ignatian *amor mortis*, the "rumination of the passions," spiritual exercises, Jesuit probabilism, and the theories of simulation and dissimulation (the passions are thus analysed as expression – that is, to the extent they are reflected or concealed in the face, in gestures, or in conduct: the case examined most closely is that of Baltasar Gracián). On the other hand, these ethics pursue the sceptical doubt in Montaigne and the Pascalian assumption of risk through the rationalization of hope, fear, and expectation. Pascal shows the establishment of a "civil war" between the passions and reason, of a struggle that presupposes the identity between them and an identity that endlessly reproduces the schism. For the first time, reason explicitly takes on the cross of the passions' conflicting character. In compensation, however, these also cease to be completely opaque. In fact, as is clearly spelled out in a pamphlet authoritatively attributed to Pascal, the *Discours sur les passions de l'amour*, love and reason are inseparable, and it is wrong "to portray love as a blind man. It is necessary to remove the bandage from him and restore the joy of his eyes."[33] Abandoning the solitude of the "hateful *I*," love accepts the "great void" in the world and tries to tame it in an undefined process where it is reborn in every moment.[34] Like reason, it now shows itself to be baseless, and it is as much stronger as it is more fragile. Ambition – love of oneself – is base love, turned in upon itself, barricaded in a false security, incapable of betting on and accepting the risk of the present.

2. The ellipse's second, and problematic, focus – the one not named previously – consists of the idea of "intellectual love" (or, to a lesser degree, of reason innervated by liberating passions), here presented according to a very specific connotation. This love must not be understood either in an emotional sense or as mere harmony, sweetness, or peace (as "food of the heart"), but as a simultaneously emotional-cognitive structure: knowledge that moves and movement that knows, an open structure, at once subversive and healing, endowed with special ways

33 See Pascal, *Discours sur les passions de l'amour*, in *Œuvres complètes*, ed. J. Chevalier (Paris, 1954), 545.

34 Ibid., 541: *Il est toujours naissant.*

of understanding and acting on (in a Spinozan manner) the *transitiones* – that is, for resolving conflicts through innovative solutions that may increase rationality without mutilating the inventive power of desire.

In this sense, love is intransigent and indulgent, binding and emancipating, destabilizing and full of hope. It becomes *pathos* of reason, "fire in the mind of men," a premise of solidarity among equals during religious and political revolutions. In essence, it brings together the sword and the olive branch, the guillotine and brotherhood. It can always become corrupt, but it appears – at least in moments of the most intense individual and social transformation – more gratifying than the *rigor mortis* of petrified laws, extinguished traditions, confused compromises, and responses that do not correspond to collective expectations.

Although often underestimating the problem of fragmentation of moral values and the conflict between the various authorities that issue them, the order of love, in continual metamorphosis, does not resign itself to remaining ensnared among those that appear to be inextricably tangled, even if it is fully conscious of the constraints placed on innovation (i.e., it knows that it is demanded that the individual struggle inventively to understand the specificity of situations and, consequently, to act: faced with a specific choice, no handbook of rules is sufficient). Love thus opens the obtuse rigour of limiting rules without removing their character of universality; it resolves disagreements without humiliation or bargaining, avoiding leaving a perpetual contentiousness behind it. It shows the boundaries of the individual dimension just as it expands that dimension's power. It heals the lacerations and the *double bind* of will, dethroning it – not in favour of divine grace but of more satisfying criteria of conduct, aimed towards increasing joy. It proceeds beyond laws and justice without suppressing them as such and without attributing to them any supererogatory character. On the contrary, it implements them and makes them creative, multiplying their effects. (Justice assumes giving to each his own, the *unicuique suum tribuere*, the exchange of equals. Love, loosening itself from this logic, assumes an excess: with it, the more given, the more received.)[35]

The Spinozan logic of *amor intellectualis* is juxtaposed both with that of the passions, which tend towards an analogous generalization, and with that of reason, which elaborates universals that can be known with

35 Even in other cultural traditions, it is not necessary to juxtapose love and justice directly, to the extent it is, itself, "creative justice." See P. Tillich, *Love, Power, Justice* (Oxford, 1954), 71.

certainty but cannot yet articulate itself in the concrete cognition of the *res particulares*. It indirectly belies the widespread conception that the passions constitute uncontrollable energies, released as a result of the impact with specific events and contexts and strictly bound to them as their origin. Spinoza's position seems, rather, to confirm an intuition, arising from something in the field of "bi-logics."[36] In this latter, the passions assume the character of universality instead of specificity, to the extent that every emotion, transcending the determined scope of its motivations, refers back to an "infinite set" – that is, to a general class of events and of assimilable situations. In turn, reason – as an organ *par excellence* of "asymmetrical" universality thanks to ideas, concepts, and principles – comes, on the contrary, to acquire a nature analogous to that which Spinoza attributes to "intellectual love": that is, of being individualizing faculties, knowledge of "particular things."

Some examples, dealt with in the sphere of "symmetric logic," will help clarify the point. Every particular passion (fear, rage, sadness, love) carries the element of exaggeration, of "excess" or "delirium," that had induced many philosophers – from the Stoics to Descartes and beyond – to consider it as its principal characteristic. Thus, indiscriminately, all the possible faceless dangers that torment us come together in our fear of the dark, in our anger over the destruction of something we desire or the loss of an expected good or advantage. The accumulated frustrations, discontent, and disappointments over the unpleasant surprises that life has held for us and that we fear it still holds vent themselves instantly in an aggressive way. In the sadness derived from a specific circumstance that has happened to us, all the sadness of the world suddenly preciptates,

36 I am referring to the implications of "bi-logic" of Ignacio Matte Blanco, who frames the "emotions" within the "symmetrical logic" of the unconscious, which abolishes not only every "asymmetric" contradiction and distinction, but also every element of singularity. That is, like in a dream, A – who is the father of B – can present himself "symmetrically" as his son, and just as, in him, the causal and temporal relations can reverse themselves and end up equivalent (repeating the images of Freud: the hare shoots the hunter or a subsequent event happens in precedence, like a bad actor who falls in the scene before the trigger of the pistol is drawn), so in love, for example, all the differences and the separations invert themselves and disappear: two people feel interchangeable with each other, cancelling in this way the special and temporal distances between them, basing themselves on the desire for a single body and soul. But emotion also cancels the specificity of the situations, transforming an episode that is singular and narrow in its generality, in the "infinite sets" or in the class that includes all the possible analogous episodes. See I. Matte Blanco, *The Unconscious as Infinite Sets: An Essay on Bi-Logic* (London, 1975).

tinging every event with its tragic colouring and modifying the perception that a little earlier or later we would have judged with a different heart. Finally, in love, every perfection and every promise of happiness crystallizes in the loved being so that – for example – in every individual woman one loves all women or even love itself. Passion tends to become *ab-soluta*, loosened from the context of immediate relevance and capable of capturing, making collapse, or disintegrating anything that crosses its orbit, generating a confused order as powerful as it is paradoxical.

Active passion reactivates, exasperates, stirs up, and "earthquakes" all those that had previously sedimented, modifying the now unconscious "gyroscopic" orientations of action and character, invisible but not inert. It invokes them instantly, clearing their differences and their history, sharpening their intensity, and increasing their specific weight in the moment that functions as a detonator of deeper charges. In this sense, the passions are absorbent and tyrannical, clear to excess but not distinct, capable of "enlarging" their objects but not of focusing on them in their peculiarity. They are not at all blind, as the popular proverbs say.[37] If anything, they see too well, since they overflow the context, taking on whatever would "rationally" be beyond and outside what is otherwise held to be pertinent (from this comes the effect of being dazzled by too much light). The attribute of blindness derived from the passions comes from the fact that for millennia, rage was considered paradigmatic,[38] while patience and perseverance were its antidotes (nearly synonyms of dilatory virtue, self-control, and quiet wisdom).

Any object of passion and every person, thing, ideal, or event is substantially a vehicle, symbol, or opportunity that refers back to the universal. This causes instantaneous conversion of the whole genre into the individual case, thus emphasizing the "surplus" or showy residue, present in all the passions, that never ceases to scandalize reason because of the "evident" excess of instantaneous emotional reaction compared to the magnitude of the cause that generated it.[39]

"Passion," then, seems to function as a synecdoche with a logic (or a rhetoric) of the *pars pro toto* but also of its symmetric opposite, the *totum*

37 For example, "affection blinds reason" and "rage, madness, love, the shortest is the best." See J.-L. Flandrin, *Les amours paysans (*XVIe–XIXe *siècles)* (Paris, 1975).

38 Beyond being the canonical passion of antiquity, rage has once again become a centre of attention through a "*timica*" or "semiotics of the passions." See A.J. Greimas, "De la colère: Étude de sémantique lexicale," in *Du sens* II: *Essais sémiotiques* (Paris, 1983), 225–46.

39 This convergence corresponds symmetrically to the "radiation" by which from the individual fact one passes to its generalizing extension in a class with which one identifies.

pro parte. On the other hand, "reason" circumscribes and distinguishes, bringing the passionate event back (almost in the sense of Spinozan "intuitive science") to adequate understanding of the particular cause and avoiding an indiscriminate mix of good and bad. It could be said that because of this, "passion" is equalizing, condensing, and "symbolic" (because etymologically, it "throws together," "puts together," or "stores up"), while "reason" is distinguishing, analytical, and distributive.[40] The core problem is whether it is possible or desirable (and under what conditions, times, circumstances, and places) that one of the two logics tries to destroy or subject the other, or whether it might not be better to identify, in each field, each one's optimal forms of expression, separated either by gradation or reciprocal hybridization. Might not reason become stronger the larger its active involvement (and not its separation) is in the world of the passions and "desires," the more it becomes strengthened by *cupiditas*, the more it is susceptible to rebalancing the other logic in a superior, more hospitable order, while preserving its distinctive traits? And conversely, might not the opposite be seen more easily? That is, might not passions and desires appear more "reasonable" once they have been elaborated by a "reason" that does not pretend to uproot them, but that respects their physiognomy and motives and that places itself in their path as they place themselves in its – introducing a history of vicissitudes into their apparent neutrality?

3. Although being, as experience demonstrates, a remedy that rarely appears effective in the course of the history of large human aggregates, intellectual love offers a model of "trans-logic" or of logic of furthering (*ulteriorità*), making a sort of bridge between the "symmetrical logic" of the passions and the "asymmetrical" logic of rational thought. In fact, it is capable of completing transitions to a greater *cupiditas* (i.e., towards that suitable "knowledge of things in particular" of which Machiavelli speaks),[41] because it is not content with fetishistically respecting the inert universal of the law, whose strength is presumed. It does not place itself on this side of the universal, but beyond it.

Something analogous happens in grammatical and syntactic rules, where someone who possesses *competence* in them can produce myriad *performances* or unpredictable sentences. But in our case, it is ethically relevant cognitive and affective acts performed at the same time. If one is capable, he can enucleate from "codes" the most remote, latent, and

40 Because of this, perhaps, passion and rush of feeling are also related to artistic expression, even if they many not cancel its formal, ordering, selective, and "polished" side.

41 *D* I, 47, 236.

unimagined possibilities. Consequently, one is not merely forced but supported and directed by the ties between assimilable norms and the universal norms of grammar for speakers who learn a foreign language. At the beginning, they endure them as impositions whose meaning they cannot yet grasp. However, once they have learned to make use of them in a loose and fluid way, they transform the previous passivity into activity. In the end, the element of constriction no longer belongs to the nature of the rule, which breaks off and becomes independent of it. In fact, they absorb the premise of the freedom to construct many individual sentences that are true (or at least "well formed") in that creativity does not occur through the violation of the linguistic code's objectivity, but through the most knowledgeable and bold use of it. In this sense, intellectual love could be imagined as the *parole* of that *langue* that is reason, with its norms that are already codified and understood to the letter.

Someone who has firmly accepted and elaborated the law to the point of "somatizing" it does not need to cling to it anxiously. He is nimble, free, and innovative, precisely because he does not feel any compulsory need to deny it. In fact, he not only feels obligated and constrained by it but also supported and guided by rules that have finally become operational, capable of removing him from his own will, precisely while they open spaces of unforeseen intervention (even placing him face to face with the problem of how to organize such an excess of meaning).

Love does not require burying one's own talents or proceeding to a pure exchange of equivalents (nor does it require entering into a spiral of negative retaliation in which one evil is exchanged for an even bigger one: revenge). Rather, it desires that talents multiply themselves, that the exchange grows on its own, possibly producing "richness" and reciprocal advantage. It is supererogatory, even in an etymological sense. *Supereorgatio* means, in fact, to pay more than is owed. It is therefore different from simple *paying off*, in the sense of "purchasing."[42] But in Spinoza, this love does not at all imply the sacrifice of oneself but, on the contrary, maximum self-affirmation. In this, the separate currents

42 This can be seen in the gospel of Luke, 10:35, where the Good Samaritan – after having paid two denarii for the care of a man robbed and wounded – says to him: "When I come back, I will repay you whatever more you spend (*quodcumque supererogaveris*)." See D. Heyd, *Supererogation: Its Status in Ethical Theory* (Cambridge, 1982), 7 et seq. It is a choice, not an obligation. Unlike the Greek virtue, from the *arête* that is "excellence" and therefore is not subject to increase, Christian virtue is open and tends, more than to moderation, to excesses: "Greek self-affirmation is replaced by Christian abnegation" (see Heyd, 37).

of activity and passivity, of knowledge and emotion, of the "hot" and the "cold" of the passions and of reason come together (within a socializing dimension, such that intellectual love reveals the one-sidedness both of universalistic claims that oppress individuality and individualistic claims that profess to assert themselves in a petty manner through rejection of the highest forms of desire).[43]

The results of Spinoza's research into the role of the passions, reason, and intellectual love contrast substantially – "radially" – with all the other exemplary positions present in the story of ethics. Explicitly or implicitly, they oppose the separation of the intellect from love, the mind from the body, will from desire, and altruism from love for oneself. Spinoza intends to lead men towards happiness and fullness through clear rejection of *amor mortis*, melancholy, *vanitas*, and the feeling of transience, arguing in favour of "meditation on life," also because it is happiness that produces virtue and not vice versa. For Spinoza, we do not enjoy because we repress our desires, but we are capable of holding in check the less satisfying ones and ordering them according to a hierarchy of choices that are ethically more elevated and autonomous when (and because) we enjoy that which most fulfils us. For this reason, however, his *cupiditas* is still supported and guided by a sound plan aimed at reaching that which one knows to be the greatest happiness (or, better, satisfaction or *acquiescentia*) for man: wisdom. It is not animated, then, by the logic of the incommensurate and dissident desire that shines through the multiple and changing aspirations of so many of the men of contemporary societies (Spinoza knows that for most of them, the happiness achieved is precious little).

In attempting to reconcile – without confusing – the two traditions of thought that have separated *amor* from the *intellectus*, the solution put forth here also indirectly involves a different image of philo-sophy, as love of knowledge, activity of thought tied to the dimension of the *philia*, often neglected to the exclusive advantage of the *sophia*. The decisive role carried out by *cupiditas* in its ascendant process towards rational joy is opposed, then, to "thanatosophy," to the wisdom that (from Plato to Heidegger) traditionally derives from *meditatio mortis*.

43 From this point of view, the ancient and pagan element of "utility" without abnegation (a concept dear to Descartes and to Hobbes, among others) is inserted by Spinoza both in the dynamic of the *plus ultra* moral philosophy exploited by Christianity, and into the new forms of mentality and emerging knowledge on the part of mercantile and active societies, directed towards the progress and advancement of the sciences.

Thus, Spinoza's *amor intellectualis* (which reveals itself in concrete things, in perfect conformity with the laws of necessity) and revolutionary "fire" (dictated by intransigent and despotic love for justice and for the ideals of emancipation from political oppression and of liberation from need) provide the outline for placing under discussion the general notions of "passion," "desire," "happiness," and "instrumental use of the passions" – for getting to the root of classifications and oppositions often accepted uncritically, creating the theoretical bases for a double revision of the concepts of reason and passion.

It is necessary to take seriously the image of the ellipse and its two "foci." This means, first, that such a geometric figure organizes the subjects according to a gravitational field that holds them tightly conjoined despite their difference, so that there results from it a single and organic treatment within a book rigorously articulated in interdependent parts. Second, it means that there is not expressed here a simple option in favour of Spinoza (of *securitas*, of the modern exponential growth of desires or the negation of hope) and against the Jacobins (or, more generally, against a sacrificial conception of ethics justified by the expectation of a better world). In fact, it is not a case of praising one of the two solutions to the detriment of the other or of mediating them abstractly in the search for improbable reconciliations or points of balance. If the adopted theoretical choice proceeds without question in the direction of an ethics far from renunciation and sacrifice, social repression, and individual transgression, this does not mean that it ignores the fact that the majority of men continue even today to live in insecurity, need, and fear, nor that sacrifices are often imposed by circumstances on which goodwill has little hold, by the bitter humiliations of history. Nor does it ignore, finally, the great merit of the Jacobins in undertaking an experiment that we know today to have failed as a response but whose questions we must still consider to be unavoidable and, in part, unavoided.

All of the problems noted, and those still to be developed, help reformulate the frame of the categories we are accustomed to using, and they throw more light (through a theoretical undertaking that presumes articulated, well-organized, historical, and semantic investigation) on a complex of ethical and political questions that today acquire new meaning and that should be examined in their specificity. That is, we are led to ask ourselves more directly about the opposition between the increased search for happiness and the inevitability of certain sacrifices and disappointments; between moral consistency and the assumption, with reservation, of commitments that can be continuously renegotiated; between responsibility for the present and actions favouring generations to come;

between different orientations towards desires that are imponderable and partly "superfluous" and priority demands for the satisfaction of basic needs for survival; between the old landscape of passions and desires and the new one that is about to be redesigned by biotechnologies, now capable of upsetting and damaging even the pluri-millennial rocky base of familial relationships (e.g., how will passions and feelings change because of the already noticeable effects of artificial insemination, in the absence of a living or identifiable father, and what will the results be of the spread of the figure of the surrogate mother, of euthanasia, and of the cloning of organ transplants?); between the necessity of loosening the disturbing Jacobin knots of freedom and despotism, of justice and violence, and the creation of real material resources and ideals that might contribute to allowing billions of men to escape scarcity, oppression, and traditional or induced ignorance through the instrumental use of the means of mass communication; between life plans of individuals of limited existence and political and religious projections towards distant and eternal goals (with the consequent renunciations of enjoyment of the present and the massive investment of meaning in events situated beyond the visible and imaginable horizons). These are questions, of course, of frightening complexity, and yet they are impossible to avoid and their silent *memento* must not be forgotten by philosophy today, even when it does not talk about it.

The itinerary of thought put forth in this volume tries to open a passage between the positions and concerns only alluded to up to this point. This does not happen through inadmissible attempts to revive ideas of the past (even if the classic ones may be like vigorous stumps from which new shoots branch out every season) but, on the contrary, through measuring their distances with exactitude with respect to the tasks of the present, making the differences sharper and identifying, in knots yet to be loosened, the problematic points from which to begin new reflections.

Into the analysis of "classic" themes of the history of thought, therefore, is woven the argumentative thread of peaceful and discrete polemic against every form of rigid control, repressive containment, and simple moral or religious debasement of the passions; against every absurd apology for absolutist will; against the preconceived, ready-made opposition between cold and hot passions, between egoism and altruism. However, rejected are the compromises, the Pilate-like softness of moral *deregulation*, and "Dionysian" attitudes (that have characterized recent decades and that are founded on mere transgressiveness of desire and the emphasis of impulses and passionate forces that become evasive, intoxicating, and dilatory in their pretext of casting "the heart beyond the obstacle").

The project pursued here aims at an ethics (inevitably as distant from that of Spinoza as it is from that of the Jacobins) that would not bureaucratically harden principles and rules, but nor would it recede behind the lines of rationality, towards the case-by-case, empirical, or opportunistic solutions, or purely arbitrary preferences. In other words, this plan of research tends towards an ethics and a philosophy that might tighten and not loosen the relationships with the factors of universality. However, this also requires the elaboration of a logic of furthering (*logica dell'ulteriorità*) that is credibly tied to an affective reopening of the mind in the direction of a world where every objective unit of measure of values and actions inevitably seems to have failed. Thus, there is a difficult theoretical task and a still longer journey that must still be completed. It would require, however, ensuring that such an ethics – and the logic of the singularity that orients it – does not reject either the innovative and regenerative power of desire or the demands of norms but is also conscious of the fact that every universality arises and forms through conflicts and inequalities, and also considers the different modalities in which the passions are elaborated and expressed (because the great cultures of our planet have not yet really met, and so the universality we are thinking of here risks preserving provincial traits, even when it appears hegemonic, and of generating, in reaction, particularism as its evil twin). If this picture were complete, the passions would appear as symbolic and expressive forms transmitted and refined (in their own way) by specific traditions and not, on the contrary, as simple impulses that are natural, primitive, and immutable. Consequently, they would not have any absolute need of being only repressed or elevated to the sublime realm of magnificent or merciful reason, but understood and elaborated in depth (today, for the most part, through the prevailing method of desire).

Except for the elimination of some misprints, this book is the same as the fourth (Italian) edition of 1994. The framework still seems to me to be solid, and the incidental bibliographical additions, however conspicuous, would not modify it. I note just two essays in which I further developed some of the topics addressed here: "Il rosso, il nero, il grigio: Il colore delle moderne passioni politiche," in *Storia delle passioni,* ed. S. Vegetti Finzi (Rome-Bari, 1995), 315–55; and "Passione e ragione: Come le spiega l'Encyclopédie di Diderot e D'Alembert; Come le riscrive Remo Bodei," in *Le parole nel tempo: Ventisei voci dell'Encyclopédie riscritte nel Duemila,* ed. D. De Masi and D. Pepe (Milan, 2001), 325–35.

Pisa, December 2002

PART 1: PASSIONS OF EXPECTATION

1. The Disorder of the Passions

The Atmosphere of the Soul

At the beginning of his *Political Treatise,* Spinoza establishes an indirect parallel between the passions that modify and act upon human beings and the phenomena, even the unpleasant ones, that characterize the atmosphere: "I have regarded human emotions such as love, hatred, anger, envy, pride, pity, and other agitations of the mind not as vices of human nature but as properties pertaining to it in the same way as heat, cold, storm, thunder, and such pertain to the nature of the atmosphere."[1]

However unexplainable, unruly, capricious, or disturbing they might appear at first glance, the passions – wisely observed – not only reveal an intelligible story and a consistent articulation, but they can also become the object of an agreeable show. Behind their chaos, we discover a precise order. Within their imperceptible or sudden swerves and excesses, there is a cogent logic; in their sometimes frightening aspect, there is a specific beauty. There is reserved, for those who may be capable of penetrating their covering, not only the joy that knowledge traditionally bestows but also the satisfaction of contemplating, from the point of view of a "meteorological science" of the heart, the varied landscape of their metamorphoses against the background of the theoretical horizon of necessity.

1 *TP* 1.4. In *Meteorologica,* Aristotle had already spoken of the *pathe* of nature with regard to thunder, hurricanes, earthquakes, and drought. See *Meteor.* 363a, 382a, and passim, generally understanding *pathos* as the "quality according to which alteration is possible" (*Met.* 1022b15–16).

The passions offer the most convincing testimony of the fact that "man" is not master of himself, let alone of the world. Even if accustomed by now to considering himself an "empire within an empire"[2] – citizen of an extra-territorial *regnum hominis* with respect to the rest of the universe – he discovers himself, through the passions, to be instead rigidly subjected to nature, the only thing that is truly free. Conditionings of every sort, they shape him like "clay in the hands of the potter."[3] To imagine escaping from them, the laws of this world remaining firm, appears as absurd and undesirable as living under an eternally calm sky. Recognizing the inevitable power of the passions (incommensurably larger than all of nature over every man) does not, in itself, imply the preventative acceptance of a servitude that is irredeemable and always the same. To be able to free himself from absolute passivity with respect to the passions, it is at least necessary to admit (preliminarily) their supremacy. Reducing our excessive pretences of control and self-control with respect to the passions, we paradoxically multiply the chances of success in confronting them. We also discover in the imagination a side of *potentia* that consists of the capacity to evoke absent things (see *E*, especially 17, schol.).

The child also grows until reaching stages where subordination to external causes diminishes, though without ceasing, and awareness of self grows, though without ever becoming complete.[4] In an analogous way, it is also possible to identify for adults the suitable path for a further "growth" that – elevating its *vis existendi* or *agendi* – might modify (in favour of individuals and of the collective) the inevitable equilibrium with respect to external causes and that may act as a barrier to our total ignorance of them.

There exists, between the level of dependence on the passions and the level of awareness reached, a relationship of inverse proportionality (i.e., the more that this grows, the more that decreases, and vice versa). However, wanting or planning such an increase in knowledge – which is, at once, an increase of happiness, "virtue," and even health – is not enough. Consequently, those who try to suffocate the passions through energetic intervention of the will or of reason, propelling or expunging them through the force of human nature, delude themselves. No one, not even the most wise, can be exempt from them completely and in

2 Spinoza, *E* 3, pref.; *TP* 2.6.
3 See *TTP* 16.*581* (note 34); *TP* 2.22; *Ep.* 75.900.
4 *E* 5.39, schol.

every moment. Those who try to bend the passions' violence or tenacity – exhorting, cursing, imploring, and making propitiatory gestures, instead of finding the means for reducing their impact and rootedness or possibly changing their disadvantages into advantages – resemble those who pretend to magically impose themselves on atmospheric phenomena – that is, impeding the variation of cold and warmth, of wet and dry, or prohibiting lightning from flashing and wind from blowing.

The Separate Empire

Spinoza marks the end of the Renaissance model of "man" as "microcosm," a being harmonically set within the whole and capable of embracing it, despite his own smallness. Such a man would have been able to reflect upon himself, in "sympathy," some fundamental changes of the structure of the world, transforming himself – through imagination and thought – into a "chameleon" capable of imitating all of its forms, while his heart, traditionally the seat of the passions, would have played the role of the "sun of the microcosm."[5] Instead, Spinoza considers mankind and every single individual only one part of the universe, inseparable from its processes, but lacking the faculty for reflecting it fully. Man must thus adapt himself both to the marginal role attributed by modern astronomy to the planet on which he lives, and to the idea of the ineluctable and anonymous necessity that governs all events. Illusions of an essentially unconditional freedom and of a Providence that benignly watches over the world are thus damaged. The philosopher turns to his reluctant readers, almost inviting them to renounce what, by now, appears to be a delusion of omnipotence and separateness, alternating in depressive phases of total inertia and self-denigration. Simple surrender to the passions and the obstinate desire to dominate them are complementary, and both end up rendering the slavery even more onerous. For each person in his own space and time, solidarity with the nature that lives in every thing, self-knowledge inserted into a thick network of necessary causal links, and the taking leave of Providential finalism present positive aspects that few are disposed to notice. Thus, even the apparently inexorable necessity of the passions presents itself to them, above all, as a sign of painful humiliation, impotence and chaos. Not

5 See Giovanni Pico della Mirandola, *Oratio de hominis dignitate*. For the human heart *sol Microcosmi*, like that of the animals, see W. Harvey, *Exercitatio anatomica de motu cordis et sanguinis in animalibus* (Francofurtii, 1628) (dedicated to King Charles I).

immediately identified and valued are the precious resources offered to those who might know how to understand that individuals can intervene in the processes of nature and modify them according to their (i.e., the resources') laws, exactly as men constitute part of nature or, even better, are nature themselves.

Spinoza's choice consists of finally decentralizing man and his conscience with respect to the totality of this world, purged of a personal God that looms over and directs him, in order to restore (through thought) the sense of man, of nature, as everything. Towards this end, he rejects, simultaneously, both anthropocentrism and theocentrism, denouncing those who ignore or obscure the relativity of their own point of view and who trust in superior beings as guarantors of an absolute physical and moral order.[6] Nonetheless, for Spinoza there is no fixed or unconnected order, nor any undisputed and untouchable hierarchy whose sacredness would be upset by human appetites and desires. Order and disorder, good and bad, justice and injustice are concepts lacking in value if they are not considered both from the perspective of those who judge them and from the moment when this happens. What is good for the wolf is bad for the lamb; what is order for some is disorder for others; what is justice for those who oppress is irrational power for those who are oppressed.

The question, at once naive and embarrassing, that could be posed to Spinoza is: for what reason did he write an *Ethics* if every point of view, for him, is relative? The provisional response rests on the observation that there exists for us, in effect, a point of view that is unavoidable and not arbitrary (the one in which we find ourselves: the point of view of man) and a criterion of moral preference that, in principle, may be shared by anyone (choosing that which best increases the power of existing – that is, at once, happiness, "virtue," and the satisfaction of one's own *utilitas*). The usual viewpoint is thus reversed, in that "we do not endeavor, will, seek after or desire because we judge a thing to be good. On the contrary, we judge a thing to be good because we endeavor, will, seek after and desire it."[7] It is desire, reaching its maximum awareness, that

6 It is no longer a case of denouncing the abuses of the imaginations of men, which may, in fact, forge the gods in their image and likeness, as much as showing as they incessantly and inevitably shape the entire world to their own passions. Knowledge presumes this unavoidable background, that can and must be refashioned, but not forgotten or abandoned.

7 *E* 3.9, schol.

produces for man an order that renews and reformulates itself under the guidance of the *amor Dei intellectualis.*

The "Universal Wolf"

Spinoza's distance from tradition may be calculated exactly through a comparison between some famous literary tests, in which different motives and fears come together just a few decades before the Dutch philosopher's birth. For example, Shakespeare's *Troilus and Cressida* describes, with effective incisiveness, the evil consequences of subversion of natural order because of the passions.

The cycle of disorder ends in the generalized conflict that sees, lined up in opposing camps, not only men and institutions but also the divisive factions of will and the teeming world of the passions and desires harboured in individuals. If this anarchy were to establish itself stably, bringing to an end its own work of corruption, "each thing meets/in mere oppugnancy: the bounded waters/should lift their bosoms higher than the shores,/ and make a sop of all this solid globe;/strength should be lord of imbecility,/and the rude son would strike his father dead."[8] Justice would then degrade into power and power into arbitrary acts, until it undergoes its final metamorphosis, reducing itself to "appetite," which would finally even tear itself apart, autophagically: "Force should be right; or rather, right and wrong,/(between whose endless jar justice resides),/should lose their names, and so should justice too./Then every thing includes itself in power,/power into will, will into appetite;/and appetite, an universal wolf,/(so doubly seconded with will and power),/must make perforce an universal prey,/and last eat up himself."[9] Touching bottom, the degradation thus dissolves in a *destructio destructionis.*

Fear of chaos – attributed to the collapse of the ancient and consolidated hierarchies and paralleling the rise of an individuality that affirms itself, triggering its own passions – spreads widely in England in this period, partly attributed to the diffusion of *New Philosophy,* partly derived from the political tensions connected to the beginning of the reign of James I. In fact, in 1611, just two years after the publication of *Troilus and Cressida,* John Donne states, in a justly famous move: "'Tis all in pieces, all coherence gone:/all just supply, and all relation:/prince, subject,

8 W. Shakespeare, *Troilus and Cressida,* act 1, scene 3, vv. 569–74 (Ulysses's speech to Agamemnon). Original edition published in 1609.

9 Ibid., vv. 575–83.

father, sonne, are things forgot,/for every man alone thinks he has got/ to be a Phoenix."[10] Each prefers his own judgment to that of the authorities, so in the end no comparison is possible, because, in the "discord and rude incongruity" of this universe, any sort of benchmark is lacking.

From the ashes of miserable hierarchies and from the remains left by the cannibalism of their appetites, individuals dream of being reborn in renewed form. If they were to look at the irreversibility of time, however, and at the progressive aging of the world and the vanity of all things, they would be struck, like Henry IV, by a melancholy and paralysing fear: "O God, that one might read the book of fate/and see the revolution of the times/make mountains level, and the continent,/weary of solid firmness, melt itself/into the sea, and other times to see/the beachy girdle of the ocean/too wide for Neptune's hips; how chances mocks/and changes fill the cup of alteration/with divers liquors! O, if this were seen,/the happiest youth, viewing his progress through,/ what perils past, what crosses to ensue,/would shut the book, and sit him down and die."[11]

The collapse of an absolute hierarchical order (projection of the human imagination), regret for the destruction of the prerogatives of rank, ethical nostalgia for the past, attachment to the "new philosophy" and to the triggering of individual appetites, melancholy vision of the transience of all things and the unstoppable deterioration of the universe: nothing could be more diametrically opposed to Spinozan theory.

Definitions and Limits

Since Spinoza is a rigorously systematic philosopher, in order to understand him it is necessary to take seriously the definitions of some key concepts, even at the cost of departing, somewhat pedantically, from the principal elements of his thought.

Of the forty-eight emotions that this Linnaeus of the passions considers in his *Ethics*, only three are fundamental: desire, sadness, and joy (*cupiditas, tristitia, laetitia*).[12] Desire, in its continuous variation in intensity

10 See J. Donne, "An Anatomy of the World: The First Anniversary," vv. 213–17, in *Poems of John Donne*, ed. J.C. Grierson (Oxford, 1963), vol. 1, 237–8. For a comment, see vol. 2, *Commentary*, 190. For the causes of this anarchy and the role of the New Philosophy, see C.M. Coffin, *John Donne and the New Philosophy* (New York, 1958).

11 W. Shakespeare, *Henry IV, Part 2*, act 3, scene 1, vv. 45–56.

12 See *E* 3.11, schol.; *E* 3 defs. of the emotions 4, expl.; 4.59, dem.

and orientation, is constitutive of man, who is pushed every moment by it towards the future. Sadness and joy, on the other hand, are passions through which the mind passes, respectively, in its *transitio* to a lesser or greater "power of existing." If desire may not subsequently expand because it encounters insurmountable impediments, it can turn its own strength back against itself, spiraling in a descending *tristitia*, or stabilizing on a relative maximum of *laetitia* or *acquiescentia*, in which it feels fulfilled thanks to intellectual love.[13]

Another notion that cannot be avoided is that of *conatus*, the effort "with which each thing endeavors to persist in its own being" for an indeterminate time.[14] When *conatus* "is related to the mind alone, it is called Will [*voluntas*]; when it is related to mind and body together, it is called Appetite [*appetitus*], which is therefore nothing else but man's essence, from the nature of which there necessarily follow those things that tend to his preservation, and which man is thus determined to perform. Further, there is no difference between appetite and Desire [*cupiditas*] except that desire is usually related to men insofar as they are conscious of their appetite. Therefore, it can be defined as follows: desire is 'appetite accompanied by the consciousness thereof.'"[15]

This *conatus* must be situated in the environment of a dynamic (and not just mechanical) contrast between forces of activity and forces of resistance internal to the nature of every single being. In man, the growth of *conatus* expresses the levels of his power of self-preservation that manifests itself, even in knowledge, according to three moments: imaginative, rational, and intuitive.[16] The passions are only the *verso* of the medal of imagination; on its *recto*, it bears inadequate and incomplete ideas, manifestations of the lowest level of knowledge, a *mutilata cognitio* (*E* 4.2).

---

13 We will return to all these points more fully later.

14 *E* 3.7–8. For *conatus* (a term that can be also translated as "force" or "power") and its original relationship with the idea of self-preservation, see, in the present volume, pp. 301–4. For its link with the hylozoic tradition and the notions of "activity" and "life," see H.A. Wolfson, *The Philosophy of Spinoza: Unfolding the Latent Process of His Reasoning* (Cambridge, MA, 1934; rpt., New York, 1960), vol. 2, 195 et seq.

15 *E* 3.9, schol.

16 On the imagination as the first kind of knowledge, see C. de Deugd, *The Significance of Spinoza's First Kind of Knowledge* (Assen, 1968); R.G. Blair, "Spinoza's Account of Imagination," in *Spinoza: A Collection of Critical Essays*, ed. M. Grene (Notre Dame, 1979), 318–28.

The passions as such do not depend, however, on purely psychological character traits, nor do they belong exclusively to the subjective and private sphere (inasmuch as they also delimit the field of politics, as we will see). Rather, they demonstrate the working preponderance of forces "external" or "internal" to the individual, towards which he appears passively malleable and of which he possesses an insufficiently or partially glimpsed idea.[17] Once understood, however, the passions can also be considered natural energies that are hypothetically at the disposition of those who know how to elaborate them. Thus, they cease being absolutely "intractable,"[18] because knowledge itself modifies them and strengthens the *appetitus.*[19]

With respect to the image he would later have of them, they are not characterized so much by spontaneity as by necessity or, to put it better, by a sort of paradoxical necessary spontaneity. Unlike what many philosophers thought and would think, for Spinoza the soul works always according to certain laws and shows itself *quasi aliquod automaton spiritualis.*[20]

The Powers of the Imagination

As for the side of the imagination, the nature of the passions does not depend on chance. If examined well, nothing in that nature ends up being arbitrary, since "inadequate and confused ideas follow by the same necessity as adequate, or clear and distinct, ideas."[21] Springing from mutilated

17 On the link between passions and inadequate ideas and, more generally, on the nature of the passions (beyond the classic essay of A. Labriola, "Origine e natura delle passioni secondo l''Etica' di Spinoza," in *Scritti vari editi e inediti di filosofia e politica* [Bari, 1906], and the old article of G. Jung, "Die Affectenlehre Spinozas: Ihre Verflechtung mit dem System und ihre Verbindung mit der Ueberlieferung," *Kant-Studien* 32 [1927], 325 et seq.), see M. Wartopsky, "Action and Passion: Spinoza's Construction of a Scientific Psychology," in *Spinoza: A Collection of Critical Essays,* ed. M. Grene, 329–53; and A. Negri, *L'anomalia selvaggia: Saggio su potere e potenza in Baruch Spinoza* (Milan, 1981), 114 et seq.

18 I use the expression in the sense of J. Houssoun, *Les passions intraitables* (Paris, 1989).

19 For the extent to which *potentia essendi* and *potentia cognoscendi* are in this case narrowly suitable, see P. di Vona, *Studi sull'ontologia di Spinoza* (Florence, 1969), vol. 2, 142 et seq.

20 Spinoza, *TIE,* in *OS* II, 32.

21 *E* 2.36.

knowledge, the order set out by the imagination proceeds through tireless work of restoration and integration of fragments of meaning that present themselves to it, so that – based on conclusions and on analogous generalizations dictated by the passions – the uncertain ends up becoming certain and the unclear, evident.[22] In some way, we all talk nonsense (i.e., we are subject to perturbations of the heart that twist the "truth") in that we integrate, according to conjectural connections, the little that we know with relative certainty with an enormous quantity of inference and unknown elements.

Nevertheless, the imagination or the passions do not offer only a form of inferior knowledge that would culminate in *ratio.* As already alluded to in the Introduction, this latter is none other than the second level of *cupiditas* – that is, an expression of desire that is still partial and imperfect. There remains in it a trace of the efforts directed towards repression of the passions. Since a passion can, in a Spinozan sense, be conquered only by a stronger passion, reason itself (in this guise) is only the most potent and illuminated passion of command and order. The summit of desire – desire fulfilled – is represented by "intuitive science" or *amor Dei intellectualis,* knowledge of "particular things" (*res particulares*) and maximum expression of the *vis existendi.*

Acknowledging the impossibility of extracting order from the imagination and assuming, instead, that there exists the opportunity to reduce its range by knowing it, another problem arises. Can it be asserted that the imagination, as the first step of knowledge, is genetically the basis of the pattern of linking rational ideas together or that – as soon as an argument is formulated – the imagination also, in turn, follows its tracks? Spinoza accepts this latter position,[23] without excluding the former. Only with respect to a higher level of truth, and to a linking together that is

22 This progressive rationalization of the narrow environment of the partial knowledge that we possess is well illustrated in the hypothesis of a worm that lives in the blood, "capable of distinguishing by sight the particles of the blood – lymph, etc. – and of intelligently observing how each particle, on colliding with another, either rebounds or communicates some degree of its motion, and so forth. That worm would be living in the blood as we are living in our part of the universe, and it would regard each individual particle of the blood as a whole, not a part, and it could have no idea as to how all the parts are controlled by the overall nature of the blood and compelled to mutual adaptation as the overall nature of the blood requires, so as to agree with one another in a definite way" (*Ep.* 32.849).

23 See *Ep.* 17.802 (letter to Balling of 20 July 1664).

"objectively" more binding and explanatory of the connections between ideas and things (that is present, however, as "subjectively" freer and more creative), can we rightfully equate intellect to "true ideas" and imagination to the "fictitious, false, [and] doubtful."[24]

The same reasoning may be applied to the passage from the second type of knowledge to the third. In intuitive science, which abandoned the hyper-defensive attitudes of reason, there remain, however (and significantly), characteristic components of the imagination. This not only "accompanies" adapted knowledge or is "auxiliary" to it, but also demonstrates, despite itself, the calm power of the third type of knowledge, so strong and sure of itself as to give open access – because it no longer considers them dangerous – to those powers of the imagination that reason still rejects as a trap for its solidity and integrity.

The Ghost in the Mirror

Several important consequences derive from this Spinozan foundation: that the products of the imagination – or the passions[25] – can be known with a need equal to that of rational ideas; that not having to consider the passions "as vices, but as properties of human nature," their internal consistency does not eliminate their conflicting character, just as the identification of the laws that govern atmospheric turbulence or the formation of lightning does not erase their danger for man; that, if consistency and conflict concern affections as well as representations (or better yet, emotionally invested representations and emotions understood through inadequate ideas), there are also generated orders of emotions (and not only representations) that are consistent and conflicting at the same time.

Just as they are not vices, the results of the imagination also, from the point of view of unsuitable ideas, do not constitute simple falsehood. In fact, imagining things means having them really present, just as the imaginations of the spirit, if considered in themselves and not

24 *Ep.* 37.861. The contrast between *intellectus* and *imaginatio* is attributed by some scholars to the intellectual heritage of Maimonides. See, for example, G. Semerari, "La teoria spinoziana dell'immaginazione," in *Studi in onore di A. Corsano* (Bari, 1969), 759–60.

25 The products of the imagination (that do not all have an "iconic" nature) correspond in general with the passions, insofar as they may also give representations (apparently?) lacking emotional charge.

contradicted, do not contain errors.[26] Thus, Spinoza does not contrast the real to the imaginary, but the reality of the imaginary to the reality conceived by rational knowledge and to the reality conceived by intuitive knowledge.[27] We know according to different orders corresponding to a different power of existing, but we do not access different worlds. Rather, each successive level transliterates and reformulates, making the contents of the stages that proceed it more convincing, incorporating them in its own specific order.

In general, the imagination is much more robust and despotic as knowledge of things is reduced. At this level, individuals and peoples are forced to think in a mythological or superstitious way, so that "they can feign many things, such as trees speaking, men instantly changing into stones and into springs, ghosts appearing in mirrors, nothing becoming something, even gods changing into beasts and into men, and infinitely many other things of that kind" (*TIE* II.58, 29). Perceiving phenomena that function as flint for the mind and then re-elaborating them in a dizzying way with a heart that (Vico-like) is "disturbed and moved" in order to extract full sense from it, the imagination catches fire and flares up, extending its own power and finding sustenance in the more-or-less vast zones of uncertainty in the lives of men and in the consequent ignorance of the causes of events.

However, as soon as adequate ideas are conceived, the imagination is weakened. So, for example, once the nature of bodies is noted, it becomes impossible to imagine oneself "an infinite fly" (ibid.). Limiting the omnivorous power of the imagination, men adapt themselves better to the world and more frequently find motives for satisfaction there. After all, if the word were not conditioned by polemics to which Spinoza himself offered his own contribution, we could say that man becomes more "free" (if that's what we call someone who – having increased his own knowledge of things, that is, the number of suitable ideas – simultaneously reduces his own dependency on passions and on external causes).[28] He does not accept, therefore, mere fatalism, the lazy surrender to destiny, as it is often called. He recognizes that men are often subject to

26 See *E* 2.17, schol., and particularly 2.49, schol., which presents, as an example, the image of the "winged horse," which can be held to be true only as long as the mind does not proceed to limit it through another image. On this point, in a different context and from a different angle, see, in the present volume, p. 249.

27 See M. Bertrand, *Spinoza et l'imaginaire*, 15 et seq.

28 In fact, considering the question from an opposite viewpoint, "the more the mind has inadequate ideas, the more it is subject to passive states [*passionibus*]" (*E* 3.1, cor.).

forces beyond their control (passions or unsuitable ideas, earthquakes, illnesses, etc.), but, forcing himself to adequately understand the causes, he adds that he is also in a position to reduce his dependence on their effects, even if he is unable to counter them.

This effort implies that individuals – separated and often rendered enemies by the variety and entanglement of the passions – may move forward in the territory of the common and shared order of reason, becoming consciously more active and holding back what now clearly appears to be the arbitrary vehemence of the imagination and of the passions. In the last and highest step of knowledge and desire – intellectual love – reason finally reveals its own necessary limitation and inadequacy: its order appears too binding and too inelastic, capable of including the universality of the law but not of rendering justice to the intrinsic knowledge of the *res particulares* that assumes an open order and innovative consistency.

The victorious force of desire that passes through resistance metabolizes the passions into emotions, transforming them into energies that lead towards a greater security, joy, and bliss, without useless sacrifices. At the same time, it loosens the stiffened "musculature" of reason and will, modifying their substantially closed attitude, still marked by fear in the face of the passions' disorder. Thus, the *transitio* of a lesser perfection to a greater one does not occur through recourse to either divine grace or fate, nor through repression, asceticism, mystical energy, or pure force of will. In virtue of the intrinsic power of a desire that, the more it increases its own lucidity, the more its power grows, we pass in fact successively from the confused and mutilated ideas of the imagination to the general and abstract ones of reason and, finally, from these to the superior clarity and distinction of intuitive science (which does not, however, renounce the advantages and tools of the phases it has passed through). The same process appears, in another guise, as an "emendation" of the passions and of the intellect – that is, a reintegration of the lacunae and mutilations of sensation, elimination of the obscurity and confusion, restoration of articulations and connections that are more secure and demonstrable. Analogous to the reading of a text that was seriously corrupted and subsequently restored, the vision of the dynamic complexity of one's own desires and the understanding of the possible avenues of their realization, in an unrestricted arc of time, thus appears more clear. The tumult of the passions calms down not because it stagnates, flowing into a sort of stagnant pond, but because, on the contrary, the *conatus* that animates it – instead of scattering fruitlessly or cancelling itself through elision in a paralysing and depressing struggle – projects itself upward, tracing a curve that shows oscillations, yet still stabilizes on the elevated peaks of the *vis existendi.*

2. Hope and Fear

Two Passions of Uncertainty

Among all the passions, fear and hope assume, in the later works of Spinoza, the highest strategic value, and they constitute the key to the understanding of different ethical, religious, and political problems.

It is a case of eminently unstable emotions that never crystallize in form or in virtue and therefore make the mind restless and unsettled: "Hope is 'inconstant pleasure, arising from the image of a thing future or past, of whose outcome we are in doubt.' Fear is 'inconstant pain, likewise arising from the image of a thing in doubt.'"[1] All the passions appear changeable and unpredictable, but hope and fear figure among the most violent.[2] In fact, they are uncontrollable, raging, destructive, contagious, intractable, and refractory of every direct intervention of reason and will; they clash with a mobile and unknown adversary. They imply (non-methodical) doubt, hesitation, uncertainly, negative turbulence, danger, or the hope for salvation in the face of an evil or good considered in advance. In any case, they implicate the awareness of finding oneself before inscrutable powers, men and events that are stronger than the resistance with which one can oppose them. From this derives, on one hand, resignation and paralysis of will and, on the other, as antagonistic compensation, the most virulent forms of fanaticism, impermeability to criticism, enthusiasm, and unrest.

---

1 See *E* 3.18, schol. 2.
2 See *E* 4.33.

Their inconstancy is diametrically opposed to "constancy" and the clarity of the ancient (particularly the Stoic) example.[3] Unlike pleasure and pain from joy or sadness, which concern the certainty of the present, the instability of fear and hope is tied to projection towards the uncertainty and risks not only of the future but even of the past; that is, to the alternation of the conjectures between undecidable probabilities and consequences of irremediable acts. Thus, *metus* is not connected directly to the present, nor is *spes* connected to imminence.[4]

Spinoza is not opposed to fear and to hope because they distract – according to the opinion of the Stoics – from enjoyment of that which is part of the horizon of the present, enfeebling the heart in vain regrets and endless expectations,[5] but because they block the development of themselves towards states of greater perfection. This is why there is not in Spinoza, as there is in Hobbes, an instrumental relationship between the expectations of the future and the plan of arranging power in the present in order to carry out the contents of expectations,[6] but rather indication of the ways through which real attainment of greater perfection

3 In Spinoza, however, *laetitita* remains a passion: "pleasure is not perfection itself. If a man were to be born with the perfection to which he passes, he would be in possession of it without the emotion of pleasure" (*E* 3 defs. of the emotions 3, expl.) For the evaluation of fear and hope as forms of *inconstantia*, from the *De Constantia sapientis* of Seneca to the *De Constantia* of Justus Lipsius or to *La constance* of Guillaume Du Vair, see, in the present volume, p. 206–8.

4 In discussing uncertainty and unpredictability, even in the past, Spinoza clearly departs from earlier traditions that tied them to the future. See, for example, Cic., *Tusc.* III, 11, 25, where *metus* is an *opinio magni mali impendentis*, while *spes* is an *opinio venturi boni quod sit ex usu iam praesens*. According to Spinoza, these two passions are more generally connected to inadequate ideas of a distant joy and a distant pain. In tragedy as well, there appears the fear that one could have done something horrible in the past without knowing it or something horrible may have happened whose effects must still reveal themselves. Fear is not, however, necessarily tied in Spinoza to the "places" of what is different and potentially hostile or to objective factors (described by C. Jacob, "La topographie de la peur," *Traverses* 25 [1982], 51–60, and by Y. Tuan, *Landscapes of Fear* [New York, 1979]), but to the imagination that, within us, continuously creates otherness and reproduces the phantasmal presence of what is absent with respect to the data of perception and the conceptions of the intellect.

5 The temporal dimension does not, in itself, affect the intensity of a passion (see *E* 3.18 and dem.), even if the image of a present thing produces greater stability of the emotion, while that of a past or future thing, being uncertain, makes the heart more exposed to fluctuations.

6 See Hobbes, *El.* 58.

will fall by itself, making both fear and hope useless, against which reason can battle with difficulty, using its only weapons.[7]

What makes these passions important for philosophical reflection is their being common to all men, as threats or promises that touch and implicate the life of everyone and because they contribute to forming and influencing, in a way that is constructive or "seditious" to the prevailing powers, the orientation of weak wills, always balanced between present and future obedience and the desire to rebel, between the propensity towards faith and lacerating doubt.

Opposing Fronts

The most ancient tradition – with Plato, Aristotle, or Greek Stoicism in particular – considered fear in isolation, either as an expectation of a future evil or as one of the four fundamental emotions, along with pleasure, pain, and desire.[8]

For Spinoza, however, fear and hope constitute an indivisible pair.[9] This happens, on the one hand, according to a historiographic model dating back to Sallust, Livy, and Tacitus. On the other, it happens according to philosophical doctrines partially elaborated by Seneca and by the Neostoicism of Justus Lipsius, in which the interweaving of *metus* and *spes* is by now canonical and falls under the sign of a common condemnation.[10] Such opposition appears in general in Roman historiography to describe the state of heart of soldiers before battle, individual and collective fluctuation between fear and hope in the face of a mortal test.[11]

---

7 A greater future good is certainly rationally preferable to a lesser present good, and a present lesser evil, as the cause of a greater future good, certainly must be accepted (see *E* 4.66 and schol.). However, most men behave in a manner diametrically opposed to these criteria that they approve of in words (see *E* 4.12 and dem.).

8 See Plat., *Lach.* 198 B (in opposition to courage); *Prot.* 358 D; Arist., *Eth. Nic.* III, 9, 1115a9; *Rhet.* II, 5, 1382a et seq., where fear is tied to the "approach of a terrible thing" and opposed to trust or to certainty: "Hope of safety is accompanied by an imagination that it is near, while fearful things either do not exist or are far away" (*Rhet.* II, 5, 1383a); *SVF* III, 386; Cic., *Tusc.* III, 11, 24; IV, 6, 11; *De fin.* x, 35.

9 See *E* 3.50 and schol.

10 So for Seneca, *spem metus sequitur,* while for Lipsius, both represent the most terrible sickness. See Sen., *Ep.* 5, 7, and J. Lipsius, *Manud.* 3.1. For Descartes see, instead, *PA*, art. 165. Some notes on the link between fear and hope are already present in Arist., *Rhet.* II, 5, 1383a: "[For fear to continue,] there must be some hope of being saved from the cause of agony. And there is a sign of this: fear makes people inclined to deliberation, while no one deliberates about hopeless things."

11 See Livy, XXX, 32, 4; XXX, 33, 1; Sall., *Iug.* 105, 4.

From Xenophon's *Hieron* to the *Histories* of Sallust, the reflection on politics takes fear into consideration from the point of view of both those who command and those who obey, of the tyrant and of his subjects.[12] In Tacitus, on the other hand, *metus, pavor,* and *terror* (from the first term is derived the Spanish *miedo,* from the second, the Italian *paura* and the French *peur*) appear for the most part interwoven with the conditions of uncertainty of those who endure it: single individuals or, more often, great human masses such as the army or the plebes. After some nods to Thucydides and Sallust, Tacitus is the first to identify, in a systematic way and with much clarity, the eminent political role of fear (and, albeit in lesser measure, of hope) in imperial despotism, highlighting the mechanisms and subtleties in the daily practice of governing and in the psychology of individuals and crowds.

Spinoza fights on two fronts, trying to decapitate the two-headed eagle of the theological-political empire. He fights against fear, as passion hostile to reason (see *E* 4.52), and against hope as, normally, it flees from the world, an excuse for life, an instrument of resignation and obedience. As long as they last, fear and hope dominate not only the bodies but the imaginations and minds of individuals, casting them at the mercy of uncertainty and making them inclined to resignation and passivity. As soon as they stop, individuals become free again (see *TP* 2.10, 3.8).

In this choice of simultaneously attacking hope and fear, Spinoza is surrounded by a few allies (who use much weaker theoretical arms) and by formidable adversaries, and he is forced to confront not only established and well-known traditions but also real threats to his life and freedom. Therefore, Spinoza is consistent in rejecting, with equal energy, both fear and hope: *Spes et metus affectus non possent esse per se boni* (*E* 3.40–7) unless they serve to suppress an excess of joy or constitute the lesser evil, with respect to men of powerless and proud heart, that would not otherwise lead to obeying the law.[13]

If his thought is compared to, for example, religion, theology, and Christian and Jewish philosophy, Spinoza lacks any sort of apology for

---

12 In fact, this work not only highlights the fear of citizens, but also of the tyrant himself (who fears even his bodyguards). See Xen., *Iero.* 6, 4 and Sall., *Hist.* i, 55, 9; *serviendum aut imperitandum, habendum metum est aut faciendum.* And see L. Strauss, *On Tyranny: An Interpretation of Xenophon's Hieron* (New York, 1948).

13 See *E* 4.47, dem., and 4.54, schol.: "As men seldom live according to the dictates of reason … hope and fear bring more advantage than harm."

the "hope principle."[14] The common rejection of *spes* and *metus* constitutes – indirectly – the most powerful attack on Christianity, and in particular on the Pauline message and that of John of the *Apocalypse*, according to which evangelical hope constitutes victory against fear and death. Those who hope in God will not not have to fear death, which was the "wages of sin" (Rom. 6:23), and Christ – who, as a man, had experienced "distress and agitation" (Mark 14:33) about it – had redeemed it with His resurrection. Now, following Him, whoever has faith can rise again in a glorious body. This "last enemy" (1 Cor. 15:26), would, in fact, be definitively defeated after the second coming of the Lord. In heavenly Jerusalem, there would then be heard a powerful voice that, speaking from the throne, would proclaim in the most solemn way that God Himself, for mankind, would "wipe every tear from their eyes./Death will be no more;/ mourning and crying and pain will be no more,/for the first things have passed away" (Rev. 21:4).

For Spinoza, opposing fear means, in political terms, rejecting absolutism and *raison d'état.* In religious terms, it means repudiating the biblical precept of *timor Domini, initium sapientiae*,[15] the "reason of the Church." In philosophical terms, it means virtually abolishing the Pascalian distinction between bad fear and good fear.[16] Neither the state, faith, nor – least of all – philosophy and wisdom must be based on fear.

On the other hand, opposing hope means striking at the "heart" of religion, denying that which makes it different from the state in its promise of a kingdom that is not of this world, of a "new heaven and a new earth": discovering its dogmas and practices behind its hopes and promises, the chain of the painful mystery of obedience and, often, of servitude.

---

14 For the last great philosophical defence of hope, see E. Bloch, *Das Prinzip Hoffnung*, in *Gesamtausgabe* (Frankfurt, 1962–77), vol. 5, 2. For a broader framing of the problem in Bloch, see R. Bodei, *Multiversum: Tempo e storia in Ernst Bloch* (Naples, 1983).

15 I don't believe that Spinoza could have interpreted the *Domini* of this expression in the sense of a subjective genitive (that is, that it is God who has fear or could have fear of men), as has been proposed. See H. Blumenberg, *Matthäuspassion* (Frankfurt, 1988), 28–33.

16 See Pascal, *P*, n. 282: "Evil fear; fear, not such as comes from a belief in God, but such as comes from a doubt whether He exists or not. True fear comes from faith; false fear comes from doubt. True fear is joined to hope, because it is born of faith, and because men hope in the God in whom they believe. False fear is joined to despair, because men fear the God in whom they have no belief. The former fear to lose Him; the latter fear to find Him."

Ideally, once man is liberated from both earthly and ultramundane fear and hope (from the absolute monarch and from the personal God *pantokrator*), Spinoza can pose the problem of the limits of his action and thought. The *Deus seu Natura* is not an *Ersatz-Gott*, a more sophisticated substitute for the divinities adored by positive religions; because he is impersonal, he ends up lacking any sort of intelligent plan for governing the world. Lacking Providence, man is therefore theoretically free to broaden the sphere of his participation beyond this incarnate ghost of the impotent imagination: *mors Domini, initium sapientiae.* With the disappearance of the personal God (Spinoza's attitude towards Jesus and the religion of the "ignorant" and "unaware," however, is more complex), there is also an end to theological-political morals based on a duty to account to Him, or to His earthly representative, for the conduct of each person. Obedience to God's commandments thus ceases to represent the basis of ethics. They are replaced by individuals' making of themselves according to the level of each person's *cupiditas.* Spinoza, then, does not assert "Become what God wants" as much as a more developed version of the Aristotelian paradox, "Become what you are." His position could be stated in this way: "Become all that you necessarily can become, developing your passions and your reason." As soon as man ceases to be subject to the investigatory gaze of a personal God, he is aware of being – himself – observer and observed, as God and part of God. And when he is capable of shaking off the *tristitia* connected to the idea of transience, he realizes that the eternal is perhaps not situated in another world or another time, but is accessible even here and now, because (being outside temporal parameters) it does not involve any other expectation: *sentimus experimurque nos aeternos esse.*

From the beginning of his *Political Treatise*, then, Spinoza simultaneously strikes at the champions of hope and those of fear: the utopian philosophers who consider men as they wish they were and the politicians who accept them as they are. To both (the theoretical dreamers who look down upon "the actual reality of things" and the *callidi* [cunning] politicians, taught by experience, who hold that one can govern only through fear and shrewdness), Spinoza shows how one can avoid the dilemma, judged to be insolvable, between the dream of a golden age and brutal, presumed realism; between the opportunism of the concrete and the reality of the universal. Neither perspective is more true than the other; on the contrary, their complicity is analogous to that of *spes* and *metus* or – on a parallel plane – of *ridere* and *lugere,* of sarcasm or the painful condemnation of human behaviour on the part of those "who know how to censure vice rather than teach virtue, and who are eager not to guide men by reason but to restrain them by fear so that they may shun evil rather than love virtue" (*E* 4.63, schol.). In this sense, in realist politics, fear transforms prudence into cunning and hate into derision, which "is pleasure arising from our imagining that there is in the object of our hate something that we despise" (*E* 3, def. 11), while, in the utopian and the "Saturnine" melancholy, the alternation between fear and hope leads to political paralysis or – Benjamin-like – to the *melancholia illa heroica* of *Trauerspiel*, of Baroque German drama. Similarly, weeping becomes sadness born from imagining that something we hate recalls that which, if things were different, we could love.

The space for an effective, albeit partial, exit from the horizon of fear and hope can be found, then, only in the abandoning of such a cage dictated by the same logic of the imagination and of political and religious obedience that contributes to keeping men prisoners.[17] The very evaluation of the passions, not as "vices" to be eradicated or subdued but as expressions of nature to understand and, under certain conditions, emancipate, constitutes the Spinozan alternative to a path blocked both on religious grounds and on that of traditional philosophies. In fact, it is useless to abolish the passions with just the decree of reason or of will, placing oneself above the possible, or to content oneself with combining those carriers of physical energies (with their points of application, intensities, ways, and directions), placing oneself below them. Demonizing or manipulating the passions absolutely is an infallible method for remaining embroiled in the eternal, insolvable dispute between being and having-to-be, an abstract utopian realism that is all too concrete for inferring, from how things have gone up to now, either their reverse-mirroring or their immutability. Instead, Spinoza favours a more elevated connection between politics and civic virtues and a "become that which you are" that removes from the precept its evident paradoxical nature. That is, if the *callidi* reduce man to those minimal terms in which the "spring" of his potentiality is contracted by the effect of the enormous and age-old weight of theological-political oppression,

17 In Judeo-Christian religious terms, fear of death is placed by Spinoza in relation to the warning given by God to the "free man," Adam, to not eat the fruit of the tree of the knowledge of good and evil. As soon as he did so, "he would straightaway fear death instead of desiring to live" (*E* 4.68, schol.).

and if the utopians, on the contrary, imagine that such a spring may expand without limits and determinations-negations, for Spinoza the problem becomes, instead, to determine the most effective methods for reducing the burdens of conditioning and, in parallel, for increasing the associated individuals' power of existing. So, while *raison d'état* presumes a levelling of reason on the existing, a freezing of necessity that sacrifices the power of the imagination to depict the different, utopia appears as an attempt to rationalize the imaginary, a leap beyond the "realm of necessity."

Contra spem

Philosophically, hope is not, as in Cicero and Thomas, turned by necessity into a future good, nor is it contrasted with *acedia*, which is a *species tristitiae.*[18] It cannot be controlled, according to Plutarch's principles, operating "as sailors do their sails, to correspond to our capacity" (Plut., *De tranq.* 471 D) or adapting our expectations to the situation and degrading reality, like the fox of the fable who declares the grapes that he cannot reach to be "unripe." If, in medieval language, hope was an *extensio animi ad magna*, it can be said that for Spinoza, instead, it is a *contractio animi ad parva.* With joy and bliss we achieve simultaneous victory over fear of death and its supposed remedy, hope.

As I pointed out previously, in condemning both hope and fear, in some aspects Spinoza connected himself – in an original way – to part of the ancient tradition and to some branches of the modern one, particularly Stoicism and Neostoicism. In fact, for the Greeks, *elpis* was ambivalent; it did not possess any particular positive or negative quality. At various times, it designated hope, expectation, conjecture, and probability of good or evil.[19] In particular, it could be insubstantial, like that

---

18 See Cic., *Tusc.* IV, 80: *Spes est expectatio boni,* and Thomas, *Summa Theologiae,* I–IIa, q. 40, a. 2: *Spes est motus appetitivae virtutis consequens apprehensionem boni futuri ardui possibilis adipisci, scilicet extensio appetitus in huismodi objectum.* For its contrast with *acedia,* see *Summa Theologiae,* Ia–IIae, qq. 35, 8, 2. For hope as a theological virtue see Ia–IIae, qq. 17–22 and 52–7.

19 See P. Lain Entralgo, *La espera y la esperanza: Historia y teoría del esperar humano* (Madrid, 1962), 27 et seq.; O. Lachnit, "Elpis," diss., Tübingen, 1965; H. Desroche, *La sociologie de l'espérance* (Paris, 1973) (English trans. *The Sociology of Hope* [London, 1979]), 12, 180. The root of *elpis* would seem to be tied to the root *vel,* from which comes *velle* and *voluptas.* See A. Walde and J. Pokorny, *Vergleichendes Wörterbuch der indogermanischen Sprachen,* vol. 1 (1930; rpt., Berlin, 1973), 295.

contained in the Hesiodic Pandora's box, or treated negatively by Greek poets and philosophers.[20]

Following the Hellenic tradition, two great admirers of Spinoza – Goethe and Nietzsche – would subsequently condemn hope (together with fear). In Goethe, the subject is recurring, almost obsessive, and precisely in relation to the myth of Pandora. In 1807, he wrote the poem "The Return of Pandora," which preceded *Pandora*, a drama of "renunciation," explicitly connected to *The Elective Affinities.* In a letter from 1809 to Zelter, he declares, "Hope and fear are two hollow entities"; in the *Zahme Xenien* he defines the philistine as "a hollow gut/stuffed with fear and hope"; in *Writings on Literature*, he speaks of strong spirits, like Lucretius, who "as they rejected hope, they also sought to liberate themselves from fear." Finally, in the *Second Faust*, he lets Fear and Hope appear on the scene, introduced by Prudence like this:

> Two of human foes, the greatest,
> Fear and Hope, I bind the faster
> Thus to save you at the latest.[21]

20 For a negative evaluation of hope as deceptive expectation or blind prediction, see Pind., fr. 24 Sn.; *Theogn.*, 637 et seq.; *Antiph.*, 6, 5; Aischil., *Prom.*, 250; Soph., *Ai.*, 477 et seq.; Euro., *Tro.*, 681 et seq.; *Suppl.*, 479 et seq.; Plat., *Gorg.*, 523 D–E. For the ability of the wise to grasp things hoped for and of those who do not understand to ignore them, see Democr., fr. B 58 D.-K. = II, 157, 14.

21 Goethe, *Faust, der Tragödie zweiter Teil*, II, 1, vv. 5403–544. The verses cited are 5441–3, *Faust, Part* 2, trans. Bayard Taylor (London, 1969). On these texts, see G. Diener, *Pandora: Zu Goethes Metaphorik* (Berlin-Zürich, 1968), and K.A. Wipf, *Elpis: Betrachtungen zum Begriff der Hoffnung in Goethes Spätwerk* (Bern, 1974), particularly 42–58.

3. Hobbes: Politics and Fear

A Passion for Order

The most direct philosophical target of Spinozan criticism of the political use of the passions is the function of fear in Hobbes.[1] Hobbes attributes to fear – and particularly to "fear of agonizing death" – an essential civilizing mission, placing it not only at the (false and "plebian") origin of reason and of the state, but also attributing to it the task of their actual preservation against every possible relapse into the social inferno of extreme violence and the state of nature.

Primitive fear, which is shared with the other animals, in man sublimates itself in rational fear, and it constitutes the prime source of every calculation of reciprocity – that is, of *ratio* as such, born from the understanding of reversibility and the mirror-like symmetry of all threats of violence.[2] In fact, reason and the state are not based, in positive terms,

1 Fear was traditionally considered to be the basis of despotic regimes, from the *phobos* attributed by the Greeks to the Orientals, whose sovereigns treated their subjects like slaves (within the *oikos*, fear is, together with cowardice, the servile passion *par excellence*, the opposite of courage, and *despotes*, strictly speaking, is the slave master), up until the *crainte* that Montesquieu found in his time dominating in the Ottoman empire and in Persia. In Hobbes, on the other hand, this is an inseparable characteristic of every regime, when it is exercised in the context of the law of sovereign will, and of anarchy, when it is transformed into widespread terror. On knowledge of Hobbes on Spinoza's part, see C. Gallicet Calvetti, "In margine a Spinoza lettore del 'De cive' di Hobbes," in *Rivista di filosofia neo-scolastica* 73 (1981), 52–84, 235–63. On the passions in Hobbes, see L. Strauss, *The Political Philosophy of Hobbes* (Chicago, 1963 [1936]).

2 Dedicated to the subject of fear in Hobbes is the work of J. Freund, "Le theme de la peur chez Hobbes," *Cahiers Vilfredo Pareto: Revue européenne des sciences sociales* 13 (1975), 57–64 (see also "La peur et la crainte," in *L'essence du politique* [Paris, 1981],

on the principle of self-preservation, but largely on its opposite: on a negative passion, the fear of violent death.[3] An indivisible pair is formed, a complicity between reason and fear. Reason is impotent without fear and terror (since in the civil state, political, moral, and religious commandments are merely buried chains of power, temporary rules with respect to the ultimate end of avoiding the death of the great Leviathan). In turn, fear is blind without the light of rational calculation, the only means (also negative) by which men may prepare "to recognize their own darkness."

Since it represents the conflicts' only margin of modularity – an alternative that should be preferred over the triggering of incontrollable violence – reason itself could be defined as an ordering, "denatured" passion, placed in the service of all the others in defence of life and against an always impending death. A formal and abstract activity, filtered by specific contents, it is only the (continuously discussed) result of an auto-immunizing fear. *Ratio* is thus formed – in the sense of tragedy – by the "catharsis" that the individual and the collective undergo by means of the fear of death that is never erased, a fear that ends up restraining itself and, at least in part, twisting back upon itself (without, however, repudiating its own pre-rational origins). Although responsible for the isolation of individuals,[4] fear matured into reason still constitutes the best bond of the civil state. Unable to transubstantiate itself into an existing, chimerical *summum bonum* (see *El.* 50), the theoretically avoidable *summum malum* of the violent death of the body transforms into

524–37, where the first would indicate an attitude that refers to reason, interests, or expectations, while the second would refer to a state of heart, of apprehension and alarm). Even if criticism tends today to emphasize those aspects of rationality and consensus that establish, in Hobbes, the modern state even in its individualistic, liberal, and democratic prospects – this is also the view of D.P. Gauthier, *Morals by Agreement* (Oxford, 1986), regarding which see T. Magri, "Fuga dalla strategia: A proposito del neo-hobbesismo di D.P. Gauthier," *Teoria politica* 3, no. 2 (1987) – I am of the opinion that this does not at all diminish the role of fear and power in Hobbes's thought.

3 In fact, Hobbes recognizes that the fears of life can be worse than death itself – just as it is worse to be vilified and to live "infamous and hated of all the world" – and that those who kill themselves are moved by some internal torment or by some apprehension that it is "worse than Death." On this aspect, see G.S. Kavka, *Hobbesian Moral and Political Theory* (Princeton, 1986), 80–1 and, more generally, A. Alvarez, *The Savage God: A Study of Suicide* (London, 1971).

4 See E. Voegelin, *Order and History*, vol. 3 (Baton Rouge, 1957).

an aggregate of the divergent goals dictated by individual appetites, held together and, for the most part, made consistent enough by political power.[5] But precisely because of the close solidarity between passion and reason, even this latter can provoke in individuals erroneous calculations and distorted or myopic conceptions, relentlessly recalling the state of nature's threat of bursting, disastrously, into the civil state.

Starting from its first and elementary origin, in which it is connected to the physical sensation of cold,[6] fear translates and styles itself into a calculating, "universal passion." From such a point of view, it is distinct both from "dread," as a mere "foresight of future evil" (*DC* I, in *EW* II, 2), and from "terror." In the absence of further specifications, the latter presents itself as the force of inhibition of citizens' impulses and passions, which is exerted by political power. With the addition of the adjective "panic," on the other hand, this fear separates from apprehension of the causes that generated it, "of the why or the what." *Terror panicus* relates only to the individual, as part of "a throng or multitude" (*L* I.6, in *EW* III, 45), in the moments of dissolution of these unstable components when – in the most complete disorientation – each person follows by chance the example of the first who seems to him to act based on some criterion.[7]

Hope and fear have a decisive weight also because they constitute the substance and the root of will, according to the (typically Hobbesian) polarity of appetite/aversion and, spatially, of coming closer/distancing or attraction/flight: "Appetite and fear ... are the first unperceived beginnings of our actions ... In deliberation, the last appetite, as also the last

5 For Hobbes, however, such power, unlike modern absolutisms, stops in principle at the threshold of the home, where it gives way to the delegated authority of the father, heir to a more ancient sovereignty.

6 Fear appears, in its initial state, as a conversion of cold into frightening images and of fear into cold: "Cold doth in the same manner generate fear in those that sleep, and causeth them to dream of ghosts, and to have phantasms of horror and danger," just as, in turn, "fear also causeth cold in those that wake" (*De corp.* IV, 377–8; Engl. trans., 401).

7 In the second edition of *De cive,* responding to the objection that reciprocal fear would push men to flee rather than come together in society, Hobbes observes that his critics confuse fear with terror: *sentiunt, opinor, nihil aliud esse metuere, praeter quam perterri* (*OL* II, I, 2, p. 161, and see *EW* II, 1, 2, p. 6: "They presume, I believe, that to fear is nothing else than to be affrighted"). The *metuere* or the *to fear* presume, in fact, a certain dose of lucidity induced by the danger, the source of cautions and the formulation of guesses, while the *perterri* or the *to be affrighted* implies, on the other hand, the complete loss of control over oneself, the disappearance of every behavior directed toward self-preservation."

fear, is called will, viz. the last appetite, will to do, or will to omit" (*Human Nature* XII, in *EW* IV, 67). Hope is appetite "with an opinion of attaining," while fear is aversion, "with opinion of hurt from the object" (*L* I.6, in *EW* III, 43). Their fluctuations are so rapid that "almost no time is so short that it cannot encompass their interchange" (*DH* XII, 603; *OM* 56).

With a similar approach, Hobbes distinguishes himself both from the Thomist tradition, in which the *appetitus delectationis fortior est quam fuga tristitiae* (for a complete account, see Thomas, *Summa Theologiae,* Ia–IIa, qq. I–XXI), and from the two fundamental concepts that mark the renewal of Stoicism in the modern age. The first is represented by the affirmative and indefeasible right and duty of each individual to *sese conservare,* which Hobbes, instead, demonstrates negatively, referring to the presence in every organism of hunger, thirst, and other yearnings (that are certainly not voluntary and that push him incessantly towards the future).[8] More precisely, the connection between individuality, appetites, death, and time is clear to Hobbes, who renounced the scholastic "fable" of the immobile and extraterritorial moment to time (to *nunc stans*) and who believes only in the rapid and incessant transformation of the conditions of being in time, all directed towards the satisfaction of their own impulses. Unlike that of Stoicism and Spinoza, Hobbes's emphasis falls on the future, also because the figure of the wise man dedicated to contemplation (in his blessedness), and intimately immune to the violence of the world and political struggles, by now seems unacceptable to him.

The second concept that separates Hobbes from ancient and modern Stoicism consists of the fact that for Hobbes, there do not exist natural laws to follow, given that men would already be – by nature – rational beings. There exist only laws established by agreements: one becomes rational; one is not born that way. Further, one becomes rational not starting with the classic superiority of vision (from the etymological analogy of *idea* and of v-*id*-ere) but from sensibility in all its aspects, from the body capable of suffering and rejoicing, connected to the world through various channels of communication, having become capable of imagining and making signs.

Although Hobbes declares that the good of the citizens must be not be understood simply as "their own preservation and of a more contented life thereby" (*DC* XVII, in *EW* II, 153), every security that is too marked, diminishing the fear of death, gives strength and voice to vanity,

8 Thomas, *Summa Theologiae,* Ia, IIae, q. 33, art. 6 to resp.

pride, presumption, hypocrisy, and the propensity to realize one's own interest to the detriment of others'. All of these are factors that weaken the collective agreement of union and subordination.[9] If the sense of relative calm promoted by reason were to prevail in this form, it would provoke insidious invitations to sedition precisely among those who enjoy the greatest social advantages, the cultured and well-off classes – as happened, in fact, in the years preceding the decapitation of Charles I.

From the Devil's Mountain

Hobbes notoriously not only lived through tumultuous historical situations, he analysed them, beginning with his introduction and translation at a young age of *The Peloponnesian War* by Thucydides to the *Behemoth* later in life. In the first work, he already seems to address strongly the idea of mutual fear (*antipalon deos*) necessary for maintaining the balance between states,[10] and fear continues to be dominant even in his last essay (at the time of its publication, in 1679, with a delay of ten years from the period in which it was composed), fear of a "papist plot." In an exemplary way, The *Behemoth* preserves the flavour of an entire era placed under the sign of fear and of rebelling. "If in time, as in place, there were degrees of high and low, I verily believe that the highest of time would be that which passed between 1640 and 1660. For he that thence, from the Devil's Mountain, should have looked upon the world and observed the actions of men, especially in England, might have had a prospect of all kinds of injustice, and of all kinds of folly, that the world could afford, and how they were produced by their hypocrisy and self-conceit, whereof the one is double iniquity, and the other double folly" (*B* I, in *EW* VI, 165). This is also why, in the same work, Hobbes condemns the study in English universities of those ancient classics that, praising republican liberty against monarchical despotism, destroy the root of authority and place obedience under discussion.[11]

9 On the desire for security, see *DC* 211. The question posed by T. Sorel (*Hobbes* [London, 1986], 118–23) is fair: "Safety at what price?" On the relatively contemporary theories of sedition, Francis Bacon's essay "Of Seditions and Troubles" is noteworthy.

10 Regarding this work, see R. Schlatter, "Thomas Hobbes and Thucydides," *Journal of the History of Ideas* 6 (1943), 337–61.

11 See Hobbes, *B* 7. Hobbes is perhaps one of the first modern authors to present, as a source of political subversion, not religious sects or individual philosophies but intellectual groups inspired by the republican ideals of the classical world.

Complete happiness and freedom are not, after all, of this world: "The greatest good, or as it is called, felicity and the final end, cannot be attained in the present life. For if the end be final, there would be nothing to desire; whence it follows not only that nothing would itself be a good from that time on, but also that man would not even feel. For all sense is conjoined with some appetite or aversion; and not to feel is not to live" (*DH* XI, 600; *OM* 53). Even our absolute freedom, which we consider a necessary tool to pursue happiness, is only a simple show, a toy with which we like to amuse ourselves like a child, to feel like we are protagonists of the events that we happen to witness. It is "a wooden top that is lashed by the boys, ... sometimes spinning, sometimes hitting men on this shins, if it were sensible of its own motion, [it] would think it proceeded from its own will, unless it felt what lashed it" (*The Questions Concerning Liberty, Necessity, and Chance,* in *EW* V, 55).

Unlike the aristocratic feeling of honour, fear is common to everyone. Further, unlike vanity or the degeneration of desire for glory into vainglory, pride, or spiritual dejection, it only blinds the presumptuous and arrogant, including the melancholy – those who, pushed by "causeless fears," continue to praise themselves for their presumed superiority, only to then depress themselves, pushing themselves to "haunting of solitudes and graves."[12] It remains true, however, that vanity – which, although held in check, hides in all those Narcissuses in love with themselves (i.e., men)[13] – does not have the same power of incivility and development that fear possesses. The latter, in fact, is the force that makes one far-seeing and is almost "Providential," even for the vain.[14]

Reason, then, sets forth its roots in fear and continues to receive nourishment from it, accumulating life, distancing individual and collective death, and exorcising the destiny that impends upon every human society, incessantly exposed to the risk of decomposition of the political body in its "elements." Precisely because fear – in a Spinozan way – depresses the power of existing, it is compensated for in Hobbes by a hyperactivity, a "race" by the subject that lasts until death.[15]

12 *L* I.8 in *EW* III, 62. See also *El.* I, IX, 12 and IX, 11.

13 On the Narcissus that vanity reproduces in every man, see A.M. Battista, *Nascita della psicologia politica* (Genoa, 1982), 17.

14 For the expression, see F.C. Hood, *The Divine Politics of Thomas Hobbes: An Interpretation of Leviathan* (Oxford, 1964), 80. M.M. Goldsmith, *Hobbes' Science of Politics* (New York, 1966), 73, speaks appropriately of *timor mortis initium sapientiae.*

15 On this point, see, in the present volume, pp. 381–4.

And so, while vainglory leads men into conflict and discord, since each one searches to raise himself above the others, to "swell" his own *I*, fear – which is born from equality – helps to preserve the stability and duration of states.[16] And yet a residue of Aristotelian mean or *mesotes* stubbornly remains in Hobbesian philosophy, since the magnanimous man diametrically opposes both the pusillanimous and the vainglorious.[17]

In Hobbes, it is not a case of highlighting the fear of death in the face of divine judgment,[18] of eternal death of the soul, nor of beginning a melancholy and sophisticated *meditatio mortis* that – reflecting on the transience of all things – should lead to the sad science of wisdom. Rather, such fear is an articulation of the spontaneous and pre-reflexive attitude of all men: "And forasmuch as necessity of nature maketh men to will and desire *bonum sibi*, that which is good for themselves, and to avoid that which is hurtful; but most of all the terrible enemy of nature" (*Elements of Law* I, in *EW* IV, 83). In effect, death lays the basis for sovereign power, because it keeps the living in *insecuritas* and because it takes from each person the share of power that could have still been due him.[19] From this point of view, probably, every victory of power that lasts could be configured as an open or hidden victory over death, which acts as a spring or catalyst of political processes. It builds itself by destroying or dominating. How far this position is from the more serene one of Descartes, who, asserting the immortal soul with certainty, considered the difference between a living body and a corpse to be as similar as that between a clock or machine that works and one that is stopped or broken (see *PA*, art 6), the same Descartes who had endured the sarcasm of Queen Cristina of Sweden because he believed that – through better knowledge of the body and an appropriate diet – the life of man did not have to be unhappy, short, and brutal (as in Hobbes's state of nature) but serene and even as long as a couple of centuries![20]

16 See *DC* 161 = 82; *Statuendum igitur est, originem magnarium et diuturnarum societatum non a mutua hominum benevolentia, sed a mutuo metu existisse.*

17 See Hobbes, *El.* I, IX, 20.

18 In *DH* 605 et seq., Hobbes narrowly ties fear of God to love of God, placing the accent more on fear than on love (a position that Spinoza would never have accepted and that, in any case, appears softened in the *Elements* in relation to evangelical law. See *El. i*, 152–5).

19 After all, the threat of inflicting death or the suffering of the body or the soul (or of bestowing grace like God, which is the same thing) is one of the oldest tools of power of the political Leviathan.

20 This episode is noted by D. Choron, *Der Tod im abendländischen Denken* (Stuttgart, 1967), 67.

The Effectiveness of Fear

Completely opposite is the conception of Spinoza, according to whom the purpose of the state

> is not to exercise dominion nor to restrain men by fear and deprive them of independence, but on the contrary to free every man from fear so that he may live in security as far as is possible, that is, so that he may best preserve his own natural right to exist and to act, without harm to himself and to others. It is not, I repeat, the purpose of the state to transform men from rational beings into beasts or puppets, but rather to enable them to develop their mental and physical faculties in safety, to use their reason without restraint and to refrain from the strife and the vicious mutual abuse that are prompted by hatred, anger or deceit. Thus the purpose of the state is, in reality, freedom. (*TTP* 20.*567*)

Besides (as is shown by chapter 6 of his *Political Treatise*), an absolute monarchy is impossible and is actually an aristocracy, in that if the law is determined by power alone, the power of just one man is largely inadequate to support such a weight: *unius hominis potentia longe impar est tantae moli sustinendae.*[21]

Fear and violence cannot dominate the states in a stable manner, because they bar men from the mutual cooperation that is at the base of communal life and of *utilitas* understood properly:

> All men do, indeed, seek their own advantage, but by no means from the dictates of sound reason. For the most part the objectives they seek and judge to be beneficial are determined only by fleshly desire, and they are carried away by their emotions, which take no account of the future or of other considerations. Hence no society can subsist without government and coercion, and consequently without laws to control and restrain men's lusts and their unbridled urges. Yet human nature will not submit to unlimited repression, and, as Seneca says in his tragedy, rule that depends on violence has never long continued; moderate rule endures. For as long as men act

21 On the evaluation of absolutism and the differences between the political philosophy of Hobbes and that of Spinoza, see L. Strauss, *Die Religionskritik Spinozas* (Berlin, 1930), 222 et seq., and E. Giancotti Boscherini, "La natura del assolutismo in Hobbes e Spinoza," in *Studia Spinozana* 1 (1985), 231–58.

> only from fear, they are doing what they are most opposed to doing, taking no account of the usefulness and the necessity of the action to be done, concerned only not to incur capital or other punishment.[22]

Of course, since men rarely live "under the dictates of sound reason," when it is not possible to guarantee their security, they can make use of hope and fear – as lesser evils – in addition to humility and regret. Even if all of these passions derive from *tristitia* and are harmful to *utilitas*, in this case they

> bring more advantage than harm ... For if men of weak spirit should all equally be subject to pride, and should be ashamed of nothing and afraid of nothing, by what bonds could they be held together and bound? The mob is fearsome, if it does not fear. So it is not surprising that the prophets, who had regard for the good of the whole community, and not of the few, have been so zealous in commending humility, repentance, and reverence. And in fact those who are subject to these emotions can be far more readily induced than others to live by the guidance of reason in the end, that is, to become free men and enjoy the life of the blessed. (*E* 4.54, schol.)

Precisely because these men do not know how to assert themselves by means of positive feelings of joy, they sanctify their weaknesses in moral form, weakness exalted and transformed into virtues that are positive in themselves. In this sense, they are more like the ill who eat something towards which they have an aversion "through fear of death" than they are like the healthy man who "takes pleasure in his food and thus enjoys a better life than if he were to fear death and directly seek to avoid it" (*E* 4.63, schol.). They do not realize that a "good that prevents us from enjoying a greater good is in reality an evil" (*E* 4.65, dem.). That is, they forget that good and evil, virtues and vices, do not have a value in themselves, but they are always derived from a comparison. Fear and hope can thus be a lesser, acceptable evil in conditions of weakness of the individual and collective *conatus* (in which they can carry out an orthopedic, so to speak, function of support), but they become a cage and a restrictive armour when the power of existing or of the society has grown overall.

22 *TTP* 5.*438,* and see Sen., *Troades* 258–9.

4. Evil Because Unhappy

Freedom, Fear, Necessity

In Hobbes, true freedom coincides with fear and necessity, however subjectively our choice could have been different from what we actually did:

> Fear and liberty are consistent: as when a man throweth his goods into the sea for fear the ship should sink, he doth it nevertheless, very willingly, and may refuse to do it if he will. It is therefore the action of one that is free ... Liberty and necessity are consistent: as in the water, that hath not only liberty but a necessity of descending by the channel, so likewise in the actions which men voluntarily do, which, because they proceed from their will, proceed from liberty. And yet, because every act of man's will and every desire and inclination proceedeth from some cause, and that from another cause, in a continual chain (whose first link is in the hand of God, the first of all causes), they proceed from necessity. So that to him that could see the connection of those causes, the necessity of all men's voluntary actions would appear manifest.[1]

Without considering the different style and reasons adduced, in this passage we can see a coexistence, that could not be more jarring, of one element of absolute divergence and another of absolute convergence of the thought of Hobbes and of Spinoza. While Spinoza cleanly rejects the first "concordance" proposed by Hobbes (that fear and liberty as exact

---

1 *L* II.21, 162. In *On Liberty and Necessity*, Hobbes offers a concise definition of liberty: "Liberty is the absence of all the impediments to action that are not contained in the nature and intrinsical quality of the agent" (*EW* IV, 273).

opposites is true – that is, that man is free only if he does not act on the basis of fear of death), the consensus on the second point, on the other hand, seems complete.

Even in Spinoza, liberty and necessity coincide, and the awareness of one's own *conatus* – that is, of the actual struggle to preserve one's own being[2] – does not at all imply that one is free. Thus, the primacy attributed by tradition and Descartes to the conscience and to *cogito* falls in both Spinoza and Hobbes.[3] Instead, it is necessary – in a Spinozan sense – to pass from the level of conscience to that of the knowledge of causes. Being aware of something does not mean that the reasons for it are known. *Sapiens* is distinguished from *ignorans* precisely because one knows something better than others (even if his knowledge is also inevitably limited by the infinite power and variety of nature, of everything of which it is a part).

In addition to the pages noted in *Ethics* (*E* 3.2, schol.), this point is well illustrated by Spinoza's more neglected letter 58, to Schuller. There, the hypothesis is formulated that a stone, like all things that are finite and subject to external causes,[4] receives a fixed amount of movement from another body or force. Moreover, Spinoza adds, we assume that – while its movement continues, even when the impulse of the external cause has ceased – it thinks, "and knows that it is endeavouring, as far as in it lies, to continue in motion." Through merely being "conscious only of its endeavour," such a stone may be persuaded of its own absolute freedom and may believe that it continues to move only because it wants to. In this presumption, men do not differ at all from such a hypothetical stone. Consciousness of their appetite and of their acting is accompanied by ignorance of the causes that push them to behave in the way they essentially behave.[5] Spinoza then presents some examples that reappear almost exactly, along with others, in his *Ethics*:

---

2 See *E* 3.7, where *conatus* is defined as *ipsius rei actualis essentia*, "the actual essence of the thing itself."

3 In Hobbes, this also happens on the political level, where the primacy of the inner forum is vigorously rejected as seditious. See *L* 364–5.

4 And thus it may not be, in a Hobbesian sense, the First Cause.

5 *Ep.* 58.909, and see *E* 3.2, schol. One of the reasons for the interest that Freud shows in Spinoza could derive from this very aspect: that behind consciousness, or awareness, there are causes, impulses or *conatus*, of whose unconscious motivations we are ignorant, even if we clearly perceive their effects. For Freud, as for Spinoza, the task of science consists in the discovery of such causes, without renouncing an explanatory

> In the same way a baby thinks that it freely desires milk, an angry child revenge, and a coward flight. Again, a drunken man believes that it is from his free decision that he says what he later, when sober, would wish to be left unsaid. So, too, the delirious, the loquacious, and many others of this kind believe that they act from their free decision, and not that they are carried away by impulse. Since this preconception is innate in all men, they cannot so easily be rid of it. For although experience teaches us again and again that nothing is less within men's power than to control their appetites, and that frequently, when subject to conflicting emotions, they see the better course and pursue the worse, they nevertheless believe themselves to be free, a belief that stems from the fact that in some cases our desire has no great force and can easily be checked by the recurrence to mind of some other thing which is frequently in our thoughts. (*Ep.* 58.909)

The divergence on this point emerges when Hobbes refuses to proceed beyond *ratio* as calculation towards the third type of Spinozan knowledge: the *scientia intuitiva* that would surely have appeared to be a remnant of medieval mysticism to the English philosopher.

The Mouse and the Angel

Through this solution in which liberty and necessity are not opposed to one another,[6] Spinoza sidesteps both the so-called "ethical intellectualism" of Socrates and Plato, in which good and evil depend, respectively, on knowledge or ignorance (as evidenced by conscience or even by one's *daimon*),[7] and the idea that men may work on a range of choices, all abstractly possible. Like a drunkard, each of us says every time what in that moment "is pushing" him, that which possesses the impulse to express itself. Only afterward, when the *conatus* is transformed and everyone has

---

structure of a rigorously deterministic sort, where everything that appears incidental is, instead, obligatory (see *E* 1.29 and, for some final remarks on the relationship between Freud and Spinoza, in the present volume, pp. 288–9.

6 See *Ep.* 56.903 (to U. Boxel): "That 'necessary' and 'free' are contraries seems no less absurd and opposed to reason."

7 It is a position that extends also to some Stoics like Epictetus; see *D* 1.3–4. For Spinoza, understanding the error is not enough if this comprehension remains passive – that is, if it is not accompanied by a *transitio* towards a greater power of existing (on this problem see, in the present volume, pp. 281–4).

a different disposition of body and mind, will it possibly lead to regret for the words that escaped from his mouth and for not having remained silent. As in Hobbes, good and evil – apart from positive law – are considered just names. Similarly, in Spinozan "immoralism," they exclusively represent relative points of view, in that each person calls good or bad that which he believes may be good for or harm his own preservation.[8]

The wise man will struggle, then, to have neither external masters (he will be free and not a servant) nor internal masters (commandments of passive obedience to precepts or passions that depress the power of existing). In this way, he will limit himself to following his own nature, endowed with greater awareness and perfection with respect to others and incapable, normally, of conforming to presumed, final, and mysterious decrees, both divine and human.

Of course, even evil men, sinners, and the impious – to the extent they follow their own nature – express the will of God in their own way and are perfect, each at his own level.[9] This is why, if we take the first infraction of law, Adam's decision to eat the prohibited fruit, and examine it in isolation, we will not find any imperfection:

> This resolve or determinate will, considered solely in itself, contains in itself perfection to the degree that it expresses reality. This can be inferred from the fact that we cannot conceive imperfection in things except by having regard to other things possessing more reality. For this reason, when we consider Adam's decision in itself without comparing it with other things more perfect or displaying a more perfect state, we cannot find any imperfection in it. Indeed, we may compare it with innumerable other things much more lacking in perfection in comparison with it, such as stones, logs, and so forth. In actual practice, too, this is universally conceded. For everybody beholds with admiration in animals what he dislikes and regards with aversion in men, like the warring of bees, the jealousy of doves, and so on. In men such things are detested, yet we esteem animals as more perfect because of them. (Ep. 19.808)

---

8 See *E* 1, app.; 4.8 and dem. On the professed "immoralism" that is, in reality, an amoralism, or an ethic directed not to persuading, ascetically, towards virtue, but to increasing one's own joy and power of existing, see G. Deleuze, *Spinoza: Philosophie pratique* (Paris, 1981), 27.

9 In fact, "whatever is, when considered in itself without regard to anything else, possesses a perfection coextensive in every case with the thing's essence" (*Ep.* 19.808).

But this does not mean that, given the greater happiness of man, there do not exist differences between goods and evils: "For although a mouse is as dependent on God as an angel, and sorrow as much as joy, yet a mouse cannot on that account be a kind of angel, nor sorrow a kind of joy."[10] These are differences not only of degree but of nature.

Crimes without Guilt

If every act is perfect in itself and demonstrates the necessary presence of a God without anthropomorphic or personal characteristics, then the Augustinian question, *unde malum?*, makes no more sense than the one later posed by Leibniz in his *Essays de Théodicée sur la bonté de Dieu*: "*Si Deus est, unde malum, si non est, unde bonum?*" Even the most atrocious crime, when the power of existing of the person who commits it is low, ceases to be such and appears in a favourable light:

> For example, Nero's matricide, insofar as it contained something positive, was not a crime; for Orestes too performed the same outward act and had the same intention of killing his mother, and yet he is not blamed, or at least not as Nero. What then was Nero's crime? Nothing else than that by that deed he showed that he was ungrateful, devoid of compassion and obedience. Now it is certain that none of these things express any essence. Therefore neither was God the cause of any of them, but only of Nero's action and intention. (*Ep.* 23.833)

Radical and absolute evil does not exist and, in itself, no action is good or bad in an unrelated way. Therefore, even if Spinoza certainly does not propose a "cheerful" ethics, one cannot place moral blame per se under the sign of joy commonly interpreted as "Dionysian." Wasting away is of no use. Instead, it makes the soul weak and drives back every attempt to increase one's own perfection. Man, by nature, is the being that – within

10 *Ep.* 23.833. If there were not differences between goods and evils, one could revive the question, which has already been noted, why Spinoza would have had to write an *Ethics*. Spinoza did not seek consolation in faith, nor did he consider the "science of external things" separable from morality or the knowledge of divergent causes from the search for wisdom, of the highest form of good life. However – if we think, in contrast, of Francis Bacon – we see that Spinozan ethics proceeds not towards "the science of external things" as mastery of nature and of the world, but as their specific and special comprehension in the sphere of the usefulness of every being.

a band of oscillation that is not very wide – can rise and descend endlessly between levels of greater or lesser perfection, increasing or diminishing his happiness – a happiness, to paraphrase Peter Handke, "with desires" and not, like that of the Stoics, without desires.[11] It is the passions – of the sort that are often incompatible with their objectives, in the conflicts and differences of power of existing that they bring to light – that make men different and enemies of one another. Their ineradicable permanence supports, and again makes plausible, the idea of searching for absolute domination over them. From this idea one infers the corollary (from the indisputable appearance, given the conditions) of an eternal need for terror, violence, crime and, in a complementary way, the hope that all of those things will end. We do not take into account the fundamental fact that fear and hope, crime and punishment, terror and flight adapt and flourish only where the "perfection" of individuals and communities cannot increase, because it does not find a solution at higher levels – that is, greater satisfaction and happiness. This explains not only the widespread violence directed towards others but also that – which seems deceptively more rare – twisted against themselves. With a final hyperbole or (better still) a final taking of things to extremes, which has the function of unambiguously clarifying his thought, Spinoza formulates the hypothesis that people may exist who are so self-injured that they prefer the most horrible tortures to pleasure or to the simple absence of pain. Following their own *conatus* would not be a crime for them, but a virtue. "However, suppose it possible that there could be such a nature. Then I say (whether I grant free will or not) that if anyone sees that he can live better on the gallows than at his own table, he would be very foolish not to go and hang himself. And he who saw clearly that he would in fact enjoy a more perfect and better life or essence by engaging in villainy than by pursuing virtue would also be a fool if he did not do just that. For in relation to such a perverted human nature, villainy would be virtue."[12]

Men are evil because they are unhappy, because they are racked by *tristitia* that diminishes their joy or power of existing and casts them ever

11 According to a criterion common to Hispanic culture that derives from Miguel de Unamuno (see, in the present volume, pp. 313–14), a contemporaneous author who supports the thesis that Stoicism culminates in Spinoza.

12 *Ep.* 23.834. From this perspective, it is not surprising that – although twisting his intentions – the Marquis de Sade considered Spinoza the first of his teachers. See D.A.F. de Sade, *Histoire de Juliette ou les Prospérités du vice* (Sceaux, 1954 [1797]).

lower, twisting them in a spiral of destruction and self-destruction. But how do they get out of it?

Spinozan ethics aims at the emancipation of man from personal and political servitude by following a path that separates freedom from will and does not accept, as an endpoint, submission of the passions to the yoke of a will that is only repressive and to a reason that judges on the basis of universal laws that set aside the sudden and continuous variability of the *conatus*. If one really intends to limit the fear caused by the apparent harmfulness of men towards themselves and others, and if one really wants also make superfluous the thrust of hope towards an imaginary world without evil, it is necessary to find solutions to successfully diminish the power of these depressing passions and increase – in parallel measure within the limits of the possible – the world of reason and "intuitive science." In this way, both the "heuristics of fear"[13] and the "hope principle" will finally lose their value.

13 I am referring to the theory of Hans Jonas, according to which, in a world that has become more complex and where the power of self-destruction of the human species and of the entire planet is no longer an illusion, it is necessary to abandon dangerous, destabilizing utopias because of their insistence on plans for radical change, with unpredictable results, and to no longer look at the attainment of the *summum bonum*, but rather at the task of the *summum malum*. From here, by means of a "heuristics of fear," there would need to start the search for possible escape routes from the crises we are currently experiencing. See H. Jonas, *Das Prinzip Verantwortung*; Ital. trans. *Il principio responsabilità* (Torino, 1989), 34–5.

5. *Amor mortis*

Virtuosity of the Imagination

Spinoza was not prejudiced against processes of self-immunization and self-prohibition of reason and will with regard to the passions. The imagination can sometimes educate by means of anticipatory exercise and enumeration, in the style of Seneca, of possible and imminent dangers: "We ought, in the same way, to reflect on courage to banish fear; we should enumerate and often picture the everyday dangers of life, and how they can best be avoided and overcome by resourcefulness and strength of mind" (*E* 5.10, schol.). These attempts succeed, however, only provided that the imagination is not abandoned to itself, and that a firmer and freer order (however much it might not be immediately understood) is substituted for the order of the imagination, substantially created by a crystallization and combinatorially changeable stabilization of individual feelings and special situations. The passage from the regime of the imagination to that of the intellect requires a transitional phase: the anticipation, without immediate advantages, of a greater effort, a more intense *conatus.* This, however, may be born only of a need that is actually felt and not by unrealistic proposals. Subsequently, it will be compensated for by the greater satisfaction obtained through a similar strategy. In fact:

> greater force is required to check emotions arranged and associated according to intellectual order than emotions that are uncertain and random. Therefore, the best course we can adopt, as long as we do not have perfect knowledge of our emotions, is to conceive a right method of living, or fixed rules of life, and to commit them to memory and continually apply them to particular situations that are frequently encountered in life, so that our

casual thinking is thoroughly permeated by them and they are always ready to hand.[1]

Those who subject themselves to "rules of life," to intellectual maxims fixed by means of the memory and the imagination, will thus succeed more easily in ordering the passions so that, faced with an offence, they will not follow the impulse for revenge, exchanging hate for hate, but will make the virtue (i.e., the excellence, strength, and habit) of generosity prevail. Only then will the offence "occupy just a small part of our imagination and will easily be overcome" (*E* 5.10, schol.).

Pondering the Passions

With regard to the ethical training of individuals, Spinoza does not withdraw into the first type of knowledge – that is, he does not appeal directly to the powers of imagination. For the transitional phases, he relies upon a variation of the Stoic model frequently proposed by Marcus Aurelius: the one that suggests, for separating opinion from feeling, letting the attitude or words of others occupy a narrow zone of the imagination and letting the "best part of ourselves" – intelligence – prevail. However much Spinoza was a pupil and friend of the ex-Jesuit Franciscus van den Enden,[2] and however well he knew Spanish literature of the *siglo de oro*, often marked by the mentality of, or by explicit references to, Stoicism and the values supported by the Company,[3] his method departs cleanly both from that of the Stoics and, in particular, from that presented by Ignatius of Loyola in his *Spiritual Exercises*. Because it can highlight important differences, a (merely theoretical) comparison of their respective positions can prove fruitful in the present context.

---

1 *E* 5.10, schol. See also *Ep.* 17.803.

2 On this notable character, see G. van Suchtelen, "François van den Enden, precepteur de Spinoza," *Bulletin des Amis de Spinoza* 1 (1979), 3–14; W. Klever, "Proto-Spinoza: Fanciscus van den Enden," *Studia Spinozana* 6 (1990), 281–9 (which, on the basis of some writings recently attributed to him, sees some of the most radical ideas of the author of the *Ethics* at work in his thought).

3 Spinoza, who spoke better Spanish than Dutch, showed a marked interest in Iberian texts (Castilian, Portuguese, and Sephardic Hebrew), particularly those of a literary character. On Spinoza and Spanish culture, it should be noted, among the books of his library, the presence of Góngora (in two different editions), Quevedo, Cervantes, and Gracián. See S. von Dunin-Borkowski, *Spinoza* (Munster, 1933–6), vol. 1, 47, 53, and P. Vulliaud, *Spinoza d'après les livres de sa bibliothèque* (Paris, 1934), 99–103.

Spinoza bases his ethics on principles of life (*vitae dogmata*) linked according to the order of the intellect, and he makes use of the imagination in propaedeutic form and under the careful control of reason. Only at the next step, that of the third type of knowledge, is it possible to abandon the rigid order and the inelastic connections of reason concerned with training the passions and finally reach the *ordo* of *amor intellectualis.*

Ignatius, on the other hand, makes use of the imagination to "ponder" the passions, to scrupulously elaborate them, distilling them to the point of producing the firm determination to defeat sin. Ignatian precepts aimed to modulate the passions, starting from some real (or at least imagined) sensations, as well as from words and ideas, possibly chosen from the sphere of his own past or present existence, so as to disarticulate that sphere from its current agglomeration and then reassemble it in a different way, by means of conclusive "exercises" carried out at the end of every retreat under the guidance of a spiritual director. Thanks to a genuine virtuosity of the "internal senses,"[4] such sophisticated rhetoric of fleeting images, stuck in the mind and taken to their extreme limits of expressibility, succeed in making the "practitioner" relish the taste of the unimaginable, and they make him have a premonition of the delicious aroma of heavenly blessedness and the sulfurous stench of eternal damnation.[5] Besides a sort of *Gradus ad Parnassum*, so to speak, for "playing" the great keyboard of the imagination, Ignatius also presents a *Gradus ad Golgotham* or an *Itinerarium imaginationis in Deum*: a series of ever more meticulous, complex, and branching depictions of sorrow, death, and future joy (tempered by techniques aimed at "de-obsessing" the meditation itself, at preventing it from imploding as a result of excessive concentration). As would happen later for pedagogical purposes,

4 On the origins of the theory of the internal or spiritual senses, see H.A. Wolfson, "The Internal Senses in Latin, Arabic, and Hebrew Philosophical Texts," *Harvard Theological Review* 28 (1935), 69–133.

5 On the theory and technique of the Jesuit method of exercising the imagination, see L. Zarnke, *Die Exercitia Spiritualia des Ignatius von Loyola in ihren geschichtlichen Zusammenhängen* (Leipzig, 1931); I. Iparraguirre, *Práctica de los Ejercicios de San Ignacio de Loyola en vida de su autor* (Bilbao, 1946); J.A. Hardon, *All My Liberty: Theology of Spiritual Exercises* (Westminster, 1959); and A.T. De Nicolas, *Powers of Imagining: Ignatius de Loyola: A Philosophical Hermeneutics of Imagining through the Collected Works of Ignatius de Loyola, with a Translation of These Works* (Albany, 1986).

the end on which Jesuit theatre or organization of studies[6] focuses still remains the use of massive doses of imagination (along with all the tools offered by the arts of persuasion and scenic illusion) to bring order to the "unregulated feelings," subjecting them to obedience to an authority of the soul that has internalized that of God and His Vicar. The value of the rules endorsed by such a voice (otherwise hardly justifiable) is supported, however, by a penetrating analysis of the psychological and social motivations of action and by careful consideration of the complexity of situations and facts (including the relationships between prevailing forces).

Such a sophisticated attitude can be judged as purely opportunistic (and it often was, as Pascal's *Provincial Letters* clearly show). However, one point must not be underestimated: that the Jesuits' "probabilism" and "laxness" tended to give a moral and religious meaning to the things of a world that was expanding geographically (and of whose differences they were attentive observers) and that, historically, was changing at an accelerated pace. They sought to find a criterion that was pliable and adaptable to circumstances, one that would be capable not simply of measuring the great variety of the world's situations, but also of contributing to "building it" on the basis of "practiced passions," techniques and new wisdom that unconventionally rotated on a rigid axis of authority embodying an indisputably sacred tradition. This is why they organized the training of young men and transplanted their missions to the most remote corners of the globe, from Japan to Paraguay, using the experiential data of every individual and culture as material for "constructing" its soul and, at the same time, for strengthening the power of the church (and often of the state as well). The good that could be achieved in the uncertainty and variety of this world is split into so many small fragments of duties and of practices. Morality seems to become tolerant and "soft" and seems to abandon the ethical absolutism of the supreme good. This, however, is only because it had already chosen the will of the pope as a fixed and unyielding basis.

6 On Jesuit theatre as an auxiliary of the imagination, see R. Wimmer, *Jesuitentheater, Didaktik and Fest* (Frankfurt, 1982). On the method of studies that, through examination not of conscience but of knowledge, imposes discipline also on wisdom, see F. Lebrun, "Un aspect de la pédagogie jésuite: Contrôle des connaissances et examens d'après la *ratio studiorm*," in *Les Jésuites parmi les hommes aux* XVIe *et* XVIIe *siècles* (Clermont-Ferrand, 1987), 385–94.

In this sense, thinking for contrast of the Pascalian *pari* – where the propensity for risk is very high (all or nothing) and the stakes at their highest – the Jesuits' propensity towards risk appears lower only because the stakes and bets are subdivided and distributed in smaller parts, shares to be doled out with the "art of prudence" – that is, with a mixture of calculation, caution, and shrewdness. In the end, however, the totals still must be dealt with, and from them, it is also necessary to start making radical choices. Once an accounting, a *redde rationem*, is reached, a sort of fatalistic obedience to providentially conceived destiny (or to an entity that represents it) indicates the path of decisions. Once again the hints and the signs of the imagination occupy the post left vacant by subtle reasoning. Something of the fiery Basque soldier, of the passionate reader of Amadis of Gaul and other chivalrous novels, of the man who trusts in the direction of events and the impulsive bets on the outcome of the match, was transmitted from the order's founder to many of his followers, called to decide quickly when faced with alternative shoals. Where *veritas* was no longer enough, he resorted to the most iron-like sort of *auctoritas*, to discipline of a military sort. When one rejected substantially rational choices, one trusted inevitably in those of others, whoever they might be, overloading incidental events with meaning – according to the logic of the imagination.

In this regard, one episode of the biography of Ignatius is revealing. Having recovered from the wounds received during the French siege of Pamplona, he was going on a pilgrimage to Jerusalem when, having come close to his point of embarkation, he met a Moor who doubted the virginity of the Madonna after having given birth. Ignatius spoke with him at length without succeeding in shifting his convictions, until his interlocutor changed course. At that point, after having meditated for a good part of his journey on what had just happened, he was suddenly struck by the irrepressible impulse to defend the "honour" of Our Lady:

> Thereupon he was seized with a longing to go and seek out the Moor and dispatch him with his dagger, on account of what he had said of our Most Blessed Lady. After long wrestling with these thoughts he was still doubtful, nor could he distinguish what he was bound to do in the matter ... Wearied with debate and being unable to come to any certain conclusion, he decided to give the mule her head; if, when they came to the parting of the ways, the beast turned towards the place where the Saracen was, then he would find him and stab him; if she kept to the highway, he would let him go. He followed this plan, but by the mercy of God it happened that the mule kept to the highway and avoided the other, although the spot was little more

> than thirty or forty paces from the road, and the way leading to it was very broad and easy.[7]

In a sort of "animal kingdom of the spirit," the magical authority of a mule decided his future sanctity, and an insignificant sign was thus filled with meaning. When the criteria of choice appear dim, the propensity towards risk becomes pronounced. In the end, they succumb to the fatalistic obedience to a providential destiny, to a surrogate for reason.

Speaking in Spinozan terms, the apparent freedom of the passions in Ignatius is regulated by the iron logic of an order understood as obedience. This, in turn, is connected to the lack of surpassing the imagination's barriers and its *tristitia*, to the desperate need for salvation that clings to the feeling of death and the vanity of all things, which the imagination dissolves in the depth of their reality and in their horrifying presentation to the senses, transforming them into celestial visions. *Amor mortis conturbat me* and the unbreakable obligation to the most complete passivity are also the induced result of the imaginative exercises of submission to the ineluctable, the Catholic *pendant* of Luther's "bondage of the will," a voluntary servitude to the benefit of a kingdom that is not of this world but that, under the bitter humiliation of this world, it must still pass. They are the result – to use a Spinozan expression in reverse – of a regressive *transitio* from the *ordo rationis* to the *ordo imaginationis*; from the *meditatio vitae* to the *meditatio mortis*. They represent the recognition of a *fatum* within the superficial chaos of the imagination, or even a leap into the *ordo amoris* made possible by the conviction that the arms of criticism may have to give way to the military discipline of the spirit. Life, rather, is a soldiering – as in Seneca or in the Christian martyrs of the early church – but one no longer soldiers for himself or directly for God, but for the religious absolute sovereign, the pope, who represents him on earth.

Philosophy as Meditation on Death

Spinoza fights, however, not so much against the *amor mortis* of Ignatius, fomented by the imagination, or against the *De meditatione mortis* of

---

7 *Acta patris Ignatii*, in *Fontes Narrativi de Sancto Ignatio de Loyola et de Societatis Iesu initiis* (Rome, 1943), vol. 1; Engl. trans. *The Testament of Ignatius Loyola* (London, 1900), 67–8.

Thomas à Kempis, but against the whole of a long and venerated tradition of thought accustomed to consider philosophy as an "exercise of death." This solemn funeral march of philosophical thought – whose beginning is made up of the *melete thanatou* of Plato, who considers such an exercise of thinking about death as a means to free oneself from the "passions of the body," "fears and imaginings of every sort," and the egotistical link to one's own individuality – represents one of the constituent moments of the ideal of a life dedicated to knowledge of the truth. To cite only the exemplary cases and the authors who had the greatest influence, the subject was further enriched by Cicero (for whom the life of philosophers is just "a comment on death") and by Seneca, to the point of permeating through all of Western thought for centuries, interwoven with Christian motifs.[8]

But it is in eras closer to him (and to us, if one thinks that Tolstoy still held that "one mustn't be afraid of death. One should think about it as often as possible" or that Freud, in 1915, was still a supporter of the principle *si vis vitam, para mortem*)[9] that Spinoza – for whom the motto *si vis vitam, para vitam* might be valid – can observe a strong renewal of this almost thanatophilic vision of philosophy, from the most obscure writings of Erasmus in *De preaeparatione ad mortem* and from Ronsard's *Hymne de la Mort* to Montaigne's closer, ambivalent, and complex *Essays.*[10]

8 See Plato, *Phaedo,* 64 A et seq. and 67 E: "'In fact, then, Simmias,' said he, 'the true philosophers practice dying, and death is less terrible to them than to any other men'" – precisely because it is a way to a higher life, and philosophy is a progressive reawakening, a habituation – like at the beginning of Book VII of the *Republic* – to asserting the light of the "sun" and, at the same time, almost Hegel-like, a "lingering," a *verweilen,* at the sight of that "black sun" that is death. For Cicero, see Cic., *Tusc.* I, 74: *philsophorum vita … commentatio mortis est;* and *Tusc.* I, 29, 71; I, 31, 75; Epict., *Ench.* 21: "Keep the prospect of death, exile, and all such apparent tragedies before you every day – especially death – and you will never have an abject thought, or desire anything to excess."

9 See S. Freud, *Zeitgemässes über Krieg und Tod,* in *GW,* vol. 10, 255. On the other hand, we can observe, Weber-like, how with the decline of religions, the loss of the meaning of death, may seem to imprint the definitive accent on the lack of meaning of life.

10 See, for Erasmus, E.W. Kohl, "*Meditatio mortis* chez Pétrarque et Erasme," in *Colloquia Erasmiana Turonensia* (Paris, 1972), vol. 1, 305 et seq.; for Ronsard, see his "Hymne de la Mort," in *Oeuvres complètes,* ed. P. Lemonnier (Paris, 1914–19), vol. 6, 205–38. For a broader picture of references, see R.R. Post, *The Modern Devotion: Confrontation with Reformation and Humanism* (Leyden, 1968), and J. Delumeau, *Le péché et la peur: La culpabilisation en Occident* (XIIIe–XVIIIe *siècles)* (Paris, 1983).

A few pages after having dedicated a chapter to fear, Montaigne writes another about it – titled "That to Study Philosophy Is to Learn to Die" – in which he holds precisely that "all the wisdom and reasoning in the world do in the end conclude in this point, to teach us not to fear death," following the counterintuitive way of removing the *étrangeté* of death and of representing it *à notre imagination en tous visages*: in the discarding of a horse, in the falling of a roof tile, in the smallest prick of a pin.[11] This is another work thick with classical citations, particularly Senecan, according to which meditation on death is meditation on liberty.[12] But from here on, the idea of philosophy elaborated by Montaigne has nothing sad or austere about it:

> The most manifest sign of wisdom is a continual cheerfulness ... She has virtue for her end – which is not, as the schoolmen say, situate upon the summit of a perpendicular, rugged, inaccessible precipice. Such as have approached her find her, quite on the contrary, to be seated in a fair, fruitful, and flourishing plain ... 'Tis for not having frequented this supreme; this beautiful, triumphant, and amiable; this equally delicious and courageous virtue; this so professed and implacable enemy to anxiety, sorrow, fear, and constraint – who, having nature for her guide, has fortune and pleasure for her companions – that they have gone, according to their own weak imagination, and created this ridiculous, this sorrowful, querulous, despiteful, threatening, terrible image of it to themselves and others, and placed it upon a rock apart, among thorns and brambles, and made of it a hobgoblin to affright people.[13]

In the last years of his life, Montaigne assumed an ever "more relaxed" attitude towards death. Let us not disturb our life, he says, with the worries that it causes us. Rather, let us learn to associate with joy, rather than sadness. Let us imitate Democritus, who found the human condition "vain and ridiculous," rather than Heraclitus with his "piety and compassion" for it.[14] At the right moment, nature will know how to instruct us,

---

11 Montaigne, *ES* I, XX, 80 (*ESe* I, XIX, 65) and passim in the same chapter. For the context, see *ES* I, XX, 79–93 (*ESe* I, XIX, 64–84). On fear, see *ES* I, XVIII, 74–7 (*ESe* I, XVII, 58–61).

12 On Montaigne and Seneca, see P. Villey, *Les sources et l'évolution de la pensée des Essais de Montaigne* (Paris, 1932), and A. Grilli, "Su Montaigne e Seneca," in *Studi di letteratura: Storia e filosofia in onore di Bruno Revel* (Florence, 1965), 303–11.

13 Montaigne, "Of the Education of Children," *ES* I, XXVI, 160 (*ESe* I, XXV, 165).

14 On this point, see p. 97 et seq. in the present volume.

so that often even the lowly will show themselves to be courageous: "To say the truth, we prepare ourselves against the preparations of death. Philosophy ordains that we should always have death before our eyes, to see and consider it before the time, and then gives us rules and precautions to provide that this foresight and thought do us no harm: just so do physicians, who throw us into diseases, to the end they may have whereon to employ their drugs and their art."[15] One could assert, in this sense, that the later Montaigne trusts, more than in a *meditatio mortis*, in a homeopathic cure that inures us to it, to an immunization with regard to that death that is within us and that poisons our life. He thus ends up living in the *arrière boutique* of his soul, in an interior solitude populated by a "crowd" of interlocutors and voices that come from books (based on the maxim of never judging others according to his measure, so that it may be easy for him to believe "there may be things that are different from me"), voluntary prisoner of a string of precautions that prevent him from enjoying fully some feelings directed cautiously towards persons and things out of fear of the disappointments that may come from their subsequent loss: "Wives, children, and goods must be had, and especially health, by him that can get it; but we are not to set our hearts upon them that our happiness must have its dependence upon them; we must reserve a backshop, wholly our own and entirely free, wherein to settle our true liberty, our principal solitude and retreat."[16]

Beyond exclusively philosophical models, Montaigne now also begins to make use – with an expression of Lucien Febvre – of the *outillage moral* of the people of more humble class who surround him, turning with ever greater attention to the wisdom (hardly apparent and even less transformed into theory) of his peasants and attendants, to an ethics that one acquires with the direct knowledge of sorrow, with the experience of those who have the calm strength to accept the inevitable, the courage to change what little depends on him, and the capacity to distinguish the first attitude from the second. All of Seneca's declamations on preparation for death – he says – could have diminished his esteem for the great moralist if his own courage, put to the test in the moment of coolly and

15 Montaigne, "Of Physiognomy," *ES* III, XII, 1028 (*ESe* III, XII, 302) and, for the complete reasoning, see the entire chapter, 1013–41 (*ESe* 286–317). On Montaigne's change of attitude when faced with the fear of death, see J. Starobinski, *Montaigne en mouvement* (Paris, 1982), 96 et seq., and J. O'Neill, *Essaying Montaigne: A Study of the Renaissance Institution of Writing and Reading* (London, 1982), 127 et seq.

16 Montaigne, "Of Solitude," *ES* I, XXXIX, 235 (*ESe* I, XXXVIII, 256).

resolutely confronting death, had not shown him its consistency with the professed doctrines.[17] And yet, how much more more modest and admirable are those who exercise a hidden virtue, who do not boast because of their science and their intrepid determination, who do not highlight the control exerted by reason and will over the fear of their own death! In this regard, even the miserable peasants whom he sees around him or his own gardener offer examples of conduct worthy of a Stoic:

> Let us look down upon the poor people that we see scattered upon the face of the earth, prone and intent upon their business, that neither know Aristotle nor Cato, example nor precept. From these, nature every day extracts effects of constancy and patience, more pure and manly than those we so inquisitively study in the schools. How many do I ordinarily see who slight poverty? How many who desire to die, or who die without alarm or regret? He who is now digging in my garden, has this morning buried his father or his son.[18]

Sadness and meditation on death also become a dialogue with the dead, with the great or humble spirits of the past and with friends who have died, like La Boétie, in order to escape the obsessive self-control of reason and to surrender to the *ânerie si elle m'apporte plaisir*: "I am therefore angry at this trouble-feast reason, and its extravagant projects that worry one's life, and its opinions, so fine, and subtle, though they be all true; I think too dear bought and too inconvienient. On the contrary, I make it my business to bring vanity itself in repute, and follow too, if it produce me any pleasure; and let myself follow my own natural inclinations, without carrying too strict a hand upon them."[19]

Inserting the problem of death into the larger framework of the vanity and fragility of all things, Montaigne – ever more convinced that life may be supported more by luck than by wisdom (see Theophr. in Cic., *Tusc.* v, 9) – now realizes that sadness, grief, and the battle with the inevitable do not make sense. He chooses "wisdom of vanity" over tragic wisdom and *confidence avec le mourir* over any sort of exorcism: "I wrap and shroud

17 See Montaigne, "Of Physiognomy," *ES* III, XII, 1017 (*ESe* III, XII, 290).

18 Ibid.

19 Montaigne, "Of Vanity," *ES* III, IX, 974–5 (*ESe* III, IX, 241). Symptomatic is the preference given by Montaigne to Plutarch's *Moralia* (*la plus belle partie et la plus proufitable*) compared with the heroic *Parallel Lives* and to Plutarch in general with respect to Seneca (cf. *ES* II, X; III, XII; and M. Lamotte, "Montaigne et Rousseau lecteurs de Plutarque," diss., New York, 1980.

myself in the storm that is to blind and carry me away with the fury of a sudden and insensible attack."[20]

Everything is subject to the law of transformation, which can be consoling: "All things therein are incessantly moving, the earth, the rocks of Caucasus, and the pyramids of Egypt, both by the public motion and their own. Even constancy itself is no other but a slower and more languishing motion.[21] I cannot fix my object; 'tis always tottering and reeling by a natural giddiness. I take it as it is at the instant I consider it. I do not paint its being; I paint its passage."[22] His strategy towards death and life, fear and hope, changes objective. It is no longer a case of waiting for the end of existence, of preparing oneself for that single fatal moment that will conclude it, but of dividing it into separable and autonomous modules, of decontextualizing the days of life from their whole: "My design is divisible throughout; it is not grounded upon any great hopes. Every day concludes my expectation, and the journey of my life is carried on after the same manner."[23] Paraphrasing Terence, an author who would be dear to Spinoza, Montaigne, renouncing great hopes, places every expectation back within himself: *In me omnis spes est mihi.*[24] And finally, even every fear, because (from Quevedo's "Dream of Death" to Shelley's poem "Death," to Pavese's "Verrà la morte e avrà i tuoi occhi" [Death will come and it will have your eyes]) it is known that we are the death of ourselves and that it has our features.

This attitude would scandalize Pascal, who in *Entretien avec Monsieur de Saci* will reproach Montaigne for having created a dangerous mixture of pagan "proud reason" (though "knocked about with its own arms" by scepticism) and softness of heart that professes to base itself on the uncertainty of every question. From all that, Montaigne would pull the instruction to leave the worries of others and remain, in the meantime, "at rest, touching lightly upon those subjects for fear of emphasizing and supporting them … And so he escapes pain and death, because his

---

20 Montaigne, "Of Vanity," *ES* III, IX, 949 (*ESe* III, IX, 211).

21 *La constance mesme n'est autre chose qu'un branle plus languissant* (on the governance of one's own will, see *ES* III, X). This devaluation of constancy contrasts not only with the entire tradition of ancient and modern philosophical Stoicism, but also with its theatrical transpositions, deliberately accentuated, in Corneille or in the *Constant Prince* of Calderón de la Barca.

22 Montaigne, "Of Repentance," *ES* III, II, 782 (*ESe* III, II, 19).

23 Montaigne, "Of Vanity," *ES* III, IX, 955 (*ESe* III, IX, 218).

24 *ES* III, IX 946 (*ESe* III, IX, 211) and see Ter., *Adelph.* iii. 5, 9: *Nostram vitam omnium, in quo nostrae spes/opesque omnes sitae erant.*

instinct pushes him to do so, and he does not want to resist for the same reason."[25] The moral conduct of following his own country's customs would descend from the same compromising premises, "since example and comfort are the counterweights that drive him." And this would be the reason why Montaigne distances himself from "Stoic virtue," denigrating it and painting it "with a severe expression, a fierce look, bristly hair ... absorbed in a gloomy silence and alone at the top of a cliff." His virtue, gay and "frolicsome," would instead follow what attracts him from time to time: considering good and evil with benevolent detachment. From the soft bed to which he idly surrenders, he would have the impudence to show "those who search for happiness with much pain that it can be found only there and that ignorance and the absence of curiosity are two sweet pillows for a well-made head, as he himself says."[26] Pascal's harsh judgment indicates the shallowness, according to him (even with respect to Epictetus), of the *meditation mortis* undertaken by Montaigne and then transformed into *ânerie* and *folâtre* virtue.

That Which Enslaves

In the face of such positions, the Spinozan rejection of the cult of death is complete. With a significant difference of tone with respect to some of the assertions of libertine thought, particularly those contained in the then-unpublished *Theophrastus Redivivus*, the wisdom of the free man does not consist simply of making life happy by using the idea of death as proof of the fact that one should not worry about the future. It is, precisely, *non mortis, set vitae meditatio.*[27] In fact, only a grim superstition condemns the enjoyment of life: *Nihil profecto nisi torva, et tristis superstitio delectari prohibet.* Enjoyment is calm self-possession on the part of the mind and the body, which do not let themselves become depressed by the inevitable difficulties of existence. The mind of the individual is certainly not eternal like that of God, but it lives in eternity as knowledge of the truth, of that which it necessarily is. In fact, eternity and truth are synonyms: *aeternitas seu veritas.*[28] The eternity of the truth, in which we take

---

25 Pascal, *Entr.* 569–70, and see, on this work, P. Courcelle, *Entretien de Pascal et de Saci, ses sources et ses enigmes* (Paris, 1960).

26 *Entr.* 570–1.

27 See *E* 4.67 and *Theophrastus Redivivus*, in the citation from the manuscript (p. 1033) in T. Gregory, *Theophrastus Redivivus: Erudizione e ateismo nel Seicento* (Naples, 1979), 193.

28 *E* 4.62, dem.

part, is outside of time and always valid but not outside of this world that is ours alone. Particularly in intuitive science, we do not vanquish death as single and unique individuals. Rather, we defeat the fear of death that fantasy brings to us, the passionate knowledge that obfuscates the mind, hiding there the consistency, necessity, and eternity of the truth: "The greater the number of things the mind understands by the second and third kinds of knowledge, the less subject it is to emotions that are bad, and the less it fears death."[29] In knowing, we draw upon the highest joy, *beatitudo*, which is perfection itself without further *transitiones*, full satisfaction, the *animi acquiescentia*. In knowing, our entire life, the God that is nature, and all things are illuminated with meaning.[30] Hope and fear disappear, as well as insecurity and desperation and every form of sadness, not because we feel omnipotent and indestructible but because we experiment, from time to time, with having reached the limits of that power of existing that is precisely our nature.

The fact is that men, for the most part, do not feel capable of surrendering to the time of dissipation and the logic of the imagination – all signs, generally, of a low power of existing – in favour of the most difficult intra-worldly eternity, of *carpe aeternitatem in momento* and intuitive science, that shows the specific necessity of *res singulares* in the articulation of the whole. This is why they are obsessed with fear of death, with the idea of time that flees inexorably, with unsatisfied yearnings and hopes, with the frustrations that follow failures and with regrets for missed or failed actions that they drag with them. This is why they are not free men, and they show a servile heart: because in relying on what is incidental and that, as such, cannot give constant satisfaction, and by surrendering not to themselves but to their more-or-less permanent passions, they end up fearing death or meditating obsessively on it (through weakness, cowardice, or sadness). In fact, servitude is just a juridical or political condition that is natural and necessary. Neither Spinoza nor Hobbes reason, like Aristotle or Sepúlveda, according to the concept of a difference by nature between free men and slaves. Rather, they continually (for good or ill) emphasize equality, the reciprocal benefit – or even the harmfulness – of all men. In Spinoza, "servitude" means that one is not master of oneself when he abandons himself to external powers that, although provoked by external causes, live with us and "within" us when

29 *E* 5.38.
30 *E* 5.42, schol.

he obeys the passions in an indolent manner or resists them with weak effort. Servitude is, in fact, "man's lack of power to control and check the emotions. For a man at the mercy of his emotions is not his own master but is subject to fortune, in whose power he so lies that he is often compelled, although he sees the better course, to pursue the worse."[31] He is thus condemned to live outside of active and life-giving knowledge of the eternal and of the truth, remaining caught in passivity and the relative weakness of the passions and the imagination.

31 *E* 4, praef. See also *E* 4.67, dem.

6. *Vanitas*

Et in Arcadia ego

For Spinoza, the most difficult obstacle to overcome, that which impedes the realization of usefulness and happiness, is represented by the behaviour of men. In fact, they are their own worst enemies. They yearn for life, but – like Ignatius of Loyola or the melancholy – they are attracted by *amor mortis*, by the perverse pleasure of pain or desperation for their own future fate, in this world and the next. They all desire, in a word, liberty; they appear inclined to follow their own *utilitas*, but they end up for the most part resigned to live in terror of Leviathan and of Hell or to die for the glory of an individual or a God who watches over their own passivity and nothingness. They complain continuously of the transience of their own existence, but then they do not know how to make good use of it, and they seek recompense in its brevity and in the hope of an eternal life. However, as long as they act this way, they are still servants. In fact, as we know, "a free man thinks of death least of all things."[1] Consequently, a meditation is useful to him, so that he may exercise the passions to develop life, loosening it from passivity, starting with imagination itself.[2] Philosophy does not require a detachment from existence, a renunciation of joy. It is not melancholy, the tendency to see things under the sign of loss, as much as a way of considering them *sub specie aeternitatis*.

Instead, melancholy people (heirs to the medieval attitude of contempt for the world, awareness of the vanity of all things) desire to

1 *E* 4.67: *non mortis sed vitae meditatio est.*

2 *E* 3.12: *Mens, quantum postest, ea imaginari conatur, quae corporis agendi potentiam augent, vel juvant.*

separate themselves from other men and take leave of all pleasure, judging it to be impossible. They therefore seek refuge in a pastoral utopia so that they can be completely alone, so as not to meet (paradoxically) even themselves. "Let the misanthropists [*melancholici*] heap praise on the life of rude rusticity, despising men and admiring beasts. Men will still discover from experience that they can much more easily meet their needs by mutual help and can ward off ever-threatening perils only by joining forces, not to mention that it is a much more excellent thing and worthy of our knowledge to study the deeds of men than the deeds of beasts."[3]

Melancholy is tied to the "uncultured and rural life" of bucolic poetry and the pastoral landscape, to the death that is always present within it, from the odes of Theocritus to Poussin's painting *Et in Arcadia ego* – even in the seeming happiness of the solitude of the forests and the simple life of the shepherds, even in Arcadia, there is death.[4] The transience of all things ("Every thought flies" is written on a large mask with an open mouth decorating the garden of Bomarzo, with deliberate ambiguity) and the disappointment that comes over us in the moments when we attain the objects of our desire (well tended at first, with their newness and differentness that, nonetheless, do not succeed in eliminating the uneasiness) reveal themselves precisely in the aspiration to a more perfect solitude. They also reveal themselves, paradoxically, in the most idyllically peaceful landscape. Solitary life and fear are, after all, characteristics traditionally attributed to the melancholy man.[5] Piety or scorn towards men push him to isolation, evoking in him crying or derision. Even in this case, an old *topos* – reprised in the modern age by Montaigne and Burton – sees the condemnation of human vices represented by two wise men who depict, in turn, the double face of melancholy: "Democritus

3 *E* 4.35, schol. See also 4.67.

4 On the presence of the subject of death in the earliest bucolic poetry, see C. Segal, "Death by Water: A Narrative Pattern in Theocritus (*Idylls* I 12.22,23)," in *Poetry and Myth in Ancient Pastoral: Essays on Theocritus and Virgil* (Princeton, 1981), 47–67. On the subject of melancholy and death in the pastoral landscape, see E. Panowski, "*Et in Arcadia ego:* On the Conception of Transience in Poussin and Watteau," in *Philosophy and History: Essays Presented to E. Cassirer* (Oxford, 1936; rpt. New York, 1963), 224 et seq.

5 Against the transience of the things of the world, Spinoza could not have repeated – with Michelet and against Marcus Aurelius or the melancholics – that *histoire est une resurrection*, because he lacks the sense of history. However, he could refer to *tristitia* as a state that can be defeated, creating the conditions for an increase in the power of existing.

and Heraclitus were two philosophers, of whom the first, finding human condition ridiculous and vain, never appeared abroad but with a jeering and laughing countenance; whereas Heraclitus, commiserating that same condition of ours, appeared always with a sorrowful look, and tears in his eyes."[6]

Like Montaigne, Burton (a new Democritus or "Democritus Junior," as he called himself) juxtaposes the philosopher from Abdera to Heraclitus accustomed to crying over the evils and defects of his peers:

> A mere spectator of other men's fortunes and adventures, and how they act their parts, which methinks are diversely presented unto me as from a common theatre or scene. I hear new news every day, and those ordinary rumors of war, plagues, fires, inundations, thefts, murders, massacres, meteors, comets, spectrums, prodigies, apparitions, of towns taken, cities besieged in France, Germany, Turkey, Persia, Poland, etc., daily musters and preparations, and such like; which these tempestuous times afford, battles fought, so many men slain, monomachies, shipwrecks, piracies, and sea-fights; peace, leagues, stratagems, and fresh alarms.[7]

Burton immediately indicates *supersitiosus* and *solitudo* as signs of melancholy.[8] Although laughing and crying are its complementary aspects, he takes the side of derision and indignation, typical of the satirical genre. In the pseudo-Hippocratic *Letters to Damagetos* – widely cited by Burton – it is asserted: "If men would govern their actions by discretion and providence, they would not declare themselves fools as now they do, and he should have no cause of laughter; but (quoth he) they swell in this life as if they were immortal, and demigods, for want of understanding. It were enough to make them wise, if they would but consider the

---

6 Montaigne, "Of Democritus and Heraclitus," *ES* I, L, 291 (*ESe* I, L, 348). On misanthropy and the condemnation of the vices of men, through the smiling of Democritus and the crying of Heraclitus, see J.N. Shklar, *Ordinary Vices* (Cambridge, MA, 1984); Ital. trans. *Vizi comuni* (Bologna, 1986), 227–65. For an interesting discussion of crying, see A. Vincent-Buffault, *Histoire des larmes,* XVIIe–XIXe *siècles* (Paris, 1986).

7 Burton, *AM* 30.

8 See Burton, *AM,* frontispiece of the third edition of 1628. On this subject, see J.R. Simon, *Robert Burton (1577–1640) et l'*Anatomie de la Mélanconie (Paris, 1964). That utopia might assume a melancholic character is shown by J. Shklar, "The Political Theory of Utopia: From Melancholy to Nostalgia," *Daedalus* (Spring, 1965), 367–81, and J. Starobinski, *Democrito parla (l'utopia malinconica di Robert Burton),* introduction to Burton, *AMi* 7–45.

mutability of this world, and how it wheels about, nothing being firm and sure."[9] The passions disturb hearts, taking from them absolutely every capacity to reason and transforming men into "brutes" (no security can therefore redeem them and raise them to the civil state): "All men are carried away with passion, discontent, lust, pleasures, etc.; they generally hate those virtues they should love and love such vices they should hate. Therefore, more than melancholy, quite mad, brute beasts, and void of reason, so Chrysostom contends; 'or rather dead and buried alive,' as Philo Judeus concludes it for a certainty, 'of all such that are carried away with passions, or labor of any disease of the mind.' 'Where is fear and sorrow,' there, Lactantius stiffly maintains, 'wisdom cannot dwell.'"[10]

The Antidote for Melancholy

In his famous statement "I have taken great care not to deride, bewail, or execrate human actions, but to understand them," Spinoza seems to be referring paradigmatically to the two figures of Democritus and Heraclitus.[11] Understanding means defeating both faces of melancholy. In theoretical terms, this means cutting "the thread of the Parca" that unites death, *tristitia*, and philosophy. In political terms, it means surpassing the complementary and involuntary connivance of the cunning politicians and the utopians.

Of course, the Spinozan wise man does not arrive at an anesthesia of feeling or complete ataraxia. Through knowledge and *constantia* of the character – and not self-punishment – he tries not to distance himself too much from the bliss that he can reach even amid the evils of the world. Thus, he "suffers scarcely any disturbance of spirit, but being conscious, by virtue of a certain eternal necessity, of himself, of God and of things, never ceases to be, but always possesses true spiritual contentment."[12] And although he may not be as unfeeling as the Stoic, who remains imperturbable and endures the torments within the "bull of Phalaris," the free man ends up capable of preserving his own joy even in difficult situations, and he displays a serene courage because he loves life. The ascending *transitiones* of the *conatus* are, for him, the antidote

9 Cited in Burton, *AM* 68.

10 Burton, *AM* 101. The quotation of Lactantius, *Lib. de sept.*, whose meaning would not be rejected by Spinoza, reads: *Ubi timor adest, sapientia adesse nequit.*

11 See *TP* 1.4 and *E* 3, praef.: *nec ridere, nec lugere, sed intelligere.*

12 *E* 5.42, schol.

to melancholy, to desire that does not devalue the object even before reaching it or as soon as it has reached it. The melancholic man is, instead, led to contempt for life, to the self-destructive cult of death, to a negativity that (in becoming a firm point, however) at least offers him this single certainty: all is vanity. What the man who is struck by melancholic *acedia* lacks most, in fact, is steadfastness and determination, constancy and the capacity to concentrate his own energies. Instead, he has pronounced his disgust for the end that he is about to reach. As soon has he gets near it (although he perhaps wanted it) every effort of will or intelligence seem in vain to him. His desire, lacking intellectual life, remains weak and hesitating.

Showing himself averse to melancholy, Spinoza says he is not trying to pass through life in sorrow and moaning, but rather in peace, joy, and happiness.[13] The wise man allows himself laughter (not melancholic derision like Democritus) because the greater the *laetitia* by which we are affected, the greater the perfection to which we pass – that is, it is all the more necessary that we participate in divine nature.[14] Laughing in moderation, being content with oneself, is therefore a good, the symptom of an ethical virtue that does not rise from the ascesis and the mortification of the spirit and the body.[15] It is therefore worthy of the wise man to make use of things and to draw pleasure from them as much as possible (i.e., not to the point of nausea, because that means, precisely, not enjoying them). "It is, I repeat, the part of a wise man to refresh and invigorate himself in moderation with good food and drink, as also with perfumes, with the beauty of blossoming plants, with dress, music, sporting activities, theaters, and the like, in which every man can indulge without harm to another."[16] Spinoza refers to "blossoming plants," but

---

13 See *Ep.* 21.823: *vitam non maerore et gemitu, sed tranquillitate, laetitia et hilaritate transigere studeo.*

14 In Hobbes, laughter is often born from the presumption of one's own superiority over others. See *DH* XII, 7. The position of Descartes is different – see *PA*, art. 149 et seq.

15 "Certainly nothing but grim and gloomy superstition forbids enjoyment. Why is it less fitting to drive away melancholy than to dispel hunger and thirst? The principle that guides me and shapes my attitude to life is this: no deity, nor anyone else but the envious, takes pleasure in my weakness and my misfortune, nor does he take to be a virtue our tears, sobs, fearfulness, and other such things that are a mark of a weak spirit. On the contrary, the more we are affected with pleasure, the more we pass to a state of greater perfection; that is, the more we necessarily participate in the divine nature" (*E* 4.45, schol.).

16 Ibid.

certainly not stylized nostalgia or solitude, a fictitious desire to regress to a pastoral life or the simplicity of the golden age. Imposing or enduring privations, the *meditatio mortis* and melancholy confirm for the most part a devaluation of the body and the pleasures that derive from it. This is another reason why Spinoza rejects the temptation to see things under the sign of transience.

Living Nature

In looking at the world in this light, Spinozan thought shows affinities and differences with respect to the images of the world offered by the painting of the time. If we consider one of the subjects typical of Dutch paintings, we might realize how much the expressions "still life," *natura morta,* and *Stilleben* are partly misleading, because in reality they deal with vegetables and animals (flowers, fruit, game, oysters, fish – all things thought of for the joy and enjoyment of man) that appear suspended between life that is ephemeral or just ended, and death; between mobility and immobility, between their visible form and the coming consumption or decomposition. Together, they give evidence, with equal force, of the pleasures of life and their vanity, joyous moments and their passing, the utility and beauty of daily goods and their brief fate. These beings are represented at their *toppunt,* at the zenith before the fall, in the moment of perfect maturity that precedes their corruption.[17] Subjected to the Spinozan perspective that considers them *sub specie aeternitatis,* they would appear, however – in their nature as "particular things" intuitively known by intellectual love – to be "living life" rather than "still life." After all, the tendency to save the *res particulares* in the complexity of their relationships to a whole without a centre and without a periphery seems to be one of the specific traits of the great European painting of the seventeenth century.[18]

According to Spinoza, the imagination can, if properly directed, also become the fulcrum for an initial rising to the knowledge of necessity that defeats the mournful feeling of melancholy *vanitas* and begins to

17 See W. Burger (T. Thoré), *Les Musées de Hollande* (Paris, 1858), vol. 1, 323. On Spinoza and the Dutch pictorial environment of the time (within the circle of Spinoza's closest friends figures a painter), see D. Regin, *Traders, Artists, Burghers: A Cultural History of Amsterdam in the 17th Century* (Assen, 1976), and G. Aiullaud, *Vermeer et Spinoza* (Paris, 1987).

18 On the interest of Velásquez in concreteness and individuality, see J.A. Maravall, *Velásquez y el espíritu de la modernidad* (Madrid, 1987).

placate the soul: "For we see that pain over the loss of some good is assuaged as soon as the man who has lost it realizes that that good could not have been saved in any way."[19] Showing the dimension of the eternal, the *intelligere* is lifted by the prospect of transience, thus reducing and stabilizing the fluctuations between fear and hope. Philosophy ceases to be a mere "lingering" on the cognition of sorrow or on suffering understood through pain. With *tristitia* reabsorbed and the passions transformed into positive feelings, it can proceed towards a bliss that is of this world and that is, in itself, truth and life. What Fichte would continue to repeat – that is, he who philosophizes does not live and he who lives does not philosophize – does not possess any validity in Spinoza.

In this way, philosophy loses the accomplice-enemy that it has in common with religion and that, since Parmenides, it has tried to exorcise through wisdom and the eternal solidity of being: that is, death and non-being.[20]

19 *E* 5.6 schol.

20 See K. Heinrich, *Parmenides und Jona* (Basel, 1982). Parmenides wants to transform the *me on* into *ouk on* – the not-being into something that has no value. The "man who knows" ascends to heaven in a luminous chariot, and Dike reveals to him the immobile unity of being, eternally present and without purpose. For Heinrich, there are three paths: that of being, which the wise man already knows; that of not-being, which is unfeasible; and that – typical of the "two-headed" (*dikranoi*) multitude and of Heraclitus – which wavers between being and not-being or proclaims its modularity and harmonic equivalence (in a theology of Apollo, the bow, death, and the lyre).

7. Fear and Rejection

The Mass of the Unaware

Spinoza soberly notes that "everyone knows to what wickedness men are frequently persuaded by dissatisfaction with their lot and desire for change, by hasty anger, by disdain of poverty, and how their minds are engrossed and agitated by these emotions" (*TTP* 17.*538*). But to such passions and "common vices" men react differently, because they are divided between the few who live "according to the laws of reason" (*TTP* 16.*527*) and the many who "are led more by blind desire than by reason" (*TP* 2.5).

The first are those who have undertaken the *perardua* (extremely arduous) but navigable path of wisdom. The second consists of the *multitudo*, the *vulgus*, the *populus*, or the *plebs*[1] – that is, the *maxima humani generis pars* (*TTP* 5.*441*). Unlike the wise men, this majority makes up the crowd of the unaware, those who ignore the causes of their situation.

Certainty, the relationship between truth and authority is different in the two groups. Among wise men, it rests on rational or intuitive knowledge, which is greater the more that men participate in enjoyment of it (see *E* 5.20 and dem.) – that is, the greater the number who think as much as possible.[2] In the crowd, it clings to faith, which is imaginative

---

1 For a terminological analysis, there are several excellent tools available, such as the *Lexicon Spinozanum*, ed. E. Giancotti Boscherini, 2 vols. (The Hague, 1970–1); *Spinoza: Ethica, concordances, index, liste des fréquences, tables comparatives*, ed. M. Gueret, A. Robinet, and P. Tombeur (Louvain-le-Neuve, 1977); and *Spinoza: Traité politiques: Index informatique*, ed. P.F. Moreau and R. Bouveresse (Paris, 1979).

2 For this formulation, see E. Balibar, *Spinoza et la politique* (Paris, 1985), 118. For Spinoza, from the *Tractatus de intellectus emendatione* forward, effort is necessary – for the

knowledge necessary for obedience, order of the passions' submission to the social body, and a collective usefulness again based on the low intensity or virtual erasure of individual *utilitates.* In fact, most people lack the capacity to follow the "long series of connected propositions" and the "greatest caution, acuteness of intelligence and restraint" required for superior types of knowledge and that are "rarely to be found among men" (*TTP* 5.*441*).

That is, lacking insight, most men are forced to subject themselves to impositions and obligations dimly carried out as foresight, but that have on their part, however, all the power and authority of a theological-political oppression institutionalized and internalized for millennia. They consider them

> burdens which they hope to lay aside after death, when they will receive the reward of their servitude, that is, of piety and religion. And it is not by this hope alone, but also and especially by fear of incurring dreadful punishment after death, that they are induced to live according to the commandments of the divine law as far as their feebleness and impotent spirit allows. And if men did not have this hope and this fear, and if they believed on the contrary that minds perish with bodies and that they, miserable creatures, worn out by the burden of piety, had no prospect of further existence, they would return to their own inclinations and decide to shape their lives according to their lusts, and to be ruled by fortune rather than by themselves. (*E* 5.41, schol.)

The Fear of the Common Man

The mob, conceived as a mass that cannot be disassembled atomistically in the social contract, inspires fear and terror in those who command: *Multitudo imperantibus formidosa est* (*TP* 8.4). But it is also afraid: *Terret vulgus nisi metuat.* Fear, both endured and exercised, is its most customary horizon of expectation. Like all theorists of politics contemporaneous to him, accustomed to dealing with the *tumultus* and with the *seditio,* Spinoza also knows the fearsome fury of the masses. He had present

---

happiness of man – to ensure that the many understand what the wise man understands, so that their desires and their intellect agree with his desires and his intellect (on this requirement, see A. Tosel, *Spinoza ou le crépuscule de la servitude: Essai sur le Traité Théologico-politique* [Paris, 1984], 21).

the canonical example of the crowd of the Jews who – instigated by the Sanhedrin – preferred to condemn Jesus rather than Barabbas, thus marking themselves with a "guilt" that would traditionally be attributed to them by Christians. Moreover, he was directly struck by the effects of an act completed in his time by the masses of a nation then famous in Europe for its tolerance and civility – an act that suddenly became cruel: by the furious action of the Dutch common people who, in 1672 (incited by the faction guided by the *Stadhoulder* William of Orange, resorting to superstition), had literally torn the Grand Pensionary, Jan de Witt, to pieces, along with his brother.

Unlike Lipsius and Hobbes, however, Spinoza did not stop at condemnation of the sedition and riots, nor did he limit himself to emphasizing only the hypothetically positive aspects in increasing the potential energies of the state, as had been suggested by Machiavelli for the Roman republic.[3] Against the detractors of democracy and the rights of the masses – that is, against those who assert that "'the common people is either a humble servant or an arrogant master, there is no truth or judgment in it,' and the like" (*TP* 7.27), he limits himself simply to observing that nature is equal in all men. They behave with greater or lesser rationality in relation to the passions to which they are prey and to the appropriate or inappropriate ideas within which they frame their reciprocal relationships. If the excesses of the people are condemned, almost always *servituti adsuetus*, what should then be said about the overbearing manner of the nobility, whose boundless pride and wild ambition seem less severe only because they are consecrated by being long-accustomed to power? "But their arrogance is bedecked by an air of disdain, by magnificence, by lavishness, by a certain blending of vices and a kind of cultivated folly and a refined depravity, so that vices, each of which when taken separately and thus rendered conspicuous is seen as foul and base, appear to the naïve and the ignorant as honorable and becoming" (ibid.).

The common people behave in a passionate, superstitious, and passionate manner precisely because they have often systematically been kept far from politics and the exercise of power, limited to guessing, from a few signs and from indemonstrable hypotheses, what is happening at the level of the state: "Finally, that 'there is no truth or judgment in the common people' is not surprising, since the important affairs of state

3 See the following section, "Rioting."

are conducted without their knowledge, and from the little that cannot be concealed they can only make conjectures."[4]

But a politics that – combining rationality and passion, calculation and imagination – is carried out in the shadow of the cabinet of the princes who let only obscure messages or mimed passion filter out is "the height of folly." It is one of the principal causes that push the people to incite or live in fear. It is not, however, only the masses that provoke terror when they are not frightened: "All men have the same nature – all grow haughty with rule, terrorize unless they are frightened – and everywhere truth becomes a casualty through hostility or servility, especially when despotic power is in the hands of one or a few who in trials pay attention not to justice or truth but to the extent of a person's wealth" (ibid.).

Rioting

On this crucial point of the advertisement of affairs of state as a means for educating the common people, Spinoza again makes a clean break both from "that keen observer, Machiavelli"[5] and from Justus Lipsius. In the *Prince* in particular, Machiavelli had asserted the necessity to use and flaunt appearances in politics. Most men are satisfied with how much they are permitted to see, and those who are not content can be intimidated, forced to pretend that they believe in the staging of political power.[6] Spinoza is opposed to the theory and practice of the double truth and the *raison d'état* (a term introduced by Guicciardini) explained in the *Prince*, in that he contrasts, to the shrewd politicians' game of appearances and being, the idea that an order can be perceived in the world that is superior to the one depicted by the theatre of the imagination. The effective reality of the thing – life itself – is the world's stage. A political regime is better the less it needs to resort to duplication of the

4 *TP* 7.27. The common man thus develops, through the imagination, a series of fantastic conjectures that have (as we will see) the same structure as superstition at the religious level.

5 *TP* 5.7.

6 *P* XVIII: "Men in general judge by their eyes rather than by their hands; because everyone is in a position to watch, few are in a position to come in close touch with you. Everyone sees what you appear to be, few experience what you really are. And those few dare not gainsay the many who are backed by the majesty of the state ... The common people are always impressed by appearances and results. In this context, there are only common people."

real in appearances – that is, of basing itself on imagination to appeal to men's weakness, of dazzling them with pomp to better hide its own secrets. Despite the desire for its own transparency, even Lipsius knows and asserts that political power needs to mask itself.[7]

For Machiavelli, however, the most solid states are those that, although imaginatively hiding the break between new and old orders, do not hide the "horizontal" conflict of the present. From this point of view – even if he does not approve of rioting in principle – Spinoza agrees with the sense of those chapters of the *Discourses* that show the common Roman capable, in his struggle against the patricians, of not degenerating into the corrupt common man and not organizing himself in factions, just as had happened in Florence at the time of Savonarola and Pier Soderini.[8] In ancient Rome, such harsh conflicts made the republic "free and powerful":

> I maintain that those who blame the quarrels of the Senate and the people of Rome condemn that which was the very origin of liberty, and that they were probably more impressed by the cries and noise which those disturbances occasioned in the public places, than by the good effect which they produced; and that they do not consider that in every republic there are two parties, that of the nobles and that of the people; and all the laws that are favorable to liberty result from the opposition of these parties to each other." (*D* I, 4, 119)

While, in fact, the nobility "wish to be free for the purpose of commanding," the Roman plebes "desire liberty so as to be able to live in greater security" (ibid., I, 16, 163) – that is, without fear. But in this "conflictual republic," the struggle is not always triggered by the little people or the "proletariat." On the contrary, "it seems, however, that they are most frequently occasioned by those who possess; for the fear to lose stirs the same passions in men as the desire to gain, as men do not believe

7 The seventeenth-century poet Georg Philipp Harsdörffer relates these words of Lipsius: "Just as we see the hand of the clock and we read the time without having any idea of the ingenious functioning of its complicated workings, so can we observe the blessings and the punishments of God without knowing their secret causes. Similarly, the actions of princes and of nobles are before our eyes, but their intentions and their motivations are hidden" (*Delitiae mathematicae et physicae* [Nuremburg, 1651], 348–9).

8 By non-corrupt Roman society, Machiavelli means "flowering from collective energies" (F. Chabod, *Scritti su Machiavelli* [Turin, 1964], 33).

themselves sure of what they already possess except by acquiring still more" (ibid., I, 5, 124).

The "bad contentment" with what one possesses then propels to the conflict of ambitions, motivated by insecurity: "The reason of this is that nature has created men so that they desire everything, but are unable to attain it; desire being thus always greater than the faculty of acquiring, discontent with what they have, and dissatisfaction with themselves result from it. This causes the changes in their fortunes; for as some men desire to have more, whilst others fear to lose what they have, enmities and war are the consequences; and this brings about the ruin of one province and the elevation of another" (ibid., I, 37, 208). It is precisely within this space of "*mala contentezza*" (regarding which see also the *Proemio* to the second book of the *Discourses*), within the gap between "desiring everything" and not being able to achieve it, that politics – particularly modern politics – takes over, in its resorting to illusions and necessary appearances.

In the same way, factions do not normally emerge from below. One certainly unforgettable example is offered by the still-young Machiavelli during the convulsive period in which he entered public life, when Fra Girolamo Savonarola stirred the hearts of Florentines with fear of eternal fire and with hope for their regeneration in this world and the next, promising the imminent descent of a Reign of God on earth according to a model of celestial perfection and overheating the crowd's imagination. In his doubt over having few proselytes and not finding the Signoria on his side, he tried to create his theocratic republic with threats and promises:

> He began his talk by frightening everybody; he used arguments that were very convincing to those who did not examine them carefully, showing how his followers were the most excellent of men and his enemies the most wicked, using every rhetorical device that existed to weaken his opponents and to strengthen his own faction. Since I was present, let me tell you briefly about a few of these devices.[9]

In the church of San Marco, he held a fiery sermon in which he asserted that "the honor of God" and the times required that people give in

9 Niccolò Machiavelli to Ricciardo Becchi, Florence, 8 March 1498, in *PM* 55.

to rage: "And having given this brief speech, he described two groups of people – one that fought for God, and this was himself and his devotees, and the other commanded by the Devil, which was his opponents."[10]

In the case of the Roman republic, the liberty of the masses is based on the absence of external impediments to the achievement of their own ends – that is, on the explicit desire to not permit the "greats" to subjugate the people. Even in the modern age, "those republics which have thus preserved their political existence uncorrupted do not permit any of their citizens to be or to live in the manner of gentlemen, but rather maintain amongst them a perfect equality, and are the most decided enemies of the lords and gentlemen that exist in the country" (*D* I, 55, 254).

The liberty of the individual is possible only in the "free living" of the entire community that governs itself and that tends towards equality and the common good. Necessary for this purpose are the republican virtues of prudence and magnanimity that alone preserve and consolidate liberty. Precisely because men are "wicked," they can achieve the best form of communal life only provided that their interests and their duty coincide. It is necessary to give them egotistical reasons to be virtuous.[11]

In the long term, fear alone is not, in fact, sufficient to link special interests with general interests. Once again – thinking of Hobbes, in whom the role of fear is certainly not absolute but certainly remains central – the liberty of the individual is not assured (according to the Machiavelli of the *Discourses*) by a regime that bases itself upon it, but only by a free state, the only thing that manages to reconcile (and even reciprocally strengthen) the *utilitas* of the individual with that of the collective, with the common good. Thus, the general interest ceases to represent, on one hand, a utopian objective, a must-be, and on the other, the result of a pact in which the particular egoisms and forms of their compatibility are negotiated and in which obedience to laws is placed under the aegis of reason governed by fear, rather than by *utilitas*.

---

10 Ibid., in *PM* 56.

11 See Q. Skinner, "The Idea of Negative Liberty: Philosophical and Historical Perspectives," in *Philosophy in History*, ed. R. Rorty, J.B. Schneewind, and Q. Skinner (Cambridge, 1984), 193–221 (particularly 24 et seq.). Unlike Spinoza, Machiavelli still appreciates hope, since it strengthens the trust of individuals in the controlling *fortuna*. See *D* II, 29, 367.

Men and Fish

Spinoza is close, then, to the republican Machiavelli, who does not consider the people, the masses of the unaware, as necessarily corrupt. Both think of individuals as potentially capable, in specific circumstances, of simultaneously following their own *utilitas* and the general interest, provided that these coincide for the most part. But in Spinoza, another element is added: "democracy," which makes possible not only a relative balance between self-preservation of individuals and the life of the state, but also a parallel increase in the power of existing of both the individual and the community.

Every state being an individual compound, a structure of well-defined order in which individuals "are all guided, as it were, by one mind" (*una veluti mente ducuntur: TP* 2.16), democracy is the most equitable, coherent, and differentiated form of accumulation and redistribution of power and rights between the citizen and the state: "Such a community's right is called a democracy, which can therefore be defined as a united body of men which corporately [*collegialiter*] possesses sovereign right over everything within its power" (*TTP* 16.*530*). In it, the *conatus* of each person comes together, generating a single and joint process of dual and reciprocal growth, where the obeying of laws is theoretically free from fear and where feelings and ideas can develop in the direction of greater joy and power of existing. Since the right of nature extends to the point where it reaches the power of every being (and it is therefore right that the big fish eat the small; see *TTP* 16.*527*), the achievement of democracy presumes that men associated with one another become so strong, standing together, as to no longer be forced by fear and hope to renounce their own self-preservation properly understood. It thus requires that everyone's power be developed, that they be transformed, so to speak, into fish more or less of the same size (but, still speaking figuratively, what would these fish eat?). In this sense, democracy is the absolute form of governance[12] – that which develops the greatest individual and collective power of existing and guarantees the maximum security as the entire society, the *communis multitudo*, maintains the power collectively (*TTP* 5.*439*) and therefore has less fear of external attacks.[13]

12 See *TP* 11.1: *Transeo tandem ad tertium, et omnino absolutum imperium quod Democraticum appellamus.*

13 On the concept and the extension of democracy in Spinoza, see A. Negri, *L'anomalia selvaggia,* 299 et seq.

Security sets itself against both fear and hope and creates a basic human aspiration: "Furthermore, there is nobody who does not desire to live in safety free from fear, as much as is possible" (*TTP* 16.*529*).[14] Politically, it is not only the opposite of anarchy (which, in turn, generated and increased the need for it) but also of chance, of chivalous risk whose loss the heroic aristocratic ethics and the imagination of Don Quixote did not know how to accept. The development of adequate knowledge and the broadening of the area of certain and shared knowledge, reducing the margins of the unknown and the impact of uncertainty about the future, limit the space of *insecuritas.*[15]

From the citizens' point of view, however, as long as individuals do not collectively become stronger, all moralistic derision or compassion for their impotence is futile and damaging. In fact, there is no "guilt" either on the part of those who actively oppress and know how to make their own power count or on the part of those who passively suffer the will of others. And this applies both with respect to other men or groups and with respect to the collective itself, as it may profess simply to impose itself with force or with the authority of law, pushing individuals to sacrifice (not consciously or reciprocally) their own *utilitas*[16] or, in the case of rebellion, to exercise a mere pipe dream of power.

Spinoza suggests a dynamic, collective model of politics that subverts all ideas that are static, harmonic, or intent on masking changes. Therefore, he would not have approved of the fear of the *rerum novarum cupiditas* that Montaigne, who lived in the era of violent political and religious

---

14 Since *De intellectus emendatione,* Spinoza was searching for a *fixum bonum* capable of providing security, placating the conscience of human weakness, of the *humana imbecillitas* (*TIE* 8) in its inability to always satisfy *cupiditas.*

15 More generally, the problem of *se-cur(itas),* also understood as care of oneself, is enlightened, in relation to our times, by the essays of F.-X. Kaufmann, *Sicherheit also soziologisches und sozialpolitisches Problem* (Stuttgart, 1973); A.F. Fritzsche, *Wie sicher leben wir?* (Cologne, 1986); U. Beck, *Risikogesellschaft: Auf den Weg einer anderen Moderne* (Frankfurt, 1986); and H. Lübbe, "Sicherheitskultur: Unsicherheitserfahrung in der modernen Gesellschaft," in *Wieviel Sicherheit brauch der Mensch* (Zurich, 1989), 5–29.

16 Against those who assert that in his *Political Treatise* Spinoza would have abandoned his support for democracy, amply expressed in the *Theological-Political Treatise,* see the pertinent objections of R.J. McShea, *The Political Philosophy of Spinoza* (New York, 1964), 123 et seq. On *utilitas* see pp. 113, 115, and 135 of this volume. But see also, for example, *E* 4.57, schol.: "I am going on to point out what features in our emotions bring advantage or harm to men."

rifts, abhorred more than the plague. The author of the *Essays* realized the relativity of different peoples' customs, but he was in favour of obedience to the laws of his own country, the only anchor of salvation in the face of the abyss of anarchy: "I have a great aversion from novelty, what face or what pretense soever it may carry along with it, and have reason, having been an eyewitness of the great evils it has produced … They who give the first shock to a state are almost naturally the first overwhelmed in its ruin. The fruits of public commotion are seldom enjoyed by him who was the first motor. He beats and disturbs the water for another's net."[17] Spinoza no longer feels even the need, asserted by Machiavelli in the *Discourses*, of ensuring that free states "at least retain the semblance of the old forms; so that it may seem to the people that there has been no change in the institutions, even though in fact they are entirely different from the old ones." In fact, for Machiavelli, most individuals do not distinguish the reality from the appearance and even let themselves be more easily seduced by this latter: "For the great majority of mankind are satisfied with appearances, as though they were realities, and are often even more influenced by the things that seem than by those that are" (*D* I, 25, 182).

Obedience and Sacrifice

Self-renunciation for the benefit of other individuals is one of the most widespread attitudes and one of the most constant targets of Spinoza's *Ethics*.[18] But what now seems like intolerable oppression to those who enjoy the security offered by a democracy is, instead, merely the ripe fruit of the connivance and collaboration of a double fear and a double hope, of a conjoined servitude (theological-political, religious, and state) that corresponded and corresponds to "just" and real imbalances of power and rights.

Unlike what would happen with Rousseau and the Jacobins, the Spinozan conception of democracy had nothing to do with the model of the ancients, which is often based on the sacrifice of individuals to the common good and, in general, fruit of mere obedience to traditions or to the *mos maiorum*. This also allows him – in addition to the rejection of sacrifice – the theoretically more radical attack that until then

17 Montaigne, "Of Custom," *ES* I, XXII, 118 (*ESe* I, XXII, 112).
18 See *TTP*, praef.

had been launched against the motivations of obedience. If each person has reached a power of existing not very dissimilar from that of his fellow citizens and has become master of himself, he has the power (and therefore the right) to reject obedience to a state and an authority that present themselves as absolute, indisputable, and superior to the power resulting from the collectivity of the constituent individuals. Therefore, Spinoza does not grant any substantial premium to any form of government in itself, not even to democracy. The only metric he uses is one that measures the capacity of a political regime to increase as much as possible – in given circumstances – its members' power of existing. Implicitly denied, then, is the Aristotelian recognition (subsequently reprised and condemned by Hegel) of the supremacy "by nature" of the whole over its parts, of the state over its citizens. In this way, it also becomes possible, concurrently, to reject any type of social contract that may provide for alienation or that delegates, revocably or irrevocably, some of the powers and rights of individuals.

Still, even if the conditions exist, no one is required to yield passively to any sort of "general will" that may present itself as an entity incomparably higher than the ordered sum of its parts, of the *conatus* of the individuals. In this sense – despite the opinion of some great interpreters – I do not believe that Spinoza's solution approaches that of Rousseau, however true it may be that Rousseau had in mind the Spinozan assertion that a democratic government is one "approaching most closely to that freedom which nature grants to every man. For in a democratic state nobody transfers his natural right to another so completely that thereafter he is not to be consulted; he transfers it to the majority of the entire community of which he is part. In this way all men remain equal, as they were before in a state of nature" (*TTP* 16.*531*). The essential difference lies precisely in the fact that Spinoza does not ask individuals for preventive renunciation and thus does not risk the unequal exchange that inevitably is set up between completely surrendering one's own liberty to the general will and receiving in exchange only a portion. In this latter case, liberty and power alienated from the general will are restored, so to speak, with the subtraction of the political surplus value that the state retains for itself, like a sort of tax for its own autonomous survival with respect to the possible whims of the "will of all together" (*TTP* 16.*528*).

If no one is obligated to obey a democracy that expects unjustifiable sacrifices of individual *utilitas* (since it is precisely on this that the equation between power and rights justifies itself), still less should one bend to tottering political supremacy, having the means to do so, and to the declining *vis existendi* of a previously ruling despot, king, or aristocracy.

Spinoza's logic thus ends up being the complete opposite of Hobbes's. Spinoza places himself in the point of view of someone who struggles to reduce the passivity of men and not in that of the monarch's sovereignty. He is as familiar as Hobbes (despite his insistence on joy) with the drama of the sacrifices that demand organization of associated life and the maintenance and increase of order and power. His view, however, comes from below, from the assumption of the viewpoint of the individual who tries to save himself and others, collectively growing in power, so as to be able to counter the bullying of others. Hobbes's view, on the other hand, generally comes from above (once the natural state is abandoned): from the more strongly emphasized need for rigorous control of the centrifugal and disintegrating forces represented as much by the passions as by citizens' consciences. In contrast, Spinoza's problem from his earliest works is that of teaching directly, to a few people, the science that leads to wisdom and indirectly, to the majority of men, the way of liberty and reason. Because, he says, "my own happiness involves my making an effort to persuade many others to think as I do, so that their understanding and their desire should entirely accord with my understanding and my desire. To bring this about, it is necessary (1) to understand as much about Nature as suffices for acquiring such a nature, and (2) to establish such a social order as will enable as many as possible to reach this goal with the greatest possible ease and assurance" (*TIE* 14–15). But these intentions are not expressed in the form of the Stoic or Christian imperative, nor in that of the utopian optative, but rather in the "if-then" schema of the conditional. But the behaviour of men in search of the conditions for greater liberty and rationality does not depend exclusively on their will; a sudden natural or social catastrophe or even a slow decline of a community can make individuals and groups regress to the logic of imagination and superstition.

From the equal right/power of men, which for Spinoza continues beyond the natural state, one cannot deduce the need for a centralization of sovereignty, for the further strengthening of the *vis existendi* of a single individual but, at most, for its more collective, fair distribution. Consequently, no Leviathan (however that might be interpreted: whale, sea snake, or crocodile) exists for him that could devour his subjects on the whims or exclusive interests of those who command: "Granted, then, that the supreme mystery of despotism, its prop and stay, is to keep men in a state of deception, and with the specious title of religion to cloak the fear by which they must be held in check, so that they will fight for their servitude as if for salvation, and count it no shame, but the highest honor, to spend their blood and their lives for the glorification of one man. Yet no more disastrous policy can be devised or attempted in a free commonwealth."[19]

From this observation, Spinoza does not, however, draw the conclusions of the melancholics when they note – with Burton – that for the guilt of one, "thousands of men" were slain in battle, shedding "streams of blood able to turn mills," or that "a poor fellow" as soon as he is hired will "venture his life for his new master that will scarce give him his wages at year's end."[20] If the power of the masses remains firm and consistent, it is possible – at worst – to organize it in monarchical form as well, even if this generally favours the maintenance of servitude (see *TP* 6.4) – provided, however, that the power that must be granted to the monarch is determined precisely by the power of the masses and guaranteed by them (see *TP* 7.31).

This was certainly not the case of the absolutist state desired by Hobbes or the desire for glory and grandeur of Louis XIV who, in the period of Spinoza's adulthood, had made his own subjects fight his wars of conquest in Europe and who, in the years immediately following the publication of the *Theological-Political Treatise*, had tried to invade the Netherlands.[21]

The masses are usually turned to the universal not by reasoning but by feelings (and by the passions of fear and hope in particular). The desire is to extort from them an obedience that often borders on servitude.

Even if it becomes spontaneous over time, obedience has always initially been introduced from the outside, even in the case (illustrated by Étienne de la Boétie) of voluntary servitude. The renunciation, apparently against nature, of one's own *utilitas* implies not only a noteworthy plasticity of human nature – every man is different according to the combination and intensity of the passions by which he is moved (see *E* 4.33) – but even the existence in society of an organic system of coercion and obedience that religion and politics gradually developed and perfected over the course of millennia, using the passions and imagination, violence and fear, hope and promises, the spectre of a worse condition

19 *TTP*, praef. *389–90*. It is appropriate to note how Hobbes, alternately, considered the ability to "command and understand commands" one of the principal benefits of the discourse (*DH* x, 588; *OM*, 40).

20 See Burton, *AM* 76, 191 (regarding which also see pp. 95–8 above). On Burton's insistence on the disorder of the world, see R.A. Fox, *The Tangled Chain: The Structure of Disorder in* The Anatomy of Melancholy (Berkeley, 1976).

21 On this war and its political and emotional consequences, see P. Sonnino, *Louis XIV and the Origins of the Dutch War* (Cambridge, 1988).

and the mirage of a blessed life, and then propping up everything with specious arguments in which reason is assigned the task of legitimizing the order of the imagination (a stranger to it, even if necessary as a condition).

However, the great political and religious heads (the same ones noted by Machiavelli in chapter 26 of *The Prince*) are those who, like Moses, sometimes knew how, in the short term, to lead a people, *servituti adsuetus,* to obedience "willingly rather than through fear" (*TTP* 5.*439*), favoured in this by their virtues and by extraordinary conditions.[22] Therefore, maintenance of the social order by means of religion and politics can, in some circumstances, remove the odiousness of servitude, but not the necessity for obedience. The hierarchical element of command remains quite firm even in Spinoza. However, his worry consists now in reconciling the free access of the few to the path of wisdom with the education of the *unaware* in an obedience lacking servitude, in the common perspective of a "satisfied life."

22 The threats and fear were, however, generally projected into the future (if we exclude the slaughter of the worshipers of the Golden Calf). See *TTP* 14.*515*: "the aim of Scripture is simply to teach obedience, a statement which surely no one can deny ... Moses' aim was not to convince the Israelites by reasoned argument, but to bind them by a covenant, by oaths and by benefits received; he induced the people to obey the Law under threat of punishment, while exhorting them thereto by promise of rewards."

8. The Lynx and the Cuttlefish

Raison d'état and Honest Dissimulation

In Spinoza, there falls apart the justification adopted by theorists regarding *raison d'état* and dissimulation, according to which politics is constitutively reserved to the few as an occult science, a rationality that must not be divulged to a throng that is by nature irrational, passionate, and not suited for self-governance.

However, it would be reductive (and would take us back to an archaic hermeneutic cliché) to consider the phenomenon of dissimulation – particularly the "honest" sort – under a purely moralistic profile. In fact, if we presuppose a meta-historical ideal of authenticity in relationships between man, it would end up inflicting on agent subjects an explicit censorship, almost as if they had all arbitrarily decided to complicate their own lives and those of others with the view of meeting illicit ends. In fact, not only is the same "honest dissimulation" conceived by many authors of the sixteenth and seventeenth centuries almost as a shadow that brings out the light and promotes truth (or at least a "repose of truth"), but also as a formal, rational, and creative resistance to the impression of a power that had begun to infiltrate directly into their consciences and for filling the void of interior hegemony left by the theological schisms and religious wars that had lacerated Europe.[1] If "one is not allowed to sigh when the tyrant does not let you breathe,"[2] there remains no other way out for resisting the persecutions of "unjust power."

1 See G. Macchia, *Il paradiso della ragione* (Bari, 1960); Macchia, *Introduzione al Breviario dei politici secondo il Cardinal Mazarino* (Milan, 1981); and R. Villari, *Elogio della dissimulazione: La lotta politica nel Seicento* (Rome, 1987).

2 T. Accetto, *Della dissimulazione onesta* (Genoa, 1984 [Naples, 1641]), ch. 19, 76.

Despite all its appeals to consistency, not even Neostoicism is immune from a similar attitude. Previously, Lipsius had defended (against what have since come to be defined as *anime belle*, beautiful souls) the necessity of both simulation, or showing what is not, and dissimulation, or hiding what is: "Some upright soul is certainly going to dislike these ideas, and will exclaim, 'Feigning and dissimulation must be removed from every part of life.' Which I agree with as regards the private life, but totally deny with respect to the public life."[3] Had not Jesus said to his disciples: *Ego mitto vos sicut oves in medio luporum* (Matthew 10:16)? The practice of dissimulation, however, produces unexpected positive effects. In fact, it increases the individual's wisdom and introspective capacity, making him more familiar to himself, to his own ideas and motivations. It accentuates detachment from the temporal immediacy of experiences and encourages the split between one *I*-object and another *I*-subject of the observation, facilitating self-control and sovereignty over one's feelings: "It is important to anticipate with consideration how much more of a delight it is to master oneself while waiting for the tempest of feelings to pass and not to deliberate in the confusion of one's own storm."[4] The interior eye of the *I* thus tends gradually to replace the primacy of God's. Even dissimulation ends up becoming a way (to be honest, one that is hardly Socratic and that Spinoza would truly not have shared) of knowing oneself.[5]

After all, the perfect dissimulator does not exist or – if he really is one – always remains unknown. Most men are betrayed by showing their passions. Among these, rage is the most dangerous, because classically, it can become irrepressible, leaking out like a flash of lightning through the face or voice and "making the words fall almost with abortion of the concepts," revealing an imperfect mastery of oneself.[6] In this era, Richelieu was much admired precisely for the fact of never losing the calm expression of his face, *que la crainte ne fit jamais pâlir, et que la colère ne pût jamais troubler.* While even the most astute dissimulators let themselves be betrayed by their passions, when those passions, troubling the spirit, shine through their faces, Richelieu's face "*qui ne change jamais* [says Senault, addressing himself to Monseigneur], *est une preuve assurée de la*

3 J. Lipsius, *Pol.* IV, in *Politica: Six Books of Politics or Political Instruction*, ed. and trans. J. Waszink (Assen, 2004), 517.

4 Accetto, *Della dissimulazione onesta*, XV, 68.

5 Ibid., ch. 12, 60–1.

6 Ibid., ch. 16, 67.

paix dont vous jouyssiez, et de la victoire que vous avez remportée sur toutes vos Passions."[7] Unlike the Stoics, who wanted to become impassive, abolishing desire and hope, the good use of the passions transformed this great man into a superior being. Even Senault had to confess "*que l'insensibilité ne peut faire que des Idoles, et que les Passions bien mesnagées peuvent faire des Anges ... Le Desir et l'Espérance que vous trompent par leurs promesses, vous eslevent au dessus de la Terre, et vous portent au delà du temps.*"[8]

Faces, Gestures, Passions

In his 1659 book *L'art de connaître les hommes,* Cureau de la Chambre articulates, as a function of politics and the physical expression of the passions, the old physiognomic tradition that considered the body's traits to be adequately interpretable signs. Since everything that is internal tends to spread to the external, even if in a deformed and camouflaged way, this art *apprend à découvrir les desseins cachés, les actions secrètes et les auteurs inconnus des actions connues.*[9] The face is no longer simply the mirror of the soul but the corporeal expression of the passions and the more or less active control over them. Passions and emotions are tamed when the individual is able to organize himself and repress what he immediately feels in his "innermost part." Then, what he expresses is the result of an elaboration that becomes almost a third nature, a vigilant habit with respect to the torpid and relatively spontaneous habit of someone who is unable to impose himself on himself.

The double ability to make one's own mask impenetrable and read others' intentions in their faces and behaviour is once again attributed most strongly to Cardinal Richelieu.[10] He reached virtuosity in interpreting the language and silent or involuntary signs of others and in the distortion of his most hidden intentions. Through perfect self-control,

7 J.-F. Senault, *De l'usage des passions* (Paris, 1641; rpt. Paris, 1987), *Êpître à Monseigneur l'Eminentissime Cardinal Duc de Richelieu,* 2–3.

8 Ibid., 3–4.

9 See M. Cureau de la Chambre, *L'art de connaître les hommes* (Paris, 1659), 1 and 6–7 passim. Descartes sent him a copy of the *Passions de l'âme* – see J.-M. Monnoyer, "La pathétique cartesienne," preface to Descartes, *Les passions de l'âme* (Paris, 1988), 11.

10 On the eyes with which Richelieu was accustomed to scrutinize the passions and sentiments of his interlocutors, see O. Ranun, "Courtesy, Absolutism, and the Rise of the French State, 1632–1660," *Journal of Modern History* 52 (1980), 432, and, more generally, P. Ansart, *La gestion des passions politiques* (Lausanne, 1983).

he would transform himself into a "man without passions" or (which is the same thing) into a protean individual, capable of simulating or dissimulating almost all of them under the veneer of courtesy and politesse.

The science of the passions thus becomes an "invisible science"[11] that proceeds to the simultaneous translation of the visible and invisible and vice versa. The face – always exposed without the intermittences of the voice, to the examination of others – appears to be the principal means of indirect communication of the Baroque *homo clausus.* It is the window through which one is capable either of releasing more or less coded messages, the privileged site of expression or distortion of the meaning of the passions according to experimental techniques of self-representation and to oblique hermeneutics of others' manifestations. Unlike the tradition of classical ethics, which called for a deep and endogenous change in the passions, their control stops here – and not without effort – at the external behaviour towards a second person or towards oneself, considered as actors who try out a show destined to take place later before an audience.[12] The "Delphic" knowledge of oneself and the Christian introspection of spiritual exercises and meditations is joined by an ever-growing interest in the knowledge of the other in his most hidden "recesses." And yet every form of active self-control, in appearance only superficial, cannot not also find corroboration in the "interior" of the individual, and every way of opening can only modify the forms of hiding himself, of avoiding the scrutiny of the other. After all, as Lipsius had already observed, the subject knows himself only by splitting and externalizing himself, like in a mirror, *quodam reflexu.*[13]

Profane Divinations

> The passions are the gates of the soul. The most practical knowledge consists in disguising them. He that plays with cards exposed runs a risk of losing the stakes. The reserve of caution should combat the curiosity of inquirers:

11 See. J.-J. Courtine and C. Haroche, *Histoire du visage,* XVI*e–début* XIX*e siècle* (Paris, 1988), 43. It should not be forgotten that in the face, there is a simultaneous spatial condensation of the signs that time, events, and passions have deposited there.

12 From this comes the contrast with Socrates who – faced with the indignation of his disciples who had heard it said by the physiognomist Zoppiros that their teacher was a shrewd and sensual deceiver – responded calmly that that corresponded effectively with his character, but then it succeeded, through reason and philosophy, to defeat his bad inclinations to change (see Cic., *De fato* V, 16).

13 See Lipsius, *Phys. Stoic.* I, III diss. 3.

adopt the policy of the cuttlefish against those who have lynx's eyes. Do not even let your tastes be known, lest others utilize them either by running counter to them or by flattering them.[14]

In Baroque culture, the lynx rises to become the allegory for insight, for *agudeza* – that is, a big capacity for knowledge that penetrates appearances, reduces the distortions and disruptions of judgment caused by the passions, uncovers and deciphers the most hidden meaning of things, and stretches to eliminate ambiguities, analysing both human behaviours and natural phenomena.[15] Because of its ink, the cuttlefish, on the other hand, is the symbol of stratagems and camouflage, of coding, of concealing and manipulating of information aimed at everyone to make indistinguishable truth and lie, reality and appearance, communicative action and strategic action. They thus deliberately confuse potential enemies, or they are challenged to exceed a higher threshold of complexity and risk. War and the duel, changing the battlefield, acquire new dimensions.

"Hesitation" is that moment of "mysterious reflection" in which the destiny of an action and of a person can be decided, in a world that is "filthy" and full of dangers,[16] in a sort of Hegelian "animal kingdom of the spirit" in which the rules of survival that the ancients had applied to the animals are followed."[17]

When uncertainty and risk dominate the environment, this simple *recta ratio*, directed towards univocity and direct comprehension, is no longer enough. In fact, it assumes that one may stick to common rules for finding solutions of mutual advantage. But what happens if we lack any sort of trust in another or if, lowering our guard even for one moment, we place in danger what is most dear to us? It happens that in human relationships guessing is ever more often substituted for reasoning, the

14 B. Gracián, *Or.*, n. 98.

15 It is not by chance that the scientific institution founded in Rome by Federico Cesi in 1604 is today still called the Academy of the Lynx-like Men (Accademia dei Lincei).

16 B. Gracián, *El Criticón*, in *Ob.*, part I, Crisis VI, *Estado del siglo.*

17 This line of thought that emphasizes the shrewdness and intelligence or *sollertia* of the animals can be traced back to the last books of the *Historia animalium* (written perhaps by Aristotle and not by his pupils), with the *De sollertia animalium* or the *Bruti ratione uti* of Plutarch, or with the *Alieutica* of Oppian. See M. Detienne and J.P. Vernant, *La mètis des Grecs* (Paris, 1974). The image of the lynx and the cuttlefish comes to Gracián, after all, from Tertullian, who is part of this more ancient tradition.

instant blink of an eye for structured and methodical reflection. Taking on the risks, thought gambles and, without repudiating itself, finds its completion in a sort of profane divination that stretches from signs and symptoms to their probable interpretation: "It was once the art of arts to be able to discourse; now it is no longer sufficient. We must know how to take a hint ... The very truths which concern us most can only be half spoken (*Or.*, n. 25).

In Gracián's universe, the transition from the natural state to the civil, from the feral to the human, from ambiguity to the logic of consistency (just as they are presented by Grotius or Hobbes) has not yet come to pass. An intermediate realm can be found there, one with a sort of profane divination, that from signs stretches to a probable interpretation, one that tries to stop "Proteus" at least for a moment. This is certainly one of the reasons for the title of Gracián's work, *Oracolo manuale*: advice within reach for extricating oneself from the complexity of the world, in navigating a life ever more exposed to the deceit of natural and artificial appearances and always subject to ruin.

But there is not only one "rhetoric of the chameleon," which consists of camouflaging oneself and persuading others to act according to our own intentions. Even more important is disorienting them, misinforming them by means of the practice of unpredictability. For this, it is not necessary to speak or act always with deceit or always with frankness. The truth – which is "dangerous" – must come from time to time suitably mixed with falsehood, so as to forge an artefact of the truth, its simulacrum. Similarly, it is necessary to use the senses – normal ways of accessing the truth – in a differentiated way, colouring with passion everything that one wants to have perceived, particularly through words: "The ear is the gate-area of truth but the front door of lies. The truth is generally seen, rarely heard" (*Or.*, n. 80). In military terms, it is not necessary to further humiliate and crush the adversary completely, because this may make him more furious and uncontrollable: one may be congenial and kind to him so as to act "as a magnet on all hearts" (*Or.*, n. 79); one may show some small defects to save oneself from the ostracism of resentment, so as to "leave your [bullfighting] cloak on the horns of envy" (*Or.*, n. 83).

The intellectual activities spurred by human behaviours classifiable under the rubric of the lynx and the cuttlefish are not limited to simulation and dissimulation. They also contain an enormous cognitive potential in itself. Specificallly, they elicit the capacity to discriminate, separate, and articulate differences and similarities. From this point of view, such a faculty does not have any relationship with the realm of shadow or chiaroscuro. It is radiant and Apollonian power, since Apollo is *dios de la discreción.*[18]

In order to include a universe that has greatly extended its boundaries and points of reference, it is necessary, on one hand, to erase the previous code of identification of objects (based on parameters that are now unusable) and, on the other, to restore differences to unity without ever pretending to exhaust their number or level of complexity. To the careful observer, differences reveal themselves as figures and constellations of meaning that allude to a richness greater than we are capable of expressing, but whose glow needs, in order to be limited, all that we have the capacity to show. Understanding means, then, inserting every individual phenomenon into a network of similarities open to the possible and even to the improbable, similarities that refer to a mysterious totality, a *verdad escondita, recondita.*[19] This eludes, in its essence, every definition. But in Gracián, mystery plays a role that is not exclusively religious; it is also epistemological. It attracts attention to the totality of imponderable factors that no *ponderación* will succeed in eliminating but that requires being taking into due account, because the hidden and ignored truths bend and determine the structure and the indication of certainty of those notes.

Knowing How to Distinguish

The truth appears, after all, as the fruit of cognitive strategies by means of which artifice enriches the nature of innovations. To all appearances, Gracián appreciates variety, not only as the antidote to the monotony and order of the repetitiveness of forms, but also as the expression of that which is more perfect: *La uniformidad limita, la variedad dilata; y tanto es más sublime, cuanto más nobles perfecciones multiplica.*[20] The variations (the *petites différences* that will return in the "Baroque" Leibniz) establish an independent and inextricable network between the identical and the different.[21] To know the world, it is necessary also to know the thickness of the cultural diaphragm that every generation adds to it, separating individuals from their natural immediacy. Thus, the truth ceases to represent a simple *adaequatio* of understanding of the thing, and the

18 Gracián, *El discreto,* in *Ob.* 78.
19 Gracián, *Agudeza y arte de ingenio,* in *Ob.* 260.
20 Ibid., 240.
21 I am referring, naturally, to G. Deleuze, *Le pli: Leibniz et le Baroque* (Paris, 1988).

individual finds himself forced continually to learn, to take into account the series of rejections with respect to the obvious and to the past – i.e., to take into account new experience: "There is more required nowadays to make a single wise man than formerly to make seven sages, and more is needed nowadays to deal with a single person than was required with a whole people in former times" (*Or.*, n. 1). Culture is the means within which Gracián's reflection moves. Every thought, every action, and every evaluation presumes it in its growing complexity, ambiguity, and local expression. Thus, over time, variety constitutes a challenge that the mind can win, finding or inventing a structure of meaning within which to insert it, just like judgment (*juicio*) can establish, on a case-by-case basis, through *prudencia* (not to be confused with mere shrewdness[22]), what the best behaviour might be. Cunning, *agudeza,* and *discreción* are products and factors of civility in that they prevent men from becoming dim-witted and from keeping their talents hidden. And yet each person must find his way on his own, because no advice is ever appropriate for the range of situations, and experiences cannot always replace instinct nor reason replace passion (and this is the meaning of the *Criticón*'s peregrinations: we do not turn back from them with greater loads of positive wisdom or usable knowledge). We do not learn from books or from the examples of others – and not even, suggests Gracián, from the books that he himself composed; their utility consists only in a warning, in the negativity of the admonition. Therefore, it is useless to turn to them to receive a well-constructed system of rules that may indicate to each person which course to establish or where he might find the North Star on which to orient himself. Stoic consistency or Seneca's doctrines are not much help.[23] Each person, then, must confront – alone – the scene of the *Gran teatro del mundo* as painted by Calderón de la Barca, tormenting himself with the illusions, doubts, and risks that it entails and subsequently passing between *dos portas: la una es la cuna/y la otra es sepulcro* (vv. 241–2).

Gracián succeeded in describing and illustrating the not-yet-perfectly catalogued forms of *agudeza,* cunning, or *discreción,* of the capacity to distinguish and discriminate, and he led them back to a synoptic frame where each one finds its position and its name.

---

22 On "prudence" and its transformations, also with respect to Gracián, see R. Bodei, "Fra prudenza e calcolo: Sui canoni della decisione razionale," in *Ricerche politiche due: Identità, interessi e scelte collective* (Milan, 1983), 59–85.

23 See Gracián, *Or.*, n. 36, 51.

Even in his seemingly most wild manifestations, in the use of the most complicated linguistic registers or the most daring and curious images, Baroque culture is generally subject in Gracián to an intellectual regime analogous to the one in which the scientific research of the time functions – i.e, a systematic propensity to experiment that uncovers complex symmetries, contrasts, and recurrences between phenomena. It is a *curiositas* that is no longer condemned, one that moves the mechanism of discovery and the shaping of experience. Curiosity and ingenuity can certainly be ends in themselves. But the spirits of scientific knowledge and literature present surprising similarities. Obviously, the parallels are achieved in a different manner in the first field than in the second, where the demon of analogy prevails but where, despite everything, the push towards new structures of order is consistent and firm. It finds its limit in the unspeakable in literature (where it reaches the boundaries of the ineffable) and the unknown in science.

From this standpoint, *agudeza*, a product of *injenio*, is simply the attempt to show in the work the extreme flexibility of language and thought in forging pointed and expressive weapons and in giving beauty its sharp-edged aspect – how it might be detected, at the moment of its creation, in the shine of new combinations and in the spark that its game of friction produced.

An Exponential Hermeneutics

And yet the work of deciphering the world does not at all imply a rejection of the search for the "true." Rather, it requires a "supplement of soul," an exponential hermeneutics of power that is always superior to the complexity of the questions or of the adversaries to be confronted. And what is more important, it is a hermeneutics not of what remains hidden or absolutely secret, but of the depth on display, of the visible that is carefully observed in the smallest details, in order to find there a thread that may connect it to the presumed invisible that is nonetheless exposed to the view of those who know how to make themselves be a "lynx." Living in places governed by subtle rules, travelling and knowing the different customs and the changing multiplicity of the real helps the individual to distinguish crucial nuances, to know the variety of phenomena and characters, to become a "man of the world,"[24] open to the

24 On this concept, see C. Ossola, *Dal "cortegiano" all'"uomo di mondo"* (Turin, 1987).

richness and the dangers of experiences. It contributes to teaching him how to move in environments governed by specific and variable demands and rules – that is, to conquer the *imperium* over himself and the control over his passions by means of a parallel development of intelligence and the sense of the proper distance from himself and others.

Describing nature by means of new instruments (particularly the microscope and telescope) thus means pushing oneself further into unknown territory too close or too far to have been previously explored, becoming accustomed to the astonishment of strange and disturbing images, discovering unconnected parts of a whole whose boundaries become, paradoxically, more uncertain with the advancement of partial knowledge, thus hyper-compensated – through a rebound effect – by the pathos for unconditional certainty, for systems demonstrated *more geometrico*.

The individual now makes use of an ever wider stage within which to move and scenarios that simultaneously require both remarkable inventive capacity and firm control over oneself and one's own faculties of comprehension and expression. Invention, by its nature, is unpredictable, and intelligence is not acquired only with discipline. And yet there exists an *ars inveniendi* and an *ars combinatoria* at whose school acumen can learn to become sharper, and intelligence can learn to exercise itself. In the presence of such risky arts, Baroque hermeneutics does not develop according to the quiet and relatively peaceful form of circularity. The "hermeneutic circle" of the nineteenth century can be contrasted now, in anticipation and in fact, to the presentation of a challenge and provocation that forces an adversary to continually raise the stakes of the confrontation or that obliges a "scientist" to react to the obscurity of a problem, raising – starting from the response given – the level of general complexity of a specific field of knowledge or individual social practices. In this way, in being presented with opacity and anomalies greater than foreseen, or by a "squared" movement or cunning (disconcerting because it reformulates or reframes the questions in a different way), we reply with a "cubed" move, so to speak, one that restates the problem, highlighting further difficulties in the sphere of its own consequences or inducing the virtual antagonist to elaborate ever more perfect strategies of defence and offence, according to the complementary strategies of the lynx and the cuttlefish.

In this unspoken or acclaimed duel of questions and responses, there are often leaps, fractures, discontinuities, and surprises that events and investigations continually bring to light and that, for us, constitute a not insignificant factor of fascination with the Baroque. In the space that extends between method, repetitiveness, and simplicity on the one hand and creativity, innovation, and complexity on the other, there unfolds, in effect, the allegorical representation of a show that (repeated down to our times) still refers allusively to knots unresolved since the time of its original staging. On this stage, fear and hope continue to play an irreplaceable role and produce effects on their spectators that are not always cathartic.

9. Superstition

Voices and Signs

In Spinoza, *metus* and *spes* often enter into a conceptual constellation that includes *superstitio*, connecting these passions to the religious dimension and, more generally, the theological-political one.

Superstition arises spontaneously in the human heart. At the beginning, it is not the fruit of shrewd machinations or plots of power to keep the people submissive. Rather, it springs from uncertainty and fear, from the need to exorcize the ever-pending natural and social dangers. If all individuals were to let themselves be guided by reason, of course, superstition would not exist. But reason, in turn, to rise and preserve itself, needs a precondition, the security of existence: "If men were able to exercise complete control over all their circumstances, or if continuous good fortune were always their lot, they would never be prey to superstition. But since they are often reduced to such straits as to be without any resource, and their immoderate greed for fortune's fickle favors often makes them the wretched victims of alternating hopes and fears, the result is that, for the most part, their credulity knows no bounds" (*TTP*, praef. *388*). All individuals and peoples are, therefore, naturally exposed to superstition, even if to different degrees, according to their greater or lesser incapacity to comprehend and adequately control real processes, to stop themselves or exit from passivity, a more-or-less wide sphere of control of the imagination. In fact, it is easy to be rational and "rich with wisdom" when things go well, but then, in adversity, lend faith to the most absurd suggestions imparted by others or by one's own excited fantasy.[1]

1 Even cultured people, like Spinoza's correspondents P. Balling and U. Boxel, were inclined to believe in premonitions, ghosts, and witches. For the rational explanations offered by Spinoza to these phenomena, see *Ep.* 17 and 54 and A. Billecoq, *Spinoza*

As a product of the imagination, superstition is, in its way, a form of knowledge, often accompanied by the claim of modifying the course of events with the magic force of desire or with the help of superior powers. In fact, it is a mutilated knowledge that, from fragments casually collected or from dark, partial, and undeveloped intuitions creates a coherent order of images according to a logic dictated by the passions that dominate from time to time (consequently, it is wrong to believe that the only existing order is the one dictated or imposed by reason). From this point of view, superstition expresses both the attempt to explain the state of passivity in which men find themselves and the effort to identify an initial, weak form of security that supports itself on an order that is even more cogent than that of reason, since it obeys – through fear and hope – a faith in external and inexorable powers. It is a way (apparently rough, but effective and, in any case, insurmountable) to frame opaque and uncertain events over which, in the moment, it is impossible to exercise any other type of influence or comprehension. Through the power of imagination, men give hallucinatory form to the unknown, thus reading "extraordinary things into Nature as if the whole of Nature were a partner in their madness" (*TTP*, praef. *388*). But the order of the hallucination (which crazily recombines perceptible signs and makes some individuals perceive voices or visions that others do not notice) or that of delirium (which combines ideas according to a private logic not shared by common reason) constitute powerful mechanisms of meaning that are not in the least damaged as long as they do not change the conditions of life and the need for security of those who experience them.

Although superstition adds fear to error, the kernel of truth enclosed within it is represented by the real insecurity of life and the effort to comprehend and transform it according to laws that obey a sort of fantastic necessity, where what is incidental acquires a hidden meaning to be deciphered.

Superstition and religion, *ex auditu et ex signis*, interpret voices and clues, and even on this basis they demand obedience on the part of those

---

et les spectres (Paris, 1987). In his letter to Balling (17), Spinoza seems to admit to the existence of a *verum omen*, an authentic omen, because of the tie of love that unites – at the level of the soul – a father and son such that they are "as it were, one and the same" (on this position, later abandoned in his *Ethics*, see J. Domingues Sanches-Estop, "Des présages à l'entendement: Notes sur l'imagination et l'amour dans la lettre à P. Balling," *Studia Spinozana* 4 [1988], 57–74).

not held to be capable of reading and correctly understanding the divine commandments transmitted in that way (after all, Paulistically, one believes precisely by hearsay, based on faith in a worthy witness: *fides ex auditu*). Superstition (as a private, non-recognized religion) creates an individual hermeneutic, while religion (public superstition necessary to ensure the obedience of people to laws through fears and hopes)[2] professes to possess the monopoly on interpretation of signs and collective needs. It thus raises the most grandiose symbolical systems of imaginative granting-of-meaning that have ever been constructed, and it proceeds uninterrupted to consolidate, restore, renovate, or prop up these systems of belief, making them ever more consistent according to the logic of the *ordo imaginationis.* It thus organizes the collective insecurity and exorcises the nameless worry of an uninterpreted world. It does not cancel the swinging of the heart between fear and hope, but it muffles those swings and regulates their extent, causing the panicked terror to diminish and allowing a moment's rest for men incapable of abandoning the powerlessness of their own hearts. The rituals of fear and the show of intimidation and death that religions establish are balanced by the promises of a future happiness, of the consolatory response to the thought (which had become intolerable for many) of the eternal "nothing," of the sharp loss of life and the world, of not being able to continue to exist after death.[3] This judgment by Spinoza of religion is also valid – it seems to me – in the case in which religion, to the extent it belongs to men and to the "ignorant," succeeds in forming autonomously in all its power.[4]

---

2 See *Ep.* 19: "I say that Scripture, being particularly adapted to the needs of the common people, continually speaks in merely human fashion, for the common people are incapable of understanding higher things. That is why I think that all that God has revealed to the Prophets as necessary for salvation is set down in the form of law."

3 See the letter of W. de Blyenberg to Spinoza (*Ep.* 20) or Pascal, *P*, n. 352: "It is horrible to see all that we possess disappear."

4 *Superstitio* is traditionally connected to fear or to the terror of the divinity. Originally, in the Roman world, the term *superstitio* alluded to the divinatory practices (*superstitiosus* is he who *vera praedicat*). Only later, when anti-magical philosophical concepts asserted themselves, did it become a type of degeneration, characterized by an excess of exterior scruples and by the obsessive insistence on specific cult rituals, precisely because of the incessant servile fear of not having been sufficiently deferential towards the divinity and finding oneself, therefore, always exposed to its punishments and vengeance. See E. Benveniste, *Le vocabulaire des institutions indo-européennes,* 2: *Pouvoir, droit, religion* (Paris, 1969).

Signs and Dreams

Although at first sight Spinoza may appear closer to the line that leads from Epicurus to Lucretius to the libertines and highlights superstition's dependence on fear (a thesis shared both by the Stoics and by some of their adversaries, like Plutarch), he is not satisfied by any of the interpretations proposed up to his time.[5] Although accepting the Stoic doctrine by which nothing in the world happens by chance,[6] he rejects, in an implicit way, its consequent theoretical justification of superstitious practices through the crediting of divinatory art, which ends up legitimizing the most baseless popular beliefs. The arguments used by the Stoics begin, precisely, from the assumption that nothing accidental exists in reality. Consequently, if all events fall under the government of necessity, they must find a specific and appropriate place within its frame. Thus, this semantic and individualizing hyper-rationalism, which points to phenomena, in their punctual and unrepeatable specificity, as being all equally meaningful, inserts signs, dreams, and premonitions into the inexorable chain of destiny, asserting that it is not a case capricious phenomena but – as divination shows "the foreseeing and foretelling of events considered as happening by chance"[7] – a case of seemingly random events, theoretically endowed with a rational explanation. Spinoza aligns himself with Cicero in condemning superstition, even if he rejects the explanations that Cicero offered. That is, he considers true the fact that "superstition, which is widespread among the nations, has taken advantage of human weakness"[8] but he does not believe

5 See *SVF* III, 394, 408, 409, 411.

6 This would be the legacy of the Stoics that, through Spinoza, will later come to consolidate Freud's psychic determinism, according to which no symptom lacks meaning, and Einstein's conviction that, in the universe, "God does not play dice." In general terms, for the interest that Einstein nourished regarding Spinoza, see B. Kouznetsov, "Spinoza et Einstein," *Revue de Synthèse* 88 (1967), 31–52.

7 Posid. in Cic., *De div.* I, 9. This is the subject classically addressed in Cicero's *De divinatione* in a double polemic against Stoic determinism and popular beliefs (see Cic., *De div.* II, 150) that will subsequently be reprised by the Fathers of the Church and by Augustine.

8 Cic., *De div.* II, 148, and see, on this subject. J.-P. Vernant, *Divination et rationalité* (Paris, 1974). In the field of divination on the religious and popular level, we can suppose that "in Cicero's time, philosophers had considered with great favor all of the uncertainty present in those beliefs, uncertainty that permitted wise men a great liberty" (G. Boissier, *La fin du paganism: Études sur les dernières luttes religeuses en Occident au quatrième siècle* [Paris, 1891]).

in its total arbitrariness. Against the Stoics, he asserts that the necessity found by the superstitious does not have any objective character. There exists, but only within the internal consistency of the human imagination, some psycho-physical determinism (to use a modern term), but this varies in its contents according to the individuals and the society (in representing, precisely, the *conatus* striving to devise an order that might connect them, through relationships of "magic causality," scattered and not-understood fragments of a whole). Against Cicero, Spinoza judges it impossible "to weed out every root of superstition" (Cic., *De div.* II, 149), as long as one does not search for the reasons for it outside of its own logic. To an even greater measure than the radius of uncertainty of fear and hope – passions that, in Spinoza, extend to the past – prophecy formulates temporally wide-ranging speculations. In fact, in Homer (and the order of the times may be noted), the clairvoyant Tiresias "knew what was, what had been, what would be" (*Il.* I, 69–70).

Human hearts (and this objection is valid also with respect to the Epicureans) will continue to endure the oppression of *superstitio* until they are capable of finding the means for reducing the excessive power of those causes, of which superstitions constitute only the most striking effect. Of course, fear – as the exegesis of the Old Testament shows[9] and as Spinoza affirms in the *Theological-Political Treatise* – is the first cause that "engenders, preserves, and fosters superstition,"[10] pushing men towards obedience and, in moments of greatest danger, to contempt for rationality and the instinct for self-preservation.[11] In fact, it induces them to place their own lives at risk and let themselves be guided in the most difficult choices by the slight and deceptive thread of wild interpretations of clues, signs, and omens – that is, by the hope that the circumstance may contain the secret of its necessity and may be capable of communicating that to whomever knows how to penetrate its shell. People thus exercise a sort of hermeneutic that is unlimited and impermeable to experience; they practise a type of *scientia intuitiva inferior*, that professes, in an absurd way, to deduce a valid rule of conduct or an acceptable sense of *res particulares* that is not to be filtered through the general knowledge

9 For a more wide-ranging examination of the problem, see J. Becher, *Gottesfurcht im Alten Testament* (Rome, 1965), and L. Derousseaux, *La crainte de Dieu dans l'Ancien Testament: Royauté, alliance, sagesse dans le royaumes d'Isräel et de Juda* (Paris, 1970).

10 *TTP*, praef. *388*: *Causa, itaque, a qua superstitio oritur, conservatur, et fovetur, metus est.*

11 The Pharisees, the sect of the "separated," were very careful to have "the masses as allies" (Joseph. XII, 10, 5).

of reason.[12] Superstitious practices achieve only temporary advantages, moments of exhilaration or relief, followed by phases of renewed torment and agony that are soon forgotten, and so the cycle begins again.[13]

Even when religion, custom, and the habit of obeying succeed at not driving individuals and groups "crazy" – in the cases in which they are capable of bridling the fury and making their hearts more gentle – reason reveals itself to be powerless in the face of superstition and fear. Good reasons end up useless, incapable of getting to the heart of the disposition to believe in the absurd, given that "imaginings do not disappear at the presence of what is true insofar as it is true."[14] In interpreting scripture, however, theology professes to give a rational foundation to piety and obedience, making use of images and ideas accommodated "to the understanding and the preconceived beliefs of the common people." In this way, it "defines its religious dogmas" only to the extent required by obedience, and it ends up producing a strange and dangerous hybrid of reason and imagination, a superstition barely more sophisticated for the use of whomever must wield it and the most cultured classes of society. For Spinoza, "we cannot entirely absolve ... from censure" both the sceptics who "seek the help of reason in the task of repelling reason" or the theologians who "try to employ the certainty of reason to disparage reason's certainty" (*TTP* 15.*520, 523, 525*).

Unlike the Epicureans or the libertines, however, Spinoza does not free himself from superstition or from the fear of death by denying the existence or the impact of "God" on the world, but instead by transforming fear into love (we could say that, for him, the *amor Domini* is *initium et finis sapientiae*). This is why – unlike Lucan, who emphasizes in his *Pharsalia* the fact that men fear what they themselves have imagined (see

12 And that is unlike bona fide *scientia intuitiva* (regarding which see p. 281 et seq. in the present volume), where particular events are inserted into a network of meanings that includes them – to use an expression of Simmel's that is decontextualized and apparently paradoxical – according to their "individual law."

13 The term "supplizio" (*supplicium*) – torture – is, after all etymologically tied to the idea of placating the gods (see *subplacare* and *supplex*). However, it would be necessary to ask ourselves if, in being attracted by superstition, there is not also another component, represented by those that the psychoanalyst Michael Balint calls "philobatic" needs – that is, the inclination towards the deep, dark, and threatening sides of existence – to ask ourselves if the loss of the dimension of uncertainty and risk might not be generally felt as an impoverishment of experience.

14 *E* 4.1, schol., and see, previously, on security's dependence on hope, *KV* 2.9: "For Confidence and Despair never arise, unless Hope and Fear (from which they derive their being) have preceded them."

I, 486: *Quod finxere, timent*), or unlike Cyrano de Bergerac, who called the gods *ces enfants de l'effroi* and, in the tragedy *La mort d'Agrippine*, mentions "ces beaux riens qu'on adore sans savoir pourquoi/... Ces dieux que l'homme a fait et que n'ont point fait l'homme"[15] – Spinoza speaks of his God as an object of love that can never be excessive.

The Reasons of the Many

Why can't reason get a grip on superstition and the passions? Why don't concepts defeat imagery, and why don't appropriate ideas defeat inappropriate ones? Why, in Kantian terms, does reason itself generate a sort of theological-political "transcendental illusion," impervious to every logical demonstration and blind to every proof of reality? And why, for Spinoza (and still in Kantian terms), does it not make sense to ask ourselves what we can hope? Why does the search for *utilitas* and happiness, which should be typical of man, lead simultaneously to fear of death or hope for death, in the reference to a world beyond this one? Spinoza's response is simple and good: as long as men live at the mercy of insecurity and fortune, they will always necessarily be inclined to fear and hope, and they will interpret reality not according to the criteria of reason but according to the logic of the imagination. They are subject to the seemingly total control of chance, because they are incapable of knowing and foreseeing, in a suitable way, the causes of that which acts upon them and the results of their own initiatives. Passive fatalism and superstitious faith in fortune are both the products of a weak *conatus*: the one is no more true than the other.

The world is certainly ordered, even for Spinoza, according to an iron, implacable, mathematical necessity, where the possible has no other role than to function in the imagination as an ineffective alternative or as the only antecedent of the inevitable.[16] But it is precisely its sufficient comprehension that makes us free, allowing us to insert ourselves consciously at the intersection of different causal chains. The majority of men will therefore not be capable of becoming ethically and intellectually more free, if they do not increase their power of existing through

15 C. de Bergerac, *La mort d'Agrippine*, act 2, scene 4, in A. Adam, *Les libertins au XVIIe siècle* (Paris, 1964), 186.

16 On the limits of the possible and, conversely, on the extension of necessity in its historical and theoretical bases, see the monumental work by A. Faust, *Der Möglichkeitsgedanke: Systemgeschichtliche Untersuchungen* (Heidelberg, 1931).

passage from the imaginative dimension of passivity to the rational one and, from the latter, to "intuitive science," accessible only to the wise man.[17] Only through such a process of transition – in which passivity progressively dominates, and not necessity – will the improvement of their existence produce successive feedback loops that reinforce the powers of reason, so that the latter, in a virtuous circle, will be able to recursively heap its benefits on the lives of individuals and the community, making them less unhappy. The area of passivity and servitude will be able to be reduced and it will be shown – against Hobbes – that reason emerges and flowers not from the ground of fear, but from that of security – that is, of a hope lacking doubts and of a mind that has limited its own fluctuations (see *E* 3.18, schol. 2).

Spinoza thus skirts the conflict between a cold reason (unsuited to affecting the passions, to persuading with its mere universal laws) and a set of burning passions that would be colonized by reason through tough and relentless work of discipline and subjugation, destined to end with the passions' surrender to an external master, the only one capable of keeping them at bay and cooling them. In fact, for Spinoza there are not hot or "calm" passions (in the sense of Hirschman or Hobbes) that would become "cold" following the regulatory intervention of rationality, assuming the form of "interests" or "calculation."[18] Reason and (even more) intuitive science are always hot, alive, and tense. They move feelings only to the extent they become more powerful than the feelings are. They are innervated by feelings. From the point of view of effectiveness, they are even the strongest feeling, capable of ordering and promoting the maximum development of the power of existing. In fact, reason and power are not separate, at either the political level (see *TP* 3.7) or the individual level. In Spinoza, what is rational is that which is more "real" than the simply imagined, in that it is intrinsically endowed with a greater perfection – that is, with a greater power of existing.

---

17 Pascal does not believe in the thaumaturgic power of reason in its (always losing) struggle for control of the imagination. Even if men no longer let themselves be awed by its power and its symbols, this is not why they would draw greater satisfaction and an increased power of existing: "Imagination cannot make fools wise; but she can make them happy, to the envy of reason, which can only make its friends miserable; the one covers them with glory, the other with shame" (*P*, n. 104). For him, reason is the source of greater unhappiness. Nothing could be farther from Spinoza's position (also on this point see, in the present volume, pp. 215–23).

18 See A.O. Hirschman, *The Passions and the Interests: Political Arguments for Capitalism before Its Triumph.*

This means that both the philosophical utopias (directed towards showing men how they should be) and political theories and practices (worried about leaving them in the degradation in which they find themselves) appear inadequate. The exhortations to "must be" or to the cynical acceptance of what exists – although they do not change anything – contribute in significant measure to discrediting the desirability of incisive transformation of the social order. However, liberty acquired by men in this way does not depend, as Friedrich Engels believed, on a mere and static realization of necessity but, rather, on the interweaving of liberty and happiness.

Although, until now, superstition has been the most effective means for governing the masses, they are hypothetically capable of changing – provided, however, that their existence is made secure, since "confidence is pleasure arising from the idea of a thing future or past, concerning which reason for doubt has been removed" (*E* 3, defs. of the emotions 14). *Securitas,* as the *tranquillitas animi* typical of the ancient wise man, democratizes itself in Spinozan philosophy, assuming the more general characteristic of *animus terroris liber,* previously seen in Cicero.[19] Both in Spinoza and in Descartes – although with significant differences in emphasis – hope and fear, once deprived of doubt, respectively produce "confidence" and "desperation," establishing themselves with a constant positive or negative sign – that is, becoming certainties.[20]

The absence of doubt implies both a stabilization of the passions and a calm or storm in the fluctuations of the soul, but in the presence of external causes that push and direct men towards the need for greater rationality, towards greater integration of their *conatus* – that is, towards a "reflexive organization" of desire.[21] As soon as the power of fortune is limited and the impact of need and the unpredictable diminish, reason grows stronger both on the individual level and on the social one (since *securitas*

---

19 In fact, Seneca translated the Stoic concept of *ataraxia* as *securitas* (see *De const.* XIII, 5; *Ep.* XCII, 3), to indicate a condition of absence of disturbances, tranquility, or serenity of the soul. That is the same *euthymia,* of Democritic origin, that Cicero rendered as *animus terroris liber* (*De fin.* V, 8, 23) and with *securitas, quae est animi tamquam tranquillitas* (*De fin.* V, 29, 87).

20 See *E* 3.18, schol. II. Note that in Spinoza, the problem is elimination of doubt with respect to results expected in the future. For Descartes, however, it is a problem of lesser or greater probability that depresses or raises the value of oneself with respect to others.

21 See R. Misrahi, *Le désir et la réflexion dans la philosophie de Spinoza* (Philadelphia, 1972).

is, for states, what *virtus* is for individuals; see *TP* 1, §6). In addition, superstition loses its virulence, and the passions of fear and hope weaken or are eclipsed. Thus, while for Hobbes reason is born of fear, for Spinoza it develops starting from security, which constitutes a leavening of rationality for the masses. This position is still symmetrically contrary to that of Hobbes, who held that insecurity, fear, and permanent terror are means to affirm rationality (and obedience, the only "virtue of a subject").[22]

The Determination of the Wise Man

Even for Spinoza, those who undermine superstition are attacking a social order that founds itself upon it. This is, however, a practical and political risk that the wise man must run:

> As a result, he who seeks the true causes of miracles and is eager to understand the works of Nature as a scholar, and not just to gape at them like a fool, is universally considered an impious heretic and denounced by those to whom the common people bow down as interpreters of Nature and the gods. For these people know that the dispelling of ignorance would entail the disappearance of that astonishment, which is the one and only support for their argument and for safeguarding their authority. (*E* 1, app.)

The type of *securitas* sufficient for the masses to avoid domination by the passions and uncertainty, at least in part, is not enough for the wise man. For him, it is not so much security or participation in the management of public affairs that counts – particularly in an era full of dangers and external and civil wars – but the possibility of completing positive *transitiones*, of increasing the individual and collective power of existing. He intends to take advantage of the upward currents, so to speak, generated by an increase in security in the community to increase the widespread sentiment for rationality and peace (or, which is the same thing, for reducing fear and finding, in other potential collaborators, an expanded community and not real enemies). Peace, in fact, is not the absence of hostility; it does not correspond to the apathy of the Stoic wise men or to that of a crowd of slaves. Instead, it is activity,

---

22 Hobbes, *B* I in *EW* VI, 219. However, for Spinoza himself, since currently it is difficult for masses and political men to live under the guide of reason, they preserve, de facto, civil peace and abstain from causing damage to others more from fear and threat of reprisals than from awareness of the common good (see *TP* 1.5 and *E* 4.37, schol. 2).

the positivity of internal and international relationships (see *TP* 5.4). Therefore, the more a state is powerful and independent, the more it is rational (*TP* 3.7). This means that the increase in the *vis existendi*, both among the states and in individuals, increases confidence and rationality, conversely decreasing uncertainty and fear.

It is possible, however, for the *sapiens* to transform hope into confidence, taking *inconstantia* away from *laetitia* (and indirectly limiting fear and desperation). But to what extent? Confidence is not an optimal solution, in that it still preserves latent relationships with the *tristitia* from which it originates and, further, is the sign of "a weakness of mind." "For although confidence and joy are emotions of pleasure, they imply a preceding pain, namely, hope and fear. Therefore, the more we endeavor to live by the guidance of reason, the more we endeavor to be independent of hope, to free ourselves from fear, and to command fortune as far as we can, and to direct our actions by the sure counsel of reason" (*E* 4.47, schol.).

Thinking Conditionally

Spinoza thus denies – again – the privilege traditionally attributed to conscience and to will in the processes of real transformation. Neither becoming aware nor absolute power is sufficient to create the conditions of a better social life, if its basis is not set within the "external" world of institutions and forms of life.

Incidentally, similar to that of Spinoza, in its basic framework, is the criticism by Marx and Feuerbach which says that men are not at all disposed to abandon their religious faith (or their superstitions) because it is demonstrated to them, in an exemplary logical way, that it is a matter of simple illusions, reified desires, paradises, and infernos of the imagination. First, it is necessary to eliminate, practically, the situations of need that push men to find consolation and compensation within this life in the hope of a future existence. Only then will they be ready to accept and examine with greater mental openness the criticism directed towards religious isolation and products of fantasy. They will thus see, by and large, the structure of the celestial "holy family" fade, along with that of the earthly family.[23]

23 From a merely philological point of view, it must be noted that Marx read Spinoza intensively, in the Paulus edition, in the first months of 1841, when he was preparing his dissertation on Epicurus. See K. Marx, *Exzerpte und Notizen bis 1842*, in *MEGA*, Vierte Abteilung, vol. 1, *Exzerpte – Notizen –Marginalien* (Berlin, 1976), 233–76.

Like Spinoza, Marx and Freud go "behind" human liberty to seek the (removable) conditioning of acting and imagining that make suffering inarticulate and make the expectations of the masses and individuals indeterminate, contributing to increasing their passivity. Behind the conscious nature of the *logos* and of the will, there are hidden the causes of the conditioning that, once removed, remove the effect. Knowing them means placing the assumptions for removing these "thorns," acting first and particularly at the level of efficient causes and only secondarily – when awareness of the origin of the undesirable conditioning is widespread – at the level of final causes, of the plans of men.

Fear and hope, then, will not disappear automatically and forever. That could happen, in a completely improbable way, only where (and when) they might be offered an alternative that is really felt to be better, where (and when) the security and power of existing might meet minimal obstacles to their growth. It is not a case, therefore, of utopia or optative speech, but rather – to be precise – of conditional thought. If defined optimal conditions are obtained, fear and hope will proportionally lose importance and meaning for individual and collective life. It will then be possible to really move beyond, and not by means of desires and declamations, the Hobbesian images (now true) of the man, "famished even by future hunger," who surpasses "in rapacity and cruelty the wolves, bears, and snakes that are not rapacious unless hungry and not cruel unless provoked" (*DH* x, 588; *OM* 40). The possible lessening of the functions of fear and hope (in both the individual and the social field) does not imply, however, a general weakening of the imagination. If passions become "feelings" (i.e., passions of which one has a clear and distinct idea – see *E* 5.3 and cor.), reason and understood passions will develop together.

The knowledge of the philosopher, even in the political realm, is knowledge of necessary relations, but the necessity is always situated within a context, a system of ties. If some of them become altered or weakened – so as to find the needs of men ever more capable of being satisfied – then realities that appeared inalterable will also be able to change within the framework of a new interweaving of ties, necessities, and possibilities.

After Fear …

Precisely because "the multitude remains ever at the same level of wretchedness" (*TTP*, praef. *389*), it is the most exposed to the passions and to superstition. Its lack of rationality does not depend, therefore, on the intrinsic nature of the crowd, which is passionate in itself (as Le Bon and even Croce thought), but on its conditions of more frequent and difficult struggle against insecurity. It is much more exposed to risk, then, both with respect to the man who lives largely protected from power and external things, and with respect to the wise man who made himself invulnerable to fortune and its random rolls of the dice.[24] The mass of the unaware, in fact, does not disrupt "the order of nature," but follows it, like everyone (see *TP* 2.6). From the reduction of fear, security can be born – and from that, reason, which will retroactively weaken both fear itself and hope. Of course, we cannot pretend that all men will become fully rational or wise, but after all, even in the most orderly states – those that better guarantee the peace and security of life – one is born a man, but becomes a citizen (see *TP* 5.2).

In this sense, Spinoza's attitude differs strongly from that of Charron or the libertines, for whom contempt for the common man and his superstitions represented a full stop. The wise man must keep his distance from the crowd and look with derision at its beliefs and at the rise and fall of its passions, dictated by fleeting fear and hope. Thus, for Charron (who is quoting Horace), as we will see, there is "a precondition of withdrawing and diverting [from people], if one wants to cross the threshold of the holy sanctuary of wisdom: *Odi prophanum vulgus et arceo.*"[25] The crowds are fickle, as Gabriel Naudé effectively shows in a lively and significant work, *Discours sur les divers incendies du mont Vesuve, et particulièrement su le dernier, qui commença le 16 Decembre 1631*, published in Paris in 1632. On the occasion of the eruption of Mount Vesuvius, Naudé, who witnessed it, recalls the fear that gripped all the citizens, from the most noble and powerful to the most miserable (this time brought together by the collective *insecuritas*). Some fled as rapidly as if the fear had added wings to their feet (*pedibus timor adderet alas*). Others, forced to remain in Naples or massed around the city's ports, resorted to every sort of superstition and religious practice to save themselves. It was thus possible

24 See Plut., *De tranq.* 467 A–B; Engl. trans., 183 (and Plato, *Resp.* X, 604 C): "Plato, for instance, compared life to a game of dice in which we must try not only to throw what suits us best, but also, when we have thrown, to make good use of whatever turns up. But with circumstances, though it is not in our power to throw what we please, yet it is our task, if we are wise, to accept in a suitable manner whatever accrues from Fortune and to assign to each event a place in which both what suits us shall help us most and what is unwanted shall do least harm."

25 P. Charron, *Petit traicté sur la sagesse* [1606], in Charron, *De la sagesse* (Paris, 1824), vol. 3, 276. See also, in the present volume, pp. 202–3.

to witness a multiplicity of practices of mortification of the body and soul, based on different penitential rites. Disheveled women could be seen scratching their faces, monks laden with heavy crosses and wearing crowns of thorns, processions of San Gennaro, prostitutes who withdrew to churches, determined to vow chastity for the rest of their lives, and assassins who resolved to declare their crimes in public.[26] Naudé observes caustically that all this show of piety is destined to last as long as the fear. Once this has passed, everyone will return to their previous behaviour, forgetting their proposals and their piety (an analogous observation on the sudden changes of the "furious" crowd was made in Holland by a contemporary of Spinoza in describing the revolt of Masaniello in 1647 – that is, of the same Neapolitan leader, tribune of liberty, in whose capacity Spinoza would have himself portrayed).

Naudé does not believe, however, that the common man is superstitious because he lacks reason. On the contrary,

> being endowed with reason, he abuses it in a thousand ways and through it becomes the theater where orators, preachers, false prophets, imposters, crafty politicians, rebels, seditionists, the angry, the superstitious, the ambitious – in short all those who have some new plan – act their most furious and bloody tragedies. And so we discover that these people can be compared to a sea subject to every sort of wind and storm; to the chameleon that can assume every color except white; and to the bilge and sewer into which flow all the filth of the house. Their best part is being fickle and variable, approving and disapproving something at the same time, always dashing from one extreme to the other, believing easily, rebelling quickly, always grumbling and murmuring.[27]

According to the tradition of Epicurus, Lucretius, and the Seneca of the *Quaestiones naturales*, revived by *Theophrastus Redivivus*[28] and libertine

26 See G. Naudé, *Discours*, 29–30, and L. Bianchi, *Tradizione libertina e critica storica: Da Naudé a Bayle* (Milan, 1988), 78–81. On the relationship of religion and superstition to fear, Naudé sometimes refers to the subject of *metus*, just as it was treated by Seneca (see, for example, Sen., *Nat. quaest.* II, 42–3; VI, 3, 3; VI, 29, 3; VII, 1, 2).

27 G. Naudé, *Considerations politiques sur le coup d'état* (Rome, 1639), and (Italian trans.) R. Villari, *Elogio della dissimulazione: La lotta politica nel Seicento*, 10.

28 See *Theophrastus Redivivus*, ed. G. Canziani and G. Paganini, 2 vols. (Florence, 1981–2) and, on this anonymous writing, the fundamental study of T. Gregory, *Theophrastus Redivivus*, which cites further from the manuscripts. Almost as a heraldic motto of these trends, this verse sometimes recurs: *primos in orbe deos fecit timor* (from the

thought in general, it is notoriously fear – in its various gradations, like *timor, metus,* or *terror* – that creates the gods, thereby underpinning power on earth as well. Fear, multiplied by superstition, has been accused (echoing Seneca) of making many lose their senses, of provoking effects more deleterious than cataclysms.

It is the occurrence of unexpected individual and collective events that prove disastrous for the mind. This happens, for example, in the case of earthquakes or wars:

> It is not easy to stay sane in the midst of great disasters. So the weakest temperaments generally reach such a pitch of terror that they lose their heads. No one can panic without some loss of sanity, and anyone who is afraid resembles a madman. But fear soon restores some people to their normal selves, while it disturbs others more deeply and drives them mad. That is why in time of war people wander around distraught, and nowhere will you find more cases of people prophesying than when panic blended with religion has attacked their minds.[29]

Seneca's wise man succeeds in differentiating himself with respect to other men, who are more subject to the passions and who are strongly and suddenly attacked by fits of madness. But this undertaking of nature, which guides the course of the heavens with inflexible hand and varies with the seasons, generally does not favour other men. Turning to the ruler of Olympus as his guarantor, in verses that today can seem to us encrusted with a moralistic patina, Seneca – through the mouth of Medea – brings to light the innermost nucleus of the *paradoxa storicorum* – that is, the drama and scandal of a rationality that sees faith (continually belied by events) in its own inalienable strength and ubiquity, that question of

Thebaid of Statius – III, 661 – but previously present as an expression in a fragment of Petronius, and along the lines of some ideas of Lucretius, regarding which see *De rer. nat.* V, 1218 et seq.). On the impact of the Seneca of the *Quaestiones naturales* in *Theophrastus Redivivus,* see, in the edition cited above, 37, 74, 123, 269, 289, 287, 740.

29 Sen., *Nat quaest.* VI, 29.1–3; *Natural Questions,* trans. H. Hine (Chicago, 2010), 134. Seneca considers the phenomenon within his analysis of the destructive and subversive power of nature, which opens the ground and causes rivers and cities to collapse: "An earthquake produces a thousand strange things and changes the appearance of places and carries away mountains, elevates plains, pushes valleys up, raises new islands in the sea" (VI 4, 1). Madness as a result of earthquakes was previously described in Posidonius (*FGRHist* 87 Fr. 88 Jacoby) and would be noted also by Pliny the Younger (*Ep.* VI, 20, 19).

the origin of evil that tormented him in the work *De providentia.* In fact, for those who – rising above the level of sentiment – did not acquire the strict awareness on the basis of which the *logos* has no other enemy than itself, the way that human societies function and the individual experience of pain or nausea seem to refute definitively the idea of a reason that lacks boundaries:

> But why, again, dost thou, who holdest so wide sway, and by whose hands the ponderous masses of the vast universe are poised and wheel their appointed courses – why dost thou dwell afar, all too indifferent to men, not anxious to bring blessing to the good, and to the evil, bane? Fate without order rules the affairs of men, scatters her gifts with unseeing hand, fostering the worse; dire lust prevails against pure men, and crime sits regnant in the lofty palace. The rabble rejoice to give government to the vile, paying high honors even where they hate. Warped are the rewards of uprightness sad virtue gains; wretched poverty dogs the pure, and the adulterer, strong in wickedness, reigns supreme. O decency, honor, how empty and how false![30]

Superstition triggers political disorder, fomenting fear and, with it, wickedness and injustice.

But it is true that the ancients distinguish *deisidaimonia* or *superstitio* (fear of the gods, cowardice towards them justified by the expectation of punishment or reward) from *religio* (veneration of the gods, disinterested respect and filial obedience towards them).[31] Legislators take advantage of precisely this passive and servile side of fear, *superstitio,* to govern the masses in a more docile manner. As Seneca observed with regard to the ancients who imagined Jove with lightning bolt in hand:

> So what was their purpose when they said this? In order to control the minds of the ignorant, those very wise men pointed to an inescapable object of fear. In order that we should be afraid of something superior to us,[32] it was

30 *Phaedra,* 972–88, and see, in the present volume, pp. 194–7.

31 See Varro, in August., *civ.* VI, 9: "But what kind of distinction is this which [Varro] makes between the religious and the superstitious man, saying that the gods are feared by the superstitious man, but are reverenced as parents by the religious man, not feared as enemies." See also Cic., *De nat. deor.* II, 28).

32 *Ad coercendos imperitorum animos sapientissimi viri iudicaverunt inevitabilem metum, ut aliquid super nos timeremus.* For the contrast between *sapiens* and *imperitus,* which also establishes a discriminating politics between he who is governed externally through fear and he who governs himself through reason, see also Cic., *De nat. deor.* I, 77.

expedient, in the face of such audacious wickedness, for something to exist that nobody thought himself powerful enough to oppose; and so, to strike terror into those for whom innocence has no attraction unless fear is the driving force, they placed overhead an avenger, and one who was armed.[33]

In a more general form, this idea is represented in Spinoza's *Theological-Political Treatise*, when both *religio* and *superstitio* are based on obedience towards those authorities who succeed, from time to time, in imposing their greater power in the field of imagination as well, as happens in the case of the prophets of the Old Testament, whose ideas corresponded to the dominant passions within them (see *TTP* 1, 2, 5).[34]

The difference between superstition and religion essentially disappears in Naudé and in the libertines in general (divisible into atheists, deists, and sceptics), but even in Spinoza it no longer has reason to exist. An impersonal God does not ask to be the object of either veneration or bizarre cults, fruit of the imagination and human powerlessness. It is precisely the men who are not guided by the dictates of reason who need religion to restrain their whims and their restless passions and to impose themselves on others. Both the libertines and Spinoza subscribe (or could have easily subscribed) to the tenth of Epicurus's *Capital Maxims*: "If the things that produce the pleasures of the dissolute were able to drive away from their minds their fears about what is above them and about death and pain, and to teach them the limit of desires, we would have no reason to find fault with the dissolute; for they would fill themselves with pleasure from every source and would be free from pain and sorrow, which are evil."[35]

However, according to the libertines – diametrically opposed to Spinoza on this point – it is useless to reveal to the common man the trick of religion and superstition. Following in a restrictive manner the core of Epicurus's "gospel,"[36] which potentially had been preached to all men, only the *esprit fort* is capable of freeing them – through contempt for death and a knowledge hidden to most – not from their sins, but from the ghosts of divinity. However, it is without doubt, even for Spinoza, that

33 Sen., *Nat quaest.* II, 42.3; Engl. trans., 207–9.

34 If men followed reason, there would be no need for laws. See, in the present volume, pp. 70–1.

35 Epicurus, *Cap. Max.* x; Engl. trans., 61.

36 See A.J. Festugière, *Epicure et ses dieux* (Paris, 1985).

the crowd will only understand with difficulty the distinction between obedience to divine and human precepts through conviction and gratitude on the one hand and obedience through fear or hope on the other. But from this, he does not draw the conclusion, also asserted by the libertines, that people always still need to be guided by laws that are not publicly justified by reason.[37]

37 See T. Gregory, *Theophrastus Redivivus*, 185 et seq.

PART 2: THE ARCHAEOLOGY OF WILL

SECTION 1

Consistency and Self-Control

1. Itineraries, Deviations, and Crossroads

The Inner Master

The meaning attributed to the passions in Spinoza's theoretical system shows clear and symptomatic differences with respect to the orientation of the other principal traditions of thought. In fact, he contradicts a wide-ranging array of ancient and modern philosophies that claimed to master, steer, exhaust, and channel the passions through commands of reason, decrees of will, or spiritual exercises.

The polemical targets of the *Ethics* explicitly consist of Stoicism and of Descartes, joined by the fact that both try in vain to repress the passions and achieve perfect self-control through the rule of *logos* and *volonté.* Their efforts, however, are destined to fail, because – despite "no little practice and zeal"[1] – complete supremacy over feelings generally cannot be achieved (nor is this the way to achieve satisfying solutions).

Among the ancient Stoics,[2] the author who turns out to be most congenial to Spinoza is certainly Seneca. Although he does not ignore the ideas of the Greek philosophers of the ancient and middle Stoa, he knows much better (and directly) the sources of the Roman age: certainly Epictetus and probably Marcus Aurelius. Spinoza uses and cites not only Seneca's theoretical texts, but also his tragedies, which effectively integrate and illustrate some fundamental philosophical assumptions,

1 *E* 5, pref.: *usum et studium non parvum.*

2 On Spinoza's relationship with Stoicism, a subject generally little explored, see P.O. Kristeller, "Stoic and Neoplatonic Sources of Spinoza's *Ethics*," *History of European Ideas* 5, no. 1 (1984), 1–16, and R. Schottlaender, "Spinoza et le Stoïcisme," *Bulletin de l'Association des Amis de Spinoza* 17 (1986), 1–8.

demonstrating, in particular, the disastrous consequences produced by perversion of reason itself into passions, into the lucid madness of Medea or the fury of Phaedra.[3]

Against the Stoics and Descartes,[4] Spinoza rejects the idea that man is free only when he is not obeying an external master. If will and reason assume a peremptory tone, if they expect to subdue the passions by means of simple *diktat* (by an "I want" or an "I think that one must"), they themselves become an internal master, as despotic as the external one. If the passions are denied every right to validate their own "reasons," the eventual obedience and submission that they extort will necessarily be a weak, fleeting herald of continuous fluctuations of the soul and of new rebellions. Moreover, they will inevitably lead to the demotivation of behaviours and the alternation of phases of desperation and exhilaration – and always to a decrease in the individual's power of existing. The governing of the passions imposed in authoritarian form – supported by threats or flatteries, fomented by fear of punishments or by promises of rewards – will certainly obtain its victory, but only at the price of rendering man a slave and accomplice of his own oppressor, torn by a renewed and unsolvable struggle between one part of himself that is restricted to commanding and another that is restricted to obedience, without collaboration, "friendship," or consistency existing between the two.

The "internal" master bears down upon almost all individuals. In the worst case it presents itself almost physically, not as a Greek slave owner or an Asian despot but as a cacique, the notable American Indian who had himself transported on the shoulders of his subjects, using them

3 On the significance that Seneca's tragedies assume for Spinoza (present in his library in a small volume in duodecimo: *Senecae Tragediae*) and on his deep interest in comedies, tragedies, and literary works in general (from Terence, Plautus Virgil, Martial, Ovid, and Petronius to Petrarch, Cervantes, Quevedo, and Góngora) in light of his study of the passions and the mechanisms of the imagination, see, in the present volume, pp. 70–1 and 300–1. In fact, the philosophers often treat the passions in a schematic and classificatory way, lacking the concreteness of vision that the theatrical exempla succeeded in translating imaginatively into well-organized, incisive form. Seneca – philosopher, dramaturge, and satirical poet in one – enjoyed the advantage, even theoretically, of a conception made ever sharper by the breadth of the passions and the ways of their expression – an analysis, so to speak of their thickness and not their thinness. On Spinoza as a reader of Seneca and of Latin classics, see also A. Akkerman, "Studies in the Posthumous Works of Spinoza, Earliest Translation and Reception, Earliest and Modern Edition of Some Texts," diss., Groningen, 1980, 14–17.

4 On Descartes, to whom Part 2, Section 2 of this book is dedicated, see pp. 227–73.

as a means of animal locomotion, before the Spanish colonists introduced the use of the horse. In the best case, it weighs upon them like an Anchises on Aeneas, like a venerating father whose weight one continues to support. Whether the master, tyrant, or cacique are called *will* or *reason* does not make much difference, nor does it serve to ennoble their demands.

Unlike ancient Stoicism,[5] for Spinoza there are not, therefore, only the passions that represent the despots or tyrants of men. Despotism and tyranny can come from two sides: we can become servants or passive subjects of the passions to the point of suffering their domination and of becoming deprived of the power to reach a higher *utilitas* and happiness. But if reason and will are limited to breaking the *cupiditas* of man (i.e., that which defines him as a "desirous animal," even if capable of following "virtue and knowledge") without offering him a new order in exchange where his passions may find satisfaction, they end up oppressing his nature. They do not permit the semi-spontaneous order of the passions to pass to the more rigorous and stable order of reason, let alone to the freer and more joyful one of intuitive science. That is, they do not allow a *transitio* from the *ordo imaginationis* to the *ordo rationis* and from this – to use an Augustinian expression – to the *ordo amoris*.[6]

Spinoza's philosophy has as its objective the formation of free men both "internally" and "externally," not the formation of servants or automatons. He thus deals with the passions – which are already forms of imaginative knowledge – not, on principle, as riotous subjects but as inferior energies and forms of knowledge that can be guided to their metamorphosis into feelings (i.e., to the abandonment of the side of passivity) through an increase of knowledge.[7] It is not necessary, however, for them to predicate the suitability of the rational order on the linking

---

5 See, for example, Andronicus in *SVF* III, n. 391.

6 For Augustine, see R. Bodei, *Ordo amoris: Conflitti terreni e felicità celeste* (Bologna, 1991). Another relevant difference with respect to Stoicism is that according to such a doctrine, nature had provided for the self-preservation of living beings, giving appetites to the animals and reason to men. Therefore, it considered the surrender of men to the passions to be unworthy conduct, particularly for the wise man. In fact, it represents the rejection of using the *logos*, the only instrument suitable and specific to the happiness of the rational animal that is man.

7 If some individuals or communities are, however, endowed with such great passivity and turbulence of imagination as not to allow any increasing upward *transitio*, only then is it permissible even for Spinoza to preserve (temporarily?) the coercive character of reason and of will.

of feelings and, least of all, on the order founded by intuitive science. The same noticeable increase in satisfaction and happiness eventually constitutes both its proof and confirmation.

Compensations

If desire forms the essence of man, no external or internal force can bend its nature or erase its force unless obvious or hidden compensations are sought elsewhere. Why, then, do men tolerate oppression and unhappiness? Perhaps because they love "voluntary servitude" (in the words of La Boétie) or the "state of minority" (in those of Kant)? Spinozan ethics aims at the emancipation of man from servitude by following a method that does not hinge on the mere strength of reason and of will and that even rejects any sort of titanic conception of liberty as unconditional power of self-determination. Experience itself bears witness to how violent, polite, or cunning repression of the passions may contribute to further entangling the knots of will, to paralysing its movements or transforming it into a fetish to which to sacrifice life and effort. Through it, one attains the opposite of that to which one aspires: the intensity of the heart's conflicts sharpens, their duration lengthens, and the sufferings to be eliminated increase, to the point that resignation or stagnation end up seeming the most tolerable and practicable solutions.

All the compensations of desire blocked from more satisfying goals and redirected towards surrogates – as happens to products of the imagination or to their hybridization with reason – gain credit and fascinate as a response to the real unhappiness of the overwhelming majority of men. From this spring both evil and its remedies, that is to say superstitions, positive religions, and laws. Bearers of certainties and consolations valid for those who possess a weak power of existing (e.g., see *E* 5.41, schol.), these latter act retroactively on the reasons that elicit them, as they tend not to eliminate but to preserve them. Thus, they also represent, at the same time, the forces that perpetuate and circularly self-eliminate unhappiness, insecurity, and wickedness – as they fight according to a "double-binding" connection.

Without moving far from the criterion of consistency of choices and without repudiating reason in the search for mystical or miraculous solutions, it is necessary for Spinoza to identify processes that may encourage the solution of conflicts, heal the blockage of the passions, and may at the same time increase joy and each person's power to act, to know, and to feel. In fact, "we do not enjoy blessedness because we keep our lusts in check. On the contrary, it is because we enjoy blessedness that we are able to keep our lusts in check" (*E* 5.42). However, one clause must be respected without fail: that which prohibits (to those who are capable of training themselves) retreat to the domain of passivity of the imagination, acceptance of support or salvation from the "low" of fear and hope or from the "high" of divine grace. If it is true that only man can be a god for man, then everyone must learn to count on himself and to strengthen with his peers his own *vis existendi,* so as not to be induced to think up substitutes for his own happiness and endure oppressive authorities.

Pathways

Beyond the Stoics and Descartes, however, Spinozan criticism involves, indirectly, all of the most noted and influential ethical models, both ancient and modern. In the field of philosophy, intrinsically involved are: (a) the Platonic ideal of separation between the rational and irrational soul, with the consequent condemnation of the "concupiscible soul" and of the lowest social class to which it corresponds in the *polis*; (b) the Aristotelian project of education and persuasion of the feelings that is the prerequisite of a "good life" and consistency with oneself; (c) the proposal of Justus Lipsius, in the sphere of Neostoicism, of maintaining a steady heart in turbulent and calamitous times through a strict but already, in some ways, opportunistic discipline of the passions; and (d) finally, albeit indirectly, the thought of Pascal himself, which continues – unknown to Spinoza, despite the common condemnation of Descartes, in the sphere of the moral, and some aspects of classical Stoicism, excluding Epictetus – to trust in hope and in fear of God to fight the effects of the imagination and the disorder of the passions.

At the religious level, they then end up struck (perhaps not accidentally, albeit never named) both by the "soft" line of Catholicism and the "hard" one of rabbinical, Jansenist, and Protestant rigour in general. In the first case, the Spinozan arguments damage – as we partly know – trust in the validity of the Jesuit virtuosity of the imagination. With difficulty, this instrument of dramatization of the conflicts in the interior theatre of the conscience will produce (beyond the renewed death and illusory transfiguration of the passions) an effective liberation from their grip. However, laxity also appears undermined at its foundations, in its conviction (in part still humanist) that man has the power to remain master of his own external destiny (despite the chain of sins, regrets, and relapses), because he has not lost his free will. It is similarly clear in the second case, the contrast with Protestant confessions: with Lutheranism (in its idea of "bondage of the will" that, while releasing man from the impossible perfect obedience to divine law, ties him to a contest of faith against sin, a sort of *potlàc* in which one reacts to every inevitable capitulation to evil with an ever stronger faith that redeems: *pecca forte, sed crede fortitre*) and with Calvinism, more familiar to Spinoza in a Holland where the horrible doubt over predestination of the individual is accompanied, without apparent contradictions, by the cult of pleasure of the senses and of the commodities of life.

Finally, at the political level, a previously encountered double argument is reprised, modulated in other registers: an argument against the utopians and the abstract reformers who claim to extirpate the passions and the "vices" by transforming men into citizens of an ideal state (that has the only fault of not existing anywhere), an argument against the instrumental and astute use of feelings towards maintenance of the status quo, justified by the presumed inalterability of evil and egotistical instincts.

At any level (philosophical, religious, or political), however, Spinoza declares his own rejection both of the primacy of reason and will – that presupposes individuals who are substantially free, convinced of being able to govern the passions despotically – and of the passive acceptance of theories that condemn men to powerlessness, abandoning them to the whims of grace and the predestination of a personal God, or attributing to them by nature a weak *vis existendi* (i.e., leaving them always at the mercy of forces that make life sad and miserable, even independently of social conditions). From this comes the strong claim of the correspondence of liberty and necessity, but also of individual *utilitas* and the common good.

For opposite and complementary reasons – without any desire for equidistance or mediation, and in fact through forms of philosophical "extremism" that will soon bring him fame as an atheist and destroyer of every moral criterion – Spinoza attacks, with calm resolution, different adversaries: the advocates of the omnipotence of will and those of the bondage of the will (as both reveal the two sides of a single passivity); the representatives of philosophies and religions based on attraction to death and the mortification of the spirit and the body; those who immoderately seek pleasures in the swirl of social relationships, dissipating their own existence in the disordered tangle of the passions to then take refuge, perhaps, in sadness and forgetfulness of themselves to find asylum in rural solitude, like wild animals; the cunning politicians, pretenders, and dissemblers who made an art of duplicity and cynicism; and the severe critics of customs, the constructors of dreams whose candour is as evil as the dark machinations of the representatives of the *raison d'état.*

To make sense of such questions, I will proceed according to an itinerary that – beyond historical and philological reconstruction, which I have nonetheless tried to complete with rigorous exactitude – does not claim to relate events of such long duration in a cursory way. Rather, the goal is precisely that of clarifying problems. As these may be endowed with a relative theoretical autonomy with respect to their original contexts (while maintaining their side of historical and cultural conditioning), it then becomes possible to articulate them on the basis of an internal logic in which their fracture lines and turning points also appear. Finally, from an expository point of view, the results will converge at first on that "focus of the ellipse" named Spinoza to subsequently radiate out from it again in another direction, so that the historical experience accumulated along the way may be more easily put to the interests of theory.

The path unfolds into its different results within a complex space, rutted by articulations and junctions that, through contiguity and exclusion, establish the isolated peculiarity of Spinoza's position. Thus, I will start from the "retroactive" examination of some exemplary theses of Greek and Roman Stoicism (with particular attention to Seneca), considered as well for the background of motives that pushed it to compare Platonic and Aristotelian positions and to take up themes drawn from the literary repertoire (and from tragedy in particular). From here I will go back to modern Neostoicism, dwelling particularly on Justus Lipsius, to then pass on to Pascal. Finally, a broad treatment will be dedicated to Descartes in the second section of this part.

2. Persuasion and Toughness

"Patience, My Heart"

Menis is the "first word in all of European literature."[1] It designates the "rage" of Achilles, that "brought woes numberless upon the Greeks"[2] with which the *Iliad* opens. In the "heroic" code, when the son of a goddess suffers a grave injury from Agamemnon, the *menis* is just a sacred rage, parallel to the wrath of Apollo, who decimates the Greek army with the plague. Achilles must resist – according to the heroic code of honour – the bullying of the supreme commander of the expedition against Troy. When he refuses to accept the gifts offered in reparation by his antagonist, however, he passes, based on the same values by which he is inspired, to the side of wrong, debasing his own *menis* in human rancour ("bile" or *cholos*) that poisons the soul.

Closed in his tent, angry over the offence suffered, fighting in his heart, he witnesses the spectacle of his companions who succumb in great numbers because of his absence. Despite the wise advice and the arguments that he is capable of addressing even to himself,[3] the *thymos* (the irrepressible and "leonine" impulse to antagonism, glory, and revenge, the unreasonable desire of Achilles's vengeance, not yet well distinguished in Homer from the *phren*, from thinking or reflecting) prevails within him immediately. When the decision to return to fight beside Agamemnon has matured, the death of Patroclus only changes its

1 For the ethical and philological context, see G. Nagy, *The Best of the Achaeans* (Baltimore, 1979).

2 *Il.* I, 2–3.

3 Accompanied by the recognition that "I could not rage forever" (*Il.* 16, 60–1).

goal. The *thymos* becomes ever wilder in his turning to Hector and in the horrendous tearing apart of his corpse.[4]

Since the beginnings of Western culture, the problem of the passions and self-control has been crucial for poetic and ethical reflection. The ability to keep at bay *menis, cholos, thymos*, or *orge* – that is, the intense "rage" (*ira*) broadly understood, that overflowing vehemence of the psyche – immediately divides men into different categories. The Homeric poems had already implicitly contrasted the divine and human instability of the conduct of Achilles – who does not know how or does not want to restrain the kindling of passion – to the mastery that Odysseus achieves over himself. In a decisive scene, Odysseus succeeds in repressing the violent desire to kill the insolent servants, friends of the Proci, who – without recognizing him – mistreat him in his own palace. So, having disguised his own internal agitation, the new hero of a world bound towards the civilization of self-control (of the interruption or deferment of the immediacy of impulse) learns with difficulty to command himself. And while *thymos* or *kradie*, the "heart," "howl[s]" at him in his chest "like a brach with whelps," he is capable of imposing himself on it and beating it, saying: "Down; be steady."[5] Vengeance will come, but only subsequently: calculated and cold, with all the doors barred so that none of the Proci or the unfaithful servants can escape him, the embittered and patient heart will finally be able to unload its tensions and find fulfilment in an effective action.

With the increased demand for self-control, reflections on *thymos* and treatises on rage, on *orge*, will multiply – particularly starting from the fourth century BC. These are subjects that will pass from philosophical writing to theatrical representations. From Plato to Aristotle, from Theophrastus to Menander, but particularly in the sphere of Stoicism, Epicureanism, and Neoplatonism, the presence of these subjects will, revealingly, become almost obsessive.[6]

---

4 He is thus at the mercy of the same fluctuations of the soul, similar to the waves of the sea, to which even the wise Nestor is sometimes subject. See Homer, *Il.* 14, 16–21.

5 See Homer, *Od.* 20:13–30. This will then become paradigmatic for the theory – that reaches as far as the Stoics – according to which wisdom is identified with the triumph of reason over desires and over uncontrolled impulses of the soul. For some elements of this strategy in the literary tradition, see H. North, *Sophrosyne: Self-Knowledge and Self-Restraint in Greek Literature* (Ithaca, 1966).

6 Just think of the first comedy of Menander, entitled *Orge*, or of *Peri orges* by Philodemus of Gadara (chronologically, this is the first work to reach us in which such passion is presented systematically. See the critical edition and the Italian translation edited by G. Indelli, *L'ira* [Naples, 1988]), or *De ira* by Seneca and *De cohibenda ira* by Plutarch,

Animosity or rage continues to be tied both to a generous feeling of vengeance and blocked revenge towards a real or presumed insult of which one feels a victim, as well as to a form of bursting and savage justice. With the weakening of traditional values that referred back to aristocratic and heroic ethics – which has become more idealized than felt previously in the Homeric poems – and with the rise of different conceptions of justice tied to a common law, the interest in this phenomenon assumes more analytical and descriptive traits. The man in the grip of rage was often presented as subject to a temporary madness: "he has the eyes of the insane, which sometimes emit flashes," "he has a face that is largely flushed; some have a tense neck and swollen veins and bitter and salty saliva."[7] He does not care about social conventions; he is quick to have a fit of nerves for the most diverse and useless reasons, since by now he does not know how to distinguish truth from falsehood. He transforms himself into a madman, in contrast to the wise man, as can be easily seen by observing (according to widespread physiognomic and descriptive models) his appearance and conduct: "a bold, fierce, and threatening countenance ... a wrinkled brow, violent motions, the hands restless and perpetually in action ... deep and frequent sighs, and ghastly looks."[8] The effects of rage are disastrous because it is contagious; the words said or the example displayed excite the crowds and sometimes induce them to crime or to war.[9] The question now is generally examined both from the point of view of the effects the "rage" – it would be better to say the loss of control of oneself – produces on others and from the viewpoint of the man overcome by it. Against Aristotle and the Peripatetic school, the Stoics and Seneca soften the distinction between morally justified rage and blind fury, the complete loss of lucidity. For the former – who intend to preserve in this case traces of heroic ethics – the inhibition of rage would be not only a sign of baseness but an invitation to have oneself trampled and defeated without arms, so as to sever "the nerves of the soul" and reject the "prod of virtue." He who does not inflame himself

down to the late formulations by John Chrysostom (*De ira et furore*, in *PG* 43, 813–51). For a history of this passion in the philosophical, literary, and religious spheres, see J. Sarocchi, *La colère* (Paris, 1991).

7 Philodem., *De ira*; Ital. trans., 111.

8 Sen., *De ira* IV, 1.

9 See ibid., III, 2, 3. Rage is often seen as a sort of temporary madness (for the conception of which, the framing offered by B. Simon, *Mind and Madness in Ancient Greece: The Classical Roots of Modern Psychiatry* [Ithaca, 1978], is useful).

with rightful indignation in the face of the offences or wickedness of others appears endowed with a servile heart and lacking in dignity.[10]

The Black Horse

Only in Platonic philosophy does the problem of the *thymos* find its first theoretical arrangement. The psyche is at first divided in two parts, the rational (*logistikon*) and the arational (*alogon*). This latter is articulated, in turn, in the "concupiscible" soul, capable only of low desires (*epithymetikon*: "with which [one] loves and hungers and thirsts and feels the flutterings of any other desire ... the ally of sundry pleasures and satisfactions") and the irascible or impulsive or courageous soul (*thymoeides*).[11] According to the animal metaphors used by Plato, "man" is a composite being formed by a real man (the *logistikon*), a lion (the *thymoeides*), and a many-sided or chameleon-like monster that assumes every aspect (the *epithymetikon*). The arational soul and the rational one are united and separated by Eros, who tries to unite them with tireless effort.

These three real parts of a fundamentally binary division can be translated "from below" into three forms of desire in general: the unrestrained, bent on satisfaction of the basest instincts; the generous and educable; and finally the rational, where reason presents itself as "desire

10 In this sense, there is nothing scandalous or unseemly in the sublime nature of the place and the majesty of the character if Dante "dares" to describe, in Paradise, Peter – the first of the apostles and the popes – while he flares with rage and pronounces fiery words at the memory of the misdeeds performed by his unworthy successors in guiding the church. Therefore, even in the afterlife, some passions continue to be good.

11 See Plat., *Rep.* IV, 439 D–E. On the concept of *thymos*, see G. Concato, "*Thymos*," *Atque* 2 (November 1990), 107–24. According to G. Dumézil (*Mythe et épopée*, vol. 1: *L'idéologie des trois fonctions dans le épopées des peuples indo-européens* [Paris, 1968], 396), such tripartition refers to the Indo-European triad of political, military, and productive functions. Moreover, it conforms to the tripartition of the types of life that Plato establishes: that of the *philosophos* who seeks wisdom, the *philotimos* who pursues honours, and the *philokerdes* who greedily aims for profit (see Plato, *Phaedo*, 68, 82; P. Joly, *Le thème philosophique des trois genres de vie* [Paris, 1956]; and A.J. Festugière, "Les trois vies," in *Études de philosophie grecque* [Paris, 1971], 117–56). In Plato, the conflict or the possible agreement are not between the soul and the body, but within the soul itself. It follows "that drives and desires do not have their root in corporeality (which this way ends up being neutral)" (M. Vegetti, "Platone e l'origine della psicologia," in *La qualità dell'uomo* [Milan, 1989], 90).

for good" (later, in Aristotle, it will become desire made reasonable).[12] In the best way, virtue coordinates the conduct of the soul, channeling its desires towards rationality, so as to reduce the energetic cost – whose quantity appears finite – directed towards the worst impulses.[13] As the desires anchored by reason are strengthened, the power over the soul firms up as a consequence. Therefore, it is not exactly as it is commonly said – that is, that poetry and art in general are condemned absolutely by Plato. If anything, that is valid from the higher point of view of reason and morality (because of the bad examples offered by the poems of Homer). But poetry also represents the distorting (and thus, paradoxically realistic) mirror of the protean aspect of the soul's desirous part. Thanks to this function, art in general can become one of the most suitable sources for knowledge of the passions. This is the reason why, among other things, in the third book of the *Republic* (400 E, 402 A), beauty (of the gardens, statues, and buildings of the city) is shown as the instrument for purifying and calming the *thymos* of the "guardians," men capable of dominating their desires that aim towards the low but whose reason is still entangled in competitive conflicts dictated by the search for honour and glory.

The arational parts of the mind become irrational when desires harden and structure themselves over time into conglomerations that are relatively coherent and difficult to disaggregate, assuming the aspect of traits of "character" and joining forces permanently against reason. The most effective weapon to fight them is self-control, moderation, or

12 The image of the conflict between the indeterminateness and unshakability of desire and the need for harmony and precision of the *logos* seems to reproduce, by analogy, the problems tied to the discovery of incommensurability in Greek geometry (regarding which, see D. Kurz, *Akribeia: Das Ideal der Exaktheit bei den Griechen bis Aristoteles* [Göttingen, 1970], and K. von Fritz, "The Discovery of Incommensurability by Hippasus of Metapontum," in *Studies in Pre-Socratic Philosophy* [London, 1970], 382–442). On reason as desire for good in Plato – which is connected to *logismos*, as a "large and vigorous" part of the soul (*Resp.* IV, 442 A) – see S. Skolnikov, "Reason and Passion in the Platonic Soul," *Dyonisos* 2 (1978), 35–49, or, as desire for reason in Aristotle, see *Magna Mor.* 1187b and *Top.* 126a.

13 See *Resp.* VI, 485 D: "But then again, as we know by experience, he whose desires are strong in one direction will have them weaker in others; they will be like a stream which has been drawn off into another channel." Some analogies between this statement and the "hydraulic model" of the Freudian psyche were highlighted by C. Kahn, "Plato on the Unity of the Virtues," in *Facets of Plato's Philosophy*, ed. W.H. Werkmeister (Assen, 1976), 27 et seq., and G. Santas, *Plato and Freud: Two Theories of Love* (Oxford, 1988).

enkrateia (*Resp.* IV, 430 E), which implies a rational strengthening of the "will" or *boulesis* (note, incidentally, how in Spinoza evil does not at all derive from the prevailing of the irrational parts of the soul). The tyrant – despicable as he pursues to the end the realization of his own wild and inflated desires, demonstrating himself to be the direct opposite of the philosopher – lacks any sort of self-control. He carries out, while awake, those illegitimate impulses (*paranomoi*) that all other men pursue since childhood but have learned to repress during their waking hours "by the laws and by reason" or that they satisfy in a hallucinatory way in their dreams, when the rational part of the soul sleeps and man's feral element takes the upper hand. It is then that every individual surrenders – involuntarily, like a sleeping Oedipus – to terrible, chaotic, and wild desires "not excepting incest or any other unnatural union, or parricide."[14]

The *boulesis* transforms the individual into a small, deliberating assembly obligated to keep in mind psychic needs that are unyielding to rationality. Substituting for the Socratic *daimon*, the *logos* gathers advice and chooses its line of conduct. In this sense, Plato's strategy aims at a *logokratia*, directed towards making power wise and wisdom powerful (which also happens, indirectly, according to the double register of persuasion and coercion: educating the *thymos* and the "custodians" to goodness and inciting them at the same time, as faithful guardians of reason, against the *epithymetikon* and the lower strata of the *demos*). In the famous Platonic myth of the winged chariot (see *Phaedr.* 266 A et seq.), the *logos*, charioteer of the soul, directs towards the heights the animal element of the fiery white horse and, with more effort, that of the untamed black horse made up of rebellious desires directed downward.

The Voice of the Shepherd

At the command of the *logos*, the generous passions calm down, like a dog at "the voice of the shepherd."[15] It is a "pastoral power," protective and coercive at the same time, that lasts until some individuals, destined to command, have reached full autonomy. To tame the beasts and the

14 See Plato, *Resp.* IX, 571 A–D. In the *Interpretation of Dreams*, Freud alludes to this Platonic passage. See S. Kofman, "Freud et Platon," in *Séductions: De Sartre à Héraclite* (Paris, 1990), 65–86.

15 Plato, *Resp.* IV, 440 D.

irreducible animal part of man, what is necessary is authority and the bit, reason armed by proxy – defended by the safety belt of the guards and fed materially, in its political representatives, by the activity of the producers, the men of that third class who do not know how to adapt themselves to the radical transformation of the impulses and desires (including meanness and jealousy) that rise from the abolition of the propriety of things and women in the just city.[16] Reason commands the use of strong measures only when one is forced to, as in the case of horses or draft animals, if you are talking about eliminating their deviations and abrupt movements without impeding the energy of their impulses and desires.[17]

As is well known, even Aristotle follows the tripartite scheme of the subdivision of the soul, preserving, in much weaker form, the analogy between *psyche* and *polis* and distinguishing the "vegetative" arational soul, which presides over vital functions of the organism, and the "concupiscible" one. Unlike in the oriental traditions of the "Gymnosophists," the vegetative soul for Aristotle ends up deaf to the dictates of the rational part. The "naked philosophers" that Alexander and his army had encountered in India and tried to bring to the West were, in fact, capable of influencing – through meditation, ascetic exercises, and will – the spontaneous (for us) functions of the body, like breathing or heartbeat. Instead, in the Aristotelian sense, the "concupiscible" soul participates, within certain limits, with the rational soul, "in so far as it listens to and obeys [reason]; this is the sense in which we speak of 'taking account' of one's father or one's friends, not that in which we speak of 'accounting' for a mathematical property" (*Eth. Nic.* I, 13, 1102b).

16 See Plato, *Laws* VII, 808 D–E: "For neither sheep nor anything else ought to live without a shepherd, nor boys without some boy-leaders, nor slaves without masters. Now a boy is of all wild beasts the most difficult to manage. For by how much the more he has the fountain of prudence not yet fitted up, he becomes crafty and keen, and the most insolent of wild beasts. On this account it is necessary to bind him, as it were, with many chains."

17 In arguing with the Stoics, Plutarch explained this aspect of the Platonic tradition well: "With oxen and horses people try to restrain their mad bounds and restiveness, not their movements and powers of work. And so reason makes use of the passions when they have become tame and docile, not by cutting out the sinews or altogether mutilating the serviceable part of the soul" (Plut., *On Moral Virtue*, 451).

The Aristotelian "moral family spirit" establishes a rhetoric connected to a model of reason that is much more plastic than the Platonic and particularly the Stoic, one that exercises the passions that it lets convince and educate but becomes equally repressive when it meets similarly insurmountable resistance: "argument and teaching, we may suspect, are not powerful with all men ... For he who lives as passion directs will not hear argument that dissuades him, nor understand it if he does; and how can we persuade one in such a state to change his ways? And in general, passion seems to yield not to argument but to force."[18]

---

18 *Eth. Nic.* x, 9, 1179b. In this regard, the *logos* is presented as an ability to modify feelings that are external, even if in part educable.

3. Consistency and Constancy

Enemies of Themselves

To live according to reason, man must maintain consistency with himself over time, even when he must do so through the hardest trials. He must tell himself – paraphrasing Odysseus – "patience, my *logos*!" In fact, constancy and integrity are for Aristotle the distinctive traits of the virtuous person, whose heart is friendship with itself, and of the *eudaimonia* as the capacity to follow one's own *daimon*:

> For [the good man's] opinions are harmonious, and he desires the same things with all his soul ... and he wishes himself to live and be preserved, and especially the element by virtue of which he thinks. For existence is good to the virtuous man, and each man wishes himself what is good, while no one chooses to possess the whole world if he has first to become someone else (for that matter, even now God possesses the good); he wishes for this only on condition of being whatever he is. (*Eth. Nic.* IX, 4, 1166a)

Therefore, no good man would like to become another, even if he were offered all the goods of the world. The desire to be different from what one essentially is is condemned by Aristotle as typical of evil. Incidentally, this attitude by which the good man wants himself as he is ("become what you are") clearly contrasts with some characteristic aspects of our contemporary sensibility in which many man, certainly not "bad men," have often cultivated fantasies of otherness, regrets for what they could have been and were not, or they demonstrated the aspiration to live other lives "parallel" to their own. Faithfulness to oneself – *constantia* or *firmitas* – constitutes, instead, the genuine cornerstone of classical ethics. He who intends to remain equal to himself has constant desires and attitudes, precisely because he enjoys such consistency and continuity with his own being: "And such a man wishes to live with himself; for he does so with pleasure, since the memories of his past acts are delightful and his hopes for the future are good, and therefore pleasant … And he grieves and rejoices, more than any other, with himself; for the same thing is always painful, and the same thing always pleasant, and not one thing at one time and another at another; he has, so to speak, nothing to regret" (ibid.). Continuity with one's past becomes a dominant value.

Dysdaimonia or *kakodaimonia*, being in disagreement or the enemy of oneself, derive from the violation of this value. The wicked man lacks integrity and equality with himself, as he would gladly exchange his identity to obtain some goods. Above all, however, he is a deeply torn man. His soul, dragged in opposite directions, is subject to the turmoil of opposing factions. Within it, one part always fights the other, dividing their strengths. Therefore, bad men – not being consistent and desiring some things while in abstract terms they might want others – always try to amuse or distract themselves to avoid remaining alone with their own thoughts:

> Wicked men seek for people with whom to spend their days, and shun themselves; for they remember many a grievous deed, and anticipate others like them, when they are by themselves, but when they are with others, they forget. And having nothing lovable in them, they have no feeling of love to themselves. Therefore, also such men do not rejoice or grieve with themselves; for their soul is rent by faction, and one element in it, by reason of its wickedness, grieves when it abstains from certain acts, while the other part is pleased, and one draws them this way and the other that, as if they were pulling them in pieces. If a man cannot at the same time be pained and pleased, at all events after a short time he is pained *because* he was pleased, and he could have wished that these things had not been pleasant to him; for bad men are full of regrets. (ibid., 1166b)

The Man of Tomorrow and the Man of Today

The distinction between good and evil also passes through temporal parameters. The good man is always present to himself, whole in every moment, even when he enjoys "memories of his past acts" and "his hopes for the future are good."[1] The lived story of his life is made consistent by a continuity that is temporal and ethical at the same time.

---

1 *Kalai elpides*: the term *elpis* denoting an uncertain expectation, "good hopes" means nothing other than "hope" as we understand it. In the *Nicomachean Ethics*,

The evil man, however, wavers because of the fluctuations of his soul. In the most serious cases, it is as if he were cut up by desires that push in different directions. His regret is not a symptom of reformation but of further wickedness. He avoids both himself and his past without, however, succeeding in enjoying his own future. His *I* is essentially divided[2] and is an enemy of itself, because it ignores the nature of *philautia* or self-esteem.

In the later language of Plutarch, who remained absolutely faithful to the spirit of Aristotle on this point, men in general, seeing "their own life is unsmiling and dejected and ever oppressed and afflicted by the most unpleasant experiences and troubles and unending cares,"[3] do not get a reprieve and do not listen to advice. Thus, they refuse to accept all reasoning that would lead them to "acquiesce in the present without fault-finding, remember the past with thankfulness, and meet the future without fear or suspicion, with their hopes cheerful and bright."[4] Unlike these, only the honest man is capable of remaining faithful to himself in an intelligent way, as integrity is nothing more than presence to oneself, at every moment, of all of oneself, a connective tissue of the soul that establishes an uninterrupted continuity between past and future. The good man recalls with gratitude the past time and discerns its extension into the present.[5] Being good does not constitute a supererogatory act, but is the condition itself of happiness and of fullness of being.[6]

---

the only reason why childhood is considered in positive terms is because it is open to the possibilities of the future: "A boy is not happy; for he is not yet capable of such acts, owing to his age; and boys who are called happy are being congratulated by reason of the hopes we have for them" (*Eth. Nic.* I, 10, 1100a).

2 Not only in the sense of the famous work of that name by R.D. Laing, *The Divided Self* (London, 1959), but also in that of William James's "Lecture VIII: The Divided Self and the Process of Its Unification," in *The Varieties of Religious Experience* (New York, 1982 [1902]), 166–88. The "divided *I*" does not often enjoy the Christian promise of regeneration and rebirth of the individual in the form of a new man, the possibility of being "twice-born" (166).

3 Plut., *De tranq.* 477 F; Engl. trans., 241.

4 Ibid.

5 Meanwhile, "thankless forgetfulness steals upon the multitude and takes possession of them, consuming every action and success, every pleasant moment of leisure and companionship and enjoyment; it does not live to become unified, when past is interwoven with present, but separating yesterday, as though it were different, from today, and tomorrow likewise, as though it were not the same as today, forgetfulness straightaway makes every event to have never happened, because it is never recalled" (ibid., 473 C–D; Engl. trans., 217).

6 "Those who do not preserve or recall by memory former events, but allow them to flow away, actually make themselves deficient and empty each day and dependent on

The Ages of Life

Being consistent with one's history, remaining exactly like oneself throughout passing experiences, represents the ethical model to which classical culture constantly aspires, albeit in different forms. In modern terms, this means that personal identity is something that one creates and not only that happens. In the Aristotelian perspective (shown by *Rhetoric*, II, 12–14, 1388b–1390b), it is tied to stages of an individual's life. Aristotle distinguishes three ages: youth, maturity, and old age – two extremes and a middle. Virtue, consistency, and fullness of identity stand in the middle, in maturity, while youth errs through excess and old age through deficiency. According to analysis that, for its penetrating vividness, merits being related extensively, for Aristotle, a characteristic of young people is the force of their desires, but also their inconstancy: "In terms of their character, the young are prone to desires and inclined to do whatever they desire. Of the desires of the body, they are most inclined to pursue that relating to sex and they are powerless against this."[7] The old are the mirror opposite of the young, "for through having lived for many years and having been more often deceived and having made more mistakes themselves, and since most things turn out badly, they assert nothing with certainty and all things with less assurance than is needed" (ibid., 1389b). In the old, the contradictory nature of desires is substituted for the youthful force of desire: "they love as if they would one day hate and hate as if they would one day love … And they are fond of life and more so on their last day because of the presence of

the morrow, as though what had happened last year and yesterday and the day before had no relation to them nor had happened to them at all" (ibid., 473 D–E; Engl. trans, 217). Even for the wise Epicurean, the goods of the past are not lost: he always remains "young of goods through the grateful memory of the past" (*Epistola a Meceneo*, 122).

7 Arist., *Rhet.* 1389a. Aristotle continues: "They are changeable and fickle in desires, and though they intensely lust, they are quickly satisfied; for their wants, like the thirst and hunger of the sick, are sharp rather than massive … And they live for the most part in hope; for hope is for the future, and memory is of what has gone by, but for the young the future is long and the past short … And they are magnanimous; for they have not yet been worn down by life but are inexperienced with constraints, and to think oneself worthy of great things in magnanimity and this is characteristic of a person of good hopes."

desire for what is gone, and people most desire what they lack" (ibid.). Further, "they are small-minded because of having been worn down by life; for they desire nothing great or unusual but things necessary for life ... Their outbursts of anger are sharp but weak; and some of their desires have failed, others are weak, with the result that they are not spirited and do not act on the basis of desire, but for profit ... And they live more by calculation than by natural character; and calculation is a matter of what is beneficial, character of virtue. And the wrongs they commit are from malice, not insolence" (ibid., 1389a, 1390a). Those in the prime of life "will be between the young and old in character, subtracting the excess of either ... To speak in general terms, whatever advantages youth and old age have separately, [those in their prime] combine, and whatever the former have to excess or in deficiency, the latter have in due measure and in a fitting way" (ibid., 1390a–b).

The importance of this line of development of the problem of identity consists not only in its genetic character (i.e., in the fact that identity changes with time), but also in the historical one. Looking forward, we can observe how the division of the age brackets in Western societies remained substantially the same for centuries and millennia as that described in the *Rhetoric* (so that Schopenhauer, in his description of the ages of life, or Vico, in his hypothesis of the ages of the human race, are theoretical contemporaries of Aristotle more than of us). In little less than a century and – in a more accelerated form – in little less than a few decades, things have changed for us. Childhood had already separated from that conglomeration that Aristotle indicated instinctively as "youth," but currently it is, in many countries, prolonged in time. Adolescence is often protracted even longer, invading the period previously reserved for the adult age. Maturity, to paraphrase Shakespeare, is no longer "all" and old age does not represent only *gravitas* or the harbinger of death, but the position reached by a now numerically strong army of men who often desire to recuperate what they lost over the course of years. The expansion of the "extremes" restricts, even ethically, the area of influence of the "middle," of the *mesotes* in the Aristotelian sense.

Now, one does not aspire any longer (or only) to the consistency indicated by classical ideals (to the granitic determination to remain the same over time to oneself and in friendship with oneself), but to the continuous opening of oneself to the possibility of being others, making the *I* not bound by its past choices, restricting the number of prerequisites necessary for personal identity, by which one can be "oneself" even by passing through possible changes to the body's organs or the brain or even becoming replicas of oneself, token persons.[8] Wanting oneself as one is, and avoiding the conflict of the soul as an evil, are distinctive characteristics of the classical world with respect to the Christian and the modern ones, which are often driven to praise either the soul that is renewed, defeating the "old man" within each of us, or the split and inevitably multiple consciousness (aimed at imagining other lives) in the search for possible changes and an elastic integrity and identity.

The Stronghold of the Soul

With ancient Stoicism, starting with Zeno and Chrysippus, the centre of gravity of ethics moves. The harsh and clear conflict between reason and the passions replaces the Aristotelian analysis of the modularity and adaptation of the virtues according to the midpoint between vices extreme in their excess and deficiency (which does not at all imply an algebraic elision of the two opposing vices, but the priority of this "peak" that contemporaneously disqualifies the extremes and that, as the pre-eminent or standard, cannot have a "more" or a "less"). The symmetry of useful and good breaks both in individuals and in the cities, and we pass, in the field of ethics, from common political education to the personal and solitary (in large part) education of the wise man, from "gyroscopic" mechanisms of custom interpreted by practical wisdom[9] to the application of universal norms.

Thus, the strictest self-control separates the tradition of old Stoicism from the measure or temperance of the passions (*metropatheia* and *temperantia*) typical of the Platonic-Aristotelian tradition in all its variants and offshoots.[10] It is no longer a case of "pruning" or "bridling" feelings through technical means of persuasion and domestication – reducing

8 Today this value of consistency seems to be in decline in some sectors of ethics. Just think of the theory of non-binding commitments in R. Nozick, *Philosophical Explanations*, (where one need not feel bound to obligations previously assumed, as the weight of the reasons for a particular choice varies over time), or of the problem of personal identity transformed into a problem of survival through a series of "successive I's" or, further, of its complication in different ways in P. Berger, B. Berger, and H. Kellner, *The Homeless Mind* (Harmondsworth, 1973); T. Nagel, *Moral Questions* (Cambridge, 1973); D. Parfit, *Reasons and Persons* (Oxford, 1984); or J. Elster, ed., *The Multiple Self* (Cambridge, 1986).

9 Starting from childhood, since children are controlled, from birth, by rage or temper. See Plat., *Resp.* III, 411 B.

10 Even if, in Aristotle, virtue is not simply a habit but an intelligent disposition to aim high, and "men, through it, perform the best things, ... according to which they are disposed in the best manner toward what is best" (*Eth. Eud.* II, 5, 1222a), it is still true

their virulence and keeping the soul in an intermediate state between indifference and intemperance – but of fighting them head on, generating, in a recursive manner, a struggle and a "collision of duties." If he does not succeed in keeping the conflict between reason and passions under control, the wise Stoic, remaining in conflict with himself, risks acquiring some of the characteristics that Aristotle attributes to evil.

The effort of the soul to dominate and continually watch over the passions and desires is commanded by its central part, by the *hegemonikon*, which generally has its seat in the heart (*cuore*) or in the *pneuma* around the heart. It stands within us like God or the sun in the universe.[11] The *hegemonikon* is compared sometimes to an octopus that extends its eight tentacles from the centre to the periphery of the individual[12] and – from the point of view of comprehension – of the world. At other times, it presents itself as a citadel that controls the civil-built environment militarily, from above and from within, or as a fortified acropolis of reason, free of passions, that defends the security and the inner life of the wise man – a place from which to return, restored to the battle.[13] This implies in its name the idea of rigorous control of the will[14] and intelligence over

---

that the criterion of the ethical choices is never abstract, because it is offered by those who possess prudence. Another defender of custom against general (but uncertain) rules – Michel de Montaigne – was able in this sense to tell this significant anecdote: "Plato reprehending a boy for playing at nuts, 'Thou reproves me,' says the boy, 'for a very little thing.' 'Custom,' replied Plato, 'is no little thing'" (*ES* I, XXIII, 107 [*ESe* I, XXII, 100]).

11 On the *hegemonikon* (an adjective-turned-noun whose meaning, "capable of commanding," slips into the "supreme and sovereign part of the soul"; see Diog. Laert., VII, 159) that assumes control of the feelings, see *SVF* I, 143; II, 827, 836, 838, 843. For its comparison with God on the part of Chrysippus, see *SVF* II, 885. For the Stoics, only the *phaulos* (the fool, the unimportant man, the ignorant one or the evil), as lacking *enkrateia*, temperance or control of himself, feels all the force of desires (see *SVF* III, 355, 441, 593, 599). For the Stoics, not having irrational parts (beyond the soul), it is possible to know of its existence (in the words of Chrysippus, "the power of acting and of suffering"; see Plut., *Stoic. rep.* 1042 E) in all its aspects. In the language of Leibniz, one could say that there does not exist for the Stoics a truth of fact that is ontologically distinct from truth of reason.

12 On the comparison to an octopus, see Aetius, *Placita* IV 4, 4; IV 2, 21 (= SVF II, 836).

13 On the image of the citadel of the soul, see also Marc. Aur., VIII, 48.

14 On the corporeal nature of the soul, see Nemesius, *De natura hominis,* 2. On the medical tradition that places the passions in relation to corporeality and indicates a not always repressive path with regard to them, see Galen, *Le passioni e gli errori dell'anima: Opere morali,* ed. M. Menghi and M. Vegetti (Padua, 1984) (with the accompanying essay by M. Vegetti, "La terapia dell'anima: Patologia e disciplina del soggetto in Galeno," 131–55). See also Spinoza (among others), *Ep.* 17.

action[15] and over the continual mutiny of the *demos* of the passions.[16] Like the Stoa Poikile of Athens, where the school arose[17] – this acropolis is also visible to everyone, and deliberately participates in the public and political sphere, in that it houses a dimension of inwardness directed towards the *kosmos,* which holds the *polis* itself.

While in Plato the *psyche* is structurally analogous to the *polis,* in the Stoics it assumes the form of the *akro-polis.* This is another sign that reveals the change that occurred from a system of "horizontal" containment of impulses and desires to a "vertical" system in which reason tries to impose itself upon itself.[18] Closed within its fortress, the "charioteer" of the *logos,* the *hegemonikon,* now corresponds to the same "horses" of the brave impulses and of dissenting and rebellious desire. Given that rationality is not external to passion, the fight to establish the liberty and tranquility of the wise man becomes painful. The errors caused by passion should be "entirely plucked up and destroyed, not pared and amputated" (Cic., *Tusc.* IV, 27).

Therefore, the tranquility of the soul is not idleness, but an armistice continually renegotiated after every war of attrition of the passions, even if the rejection of the things that are not in our power does not weaken, but strengthens, the directive function. The *hegemonikon* is a centre of self-control that restrains one's own excess, not a separate reason. It

15 On the theory of action in early Stoicism, see B. Inwood, *Ethics and Human Action in Early Stoicism* (Oxford, 1985).

16 The *hegemonikon* "appears as a craftsman who forges impulse" (Diog. Lert., VII, 86). This latter – *horme,* instinct, or inclination, a term rendered by Cicero as *appetitus* (*De fato* XL) and by Seneca as *impetus* (*Ep.* CXIII, 10–11) – is characterized by a particular *tonos,* by the tension or by the expansive and attractive force possessed by each individual that assents to its *pathos.*

17 The portico chosen by the ex-merchant Zeno of Citium that ran along the north side of the agora – a place of philosophy near the voices and noises of the marketplace and not, as in Parmenides, a "path far from the life of men" (see B 13 D.-K.).

18 On the similarity between psychic *mikropolis* and political *makropolis,* see *Resp.* 435 B–C. In Platonic physiology, the acropolis was represented by the head (see *Tim.* 69 et seq.). Near it, between the diaphragm and the neck, the *thymos* had its seat so that "it might be within hearing of the reason and might join it in forcibly keeping down the tribe of lusts, when they would in no wise consent to obey the order and word of command from the citadel" (*Tim.* 70 B). In Aristotle, on the other hand, the acropolis – from a biological point of view – is already situated in the heart (see *De part. an.* III, 7, 670). The nature of the Stoic *hegemonikon* did not permit any mediation of the *thymos* between the acropolis of the *logos* and the passions and desires.

is the *hegemonikon,* "by the alterations which habit or disposition have brought about, [that] becomes vice or virtue, without having in itself any unreasoning element, but it is called unreasoning when, by the strong and overpowering force of appetite, it launches out into excesses contrary to the direction of reason. For passion, according to them, is only vicious and intemperate reason [*logos*] getting its strength and power from bad and faulty judgement."[19] Therefore, passion ends up being voluntary and derives from a false judgment of reason that, through weakness, marries a false opinion.[20] From this point of view, it is possible to think and act not only, Aristotle-like, in friendship with oneself, but in full consistency with oneself, because consistency of duty is simply living according to reason[21] or a *vita concors sibi* (Sen., *Ep.* 89.15), in which moral interior logic aspires to reflect cosmic material logic. Stoic ethics is the locus of the precision and rigour that organizes itself according to an order promoted and recognized by the wise man. Controlling the self and the world or (better still) feeling at home in the cosmos: this is the "desire of desires."[22] But doesn't such an obsession with consistency and rationality contain, perhaps, a secret fear of losing oneself in chaos?

Passion is simply *diastrophe* (distortion or diversion) of reason, delirium that overflows beyond its established limits. Man, for the most part, is a depraved – or easily corruptible – animal who does not understand what his true interest might be, and because of this he becomes evil or continually becomes stuck in paradoxes.[23] It is a matter of healing him,

19 Plut., *On Moral Virtue* [*De vit. mor.*], 441 C. However, for Plutarch, to say that reason and passion are the same thing according to two different orientations is the same as saying that "the hunter and the animal he hunts are one and the same person, but alternately changing from hunter to animal, from animal to hunter" (447 C). On Plutarch and the sense of his aversion to Stoicism, see R. Flacelière, *Sagesse de Plutarque* (Paris, 1964), and D. Babut, *Plutarque et le Stoïcisme* (Paris, 1969).

20 See Cic., *Ac. post.* I, 38, and *SVF* III, 473.

21 See Cic., *De fin.* III, 58, and Diog. Lert., II, 89.

22 See A.A. Long, *Hellenistic Philosophy: Stoic, Epicureans, Sceptics* (London, 1974).

23 See A. Grilli, "Diastrophe," *Acme* 16 (1963), 87–101, and M. Forschner, "Die pervertierte Vernunft: Zur Stoischen Theorie der Affekte," *Philosophisches Jahrbuch* 87 (1980), 258–80. In this sense, "the definition of man as a rational animal can, effectively (if not directly) be converted into that of a 'passionate animal.' The paradox lies in this: the reduction of passion and reason aimed at liberating the subject from servitude to the irrational side of his soul, to voluntary and responsible conduct. But since it happens in men that the *logos* may degenerate into passion, there is no force that can challenge it, since it produces a total subjugation of the *I*" (M. Vegetti, *L'etica*

straightening out his reason through a sort of orthopedics of the soul, thus making him indifferent towards what is not the true good (see *SVF* I, 83). In this way, however, the wise Stoic often risks extracting from his own soul the root of desire and affectivity. Precisely from neither fearing nor aspiring to anything,[24] his desires shrink, "laid at the voice of reason."[25] In many respects, in this he appears close to Kantian "rigorism," while he is, instead, at the poles both of the Epicurean model and the Spinozan one, where it is necessary to pursue pleasure, seek happiness, and keep desire alive.[26] Between the two basic strategies explained here (that of soothing, taming, or educating the arational parts of the soul by means of desire and that of repressing and fighting perverse reason transformed into passion), Spinoza elaborates a third one, intent on reformulating the passions from within and without through a reinvestment of desire at higher levels and an increased security of existence. Against every "master's voice" and every asceticism, the separation between the arational and rational parts of the soul collapses. Every moment of the power of existing is endowed with its own logic, and reason is only an intermediate step of desire. What counts is not taming the passions, via proxy, as irrational means, nor keeping them at bay through a reason armed and fortified against itself. Rather, it is necessary to offer them an outlet, transforming their dissipative energy into activity targeted towards the good, making men more secure and happy.

Passions and Desires

Stoicism shows a new interest in the passions, their expression, and their leaking out (or not) through the body. The wise man sculpts himself into a living monument of imperturbable self-control and marble-like plasticity. With the strength of reason, he must balance the weakness of

---

degli antichi [Bari-Rome, 1989], 230). Not being opposed to one another, passion and reason produce together "the continuous man" of whom Chrysippus speaks (*SVF* 885). On the Stoic concept of evil, see A.A. Long, "The Stoic Concept of Evil," *Philosophical Quarterly* 18 (1968), 329–43.

24 See *SVF* III, 109, 18: *nihil timere nec cupere summum bonum est.*

25 Plut., *On Moral Virtue,* 442 E.

26 On this subject, see W. Schick, "Kant und die Stoische Ethik," *Kant-Studien* 18 (1913), 419–75. On desire in Stoic theory, however, see J. Bels, "A Note on Desire in Stoic Theory," *Dialogue* 21 (1982), 329–31.

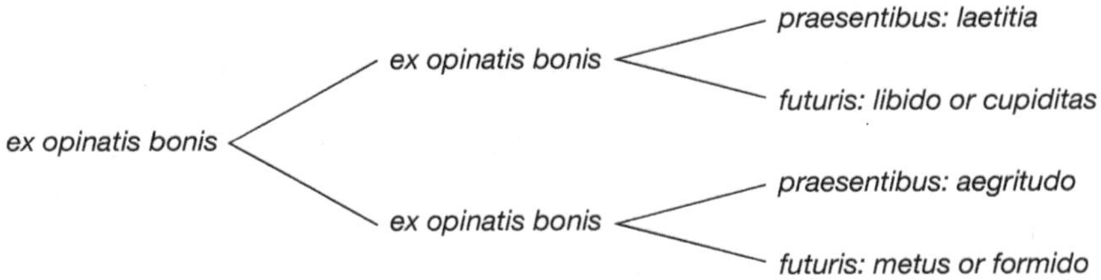

the body[27] and, as a good actor, be capable of indifferently playing both the tragic role of Agamemnon and the comic one of Thersites.[28]

The classification of the passions – previously initiated in a sufficiently methodical way by the Aristotle of the *Rhetoric* and the *Nicomachean Ethics* – crystallizes in Stoic philosophy according to the diagram above, of which Cicero offers a rich, mediated, and clear version.[29]

Passion (as we already partly know) is in general an unreasonable movement of the soul, a natural and overabundant impulse that arose from a judgment that assumed force and relative autonomy.[30] In the Ciceronian re-elaboration of these subjects, *desiderium* is distinguished from the other passions because it is a rebellious inclination towards someone or something, an uncertain future: *libido eius, qui nondum adsit, videndi* (Cic., *Tusc.* IV, 21, and see IV, 14). Fear, on the other hand, is presented as an inclination contrary to reason, or expectation of an evil thought to be approaching, and is divided into "fright, hesitation, shame, dismay, terror, anxiety."[31] Fright consists of a fear that causes the

27 On the new sensibility that arose at the end of the fourth century BC for the expression of the passions in relation to the body, as well as for the imbalance between the greatness of the soul and the decadence of the body, see P. Zanker, *Die Trunkene Alte: Das Lachen der Verhönten* (Frankfurt, 1989), which considers both the statue of an old drunken prostitute who shows happiness in Dionysian drunkenness and that of Diogenes the Cynic in his struggle to maintain control over a body that had become deformed because of age (see, in particularly, 62 et seq., 69 et seq.). On the new interest in the passions on the part of the literature, painting, and plastic arts of this period, see B.H. Fowler, *The Hellenistic Aesthetic* (Madison, 1989), 79–91.

28 See *SVF* I, 351, and M. Vegetti, "La saggezza dell'attore: Problemi dell'etica stoica," *aut-aut* 195–6 (1983), 19–41.

29 See, for example Cic., *De fin.* III, 35; *Tusc.* IV, 11 et seq.; but compare *SVF* III, 377–490 (on the passions in general) and *SVF* III, 387, 396, 400, 412, 498 on such a subdivision.

30 See *SVF* III, 377, 378, 386, 389, 394.

31 See *SVF* III, 394; Cic., *Tusc.* IV, 13; Diog. Laert., VII, 112–13.

loss of self-control, the hesitation in fear relative to an act to complete. Shame, on the other hand, is the fear of infamy, just as anxiety is fear that derives from an unusual or unknown thing.

The wise man succeeds in controlling the four greatest types of passions, even if he is certainly not "apathetic" in the sense of complete insensitivity towards the events that happen to him or to others. On the other hand, he undoubtedly feels *eupatheiai*, forms of joy or emotions of reason (see *SVF* III, 431). He simply does not want to grant moral value to the disruptions of judgment and behaviours induced by the passions. At the same time, he rejects the academic and peripatetic theory of the separation of a rational part from an arational part of the soul[32] – that is, of a division between reason and passion (and this also to not offer excuses of powerlessness of reason in a struggle against an element that is foreign and, by definition, a reflection of his influence). Because of this, on one hand, he holds possible (even if it is a matter of privilege reserved to very few, whose figure represents a criterion of judgment) complete control of the passions on the part of reason. On the other, he is fully aware of the fact that this can happen at the price of a struggle much stronger than in Plato or in Aristotle, precisely because it is carried out in the arena of a unique soul, within which reason not only coexists with the passions, but possesses their same range.

Therefore, the passions are nothing but aberrations of reason – a reason that is deteriorated and diverted from its natural course (see *SVF*, I, 216; III, 459, 461). There are incandescent passions and dark and obscure passions, but all are rooted and lasting. However, they do not (yet) constitute an external enemy to fight or one with whom to come to terms. They are, so to speak, a *ratio lapsa*, a fallen and guilty reason that must be suspicious of itself and remain untiringly in operation in order to best address its plans (despite the fact that such efforts are generally destined to fail). This, however, poses the problem, confronted on another level by Augustine as well, of how it is possible that in a rationally ordered nature – supported by a universal *logos* or by a God-Providence – men are almost all depraved, a true mass of fools and of the damned. How can nature conflict with itself and err in such a massive way from excess of impulse?

32 See M. Frede, "The Stoic Doctrine of the Affection of the Soul," in *The Norms of Nature: Studies in Hellenistic Ethics*, ed. M. Schofield and G. Striker (Cambridge, 1986), 93–110.

In Chrysippus (author, in addition to *On the Soul*, of a treatise and a therapeutics on the passions), there is no paradigmatic duality between reason and passions.[33] It will be reintroduced among the Stoics, in a Platonic-Aristotelian way, by Posidonius and Panaetius, who recognize the double nature of the soul, which, in addition to the *logos*, possesses a part that is *alogon* – instinctive and saved from our power.[34] Over this bipartite soul, united with but no longer identical to the body, looms the shadow of death, since every being subject to the passions is mortal. This makes the interior struggle and the physical degradation inevitably more tragic and painful. The sculptural grouping of Laocoön and his sons, desperately engaged in fighting the suffocating grip of the snakes, if it truly derives from a group of artists from Rhodes who were inspired by Panaetius,[35] could be an allegory of his ideas.

Cicero will subsequently codify and study this separation in depth. His *coup de génie* consists of offering a dualistic reading of a monistic philosophy like that of the Stoics.[36] He does not, however, reject the Stoic ideal of full self-control of the individual over himself. In fact, he observes, regarding the *animi perturbatio*,[37] that all the passions are within our power: *omnes esse in nostra potestate, omnes iudicio suscepta, omnes voluntarias* (*Tusc.* IV, 31, 65).

---

33 On Chrysippus, see *SVF* III, 461. (Seneca follows him when he asserts, in *De ira*, I, 8, 3, that *non enim, ut dixi, separatas istas sedes suas diductasque habent, set affectus et ratio in melius peiusque mutatio animi est.*) See also E. Bréhier, *Chrysippe et l'ancien Stoïcisme* (Paris, 1951), 245 et seq.; A. Glibert-Thirry, "La théorie des passions chez Chrisippe et son évolution chez Posidonius," *Revue de Philosophie, Littérature et Histoire* 75 (1977), 393–435; A.M Ioppolo, "La dottrina della passione in Crisippo," *Rivista critica di storia della filosofia* 27 (1972), 251–68; and, more generally, J.B. Gould, *The Philosophy of Chrysippus* (Leiden, 1970).

34 On this, see I.G. Kidd, "Posidonius on Emotions," in *Problems in Stoicism*, ed. A.A. Long (London, 1971), 200–15.

35 See M. Pohlenz, *Die Stoa: Geschichte einer geistigen Bewegung* (Göttingen, 1959).

36 See J. Pigeaud, *La maladie de l'âme: Étude sur la relation de l'âme et du corps dans la tradition médico-philosophique antique* (Paris, 1981), 275 (245–371 on "Stoïcisme et maladies de l'âme"); R.J. Rabel, "Diseases of the Soul in Stoic Philosophy," *Greek, Roman, and Byzantine Studies* 22 (1981), 385–93; and J. Fillion-Lahille, *Le* De ira *de Sénèque et la philosophie stoïcienne des passions* (Paris, 1984), particularly 18 et seq. On the Ciceronian duality of soul and body, see *Tusc.* IV, 5 et seq. Pigeaud's book, sometimes disorganized and vague, nonetheless has the merit of highlighting Cicero's importance in the formulation of the theories of Pinel (see P. Pinel, *Traité médico-philosophique sur l'aliénation mentale* [Paris, 1800; rpt. Geneva, 1960], XII n).

37 This is how he translates the Greek *pathos*, which could not have been directly rendered in Latin with *passio*, which then indicated simply "pain."

Unlike Spinoza, for whom these are forces naturally endowed with their own logic (from which one can nevertheless partially emerge via internal lines, harnessing their energy), the passions are considered by the Stoics (and, to a lesser degree, by Cicero) to be completely useless. They appear to them as genuine voluntary illnesses of the soul.[38] One preventative therapy, made up of "spiritual exercises" – and in particular by the anticipatory consideration of death – thus joins a repressive intervention that has the goal of uprooting and not moderating them (see *SVF* III, 443–5).

Through long and varied vicissitudes, from this theoretical stock will be born a tradition that will lead from Chrysippus to Panaetius, Cicero, and Seneca and finally to Pinel and Esquirol, founders of modern psychiatry (on which it is worth lingering briefly).

The Philosopher in the Madhouse

Madness for Pinel, in fact, is intemperance and disorder of the passions, blocked and impeded in their release by the presence of obstacles. In it, there appear *les passions humaines devenues très véhémentes ou aigües par des contrarietés vives.*[39] Without giving any obviously decisive weight to the classical tradition and, in particular, without forgetting the long history of the explicit development of the subject, from Aristotle's *Rhetoric* to the *Idéologues* in the philosophical field, or from the *Corpus Hippocraticum* to the medieval School of Montpellier and beyond in the field of medicine, it is nonetheless interesting to observe how madness is treated by Pinel and his student Esquirol not only in the framework of a theory of the passions, but also in an intermediate – almost "Ciceronian" – position between the Platonic-Aristotelian line (of persuasion of the irrational soul through a *shock* and an authority, in this case purely moral and emotional, that imposes itself on the passions) and that of a very attenuated Stoicism (that does not consider them a negation of reason,

38 On the medical tradition that establishes a relationship between the passions and corporeality, but combats the Stoic monism of the soul and body and identification of reason and passion, reintroducing to the Platonic-Aristotelian way both the idea of an irrational part of the soul and a non-repressive model of conduct towards them, see P.W. Harkins and W. Riese, ed., *Galen on the Passions and Errors of the Soul* (Ohio, 1963); Galen, *Le passioni e gli errori dell'anima: Opere morali,* 131–55; and Spinoza, *Ep.* 17.

39 P. Pinel, preface to *Traité médico-philosophique sur l'aliénation mentale,* ii. On Pinel's view of the possibility of curing the mentally ill, see M. Gauchet and G. Swain, *La pratique de l'esprit humain* (Paris, 1980), 458 et seq.

but a perverted reason difficult to deter from being sidetracked through words). Madness can thus be cured through a proper dose of persuasion and constriction of the soul. If mental illnesses are the result of the passions, it is possible, in principle, to cure them. However, it is necessary to start from a "moral shaking" because, according to the Platonic-Aristotelian tradition, you cannot reason with some of them. They can only be confronted subordinately on another level, that of persuasion.

In this sense, the aspect of madness changes clinically or, better still, its care develops some classical insights: the exclusive use of force and the treatment of the sick as incomprehensible beings lacking reason are not only declared to lack effectiveness, but to damage patients and weaken the possibility of curing them, since "the mad, more or less all of them, reason." Thus, psychiatry is introduced, first in a very small way, to the *logos* and the *dialogos*, in the double meaning of a reasoning and of a discourse conducted by the doctor in an attempt to involve the patient (these are, however, auxiliary with respect to a treatment that appeals indirectly to the passions). But as Esquirol notes, the philosopher should strive to consider the passions as pathologically unregulated, as the other face of reason, identifying in them not only the most common cause of mental isolation, but the similarities between every passion in the sane individual and its result in the sick one:

> What reflections engage the mind of the philosopher, who, turning aside from the tumult of the world, makes the circuit of a house for the insane! He finds there the same ideas, the same errors, the same passions, the same misfortunes, that elsewhere prevail. It is the same world; but its distinctive characters are more marked, its colors more vivid, its effects more striking, because man there displays himself in all his nakedness; dissimulating not his thoughts, nor concealing his defects; lending not to his passions seductive charms, nor to his vices deceitful appearances.[40]

---

40 E.D. Esquirol, *Des maladies mentales: Considerées sous les rapports médical, hygiénique et médico-légal* (Brussels, 1838), vol. 1, 1; Engl. trans. *Mental Maladies: A Treatise on Insanity*, 19. In the nineteenth century, analysis of the passions will become a typical subject of psychiatry. See J. Starobinski, "Le passé des passions," *Nouvelle Revue de Psychanalyse* 21 (1980), 51–76. On Esquirol, see M. Galzigna, "Soggetto di passione, soggetto di follia," introduction to *Delle passioni considerate come cause, sintomi e mezzi curativi dell'alienazione mentale* (Venice, 1982), 7–51 (Ital. trans. of Esquirol, *Des passions considérés comme causes, symptômes et moyens curatifs de l'aliénation mental* [Paris, 1805]). (See also Esquirol's words, *Delle passioni* ..., 58: "It would be necessary to penetrate the recesses of the human body to analyze the passions that occupy such a large place in the study of alienation.")

It is necessary, however, to distinguish between primary needs tied to self-preservation and "fictitious" passions that depend on the development of social relationships and intellectual faculties. It is necessary to protect oneself from the latter, if one intends to preserve one's own happiness: "A thousand needs have caused new desires to be born, and the passions that these generate are the most fertile source of the physical and moral disorders that afflict man. Love, anger, terror, revenge cannot be confused with ambition, the thirst for wealth, pride, celebrity and so many other passions that are born of our social relationships."[41]

The "moral treatment" of illness consists at first of a sort of intensive care of the passions through an "aggressive therapy" aimed at producing a healthy shock in the patient, accompanied by an active effort of comprehension and an attitude of respect towards the sick person:

> If it is essential to provoke violent shocks, exciting this or that passion to subdue the alienated, to tame their pretentions, to conquer their raptures, it is no less important to be good, sensible, affable, and solicitous toward them. But it is always thanks to the moral shocks that their cure is achieved. If someone considered the moral attempt vain and illusory, it is because they did not at all understand it. It is not limited to consoling the alienated, making their courage stand out, repressing their rage, reasoning with them, or fighting the refuse of their imagination: we do not profess to cure them by talking with them. This claim would be belied by everyday experience – do the passions perhaps yield to reasoning? Treating them with dialectic formulas and syllogisms would mean disregarding the course of the passions in the clinical history of mental alienation. Without a doubt the admonishments, advice, reasoning, and consolations are means of healing – we have seen many examples of it. But one can be healed only by causing a moral shock, placing the alienated patient in a state opposite and contrary to that in which he was before resorting to this means. Do not crises, perhaps, in acute illnesses, act this way – strongly shaking the organism?[42]

41 Esquirol, *Des passions considerées comme causes*; Ital. trans., 65.

42 Ibid., 145–6. On these subjects, see M. Galzigna, *La malattia morale: Alle origini della psichiatria moderna* (Venice, 1988).

4. Fear and Delusion

Like Flowers in the Field

Contrary to the *inhumana duritia* and *superba sapientia* of the ancient Stoics,[1] Seneca prefers to subject the passions to the control of reason and will – whose role is accentuated – through a softer approach. That is, he intends to domesticate them and calm them to the point of succeeding in coexisting with them, accepting the latent threat in their induced docility:

> Animal-tamers are unerring; they take the most savage animals, which may well terrify those who encounter them, and subdue them to the will of man; not content with having driven out their ferocity, they even tame them so that they dwell in the same abode. The trainer puts his hand into the lion's mouth; the tiger is kissed by his keeper. The tiny Ethiopian orders the elephant to sink down on its knees, or to walk the rope. Similarly, the wise man is a skilled hand at taming evils. Pain, want, disgrace, imprisonment, exile – these are universally to be feared; but when they encounter the wise man, they are tamed. (*Ep.* 85.41)

Seneca asks repeatedly: *Quid praecipuum in rebus humanis est?* ("What is truly important in the life of man?"). Controlling oneself instead of being a slave to one's passions, to the fears and flatteries of fortune, is the constant response. This means acquiring a *bona mens*, a virtuous disposition of the heart that aims for tranquility, consistency, and mastery of

1 See *Ad Helv. matr.* 16.1; *Ad Pol.* 18.5.

oneself, factors that become more important as external conflicts tend more to internalize themselves and implode.[2]

To this end, the *sapiens* uses different strategies – all, however, based on reason[3] – to moderate and conquer fear, hope, and the other passions that disturb the heart.[4] It prevents *metus* and *terror* from acquiring strength in the heart, tying their everyday defeat to the ideal of perfect liberty and unbending self-presence (see *Ep.* 85.12, 75.18). It will not seek sufferings, but will confront them with a virile heart when the moment comes: "I should prefer to be free from torture; but if the time comes when it must be endured, I shall desire that I may conduct myself therein with bravery, honor, and courage" (*Ep.* 47.4). In this way one could say, along with Virgil, that the heart remains indestructible, the tears flow in vain: *Mens immota manet, lachrimae volventur inanes* (*Aen.* IV, 449).

Knowledge has the function of eradicating from the heart the fear of death and the superstitions tied to it. All eight books of the *Naturales Quaestiones* – which would exert such a diverse influence on medieval science and the morality of the freethinkers – are tied by the common thread of this idea: that in the face of phenomena of the admirable structure of the cosmos (even the most terrible among them), wise is he who strengthens his resoluteness through the search for causes, for the order that cannot be lacking even in events that seem entrusted to chance. Many men wait, however, to be liberated from fear without passing over the arduous road of knowledge. And they say, for example, "I want to have my fear of [lightning bolts] dispelled, not their nature explained," without realizing that science must serve "not so that we may escape the blows of circumstance (for weapons are being thrown at us from all directions), but so that we may endure them bravely and resolutely. We

2 Sen., *Nat. quaest.* 3, pref. 8–16, and see *Ep.* 10.4; 66.6; *De vit. beat.* 9.3.

3 See, for example, *De vit. beat.* 8; *De ben.* 1.5–6; 2.35; 5.3; and *Ep.* 16.1.

4 This happens especially in eras of political terror. Seneca notoriously knew up close, under Nero, the methods and the instruments of violence and fear. In fact, he often supported them, finding late – tired from wandering so long – that proper path that he now shows to others: *Rectum iter, quod sero cognovi et lassus errando, aliis monstro* (*Ep.* 8.3). Since *spem metus sequitur*, it is necessary to eliminate both fear and hope: "Each alike belongs to a mind that is in suspense, a mind that is fretted by looking forward to the future. But the chief cause of both these ills is that we do not adapt ourselves to the present, but send our thoughts a long way ahead. And so foresight, the noblest blessing of the human race, becomes perverted" (Sen., *Ep.* 5.8 and see 13.10). It was wisely observed how Seneca's own brother, Gallio, had in Greece judged Paul, he who announced to Christians and to the world that "in hope we were saved" (Rom. 8:24). See A. Traina, introduction to Seneca, *Letture critiche* (Milan, 1976), 15.

can be undefeated, but we cannot be unshaken, though sometimes the hope that we can also be unshaken sneaks up on us. 'How do I achieve this?' you ask. Treat death with contempt, and then you have treated all the causes of death with contempt, whether wars or shipwrecks, or the attacks of wild animals, or the weight of debris from a building that suddenly collapses."[5] In fact, fear of death prevents men from living: "He who fears death will never do anything worthy of a man who is alive" (*De tranq. an.* 11.6). But how could he not fear it, if dangers loom from every side? And yet, precisely in the observation that nothing is stable, the wise man finds serenity: "Fear without remedy is what foolish men have. Reason frees wise men from terror, and for the uneducated great confidence comes from despair … If you wish to fear nothing, consider that everything is to be feared" (*Nat. quaest.* 6.2–3).

The wise man is steady in his own determinations, because he asserts, for himself and for those disposed to follow his advice, the precept of always *idem velle atque idem nolle,* of always wanting and not wanting the same things, always remaining the same to oneself.[6] This also defeats the further dissipation caused by the new metropolitan dimension that involves haste, bustle, noise, the press of the crowd and the prevalence of the *negotia* – those occupations and preoccupations that erode the time devoted by the wise man to *cura sui* (particularly for those, like Seneca – or later Marcus Aurelius – who hold public office and want to concentrate on themselves).[7] Thus, for him it manages to be easier to control the passions and achieve a lasting happiness, not one based on the pleasure of a single moment. This happiness derives from being free from fears and hopes, from having found a solution to the two contrasting tendencies that coexist in the hearts of all men: "You have all the fears of mortals and all the desires of immortals" (*De brev. vit.* 3.4). Rejecting fear and delimiting desire, the wise man recognizes both his own dignity and his own path towards something better, his nature of being bounded by mortality (which does not frighten him) and the immortality of desire (which does not succeed in seducing him). He

5 *Nat. quaest.* II, 59.1–3; Engl. trans., 213–15.

6 *Ep.* 109.16. See also *Ep.* 120.22 (*magnam rem puta, unum hominem agere*), 71.36, 114.26, and more generally, *De const. sap.* Following the precept of constancy of will represents the best aid to total consistency with oneself – see *Ep.* 31.8: *Aequalitas ac tenor vitae per omnia consonans sibi* (There should be an even temperament and a scheme of life that is consistent with itself throughout).

7 On the dissipation of the mind in the *negotia,* see Sen., *Ep.* 1, 7.1, 10.1, 25.7, *De brev. vit.* 2.4–5; *De vit. beat.* 1.4; *De tranq. an.* 17.3.

will confront dangers by not limiting himself to survival, floating in the *mare mortuum* of an existence not exposed to the attacks of fortune (see *Ep.* LXVII, 14), and at the same time he will avoid falling into illusions and mirages of an infinite and unsatisfiable desire, conscious of the fact that happiness consists in not being frustrated in one's own desires. Far from fear and hope, he will recognize the name that we give to unknown causes: fortune (*SVF* II, 967). Without being surprised by it, "struck, as it were, off our guard" (*Ad Marc.* 9.3), he will act with the same steadiness of heart in the face of all the other side setbacks of fate, resigning himself to them and considering them imaginary evils compared to the only thing that counts, liberty.[8]

For someone who has conquered fear, joy and pleasure are not at all excluded – though they are not intentionally sought out, because telling oneself "I want joy or happiness" constitutes an impracticable and self-contradictory command. Instead, they arrive spontaneously, like certain flowers that emerge unintentionally from the ground cultivated by virtue: "As in a ploughed field, which has been broken up for corn, some flowers will spring up here and there, yet it was not for these poor little plants, although they may please the eye, that so much toil was expended – the sower had a different purpose, these were superadded – just so, pleasure is neither the cause nor the reward of virtue, but its by-product, and we do not accept virtue because she delights us, but if we accept her, she also delights us" (*De vit. beat.* 9.2, and see *Ep.* 23.3).

This is how the wise Stoic makes himself invulnerable not only to the flatteries of pleasure but to the attacks of fate, impermeable to fear and hope, to aversion and desire, to all that is negative in existence (death, pain, humiliation). He reacts to the instinct to flee; bravely, he awaits the

8 Seneca, *Ep.* 85.26–8: "'What then? Is he not to fear death, imprisonment, burning, and all the other missiles of Fortune?' Not at all; for he knows that they are not evils, but only seem to be. He reckons all these things as the bugbears of man's existence. Paint him a picture of slavery, lashes, chains, want, mutilation by disease or by torture, or anything else you may care to mention; he will count all such things as terrors caused by the derangement of the mind. These things are only to be feared by those who are fearful … Liberty is lost unless we despise those things which put the yoke upon our necks." He will confront death with the same peaceful joy of Leonidas prior to the battle of Thermopylae: "But take Leonidas: how bravely did he address his men! He said: 'Fellow-soldiers, let us to our breakfast, knowing that we shall sup in Hades!' The food of these men did not grow lumpy in their mouths, or stick in their throats, or slip from their fingers; eagerly did they accept the invitation to breakfast, and to supper also!" (ibid., 82.21).

danger. Seneca himself gave the example when, *interritus*, he waited to be put to death.[9]

What Makes Us Poor

In Seneca – to whom, according to Tacitus, it was a true *assidua praemeditatio futurorum malorum* (*Ann.* xv, 62) – the meditation on death assumes the character of a "technique for not suffering."[10] It becomes an *ars moriendi* for finding peace "in the face of the unavoidable"[11] and for abandoning the world with dignity: *egregia res est mortem condiscere* (*Ep.* 26.8, and see *Nat. quaest.* 6.32.12): "Meditate upon this one thing: so that you may not fear the name of death. By long reflection make death familiar to you so that, if necessity arises, you can also go out and meet it," because it opens an easy path to freedom. It becomes the most eloquent way of demonstrating that we are not inclined to servitude: "'Think on death.' In saying this, he bids us think on freedom. He who has learned to die has unlearned slavery; he is above any external power, or, at any rate, he is beyond it. What terrors have prisons and bonds and bars for him? His way out is clear. There is only one chain which binds us to life, and that is love of life" (*Ep.* 26.10). From this also comes the acceptance of suicide in the case of necessity, since *in necessitate vivere necessitas nulla est* ("no man is constrained to live under constraint"; *Ep.* 12.10) – every vein of our body can be the path that leads to freedom.[12] The *meditatio mortis* pays off the fear of death – so to speak – early and in instalments. It dilutes that fear across the arc of a life. However, through the double strategy of continuous enhancement of the present and familiarization with death, a contradictory effect is achieved. On one hand, fear decreases and joy of living increases. On the other, fear of death risks transforming into a fear of life, into an endless elaboration and internalization of

9 This Stoic conception of the relationship between reason and passions, which aims at preserving dignity and consistency in periods of danger and political absolutism, will return with analogous functions to European culture between the end of the sixteenth century and the first half of the seventeenth.

10 See P. Rabbow, *Seelenführung: Methodik per Exerzitien in der Antike*, 160; A. Traina, *Lo stile "drammatico" del filosofo Seneca* (Bologna, 1974), 80 et seq.

11 Sen., *Ep.* 49.10.

12 Sen., *De ira* III, 15. In the *Pharsalia* (IV, 646), Lucan specifies that "the sword was given for this, that none need live a slave" (*ne quisquam serviat, enses*) – that is, even to be able to kill oneself when it is necessary. This verse was engraved, during the French Revolution, on the swords of the National Guard.

grief. And however high the peak of wisdom might be, the shadow of death continues to accompany it. Modifying the biblical saying, one could assert: *Timor mortis, dominus sapientiae.* In this sense, Spinoza's position is diametrically opposed – at least in its intentions – as it generally aims at the promotion of life, the separation of philosophy and death and, particularly, the rejection of suicide, considered for the most part as a manifestation of powerlessness and weakness of heart (see *E* 4.18 schol.).[13]

And yet in Seneca, the *meditatio mortis* and suicide are the only weapons in the hand of the free man in times of political servitude or in conditions of intolerability of existence. The Stoic principle of self-preservation is not at all negated nor even replaced by an attraction to death or the desire to give in to its destructive fascination, both of which are condemned by Seneca.[14]

---

13 On the evaluation of suicide in Stoic ethics (or, in Plutarchan terms, on "swim[ming] away from his body, as from a leaking boat": *De tranq.* 476 A; Engl. trans., 231), see J.M. Rist, *Stoic Philosophy* (Cambridge, 1969), ch. 12.

14 *Ep.* 24.25: "The brave and wise man should not beat a hasty retreat from life; he should make a becoming exit. And above all, he should avoid the weakness which has taken possession of so many – the lust for death (*libido moriendi*). For just as there is an unreflecting tendency of the mind toward other things, so, my dear Lucilius, there is an unreflecting tendency towards death; this often seizes upon the noblest and most spirited men, as well as upon the craven and the abject. The former despise life; the latter find it irksome."

The liberation given by death is real, if one looks at the sad situation of men: "Death frees the slave though his master is unwilling; it lightens the captive's chains; from the dungeon it leads forth those whom unbridled power had forbidden to leave it; to exiles, whose eyes and minds are ever turning to their native land, death shows that it makes no difference beneath whose soil a man may lie. If Fortune has apportioned unjustly the common goods, and has given over one man to another though they were born with equal rights, death levels all things" (*Ad Marc.* 20.2). And the dangers and torments to which Seneca alludes are not, in his time, the fruit of rhetorical imagination. With Caligula and Nero, he knew, up close, the fate of men struck by a terror lacking reason, by a power founded on will and, at the same time, death, the torture of the body, the confiscation of goods, and corruption: "I see instruments of torture [*cruces*], not indeed of a single kind, but differently contrived by different peoples; some hang their victims with head towards the ground, some impale their private parts, other stretch out their arms on a fork-shaped gibbet; I see cords, I see scourges, and for each separate limb and each joint there is a separate engine of torture! But I see also Death. There, too, are bloodthirsty enemies and proud fellow-countrymen; but yonder, too, I see Death. Slavery is no hardship when, if a man wearies of the yoke, by a single step he may pass to freedom. O Life, by the favour of Death I hold thee dear" (*Ad Marc.* 20.3).

In the end, a verse by Virgil applies to Seneca: "One chance the conquered have – to hope for none" – that is, to restrain oneself from hoping.[15] In a natural and political world characterized by the instability and destruction that runs through everything, the contempt for death becomes the greatest of virtues: "So we must challenge death with great courage, whether it attacks us with a cruel, large-scale assault, or with an ordinary, everyday exit ... What is it to me how great are the causes of my death? Death itself is not a great thing. So if we wish to be happy, not to be racked by fear of humans, or gods, or circumstances; to despise fortune, whose promises are unnecessary and whose threats are insubstantial; if we wish to have a tranquil existence and to compete with the gods themselves in happiness, then we must keep our soul ready."[16]

The fear of death is the only thing that takes man's dignity from him and impedes his leaning on reason, on challenging fortune and pain, on conquering its *gravitas* and its heroic, tragic "verticality": "So, Lucilius, as far as you are able, exhort yourself against the fear of death. This fear is what demeans us; this is what disturbs and ruins the very life it spares."[17]

The Days of Life

Along the whole course of existence, there is only one ability that merits being acquired: to learn how to live, which also (and particularly) means, "to learn how to die."[18] In truth, it is "a noble thing ... to round

15 See Virg., *Aen.* II, 354: *Una salus victis, nullam sperare salute,* and Sen., *Nat. quaest.* 6.2, 3.

16 *Nat. quaest.* VI, 32.3–5; Engl. trans., 134–6.

17 *Nat. quaest.* VI, 32.8; Engl. trans., 138. Only reason offers a firm point of reference to arrive at control of oneself and of others (see *Ep.* 37.4: "If you would have all things under your control, put yourself under the control of reason; if reason becomes your ruler, you will become ruler over many" (*multo reges, si ratio te rexerit*). With respect to the Platonic conception of philosophy, innervated by the upward force of *Eros,* in addition to that of the gravity of *Thanatos,* we can say that in Seneca the latter has obtained a decisive victory. The legend of the epistolary exchange between Seneca and Saint Paul – a falsehood constructed in the fourth century – responds, in addition to the need for a stylistic-rhetorical education of the Christians (see A. Momigliano, "Note sulla leggenda del cristianesimo di Seneca" [1950], in *Contributo alla Storia degli studi classici* [Rome, 1955], 13–32), to the need to ground wisdom and Stoic-pagan culture on the new models of sanctity based no longer on martyrdom but on ascesis and on a *cura sui* parallel to "*cura Dei.*"

18 *De brev. vit.* 7.3. The perspective chosen by Epictetus is different, but the inspiration is common: not only death and suffering as such must be feared, but fear of death and suffering in itself: "Rather than death or exile, if we feared fear itself, we would practice avoiding the things we believe to be bad" (*D* 2.16.19).

out your life before death comes, and then await in peace the remaining portion of your time, claiming nothing for yourself, since you are in possession of the happy life; for such a life is not made happier for being longer."[19] According to Marcus Aurelius, it is nice to die falling like an olive that is "fully ripe," grateful to the "tree that gave it growth."[20] It is nice, finally, to be master of one's own time, in all its dimensions. He who has responsibility and mastery of himself, *qui totus suus est*, has a lasting and inalienable control of the past: *perpetua eius et intrepida possessio est* (*De brev. vit.* 10.4), but he who is "busy" is incapable of assembling the days passed and going over all the parts of his own life (*in omnes vitae suae partes discurrere*) along the unitary axis of the present, to picture for himself the chain of actions, omissions, and events that have constituted it starting with the *eimarmene*, from the *fatum*, from the conditions found in being born and inherent in relationships between things and men that are independent of ourselves. The past seems easier to control, because it is the period "over which Fortune has lost control, [it] is the one which cannot be brought back under any man's power" (*De brev. vit.* 10.2). It is that period in which we have already seen a section of the "wheel" of time move or part of the "tow-rope" that symbolizes it unwind (see *SVF* II, 944). In comparison, the future seems uncertain, while the present is short. And yet it is faith in one's own past that continues to make up the nucleus of the steadiness of the wise man, the basis for all of his actions.

In this context we reach (Aristotle-like) the *eudaimonia* and (Stoically) the *euthymia* (which, from Panaetius forward, denotes the inner joy that Seneca renders as *tranquillitas animi*). In being able, on the part of the wise man, to calmly go over one's own life *in omnes … suae partes* – that which consists of consistency with oneself and the absence of conflict[21] and, at least to some degree, the sense of personal identity and happiness as "good flow of life" (*SVF* I, 184.554) – we reach the maximum contentment of virtuous men.

19 *Ep.* 32.3. This is a solution previously offered by Aristotle. In the moment (being limit and totality at once – see. *Phys.* IV, 11, 220 et seq.; VIII, 251b; and *Eth. Nic.* X, 3, 1174b) of the act, time stops and becomes a *tout télescopé* that has within it, simultaneously, the beginning and end: the beginning of time to come, the end of what was. On this aspect, see H.H. Joachim, *Aristotle: The Nicomachean Ethics* (Oxford, 1951), 258.

20 Marc. Aur., *Meditations* IV, 48.

21 For the value attributed by the Stoics to this virtue, see *SVF* I, 179: "Because the greatest good is placed in what the Stoics call *omologia* and that we translate as consistency [*convenientia*]." Democritus was the first to introduce the term into philosophical language, writing *Peri euthymies*, of which only fragments remain.

Rejecting (like Panaetius and later Plutarch) Aristippus's theory on the sudden nature of pleasure, the *monochronos edone* – and overcoming some contradictions of the older Stoics like Chrysippus[22] – Seneca brings the tranquility of the soul to the present as fluid, as a minute-by-minute construction of oneself, the core of identity, the junction point between past and future. This does not at all conflict with his repeated affirmations that "whatever years lie behind us are in death's hands" (*Ep.* I, 1) or to other of his theses on the basis of which the wise man must not worry about the future (ibid., XIII). The wise man's present is not, in fact, robbery of the moment, but continuous presence to himself in the passage of time. This permits him to look at the past without remorse and at the future without worries, equally free of fears and hopes. In this way, he constructs about himself a firm system of defence, "lofty, impregnable, godlike" walls (*De const. sap.* 6.8).

According to Seneca, death, after all, is nothing new to us. On the one hand, we have known it even before birth and, on the other, we die every moment along with the past that belongs to us. "We go astray in thinking that death only follows, when in reality it has both preceded us and will in turn follow us. Whatever condition existed before our birth, is death ... Praise and imitate the man whom it does not irk to die, though he takes pleasure in living."[23]

The death that waits for us in the future is also nothing new, because men have perhaps experienced it countless times, just as there have been countless rebirths of the world in its cycles: "As the mother's womb holds us for ten months, making us ready, not for the womb itself, but for the existence into which we seem to be sent forth when at last we are fitted to draw breath and live in the open; just so, throughout the years extending between infancy and old age, we are making ourselves ready for another birth. A different beginning, a different condition, await us."[24]

---

22 See Sen., *De const. sap.* and *De tranq. an.* Also, according to the final lines of Plutarch's *De tranquillitate animi*, virtuous men gladly accept the precept of acquiescing "in the present without fault-finding, remember[ing] the past with thankfulness, and meet[ing] the future without fear or suspicion, with their hopes cheerful and bright" (477 F; Engl. trans., 241).

23 *Ep.* 54.5, 7. In a drama attributed to him, Seneca says that "ne'er is he wretched for whom to die is easy" [*numquam est ille miser cui facile est mori*] (*Herc. Oet.* 111). In *De consolatione ad Marciam*, he asserts that "death is a release from all suffering, a boundary beyond which our ills cannot pass – it restores us to that peaceful state in which we lay before we were born" (*Ad Marc.* 19.5).

24 *Ep.* 102.23. However complex the attitude of Seneca and the Stoics is towards future life, the emphasis still falls on this life, and spiritual exercises aim precisely at it and at its good conclusion in a death that is dignified and without fear.

From death springs the ultimate consolation: being involved in the eternal transformation. Death is a return to the entire universe, to universal reason. Thus, it is a great comfort to be overcome, carried away with the events of the universe: *Magnum solacium est cum universo rapi* (*De prov.* 5.8) or – again with Marcus Aurelius – to follow "the way of nature," the turning of the heart to the linking of all things, the "common source" from which every being and event springs in its necessity, learning to "love whole-heartedly that which befalls thee."[25] This attitude is much more advisable, even according to Seneca, since life is given in usufruct by nature. In dying, we settle a debt (Sen., *Ad Marc.* 10.2).

In the Operating Room

Learning to live and to die constitutes the nucleus of the "spiritual exercises" developed by the Stoics (and by Seneca in particular). Their purpose is to guide towards a control over the feelings, however incomplete. This allows the wise man to free himself from the limitations of his own individuality and reach – in a state of clear awareness – knowledge of himself and the world disturbed as little as possible by the passions. Through such therapy – which transforms the school of the philosopher into "a hospital"[26] – the wise man, starting to practise with the simplest things, becomes master of himself, complying with universal reason and thus inserting himself into the structure of the cosmos, cutting a little space in it for himself where he can effectively be present, renouncing everything else, over which he knows he is completely powerless.[27]

Having reached independence through conditioning, the wise man will thus be blissful in any situation – in chains, like the slave Epictetus, or on the throne, like the emperor Marcus Aurelius, or even, like Seneca, in exile, or on a desert island. Of course, he can transform himself – through *cura sui* or *epimeleia eautou*[28] – into a work of art, moulding himself to the

25 See Marc. Aur., v, 4; vi, 36–9; vii, 57.

26 See Epict., *D* 3.23.30.

27 On the spiritual exercises of the ancients, and in particular of the Stoics, see P. Rabbow, *Seelenführung: Methodik der Exerzitien der Antike*; P. Hadot, *Exercises spirituels et philosophie antique.*

28 On this attitude of Stoicism, in particular in Seneca and in Gaius Musonius Rufus, see M. Foucault, *Le souci de soi* (Paris, 1984), and R. Bodei, "Foucault: Pouvoir, politique et maîtrise de soi," *Critique* 471–2 (Aug.–Sept. 1986), 914 et seq. The proposal to go beyond pure self-preservation, which mortifies life, through a continuous shaping of oneself can also be found in the later Foucault. See J. Bernauer, "Michel Foucault's Ecstatic Thinking," in *The Final Foucault*, ed. J. Bernauer and D. Rassmussen (Cambridge, MA, 1988), 45–82.

point of reaching a contemptuous or indifferent detachment towards external circumstances. But this activity directed towards oneself is also *cura rationis*, so to speak – because it concerns itself, at the same time, with adhering to the order of the world and with not recognizing any other master beyond the universal law that governs the entire cosmos.

The price paid is often that of painful renunciations and the atrophying of entire parts of life. The same insistence on the necessity of defeating fear of death, and on the looming of a multitude of expected or unexpected evils, indicates indirectly how positive happiness (capable of abandoning every defence, "lowering the guard," expanding and violating the barrier of tranquility as an absence of storms and laborious, exhausting balancing of the heart) might be considered unreachable. The wise Stoics certainly succeed in this way in modelling themselves statuesquely, establishing sensible rules of life within a society no longer capable of issuing or approving inwardly acceptable laws. They thus test themselves in a spasmodic struggle that lowers the threshold of the power of existing, because of the practice of anticipating pain and death in order to face it with courage. The Stoics oppose, to passions and opinions, rational principles, common notions (*officia* or *dogmata rationis*), and "cold" duties. But they do not succeed in ensuring that individuals feel emotionally involved, as they do not strive to comprehend the reasons for the pleasures that pure reason does not know. Every law seeks only to subsume or subjugate the particular, to obey an order without understanding it fully except in passive reference to a universal precept. The attempt to modify oneself through pure force of will, however, leads the individual to Sisyphean effort, precisely because the control that he achieves over himself is precarious in addition to painful.[29] Changing without knowing oneself in one's own specificity means falling back endlessly in an exhausting struggle with that part of oneself that does not let itself "homogenize" with the universal *logos*. Instead of becoming stronger, the individual divides, placing one part of himself against another.

29 Not all the Stoics believe in the omnipotence of will. See, for example, Epict., *D* 2.49, and G. Rodier, "Le stoïciens," in *Études de philosophie grecque* (Paris, 1926), 287 et seq. Perfection must be tirelessly sought through daily exercises, but precisely because of this, it is never reached. The wise man can force himself to follow a suitable lifestyle, constancy, and peace of mind, but that does not at all exclude that as a man – and therefore as subject also to what is not in his power – he may be dragged by the passions. Spiritual exercises aim precisely at familiarizing the individual with not giving consent to the forces that sometimes dominate even him.

Reason in Delusion

In the face of great storms, reason becomes shipwrecked: "Light is the grief which can take counsel and hide itself; great ills lie not in hiding,"[30] says Medea. Reason has a breaking point and an inversion of inclination; it is capable of controlling only small sufferings and withstanding evil as long as it does not go beyond a particular threshold. After that, it turns into passion, *furor*, or lucid delusion, which causes it to vacillate between desire and the fear of knowing causes and solutions to its own conflicts.[31] *Furor* – the voice of perverted reason that imposes itself in the end on *bona mens* – can be the result of negative spiritual exercises, sought-after and deliberate failure of self-control, a way of turning out for the worst. The struggle between *furor* and *bona mens* is the tragedy represented not only in the scenes between exceptional characters, but in the great "theater of the world," where everyone carries out his own role within the horizon of his times and his environment.[32] In a dramaturgy of reason that

30 Sen., *Med.* 155–6: *Levis est dolor qui capere consilium potest/et clepere sese: magna non latitant mala* (Light is the grief which can take counsel and hide itself; great ills lie not in hiding). For a framing of this subject, see O. Regenbogen, *Schmerz und Tod in den Tragödien Senecas* (Darmstadt, 1963). On Seneca's tragedies, see also the edition edited by O. Zwierlein (Oxford, 1986). As something common to all sentient beings, suffering has nothing noble for the Stoics. Unlike Christianity, it does not encourage any redemption. Suffering is not noble, but resistance to it is – the wise man's firm determination to deny it his consent.

31 See Sen., *Oed.* 206 et seq. Conversely, tragic consciousness arises reactively from the sight of these perversions of reason. On the internal conflicts of Seneca's characters, see C. Segal, "Boundary Violations and Landscape of Self in Senecan Tragedy," *Antike und Abendland* 29 (1983), 172–87. On the opposition between *furor* and *bona mens* see, for example, *De vit. beat.* 23.4 and *Thyest.* 380. Earlier in *Phaedra* by Euripides, the symptoms of passion are assimilated by illness (*nosos*) and described with images associated with it. See B.H. Fowler, "Lyric Structure in Three Euripidean Plays," *Dioniso* 12 (1978), 16–24. For a deep reading of this text from another point of view, see N. Fusini, *La luminosa: Genealogia di Fedra* (Milan, 1990). However, the fact remains that in the case of Medea, her atrocious act of revenge is also explained in rational terms, since – as a barbarous wife, abandoned at Corinth by a husband who can marry a younger woman whose sons will be legitimate heirs to the throne – she does not have any access to the law to redress the wrong she suffered; see S. Jacoby, *Wild Justice: The Evolution of Revenge* (New York, 1983), 24–5, and, more generally, H.J. Treston, *Poine: A Study in Greek Blood Revenge* (London, 1923).

32 On the frequent Stoic use of this metaphor, see *Ep.* LXXVI, 31; LXXX, 6–8; *De prov.* II, 9; Epict., *Ench.* 7; D 15.11–20; Marc. Aur., III, 8; XI, 6; and L.G. Christian, Theatrum mundi*: The History of an Idea* (Newport, 1987), 11–23. It is interesting to note that Cicero translates the Greek *melancholia* as *furor* and *mentis ad omnia caecitas* (see *Tusc.* III, 5).

tears itself apart, there occurs the struggle between contrary tensions that, before becoming *furor*, get stuck initially in a momentary inhibition of will, as when Medea wavers between the function of wife and that of mother. She is induced, on one hand, to revenge herself atrociously for her unfaithful husband by striking what he holds most dear, his children. "Here where thou dost forbid it, where it will grieve thee, will I plunge the sword" (*Med.* 1006).[33] As Epictetus observed, the will to destruction is born in Medea from seeing her own desires frustrated, by the belief in a "soul which possesses great energy" that does not succeed in tolerating this state of things. She says, faced with the revenge that her act causes to fall on her: "And what do I care?" (*D* II, 17, 18–21).

The drama of reason is reflected in the split between the roles of wife and mother, of a connection to the other emotionally absorbed within itself, in love and boundless hate,[34] and in relation to one part of itself (fruit of the relationship with the other) that was rendered autonomous and enjoys a separate existence. This reason promotes life and weaves links with others and with the world. The split also reflects the destructive passion that emerges from the same stock and that does not want what it wants. Medea – who already "armed herself with rage" and

33 After all, remembering his previous crimes, she calls on all her destructive energy: "Bend to thine anger, rouse up thy halting purpose, and with all thy strength drain from thy heart's very depths its old-time violence. Let all that has yet been done be called but piety. To the task; let them know how petty, of what common stamp, were the crimes I wrought to serve him. In them my grief was but practicing; what great deed had prentice hands the power to do? What, a girl's rage? Now I am Medea; my wit has grown through suffering" (Sen., *Med.* 902–10). As a mother she is led, on the other hand, to save her own creatures: "Can I shed my children's, my own offspring's blood? Ah, mad rage, say not so! Far, even from me, be that unheard-of deed, that accursed guilt! What sin will the poor boys atone? Their sin is that Jason is their father, and, greater sin, that Medea is their mother. Let them die, they are none of mine; let them be lost – they are my own. They are without crime and guilt, yea, they are innocent – I acknowledge it; so, too, was my brother. Why, soul, dost hesitate? Why are my cheeks wet with tears? Why do anger and love now hither, now thither draw my changeful heart? A double tide tosses me, uncertain of my course; as when rushing winds wage mad warfare, and from both sides conflicting floods lash the seas and the fluctuating waters boil, even so is my heart tossed. Anger puts love to flight, and love, anger. O wrath, yield thee to love" (*Med.* 929–44).

34 Love and hate convert into one another preserving invariant the character of insatiability and boundlessness. "If thou seekest," says Medea, turning to the wet nurse, "what limit thou shouldst set to hate, copy thy love" (*Med.* 397–8).

prepares herself for the slaughter with all her fury – finally loosens the knots of her heart, letting hate prevail over *pietas.*

Similar is the attitude of Phaedra, whose unsatisfied incestuous love is transformed into mortal slander towards her son, Hippolytus, and finally into suicide. The passion burns continuously and is fed by every excuse, refracted by the suggestions of prudence that remind how guilt – even if it remains unknown to others – has its punishment on conscience[35] and how love (of whose tyrannical domination Phaedra declares herself subject) is not an irresistible divinity that those who do not accept their own human responsibility want to believe in, but rather a passion that received the specious name of god. When the fragile, innocent beauty of Hippolytus lies disfigured and dismembered in the fields, after his body is dragged and tortured by horses terrorized by a divine prodigy, Phaedra, who witnessed the impossibility of uniting her own heart to his, at least manages to conjoin their deaths. The unspeakable incestuous desire confessed thusly – a crime that even wild beasts avoid through an unconscious modesty – she kills herself.

In Medea and Phaedra we see a suicide of reason that wants to succumb to loss and a turning of life against itself, collapsing into the abyss of its own conflicts. This attitude is different from that of the wise Stoic who kills himself to maintain intact the *logos* confronted with external threats to his own independence. Seneca thus confuses again (and intentionally) that dividing line between philosophy and tragedy that Plato had drawn in an attempt to render rationally decidable those conflicts that, in drama, must remain substantially unresolved. In Plato, the hierarchy of the soul and of the city breaks up the tragic conflict, as reason raises an insurmountable wall that separates it from the irrepressible impulse of the *epithymetikon* (more than from the *thymoeides,* by nature teachable and generous, which in any event disappears in the *Laws*). Once the "black horse" is neutralized, the *logos* – as a charioteer – succeeds in guiding the soul towards the better and towards loosening the knots of the conflict, because in an ethics where evil is carried out only through ignorance, the awareness of good strengthens the ability to orient oneself towards it and, in parallel, weakens *akrasia,* intemperance with respect to

35 See *Phaedra,* 159–64: "But grant that heaven's kindly grace conceals this impious intercourse; grant that to incest be shown the loyalty which great crimes never find; what of the ever-present penalty, the soul's conscious dread, and the heart filled with crime and fearful of itself?" (*quid poena praesens, conscious mentis pavor/animusque culpa plenus et semet timens?*).

desires. On the other hand, tragedy makes the *logos* powerless, since it does not contemplate any rational way out of the struggle between conflicting rights and impulses. Perhaps directly in opposition to the ethical intellectualism of Socrates, Euripides has Medea say: "I understand what evil I am about to do, but my wrath is stronger."[36] Tragic knowledge is the revelation of unknown facts (of the error of not-knowing, of *amartia*). Conversely, philosophy proceeds platonically – by means of *anamnesis* – towards the logical identification of the reasons against which it seeks a solution. It does so to prevent the impulse considered absolutely irrepressible from producing a tragic paralysis, generating an equilibrium of equivalent reasons that is released only in an irrational way. Philosophy does not, with an act of domination, cut the Gordian knot of tragedy; it tries to loosen it through an endless labour of thought.

In Seneca, the falling of the separation between the rational and irrational parts of the soul makes the dyke collapse that had held *bona mens* rigidly divided from *furor.* Consistency does not belong only to the first, but also to the second. However, he admits not only the chance possibility, but the regular reality, of a frequent defeat of reason in its attempt to control the passions.[37] *Furor* becomes reasonable madness, conscious tension towards a target that one knows to be socially prohibited and self-destructive. The madman is no longer an irrational individual, but a detour on the road of reason, whose mental journeys – at least at the dramatic level – can be analysed based on a pathology of the mind, which appears endowed with a plausibility analogous to what governs the rational study of illnesses of the body. For the Stoics, then, it follows, on one hand, that constancy and consistency are values ever more necessary, the more that reason must defend itself from itself and, on the other hand, that to *furor* is attributed a logic and a particular consistency in turning towards evil and crime.

36 Euripides, *Medea,* 1078–9.

37 See *De ira* II, 4.2: *motus … rationem evicit.*

5. Constancy: Neostoicism and Justus Lipsius

Discipline of the Passions, Order of the State

Modern Stoicism, which developed between the end of the sixteenth century and the first decades of the seventeenth, also aims, like the ancient version, at analysis and discipline of the passions (and of the conflicts that they trigger).

The emphasis, however, falls more on the compatibility between individual behaviours and the overall hold of the political organization. Constancy, methodicalness, and order are now much more lauded, the more that the traumatic destruction of the previous organization of the impulses and the political particularisms of feudal origin leave unprotected the psychic and political terrain. The stated purpose is still that of pursuing the bliss of the wise man, but the "care of oneself" becomes ever more the worry for the survival of the individual and of the community in difficult times, when the search for a minimum basis of agreement, which involves virtually all men, becomes one of the few guarantees of tolerance and coexistence between warring factions.[1]

---

1 On Neostoicism and its function in the rise of the individual and of the modern state, see the classic study by W. Dilthey, *Weltanschauung und Analyse des Menschen seit Renaissance und Reformation*, vol. 2 of *Gesammelte Schriften* (Leipzig, 1914). Dilthey highlights the debt of Renaissance and seventeenth-century culture to the Stoic analysis of the passions and its contribution to the birth of a new and autonomous personality, responsible for its own acts and omissions, strong and flexible in its behaviour (in the construction, that is, of a "living subject, full of strengths and will"; see vol. 1, 238). However, it excessively stresses Spinoza's dependence on Stoicism (see, for a sort of table of concordances, vol. 2, 51 et seq.). So, for example, the distinction between *appetitus* and *cupiditas*, although found in Chrysippus (see Diog. Laert., VII, 85), has

The theory – of Stoic origin – of the social contract strives to make the individual assume a new, politically guaranteed identity. Coming from nature, every man receives under this pact a type of lay baptism that decrees the loss of the presumed natural and spontaneous *I* (still ruled by the search for a low-profile self-preservation) to promote him to a civil man, a rational being capable of making independent decisions. The individual, centred on himself and – at the same time – tied more closely to the social organization, is called upon to translate external restrictions into self-restrictions, thus structuring in a different way his own passions and feelings and learning to control and tolerate their contradictoriness and their virtually disruptive impulses. It could be said that – through progressive rationalization of the functions and structure of the state – Neostoicism contributes to creating a political *hegemonikon* parallel to the psychic one. The insistence on the process of making conduct more rigorous and disciplined marks, even in this case, the abandonment of the Aristotelian tradition of the mean and of the equilibrium of the virtues (still dear to Melanchthon). It began a phase of hard exercises in political control and personal self-control that would lead to the strengthening of modern states, to the ideal of an *imperium* like a "certain order in commanding and obeying," with the goal of maintaining the security and safety of citizens.

The Stoicism we are looking at now is a largely politicized one, of a Roman and not Greek stamp. More than Zeno, Cleanthes, or Chrysippus, its authors are Cicero (for the sources), Epictetus, Marcus Aurelius, and particularly Seneca. What is attractive (in a world dominated by uncertainty, "fortune," and doubt) is both the universalism achieved by the Roman political and juridical tradition in the framework of a multinational and multicultural empire and the complementary values of *auctoritas* and *disciplina*, tools for organizing and focusing scattered and dissipated energies (at the individual level, this corresponds to a strengthening of *ratio* and *voluntas* before a smoother subjugation of the rebelliousness of feelings). The disciplining appears as a reaction to the centrifugal forces of an era rich in heartaches, one that witnessed the metamorphosis and collapse of the classical system of civic virtues. It therefore belongs (in the language of McIntyre) to an era that is essentially already

a longer and more complex history that that presented by Dilthey. Contrary to his theses, on a different level, is H. Blumenberg, *Selbsterhaltung und Beharrung: Zur Konsitution der neuzeitlichen Rationalität*, in *Subjektivität und Selbsterhaltung*, ed. H. Ebeling (Frankfurt, 1976), particularly 157 et seq.

after virtue. Absolutism needs to construct a new ethics, a different connection between Christian morality and the state. Once again we turn to the Roman world rather than the Greek. And again – looking towards the end of the political cycle of absolutism, with the Jacobins – its models are found in Caesar and the imperial age and not in Brutus and the republican virtues.

Control of oneself, the rigorous vigilance of the individual over his own passions in order to be able to smooth out their vehemence, the creation of peaceful areas removed from the turbulence of mental and social conflicts, are tasks that are felt as urgent. Everything that tears and risks shattering the integrity and identity of the individual must be subjected to a more coherent order, in the form of standardization of the consciousness that refers to universal rules of nature that (in their own emphasis) express repugnance before particularisms that could become the seed of new disagreements. The progressive "quartering of violence"[2] – a violence so frequent in the Middle Ages and during the phase of adjustment of the modern structures of power – allows the consequent strengthening, in Weberian terms, of new monopolies of legitimate violence, of largely "rationalized" state structures.

This process is parallel to the individual's self-discipline and the centralization of his mental functions under the protective aegis of the dominance of "reason" and "will." We must not believe that a "true" political and institutional history exists that presents, as a mere reflection, a phenomenal history of the subject's "psychology." The two processes are complementary and indivisible. Passions that were previously active atrophy and dry up, while others, previously latent, now become active and flourish in a luxuriant way. With a sort of positive and negative bradyseism, entire areas of collective behaviour and "virtues" sink into, or emerge from, the upheavals underway. Cruel international, civil, and religious wars, with the sense of insecurity that they provoke, push towards promotion of an order that elicits the need to restrict the area of conflict and to expand that of reason. It also elicits the need to find an instrument – that is, the will of the state – that can achieve this goal with the necessary energy. Thus, adding to the spread of fears, and of both lay and religious hopes, is the desire for strengthened civil and international

2 On the quartering of violence (*Die Gewalttat ist kaserniert*), see N. Elias, *Über den Prozess der Zivilisation: Soziogenetische und psychogenetische Untersuchungen*, vol. 2: *Wandlungen der Gesellschaft: Entwurf einer Theorie der Zivilisation* (Bern, 1969), 325.

cooperation and the need for growing control of the central power over the political and religious parts that are in conflict.

Neostoicism seems to contribute to producing effects that are paradoxically in opposition. On the one hand, it strengthens and validates the idea of a universal reason that unites men beyond the passions and the different and local interests that divide them. On the other, it encloses them within the rigid structures of an authoritarian state. Thus, together, it supports the birth and development of modern international law and that of national states. It revives the idea of pacts, of civil and religious tolerance, of understanding between different civilizations, peoples, and individuals, and then it preaches, in some cases, persecution and the stake. It brings back to light (against feudal particularism) the Stoic idea of cosmopolitanism and (against Hapsburg political power, already felt as extrinsic) the necessity to respect the desire for the liberty and independence of peoples. A similar tension between universalistic tendencies and demands for the foundation of the national state encourages, on one side, the strengthening of the idea in which the *jus gentium* is regulated, even in the case of war, by specific universal norms of reciprocity. On the other side, it increases the weight of the sovereignty of the state, whose role has become all the more important as religious unity has shattered. On the political level and on the personal, these two vectors produce, in interpenetration of rationality and discipline, social control and self-control of the individual passions. The emphasis placed on sovereignty finds its parallel in the dominant function attributed to consistency and individual will. Becoming dominant, however, the latter lays down the bases for its autonomy with respect to politics and for the future conflict between universalistic morals of the individual and the law of the state.

The Integrity of Will

The idea that one can order his passions through will, constructing an identity in which he commands himself against all centrifugal forces, is included (at various levels and by different authors) in the rebirth of Stoic thought. Characterized by the plan to *mesnager la volonté,* to be able to carry out its capacity to live and orient itself in the world, it is made whole (when possible) and impervious to reversals of fate, in that it does not surrender to threats or to internal and external lures.[3]

3 On the nature of integrity, defined substantially by the things that one must not do, see the theoretical reflection of L. McFall, "Integrity," *Ethics* 98 (October, 1987), 5–20.

In Charron, for example, the will constitutes the principal pillar of wisdom. Solely it is within our inalterable and inalienable possession. For the wise man, it is the fulcrum, the "point of support" with which to raise ourselves and the world without needing any other external help: "The wise man leaves aside and is free from every passion; he considers and judges every thing, he does not quarrel with nor tie himself to anyone, but lives on his own: honest, complete and happy."[4] All that we have can be taken away or can change, but our will is the thread that keeps us united with our past and our future, faithfulness to ourselves that makes us consistent and identical: *Est vrayment notre et en notre puissance; tout le reste, entendement, mémoire, imagination, nous peut estre osté, altéré, troublé par mille accidents et non la volonté.*[5]

The integrity of desire corresponds to the moral integrity of man, with *preud'hommie*, which is a value in itself, the expression of the desire to be continually present to oneself through one's own acts and their consequences. A weak will, subject to the passions and external forces, would be disoriented and painful: "Man wants all his limbs whole and healthy: his body, his head, his eyes, his judgment, his memory, even his stockings and boots. Why would he not want his will to be made in the same way, that is, completely good and healthy?"[6]

The will's autonomy from incidental circumstances and its indestructibility with respect to the forces that could break or subjugate it become accustomed to looking at men and events from above, freeing itself from the vertigo of fear and dependence produced by weakness. This is "like those those who, standing on top of a tower, are weak of heart as they look toward the bottom. Few have the strength and courage to stay on their feet; they need to be supported. They cannot live if they they are not supported or attached. They do not dare to remain alone for fear of goblins. They fear that the wolf will eat them, people born to servitude." What Aristotle says – that when there are many to judge, it is more difficult to err – is not true. Wisdom does not correspond to the widespread belief that there is "a precondition of withdrawing and diverting [from people], if one wants to cross the threshold of the holy sanctuary of wisdom."[7]

---

4 P. Charron, *Petit traicté sur la sagesse* [1606] in *De la sagesse* (Paris, 1824), vol. 3, 275.

5 P. Charron, *De la sagesse*, vol. 1, 142. For the "voluntarism" of Charron that anticipates, in some aspects, the fundamental nexus between will and intellect in Descartes, see G. Abel, *Stoizismus und frühe Neuzeit: Zur Entstehungsgeschichte modernen Denkens im Felde von Ethik und Politik* (Berlin, 1978).

6 Charron, *De la sagesse*, 287.

7 Charron, *De la sagesse*, 285, 276.

Tolerance and Torture

Neostoicism strengthens the need for a power capable of containing the lacerations that break up the "society of the human race" and the traditional universalistic "macro-communities" (like the Hapsburg Holy Roman Empire and the Catholic church) in a varied multiplicity of national states and confessions. Towards that end, it asks the individual to submit – at least externally – to a degree of obedience and self-control similar to that to which, in the past, only the members of monastic orders were held. From personal loyalty to the sovereign, we pass to an impersonal relationship, to "laws of nature" that allow the state to exist as such. And even if the wise man may withdraw into a protective membrane of a subjective happiness, his condition obligates him to an osmosis with the exterior world: he can strive to ignore the effects of the evils of the world on his own person, but he cannot exempt himself from involvement in events and cannot avoid his duties towards the state and the community.

Thus, modern Stoicism contributes, on one hand, to spreading tolerance through the conscious revival of the tradition of Erasmus and the repeated call to reason (through demonstrations of faith celebrated in private). On the other hand, it contributes to expressly preaching – with Lipsius – intolerance towards those who disturb in public the religious peace of the state and who induce the masses to follow a specific doctrine. The crude surgical metaphor employed in the *Politica* – that of the *seca et ure*, amputate and burn – essentially represents a theoretical authorization for the use of torture and the stake in the name of protecting the sick body of the state. In private – as it appears indirectly from the *De cruce* – everyone must bear his own cross. For the Christian, "passion" still means, above all, "suffering." The juridical *cause* of the torture of Jesus – based on the Roman law that punished the "instigators of seditions and riots" – seems to depend on its will to introduce revolutionary and seditious innovations: *videri innovationem et seditionem esse.*[8] If Lipsius had been able to express his own political judgment freely on this point, he, like Montaigne, would have been more on the side of the Dostoeviskian Grand Inquisitor than on Christ's.

8 See *I. Lipsi De Cruci libri tres ad Sacram profanamque historiam utiles* … (4th expurgated ed., Antwerp, 1599), 3, 33. This volume, which illustrates in detail the meaning and the means of the crucifixion, offers readers horrifying images and descriptions of the atrocities and torments to which men were (and are still) subjected.

The problem of tolerance will be set up with a temporary solution by Grotius: theoretically, through the request for a *modica theologia* that reduces as much as possible the area of religious discord;[9] and practically, through a "regionalization" of religions that will become diversified, according to territory, based on the faith of the sovereign. With the peace of Westphalia, the Grotian formula, *qualis rex, talis lex,* would achieve public sanction in the famous principle *cuius regio, eius religio* (a largely authoritarian method of resolving conflicts, which surely lowered the threshold for doing so, but that tied the form of the cult to the anagraphic destiny of the citizen). To use a Grotian expression, even Neostoic ethics is endowed with its *ius belli ac pacis,* that is, with a system of norms and procedures for regulating conflicts and finding points of equilibrium (or of tension, since despite every Pascalian and Pirronian doubt, reason cannot be easily "regionalized").

The attention to the external world and its associated life becomes, then, a characteristic trait of this philosophy. It is defended by scholars who fight the flight of the wise man from the world and from politics and by learned individuals who place themselves at the service of the states. Implicitly or explicitly rejected in this way are both the isolation of the philosopher (which is still supported, in different forms, by Montaigne or Descartes) and the melancholic or "Saturnine" propensity for a rural or misanthropically secluded life. Unlike Epicureanism, Stoicism accepted, as is well known, the political dimension as a duty and contribution of the individual to the maintenance of everything of which he is a part. Neostoicism, in turn, tried to influence public life in a similar but indirect manner, progressively modifying the function of the universities and trying to strengthen their specialized culture in the philosophical, juridical, and political spheres. They are no longer directed towards the formation of *élites* that will be chiefly absorbed by the church or by the liberal professions. A greater number of jurists, philosophers, and even theologians are created who are destined to enter into ever closer relationships with the institutional and bureaucratic expressions of the states that achieved independence or prosperity after long and bloody international or civil struggles.

9 For a description of this, see D. Nobbs, *Theocracy and Toleration: A Study of the Disputes in Dutch Calvinism from 1600 to 1650* (Cambridge, 1938).

Constancy and Calamities

Starting from the end of the sixteenth century, one of the principal forges of European culture was the Netherlands, and in particular, the Calvinist University of Leiden. Directly subject to the State of Holland and founded in 1575 – at the most difficult moment of the struggle against Philip II, as reward for the courage and self-sacrifice of its citizens – it drew scholars and students even from abroad, particularly from France and Germany.[10]

In the Netherlands – a newly independent mercantile republic, risen from the struggle against Spanish absolutism, but still in search of its own political and civil identity – Neostoicism assumed a decisive role. Through the Flemish humanist Justus Lipsius (or Joost Lips), who taught at Leiden, Holland became the point of irradiation of ideas that soon passed beyond its borders, spreading rapidly to the rest of Europe. In different countries these ideas contributed to the strengthening of a rational conception of ethics and of politics – that is, to a restructuring of the internal hierarchies of the individual and to a reformulation of the powers and authorities of the state.[11]

The fame of Lipsius as a philologist and as a philosopher spread via two paths that ultimately came together. The first is represented by critical editions of Tacitus and Seneca that he edited in exemplary fashion. They not only constitute notable monuments of erudition, but through them, the whirl of the passions and discord in the age of bondage and civil war; the endemic scourge of fear and suspicion; the continuous threats to the life, integrity, and health of the body; and the insecurity in which every being is tossed about, gripped by dark hopes and premonitions, seem to be cast from the age of Tiberius, Caligula, Nero, and Domitian

10 On Neostoicism and the Dutch philosophical and religious culture of the time (inside and outside the university and in relationship also with Spinoza), still fundamental are the volumes by S. von Dunin-Borkowski, *Spinoza*; M. Francés, *Spinoza dans les pays néerlandais dans la seconde moitié du* XVIIIe *siècle* (Paris, 1934); P. Dibon, *La philosophie néerlandaise au siècle d'or*, vol. 1: *L'enseignement philosophique dans les universités a l'epoque précartésienne (1575–1650)* (Paris, 1954); and Dibon, *L'université de Leyde et la République des letters au* XVIIe *siècle* (1975), in *Régards sur la Hollande du siècle d'or* (Naples, 1990), 31–77.

11 On the meaning of Neostoicism and of its various representatives in the Netherlands (Lipsius, Voss, Heins) and in Europe (particularly Du Vair and Scioppius), see F. Strowsky, *Pascal et son temps*, 2 vols. (Paris, 1910–13), particularly the last chapter of the first volume.

onto contemporary events, suggesting a *de re tua agitur.* From the pages of Tacitus and Seneca – the authors most cited in the writings of Lipsius – political terror, cowardice, and weakness of individuals and peoples, but also their courage, consistency, and determination, leap to the threshold of the present like an overarching background of allusions.[12] The second path is offered by works that were among the most consulted and translated in Europe: the dialogue *De constantia* of 1584[13] and the treatise *Politicorum sive civilis doctrina libri sex* from 1589.[14] Secondarily, as formidable instruments of knowledge and in-depth analysis of Stoic doctrines, are the *Manuductio ad Stoicam philsophiam* and the *Physiologia Stoicorum,* which were born following the work on the edition and commentary on Seneca's writings.[15]

Like the book by Guillaume Du Vair, *De la constance et consolation ès calamitez publiques* – written in 1590 during the siege of Paris by the future

12 See *Cornelii Taciti Annalium et Historiarum libri qui extant. J. Lipsii studio emendati et illustrati* (Lugduni Batavorum, 1576). (Spinoza possessed the edition of Lipsius published at Antwerp in 1607, as well an unspecified edition of his works. In addition, in the field of Roman historiography, there were works by Sallust, Livy, Caesar, and Quintus Curtius Rufus.)

13 See *De constantia libri duo qui alloquium praecipue continet in publicis malis* (Lugduni Batavorum, 1584); *Politicorum sive civilis doctrina libri sex, qui ad Principatum maxime spectant* (Lugduni Batavorum, 1589); *Manuductionis ad Stoicam philosophiam libri tres, L. Annaeo Senecae aliisque scriptoribus inlustrandis* (Antwerp, 1604); *Physiologiae Stoicorum libri tres, L. Annaeo Senecae aliisque scriptoribus inlustrandis* (Antwerp, 1604). Reversing the saying of Seneca – who complained that philosophy had been reduced in his time to philology (see *Ep.* CVIII, 23) – Lipsius was able to assert *e philologia philosophiam feci.* The writings of Lipsius are generally cited according to the edition of the *Opera omnia* (Antwerp, 1637) (a symptom of the reception of Lipsius: through earlier and later editions I had to integrate the parts removed by the specimen normally consulted at the Biblioteca Nacional di Madrid, where various censors, who signed and dated their operation on the frontispiece, rendered illegible the sections that were considered, from time to time, "compromising.")

14 The first edition was published at Leiden, but the expanded edition should be consulted: *Politcorum sive civilis doctrina libri sex. Qui ad principatum spectant. Additae notae auctiores, tum de Una religione liber* (Antwerp, 1604).

15 For the edition of Seneca, which remains incomplete because of the death of its editor, see *Senecae philsophi opera quae extant omnia* (Antwerp, 1605; facsimile reproduction, Paris, 1927). For Seneca the tragedian, see also *Iusti Lipsi animadversiones in tragoedias quaem L. Annaeo Senecae tribuuntur,* in *OO,* vol. 1, where there is also a hint of the connection between *metus* and *spes.* See also *Animadversiones in Thyestem, OO,* vol. 1, 371. On Lipsius the philologist and editor of Seneca, see R. Pfeiffer, *History of the Classical Scholarship from 1300 to 1850* (Oxford, 1976), 126.

Henry IV and published there four years later – the *De constantia* also has as its principal theme the function of this virtue in times that were politically troubled by public misfortunes (*in publicis malis*).[16]

The impact of the works of Lipsius reveals itself as a well-measured combination of emotional messages, theoretical norms, and instructions of prudence. A subtle sense of distress and sadness (even in the garden scene that opens *De constantia*) is transmitted to the reader, who sees reflected in its words the merciless toughness of the times, which everyone could experience every day. This sentiment is joined, in a reactive way, by an authoritarian need for order and autonomy in the conduct of one's own life (*idem velle, idem nolle*), accompanied by continuous requests for guaranties – in particular, for a *securitas* that might save the body from torture and the soul from torments. Between the consistency to be cultivated with oneself and the rationality to be instilled in politics, Lipsius knows that no perfect parallel exists; men are not capable of governing themselves apart from relationships of strength and the disappointments and bitterness with which public life generally rewards them. The states, in turn, are largely forced to intertwine rationality and violence: *necessitas omnem legam frangit,* asserts Lipsius, in a Senecan manner,[17] not without observing (see *De const.* II, XXII) how all of human history is strewn with disasters and cruelty that, instead of decreasing, had recently increased.

Nec spe, nec metu

From here the insurmountable gap opens, despite everything, between the imperative of constancy and the universalism of reason on one side and, on the other, the flexibility dictated by opportunities and by the brutal attitude rendered indispensible by the bitterness of the struggle. From this comes the ambiguously varying emphasis between the invitation to Stoic control of oneself and obedience to external authorities,

16 In fact, Du Vair's volume was modelled on the *De constantia* by Lipsius. See H. Glaesser, "Juste Lipse et Guillaume Du Vair," *Revue Belge de Philosophie et d'Histoire* 17 (1938), 27–42. On Lipsius and his relationship with Roman Stoicism, particularly with Seneca, see A.M. van de Bilt, *Lipsius' De constantia en Seneca* (Nijemegen, 1946).

17 See Sen., *De clem.* 1.9. As an indication of the wide spectrum of the diffusion of Stoicism in the sixteenth century, remember that the *De clementia* was commented upon by Calvin, that in 1535 the edition of Epictetus edited by Trincavelli appeared, and in 1558, in Heidelberg, the *editio princeps* of Marcus Aurelius. For Lipsius's admiration of Epictetus, see *Manud.* 1.19, 2.20.

between the liberty of the individual and the relative cowardice in enduring injustices to avoid worse evils.[18] Necessity and rational consistency intertwine, therefore, in Lipsius with the acceptance of will and the insufficient propensity towards risk, giving rise – in the political arena – to that *prudentia mixta* that is composed of virtue and opportunism, of activity and passivity, of clear decisions and of resignation or disappointment (*deceptio*). Constancy constitutes, at the same time, the scale and the rudder of these opposing weights and conflicting currents.

Constantia wants to reject fear, which, in collusion with hope, always holds the heart in suspension. Fear, however, rules the world, assuming many faces, particularly that of the rebellion and terror that are necessary for every government but insufficient to keep it alive.[19] Fear must therefore enter politics skilfully, mixed with joyful obedience. An *imperium* in which subjects obey willingly is very stable, while more odious forms of power do not last long (see *Pol.* II, XII). And given that love, this "nectar of the human race,"[20] is rarely found in the world, the law normally in force is that of tyranny, which governs even among the animals. It follows – according to a proverbial example, revived by Spinoza with completely different intentions in *TTP*, chapter XVI – that the big fish eats the little one (see *De const.* II, XXV).

With his subjectively voluntaristic attitude, ready to cope with the disorders and evils of a world that had ceased to be a *kosmos*, Lipsius creates an atypical Stoicism, one that is paradoxical in its novelty and not exempt from compromises. In fact, he does not entirely follow either the fundamental precepts of this philosophy nor those of Christianity (or better still, of the various denominations that were then in conflict). In the initial pages of *De constantia*, he notes how he had been driven, in constructing his thought, to make use of "stones, cement, and mortar"

18 What differentiates the notion of will formulated by Lipsius with respect to the widespread ones of classical Stoicism or by Luther in *De servo arbitrio* (where the role of human will with respect to salvation is denied) is its intimately conflicting and lacerating nature. It is not omnipotent and it is not impotent. It does not depend completely either on reason or on faith. It does not obey only nature, but also variable demands dictated by prudence, in times lived and felt to be sad and painful.

19 On fear and its connection with hope – with many references to Seneca, in particular to *Ep.* XII, 8 – see *Manud.* III, I (dissertation titled *Aliquid contra Spem & Metium*, in *OO*, vol. 4, 490–1, where the strategy is recommended of equipping the mind against both and, if necessary, playing one against the other). On rebellion and terror see, instead, *Pol.* VI, IV, 110.

20 See Lipsius, letter to H. Schultetus, in *Centurationes* III, *Miscellanea*, in *OO*, vol. 2, 167.

drawn from "this ancient and now fallen edifice of philosophy," and in the opening of the *Manuductio*, he claims his own independence with respect to the *auctores* of the tradition. The originality of the theoretical operation that he brought to completion consists precisely in this grafting of the old onto the new, of Roman Stoicism onto a modern and divided Christianity, of a conception of the state still precariously balanced between absolutist tendencies and the assertion of its citizens' liberty.

Lipsius made plausible (and to a good degree, compact) the assembly of "pieces" of theory sometimes in contrast with one another. He smoothed their sharp edges and softened their roughness, silencing or underestimating their latent or obvious contradictions. The theoretical structure raised, however, is undeniably new and functional, since it offers to philosophy a suitable shelter and creates a moral and intellectual climate favourable to the search for solutions to problems unanimously felt to be imperative. His positions are not, therefore, reducible to a flat and erudite revival of Stoicism. And this is so for two reasons. The first, of an external (but hardly minor) character, is that Lipsius has a conception of this philosophy so broad as to include within it, ecumenically, thinkers or poets who did not have the slightest historical relationship to it, but in whom he believes he recognizes a consonance with his own ideas. The second and more substantial is that he rejects, essentially, what is perhaps the most important dogma of Stoicism: the idea that nature is endowed with an intrinsic rationality and that consequently, human *ratio* – if it really wants to unite man with wisdom, peace of mind, and happiness – must simply identify and follow nature's laws. The ethics of Lipsius is based, instead, on rules that sometimes appear to be "against nature." That is, the values he proposes are centred on deaf resistance to admitting that nature may show to reason laws that are always understandable, and it is based on the consequent emphasis placed on the dramatic role of a subject who strives, rather, to think and decide based on his own will and intelligence, but who is conscious of their inadequacy.

This solution cannot be satisfactory to the Stoic, given that the inscrutability of the decrees of providence limits the powers of the *ratio* and requires the intervention of *pietas* and *fides*. But nor can it be satisfactory to the Christian, since such Stoicism – however sweetened – still always highlights the role of *ratio* and its capacity to formulate universal criteria for reaching common agreements. Accepting them means rejecting dogmatic preliminaries, thus undermining the specificity and credibility of the individual rival faiths and placing in discussion the obedience that one owes to revealed truth and to its official interpreters.

From such aporias there emerges in Lipsius the rigid contrast and nagging insistence on *constantia*, conceived almost like a shell that the will wears to protect the heart in the long term from direct exposure to the arrows of fortune, evil, and suffering (rather than as a symptom of achieved serenity). From this comes the claim of the value of reason and its steadiness, precisely because it is continuously threatened by indecision and doubt. One gets the clear impression that reason and will may try all the more to shield themselves with constancy the more they are threatened by inconstancy, uncertainty, variability, and the instability of opinions and choices in a political and religious world in which loyalties are divided and changeable. From this, finally, comes the reiterated attempt to steer clear of precise choices of ends and refusal to involve oneself in theological disputes. Beyond personal preferences and the true or presumed opportunistic and "proteiform" character of beliefs regarding religion and politics, Lipsius (first a student of the Jesuits at Louvain, then professor at the Lutheran university of Jena, then in the Calvinist university at Leiden, finally returning to the arms of the Catholic church and dying surrounded by Jesuit confessors and pardoned by the Hapsburgs for his previous opposition to Philip II) always favoured the image of himself as a scholar *totus in libris.*

In reality, he strives to avoid both fatalism and sceptic relativism, grasping, through *prudentia*, the different nature of the relationships between necessity and possibility, the linking of causes and the opportunities for human integration into their weave. To the condition of suffering the inevitable and unpredictable (but thus making a reason of things), the individual assumes a more active role that transforms him, even to a limited degree, into an assistant of destiny. This approach is supported by an ethics whose rationalism not only tolerates frequent irruptions of chance in the course of the world, but further reads its own time under the sign of melancholy, decline, and death. Cities are born, and "their day shall come at length. And thou also, Our Antwerp, that beauty of cities, in time shalt come to nothing. For this great Master-builder pulleth down, setteth up, and (if I may so lawfully speak) maketh a sport of human affairs" (*De const.* I, XVI).

This catastrophe can be postponed if, in states, there emerge the authority and discipline indispensable to cementing internal harmony and defeating external enemies. In times of war and siege in his homeland on the part of imperial troops, Lipsius seeks in the ancients those teachings of military technique and organization explained in *De militia romana* and *Poliorceticon* that would soon be applied to the Dutch army by

Maurice of Nassau.[21] It was no longer the case, in the manner of Seneca (see *Ep.* LSV, 18), of metaphorically painting the life of the wise man as one of militancy, but of showing how the systems of force and violence effectively function in a world that cannot do without them. Stoically (and Christianly), each person will have to tolerate to a large degree all the trials to which they will be subjected, the whims and follies of fortune. The difficulties and the sorrows are not to be feared; they temper the will and enliven reason, keeping them from collapsing or bending supinely to circumstances. This is why the wise man trusts in firm consistency, in the persevering presence of spirit in confronting fate, whether it be adverse or favourable. He assigns the same commitment to such a task that others dedicate to escaping death or seeking pleasures.

After explaining various religious and political peregrinations and misfortunes, the text of *De constantia* intends to lead the reader towards a peace of mind consistent with that period of fear and decline. Although he revives the Stoic ideal of cosmopolitanism and brotherhood between men, of a universe that is the common patrimony of everyone, the world still appears to Lipsius (just as it had to Epictetus) to be dominated by pain, by a general suffering that does not derive only from public evils.[22] In truth, it is governed by a *fatum* that (coinciding, however, with the inscrutable and incomprehensible Christian *providentia*) can certainly be considered but not examined and scrutinized: *fatum aspici vult, non ispici.*[23]

The wise man does not find his own bliss through the simple insertion of his acts and thoughts into the cosmic order, having himself be "drawn," in a Senecan way, by events. The Stoic imperative to strive to live in a way that conforms to nature makes little sense for the Christian Lipsius, according to whom reason asserts itself more in contrast than in harmony with the spontaneous course of things.[24] The world and

21 These works circulated widely. In 1605 *De militia romana* was already in its fifth edition, published at Antwerp, and in 1625 *Poliorceticon* was in its fourth. See G. Oestreich, *Neostoicism & the Early Modern State* (Cambridge, 1982), 5.

22 See *De const.* I, II; II, XXII; I, IX.

23 In fact, it is impious to want to investigate the designs of Providence (see *De const.* II, XII), and there is no need to forgive the Stoics too much for having subjected God to fate, thus denying human liberty (*De const.* I, XVIII).

24 *De const.* II, 11–16. On this anti-Stoic trait, see F. Borkenau, *Der Übergang vom feudalen zum bürgerlichen Weltbild: Studien zur Geschichte der Philosophie der Manifakturperiode* (Paris, 1934); Ital. trans. *La transizione dall'immagine feudale all'immagine borghese del mondo: La filosofia nel periodo della manifattura* (Bologna, 1984), 188.

men, left to their spontaneous movement, produce in fact only enormous disasters. Unable to trust in a visible natural legality, the individual does not have available resources other than those he discovers within himself, and he does not possess any other North Star than his own discernment. Transforming himself into the fulcrum of his own decisions, and on the point of condensation of his own strengths, he is capable of exercising an effective self-control over his passions and desires and of administering the economy of his own existence in a prudent manner. In these difficult situations, constancy is the virtue that most helps to maintain consistency with oneself, to give value to the course of existence and to carve out an area of meaning (*senso*) in which internal and external constrictions – individual appetites and social violence – may be progressively developed, rationalized, and examined and then be accepted or rejected. In this environment, the coercion exercised over the conscience by the needs of the organism and the demands of the associated life intersect without becoming confused. Constancy transforms the rational obligation, thus established, into habit. It regulates the flow of the passions and guarantees against their destructive rivalries. It holds worries at bay, progressively reducing the margins of uncertainty in conduct and the band of fluctuation of the feelings. The internalization of external control mechanisms strengthens the individual will, but it does not advance any claim of undermining the external authorities with which the will engages in a complex game of negotiations that are direct or indirect, explicit or tacit.

With respect to will, constancy is the quiet effort of reunifying, through reason, the conflicting *duae voluntates* of the Augustinian tradition. With respect to the passions, it is the zone that separates pride from dejection. With respect to criteria of behaviour, it is "a right and immovable strength of mind, neither lifted up nor pressed down with external or casual accidents."[25] It is born of *patientia* and grows stronger because of it (*De const.* I, IV). Like that of "some kings of this time," its heraldic motto could be *nec spe, nec metu* (ibid., I, VI). Since the source of anxiety and disorder only resides within us, from us must come the resistance to evil and activity that promotes order. The strategy of Lipsius corresponds in this case with that proposed by the Stoics through the theory of the three *constantiae*: substituting will for desire, joy for pleasure, and caution for

25 See *De const.* I, IV: *Constantiam hic appello rectum et immotum robur animi, non elati externis aut fortuitis non depressi. Robur dixi et intelligo firmitudinem insitam animo, non ab Opinione sed a judicio et recta Ratione.*

fear. Constancy becomes more necessary a virtue the more the world is felt as unstable, because it is an effective way of governing uncertainty.

But perhaps one should not take too much pride in such constancy, as Montaigne and Pascal suggest, because it could come from a misplaced pride or from desperation that tries to hide the uncertainty of every thing, freezing the *I*. We prefer man to animals, according to Montaigne, because of a prejudice. If we were to take a better look at ourselves, we would see that *nous avons pour notre part l'inconstance, l'irresolution, l'incertitude, la superstition, la sollecitude des choses à venir* (*ES* II, XII, 465, *ESe* I, 632–3), while animals are free from it and live without postponing to the future their enjoyment of life.

6. Rationalizing Hope

"So We Never Live, but We Hope to Live …"

The fluctuations of the soul also tear at individuals in Pascal, but significantly, they are no longer the *duae voluntates* that confront each other, but again – in the Stoic manner of the beloved Epictetus – reason and the passions are like opposing powers: "There is internal war in man between reason and the passions. If he had only reason without passions … if he had only passions without reason … But having both, he cannot be without strife, being unable to be at peace with one without being at war with the other. Thus he is always divided against, and opposed to himself" (*P*, n. 316; *Pe* 109). This war does not allow for definitive solutions, but only brief and precarious respite, since one cannot reject the passions and become gods or reject reason and become animals: "and reason still remains, to condemn the vileness and injustice of the passions, and to trouble the repose of those who abandon themselves to them; and the passions keep always alive in those who would renounce them" (*P*, n. 317; *Pe* 110).

Thus, the Stoics err in believing that one can do always what one can do sometimes, that those great spiritual struggles, of which the mind sometimes shows itself to be capable, may become routine through exercises of discipline and self-control: "What the Stoics propose is so difficult and foolish" (*P*, n. 376; *Pe* 99). These are words that, for completely different reasons, express the same position as Spinoza (see *E* v, praef.). And the Stoics err in dreaming of control of the will without passions, without movement, because total control and tranquility would be equivalent to death. In this sense, Pascal is close to the *Augustinus* of Jansen, whose rigorism is clearly anti-Stoic. However, it is interesting to note that one of his most lofty ethical models, the abbot of Saint-Cyran,

Basque like Ignatius of Loyola and Jansen's friend since 1610 or 1611 (i.e., immediately after the reform of the abbey at Port-Royal), had not only studied with Lipsius, but had been directed by him towards the study of Stoicism.[1]

From Lipsius to Grotius, the control of will extends to the state and to international rights, on the threshold of universalistic ethics and the Stoic model of natural law. In Hobbes, the *esprit de géometrie* tries to give artificial form, order, and rational confirmation to the force of rights and of politics. In Pascal, however, the conflict between reason and passion, between rational order and order of the imagination, remains entrusted to local and temporal balances that are extremely unstable. They require strengthening not by the power of reason, but by that of the imagination – that is, by the effects of self-legitimization that each specific power manages to produce. And since, as is well known, within human "strange justice," "three degrees of latitude reverse all jurisprudence," and "fundamental laws change after a few years," continuous parades of power and prestige are rendered indispensable, although they are ridiculous in themselves. Thus, judges are seen wrapped in red robes and ermine like "furry cats," displaying themselves stiffly before the audience of the courts, or doctors (always ready to "dupe the world, which cannot resist so original an appearance") try to impress clients by wearing "their square caps and their robes four times too wide" (see *P*, nn. 230, 104; *Pe* 84, 26).

Unlike Spinoza, Pascal does not offer any guarantee of resolving the conflict between reason and the passions through the ascending line of *transitiones*; and, in clear contrast with Descartes, he does not admit the eventuality that man may be capable of generating strings of firm certainties founded on the *ego*.[2] No one is charged with construction, through their own powers, of a consistent knowledge that may count even in "days of grief." On this basis everyone would, in fact, remain prisoner of an intra-worldly "horizontal space," stuck in the grip of a meagre wisdom

---

1 See J. Orcibal, *Jean Duverger de Hauranne, abbe de saint-Cyran, et son temps (1581–1638)* (Paris, 1947–8), vol. 2, 30–1. On blasphemous pride, see also A. Arnaud, *De la nécessité de la foi en Jésus Christe pour être sauve …* (Paris, 1701 [1641]), 109, where he blames Seneca for *le dessein criminel d'égaler la félicité de son sage à celle de Dieu.*

2 On this, see the observation of E. Gilson, *Études sur le rôle de la pensée médiévale dans la formation du système cartésien* (Paris, 1930), 235: "Descartes no longer recognizes any intermediate position between true and false; his philosophy is the radical elimination of the 'probable.'"

lacking transcendence.[3] But even the ancient contrast between "faith and knowledge" became, in turn, impracticable, since "modern reason" eroded in many of Pascal's contemporaries the traditional supports offered to the authority of the Catholic church. Once the relative indisputability of its dogmas is damaged and once the power of the imagination is restrained or otherwise disciplined, faith must place itself in the condition of metabolizing uncertainty and taking on this cross as well. The pomp of ritual and ceremony; the splendour of gold, silver, brocades, or mosaics; the inebriating scent of incense; the moving nature of music (instruments, all of them, that must raise the soul to God through the senses, suggesting to fantasy the premonition of the unthinkable, the advance of immortality) were abolished, reduced, or changed their face as a result of the Protestant Reformation. This not only broke the unity of believers, tearing their consciences between opposing dogmas and faiths, but it also made the places of worship generally bare, penalizing scents and colours, leaving only to the imagination the most spiritualized grip of a space marked by austere architectures. The simple instruction of the Bible verses to be commented upon or sung was conspicuous on the empty walls of the churches; the internalized flow of the music resounded under the vaults. Within that music, the variety of rhythms, the intensity and quality of the sound, and the structure itself mimic and modulate the impulses, the sweetness, or the melancholy of the passions and feelings in a different way in the different phases of the liturgical calendar, highlighting the time of waiting and that of achieving, the time of hope and that of joy and exultation, in the clear awareness of the intolerable suffering for a God who dies and rises again. To the tormented Pascal and his friends of the bare and severe abbey at Port-Royal, the Jesuit revanchism of the imagination is certainly not pleasing (if, in fact, God were to reveal Himself immediately to the senses and to the imagination through images, reminders, voices, and signs, the superstitious would be the majority), just as their passivity, their moral probabilism, and their shrewd mingling with the authority of the "age" are not pleasing.

Christianity, then, precisely because it is based on invisible and unprovable assumptions of faith and hope, remains for Pascal dramatically lacking in absolute credentials, both those presented by reason and those

---

3 For the expression, attributed to Lucretius, see A. Comte-Sponville, *Le mythe d'Icare: Traité du désespoir et de la beatitude* (Paris, 1984), t. 1, n. 24: *L'ascension matérialiste se fait dans un espace horizontal: le sage s'élève, si l'on peut dire, ici-bas. La sagesse est un salut sans transcendence.*

suggested by the imagination. This is also why he is unable to promise any assurance against the risks of death and of the afterlife: "All social conditions, and even the martyrs, must fear, according to Scripture. In Purgatory the greatest penalty is the uncertainty of judgment. *Deus absconditus* ... The hope of Christians to one day possess an infinite good is mixed with real joy and with fear."[4] Precisely because the "advantage" is infinite, it is worth betting on such high stakes, because the hope of achieving an infinite good also implies an infinite joy. With tones then repressed by the modern "theology of hope" of a Moltmann,[5] only the saying *Ave crux, unica spes!* is absolutely valid for Pascal. The arms of the cross appear, however, in their centrifugal divergence: starting from a point where the light, before returning, darkens, as at the moment of the Saviour's death. A blood clot and pain, if accepted, can transform for each person into a source of joy. More than in the guise of mediator or peacemaker, Christ presents himself as that rift that tears the world and the hearts of men, as happened to the veil of the Temple in the moment of death on Golgotha. But hope equally inspires the belief that "God never abandons His own, not even in the grave where their bodies, however dead to the eyes of men, are more alive in the eyes of God."[6]

However, in destroying the haughtiness of the powerful and the learned, in preaching that humility that is the enemy of pride and interests (that render the *I* detestable – a blind, tyrannical, and untrustworthy instrument of disorder that would place itself at the centre of everything and everybody), in transforming hate of oneself into a singular and true virtue, Christianity makes necessary ostentatious intervention into the affairs of the world by its presumed great men, however ridiculous, in asserting their power.[7] Precisely because the abyss of the human heart is, in the sense of Augustine, unfathomable and immeasurable, earthly

---

4 Pascal, *P*, n. 663. See n. 661 for the reference to the Paulist saying "Carry out your salvation with fear and trembling" (Phil. 2:12).

5 See J. Moltmann, *Theologie der Hoffnung* (Munich, 1965); J. Pieper, *Über die Hoffnung* (Munich, 1965).

6 Pascal, *Lettre de Pascal à Mademoiselle de Roannez*, September 1656, in *OC* 507.

7 The testimony of Pierre Nicole, in the *Logique de Port-Royal* (III, 20, 267), has been noted, but merits being reread in this context. Nicole relates how, according to Pascal, an honest man "had to avoid naming or even making use of the words *je* and *moi* and was accustomed to say, in this regard, that Christian piety wipes out the human *moi* and that human civilization hides and suppresses it." The devaluation of the *I* is accompanied in Pascal by a typical Jansenist philosophy of the "suspicious man": the philosophy that sees in everything that is high the persistence of what is low and mean, revealing the virtues as disguised vices, so as to highlight the smallness of men when they lack divine grace and are seeking happiness even in hanging themselves.

authority becomes necessary for the observance of order at its own level. When human law loses its link with the one reason and the one imagination, when it is suspended between the doubts of thought and the feeling of the fleetingness and vanity of all things perceived by the imagination, then there is no God who might cut this knot and transform mere men into guides for the life of the world. And when, in turn, the individual's reason is confused with the automatism of habit (the first nature with the second), then it is also necessary for us to follow a strategy that – still with divine assistance – rearranges the forces of our mingled natures: "We are as much automatic as intellectual ... Custom is the source of our strongest and most believed proofs. It bends the automaton, which persuades the mind without its thinking about the matter ... It is not enough to believe only by force of conviction, when the automaton is inclined to believe the contrary. Both our parts must be made to believe, the mind by reasons which it is sufficient to have seen once in a lifetime, and the automaton by custom, and not by allowing it to incline to the contrary" (*P*, n. 470, *Pe* 73). There is no Spinozan *transitio*, then, from the "spiritual automaton" decidedly conditioned by external causes to the free spirit, from the imagination to the higher faculties. Now that the Augustinian rising scale of the *ordo amoris* that leads to happiness and to God appears impassible, Pascal notes, at most, the distressing need for a leap of faith towards the abyss, together with an intense sense of powerlessness and uselessness in the face of any prospect of changing the political institutions dominated by appearance and order as an end in itself, bolstered by the profane mysticism of an authority whose impotence masquerades as omnipotence. Better, then, to preserve one's own energies for the difficult task of one's own eternal salvation and to affect, through charity, the good of those nearby who are capable of receiving our real help.

Living with Uncertainty

To seek an ultimate meaning of reality, a fullness of feeling that Cartesian certainty cannot offer him, Pascal must resort to religion. The more that faith and reason deepen feeling, however, the more men find themselves cast into paradoxes[8] that require (circularly, in turn) faith. Every increase

8 On paradox as a constituent element of religions in general, see N. Luhmann, "Society, Meaning, Religion – Based on Self-Reference," *Sociological Analysis* 46 (1985), 1–20. This article receives a more in-depth theoretical foundation in Luhmann, "Tautologie und Pardoxie in den Selbstbeschreibung der modernen Gesellschaft," *Zeitschrift für Soziologie* 16 (1987), 161–74.

of feeling seems to have to be paid for with an increase in paradoxality and further uncertainty. The solution of the paradox is not, in Pascal, the "moderate flow" of the hermeneutic circle, infinite entertainment, temporizing, and reference to an understanding that is ever wider but never definitive. The *pari* and its inexpressibility, its simultaneous constituting of the highest instalment of the gift of feeling against anomie and the nihilism that similarly would prevail, are given by the invisibility of the *Dieu caché*, to which we turn our gaze without seeing, while we know that He sees, examines, and judges us in our impotence and misery, but also in the fragile dignity of "a reed that thinks." In Pascal, Augustinian inwardness becomes tangled and goes into a spin, because there is lacking the possibility of finding within us, with certainty, the *principium* of our being, a God that reveals Himself *interior intimo meo*, in addition to *superior summo meo.*

For these reasons, in Pascal (this time as in Augustine)[9] the will is deeply torn and split. But the disappointment of hope assumes the function of an aid to reason in surpassing the passions. Pascal's invitation to live in the present (and not only to hope to live in the future) is of a Senecan character in some respects:

> We do not rest satisfied with the present. We anticipate the future as too slow in coming, as if in order to hasten its course; or we recall the past, to stop its too rapid flight. So imprudent are we that we wander in the times which are not ours, and do not think of the only one which belongs to us; and so idle are we that we dream of those times which are no more, and thoughtlessly overlook that which alone exists. For the present is generally painful to us. We conceal it from our sight, because it troubles us; and if it be delightful to us, we regret to see it pass away. We try to sustain it by the future, and think of arranging matters which are not in our power, for a time which we have no certainty of reaching. Let each one examine his thoughts, and he will find them all occupied with the past and the future. We scarcely ever think of the present; and if we think of it, it is only to take light from it to arrange the future. The present is never our end. The past and the present are our means; the future alone is our end. So we never

9 On Pascal's debt to Augustine, see, more generally, P. Sellier, *Pascal et saint Augustin* (Paris, 1970); H. Gouhier, *Cartésianisme et augustinisme au* XVIIe *siècle* (Paris, 1978); and Gouhier, *L'antihumainisme au* XVIIIe *siècle* (Paris, 1987), 75 et seq. and passim.

live, but we hope to live; and as we are always preparing to be happy, it is inevitable we should never be so.[10]

If the claims of the *Discours sur les passions de l'amour* are true, then only love allows us to live in the earthly world in the least inadequate way. It is not blind, but it corresponds to the reason that, taking the bandages from its eyes, restores its joy of seeing.[11] Only when it is mixed with ambition – that is, with the impulse of self-love – does its gaze darken, and its power is halved. But if love goes outside the perimeter of its own *I* and succeeds in establishing the *esprit de geométrie*, with its "slow, strong, and inflexible views," and the *esprit de finesse*, with the *souplesse de pensée* that applies to that which loves, then it arrives, at least in part, at filling *le grand vide qu'il a fait en sortant de soi-même*, without, however, fully satisfying the heart that is *trop vaste* (*D* 538–9).

And yet, with a new paradox, hope is rationalized by reason, by the attempt to understand insecurity and accept it by a calculation of the celestial probabilities, which is indispensable to Pascal for his bet.[12] To confront the risks of navigating life – since *vous êtes embarqués* (*P*, n. 451) – betting is necessary, however, also because the relative reduction of ignorance does not necessarily generate a positive increase in certainties, given that the number of alternatives is not known. In this sense, one

10 Pascal, *P*, n. 168, *Pe* 49. On the Senecan assessment of time, on the necessity of concentrating on the continuity of a present that constructs, moment by moment, the entire arc of our moral life (and on the consequent precept of not becoming distressed either over the future by the igniting expectations of desire or over the past through regret and bitterness), see, particularly, Sen., *Ep.* 1 and 13. For the echo of Seneca's words in Pascal, see the following passages: "While we are postponing, life speeds by" (*Ep.* 1.2) and "Most men ebb and flow [*fluctuantur*] in wretchedness between the fear of death and the hardships of life; they are unwilling to live, and yet they do not know how to die" (*Ep.* 4.5). Montaigne was more crude: "A hundred students have got the pox before they have come to read Aristotle's lecture on temperance" ("On the Education of Children," *ES* I, XVIII, 162 [*ESe* I, XXV, 168]).

11 See Pascal, *D* 545: *L'on a ôté mal à propos le nom de raison à l'amour, et on les a opposés sans un bon fondement, car l'amour et la raison n'est qu'une même chose … Les poètes n'ont pas eu raison de nous dépeindre l'amour comme aveugle; il faut lui ôter son bandeau, et lui rendre désormais la jouissance de ses yeux.*

12 For the statement of the problem in the seventeenth century and in periods immediately before and after, see I. Hacking, *The Emergence of Probability* (Cambridge, 1975). The necessity of betting on paradise corresponds, conversely, also to the diminished belief in hell or in the eternity of pain, a conviction that spread in the seventeenth century. See D.P. Walker, *The Decline of Hell: Seventeenth-Century Discussion of Eternal Torment* (Chicago, 1964).

cannot avoid fluctuations and the storms of the sea, taking refuge in the quiet port of wisdom, like the Stoics, or in the comfortable scepticism of Montaigne, with his *nonchalance du salut, sans crainte et sans repentir*:

> We sail within a vast sphere, ever drifting in uncertainty, driven from end to end. When we think to attach ourselves to any point and to fasten to it, it wavers and leaves us; and if we follow it, it eludes our grasp, slips past us, and vanishes forever. Nothing stays for us. This is our natural condition, and yet most contrary to our inclination; we burn with desire to find solid ground and an ultimate sure foundation whereon to build a tower reaching to the infinite. But our whole groundwork cracks, and the earth opens to abysses. (*P*, n. 84; *Pe* 19)

Deeply divergent are the strategies elaborated by Pascal and Spinoza (who was marginally concerned with probability calculation)[13] for controlling uncertainty and risk, not so much because the one seeks an anchorage in transcendence while the other turns to the immanent totality of nature, or because the first bases himself on a sort of *spes quaerens intellectum* while the second separates hope from comprehension (considering it, in fact, a factor in the disturbance of reason). The underlying reason is that Pascal despairs of the possibility of healing conflicts and anguish solely through the natural forces of man, unsupported by grace, while Spinoza – although knowing that wisdom is a *perardua* path – holds it possible to go beyond both the passions and reason to arrive at the happiness of the wise man through intuitive science. Moreover, while for Pascal it is the *conditio humana* as such that generates suffering and is constitutively impenetrable by reason (and thus scandalous in his eyes), for Spinoza the increase in the rate of security is accompanied by a possible, progressive limitation of the power of external causes and a parallel increase of knowledge and of the power of existing. And so while in Pascal (who had shown Monsieur de Saci his very high esteem for Epictetus) it seems that it may by definition be impossible to influence *en masse* the "things that are not in our power" and that happiness

---

13 Spinoza follows Christiaan Huygens, author of *De ratiociniis in ludo aleae*, a treatise on the calculations of the game of chance, and possessed the edition of Huygens's *Exercitationum Mathematicarum* (Lugduni Batavorum, 1657) that appears in the catalogue of his library. See also Spinoza, *Ep.* 38 (and, for a letter from Pascal to Huygens of 6 January 1656, in which Pascal promises to send him his treatise on that type of "cycloid" curve that Mersenne had already called *roulette*, see *OC* 520–1 and 180 et seq.).

itself may not depend on us (because it "is neither without us nor within us. It is in God, both without us and within us"; *P*, n. 388; *Pe* 130), for Spinoza, not only can the number and the power of external causes be reduced and limited, but happiness also depends on the external (in an incidental way and certainly not due to God who, not being a person, is indifferent to the fate of all beings), but in a more secure and constant way, by means of each of us.

The advancement achieved by Pascal – at the philosophical level as at the mathematical – consists of the implicit shifting of attention from calculation of objective probabilities to that of subjective probabilities, of the frequency with which a particular event may occur (e.g., the result of three in a die with six faces should be a sixth of the total in relation to a sufficiently high number of tosses) to the estimate of its occurrence on the basis of our expectations, guided by the amount of information possessed. He thus anticipates, in a non-formalized manner, the position of the Scottish school, and of Bayes in particular, which will ultimately lead to the "theory of rational decisions" taken on in situations of uncertainty and of risk.[14]

14 For an in-depth look at these points, see R. Bodei, "Il dado truccato: Senso, probabilità e storia in Weber," *Annali della Scuola Normale Superiore,* n.s. III, 8, no. 4 (1978), 1415–43; Bodei, "Tra prudenza e calcolo: sui canoni della decisione razionale," in *Ricerche politiche due: Identità, interessi e scelte collettive,* 59–83.

SECTION 2

Descartes, or the Good Use of the Passions

1. Masters of Themselves

Zeno Revived?

Although Descartes read the canonical texts of Roman and modern Stoicism very early (Cicero, Seneca, Justus Lipsius, and Guillaume Du Vair, ultimately arriving at Charron), their relevance is diluted from the beginning by the Jesuit teaching of La Flèche (inspired to Thomism and the Neo-Scholastics of the Coimbra school), by the edifying approach to morals that Vives and Francis de Sales offer, and particularly by his personal and independent theoretical choices.

Despite this, the image of a Stoic Descartes – revived and asserted even recently[1] – was already widespread among his contemporaries, however much he may have explicitly stated that he was not *se sévère* in the field of ethics and did not belong to the number "of those cruel philosophers, who want their wise man to be insensitive," condemning, in the style of Montaigne, the stern, Zenoan idea of a virtue "so strict and so hostile to pleasure, making all vices equal … that only the melancholy, or spirits entirely detached from the body, could have been its followers."[2] If, in general, he did not show himself inclined to follow the teachings of others, *Les passions de l'âme* opens precisely with an explicit statement of the faultiness of the ancients on these subjects. Like Spinoza, Descartes is

1 On the questionable relationship of affinity between Descartes and the Stoic tradition, see V. Brochard, "Descartes stoïcien: Contribution à l'histoire de la philosophie cartésienne," in *Études de philosophie ancienne et moderne* (Paris, 1966), 320–6; J.-E. D'Angers, "Sénèque, Epictete et le stoïcisme dans l'oeuvre de René Descartes," *Revue de théologie et de philosophie* 4 (1954), 169–96; D'Angers, *Recherches sur le stoïcisme au* XVIe *et* XVIIe *siècles* (Hildesheim, 1976), 453–80.

2 Descartes, letters to Elisabeth of 18 May and 18 August, 1645; see *Op.* IV, 138, 154.

aware of being a distinctive innovator in the territory of the passions – inherited from Neostoicism – in which ancient thought had been most practised. Despite everything, however, an admirer of his like Guéz de Balzac connects him with the ideal model of the philosopher defined by the Stoics: "When I imagine the Stoic wise man, who alone was free, alone was rich, alone was king, I see that you [Descartes] had long been predicted, and Zeno had created the image of Monsieur Des Cartes."[3] Later, Leibniz will state with finality that, in the field of morals, Cartesian philosophy is equal to that of the Stoics: *in re morali eadem est* (*PhS* IV 275).

The rise of such a stereotype must have been made more plausible, in the time of Descartes, by the deep admiration that Christina of Sweden nurtured for Stoicism long before she was instructed, at twenty-three, by the French philosopher at Stockholm. Through their letters and his sending of *Les passions de l'âme*, then still in manuscript, Descartes had previously contributed to confirming the queen's conviction that the supreme good depends solely on will,[4] and to establishing in her mind (and in that of many contemporaries) the equation between Stoicism and Cartesian morality. The genuine veneration that Christina showed for the works of Epictetus, Seneca, and Marcus Aurelius pushed her not only to speak in enthusiastic tones of the sublime value of the Stoic virtues, but also to surround herself with philological experts (who had the task of facilitating her comprehension of the authors in the original) and even to have scholars and ambassadors seek all the new critical editions that were being published.[5]

Spinoza's assimilation of Cartesian thought with that of the Stoics, however, has only a relative or partial value for us. Emphasizing the role Descartes assigned to the will in controlling the passions, Spinoza rejects

3 See *La Seconde Partie des Lettres de Monsieur de Balzac* (Paris, 1637), 473 (*AT* I, 199), also cited in E. Garin, introduction to Descartes, *PA* VIII. Apparently, the author had not been satisfied with the statements contained in a letter by Descartes addressed to him nearly ten years earlier, on 30 March 1628: "In some places I treat the Stoic philosophers – that is, the ambivalent cynics – a little badly." On Balzac, see J. Jehasse, *Guéz de Balzac et le genie romain* (Lyon, 1977).

4 See Descartes, letter to Christina of Sweden, 20 November 1647, in *AT* V, 83–5.

5 In 1648, Christina thus asked Isaac Vossius to find for her three copies of the new edition of the *Thoughts* of Marcus Aurelius, edited by Casaubon, and in 1649, she tried to get as soon as possible the just-published edition, edited by Gronovius, of Seneca's works. I take these dates from E. Cassirer, "Descartes und Königin Christina von Schweden," in *Descartes: Lehre – Persönlichkeit – Wirkung* (Stockholm, 1939), 177–278.

or underestimates its rejection of every form of rigorism, just as he does the parallel exaltation of "joy." Looked at closely, in fact, Cartesian morals shows an unmistakable physiognomy that, in many respects, clearly diverges from that of the Stoics. The project of full mastery over the passions of the soul is inserted both into the general picture of the effort to become master of one's own house (to acquire the art of a shrewd administration of one's own spiritual and corporeal resources) and *maîtres et possesseurs de la nature* (which clearly makes the undertaking different from the program of the Stoics' "care of self") and, in the field of an activity that brings men satisfaction, master of a virtue understood as the faculty to "do the good things that depend on us." The latter, however, is a case of a capacity that sometimes emerges from passion itself (see *PA*, art. 144, 161). The exercise and development of the passions strengthens the capacity for self-control of the soul, since the determination of the will is, without doubt, free and within our power (Spinoza repeats, therefore, almost to the letter, the Cartesian thesis that *si on employait assez d'industrie à les dresser,* "there is no soul so weak that it cannot, through good guidance, acquire absolute power over its passions").[6] As an example of the impact of the training of men and beasts, Spinoza uses – against Descartes – the anecdote of the two dogs whose *dressage* aimed to transform their primitive nature, so that "he succeeded in training the house dog to hunt and the hunting dog to refrain from chasing hares."[7]

Discussing Seneca's *De vita beata* (a book chosen *en regard de la reputation de l'auteur*) with Elisabeth of the Palatinate, Descartes considered it desirable to arrive at control of the passions according to three rules. The first consists of making use of one's own spirit to know how to act in life. The second consists of having "a firm and constant resolution to carry out whatever reason recommends without being diverted by passion or appetite." The third is assuring oneself that the goods that one does not possess may be beyond one's reach: "Nothing can impede our contentment except desire, regret, and repentance; but if we always do what reason tells us, even if events show us afterwards that we were mistaken, we will never have any grounds for repentance, because it was

6 Spinoza, *E* 5, pref., and Descartes, *PA*, art. 50.

7 Spinoza, *E* 5, pref. To understand the example better, it is necessary to keep in mind that, since the *Cynegeticus* of Xenophon, the techniques of training dogs had been the subject of a small literary genre.

not our own fault."[8] However, this self-control is not achieved by means of internal and external torment (because "the mistake we ordinarily make in this regard is never that we desire too much; it is rather that we desire too little" [*PA*, art. 144]) or by not knowing or not sufficiently employing one's strength of will to make the desire for a greater good triumph. In diametrically opposing all the ethics of renunciation (and in particular the suppression of desires and "temptations" on the part of religious morals and of devotional techniques),[9] Descartes is much closer to Spinoza than the latter seems prepared to admit.

Against the Stoic theory that always ties the passions to excess and to the *diastrophe* (or distortion) of reason, for *"Monsieur Teste"* – more "fiery" and less abstractly "rationalist" than might be believed – they can be, at the same time, "excessive and submissive," as Elisabeth of the Palatinate happily expresses herself when she confesses to not succeeding in understanding well how it might be possible (see *AT* IV, 322). Descartes explains, however, that this applies only to the passions subject to reason: "There are, indeed, two kinds of excess. There is one which changes the nature of a thing, and turns it from good to bad, and prevents it from remaining subject to reason; and there is another which only increases its quantity, and turns it from good to better. Thus, excess of courage is only temerity when it passes the limits of reason; but as long as it remains within them, it can consist simply in the absence of irresolution and fear."[10] Unlike many ethical traditions, in Descartes the ideal behaviour is that in which the power of the passions is accompanied by a superior strengthening of the *I* and of rationality – to an excess, one responds with an even greater excess. Even the model of the *metropathei* or *temperantia*, of Platonic origin, falls.

---

8 See Descartes, letter to Elisabeth, 4 August 1645, in *Op.* IV, 147–50 and *PL* 165. For curing the *langueur* of this sensitive and unhappy person, Descartes does not suggest either joy ("I know that it would be imprudent to want to persuade a person to feel joy when every day sends her new subjects for displeasure") (letter of 19 May 1645, in *PP*, 40) or rigid self-control, but rather thermal cures, rest, and the search for serenity through an understanding of one's own state. In some ways, he tries to "anesthetize in her heart the movements 'induced' by the body, except to tolerate their disorders, doing away with the worry of repressing them" (J.-M. Monnoyer, "La pathétique cartésienne," 31). Spinoza possessed the Dutch translation of the letters of Descartes (Brieven, Amsterdam, 1661).

9 See, for example, Saint F. de Sales, *Introduction à la vie devote*, III, XXVII: *Les desires*, in *Oeuvres* (Paris, 1969).

10 See Descartes, letter to Elisabeth of 3 November, 1645, in *Op.* IV, 173 and *PL* 185.

Achieving *maîtrise* of the passions – to which hope contributes a lot, strengthening its boldness (see *PA*, art. 173) – is marked by the affirmation of a *joye intellectuelle* at which, in general, one arrives through successive exercises of distancing oneself from emotions and saying goodbye to excessive intimacy with one's body – that is, through an ability that does not rely on the capricious gifts of fate: "Happiness ... consists, it seems to me, in a perfect contentment of mind and inner satisfaction, which is not commonly possessed by those who are most favored by fortune, and which is acquired by the wise without fortune's favor."[11] The virtues lacking in joy are ineffective and the actions undertaken with a joyful heart and without internal repugnance turn out better. Even the most socially inadmissible passions are accompanied by a secret happiness when, in the emotional conflict, the weight of joy prevails over that of sadness: "For example, when a husband mourns his dead wife, it sometimes happens that he would be sorry to see her brought to life again. It may be that his heart is torn by the sadness aroused in him by the funeral display and by the absence of a person to whose company he was accustomed ... Nevertheless he feels at the same time a secret joy in his innermost soul, and the emotion of this joy has such power that the concomitant sadness and tears can do nothing to diminish its force."[12]

It is revealing that the series of the six fundamental passions (wonder, love, hate, desire, sadness, and joy) begins with wonder and does not include fear.[13] This beginning and absence, however, maintain an indirect link. Wonder is a passion initially tied to knowledge. It is opening one's eyes to the world with innocent wonder and yearning to know in sensing the *extraordinaire* (*PA*, art. 70). The attitude described by Aristotle in the famous opening of the *Metaphysics*, according to which all men naturally desire to know, is transformed by Descartes into native passion of the soul and is indirectly re-enabled against the Augustinian condemnation

11 Descartes, letter to Elisabeth, 4 August 1645, in *Op.* IV, 148 and *PL* 164.

12 *PS*, art. 147. Even in Molière's *Amour médecin*, Sganarello insists on crying for his dead wife, despite having fought continuously with her: *Je n'était pas fort satisfait de sa conduite, et nous avions le plus souvent disputé ensemble; mais enfin la mort rajuste toutes le chose. Elle est morte: je la pleure* (in *Œuvres complètes*, ed. G. Couton [Paris, 1971], vol. 2, 98).

13 On the system of the passions in Descartes, see P. Mesnard, *Essai sur la morale de Descartes* (Paris, 1936); A. Espinas, *Descartes et la morale*, 2 vols. (Paris, 1937); G. Rodis-Lewis, "Maîtrise des passions et sagesse chez Descartes," in *Descartes: Cahiers de Royaumont, Philosophie* 2 (Paris, 1957), 208–36; in the same volume, H. Lefebvre, "De la morale provisoire à la générosité"; and G. Canziani, *Filosofia e scienza della morale in Cartesio* (Florence, 1980).

– repeated, in different form, by Heidegger in the twentieth century – of curiosity as an end in itself as *concupiscentia oculorum*, of epistemophilia, and of disinterested desire to know.

In this case, Descartes is close to the Hobbes of the *Elements*, in that he attributes to this passion (first in the logical order)[14] a driving importance for the entire economy of the soul (however much it may not appear interested in a genetic consideration of knowledge, in the sense of investigating its ultimate origin from a passion, as Hobbes does when he connects reason to fear). In his taxonomy of the passions – deliberately incomplete, because he knows that "also are many without name" (*Human Nature*, VIII, in *EW* IV, 35) – Hobbes also dedicates special attention to wonder. This assumes in him the characteristic traits of a hope for newness, where uncertainty for the future does not at all produce an "inconstant joy," tinged Spinozanly with sadness, but adding relish to the waiting. The not yet knowing, the confronting of random and bizarre combinations, here loses its traumatic and demonic nature. Each player asks what the next cards from the deck will be for him, and all of his attention is absorbed by the distillation of events:

> And this hope and expectation of future knowledge from anything that happeneth new and strange, is that passion which we commonly call admiration; and the same, considered as an appetite, is called curiosity, which is appetite of knowledge ... Because curiosity is delight, therefore also novelty is so, but especially that novelty from which a man conceiveth an opinion true or false of bettering his own estate; for in such case, they stand affected with the hope that all gamesters have while the cards are shuffling. (ibid., 50)

In Descartes, the absence of fear from the list of primitive passions (which particularly contrasts with the Stoic tradition) is secretly connected to wonder, because for him as well, uncertainty tends to turn towards meaning, lose its negative connotations, and orient itself magnetically towards the discovery, accompanied by amazement, of unverifiable evidence that will serve as the soul's stabilizing ballast against too-violent fluctuations. If it is true that, anchoring knowledge to certain and indubitable evidence, Descartes does not even suspect the possibility (already

14 In fact, in the development of the individual, according to Descartes (in this case, very far from Augustine), the first passion felt is joy, as the soul can only be united with a well-disposed body (see the letter to Chanut of 1 February 1647 in *Op.* IV, 208 and, in the present volume, pp. 269–71.

clear to Pascal) of creating a science of uncertainty, an *ars conjectandi*, or a probability calculation,[15] it is also true that he drastically reduces, on a moral level, the disruptive role of uncertainty. He thus facilitates the culmination of the original passions in joy and of the derivative passions in generosity.

Writing to Elisabeth, then struck by a "slow fever" and various sorts of illness, Descartes casts aside the "mask" and gives in to a rare moment of confidence about his private life. He hints that he himself had had direct understanding of personal and familial sorrow. Born to a mother who died shortly after his birth, because of "a disease of the lung, caused by distress," he had inherited from her and maintained until the age of twenty "a dry cough and a pale color" so marked that the doctors had already proclaimed his early end. This looming destiny, instead of leading him to sadness and *meditatio mortis*, led him to favour, also as therapy, the bright side of events rather than the side in shadow and to measure exactly his own strengths with respect to specific tasks, that is to say "to look at things from the most favorable angle and to make my principal happiness depend upon myself alone."[16] Not dwelling too much on inevitable evils and inconveniences of existence and not being afraid of death become the most effective remedies and medicines: "Instead of finding ways to preserve life, I have found another, much easier and surer way, which is not to fear death."[17] For Seneca and Tacitus, the *metus* was generally born of the political situation that almost completely eluded the control of individuals, being subjected to the will of princes like Nero and Domitian. For Descartes – who also had developed complex strategies for avoiding the annoyances and rigours of the Catholic Inquisition and Calvinist intolerance – the fear of being defeated seems more closely tied to tools that are partially within our control, like the state of health, so that he cherished the plan and hope of being able to succeed in prolonging his existence to have it reach the duration of those of Old Testament patriarchs. Challenging death translated positively into love ("the only active force: love, charity, harmony")[18] and particularly love for life ("One of the points of my ethics is loving life without fearing death").[19] Joy promotes and lengthens life.

15 See Descartes, *Reg.* II (*AT* X, 362). For Pascal and the philosophical implications of the probability calculation, see, in the present volume, pp. 219–23.

16 Descartes, letter to Elisabeth, May or June 1645, in *Op.* IV, 142 and *PL* 163.

17 Descartes, letter to Chanut, 15 June 1646, in *Op.* IV, 189 and *PL* 196.

18 Descartes, *Cogitationes privatae*, in *Op.* I, 10.

19 Descartes, letter to Mersenne, 9 January 1639, in *AT* II, 480.

Amari aliquid

At least implicitly, then, Spinoza agrees with Descartes in preferring joy. He certainly would not, however, have accepted the mixture with those forms of solemn and controlled sadness that the French philosopher claimed and that perhaps constitute the residual trace or scar of his continuous and indirect struggle against death: "Great joys are commonly sober and serious, and only slight and passing joys are accompanied by laughter."[20] Thus, while Descartes ties himself to the models of Aristotle's school, which predict, in the famous passages of the *Problemata*, a point of gravity and melancholy in every noble heart (and in a more direct way, the Senecan model of *gaudium severum*),[21] Spinoza is categorical in separating *laetitia* from *tristitia* and in considering laughter, when it is not foolish or excessive, "good in itself."[22]

Unlike Spinozan *laetitia*, *joye* does not involve soul and body at the same inseparable level. Joy is more pure the less it depends on training of the body. Descartes even adds the suggestion of a physiological *dressage* of the feelings, a sort of school of the passions, of spiritual exercises or "autogenous training" through those procedures to a progressive separation of the soul from the body and of the feelings from habit – thanks to *prémeditation* and *industrie.* In contrast with the classical and Christian tradition, he does not at all assert that the majority of men are subject to fluctuations of the soul provoked by the passions. Only "very few" individuals behave in this way. "Most" possess "determinate judgments" on the basis of which they orient themselves. And even if these are false "and based on passions by which the will has previously allowed itself to be conquered or led astray," they become, however, their "weapons," enabling a person to "resist the present passions which are opposed to them" (*PA*, art. 49). This means that the best way to fight the distorting power of the passions over will is not to attack them head on but to act on the impression left by past cooling passions, in the form of

20 Descartes, letter to Elisabeth, 6 October 1645, in *Op.* IV, 165 and *PL* 175.

21 See Arist., *Probl.* XXX (regarding which see the edition *Aristote: L'homme de genie et la mélancolie*, ed. J. Pigeaud [Paris, 1988]) and, on this subject, J. Starobinski, "La mélancolie au jardin des racines greques," *Le magazin littéraire* 244 (July–August 1987), and Sen., *Ep.* 23.4: *mihi crede, verum gaudium res severa est* ("Real joy, believe me, is a stern matter").

22 See Spinoza, *E* 4.45, schol.

false judgments. Rectifying the judgments means not only directing the passions towards the "truth," but permitting them to explain their own beneficial role, because "the function of all the passions consists solely in this, that they dispose our soul to want the things which nature deems useful for us, and to persist in this volition" (*PA*, art. 52).

Descartes has faith in the fact that "even those who have the weakest souls could acquire absolute mastery over all their passions if we employed sufficient ingenuity in training and guiding them" (*PA*, art. 50). But for this, it is necessary to have an enforcing technique and a commitment (an "industry") aimed at recombining passions and habits differently. The vital spirits and the passions incited by them tend in fact to fix themselves, opportunistically, on the first objects or events that they meet by chance. Habits then connect these incidental links, such that the existence of men is often dominated not so much by the passions as by similar bonds that transform themselves into criteria of will. To be able to be more free and happy it is necessary to split them, instituting new "judicious couplings," new habits. Descartes has not yet arrived – like Pascal, who asked himself if first nature was not, itself, also a second nature, a great habit – at placing in doubt what Edgar Morin called "the lost paradigm," the existence of a "human nature." That nature, however, is extremely plastic, and it can be forged via the same repeatable and serial techniques with which a hunter impedes the hunting dog's immediate tendency to run towards a partridge when it sees it and flee the sound of shot when it hears it, teaching him instead to control himself in both cases and thus interrupting the course of his previous reactions, which are reformulated according to a different schema. Between the *dressage* of animals and that of men, the difference tends to diminish drastically.

No "human wisdom" could resist the assault of the emotions if it did not resort to the remedy offered by "the forethought and diligence through which we can correct our natural faults by striving to separate within ourselves the movements of the blood and spirits from the thoughts to which they are usually joined" (*PA*, art. 211). Joy represents more the result of constant training of the passions (permitted by habit, which is applied to the "movements of the brain" [*PA*, art. 50]) than an inherent development of them according to the Spinozan model of comprehension. Liberty, power, and activity of man are concentrated in the will and in the mind. This requires mechanics, automatic passivity, and blind energy in linking passions with the bodily dimension. Only after such a progressive *dressage* that works, "through taking," on the elements of "communication" of the soul with the body, which are the movements of the "vital spirits,"[23] could Descartes have repeated the (Stoically proud) words that Corneille placed on the lips of Augustus: *Je suis maître de moi/ comme de l'univers;/Je le suis, je veux l'être*[24] – but only in the sense that *ethos* is no longer the result either of the adaptation to a presumed order of nature or of a political pedagogy. Each one strives – essentially alone – to change itself, to make its own will triumph.

23 On this point see, in the present volume, pp. 267–72.

24 P. Corneille, *Cinna*, act 5, scene 3, vv. 1626–7. On Corneille's Stoicism – tempered by a notion of "prudence" – and on the diffusion also through Descartes of the subject of the passions in the theatre culture of the seventeenth century in France (with Corneille, whose greatest dramas proceeded, however, the publication of the *Passioni dell'anima*, and Racine), see E. Cassirer, "Descartes und Corneille," in *Descartes: Lehre – Persönlichkeit – Wirkung*, 71–117.

2. Will and Joy

Between God and Nothing

In 1649, a year before his death, Descartes published his last work, *The Passions of the Soul.* Perhaps in addition to its pedagogical function (indirect criticism of the Stoicism of Christina of Sweden), it highlights the positive role of the passions. Breaking from a long tradition to which Hobbes also belonged (see *DH* 104 = 602), Descartes no longer considers them simple "perturbations" of the soul. Their task consists of the "attachment" or fixing of ideas, in the continuity they provide to the operations of the mind that "strengthen and prolong thoughts in the soul which it is good for the soul to preserve and which otherwise might easily be erased from it" (*PA*, art. 74; see also art. 211). In themselves, the passions are almost all good. If they present undesirable effects, that depends in large part on the lack of wisdom of the people who have not yet acquired the capacity to attenuate their potentially destructive factors or convert their energy. In fact, they lack the disposition to "control them with such skill that the evils which they cause are quite bearable, and even become a source of joy" (*PA*, art. 212).

The linchpin of these techniques of control and transformation of the passions is will, the conception of which varies in the course of the development of Cartesian philosophy. Starting with the *Discourse on the Method* and the letters to Mersenne in 1637 and to an unknown person in 1638,[1] and then passing through the positions expressed in the *Fourth Meditation* and in the *Principia,* Descartes progressively modifies

1 See Descartes, *AT* I, 350, 366, and II, 34–5.

and enriches the statement of the problem until the epistolary correspondence of the second half of the 1640s.

Given that our will tends to pursue or flee something, depending on what the mind presents to it as good or bad, Descartes limits himself in the *Discourse on the Method* to observing that *il suffit de bien juger pour bien faire.*[2] The question, however, is in the *Meditations,* four years later. Judgment and will continue to maintain their customary pivotal threefold structure – that is, articulated in affirmation, negation, and suspension of assent and in attraction, repulsion, and indifference towards something. Will "consists purely in our ability to do or not do a given thing (that is, to affirm or deny something, pursue something or avoid it); or rather, it consists purely in this: that we are moved in relation to that which the intellect presents to us as to be affirmed or denied, pursued or avoided, in such a way that we feel we are not being determined in that direction by any external force" (*M* IV, 57). By now, however, it is no longer sufficient to say that to do well, it is enough to judge well. Between will and intellect an asymmetry is produced, and the first of the soul's two functions is promoted to a superior rank. In fact, in the *Fourth Meditation* the will is extended, as is well known, to a much broader sphere than that of the intellect: *latius pate*[*t*] *voluntas quam intellectus.*[3] Its power, not circumscribed by any limit (*nullis limitibus*), justifies in Descartes's eyes the similarity between man and God.[4] Decision is an act of willpower, irreducible and simple, analogous to divine creation. It separates the subject from his previous state and puts an end to hesitation. With this, Descartes clearly distances himself from the Augustinian line of *De trinitate,* since, in its unlimitedness, the will no longer needs to complete itself through love, and the relative balance between the "persons" of the human trinity (*intelligentia, voluntas,* and *memoria*) is broken. However, this does not mean that he falls into a delusion of omnipotence of will. Rather, his concern is attributing responsibility for the error to bad use of desire. Men err when they rashly show their consent

2 Descartes, *DM,* in *AT* VI, 28. Conversely, for Spinoza, "judging well" is not sufficient for acting well. It is necessary that "intellectual love" transform into knowledge and joy the passions that push the individual to action.

3 Descartes, *M* 54–5.

4 Ibid., 53–4. A further clarification of the Cartesian position comes from a letter to Regius from May 1641 (see *AT* III, 372): *Intellectus enim proprie mentis passio est, et volitio eius actus.* But the theologian Revius will ask, maliciously, if the idea of will is "wider and more extensive" than that of God (see *AT* V, 4).

or dissent towards things they do not understand, choosing on the basis of ideas conceived in a manner insufficiently clear and distinct. He who errs does not realize that each man is "constituted as a medium term between God and nothingness, or between the supreme being and non-being." As he participates in being, man can conceive of the truth, but as a participant in a certain "share of nothingness or non-being," he is exposed to infinite errors (see *M* IV, 54). From the point of view of the passions, consent is a permitting or a not permitting them to be carried out (after having felt them). Left free, they would tend to have no inhibition and would direct themselves towards the goals of their specific appetites. The will interrupts the otherwise spontaneous automatism of impulse or habit. It introduces a pause, allowing deliberation over a longer period with respect to that requested by the immediate venting of the passions.[5]

In the attempt to reconcile free will with grace, Descartes rejects, in the *Meditations*, the idea of will as pure indifference in the face of incontrovertible truths. The unidirectional inclination towards the evidence and the good that God shows to me are more than sufficient reason to make me decide in their favour and to modify the balance between indifference and the sceptical suspension of consent. Grace does not weaken my liberty, but strengthens it: "the indifference I experience, when no reason impels me towards one alternative rather than the other, is the lowest degree of freedom, and is not a mark of perfection but only of a shortfall in my knowledge, or a certain negation; for if I always clearly saw what is true and good, I would never need to deliberate about a judgment to be made or a course of action to be chosen; and in that case, although I would be fully free, I could never be indifferent" (*M* IV, 58). With such strategies, Descartes tries to avoid the conflict established – according to the terminology of William James – between "explosive will"

5 On the presence of unconscious elements in the *co-agitatio* (on whose function, see also pp. 241–2 in this volume), compare G. Lewis, *Le problème de l'inconscient et la cartésianisme* (Paris, 1955; rpt. 1985), 9–103, which refers both to the Augustinian tradition of something concealed and secret within us that we should know; and to the *Traité de l'amour de Dieu* by Francis de Sales (Lyon, 1616), which presents the divine love that awakens *en nous sans nous*; and, finally, to the will of Descartes to not die – according to a verse of Seneca (*Thyestes*, 402) – *ignotus sibi* (see Descartes, letter to Chanut, 1 November 1646, in *Op.* IV, 202). Seneca had previously sketched out the position (*De ira* II, 3, 1) that consent may be necessary for passion to be accepted and transformed into permitted action and, thus, the will may also interfere with such action. On the role of liberty in Descartes – which is a *notion première* – see the letter to Mersenne of December 1640, in *AT* III 259. Still insightful are some observations of J.P. Sartre, "La liberté cartésienne," in *Situations* (Paris, 1947), vol. 1, 314–35.

(i.e., inconsistency, lack of self-control, of *enkrateia*) and "obstructed will" (inertia or the incapacity to deliberate because of the irresistible forces of impulses).

In the *Principia*, the will further highlights its pre-eminence over the intellect to the point of becoming the characteristic trait of man (see *P* I, 34). With man no longer compared directly to beasts – as machines – the definition of "rational animal" no longer befits him. Rather, man is a finite being endowed with an infinite power – will – that cannot and will not ever be capable of being adequately explained, but that makes him free, responsible, and different from all other beings trained by automatisms and external forces: "We do not praise automatons for accurately producing all the movements they were designed to perform, because the production of these movements occurs necessarily. It is the designer who is praised for constructing such carefully made devices; for in constructing them he acted not out of necessity but freely. By the same principle, when we embrace the truth, our doing so voluntarily is much more to our credit than would be the case if we could not do otherwise" (*P* I, 37).

In practical life, it is not permissible to linger too much to reflect and doubt. It is necessary to content oneself with the probable, accepting the idea of incurring multiple errors. In the "contemplation of the truth," each thing must always be carefully considered. We must never trust the first ideas that come to mind, because they may be the fruit of uncontrolled opinions that we have long dragged around. For Descartes, the entire existence of the person dedicated to the search for truth passes in the struggle to abandon the proximity to the body and the misleading prejudices that we acquired in childhood: "It is here that the first and main cause of all our errors may be recognized. In our early childhood the mind was so closely tied to the body."[6] The development of opinions is also development of passions founded on these false judgments.

Wisdom is the result of exercises of distancing: not only from the spatiality of the body, but from the time of one's own life. Reversing the Platonic saying according to which "knowing is remembering," in Descartes,

6 Descartes, *P* I, 71. Descartes presents two different types of indifference, then fused, regarding choice: the case where the evidence for the reasons for the decision is lacking and the case in which they are equally powerful. On *indifferentia* as a Jesuit slogan, which the Protestants countered with *spontaneitas* as *libertas a coactione,* see G. Mori, *Tra Descartes e Bayle: Poiret e la teodicea* (Bologna, 1990), 51–3, which argues against the alignment of Descartes with Jesuit theories.

knowing means (in this case) forgetting. More exactly, it means forgetting the accumulated opinions from whose fragments we then profess to construct all of our knowledge. Childhood does not at all represent paradise lost, the age of innocence or of intuition that is original and undisturbed by the truth, but rather the place where individuals risk remaining caught, even as adults, in the net of a private knowledge woven of unverified and unverifiable beliefs. Meditating means, precisely, giving up the involuntary familiarity with one's own opinions and passing – tearing at the obvious storyline – to a different and intentional familiarity with oneself. Abandoning the past does not depend so much, at first, on an extremely theoretical reason but rather on an act of will, on a courageous decision – taken once and for all – to examine oneself deeply and declare a new beginning, even for thought. With this, the *ego* loses its rarefaction of being and its casualness, and it acquires the substantial ontological weight of the *sum*. The *I*-substance ensures its permanence through the discontinuity of temporal events that would otherwise threaten its identity. In fact, the soul does not stop thinking even in the states of deep lethargy or sleepwalking, when it is absorbed elsewhere (*dum menti alio avocata*).[7]

As a student of the Jesuits who participated in the college of La Flèche in Lenten spiritual retreats,[8] Descartes makes use of the generic devotional model of "meditations" – more than the specifically Ignatian model of a "meal of the soul"[9] – to indicate to the reader repeated and planned commitment, the care and personal concentration required even in the case of philosophical reflection.[10] Meditating means becoming absorbed in oneself in the search for a *fundamentum inconcussum*, an *ubi consistam* that cannot be identified methodically but that, once discovered,

7 See Descartes, letter to Arnaud, 29 July 1648, in *AT* v, 219, and letter to Plempius, 3 October 1637, in *AT* i, 413.

8 See C. De Rochemonteix, *Un Collège de Jésuites aux* XVII*e et* XVIII*e siècles* (Le Mans, 1880), vol. 2, 140–2.

9 See I. de Loyola, letter to Antonio Enriques, 26 March 1554, in *Epistulae et instructiones* (Madrid, 1903–13; rpt., Rome, 1964–8), in *Monumenta Ignatiana* (Madrid, then Rome, 1894 et seq.), S.I., vol. 6, 524.

10 These specifications are provided by B. Rubridge, "Descartes's Meditations and Devotional Meditations," *Journal of the History of Ideas* 51 (1990), 27–49, where it is shown how – aside from some assonance with the *Spiritual Exercises* of Ignatius and from the rarity of the use of the term "meditations" outside the devotional field – the Cartesian text has more to do with a genre of writing than with a specific work.

allows the construction of a method, thanks also to a preparatory phase in which the "imagination" is properly excited (see *M* 26, 27).

To meditate, it is necessary to achieve "a space of untroubled leisure" (*M* 17) and from there launch an attack against one's old opinions, against the sins of one's thought. Descartes reports, however, that he "noticed quickly that it was not so easy for a man to undo his prejudices, as if he were burning his home," and that – in representing his spirit "completely naked" through imagination – he had to suffer "as if it had been a question of completely stripping himself." "His spirit seized by violent agitation," he dreamed that a strong wind dragged him, with a melon in his arm, towards a church where he usually prayed, to read in a book by the Gallo-Roman poet Ausonius the verses referring to his uncertainty about the future, but also about his *methodos*, his path: *Quid vitae sectabor iter*?[11]

Methodos

Modern science and philosophy often attribute their birth to an inaugural gesture: when Descartes, by basing knowledge on an atom of certainty, on the small spark of the *cogito*, finally succeeds in rescuing it from doubt, illusion, deceit, madness, and collapse – those sirens that seduced the Baroque mind and held it captivated. Descartes, then, represents the antagonist *par excellence* of Baroque sensibility.

The *iter* to be followed is one that – through struggle with the past and with one's own errors – leads to a purification of the spirit. In this way it reaches *maîtrise de soi*: not only in the field of the passions but also in that of knowledge, defeating once and for all, with strength of purpose, the resistance caused by the inertia of old beliefs, laziness, and daily life, and making individuals more known and familiar to themselves.[12]

The value of this "method" consists – in the presence of a discontinuous conception of time – in solidifying the series of sudden certainties and translating the simultaneity of intuition during speech that one may

11 See Descartes, *Olympica*, in *Op.* I, 3 et seq. The verse by Ausonius, which appears in the dream, is indicative of the path that the philosopher intends to follow. It is identified with the path (*iter, odos*) that leads to the truth, with the *meth-odos*. For the formal definition of method, see *R*, in *AT* v, 379. Regarding the voluntary excitation of the imagination, it is necessary, however, to point out that Descartes quickly understood the limits of this faculty. See D.L. Sepper, "Descartes and the Limits of Imagination, 1618–1630," *Journal of the History of Philosophy* 27 (1989), 379–403.

12 See Descartes, *M* 21, 22.

be aware of (following a line that unites the consistency of reasoning to preservation of identity and presence to oneself). Descartes finds himself faced with the unavoidable difficulty of explaining how an immobile piece of evidence, peaceful in itself, can infect similar ideas with truth and thus spread, with the same rate of certainty, to the conclusion of the demonstration, to the point where the initial evidence meets up with and strengthens itself. It is forced, therefore, on one hand to emphasize the evidence of the *cogito*, over-investing it with luminosity. On the other hand, it is forced to justify the permanence in discontinuous time, by means of "intellectual memory," of the contents and the logical passages of the argument. To thus legitimize the *iter* of the truth starting from the detailed evidence, he is driven to analytically derive the concept of the permanence of thought from that of substance, of *res cogitans*. And since, for Descartes, the *cogito* is the prototype of every sort of evidence, nothing is clearer than the fact that *ubi cogito, ibi sum*.

Certainty becomes truth when it is transmitted by primary and irrefutable evidence of other "infected" elements along the chain of demonstration. The cogency and persuasiveness of the argument depend on the transit of the evidence itself across all of the rings passed. Once an initial, absolutely irrefutable certainty is established, it acquires such power as to pass unharmed through every doubt and thus escape madness, evil genius, and a deceitful god. Truth and certainty then proceed in step, together, strengthening and guaranteeing each other, through *intuitus* or *inspectio mentis*, a panoramic view of the spirit that reassembles in synthetic form – according to the prevailing canons of unity of time and place even in the internal theatre of the *I* – that which otherwise ends up scattered through the analysis or randomly distributed in the course of experience. Madness does not strike the *ratio* as such, the system of connections and the consistency of reasoning, but the *intuitus* itself, the capacity to conceive of things clearly and distinctly. The transmission of thoughts can therefore follow the *regulae* or logical correctness and nevertheless end up false, because the premises of the reasoning are baseless and the initial evidence deceptive.[13]

13 Incidentally, it is not unlikely that, speaking of the foolish who believe they have "a body of glass" (*M* 18), Descartes was thinking of the protagonist of one of *Las novellas ejemplares* by Cervantes, of "El Licenciado Vidreira," who believed himself made of glass and who begged – "with very logical words and speech" – whomever he met to remain far away from him, because they could break him.

In comparing the factors that make the Baroque view of the world ambiguous, Descartes – searching for simplicity and ingenuity of viewpoint – traces a clear line of demarcation. He responds to the "Baroque" challenge through a will of truth, identifying in the immense jumble of possibilities an Archimedean point, a certainty removed from all deceit. "Those who seek for gold dig up much earth and find a little."[14] Descartes found a tiny and shining nugget with which he could redeem the mortgaged control of consciousness.[15] This richness will place all those who want it in the condition of reducing the incidence of illusions and hallucinations, restoring correct perceptions of them through a work of powerful disenchantment with the world. The price paid is that of eliminating, in all fields not covered by the certainty of the method, that ability to discriminate, that *agudeza y arte del ingenio* that Baltasar Gracián had theorized and that served to orient one in peregrinations and in the "great theater of the world," in a universe different from the fully Cartesian one of unbreakable discontinuities, voids, tortuous ravines of being, and secret and "negative places" where one encounters – as in Gracián's *Criticón* – the *cueva de la nada*, the "cave of nothing."[16]

But the tool used initially is still "baroque." It is a case (that comes to be asserted many times) of the "imagination" that must be excited so as to make itself master of its own beliefs, overcoming the doubt of existing

14 See Heraclitus, Fragment DK B22.

15 And, it is necessary to add, of morals, since logical consistency corresponds to constancy of character, the maintenance of identity in time.

16 See, in the present volume, pp. 85–6. For the developments of the idea of "peregrination" in this period, see J. Hahn, *The Origins of the Baroque Concept of* Peregrinatio (Chapel Hill, 1973). Incidentally, it is thought that the current rebirth of interest in the Baroque – in the form of the "neo-Baroque" (see C. Buci-Glucksmann, *La raison Baroque* [Paris, 1984]; Buci-Glucksmann, *La folie du voir: De l'estethique baroque* [Paris, 1986]; and O. Calabrese, *L'età neo-barocca* [Rome, 1987]) – is just a return of the removal, the rehabilitation of *juicio* and of *agudeza* as modern tools to understand a complexity of variants and of possibles that the Cartesian "method" excluded or weakened. Michel Serres has observed that while Descartes asked himself with worry how to pass through a forest, the place where the trees hide the whole, "we ask ourselves, on the contrary, with the same worry, how do we inhabit the desert?" (*Statues* [Paris, 1987], 61), this new *cueva de la nada.* Moreover, it has been noted how the idea of exactness and of mathematical interpretation – and arithmetic in particular, because it concerns the *multitudo* and not the *magnitudo* like geometry – of phenomena may be tied in Descartes, author of a *compendium Musicae,* to the model of music. See A. Pala, *Descartes e lo sperimentalismo francese 1600–1650* (Rome, 1990), particularly xi–xiii and 123 et seq.

itself. And not lacking dynamic and disturbing traits is the concept of *cogito*, of *co-agito*, related to the theory of vortexes in the physical world, in that it represents the whirlwind of thoughts, desires, and sensations that incessantly shake the soul, subjecting it to difficult trials of resistance and leading it to reject all that threatens its equilibrium, its duration in time, its grip and self-control, its *maîtrise de soi*. It is a conglomerate and unstable solution of different elements, since he who cogitates is "a thing that doubts, that understands, that affirms, that denies, that wishes to do this and does not wish to do that, and also that imagines and perceives" (*M* 27). And it is within this overwhelming whirlwind – similar to that in Descartes's dream mentioned above – that it is necessary to find both the path of life and the firm foundations of knowledge.

Hell on Earth?

The novelty of the *Principles* is that the power of the will expands well beyond evidence, truth, and good. Its "extremely broad scope" (see *P* I, 37) does not retreat before the responsibility of doing ill even when good can be seen clearly enough (but to what point is one convinced of that?) and of saying a falsehood even when the truth is intended (but up to what point does the truth manage to assert itself?). With man's capacity to err, however, his liberty also grows. Descartes does not have a punitive and self-restricting concept of will and reason. Therefore, he does not lean towards a defeat and painful subjugation of rebellious passions. At most, he aims at limiting the overwhelming power of external causes and the significant impact on the choices of blind impulses that can take control of us and deprive us of our *maîtrise*. That is, he intends to find a balance between desires and goodness, sublimating the former "in high passions": magnanimity, love, or wonder (which make the individual more free) and making the latter descend from its inaccessible Empyrean.[17]

17 Claude Bénichou has identified Descartes's intentions well in his classic book *Morales du Grand Siècle* (Paris, 1948). In Descartes, "moral perfection seems to consist of a harmony between desire and liberty. It materializes in magnanimous hearts, since desire, aiming at worthy objects, does not alienate the liberty of the *I*, which is only another name for its dignity ... It must not be forgotten that the principal inspirational reason for this morality is the will to fully enhance the *I* and to make it supreme, a sovereignty that would be compromised both by the exploding of desire and by its suffocation" (Ital. trans. *Morali del "Grand Siècle": Cultura e società nel Seicento francese* [Bologna, 1990], 20).

It is this attitude that Corneille – perhaps only later directly tied to Cartesian philosophy or, in any case, in a relationship of "pre-established harmony" with it – expresses most effectively in his *Oedipus*, where he demands of man the responsibility for his own actions and errors against an immense determinism, behind which the strong version of the anti-Pelagian idea of predestination shines through. And this despite the fact that the Corneillian hero, with Stoic traits, is proudly conscious of his own greatness even in defeat and would not tolerate the minimum affront to the heroic integrity of his own *I*:

> Quoi ? La nécessité des vertus et des vices
> D'un astre impérieux doit suivre les caprices.
> ...
>
> L'âme est donc toute esclave: une loi souveraine
> Vers le bien ou le mal incessement l'entraîne,
> Et nous ne recevons ni crainte ni désir
> De cette liberté qui n'a rien à choisir,
> ...
>
> D'un tel aveuglement daignez me dispenser,
> Le ciel, juste à punir, juste à récompenser
> Pour rendre aux actions leur peine et leur salaire
> Doit nous offrir son aide, et puis nous laissez faire.[18]

18 "What? The necessity of virtues and vices/of an imperious star that must follow whims? /.../The soul is thus a complete slave: a sovereign law/drives it incessantly towards good or bad,/and we receive neither fear nor desire/from such freedom that has nothing to choose,/.../Willingly, I deign to dispense with this;/Heaven, right to punish, right to reward,/in order to give actions their penalties and their rewards,/ must offer us its help and then let us be" (Corneille, *Oedipe*, 3.5. See also, for the idea of a "pre-established harmony," E. Cassirer, "Descartes und Corneille" in *Descartes: Lehre – Persönlichkeit – Wirkung*, 78, 88). On the model of the hero in Corneille, see A. Stegmann, *L'héroïsme cornelien: Genèse et signification,* 2 vols. (Paris, 1968). On the relationship between Descartes and Corneille, see R. Champigny, "Corneille et le *Traité des passions*," *The French Review* (New York) 26 (1952–3), 112–20; and M. Fumaroli, "L'héroïsme cornelien et l'idéal de magnanimité," in *Héroïsme et création littéraire* (Paris, 1974). On the importance of the Cartesian treatise and the subject of the passions that derive from it in Italian poetry of the same period, and in particular in Gregorio Caloprese, see G. Gronda, *Le passioni della ragione* (Pisa, 1984), 24 et seq.

Unlike Descartes, Spinoza considers the passions (once controlled) as a form of knowledge and not only as an instrument of liberty. He thus erases the Cartesian separation between soul and body and cuts their tenuous link, considering the increment or the decrement of the soul's power of existing to be parallels. The absolute primacy attributed to will by Descartes (and even earlier by Francis Bacon)[19] thus falls. Spinoza considers it by now only a phantom *facultas volendi et nolendi*, since there exist concretely *singulares volitiones*, not something called "will."

But, even considering the term in a metaphysical way, "will" does not have more breadth than "intellect," than the parallel abstraction that designates individual ideas.[20] In universal form, however, "will" indicates the faculty of affirming and denying – that is, the *conatus* "related to the mind alone."[21]

Ignorance of the doctrine of will ("which is essential to know both for theory and for the wise ordering of life")[22] is based on the confusion between images, words, and ideas. Those who, confusing ideas with images, portray themselves as *veluti picturas in tabula mutas*, as pictures in a painting, miss the fact that idea is activity, the power to affirm or deny – and not passivity, the pure impression of an imprint or a seal that external things leave on the senses and on the mind.[23] Those who mistake ideas for words "think that when they affirm or deny something merely by words contrary to what they feel, they are able to will contrary to what

19 On Bacon, who does not demonstrate anything and limits himself to telling, see Spinoza, *Ep.* 2.763: "Whatever other causes he assigns can all be readily reduced to the one Cartesian principle, that the human will is free and more extensive than the intellect, or, as Verulam more confusedly puts it [*Novum Organum* 1, aph. 49], the intellect is not characterized by its own light, but receives infusion from the will."

20 See *E* 2.48, schol.; 2.49, dem., cor. and schol. Very resolute is the thesis according to which *voluntas, et intellectus unum, et idem sunt,* from which it follows that "a particular volition and idea are one and the same thing" (*E* 2.49, cor. and dem.).

21 That is, that which does not correspond with *cupiditas* – which is *conatus* referring simultaneously to the mind and the body and, further, conscious of itself. See *E* 3.9, schol.

22 Spinoza *E* 2.49, schol.

23 From this point of view, Spinoza seems to connect himself with the argument of Plotinus against the gnoseology of Aristotle and the Stoics, who supported the hypothesis by which the senses, memory, and the "passive intellect" would receive something like an imprint from sensible, fantastic, or intelligible objects (see Plot. IV, 3–4). The *mentis imaginandi facultas* is, on the other hand, according to Spinoza, a *virtus*, a *potentia imaginandi,* and a power of memory (see *E* 2.17, schol.; 3.11 and schol.), not to mention reason, which is active by its nature.

they feel."[24] In reality, they "adapt themselves" (*acquiescent*) to false ideas only because they do not perceive the causes that make their own imaginations waver. Their idea or their false (or mutilated and confused) volition does not possess any certainty until it is contradicted by another.

This is the point asserted against Descartes through a series of elaborate argumentative passages. In fact, those who think, like Descartes, that "the will extends more widely than the intellect, and therefore is different from it"[25] are wrong, since our power to say yes or no or to suspend judgment would be infinite and unlimited, yet all human knowledge would be finite and imperfect. According to Descartes, only approval of the things we perceive establishes the truth or falsehood of perception. Experience seems to teach that the act of imagining something that is perceptually improbable does not at all imply the affirmation of its existence.

However, according to Spinoza, it is not in our power to suspend judgment with an act of will: "For when we say that someone suspends judgment, we are saying only that he sees that he is not adequately perceiving the thing. So suspension of judgment is really a perception, not free will."[26]

In themselves, the images of the mind, when they are not contrasted by antagonistic images, do not contain any error. Perceiving a winged horse only means affirming the wings of the horse: "For if the mind should perceive nothing apart from the winged horse, it would regard the horse as present to it, and would have no cause to doubt its existence nor any faculty of dissenting, unless the imagining of the winged horse were to be connected to an idea which annuls the existence of the said horse, or he perceives that the idea which he has of the winged horse is inadequate. Then he will either necessarily deny the existence of the horse or he will necessarily doubt it."[27]

In a climate marked by reflection on the nature of illusions and on borders between the perceivable world, dreaming, and madness, this Spinozan step will have vast and secret resonance until the end of the nineteenth century, when it served as a basis for Taine in *De l'intelligence*, for his theory of "antagonistic reducers" of contrasting perceptions, and for William James in his *Principles of Psychology*, in discriminating between

24 Spinoza *E* 2.49, schol.
25 Ibid.
26 Ibid.
27 Ibid.

the various "sub-universes of reality" in which the single compact world, the *universum* of the previous philosophical tradition, splits into different regions of meaning [*senso*], each endowed with its own charter, criteria of relevance, and temporal parameters.[28]

To explain how our will may be conditioned, Spinoza resorts again in a letter to the example of the dream. Alluding to a friend of the addressee who claimed to be absolutely free to write or not write a particular letter, he first cites a widespread experience: "the man ... who has doubtless experienced in dreams that he has not the power to think that he wants, or does not want, to write, and that, when he dreams that he wants to write, he does not have the power not to dream that he wants to write."[29] He then adds that the same phenomenon – described by the dream almost in a pure state – also manifests itself when awake, except in this case the mind is more tied to the variation of the situations and the corporeal states, and it does not reflect the images of the objects in the same way. From such variations of state and their comparison, which he considers as if they were all simultaneously possible, comes the convincing appearance of the existence of free will. Thus, when his correspondent's friend claims to have been induced but not forced to write the letter at a particular moment, Spinoza observes that "his mind was at the time in such a state that causes which might not have swayed him at other times – as when he is assailed by some strong emotion – were at this time easily able to sway him. That is, causes which might not have constrained him at other times did in fact constrain him then, not to write against his will, but necessarily to want to write."[30]

Knowledge of the proper doctrine of will, placing men under the guidance of reason, is "most useful and necessary to know," as it demonstrates "that we act only by God's will, and that we share in the divine nature, and all the more as our actions become more perfect and as we understand God more and more."[31] This is how our mind acquires freedom from fear and the servile hope of reward and recompense for virtue (and with that, full and tranquil bliss), because it places itself in the hands

28 See H. Taine, *De l'intelligence* [1870] (Paris, 1906), 24. Regarding this, see J. Maldidier, "Les 'reducteurs antagonistes' de Taine," *Revue Philosophique de la France et de l'Étranger* 30, no. 59 (1905), 474–86; W. James, *Principles of Psychology* (New York, 1890). For complementary aspects of Taine, see P.-F. Moreau, "Taine lecteur de Spinoza," *Revue Philosophique de la France et de l'Étranger* 62 (1987), 477–89.

29 *Ep.* 58.910.

30 Ibid.

31 E 2.49, school.

of divine nature and its laws; it relies on the rationality of everything and frees itself from the "genuine inferno" made up of the passions of sadness, desperation, envy, fear, and so on.[32] This further trains and supports, in an impartial way, that which is not in our power: good and bad fortune. It "assists us in our social relations, in that it teaches us to hate no one, despise no one, ridicule no one, be angry with no one, envy no one."[33] Finally, it suggests to politicians the way to govern citizens so that they do not serve "like slaves" but "do freely what is best."[34]

32 Ibid.

33 Ibid.

34 Ibid. See also Spinoza, *KV* 2.18.

3. The Key to All Virtues

The Lens of the Passions

In Descartes, the passions function like a magnifying glass: "[T]he passions almost always cause the goods they represent, as well as the evils, to appear much greater and more important than they are" (*PA*, art. 138). Therefore, one of the control strategies recommended with respect to them consists of scaling back, through judgment, the size of the images of desire and baseless opinions, so as to reduce them to adequate proportions and diminish their perturbing impact on intellect and will.

The distance that separates Descartes from Spinoza in this regard is noteworthy. It is no longer the case, in the latter, of eliminating the exaggerations of the imagination through a "pantographic" procedure. Given that the passions involve both "thought" and "extension," every stage of their greater comprehensibility on the part of the mind corresponds with parallel strengthening of the body (see *E* 4.4, cor.), a transition from passivity to activity, or an increase in knowledge and "virtue."

Spinoza, as optician and philosopher, seems to interpret the passions according to the model of the lens, albeit with different intentions than those shown by the author of the *Diottrica.* For Spinoza, the error to which the passions can lead does not depend on simple magnification of objects as much as on their distortion, the result of a mutilated and confused knowledge from which men try in vain to fully emancipate themselves.[1] This means that reason – and even intuitive science – are destined to meet unsurpassable limits, obstacles to their intention to represent themselves and the world in a perfectly corrected, clear,

1 See, for example, *E* 4.38, dem.

and distinct way. Their difficulties appear similar to those found by the theory and practice of optics. The inadequacy of the idea, attributable to the distortions of passion in the field of representation, appears similar to the spherical aberration of the optic plane.[2] Both are inevitable; no lens and no force will succeed in correcting them completely.

This "quasi-optical" method of considering the products of the imagination helps to explain the political and religious illusions analysed in the *Theological-Political Treatise.* The reasons why kings and the powerful are generally seen as being intrinsically endowed with superior qualities (or why the prophets assert that they perceive, by means of voices and visions, messages that other men cannot get directly) do not correspond, however, with those that lead to the belief that the sun may be only two hundred feet from us.[3]

In some respects, the line of demarcation between Spinoza and Descartes recalls (and clarifies) that between Marx and Feuerbach. In this sense, Marx also holds that the human passions or desires may generate, in the effect of an uncorrected optical illusion, the various divinities with all of their myths and attributes. The real images turn upside down like in a *camera oscura*: as is well-known, God, a creature of man, would be imaginatively transformed into man's creator. Unlike Feuerbach, however, Marx holds that such illusions cannot be erased purely through intellectual operations of reduction or of straightening the enlarged or reversed images. It is not at all sufficient to meddle with the instruments and the corrective techniques of vision to arrive at denying the reality of what one sees, even with its distortions. That is, it is not enough to publicly declare the *trompe-l'oeil* character of the religious phenomenon

---

2 See D. Parrochia, "Optique, mécanique et calcul des chances chez Huygens et Spinoza," *Dialectica* 38 (1984), 327.

3 Parocchia is of the opposite position; see ibid., 328; and see Descartes, letter to Elisabeth, 1 September 1645, in *Op.* IV, 159; and Spinoza, *E* 2.35, schol.; 4.1 schol. Holland, which had helped in the development of the telescope and of maritime measurement tools, becomes in Spinoza's time the most prestigious international centre of studies of the world of the infinitesimally small. The microscope – invented by Joan Zacharias Jansen, combining two strongly concave lenses with two strongly convex lenses, and then perfected by Leeuwenhoek – offers the intellectual stimulus and the most favourable artisan practice to the extension of optics to other fields. Together with Hermann Boeherhave, physician and botanist at the University of Leiden, Antony van Leeuwenhoek – by profession, a textile merchant in Delft – then raised himself to European fame as a microscope scientist and entomologist, succeeding in cutting a lens with a focus so short as to serve only as a microscope and further illustrating, with very accurate drawings, minute insects.

for it to essentially disappear. Casting light on its nature of unintentional deceipt, in order to decree its end, is an illusion of the second power, an overestimation of the strength of an intelligence that is abstract and still incapable of pitting itself against the "overwhelming" power of desire. As long as men are pushed by real conditions to find relative consolation or satisfaction in obedience to divinity or to their fellows that they consider superior, fearsome, or protective, religion and absolute authority will remain fundamentally unassailable for most people. To reiterate: the enlargement caused by passions or desires can, to some degree, be more limited, and the escape to the upside-down world more restrained, the more the causes of the projection towards heaven are eliminated. If the apparent randomness, ambiguity, and basic uncontrollability of events are limited, if the reasons that feed contempt for the world and for life disappear, even taking leave from reality will lose its fascination. Spinoza asserts, however (and here is the core of his "realism"), that because of the individual's relative impotence with respect to external forces, the imaginative dimension is essentially unsurpassable. It can be reduced but not eliminated. A human existence socially lacking "deformations" of the imaginations (not distorted by passions and illusions) seems completely inconceivable to him.

Proper Self-Esteem

To avoid having the passions enlarge their objects beyond measure, it is necessary, according to Descartes, to be endowed with *générosité* – that is, with a mind capable of evaluating itself and the feelings that engage it to a proper degree (with an autoscopic corrective lens), because it knows the extent and the limits of its own powers. A person endowed with it knows, on the one hand, that "nothing really belongs to him but this freedom to dispose his volitions, and that he ought to be praised or blamed for no other reason than his using this freedom well or badly," and on the other, he feels in himself "a firm and constant resolution to use it well – that is, never to lack the will to undertake and carry out whatever he judges to be best" (*PA*, art. 153).

If generosity then becomes a habit, he possesses the "key to all the other virtues," the "general remedy for every disorder of the passions."[4] In fact, it is not a case of a primitive passion but of the "most mature fruit" of the result of a slow cultivation of the will – in this "absolute, indivisible

4 *PA*, art. 161.

power" of ours – "to say yes or no." Closely connected to esteem for ourselves, it depends, therefore (not without a "baroque" element of stubbornness or faithfulness to one's most deep-rooted convictions, in contrast with the mutability of the inclinations of the moment), on secure control over what is essentially in our power: "the exercise of our free will and the control we have over our volitions."[5]

The difference between the generous person and the ordinary one does not imply any trace of contempt or marked highlighting of one's own superiority with respect to others.[6] However, even if it is otherwise justified, there is not lacking an element of supererogatory squandering of oneself, of *dépense.*[7] In fact, to the degree the generous man lacks the arrogance to esteem himself more than he should (since he is really humble, likable, and thoughtful with everyone), he strives to acquire a resolute character. Once he has taken a side, he thus follows scrupulously "even the most doubtful opinions" as if they were "quite certain" (*DM* III, 24). Though not at all rejecting *utilitas,* he is also disposed to sacrifice himself with *nonchalance* for something that is worth more than his own individual life.[8] Therefore, his attitude is not typical of the "demolition of the hero" employed by French morals of the *Grand Siècle.*[9] Each person evaluates himself in proportion to merits conferred upon him by his own free will and by the intensity of the efforts expended in commanding the passions. For the *homme généreux,* it is enough to be the "hero" only in his own eyes. He does not need an external license of nobility bestowed upon him. He knows himself (not only in the sense of the Delphic maxim), since his trained passions are placed under the vigilance of a firm and resolute will, assisted by a vigilant intellect and a shrewd judgment. For the generous man, the metric of evaluating his acts determined by free will is self-referential and lacking in external

---

5 *PA,* art. 152.

6 This is what constitutes the difference from the Aristotelian "magnanimous" man. See *Eth. Nic.* IV, 3, 1123b–1124b.

7 On the logics of *dépense,* see G. Bataille, "La notion de dépense," *La Critique Sociale* 7 (1933), 7–15, also in Bataille, *Oeuvres complètes,* vol. 1 (Paris, 1970).

8 On the absence, in the generous man, of jealousy (the inclination to preserve a good that belongs to us or that we believe belongs to us), see Descartes, *PA,* arts. 156, 167, and 182.

9 The generous man recognizes the fragility of human nature in good acts and attributes the errors of others more to ignorance than to evil (see *PA,* art. 156). The thesis of the "demolition of the hero" is explained – with regard to Pascal, the Jansenists, and later, La Rochefoucauld – by P. Bénichou, *Morales du Grand Siècle*; Ital. trans., 97 et seq.

conditioning. It depends on the esteem that, from time to time, he assigns to them himself.

The generous and intellectually aware man is one who, passing through the tricky forest of correspondence with things, always follows the straight line, taking the way that is shortest and teachable to everyone: "In this respect I would be imitating a traveler who, upon finding himself lost in a forest, should not wander about turning this way and that, and still less stay in one place, but should keep walking as straight as he can in one direction, never changing it for slight reasons even if mere chance made him choose it in the first place; for in this way, even if he does not go exactly where he wishes, he will at least end up in a place where he is likely to be better off than in the middle of the forest" (*DM* III, 24).

In Descartes, the method – the strategy of proceeding in a straight line, transforming (at worst) chance into desired order, into consistency of thought – replaces the wanderings and junctions, the labyrinths, and the allusive signs through which the previous and contemporary culture loved to move. Against the Baroque model of excess for the sake of excess, he introduces a common measure – a method, essentially, in which free will, the virtual uncertainty principle, chooses to define itself according to an order of facts that is no longer the Augustinian *ordo amoris*, but pure *ordo rationis*. The ex-pupil of the fathers of La Flèche also departs from the practical teaching of the founder of the Company of Jesus from this point of view: that of leaving the most important decisions to an external, rationally unjustifiable will, to a decider whose "facts" come from a superior authority through faith.[10]

Most men are often subject to losing the arrangement and course of the will because of the continuous movement, fluctuations, or *co-agitare* of the mind destabilized by the "kinetic" rush of the passions of the soul.[11] The generous man, on the other hand, like a good pilot, is capable of controlling the boat of this unique soul.[12] He does not even need to resort to the dangerous expedient of dividing and controlling his feelings.[13] In cleverly playing them against each other, he risks triggering

10 See, in the present volume, pp. 85–6.

11 For the etymology of *cogito*, offered by Varro and Augustine, see, respectively, *Ling. lat.* VI, 6, 21–4 and *conf.* X, 11, 18.

12 Descartes is opposed to the Platonic-Aristotelian tri-partition of the soul. See *PA*, art. 47.

13 Ibid., art. 48.

a new civil war of the soul, without intending to do so. The only "real arms" of the will are the "firm and determinate judgments bearing upon the knowledge of good and evil" (*PA*, art. 48) and not the inaccuracies of apprentice wizards who unconsciously foment disorder within themselves. The non-violent *dressage* of the passions on the part of the will implies that the "Cartesian chariot" of the soul also knows how to educate the "black horse," trying to understand it and smooth the reasons for its resistance, and gradually rediscovering the primitive good character that comes from a perverted impulse to self-preservation that assumed evil traits.

In achieving the calm wisdom of magnanimity and of controlled and strict joy, the philosopher, now near death, finds the response he was looking for in the agitated "dream of a night in Swabia." The upward path to take is mapped out by the will, articulating and regulating the temporal course of human conduct, establishing its rhythms in "beating down" or "lifting up," in acts or omissions. This will was slowly educated to convert the "afflictions" that exhausted others into opposite energy, delivered to increase its own happiness and radiate its light even on others:

> But it seems to me that the difference between the greatest souls and those that are lower and common consists, principally, in that common souls give in to their passions, and they are happy or unhappy according to whether the things that happen to them are pleasant or unpleasant. The others have reasoning that is so strong and powerful that, although they also have passions (and even passions that are often more violent than those of the common souls) reason always remains their mistress, and that the same afflictions serve them and contribute to the perfect happiness that they enjoy in this life.[14]

Although Descartes does not place the social hierarchy of the soul even remotely in discussion,[15] it is the good exercise of one's own passions and not birth or rank that distinguishes men on this level. The process of "democratization" of Aristotelian magnanimity – which in Spain will become a model for the "gentleman soldier" and for nobility

14 Descartes, Letter to Elisabeth, 18 May 1645, in *Op.* IV, 138.

15 See, for example, the attack against the political and religious reformers who immerse themselves in public affairs without having the right, which is legitimately reserved to the constituted authorities.

of blood – will finally be developed by Spinoza. As he can no longer base his discussion on free will, his account of generosity presupposes only the rational desire to be useful to others without pointlessly hurting oneself. Generosity comes forth from the *homo clausus*, who experienced his isolation in the world without, however, making a habit of closeness with others.[16] It is therefore distinct from *animositas*, that is to say from strength or determination in preserving one's own being according to criteria that are, themselves, rational.[17] In this sense, it contrasts with the hesitation that his contemporaries attributed to Louis XIII and that found a suitable reaction in the revival of Stoic *pathos* for will.

The Theatre of the *I*

In Descartes, generous men are capable of working, within the reality of their own lives, the catharsis of pain into pleasure experienced in the theatre. Even at an advanced age, looking calmly at events, Descartes continued to follow the path of the youthful choice that led him to enlist in the army of Maurice of Nassau and take on the "generous" risk of a war that had become ever more thick with dangers, to be able to admire the living illustrations of the "great book" of the world.[18] The perception of the vanity and the appearance of things on this immense stage – far from inducing his melancholy – strengthens in him the desire to bend "fortune" to will, to hoard the good and the joy that can be gained, seizing the opportunity for happiness, the propitious moment, the *bonne-heure* that can be distinguished from *béatitude* because it does not depend on us.[19] Once *nos volontés* are trained, it is just a matter of awaiting the results, whatever they may be, observing from without, like spectators of a show in which one is always a protagonist.

16 For the concept of *homo clausus*, see Elias, *Über den Prozess der Zivilisation*, vol. 1.

17 See Spinoza, *E* 3.59, schol.

18 Maurice and William of Nassau had introduced, in the art of war, the technique of "volley" shooting: placing men in long rows so that the first discharged their rifles and the second reloaded them, on the basis of a model derived from the continuous launching of javelins by the ancient Romans, also described by Justus Lipsius (see W. Reinhardt, "Humanismus und Militarismus: Antike-Rezeption und Kriegshandwerk in der oranischen Heeresform," in *Krieg und Frieden im Horizont des Renaissance Humanismus*, ed. F.J. Worstbrock (Waerheim, 1968), 195 et seq.

19 Descartes, letter to Elisabeth, 4 and 18 August 1645, in *Op*. IV, 147–55.

From the errors committed, one learns the lesson calmly. Moreover, one notices more easily the mixing of good and bad, the stratifications and tensions that human souls manage to keep together:

> Thus, on the one hand, considering themselves to be immortal and capable of receiving very great contentment, and, on the other hand, considering that they are joined to mortal and fragile bodies which are subject to many infirmities and which cannot fail to perish in a few years, they do nearly everything that is in their power to render fortune favorable in this life, but nevertheless they esteem this life so little with respect to eternity that they give events no more consideration than we do events in comedies. Just as those sad and lamentable stories which we see represented on a stage often entertain us as much as the happy ones, even though they bring tears to our eyes, in this way the greatest souls of which I speak draw a satisfaction in themselves from all the things that happen to them, even the most annoying and insupportable.[20]

Looking at oneself from a proper distance, through the introspective practice of meditative reflection that is almost "from without," and concentrating one's energies on the virtual focus of the reflection, increase the capacity for self-control in that they suspend the involuntary familiarity of each person with himself, weaning him from truisms and making him "almost master" of the beliefs inherited from childhood (*M* 21).

Reaching *maîtrise de soi*, and the sense of the honour and duty completed, offer to such men a compensatory satisfaction for the sufferings endured, a state of mind that makes even death "agreeable" in the name of values (like friendship or the common good) higher than mere self-preservation, which may be dictated by fear. In them, "patience" can become strength, and suffering can become activity: "When they feel pain in their bodies they make an effort to support it patiently, and this show of their strength is agreeable to them, in this way, seeing their friends under some great affliction, they feel compassion at the friend's ill fortune and do everything possible to deliver the friend from it, and they do not fear even exposing themselves to death to this end if it is necessary."[21]

---

20 Descartes, letter to Elisabeth, 18 May 1645, in *AT* IV, 202; *CE* 87.
21 Ibid.

The Goodness of the Passions

Descartes defuses the subversive potential, the disturbances, and the disorientations of the passions, turning rather to the power of will, but not to that of a tyrannical and monolithic *I.* However, exalting the propulsive function of feelings within the general economy of the soul, he places himself in contrast with some robust dogmatic traditions of Christianity (in particular, with the Calvinist orthodoxy of the Dutch church), but he also places himself in an involuntary, remote, and embarrassing agreement with the much more rash claims of the Bruno of the *Eroici furori.*[22] Although lacking immediate cognitive value,[23] the passions, for those who know how to weigh them, are the spice of life: "Examining them, I found nearly all of them good, and so useful to this life that our soul would not have reason to want to remain joined to its body for a single moment, if it could not feel them."[24]

The most zealous theologians refer to his concept of will and, later, to his theory of the passions to accuse Descartes of Pelagianism – that is, of not believing in the corruption of human nature following the original sin. Descartes does, indeed, give inordinate space to the freedom, goodness, and autonomy of the will of men and, conversely, a limited or nonexistent role to the grace and intervention of God in the world.[25]

With these attacks, Descartes touches – without being dragged to the centre – the outer rings of the vortex agitating minds because of the renewed arguments over Pelagianism. Revived indirectly by Molina at the end of the sixteenth century, it was now discussed with greater virulence following the publication of Jansen's *Augustinus.*[26] Beyond the strictly

22 On the problem of *furor* in Bruno, see S. Filippini, "Connaissance de la fureur," *La Nouvelle Revue Française* 424 (May 1988), 78–84.

23 See Descartes, *PA*, art. 28.

24 Descartes, letter to Chanut, 1 November 1646, in *Op.* IV, 204.

25 On these accusations, see M.E. Scribano, *Da Descartes a Spinoza: Percorsi della teologia razionale nel Seicento* (Milan, 1988), particularly 15–23. Also playing on the fact that the Jesuits represented the most strenuous defenders of free will, some of his adversaries were pushed to the point of slander, spreading the word that he was just a Jesuit in disguise, that he had received the charge to convert high-placed persons to the Catholic church.

26 See L. de Molina, *Concordia liberi arbitri cum Gratiae donis Divinae, Praescentia, Providentia, Praedestinatione et Reprobatione* (Antwerp, 1595 [Lisbon, 1588]). For an account of the premises of these debates by a contemporary of Descartes and Spinoza, see G.V. Vossius, *Historia de Controversiis, quas Pelagius eiusque reliquiae moverunt, libri septem* (Amsterdam, 1655).

theological contents and the revival of subjects already widely debated in the times of Augustine or Luther, now placed in play – more or less explicitly – is the right of men to "make" history, discharging God from part of His responsibilities.[27] It is a case of letting individuals, and the human race as a whole, educate themselves to become adults, relying more on their own strengths and using their own errors as experience. One senses the need to emancipate oneself from the omniscient vigilance of the divine *hegemonikon*, from the panoramic gaze that radiates from the celestial citadel.[28]

27 For this last hypothesis, see the chapter "Geschichte machen zur Entlastung Gottes" in H. Blumenberg, *Säkularisierung und Selbstbehauptung* (Frankfurt, 1974), 64–74 (a volume driven by Nietzsche's saying "Science comes into being when the gods are not thought of as good.")

28 In an age of "Christians without a church," in a Europe torn by confessional divisions and threatened in its values by the evident de-Christianization of consistent segments of the population, social and scientific "progress" is certainly eminently promoted also by the neo-Pelagian reduction of the role of grace and by the greater awareness of the liberty that results from it. Multiple elements contribute to the assertion of such progress, elements that have little in common with religion, with theology, and with the ambiguous concept of "secularization." Without doubt, however, this also passes through this traumatic episode of the *morale du Grand Siècle*: its polarization between revived "Pelagianism" and Jansenist and Heugenot rigorism. As a more general hypothesis, one could advance the suspicion that "the spirit of capitalism" – raised by Calvinist worry over predestination – may not constitute the only patrimonial axis of progress. Also playing a legitimate role is the achieved awareness of lawfulness and man's right to expand the range of subjective liberty and to learn to guide himself with greater autonomy, "trying and trying again." And all this so that the future can be better than the present and the present than the past, in the secret hope that the apocalyptic apparition of the final catastrophe and the coming of the Day of Judgment may always be put off. On these subjects, more generally, see L. Kołakowski, *Chrétiens sans Église: La conscience religieuse et le lien conféssionel au* XVIIe *siècle*, French trans. from the Polish (Paris, 1959); H. Jonas, *Augustin und das paulinische Freiheitsproblem: Ein philosophischer Beitrag zur Genesis der christlich-abendländischen Freiheitsidee* [1930] (Göttingen, 1965), particularly 36 et seq.; and F. Chanu, *La civilisation de l'Europe classique* (Paris, 1966), 458–9, which calculates that at the end of the sixteenth century, 60 per cent of the European population was Catholic and nearly all the remaining 40 per cent was Protestant. The Jesuit priest Garasse further doubled the number of libertines estimated by Mersenne to around fifty thousand for Paris alone. See F. Garasse, *La doctrine curieuse des beaux esprits de ce temps ou pretendus tels combattue et renversée* (Paris, 1623), 783.

A Small Bloodletting

In rejecting the anesthesia of the passions and supporting free will even against the evidence of truth or goodness, was Descartes really "Pelagian"? And in highlighting the primacy of *générosité* was he, as was often said, in favour of an aristocratic individualism? Or is it instead true that he considers this virtue an affection of a socializing of nature that blocks envy or "contempt for anyone" (see *PA*, art. 154)?

In Descartes, like Spinoza (yet in a much less articulated and visible way), "love which is purely intellectual or rational," disentangling itself from love as a "passion," leads the individual gradually to a joyful conformity with the good. At the highest level, he succeeds in joining his own will to divine will, to which he calmly entrusts his own life. However, this projective identification on the part of man (in whom human will becomes stronger through its adaptation to divine will) demands a long soldiering of the soul and a precise understanding, since "many other passions, such as joy, sadness, desire, fear, and hope, mingle in various ways with love and thus prevent us from discovering exactly what constitutes it."[29] Only following repeated efforts can each person begin to

29 Letter to Chanut, 1 February 1647, in *Op.* IV, 209 and *PL* 209, 211. See the other letter to the same addressee of 6 June 1647, in *Op.* IV, 229–31, which deals with the question of the reasons that push us to love someone at first sight (for which is also given as a physiological reason the permanence of certain "folds" in the brain produced by the first impression). In the same letter, Descartes tells of a cross-eyed girl that he knew and loved as a child, that led him to have immediate sympathy for people with the same defect). For other aspects of the framing of this elaborate missive of 1 February, called a *dissertation sur l'amour* (see A. Baillet, *Vie de Monsieur Des-Cartes*, vol. 2 [Paris, 1691; rpt., Hildesheim, 1972], 309) and destined to be read by Queen Christina, see F. Heidsieck, "L'amour selon Descartes d'apres la lettre à Chanut du 1er février 1647 (Commentaire)," *Revue philosophique de la France et de l'Étranger* 97 (1972), 421–36, which highlights how Descartes, going beyond Freud – in going back in time to before the "trauma of birth" and of the attachment to the mother's breast – identifies in "nourishment" the first object of love (see 427–8 and, in this volume, pp. 36–8). Further noteworthy in this letter is the Cartesian observation that one does not suffer because of love: the pain comes from the passions that accompany it, "from rash desires and from ill-founded hopes" (letter to Chanut, 1 February 1647, *PL* 216). The subject of the passion of love is treated here also through multiple references to modern and ancient literature (for example, to Seneca's *Hercules furens*). For an implicit comparison with the contemporaneous concepts of love (Descartes is, for example, far from attributing Brunian primacy to love), see G. Bruno, *De vinculis in genere*, in *Opera latine conscripta* (Stuttgart, 1961), vol. 3, 697: *vinculum quipped vinculorum amor est.* See also L.K. Horowitz, *Love and Language: A Study on the Classical French Moral Writers* (Columbus, 1977) and J.M. Pelous, *Amour précieux, amour gallant* (Paris, 1980).

distinguish sensual love from intellectual love and understand that this consists in turning to God, saying (as in the Our Father), "your will be done" (and not mine separated from yours).

In this light, pains and pleasures, seemingly distributed at whim by "fortune" (in Spinozan terms, by a necessity that is not understood, by a linking of events that eludes us), appear as a temporal series of opportunities that God offers to each person's free will, in a performance in which He certainly knows the plot and the ending, but in which He leaves full responsibility for its development to the actors.

Our ephemeral and insignificant existence is separated by an insurmountable gap from eternal divine omnipotence, just as our living suspended between being and nothing does not yet participate in the greater fullness of being that the divine ruler's mercy and justice can guarantee. Thus the attitude is absurd of those (the numerous atheists and libertines that Mersenne was complaining about?) who, instead of expressing their own gratitude, display an envy or even a will so impious as to transform itself into a desire to dethrone God, to get rid of him in order to replace him in his role.[30]

While for the ancients, piety is justice towards the gods, for Descartes it represents something more. It is a sort of humble magnanimity that actively recognizes the disproportion in the comparison between God and man and calmly admits God's invincible superiority. The generous man, therefore, has faith in it, a faith not based on passive submission, on a feudal order projected into the heavens, on respect for hierarchical authority, but on the strong will to conform to something more perfect. In following these principles, one finds *joye* more intense and "extraordinary" as the *maîtrise de soi* – giving in to the sovereignty of being – increases instead of decreases: "If a man meditates on these things and understands them properly he is filled with extreme joy. Far from being so injurious and ungrateful to God as to want to take His place, he thinks that the knowledge with which God has favored him is enough by itself to make life worthwhile. Uniting himself entirely to God in volition, he loves Him so perfectly that he desires nothing at all except that His will should be done."[31] The intellectual love of God (who is "a mind, or thinking substance" and therefore must be loved through a knowledge

30 This is probably reminiscent of the seventeenth thesis of Luther, according to which *non potest homo naturaliter velle deum esse deum*, precisely because he would like to be it himself: *Immo vellet se esse deum et deum non esse deum.*

31 Letter to Chanut, 1 February 1647, in *Op.* IV, 211 and *PL* 213.

capable of increasing gradually to infinity) can, ultimately, become passion again – solid passion, filtered by intelligence. In the letter to Chanut of 1 February 1647, Descartes "make[s] bold" to say "that with regard to the present life, it is the most delightful and useful passion possible and can even be the strongest, though not unless we meditate very attentively, since we are continually distracted by the presence of other objects."[32]

Note that God's love, supported only by the force of our nature (i.e., not elicited by grace), constitutes the most "useful" passion. In fact, it is not founded on the rejection of oneself, or absolute sacrifice. Descartes does not contrast (as happened since Plato's *Euthyphro* and Theophrastus's *De pietate*, with themes that then pass through Porphyry in Christian thought) the impiousness of those who transform the relationship with God into a utilitarian exchange of favours, into a market, with the piety of those who trust in Him and are grateful for whatever the divinity may grant them. In Descartes, utility and gratitude correspond. Strengthening oneself in joy is adapting oneself to God's will, to his "decrees" (we can clearly see here the limits of every interpretation of Cartesian thought that insists unilaterally on the Promethean "human, too human" roll of will in Descartes). The philosopher of the power of will shows here how it may rest on a broader, infinite base to become effective. Only abandoning the habit developed in childhood of loving oneself like everything and learning instead to love oneself in everything – that is, to recognize oneself uniquely as part of a whole to which one desires to be joined (and not as a totality, as little gods), is it possible to strengthen one's own will in joy: "It is the nature of love to make one consider oneself and the loved one as a single whole of which one is a part; and to transfer the care one previously took of oneself to the preservation of this whole. One keeps for oneself only a part of one's care, a part which is great or little in proportion to whether one thinks oneself a larger or smaller part of the whole to which one has given one's affection."[33]

This grateful entrusting of divine will to love will procure for events and the way of living them an additional gift of meaning, one that will make us capable of looking both faces of Fortune in the eye. Further, eliminating the fears of life and the dread of death will even make

32 Ibid., *Op.* IV, 210 and *PL* 212.
33 Ibid., *Op.* IV, 213 and *PL* 215.

earthly existence more enjoyable. The Pascalian "days of affliction" (see *P*, n. 196 = n. 174) will thus pass calmly for each person:

> Henceforth, because he knows that nothing can befall him which God has not decreed, he no longer fears death, pain, or disgrace. He so loves God's decree, he esteems it so just and so necessary, and is so fully aware of the need to subject himself to it, that even if he expects it to bring death or some other evil, he would not will to change it even if, *per impossibile,* he could do so. He does not refuse evils and afflictions because they come to him from divine providence; still less does he refuse the permissible goods or pleasures he may enjoy in this life, since they too come from God. He accepts them with joy, without any fear of evils, and his love makes him perfectly happy.[34]

This attitude explains one of the reasons why Descartes – despite being a proponent of control of self and of nature – commits in the famous third maxim of the *Discourse on Method* "to try always to master myself rather than fortune, and change my desires rather than the order of the world" (*DM* III, 25). These words do not imply any rejection of the exercise of the will and the *maîtrise* of the self (in fact, they assume them). Nor do they prefigure a planned escape from the world. Pure and simple recognition of a disorder and an irrationality of the political sphere do not descend from the autonomy of the order of the world with respect to the individual's desires.[35] It is true that in Descartes, the authority of the evidence does not yield to the evidence of authority, but the image of a Cartesian political theory that makes "possible a society composed more of *individuals* than of *members*; that is, a democracy, a concept more philosophical than political," is anachronistic or specious.[36]

---

34 Ibid., *Op.* IV, 211 and *PL* 213.

35 According to P. Guenancia, *Descartes et l'ordre politique* (Paris, 1983) (which broadens and radicalizes theses of Koyré and of Gouhier), this would fortunately allow the individual a greater liberty than what any rational regulation of the state could grant him.

36 Ibid., 6. On the negative evaluation of some widespread attitudes in democratic states, see Descartes, letter to Elisabeth, 10 May 1647, in *Op.* IV, 222, where he asserts that, in them, one respects "not the probity and virtue, but the beard, the voice, and the manner of the theologians, so that those who are the most shameless and who know how to shout the loudest have the most power … even when as to grant greater power to the impudent and to those who cry out the most … even when they are the least right."

The relatively modest development that the political dimension has in Descartes may suggest different hypotheses of integration of this presumed "lacuna" (but why should philosophers speak of everything?). In the end, Descartes thinks only that "it is up to the rulers, or to those authorized by them, to profess to meddle in the habits of others."[37] Neither the attribution of an irrational nature to the political order nor the primacy of the individual with respect to the whole of society comes from his explicit statements. He does not need to superimpose extraneous questions and different levels of speech. When, although recognizing the due dedication of the individual to the whole, Descartes denies that one must complete supererogatory or even useless sacrifices,[38] this does not mean that he wants to exempt individuals from their political obligations. According to his strong conviction, one can (and, in fact, one must) go towards "certain death" if the good being defended is greater than the individual life. Then the sacrifice requested from the individual should not be greater than the fear of drawing "a little blood from one's arm to improve the health of the rest of the body."[39] Descartes affirmatively resolves the problem posed by La Boétie: is it permissible to sacrifice oneself for others when one's own usefulness consists of the preservation of the beloved object, of loving something that is more important for the individual than life (which raises, however, the ambiguous problem of relying on a "supreme will")?

The need to be able to make use of a broader space of movement in the search for the truth meets its personal and historical limit in the adherence of the philosopher to revealed truths and constituted authorities. The still-important protection of the "negative liberty" of individuals who are generous and capable of self-control before the intrusiveness of power, then, has precious little in common with the notions of "democracy" and "individualism." It is true that the doubts about Descartes's

37 Letter to Chanut, 20 November 1647, in *Op.* IV, 233.

38 See letter to Elisabeth, 15 September 1645, in *Op.* IV, 162 and *PL* 172: "And the interests of the whole, of which each of us is a part, must always be preferred to those of our individual personality – with measure, of course, and discretion, because it would be wrong to expose ourselves to a great evil to procure only a slight benefit to our kinsfolk or our country."

39 Letter to Chanut, 1 February 1647, in *Op.* IV, 213 and *PL* 215. The discussion of sacrifice of oneself for the prince or for one's own country occurs in the environment of love – that is, in joining voluntarily with what is felt to be a good. The passage noted above continues: "Every day we see examples of this love, even in persons of low condition, who give their lives cheerfully for the good of their country or for the defense of some great person they are fond of."

"sincerity" and his stated use of "masks" lead to the belief that he may pay an homage to the polities or the traditions and laws of his own country that is lukewarm and even less keen than that given by Montaigne to the customs of the people, the caste, and the family into which he was born.[40] In the latter, the scepsis is lacking a consistent part of its targets, placing them away from a powerful taboo. For him, exorcism of chaos and civil war means – more than a mass – the partial sacrifice of the intellect and silence imposed upon doubt. A stronger attachment to local and national traditions overcompensated for the reason for this rejection. "Provisional" Cartesian morals substitutes this sacred, protective fence of laws, customs, and prohibition of criticism for the most neutral interlude of suspension of judgment: a suspension that is not only tactical or defensive, but made necessary by the intrinsic difficulty or impossibility of making use, in moments that cannot be put off, of the acting on knowledge sufficient to determine the will for something better. It is not, however, a case of eternal suspension. Reason's entry into these intervals is not prohibited. Thanks to the *Passions of the Soul*, Cartesian morals become definitive, to a large degree.

40 There is no need to exaggerate in mechanically extending to the ethical and political spheres the image of the "philosopher with the mask." More than dissimulation or a (perhaps "fake" and backwards) rhetoric of truth (as is intended, in an acute but excessively sophisticated way, by J.D. Lyons, "Rhétorique du discours cartésien," *Cahiers de la Littérature du* XVII*e siècle* 8 [1986], 125–45; H. Caton, *The Origin of Subjectivity: An Essay on Descartes* [New Haven, 1973]; and J.L. Nancy, *Ego sum* [Paris, 1979]), it is necessary to think about the desire for peace in the private search (however publicly visible it may be) compared with "the inconstancy of the worldly *habitus*" (J.-M. Monnoyer, *La pathétique cartésienne*, 102 n.).

4. Medicine of the Passions

The Fumes from the Furnace

Having cleanly separated the soul from the body, Descartes is forced to consider will as an instrument extraneous to the body – one able, however, to modify the passions and colonize the boundary zone between body and soul. The problematic link between soul and body, will and passions, is offered by the *petite glande* or Gland H, as it is called in the *Treatise of Man* (it deals with the pineal gland or *conarium*, the only solid part of the brain, which can be likened to the form of a pine cone), whose functions are still not completely clear. The particles of the animal spirits fluctuate in a cavity like a "body attached only by threads and sustained in the air by the force of fumes leaving a furnace," and they now constitute the basis of the passions.[1] Second, the small gland is called upon to build a bridge between the mechanical-pneumatic movements of the body (particularly the heart and lungs) and the free capacity of the mind to come to a stop. In this way, it becomes capable of sensing *les esprits réfléchis de l'image*, orienting itself, establishing a link between the will and the "vital spirits," and thus suspending those passions of the soul in which the movements of the spirits themselves are translated, waiting for a decision or act of consent to their being further carried. In any event, it is a vehicle and not the seat of the representations of the soul.

Spinoza asks himself how "such a great man" could have believed that, through this gland, the mind is capable of moving the body simply

1 Descartes, *Treatise of Man*, §75. See also *PA*, art. 34. The name of Gland H was derived by Descartes from the anatomical tables of Caspar Bauhin, *Anatomiae amphtheatrum* (Frankfurt, 1605), where it is indicated that way in figure x, p. 167.

because it wants to, just as he could have connected every single act of will to its movement (e.g., the will to look at a distant object is connected to dilation of the pupil). And he is almost astonished that a philosopher who had often blamed scholastics for resorting to hidden qualities "should adopt a theory more occult than any occult quality. What, I ask, does he understand by the union of mind and body? What clear and distinct conception does he have of thought closely united to a certain particle of matter?" (*E* 4, pref.).

From Spinoza's point of view, the attempt is also destined to fail because Descartes makes use of the will as *conatus*, as an effort "related to the mind alone," instead of as the wider notion of *cupiditas*, or conscious appetite, attributable simultaneously to the mind and the body (*E* 3.9, schol.). Like other men when they say that "human actions depend on the will," he is also a victim of "fragmentary and confused ideas" typical of the imagination (*E* 2.35 and schol.). In fact, separating the soul from the body, none of them realize that "these are mere words without any corresponding idea. For none of them knows what the will is and how it moves the body" (ibid.). Attributing a mysterious and weak internal "cause" to the link between soul and body, even Descartes forgot that man is not "an empire within an empire," but is subject to the overwhelming superiority of multiple external causes.

In the context of this explanation, the nature of the passions in Descartes becomes ambiguous. To what point is it permissible to speak of *passions de l'âme* and not of the body – or of both, given that there are "exterior signs" of emotions, endowed with a certain automatism (like "the expressions of the eyes and the face, changes in color, trembling, listlessness, fainting, laughter, tears, groans and sighs" [see *PA*, arts. 112–35]), that we cannot avoid hiding at first?[2]

2 See *PA*, art. 47, regarding the impulse to flee, on which the will intervenes. But the same observation could be made of blushing in the case of shame or for going pale following a fight. The separation of the soul from the body – beyond constituting a move that increases the *chances* of a more complete *maîtrise* – diminishes in Descartes the physiognomic interest shown by Cureau de la Chambre or by the traditional sources for expression of the passions. On this latter point, and on the limits attributed to Descartes's use of the method, applied to epistemology, of explaining the invisible by means of the visible, see (for some notes in a different context) P. Galison, "Descartes's Comparison: From the Invisible to Visible," *Isis* 75 (1984), 311–26. Against all reductionism, Guéroult insists rightly on the double register, physiological and psychological, of the passions (see M. Guéroult, *Descartes selon l'ordre des raisons* [Paris, 1975], vol. 2, 40), but he neglects perhaps the nature of their solidarity with the body, with which there is undoubtedly communication, such that what is passion

Furthermore, there are even prenatal passions, felt confusedly by the human fetus in immediate relationship with pure corporeal disposition. In a quadrilateral of fundamental passions that mark the individual from the time of his intrauterine life, the first passion experienced chronologically must be, for Descartes, not wonder, but joy. In the letter to Chanut of 1 February 1647, he offers for his hypothesis a metaphysical explanation, one that is hardly sustainable and to some degree "Pelagian." Highlighting the positive elements of man's existence from his beginnings at the expense of the tragic ones, he holds that it is inadmissible that the soul "was put in the body at a time when the body was not in a good condition; and a good condition of the body naturally gives us joy."[3] For the other three passions (love, sadness, and hate) the philosopher resorts, instead, to a frankly physiological model. If, in fact, "the matter of our body is in a perpetual flux like the water in a stream, and there is always need for new matter to take its place"[4] in order to be well disposed, the body must receive proper nutrition. Thus, when one is united "voluntarily" with this new material, he feels love for it. When the food is insufficient or lacking, he feels sadness. When it is unsuitable, he feels hate. The destiny of the passions is already in part foreshadowed

---

in the soul is action in the body. After all, the interaction between the body and soul of man begins in the fetus, as the lack of food affects the future attitude of the individual. See Descartes, *Primae Cogitationes circa Generationem Animalium* (1630), in *AT* XI, 505–37. As Descartes writes to Newcastle, 23 November 1646, animals, however – as machines – do not possess passions (see *AT* IV, 573–6 and, for a historical framework, P. Dibon, "Le probleme de l'âme des bêtes chez Descartes et ses premier disciples hollandais" [1954], in *Regards sur la Hollande du siècle d'or*, 662 et seq.). Besides, he adds, writing to Henry Moore in a letter of 5 February 1649, the greatest prejudice that we have retained since childhood is the belief that animals think (see *AT* V, 276–7). Separating life from the soul, Descartes clearly distances himself from traditions that made the soul a vital principle external to the body (see Plat., *Phaedo* 105 C–D; *Tim.* 69A–70A; and Arist., *De an.* II, 412a–b). Denying a soul to the animals, he tries to explain the body through the body, according to a medical model that makes of the heat that burns in the heart a "fire without light" – similar to fermenting hay or wine – "the principle of life" (see, for example, *PA*, art. 107 and, in general, A. Bitpol-Hespériès, *Le principe de vie chez Descartes* (Paris, 1990), which also insists on the Cartesian sense, since 1632, of the model of blood circulation explained by Harvey in the *Exercitatio de motu cordis et sanguinis in animalibus*, which substitutes the previous, accredited idea of the heart as an organ that, like the Nile, irrigates the tissues, depositing in them its nutritional silt).

3 Letter to Chanut, 1 February 1647, in *Op.* IV, 208 and *PL* 210.

4 Ibid.

before birth. The physical constitution of the fetus and the mother, the nutrition transmitted, and the state of health influence the fundamental texture of the future passions.

The response to the reasons why passions of the body are not given beyond those of the soul (because "what is a passion in the soul is usually an action in the body" – *PA*, art. 2) does not directly affect the dominant role Descartes attributes to the will. The fact remains, however, that the "psychosomatic" point of view of reciprocal interference between body and soul appears less reliable than the derivation of the passions from the body, justifiable by means of dependence on "animal spirits."[5] In fact, what does it mean to assert that the passions of the soul are "caused, maintained and strengthened by some movement of the spirits" or that voluntary acts are absolutely under the power of the soul and "can be changed only indirectly by the body" (*PA*, arts. 27, 41)? In this sense, Rorty's otherwise acute comparison between the passions in Descartes and the "flesh" in Paul is not completely convincing.[6]

If the reference to the Pauline idea of the "flesh" does not succeed in situating the specificity of Descartes's position, a clearer vision of it can emerge from comparison with Hobbes. In the English philosopher's materialistic monism, the passions are all passions of the body, attributable to alterations originated in the brain by images and then transmitted to the heart, the blood, and the vital spirits. They depend, then, on figments of good and evil caused by objects that are known (see *DH* XII, 1 et seq.). In a manner diametrically opposed to that of Descartes, however, they are absolutely uncontrollable, since they correspond with the will itself (in fact, this is just the final appetite or the final fear, caused by the search for pleasure or the flight from pain). Their energy derives from small movements of the internal effort (*conatus* or *endeavour*) that lead in every instant to deliberation taken under the sign of necessity, that is to the clearest repudiation of free will.[7] To the objections of the defenders of free will, according to whom in this case education and recommendations are of no use, Hobbes replies by asserting that they contribute to creating precedents and models that become de facto reasons for acting

5 For some points, see M. di Marco, "Spiriti animali e meccanicismo fisiologico in Descartes," *Physis* 13 (1971), 21–70.

6 See R. Rorty, *Philosophy and the Mirror of Nature* (Princeton, 1979).

7 See Hobbes, *El.* 96; *De corp.* III, 15 (p. 177).

(see *Quaest.* 261 et seq.). Any claim of perfect self-control over the passions is therefore contradictory, even if it may be possible to make better use of necessity by multiplying the reasons (efficient and not final causes) of acting and orienting action preventively through the totality of conjectures based on experience, *expectatio rerum similium iis rebus quas jam experti sumus.*[8] The conflict does not take place between passions and reason but, on the one hand, between adequate and inadequate means of self-preservation and, on the other, between individual needs and obedience to laws sanctioned by an authority. What interests Hobbes is removing study of the passions from traditional rhetorical patterns of classification or individual regulation to arrive at calculating and disciplining them publicly (self-control, if it does not affect political relationships, is merely a private matter). Once the passions have been placed – like Spinoza, but with opposite consequences – in relation to external causes, morals assumes "the dimension of the means and not of the end." In this way, the instrument of achieving one's desires becomes the state.[9] In Hobbes, the ruler's "thus I will and thus I command" (*DC* XIV, in *EW* II, 183) occupies at least part of the space that, in Descartes, was given to the will of the individual.

If, for Descartes, bodies are just machines, then the passions of the soul assume, as physical support, "a sort of combustion engine" represented by the heart that alternately swells and empties itself of blood or (if you will) a type of pneumatic system of transmission of the feelings similar to what, in Hellenic Alexandria, moved the automatons of Ctesibius and Hero of Alexandria or that, in the age of Descartes, were used as a propellant for the metal eagles that the artisans of Nuremberg succeeded in making fly on the occasion of the visit of the emperors. From this point of view, the passions – knowledge of which is essential to determination of the supreme good[10] – form a field of opaque forces difficult to become aware of because of its proximity to the mysterious intersection between *res cogitans* and *res extensa.* They are part, therefore, of "the perceptions which the close alliance between the soul and the body renders confused and obscure" (*PA*, art. 28). Consequently, every

8 See Hobbes, *De corp.* I, 2 (p. 3) and, on this side of experience in relation to "prudence" (the side lacking in political value), see G. Rossini, *Natura e artificio nel pensiero di Hobbes* (Bologna, 1988).

9 See C.A. Viano, "Analisi della vita emotiva e tecnica politica della filosofia di Hobbes," in *Rivista critica di storia della filosofia,* XVII (1962), 379 et seq.

10 See the letter to Chanut of 20 November 1647 in *Op.* IV, 234.

maîtrise is, simultaneously, a keeping of distance and a passage by automatisms, moved by spontaneous and repetitive forces, towards an internal system of conscious self-regulation capable of minimizing the effects of unintentional movements. The young Descartes (so full of interest in automatons that he designed several and constructed one in the form of a tightrope-walker) does not want men to be reduced to simple mechanisms "moved only by means of springs," like those figures that he observed from his window, wrapped up in long cloaks and covered by hats with wide brims and that, practicing methodical doubt, he imagined to be ghosts or automatons.[11]

Beyond appearing notoriously in parallel with the thought, the extension instead enjoys in Spinoza the characteristic of being composed, in the living bodies of each individual, of a plurality of individuals, part and whole at the same time. The reciprocal relationships of the elements that form this multiplicity are thus not reducible to the model of the pneumatic machine and if anything resemble that teeming of organisms that the microscopists were already seeing in a drop of water and that would later lead Leibniz to a *mise en abîme* of every fragment of matter.[12]

The Sounding-Board of the Body

The idea of an energy of the body that might progressively accompany growth in the functions of the soul and simply be its repercussion is completely foreign to Descartes. He therefore asserts that the will does not know the power of the desires that it is capable of mobilizing and controlling – thus often remaining weak and irresolute. On the other hand, Spinoza holds, significantly, that no one yet knows the body's unexplored possibilities (see *E* 3.2, schol.), while experience affirms the extreme imbalance between the massive use of force of will supplied by the Stoics and Descartes and the meager results obtained.

When, in *The Will in Nature*, Schopenhauer accuses Spinoza of not having known how to construct a coherent system like his own (see *WiN* 210–11), the relationship between the Spinozan unexplored possibilities

11 *M* 300. See also J. Baltrušaitis, "Descartes: Les automates et le doute," in *Anamorphoses et perspectives curieuses* (Paris, 1955), 33–43.

12 This can be depicted as "a garden full of plants and a pond full of fishes. But each branch of every plant, each member of every animal, each drop of its liquid parts is also some such garden or pond" (Leibniz, *Monadologia*, §67; Engl. trans. *Monadology* [Oxford, 1898]).

of the body and the Cartesian unlimited extension of the will would be drastically disrupted. With respect to Spinoza, every parallelism between thought and extension, mind and body would fail, and the primacy of *amor Dei intellectualis*, as a higher level of knowledge, would be destroyed. Called upon to take their place is the mysterious root of the will to live, from which knowledge then rises, like a secondary product: "Knowledge is, so to speak, the sounding-board of the will, and consciousness is the tone produced thereby" (ibid., 112, and see 28, 62, and Engl. trans., 75). With respect to Descartes, the will to live – the *Wille* distinguished from the "presumed *liber arbitrium indifferentiae*" and from the single act of will tied to "representation" or *Willkür* (ibid., 55, 53) – losing awareness as its characteristic trait, is no longer distinguished by blind impulses of the classical *epithymeticon* or by desires that animate not only the animals, but also the plants (when they grow and seek light – ibid., 122, 110) and "inanimate" matter, like crystals battling each other to contest space (see *W*, §27, 211–12). When the body becomes an objectification of the will to live and knowledge becomes a derivation of it – in Nietzschian terms, when "small reason" is made to arise from "big reason" – then no pineal gland and no parallelism is any longer necessary since, to paraphrase Augustine, such *Wille* is the cruel divinity, torn apart within itself. It is a divinity more inside each being than each person is within himself. Will and reason, the two great areas that European thought battled to conquer and colonize for millennia, are degraded. A new God, not completely foreign and unknown (because it had always been possible to feel Him acting in us in our organic functions, impulses, acts of will, and thought) scandalizes, in the words of Schopenhauer, like a paradox: "it is only in this northwestern portion of the ancient continent, and even here only in Protestant countries, that the term paradoxical can be applied to such things; whereas throughout the whole of vast Asia, everywhere indeed, where the detestable doctrine of Islam has not prevailed over the ancient and profound religions of mankind by dint of fire and sword, they would rather have to fear the reproach of being commonplace" (*WiN* 215).

PART 3: THE GRAMMAR OF LOVE

1. Transitions

Like the Waves of the Sea

In Spinoza, the passions subject men to fluctuations of the soul, preventing them from having adequate knowledge of their causes and exposing them to endless conflict: "we are in many respects at the mercy of external causes and are tossed about like the waves of the sea ... unsure of the outcome and of our fate" (*E* 3.59, schol.). Thought is undecided. It cannot find its way out and is disturbed, in the same way that Epictetus compares mental images to a ray of light that falls on a basin full of water. The more it is moved, the more incomprehensible the images are to the soul, although the ray remains immobile (see *D* 3.3.20–2).[1] From the point of view of feelings, fluctuation of the soul is similar to doubt.[2]

According to a traditional idea, someone subjected to these oscillations is always exposed to mortal risks: "As, therefore, that storm which hinders a ship from entering into the port is more dangerous than that which suffers it not to sail; so the tempests of the soul are more difficult, which permit not a man to restrain himself, nor to settle his disturbed reason, so that, being without pilot or cables, he is through tumult and deceit hurried headlong by rash and pernicious courses."[3] The fluctuations of the soul hide from our being, dominated by the things of fortune, "that is, that are not in our power," and they thus make us feel defenceless and passive.[4] Or (and this is the same thing) they are moved

1 For this aspect, see also (in addition to *E* 3, defs. of the emotions 42, expl.) Descartes, *PA*, art. 166.

2 See *E* 3.17, schol.

3 Plut., *An. an corp.* (*Whether Affections of the Soul are Worse than Those of the Body*), 501 D.

4 *E* 2.49, schol., and see *E* 4.37, schol. I.

by "causes which, although acting likewise by definite and fixed laws, are yet unknown to us and foreign to our nature and our power" (*Ep.* 37.861). From this point of view, most men are powerless with respect to fortune (since "weakness consists solely in this, that a man suffers himself to be led by things external to himself" (*E* 4.37, schol. I). Wise people, on the other hand, either strive to complete the passage *a malis ad bona* – like the Epicureans (Cic., *Tusc.* III, 16, 35; 31, 76) – or, like Plutarch's bees, they know how to take advantage of even the most unfavourable circumstances, "extract[ing] honey from thyme, the most pungent and the driest of plants."[5] Or, finally, they may share the character of Horatio in *Hamlet*: "for thou hast been/as one in suffering all that suffers nothing,/a man that Fortune's buffets and rewards/hast ta'en with equal thanks. And blessed are those/whose blood and judgment are so well commingled/that they are not a pipe for Fortune's finger/to sound what stop she please."[6] The Spinozan solution – which is exclusively from this point of view – has a classical nature, epitomized in the phrases of Aristotle, who says: "Where there is most of mind and reason, there is least chance, and where there is most chance, there is least mind" (*Magna Mor.* II, 8, 1207a).

In Spinoza, the mind, and with it the body, are not supported by any substrate – that is, by any immobile and monolithic substance. Man is, if anything, an unstable mixture, subject to the influence of innumerable causes that are inadequately known. Thus, his nature is the continuous mutation, fluctuation, and transition from a minor state to greater perfection, or vice versa. Only the wise man is capable, within narrow limits, of being constant, of reaching Seneca's *constantia sapientis* because, having known the maximum expansion of the power of existing, he anchors himself to what is most desired.

Eliminating these disruptions and fluctuations is not suitable for everyone (and particularly for the masses), because the *conatus* of the individuals from whom they are formed is weak in them. Therefore, people will swing like an uninterrupted pendulum in opposing directions – from hope to fear and back again to hope – on the basis of "external causes," inconsistent expectations, and weak clues. Only the arc of the oscillation can diminish, in harmony with the consolidation of security in collective existence. But precisely because this goal is no less difficult

5 Plut., *De tranq.* 467 C; Engl. trans., 183.

6 W. Shakespeare, *Hamlet,* act 3, scene 2, vv. 59–65.

than the arduous path of knowledge, and relapses into insecurity are not at all excluded, the masses appear subject to frequent uneasiness, since they lack the means and the opportunities to break the double bind of fear and hope. Consequently, in a strictly political sense, their complete and final submission ends up chimerical under any regime. They remain virtually indomitable and always dangerous. Sometimes prone to the most passive obedience (the result of enormous political and religious pressures), they are capable in moments of crisis (when they go seeking *nova ac insolita*) of being attracted to the *rerum novarum cupiditas* – that is, not only tension with respect to the unknown, but revolt and conflict. "Indeed, as the multitude remains ever at the same level of wretchedness, so it is never long contented, and is best pleased only with what is new and has not yet proved delusory. This inconstancy has been the cause of many terrible uprisings and wars" (*TTP*, pref. *389*).

As, respectively, *inconstans tristitia* and *inconstans laetitia*, Spinoza rejects fear and hope as sterile and damaging. Obstacles difficult to surmount in light of the *transitio* to a greater level of perfection and existence, passions characterized by the greatest variability of *fluctuations*, by instability, and by constant inconstancy, they are at the poles of the *firmitas* that constitutes the dowry of courageous and wise men, guided neither by the fear that "arises from weakness of spirit" (*E* 4, app. 16) nor by the recklessness that often springs from insecurity, greed, or desire for self-destruction. These men do not need a *caeca audacia* to demonstrate to themselves or to others that they are worth something, nor do they need to cultivate the hope of prizes or riches. Intensifying reason and rationalizing the intensity of the *vis existendi*, they are capable of evaluating the meaning of their action on their own, of being content with their own activity or "virtue" and even ready to die for a worthy cause if they are satisfied with the meaning of their lives. Yet – precisely because it is connected to the *transitio* and possible only in the dimension of progress – Spinozan constancy does not have anything of the marble-like immobility of the Stoic wise man who anesthetizes himself against feelings, or the self-limitation of the Epicurean who consciously rejects the expansion of his own power of existing.

Spinoza emphatically rejects the *homo patiens* of the Christian imagination or martyrology and suffering as virtue, as well as the ideal of the *vir heroicus* always in struggle with himself and others. The ascending *transitio* leads to wisdom, but this is not the result of mere acts of will or reflection. Thus, in Spinoza, one does not arrive at a dampening of the swings of the passions' pendulum (which may lead to tendential immobility or *apatheia*), a *metropatheia* of Platonic or Aristotelian origin (in other words, their measured equilibrium or well-tempered mixture, a balancing and counterweight), or their submission to a centralized source of energy, similar to the spring of a clock. Spinozan *transitio* is not modelled on pendulums or on the traditional symbols of balance and the clock.[7] His paradigm is the metamorphosis of the passions into feelings,[8] the strengthening of a *conatus* capable of defeating all resistance, because it is satisfied with the goals reached from time to time.

The fluctuations of the soul are analogous to regret, a sadness concomitant with the idea of an internal cause. It "is not a virtue; that is, it does not arise from reason" (*E* 4.53). He who regrets is doubly poor and impotent. Spinoza, despite the fact that he may have acutely suffered from being subjected to *herem* (excommunication) on the part of Amsterdam's Jewish community, does not seem ever to have tried (either here or in other cases) to reconsider, in another light, choices made according to reasoned convictions. However, it should not be believed that the alternative to fluctuations of the soul is a rigid (or even obtuse) fixedness and faithfulness to the opinions and ethical values previously professed, or to the past as such. Unlike the Greek Stoics, Spinoza is not an advocate of *hegemonikon,* which, like an octopus or a spider at the centre of its web, controls all the motions of the mind and the body. And he is not Seneca, who recommends to wise men *constantia* in "always desiring and always refusing the same things."[9] Of course, like Seneca, he fights the *sibi displicere,* the discontent with oneself found in many men: "This springs from a lack of mental poise and from timid or unfulfilled desires, when men either do not dare, or do not attain, as much as they desire, and become entirely dependent upon hope; such men are always unstable and changeable, as must necessarily be the fate of those who live in suspense" (*De tranq. an.* 2.7). Even through dishonest actions, they seek in vain to reach their goals:

---

7 It is not unlikely that – beyond the classical sources – Spinoza's idea of the *fluctuatio* was enriched by the model, familiar to him, of the swing of the pendulum in the interpretation that Christiaan Huygens gives it in his *Horologium oscillatorium,* now in *Opera* (The Hague, 1892–1954).

8 However, in Spinoza there is no transubstantiation of a religious sort, nor any alchemic magic, nor the philosophical "rod of Hermes" that Epictetus used in Stoically transforming everything into "moral gold," every bad into good: "Bring what you please, and I will make it good ... Whatever you shall give me, I will make it happy, fortunate, honored" (Epict., *D* III, 20, 12, 15).

9 *Ep.* 109.16 and see, in the present volume, pp. 184–5.

> Then regret for what they have begun lays bold upon them, and the fear of beginning again, and then creeps in the agitation of a mind which can find no issue, because they can neither rule nor obey their desires, and the hesitancy of a life which fails to find its way clear, and then the dullness of a soul that lies torpid amid abandoned hopes ... The desires pent up within narrow bounds, from which there is no escape, strangle one another. Thence comes mourning and melancholy and the thousand waverings of an unsettled mind, which its aspirations hold in suspense and then disappointment renders melancholy." (ibid., 2.10)

To defeat this type of inertia and passivity, it is not necessary to throw oneself headlong into action (which can be a way of forgetting difficulties) as an end in itself.

From Fluctuations to Transitions

Leaving the sphere of the imagination and rational knowledge means reaching *scientia intuitiva*, a specificity that does not sacrifice anything to the universal and a universality that not only does not cancel the specific, but captures it in its specificity. Moreover, not only does it not depress the imagination, it develops its side of *potentia*. This means transforming the fluctuations into transitions (see *E* 4.11, schol.), passing from a lesser to a greater perfection or power of existing. The classical principle *quod nunc ratio est, impetus ante fuit* could be completed with *quod nunc scientia intuitiva est, ratio ante fuit*, in the sense of a progression that preserves the autonomy of each level without erasing its genesis.

Spinoza (partially tied here to the Platonic and Neo-Platonic tradition, from the *Symposium* and *Phaedrus* to Leo the Hebrew's *Dialoghi d'amore*)[10] does not intend to reduce the weight of feelings or extinguish their energy, but only to keep under control the power of *tristitia*, of that which leads men to repress the reaching towards the better, towards a greater power of existing – paraphrasing Nietzsche, the *Wille zum Besten.*[11]

10 On the relationship to Leo the Hebrew – previously identified by E. Solmi, *Benedetto Spinoza e Leone Ebreo: Studio su una fonte dimenticata dello spinozismo* (Modena, 1903) and by C. Gebhardt in the essay "Spinoza und Platonismus," *Chronicon Spinozanum* 1 (1921), 178–234 – see, among the more recent analyses, T.C. Mark, *Spinoza's Theory of Truth* (New York, 1972), 123 et seq.

11 Unlike Nietzsche, who (in *On the Geneaology of Morals* and in *Beyond Good and Evil*) sees in asceticism and the repression of instincts a degree of development of the will to power, in Spinoza such practices would only achieve the result of lowering the threshold of human perfection. However, he would certainly not have accepted a voluntaristic interpretation of his own idea of *vis existendi* – power cannot be willed.

Ahead of the rational exchange of equivalents between men (measure for measure) or the wanting to give without receiving – an attitude typical of the Aristotelian magnanimous man, who highlights his own superiority with respect to others – a real *ordo amoris* prevails in Spinoza, the joyful yielding of the wise man not only to *nos* (to *we* and not to *I*), i.e., to other men, but to all of nature, in a growth of his intellect and feelings. (In Spinoza, understanding is not, as in modern hermeneutics, a pure modification of the intellectual perspective, but an indissoluble capacity to transform oneself and the world by enjoying it, without violating the laws of necessity.)[12] Here the concept of strength joins that of form. In the *transitio* towards greater perfection (or "striving … to improve itself," according to the expression of the *KV* 1.5), each person shapes himself through an intellectual and emotional learning that follows a model of consistent and constant imbalance in its progress. For Spinoza, "saying yes to life" is joy (not fought by a stern or envious reason) that feeds on all the energy of the passions transformed into positive feelings and that renders *amor intellectualis* similar to a harmonic orchestration of rationality and feelings, to the measure (*Takt* or "tact") fixed from time to time (in each person with respect to "particular things") by the power of his current *conatus.*

To shake their passivity and not let men waste away in hardship, he uses the ascensional energy of feelings like *laetitia* and *amor*, no longer restrained (as in the Augustinian, Lutheran, or Jansenist theological traditions) by the necessity to obtain the extraordinary help of divine grace to defeat the enormous weight of original sin, or the insurmountability of evil, by human means alone. For Spinoza, "virtue" is no longer deprivation, repression, or self-censure, but rather *fortitudo* and *gaudium* (which, for him, is joy of a past thing that occurred beyond our hopes: *praeter spem* – see *E* 3, defs. of the emotions 16). By means of the *transitio* to a greater intramundane perfection (but one that does not enjoy any ethical privilege compared to the totality of nature), the Pauline and Augustinian struggle between law and sin, between spirit and flesh, is abolished without resorting to asceticism or the intervention of supernatural powers. The tensions dissolve thanks to the intellectual love that,

12 A position closer in some ways to that of Spinoza can be found sketched in Epicurus, according to whom pleasure does not depend on the result, but on the activity: "In the study of philosophy, pleasure keeps pace with growing knowledge; for pleasure does not follow learning; rather, learning and pleasure advance side by side" (*Sent. Vat.* XXVII).

instead of blocking or repressing them, lets the natural forces of passion and the imagination develop until they find their own way towards their resolution in more satisfying conditions of existence. Life is more full of joy and has less need to transfigure itself in the hereafter, to invoke a divine order so to avoid, in an Augustinian way, the "fear of becoming lost" that torments it.

The *transitio* is measured by the *conatus*, by the continuous quantity of movement of increased or decreased impulse or *cupiditas* – that is, of the appetite that is conscious of itself. The *conatus* is not, however, only ascendant (as some interpreters assert, projecting Nietzchean models onto it). It can also follow a descending course when the prevailing passions are tied to *tristitia* – to which each is subjected by chance or by its passive surrender or acquiescence. The wise man, even with a rough or discontinuous "diagram" of the variations of his own power of existing, manages to maintain the high level of the power that has already been reached, or at least to persevere along the upward path.

The emotions undergo a never-ending transformation in two directions: either towards an increase of joy and the power of existing, a *constans laetitia* (joy simultaneously representing the journey and the means of the journey [see *E* 3.11, schol.] and not the happiness or *beatitudo* achieved), or towards a dominance of *tristitia*. In fact, "our lives are subject to continual variation, and as the change is for the better or worse, so we are said to be fortunate or unfortunate" (*E* 5.39, schol.). Consequently, Spinoza is not the forcedly optimistic philosopher that historiography has often presented. Most men experience an existence beneath their own abstract possibilities and live a life that is lacking, worn down by fear and hope, poisoned by superstition and attraction to death. For individuals, security is often just a mirage and *amor Dei intellectualis* is an unknown God. The most widespread ethical doctrines commonly limit themselves to guiding us towards the sad extinction of our desires (*libidines*), instead of indicating the way towards "blessedness," whose enjoyment allows us to "keep our lusts in check" precisely because we are happy and satisfied with ourselves (see *E* 5.42). Spinozan philosophy does not lead to mourning grief. Lacking the "dominant" will of the Stoics or the infinite will of Descartes, it also lacks their counterpart – obedience and submission. From this point of view, the passions seem like stranded feelings that make us suffer, because we cannot freely make use of their *vis* according to an order less binding than that of the imagination, or because they let us sink into forms of murky knowledge that lower their vital tone, even when they are not felt immediately, in the absence of "causes" that might make the imagination waver.

From this perspective, the secret affinities and deep differences with respect to Hobbes are revealed. Even for Hobbes, human happiness is restlessness, transition, with a minimum of impediments towards infinite degrees of relative perfection: "Felicity is a continual progress of the desire, from one object to another; the attaining of the former being still but the way to the latter" (*L* I.11, in *EW* III, 85). Thus, neither an ultimate end nor a supreme good exist. There is only an uninterrupted moment compared to a "race" that has "no other goal, nor other garland, but being foremost" and where to "continually out-go the next [person] before is felicity. And to forsake the course is to die."[13] Throughout life, this path never ends and creates a sort of circle. Reason, victorious over the fear of other men as rivals, returns to fear as its final guarantee, and from there it departs again. In Spinoza, though within the framework of a happiness without fixed and definitive goals (that may not be established by the subject's complete fulfilment), in the idea of transition the competitive and selfish element is completely absent. Happiness does not at all consist of surpassing others but, on the contrary, of proceeding forward and arriving together (the greatest number possible) at a greater satisfaction, because the joy of winning together and sociability is potentially greater than that of winning alone.

Scientia intuitiva

Knowledge is *mentis potentia* (*E* 5.20, schol.), the metamorphosis of unsuitable ideas into more suitable ones and the production of joy, as it raises each person from the oppression of an incomprehensible power: *Qui se suosque affectus clare et distincte intellegit, laetatur* (*E* 5.15 dem.). Thus, understanding means not only being aware of necessity and resigning oneself, but also increasing one's strength, broadening one's own *I* – without erasing individuality – within the *nos* of the human community or the structure of the universe.[14] And it does not even mean knowing abstractly, without mobilizing the feelings. Rather, it is necessary to filter

13 *Elements of Law*, IX, in *EW* IV, 52–3. On this Hobbesian image of the path, see T. Magri, *Saggio su Thomas Hobbes: Gli elementi della politica* (Milan, 1982), 97–8. On the idea of ambition, see K. Hammacher, "Ambition and Social Engagement in Hobbes' and Spinoza's Political Thought," in *Spinoza's Political and Theological Thought*, ed. C. de Deugd (Amsterdam, 1984), 127–36.

14 On the meaning of *intelligere* in Spinoza see, for different arguments, G. Giannetto, *Spinoza e l'idea del comprendere* (Naples, 1980).

them from their dependence on external causes, separate the impossible from the possible, reduce the disruptions of thought, at least in part. The endogenous transformation of passions into active feelings does not imply the loss of their accumulated strength, their *vis*. On the contrary, it is developed and rescued from dissipative, centrifugal, and restrained movement that is not directed towards realistically achievable ends.

Feelings are not intellectualized or sublimated but simply deprived of their opacity. Through a series of operations of sufficient knowledge that orders and links them according to a logic different from that of the imagination, they are first separated "from the thought of their external cause" and then stabilized – with respect to the fluctuations of the soul – by the "matter of time, in respect of which the affections that are related to things we understand are superior to those which are related to things that we conceive in a confused or fragmentary way" (*E* 5.20, schol.). Passing from the *ordo imaginationis* to the *ordo rationis*, and finally to the *ordo amoris intellectualis*, there is a strengthening of the linking of ideas according to internal nexuses that are, on the one hand, more consistent and logically binding, but on the other, are ever less constrictive, because necessity repositions itself from the primacy of external causes to the "free necessity" of knowledge of them. And this happens according to the two modes mutually implicated by the second and third type of knowledge but that foresee, at the culmination of the process, an individualizing vision of things within a comprehensive framework. Intuitive science "proceeds from an adequate idea of the formal essence of certain attributes of God to an adequate knowledge of the essence of things" (*E* 2.40, schol. 2).

The victory achieved does not represent the annihilation of an adversary (of the imagination or of reason as such) achieved through terror and enslavement, but the liberation of a part of them that – although in many ways continuing to remain passive and at the mercy of external causes – can reunite more deliberately with the whole, cooperating with it, and increasing its own perfection through knowledge: "the power of the mind is defined solely by knowledge, its weakness or passivity solely by the privation of knowledge; that is, it is measured by the extent to which its ideas are said to be inadequate" (*E* 5.20, schol.).

For Spinoza, then, the saying from Ecclesiastes *Qui auget scientiam, auget et dolorem*[15] (1:18) is not valid. If anything, the opposite could be asserted:

15 "Those who increase knowledge, increase sorrow."

Qui auget scientiam, auget et laetitiam. And this applies all the more, the greater the increment of knowledge that culminates in *scientia intuitiva* – we know why we love; we love because we know. Deep knowledge of sorrow is certainly not lacking in the Dutch philosopher, but completely absent is any apologia or conversion of it into moral positivity, into compassion as virtue.

Scientia intuitiva (see *E* 2.40, schol. 2) differs from the first two degrees of knowledge, based on imagination and reason, because it returns to recognition of the particular essence of things, of which common notions of wisdom sometimes lose sight (when they mistake abstract entities like the mind or the will for substances). As *amor*, it is not directed towards the whole or the general, but towards the *res singulares*, individual things (understood in a not purely numerical sense) in their concrete and visible expression with respect to the whole.[16] In this sense, the theory according to which *individuum est ineffable* is not true. Through this form of knowledge, one reaches the highest degree of "effability": we can speak of a thing in the most articulate way because we love it singularly. We accept it with joy for how it is in the framework of the universal necessity specified and focused individually in every being.

In considering all the bodies and structures of the mind as compounds within the concept of order – as a parallel of *ordo rerum* and *ordo idearum* – Spinoza avoids both random dispersion and concise holism. In fact, this order is, inseparably, organization of the multiplicity into the singular and an unfolding of unity into the multiple. Its *ordo amoris* (or the *amor Dei intellectualis*) allows knowledge not only of *entia metaphysica, sive universalia,* abstractions like "mind" or "will," but individual ideas and individual acts of will: *singulares ideae* and *singulares volitiones* (see *E* 2.48, schol.). After all, "that which constitutes the actual being of the human mind is basically nothing else but the idea of an individual actually existing thing," whose "cause" is God Himself, since "the human mind

16 On the concept of "intuitive science," compare the interpretations, from which I break away, of S. Carr, "Spinoza's Distinction between Rational and Intuitive Knowledge," *Philosophical Review* 87 (1978), 241–52 and H.G. Hubbeling, in "The Third Way of Knowledge (Intuition) in Spinoza" (*Studia Spinozana* 2 [1986], 219–31). Hubbeling asserts that in some ways, there would not be substantial differences between the second and the third way of knowledge, because the latter would countinue to resort to reasoning. Hubbeling then distinguishes one intuition, as direct knowledge, from another intuition, as "deep" knowledge that places man in relationship with everything, in the light of the eternal. If what I have said is plausible, these distinctions, which appear largely as difficulties to Hubbeling, find a simpler explanation.

is part of the infinite intellect of God" (*E* 2.11; 2.9; 2.11, cor.). Thus, Spinozan intuitive science does not correspond to the "intellectual intuition" condemned by Kant, or to the panoramic and immediate knowledge of the whole in all its expressions, but only to the understanding of individual things made possible by the passage from general ideas of reason to their concrete specification (which already happened for those who proceed "from an adequate idea of the formal essence of certain attributes of God").[17] From a moral point of view, precisely because it still connects ethics with the search for maximum happiness, Spinoza's philosophy does not trigger the rending of the soul that, in the Kant of the *Anthropology* (§§73 et seq.), is set off by the condemnation of reason practised with respect to the "illnesses of the mind."[18]

Amor intellectualis refers beyond the boundaries of an already closed *ordo* and is a construction of possible and sharable orders, all equally rigorous, because they are adapted to the intrinsic needs of the *res singulares,* once understood in their diriment characteristics. Intuitive science does not aim, then, towards solitary contemplation, but towards a superior form of community that can, however, only be reached by a difficult path. The wise man's strategy is directed towards modification of his own passions into positive feelings. For Spinoza, against the classical world's condemnation of *pleonexia,* the intensity of desire can and must be increased according to the criterion (which we have already encountered) that has its own measure in wisdom, since it strengthens the mind and promotes virtues: "The greater the number of things the mind understands by the second and third kinds of knowledge, the less subject it is to emotions that are bad, and the less it fears death" (*E* 5.38). Enjoying a well-designed life, the wise man does not seek exceptional moments of mystical ecstasy and knows how to tolerate all adversities with a calm heart, when he convinces himself that he cannot avoid them, since they derive from a necessary order of reason that – once understood – compensates for suffering, preventing those adversities from sublimating themselves in sacrifice and apologia of suffering:

> If we clearly and distinctly understand this, that part of us which is defined by the understanding, that is, the better part of us, will be fully resigned and will endeavor to persevere in that resignation. For insofar as we understand,

17 *E* 2.40, schol. 2.
18 Kant, *Anthropology,* 7:251.

> we can desire nothing but that which must be, nor, in an absolute sense, can we find contentment in anything but truth. And so insofar as we rightly understand these matters, the endeavor of the better part of us is in harmony with the order of the whole of Nature. (*E* 4, app. 32)

Being part of it and being subject to its necessity, each person can contribute to modifying its course on the basis of his own laws.

With a pleasure of metamorphosis, knowledge thus produces a transfiguration of the passions, an increasing *transitio* that corresponds to the earthly ladder of possible happiness, as a shrinking of the width of the oscillations and a suture of the lacerations caused by the tempests of the imagination and the rigid *diktat* of will and reason – tempests released by an *amor* that constitutes the maximum development of *cupiditas*: "A passive emotion ceases to be a passive emotion as soon as we form a clear and distinct idea of it" (*E* 5.3). Changing from a passion into an emotion (*affectus*), from passiveness into activity, blind force becomes conscious of itself, a "clairvoyant" energy to develop and not repress: "So the more an emotion is known to us, the more it is within our control, and the mind is the less passive in respect of it" (*E* 5.3, cor.).

If the two forms of thought must rigorously be held separate, it is impossible not to be struck, reading Freud, by the non-secondary points of contact between his positions and those of Spinoza:[19] the propositions that the soul functions as a "spiritual automaton," that the mind is in essence *idea corporis*, and (particularly) that the affections, considered quantitatively and tied to the *conatus*, are more in our power, and the mind suffers less from them, the more that we know them (so that every increment of understanding corresponds to a modification of the affections and a strengthening of the *vis existendi*).[20]

---

19 On the relationship between Freud and Spinoza and the knowledge that the former possessed of the latter (including through the mediation of Goethe, Tausk, Lou Andreas-Salome, and perhaps Rilke), see D. Alexander, "Spinoza und die Psychoanalyse," *Chronicon Spinozanum* 5 (1927), 96–103. Since then, the studies (not all of high quality) have multiplied, particularly in recent years.

20 And this despite the fact that Spinoza's name is explicitly cited only twice: once, fleetingly, in *Jokes and Their Relation to the Unconscious*, in reference to Heine, and another, more articulately, in *Eine Kindheitserinnerung des Leonardo da Vinci*, *GW* 8, 142; Engl. trans. "Leonardo da Vinci and a Memory of His Childhood," in *The Standard Edition of the Complete Psychological Works of Sigmund Freud* (London, 1957), XI, 75.

Further, as in Freud, the child is pushed to renounce the omnipotence of thought and desire because of the strengthening of the principle of reality. So in Spinoza, the formation of suitable ideas leads us naturally to abandon what we know to be mere fruit of the imagination, something rationally impossible (the childish desire to touch the moon with one's hands and draw it up from a well with a bucket).

Finally, in Spinoza as in Freud, the passage from a inferior good to a superior one does not happen as an effect of the exclusively intellectual recognition of the superiority of one idea over another, but as the effect of abandonment, by our appetite, of what previously seemed to us a good and that now we no longer desire, although not ceasing to be a potential good even if our *vis existendi* might diminish. And since desire is just appetite accompanied by conscience, it follows that conscience changes along with appetite.

Spinoza and Machiavelli: On the "Knowledge of Particular Things"

Against every fixed, stratified hierarchy of the soul, Spinoza stresses endogenous change, the endless and incremental transition of a desire whose previous resources have not dissipated. "Reason," then, is the peak of human potentiality. It is intermediate *cupiditas*, the "moderate" depth (still partly tied to the *tristitia* of repression) between the torrid and cold excesses of the exuberant passions and the "hot" disruption of intellectual love.

Therefore, if the wise man continues along his path through a sort of intellectual training of the passions (which does not lead to their domestication but to their self-immunizing recognition), the people, conversely, need to receive salvation externally.[21] In this case, the strategy aims at an exogenous modification of the passions. First, through the state, the conditions of security are created that are indispensable to the flowering of reason. Only afterward – in direct proportion to the security achieved – does the terrain of the passions and imaginative knowledge "drain." The institutional changes thus influence the development of greater rationality (one must not fall into the illusion, however, that it is possible

21 The *Theological-Political Treatise* is, in fact, dedicated to philosophers, to those who want to learn the truth, and not to the "common man." See L. Strauss, "How to Study Spinoza's 'Theological-Political Treatise,'" in *Persecution and the Art of Writing* (Glencoe, IL, 1952), 142–201.

to dry up the sea of passions). But even in the case of the masses, it is still understanding that allows a jump in level towards the second type of knowledge, except that it is activated not by *fortitudo animi*, wisdom, but by the conditions of security established by the state, or (particularly) by the maximum expansion of the collective *conatus*. The highest level still remains tied to knowledge of the *res particulares*, a synonym of wisdom.

Despite every more obvious difference, however, it is significant that even Machiavelli thinks, like Spinoza, that understanding the "essential truth of the thing" involves knowledge of the *res particulares* in their specificity. This does not exclude, but even presumes, passage from knowledge and praxis through the universal, the overcoming (and not the abandonment) of both the confused, distorting viewpoint of the imagination and opinion, and the viewpoint that is transparent and well-articulated by types, norms, and laws: dictated by reason, but not yet experienced in concrete situations. Machiavelli obviously proceeds on the grounds of practical intelligence and not *amor Dei intellectualis*. For Machiavelli, in fact, there is no need to be a "wise man" in the full sense of knowing the *res singulares*.

Consequently, bringing some structural analogies to light will help clarify the nature of the problems addressed (deliberately leaving aside here every other historical or theoretical relationship between the two authors). In one chapter of the *Discourses*, titled "Although men are apt to deceive themselves in general matters, yet they rarely do so in particulars," the reflection revolves around the situation created in Florence following the expulsion of the Medici in 1494. An ordered government having disappeared, and the political situation worsening from day to day, many of the *popolari* often attributed blame to the ambitions of the *Signori*. But as soon as one of them came, in turn, to occupy a high magistracy, he gradually began to acquire ideas more "suitable" with respect to the real conditions of the city and abandon both the opinions circulating among his friends and the abstract precepts and rules with which he had initiated his apprenticeship in public affairs:

> And when they had risen to that place, and were enabled to see matters more closely, they discovered the real causes of the disorders, and the dangers that threatened the state, as well as the difficulty of remedying them. And seeing that the times, and not the men, caused the disorders, they promptly changed their opinions and actions, because the knowledge of things in particular had removed from their minds that delusion into which they had fallen by looking at things in general. So that those who at first had heard them speak whilst they were still private citizens, and afterwards saw

> them remain inactive when they had risen to the supreme magistracy, believed that this was caused, not by the real knowledge of things, but by their having been perverted and corrupted by the great. (*D* I, 47, 236–7)

But to what extent is it possible to get a truer notion of the "things in particular" without going "to the real truth of the matter than to the imagination of it" (*P* XV) and to the imagination of laws and rules that are general but ineffective? In the introduction to the first book of his *Discourses,* Machiavelli seems to waver, in the space of two pages, between a static or palindromic conception of human events, with its endless return of the "almost the same" and the idea that it may instead be possible to introduce innovations in the sphere of thought and of the world. In fact, he asserts that some types of knowledge have not made any progress across the millennia, since they continue to follow "the judgments and the remedies" established so long before by the ancient "juriconsults" by the "ancient physicians" (*D* I, intro., 104). Immediately after, however, he adds that men – who, as is said elsewhere, are generally "won over by the present far more than by the past" (*P* XXIV, 78) – do not read stories to draw teachings from them, but to "take pleasure only in the variety of the events which history relates, without ever thinking of imitating the noble actions, deeming that not only difficult, but impossible; as though heaven, the sun, the elements, and men had changed the order of their motions and power, and were different from what they were in ancient times" (*D* I, intro., 104). And yet he had begun with the proud assertion of having "resolved to open a new route, which has not yet been followed by anyone," one that might "prove difficult and troublesome" but might also bring reward from someone who would have known how to value his effort (ibid., 103). Later, he had even observed how the past accompanies us and changes along with us with the variation of our "appetites" and "experience." This is demonstrated by the example of old men and all the "partisans" of past things, accustomed to "praise" the time that was and "blame" the present.

In Spinozan terms, Machiavelli not only avoids *ridere* and *lugere* in favour of *intelligere,* but strives to explain why such difference of appearance arises spontaneously in the mind with the variation of age. The reasoning of the man who often assesses "whether the present age be better than the past" can be corrupted by the absence of adequate awareness. But that of the old man who knew the years of his youth and can easily compare them to subsequent ones, why should that not lead to an impartial judgment? And here is his response, which recalls the Spinozan theory of the *conatus*: "This would be true, if men at the different periods of their lives had the same judgment and the same appetites. But as these vary (though the times do not), things cannot appear the same to men who have other tastes, other delights, and other considerations in age from what they had in youth. For as men when they age lose their strength and energy, whilst their prudence and judgment improve, so the same things that in youth appeared to them supportable and good, will of necessity, when they have grown old, seem to them insupportable and evil; and when they should blame their own judgment, they find fault with the times" (D II, intro., 273–4).

Things change, then, because we and our memories change with them. But it is not only appetites, passions, and opinions (both positive and negative) that are responsible for this, but the growth or decline of "judgment" and *prudentia.* From such conditions, one can deduce the reason that might even explain the weaving (so strange at first) of the role of the new and the old into Machiavelli's theory. "Heaven, the sun, the elements, and men" remain substantially the same across time, so that reading ancient and modern stories can offer the present generation models that are still valid "universally," but the "appetites," "delights," "considerations," and capacities to understand and judge change continually. Concrete situations demand, then, a "knowledge of things in particular." Knowledge can proceed along this horizon only under two conditions: that of investigating the "real truth of the matter" all the way to the end, rather than stopping at the "imagination of it," and that of not being satisfied, in considering human events and politics, with the formulation of perfect but rigidly inelastic rules. Moreover, from this comes Machiavelli's special style – thick, even proportionately, with references drawn from the past (that are exemplary and could be followed even by contemporaries) but at the same time attentive (with "a lynx's eyes") to how much was happening that was new in the course of his life and the best ways of understanding it and communicating it to others.

In normal and peaceful times, the "circumspect man" (*P* XXV), prudent and mature in judgment and age, can happily govern his state. But in troubled times, the "impetuous" man, the young man equipped with greater courage and open to the new – and with less respect for the past and present – has more success. From this comes Machiavelli's famous conclusion (which should be rethought, however, starting from the point of view just explained, almost forgetting having read it): "I hold strongly to this: that it is better to be impetuous than circumspect; because fortune is a woman and if she is to be submissive it is necessary to beat and coerce her. Experience shows that she is more often subdued by men who do this than by those who act coldly. Always, being a woman, she favors young men, because they are less circumspect and more ardent, and because they command her with greater audacity" (*P* xxv, 82). This statement – purified, for a moment, of the image of fortune as a woman and of her rape – means that boldness, and not prudence understood as caution, is the virtue required by the present to not be "subdued" (*tenere sotto*), becoming captives. And although Machiavelli does not at all exclude the need for a temporal continuity diffused by reflection on the *exempla* of the past (which are multiplied and varied) and even by a sort of theatrical education capable of initiating the young into knowledge of the passions,[22] the break that he makes with tradition is deep and lacerating.

In fact, since Aristotle, the supreme virtue of "practical science" and *phronesis* (prudence and wisdom) corresponds to middle age and maturity in the life of a man (the peak of moral and intellectual development, a privileged position equally far from the excesses of youth and the deficiencies of old age). In turn, Stoic *gravitas* prescribed consistency, constancy, and peace of mind – "mature" values with which were contrasted the passions (comparable to youthful excesses or spiteful, geriatric wickedness that reason does not manage to keep at bay), all of them signs of immature or corrupt will in its effort to tame or calm the appetites in a Senecan way.[23]

With Machiavelli, modernity chooses the virtues of the extremes – at least in the exceptional state imposed by the wickedness and turbulence of the times. We get farther from the centre and the *mesotes*, thus imparting a strong impulse of movement and change on political and ethical thoughts and behaviours, and choosing the criterion of immoderation for its own sake: "Our nature does not permit us always to keep the just middle course" (*D* III, 21, 474). With one scandal whose echo had not yet faded, Machiavelli rewrites a new and subversive table of values founded

22 See the prologue to *Clizia*: "Comedies were discovered in order to benefit and to delight the spectators. Truly it is a great benefit to any man, and especially to a youth, to know the avarice of an old man, the passion of a lover, the tricks of a servant, the gluttony of a parasite, the misery of a pauper, the ambition of one who's rich, the flatteries of a whore, the untrustworthiness of all men" (*Cl.*, trans. D. Gallagher [Long Grove, IL, 1996], 5).

23 On the young, see, with another view, C. Lefort, "Machiavel et les jeunes," in *Science et conscience de la société: Mélanges en l'honneur de Raymond Aron* (Paris, 1971), vol. 1, 193–208. On the changing of attitude and the passions in Aristotle with respect to the ages of life, see, in the present volume, pp. 170–2.

on the exuberance of force, one that must oppose the disruptive impulses currently underway with a surplus of desire for order. The dynamism of the *impetus* legitimizes the lack of measure and virtually removes the prohibition of the most severe "sin" of classical ethics, *pleonexia* or limitlessness of desire, which will later also be attacked by Descartes, Hobbes, and Spinoza.

In Machiavelli, circumspection (*respettività*), because it is tied to the idea of *mesotes*, makes prudence regress to caution. "Impetuosity," on the other hand, constitutes the new nucleus of the "virtue" destined to subdue "fortune." Rationality, abandoning its traditional reflexive balance, is placed in the service of *impetus*, from which it receives propulsive energy. There thus arises a new morality capable, in Aristotelian terms, of regulating and giving plausible meaning to the "mixed actions" or forced choices that prevail in difficult times when events "beyond human imagining" occur, as happened for Machiavelli in Italy after 1494.[24] This is now called upon to include and codify the acts that trigger internal and external conflicts, invoking decisions that cannot be completed "in friendship with themselves," but only through hate of one part of oneself (whatever the choice might be, given that the alternative is between two evils, and the canons of action appear feeble or doubtful in their formulation).[25]

The political imperatives of balance or minimal variation are replaced, particularly for the person who commands, by those founded on the dynamic of "impetuosity." Action opposes suffering, the desire for new things opposes attachment to the past, because "men get tired of prosperity, just as they are afflicted by the reverse" (*D* III, 21, 474). This conduct conforms to the inclination towards spontaneity among men,

---

24 *P* XXV. On "mixed actions" in Aristotle – that is, those that are not completed "in friendship with themselves" and that therefore involve conflict, see *Eth. Nic.* III, 1, 1110a. For an indirect theoretical framing of the subject, see M. Walzer, "Political Action: The Problem of Dirty Hands," *Philosophy and Public Affairs* 2 (1973), 160–80. Since friendship towards oneself lies at the base of Aristotelian ethics (but see Plato, *Gorgias*, 482, in which Socrates says, among other things: "It is better to be in disagreement with the whole world than, being one, to be in disagreement with myself"), the "mixed actions" represent dilemmas that once again drive action to the level of the tragic.

25 In this sense, it can be said that there begins to appear in Machiavelli the conflict that tears modern man between two souls that cohabit the same breast, but in which the one wants to separate from the other: *Zwei Seelen, wohnen, ach!, in meiner Brust/Die eine will von der anderen trennen* (Goethe, *Faust* 1.1112–13).

who become increasingly restless when religious institutions (which previously pushed them to look towards the heavens) grow weak. They also languish in the corruption of civil institutions, forcing them to distance themselves from the main path of customs and traditional laws. On more strictly political grounds, this means that Machiavelli considers unrealistic the classical, medieval, and humanistic ideal of "good government" and the ideal of the state as an instrument for concord among classes and citizens. He no longer looks with nostalgia at the state as a stable, unitary, and harmonically articulated organism.[26] Rather, he regards it, with greater radicalness than in previous theories, as a composite (and thus mortal) body that can only grow or perish, rise or descend in power, but never stand still. Its motions, "turmoils," and "fevers" assume either a character that is physiological (transforming them into a healthy jolt) or pathological (manifesting itself in slow or rapid decline). Renewal means restraining decline, diverting the current course of events through concentration of power that effectively opposes the strength and speed of the factors that produce disintegration. This task, inseparably ethical and political, can be discharged only if the state is not yet irreversibly corrupt. The unity, compactness, and internal consistency of the parts are no longer considered an intrinsic value. They would be that way once again, at the end of the century, with Neostoicism and the formation of the first rudiments of the modern, centred, and "proto-absolutist" state – that is, when the religious and political wars would shed "the blood of Europe" in abundance, raising the desire for peace (or at least long armistice) between the warring parties. After all, although he sometimes judges tears in the political fabric, dissent, and turmoil to be authentic factors in civic growth, Machiavelli does not assert that they must give way to organized factions: "Those who believe republics can be united are greatly deceived in their belief. It is true that some divisions harm republics and some divisions benefit them. Those do harm that are accompanied with factions and partisans; those bring benefit that are kept up without factions and without partisans" (*History of Florence* VII, 1).

Despite the differences, it is not impossible to follow the development of the intellectual threads that connect Machiavelli to Spinoza in their common insistence on the imbalances that are produced at every moment in the relationship between the "appetites" that modify our

26 On the meaning and modern origin of the "state," see A. Tenenti, *Stato: Un'idea, una logica: Dal comune italiano all'assolutismo francese* (Bologna, 1987).

intelligence of things and our "judgment," and the possibilities of adequately knowing individual things without cancelling laws, rules, and examples of universal value. Not all these ideas converge, however, on analogous solutions. In fact, between Machiavelli and Spinoza there is an insurmountable gap, an incompatibility of perspective that on one capital question distances them more than they are brought together on other points. This is that the *transitio* to a new state happens, in the Machiavelli of the *Prince*, through fear – a necessary resource to defeat natural human wickedness and reinforce social stability: "Men worry less about doing an injury to one who makes himself loved than to one who makes himself feared. For love is secured by a bond of gratitude which men, wretched creatures that they are, break when it is to their advantage to do so; but fear is strengthened by a dread of punishment which is always effective" (*P* XVII, 54). What Spinoza proposes, on the other hand, is identifying the causes of men's *tristitia* and their myopic attachment to the lowest level of *utilitas* (as when, in Machiavelli's words, "men sooner forget the death of their father than the loss of their patrimony"). From this point of view, not even Spinoza harbours excessive expectations. He realizes, however, that fear (based on violence or cunning) continues to be a worse remedy for evil, because it contributes to strengthening the optical illusion that, despite everything, leads to seeing men as always equal: an unreformable *massa damnationis*, incapable of extracting the entire root of his wickedness. Contrary to Machiavelli – just like, on a different level, contrary to Hobbes – Spinoza knows that the path from fear to security, from *tristitia* to joy, ends up being passable. In fact, he shows how most men's passive obedience to previous aggregates of power may not necessarily be inevitable and eternal.

2. Loving without Being Loved

Imperfect Love

To begin to resolve the conflicts raised by the passions and the tangles of will, Spinoza combines knowledge with love (so it will be effective) and love with knowledge (so it will not be blind). Transforming passion into feeling razes to the ground the *hegemonikon* of the Stoics, the fortress and the acropolis into which the wise man and laws had retreated. The Pascalian separation of the reasons of the heart (which reason does not know) and those of the mind (which the passions ignore) is thus virtually abolished, since the "order of the heart" and the "order of the intellect"[1] are identical, multiplying their effectiveness with the innovative order of intellectual love that concentrates *esprit de géometrie* and *esprit de finesse* within itself and avoids the cutting ice of abstractions and the tepid inconsistency of the "mush of the heart."

Spinoza removes, from *amor intellectualis*, the contradictory natures of hesitation and poverty that are normally attributed to human love or Platonic Eros, understood as a devil. Intellectual love is tied, instead, to a constant growth that uses the energy of desire positively: to develop towards a greater knowledge of the individual and not to waver between opposing desires in a paralysing or inconclusive way. These aspects clearly

1 See Pascal, *P*, n. 72, 1102: "The heart has its order; the mind has its own, which proceeds through principle and demonstration. The heart has another. It cannot be proven what must be loved, exposing the order of love's causes: that would be ridiculous. Jesus Christ, Saint Paul have the order of charity, not that of the mind: because they wanted to belittle, not instruct."

distinguish it from the uncertain and tormented type of human love powerfully and effectively described by the Baroque poet Villamediana:

> Determinarse y luego arrepentirse,
> empezarse a atrever y acobardarse,
> arder el pecho y la palabra helarse,
> desengañarse y luego persuadirse;
>
> comenzar una cosa y advertirse,
> querer decir su pena y no aclararse,
> en medio del aliento desmayarse,
> y entre temor y miedo consumirse;
>
> en las resoluciones, detenerse,
> hallada la ocasión, no aprovecharse,
> y, perdida, de cólera encenderse,
>
> y sin saber por qué, desvanecerse;
> efectos son de amor: no hay que espantarse,
> que todo del amor puede creerse.[2]

2 I. De Tarsis, conde de Villamediana, "Cancionero Blanco" 34, in *Obras*, ed. J.M. Rozas (Madrid, 1987), 110: "Deciding and then regretting,/starting to dare and becoming a coward,/your chest burning and your words freezing,/being disillusioned and quickly persuading yourself; // beginning one thing and changing your mind,/wanting to declare your pain and not saying anything,/in the middle of a breath, growing weak,/ and being consumed between dread and fear; // holding back with resolutions,/ finding the opportunity and not taking advantage of it,/and lost, burning up with rage, // and without knowing why, fading away;/these are effects of love; no need to be frightened,/because everything about love can be believed." The element of ambiguity and the contradictory division of desire in love were often observed in the poetic and philosophical field. Among the canonical texts, see Catullus 85: *Odi, et amo: quare id faciam fortasse requiris/Nescio, sed fieri sentio et excrucior*; and Ovid, *Amores* III, XI, vv. 33–4: *Luctantur pectusque leve in contraria ducunt:/Hac amor, hac odium: sed puto vincit Amor*; Tibullus 2.6.13–14: *Iuravi quotiens rediturum ad limina numquam,/Cum bene iuravi, pes tamen ipse redit* (and, more generally, on the contradictory nature of all the passions, see Virg., *Aen.* 6.733: *Hinc metuunt cupiuntque, dolent gaudentque*). For the medical-philosophical tradition, which connects love with the struggle between the passions of *metus* and *timor*, see, for example, Avicenna, *Liber Canonis* (Latin trans. by Gerard of Cremona) (Venice, 1555), 10 (as annotated by Andrea Alpago in Avicenna, *Liber canonis de medicinis cordialibus et Cantica iam olim quidem a Gerardo Carmonensi ex arabico sermone in Latinum conversa* [Venice, 1555], in reference to this passion of love that the Arabs call *hea*: *Hea apud Arabes est passio animae permista ex spe et timore,*

Spinoza first lays out a phenomenology of love in general, the kind that unites human beings or ties them to images or things. He then passes to the concept of intellectual love of God. The first type of love – which always remains one of the *modi cogitandi* (*E* 2, axiom 2) – is defined as "pleasure accompanied by the idea of an external cause."[3] Since it increases the power of acting and existing, love corresponds with joy (*E* 3.37, dem.). Therefore, the person who loves strives to have present, to imagine, and to preserve the person whom he loves. In turn, he tries to be freely loved in return and (normally) to exclude others through jealousy – that is, through "vacillation arising from simultaneous love and hatred accompanied by the idea of a rival who is envied."[4] Love can thus change into a hatred that is more violent the greater the initial intensity of the affection (*E* 3.38 and dem.).

This type of love does not always reach perfection, because it contains within it a charge of monomaniacal and uncontrolled passionateness: "Love and desire can be excessive."[5] This is easy to see when lovers are derided and considered crazy, because they fixate on the object of their yearnings: "no less mad are those thought to be who are fired with love, dreaming night and day only of their sweetheart or their mistress."[6] This is a love that changes into "delirium," into fixation of desire, in a whirlwind of a single passion that reduces everything to itself. It would have been difficult for such excesses to elude Spinoza, a shrewd observer of passion in the daily experience of social life (making him similar to the

sicut quando aliquis timet aliquod damnum futurum cum spe tamen aliqua, quae illud possit amoveri). See also J. Aubery, *L'antidote d'amour* (Paris, 1599), 45: "L'amour ne produit jamais une seule passion tousjours il accouche de deux qui sont contraires, la jumelle de la peur et la hardiesse autant éventée en ses légères entreprises que la peur est retenue par ses coüardises." On these subjects, see J. Ferrand, *Traité de l'essence et guérison de l'Amour, ou De la mélancolie érotique*, chaps. 2 and 19 (Toulouse, 1610), of which there is a splendid edition in English: *A Treatise on Lovesickness*, ed. D.A. Beecher and M. Ciavolella (Syracuse, 1990), in particular 373–4.

3 *E* 3.13 schol.; 3, defs. of the emotions 6.

4 *E* 3.35, schol. See also 3.33 and dem.; 3.49; 4.44 and dem.

5 *E* 4.44.

6 *E* 4.44, dem. The terms that Spinoza uses to depict jealousy towards a woman are curious and revealing: "He who thinks of a woman whom he loves as giving herself to another will not only feel pain by reason of his own appetite being checked but also, being compelled to associate the image of the object of his love with the sexual parts of his rival, he feels disgust for her" (*E* 3.35, schol.). Who knows if Spinoza knew books on delusions or on the illnesses of love, like Ferrand's book mentioned above, or that genre of literature discussed in M. Ciavolella, *La "malattia d'amore" dall'Antichità al Medioevo* (Rome, 1976).

Dutch painters of the time) and a passionate reader of theatrical works. He even performed, for fun, the comedies of Terence, whose importance to his theory of feelings is both noteworthy and overlooked. In fact, the Latin comedy writer not only is one of the authors widely cited and used in the sections of *Ethics* related to the passions,[7] but also provides an ethical model of the education of the affections. Rejecting severity and fear, however, he relies on their development through benevolence that includes proper love of self: *proxumus sum egomet mihi.*[8]

The comedy *Adelphoe* (*Brothers*) is revealing in this regard, because it shows how different life events and different upbringings lead two brothers to opposite forms of behaviour. One, rejecting fear and using persuasion, ultimately triumphs over the other, who had hardened towards himself and others (vv. 58–65 et seq.). In the end, with a sort of *transitio* towards a happy ending of the vicissitudes portrayed, even the gruff Demea is forced to recognize the superiority of the solution he had opposed: "I have found, by experience, that there is nothing better for

7 See Ter., *Heat.* 946 in *E* 3, defs. of the emotions 42, expl. (on the consternation born of "twofold timorousness" and that makes man hesitate between two evils such that he does not know "which of the two to avert"); *Adelph.* 71 in *E* 3, defs. of the emotions 48, expl.; and *E* 5.4, schol. (on the ambition of those who hope never to be discovered in their goals, as Terence says – *Adelph.* 69–76 [act 1, scene 1] – with echoes that resonate clearly in Spinoza's convictions: "He who, compelled by harsh treatment, does his duty, so long as he thinks it will be known, is on his guard. If he hopes that it will be concealed, he again returns to his natural bent. He whom you have secured by kindness, acts from inclination; he is anxious to return like for like. Present and absent, he will be the same"); *Heat.* 962–3 in *E* 4.16 (on the desire for pleasant things in the present that thwarts the expectation of future ones); *Eun.* 232–3 in *E* 4.17, schol. (on the possible difference between the foolish man and the intelligent one in governing feelings); *Adelph.* 84–6 in *E* 4.54, schol. ("hope and fear bring more advantage than harm ... For if men of weak spirit should all equally be subject to pride and should be ashamed of nothing and afraid of nothing, by what bonds could they be held together and bound?"); *Eun.* 254 in *E* 4.57, schol. (on the proud man who loves parasites and flatterers who "humor his weakness of spirit and turn his folly to madness"). The importance of Terence had previously been noted, on another level, by J.H. Leopold, "De Spinoza elocutione," in *Ad Spinozae Opera Posthuma* (Hagiae Comitis, 1902), 24 et seq., and by F.A. Akkerman, "Studies in the Posthumous Works of Spinoza," 14–6.

8 Through Terence, there is filtered the position of Menander, in whom the Aristotelian and Theophrastic theories of passions and characters are revised under the sign of a reconciliation of social and individual conflicts. For some references that indirectly frame this problem, see P. Flury, *Liebe und Liebesgespräche bei Menander, Plautus und Terenz* (Heidelberg, 1968); and C. Lord, "Aristotle, Menander and the Adelphoe of Terence," *Transactions and Proceedings of the American Philological Association* 107 (1977), 183–202.

a man than an easy temper and complacency" (vv. 860–1). The comparison with the "mild, gentle" brother, "offensive to no one" and "having a smile for all," makes him regret having been, instead, "rustic, rigid, cross, self-denying, morose" and having wasted his existence in making money (vv. 864–9); "I bear all the misery, he enjoys the pleasure" (v. 876).

Only if men manage to ensure that others may love and hate what they themselves love and hate will fluctuations of the soul not be produced (see *E* 3.31):

> Speremus pariter, pariter metuamus amantes:
> Ferreus est, si quis, quod sinit alter, amat.[9]

Loving God like Oneself

Spinoza subsequently indicates the path that leads the *conatus* to the peak of human excellence, to *amor Dei intellectualis.* At this superior level of order and consistency with which the mind expresses its affections, love – separated from the previous idea of an external cause – is conceived in a more suitable way. Free from every imperfection and the vice of "ordinary love," it no longer overflows with any excess. In fact, it can grow endlessly: *semper major, ac major esse potest.*[10] Now it has become affection and intelligence of the perfect and internal cause of the whole of which each person is part. This whole does not compel any rejection of oneself, love of God as sacrifice of man, or altruism like repudiation of self-esteem and self-preservation. In this sense, the path of *Ethics* does not conflict with the repeated claims of *utilitas* and the unwaivability of one's own power/right. Loving God does not mean subjugating oneself to others, but inserting oneself into a context of maximum self-strengthening,

9 "Let us hope while we fear and fear while we hope, we lovers. He has a heart of iron who loves what another concedes" (Ovid, *Amores*, II, XIX, 4–5, cited by Spinoza in *E* 3.31, cor., which inverts the order of the verses).

10 See *E* 5.2 and, for the step noted above, *E* 5.20, schol.: "Again, it should be noted that emotional distress and unhappiness have their origin especially in excessive love toward a thing subject to considerable instability, a thing which we can never completely possess." Conversely, the third type of knowledge, that of God's intellectual love, "begets love toward something immutable and eternal … which we can truly possess … and which therefore cannot be defiled by any of the faults that are to be found in the common sort of love, but can continue to grow more and more … and engage the greatest part of the mind … and pervade it."

intensifying the *conatus* of self-preservation to the point of making it lose all aspects of pettiness and low *vis existendi.* Spinozan genealogy of the affections does not have intellectual love derive from "egoism" in a narrow sense, but strengthens the *utilitas* in *amor,* preventing the latter from being reduced to mere appropriation or "altruism."

The Spinozan idea of *utilitas* has little to do with the modern "possessive individualism" theorized by Macpherson, granting that it effectively existed before Locke. Such *utilitas* is not at all placed under the protection of *ratio* like a calculation, nor does it correspond to the *oikeiosis* of the Stoics, understood as the legitimate right to self-preservation or as the co-belonging of all animated beings to the same great community of living things.[11] It is, above all, a tool of greater perfection: "Since reason demands nothing contrary to nature, it therefore demands that every man should love himself, should seek his own advantage (I mean his real advantage), should aim at whatever really leads a man toward greater perfection, and to sum it all up, that each man, as far as in him lies, should endeavor to preserve his own being" (*E* 4.18, schol.). Unlike what will occur in the thought and political practice of the Jacobins, *utilitas* does not foresee any conflict between self-preservation, happiness, and virtue. It does not demand sacrifice of oneself, the solemn rejection of life in the name of democracy or of a superior principle that might end up fundamentally foreign to individuals' *conatus* of existing. In fact, "the basis of virtue is the very *conatus* to preserve one's own being, and happiness consists in a man's being able to preserve his own being" (ibid.). And it does not have any individualistic dimension: "Men who are governed by reason, that is, men who aim at their own advantage under the guidance of reason, seek nothing for themselves that they would not desire for the rest of mankind; and so are just, faithful, and honorable" (ibid.). Men's impotence and absence of virtue depends on the missing

---

11 The basis of the Spinozan idea of *utilitas,* however, is certainly this key concept of Stoic philosophy, regarding which see *SVF* III, 87; Cic., *De fin.* III, 5, 16 (and later, Sext Emp., *Adv. math.* XI). The theory of *oikeiosis* (generally rendered in Latin by the term *conciliatio*) actually dates back to Theophrastus and concerns the community of all living beings, their spontaneous inclination to follow – within each species – what is useful for the preservation of its nature and the inclination of every being to be attracted by what is "right" for it, because it is considered inadmissible that nature may have made living beings strangers to themselves (see *SVF* I, 197; Diog. Laert., VII, 85), that is, incapable of loving themselves. On this point, see F. Dirlmeier, "Die Oikeiosis-Lehre Theophrasts," *Phronesis* 1 (1955–6), 123–45 (which tends to limit the analogies between Theophrastus and the Stoics). For Stoicism, on the other hand, see

pursuit of the search for one's own usefulness, from the slowed effort of preserving oneself (*E* 4.20). The *affectuum remedia* (see *E* 5.20, schol.) generally do not produce any lasting usefulness for most people, because they do not speak of the *utilitas* of individuals. Preaching morality is useless; rules and prohibitions that appeal exclusively to universal norms and concepts remain ineffective as long as they do not involve emotions. In fact, unless they become feelings themselves, "no emotion can be checked by the true knowledge of good and evil insofar as it is true, but only insofar as it is considered as an emotion" (*E* 4.14).

Finally, also absent in this *utilitas* is "possessive" nature in the narrowest sense. To the extent possible, Spinoza certainly intends to render the individual *compos sui*, endowed with a non-repressive form of self-control, but this is also within a dimension (like the Aristotelian *philautia* or, even more, the Stoic *oikeiosis*) that assumes collectivity. *Oikeiosis* is the act of appropriating oneself, feeling in some way at home in the world, the inclination in which every living being tries to reconcile itself with itself. Any animal is capable of instinctively distinguishing what is useful for it and what is harmful, of loving its own nature and how much it contributes to preserving it, of escaping destruction and whatever contributes to destruction.[12] Nature (argues Seneca, for example) offers to the animal and the child, before all experience, what life and art will subsequently teach them. There is a sort of genetic imprinting in the fact that the hen does not avoid the peacock or the goose, but runs "from the hawk, which is a so much smaller animal not even familiar to the hen" or that chicks "fear a cat and not a dog." Their instinctive love for their own preservation is not, then, "based on actual experiments; for they avoid a thing before they can possibly have experience of it."[13] Even the smallest of men, before acquiring the fullness of reason, acts by instinct, since every age has its nature: "The periods of infancy, boyhood, youth, and old age

---

particularly S.G. Pembroke, "Oikeiosis," in *Problems in Stoicism*, 216–38, and T. Engberg Pedersen, "Discovering the Good: *oikeiosis* and *kathekonta* in Stoic Ethics," in *The Norms of Nature*, ed. M. Schofield and G. Striker (Cambridge, 1986), 341–74. With regard to the Stoics, the meaning of the concept is well stated in Diog. Laert., VII 85 and VII 94, where he emphasizes that every animal is disposed by nature to be attached to itself – that is, to flee what harms it and follow what is "useful" to it or that is not contrary to usefulness (and not, however, what is agreeable).

12 See Cic., *De fin.* III, 5, 16. This is a step in which the capital importance of the concept of self-preservation in Stoic doctrine is emphasized, since "the love of self" constitutes "the first principle" in every being (ibid.).

13 Sen., *Ep.* 121.19.

are different; but I, who have been infant, boy, and youth, am still the same. Thus, although each has at different times a different constitution, the adaptation of each to its constitution is the same. For nature does not consign boyhood or youth, or old age, to me; it consigns me to them."[14]

If for no other reason than having practised commerce (like Schopenhauer), Spinoza knows up close the importance of "material" goods and the weight of "interests" and money: "Money has supplied a token for all things, with the result that its image is wont to obsess the minds of the populace, because they can scarcely think of any kind of pleasure that is not accompanied by the idea of money as its cause" (*E* 4, app. 28). In principle, however, goods and money do not set up a field of conflict with other men. It is not and will never be true that, in their Machiavellian "sadness," they will "sooner forget the death of their father than the loss of their patrimony" (*P* XVII, 54).

Like Seneca before him, Spinoza consequently rejects the cynicism-producing position of the most rigorous Stoics, according to whom the wise man does not need external conditions to achieve happiness, because he must reduce his needs to a minimum and calmly tolerate deprivations. Although not attributing to money the importance that "common" people give to it, he lacks any ascetic and monastic concept of wisdom, since joy is offered not only by the mind, but also by the body and its moderated pleasures (in a sense more medical than moral). The theoretical problem Spinoza poses, then, is that of the postulated compatibility between individual usefulness and joy and public usefulness and happiness.[15] Therefore, some concerns related to an excessively marked emphasis on the importance of social relations in Spinoza can partially be shared, and the presence in his thought of limitations tied to his time can be admitted without hesitation, but this does not imply any possessive individualism or any reduction of *utilitas* to "cynicism" (which would require the bliss of the wise man or the intellectual love of God as antidote and compensation).[16]

---

14 Ibid., 121.16 and *passim.*

15 See *E* 4.35, cor. 2: "It is when every man is most devoted to seeking his own advantage that men are of most advantage to one another."

16 For the reasons I gave above (pp. 135–8), I hold that the submissiveness that Spinoza "requires of the masses" is not at all blind or lasting. Even in the case of money, however, the emphasis falls on the idea of "mutual aid" (*E* 4, app. 28) that men offer in social exchange. It is certainly true that Spinoza, although admitting that "the care of the poor devolves upon society as a whole, and looks only to the common good" (*E* 4, app. 17), does not yet succeed in envisioning a society in which the poor may not have reason to exist. But can he be faulted for that?

Utilitas and *philautia*

Spinoza's *utilitas* does not correspond to "egoism" (a term, after all, coined only in 1718 by Wolff to identify a "sect" that professed only the existence of the *I*) and is not at odds with *amor Dei intellectualis*. Consequently, it is not a "subterfuge" at least as concerns its "immanent" character, since the "transhuman absolute" towards which the Dutch philosopher seems to aim includes the immanent being of every individual. It cannot be denied that the nature of this love is "open and temporal": open, because it grows and extends to all individual things; temporal, because it concerns corruptible beings that only knowledge considers *sub specie aeternitatis*.[17]

It was recently noted that all human values may be rooted in will, within which the mediation between being and having-to-be is done by desire (*querer*) – according to suggestions that also derive from the *Comento a las vidas de don Quijote y Sancho Panza* by Miguel de Unamuno. It is said that what counts is what man desires, but he desires what agrees with his own being in transformation. Man cannot completely invent himself, but nor can he – according to the tradition of Pico della Mirandola's *Oratio de hominis dignitate* or to a proposition of Spinoza's *Ethics* – completely stop inventing himself along the lines of a conscious effort of indefinite duration.[18] From this perspective, every virtue has a self-affirming character, and every ethics stands on selfish (even if not self-centred) grounds. It also represents a way of saying yes to life. It is of no use, then, to search for base motives in noble actions (just as is done, in the words of Miguel de Unamuno, by *stupidos bachileres, curas y barberos*), juxtaposing the ethics of self-esteem with a feeling of innate sympathy for one's fellow beings or cultivated altruism. Virtue is individualism.[19]

---

17 The defence of self-esteem itself and criticism of Spinoza are contained in the penetrating analysis conducted by F. Savater, *Ética como amor proprio* (Madrid, 1988), 30–1, 37. The book indicatively places two phrases in exergue: one by Alexander Pope ("True self-love and social are the same") and another by Walter Benjamin, from *One-Way Street*, where he observes the strange paradox in which people think they are acting according to their own narrow interest, while in reality, it always drifts according to mass instincts alien to life. The subject was reprised, by the same author, in "La critica jansenista del amor proprio," in *Humanismo impenitente: Diez ensayos anti-jansenistas* (Barcelona, 1990), 55–74 and passim.

18 See *E* 3.9: "The mind, both in so far as it has clear and distinct ideas and in so far as it has confused ideas, endeavors to persist in its own being over an indefinite period of time, and is conscious of this conatus."

19 See F. Savater, *Ética como amor proprio*, 18 et seq. and passim. For the reference to Unamuno's key text, see p. 295.

In reality, Spinoza extends some aspects of the Aristotelian tradition of *philautia* (and in particular, of the Stoic theory of *oikeiosis*) to a sphere that goes beyond social relationships to embrace virtually all the individual beings of the universe as they strive to persevere in their own being.[20] Aristotle reasons according to classical models of benevolence towards citizens of the same state (and not so much towards the poor, the needy, or the weak) – models that Christianity marred.[21] It is manifested not only in agonistically institutional form – like a contest of munificence and liberality between the most affluent in giving or increasing their obligatory contribution to well-being or the greatness of the *polis* – but also through the expansion of completely free benefits, like public works or gifts of money and goods.[22]

Aristotle had admitted that, with respect to ambition, most men prefer to be loved rather than love, but he considered the opposite attitude to be ethically superior – that is, the one expressed through friendship (which "seems to lie in loving rather than in being loved") or in maternal love. The proof of it "is indicated by the delight mothers take in loving; for some mothers hand over their children to be brought up, and so long as they know their fate, they love them and do not seek to be loved in return (if they cannot have both), but seem to be satisfied if they see them prospering; and they themselves love their children even if these, owing to their ignorance, give them nothing of a mother's due" (*Eth. Nic.* VIII, 8, 1159a). Further, he had connected this type of love to people of

---

20 In this, Spinoza also distinguishes himself from Hobbes and his insistence on mere defensive self-preservation – what interpreters call, precisely, "egoism" (regarding which see B. Gert, "Hobbes, Mechanicism, and Egoism," *Philosophical Quarterly* 15 (1964), 341–9; Gert, "Hobbes and Psychological Egoism," *Journal of the History of Ideas* 28 (1967), 503–20; F.S. McNeilly "Egoism in Hobbes," *Philosophical Quarterly* 16 (1966), 193–206.

21 On the juxtaposition of Christian and pagan values (the latter contrary to the separation between individual life and social life, between morals and strength) that recalls Nietzsche's thesis, according to which the Greeks' problem did not consist of reinvigorating weakness but of limiting strength, see M. Augé, *Génie due paganisme* (Paris 1985). Not to be underestimated, however, is the often-observed fact that the evangelical precept of loving one's brother as oneself assumes that one is also loved for being able to love one's brother. For development of this subject in the Christian philosophical tradition, with an Aristotelian stamp, see R. de Weiss, *Amor sui: Sens et fonction de l'amour de soi dans l'ontologie de Thomas d'Aquin* (Genève, 1977).

22 Arist., *Eth. Nic.* VIII, 8, 1159b. On the munificence (*megaloprepeia*) with which citizens, who tend to be properly honoured, opulently finance the arrangement of choirs, competitions, and banquets, see *Eth. Nic.* IV, 2, 1122a–23.

good and constant character, to the *spoudaioi*, denying it to the wicked, because "wicked men have no steadfastness (for they do not remain even like to themselves)" (ibid., VIII, 8, 1159b). Moreover, loving is better than being loved because it corresponds to activity and choice in favour of one's own being: "love is like activity, being loved like passivity; and loving and its concomitants are attributes of those who are the more active" (ibid., IX, 7, 1168a).

Also in Aristotle – as in Spinoza – there is no opposition in principle between loving oneself and others, between what we are accustomed to define as "egoism" and "altruism." Aristotle asserts that it is wrong to criticize those who think about themselves and label them as bad. It is necessary to reverse a view that is widespread even today: it is not love of oneself that is intrinsically bad, it is the quality of the person who practises it that makes him good or bad. Whoever lives in friendship with himself and rationally controls his own passions contributes to improving his social relationships and making them more intense, to the extent he practises *philautia*, whereas the self-esteem of the evil man, split and torn within himself, ends up damaging himself and others. "Therefore, the good man should be a lover of self (for he will both himself profit by doing noble acts, and will benefit his fellows), but the wicked man should not; for he will hurt both himself and his neighbors, following as he does evil passions. For the wicked man, what he does clashes with what he ought to do, but what the good man ought to do, he does."[23] Since *eudaimonia* is the only activity that is an end in itself, even philosophy, which offers man the highest happiness, will be "self-sufficient" (ibid., X, 6, 1176a, 1177b). Therefore, philosophy, like Spinozan *amor Dei intellectualis*, celebrates the sublimation of *philautia*, the maximum active love of self, that which does not transform reason into a simple border guard of the passions or (as opposed to Kant, who did not hesitate to define the passions as "illnesses of mind") into an immune system that fights and blocks its metastases, so to speak.

"If I Love You, What Business Is It of Yours?"

In loving oneself as an active part of nature, one loves God and understands emotionally that it represents a love object so immense and

23 Ibid., IX, 8, 1169a. On the nature of good and bad people according to Aristotle, see, in the present volume, pp. 168–70.

fulfilling as to not feel the need for reciprocation: "He who loves God cannot endeavor that God should love him in return."[24] And this is not only because God is impersonal and, consequently, does not feel any passion (joy, sadness, love, or hate – see *E* 5.17 and cor.) but because loving God is simply loving and knowing adequately (*ex abundantia cordis et mentis*, you could say) both the particular things (see *E* 5.24), and the best part of oneself, conceived as the expression of everything. *Amor erga Deum*, "the most constant of all emotions" (*E* 5.20, schol.), is intransitive and asymmetric – unlike hate, which triggers a spiral of mutual and widespread retaliation. One loves God or Nature, breaking the cycle of mere reciprocity, unbalancing oneself, precisely because this love is not indifference but lucid and aware involvement in the events of every individual being. In this way, one simultaneously re-cognizes – that is, one knows twice – two things. First, he knows his own belonging to the world according to an order that transcends the partiality of the viewpoint of passion or the indifference of pure rational universality. Second, he knows according to an order that not only passively accepted the relative perspective of all partial points of view (of the good for the wolf that corresponds to the bad for the lamb) but that actively resolves it in loving every being for itself, through the ascending metamorphosis of the *transitio*.

This concept can only appear to the Christian tradition as a sort of arrogance, almost as if man were giving grace to God and holding himself superior to Him in not requiring reciprocity, even though his existence depends entirely on Him.[25] In the Jewish and Christian religions, man's life belongs to God; it is His property. This state imposes the obligation

24 *E* 5.19 and see 5.37, cor. Goethe's well-known phrase from *Wilhelm Meister* – "If I love you, what business is it of yours?" – is recalled by Nietzsche in contrast to Christian love based on correspondence and exchange. Even under this profile, Spinoza's concept is placed indirectly in opposition to that of some exponents of libertine thought, who not only accuse "God, Nature, or Destiny" of hating men, but who reject even intelligence as an instrument of elevation towards comprehension of reality. See, for example, Vallée des Barreaux, "Sonnet," cited in A. Adam, *Les libertines au* XVIIe *siècle*, 196: *Je renonce au bon sens, J'haïs l'intelligence/D'autant plus que l'esprit s'élève en connaissance [...]/Dieu, Nature ou Destin, que tu nous fais grand tort!/De peine et de chagrin toute la vie est pleine,/Au lieu de ton amour tu nous montres ta haine,/Que tu sois des trois que conduisent la sort.*

25 A recent echo of the persistence of this aversion to an intransitive love of God can be noted in C.S. Lewis, *The Four Loves* (London, 1958), 4: "It would be a bold and silly creature that came before its Creator with the boast, 'I'm no beggar. I love you disinterestedly.'"

to give back as much as one was given and to show one's gratitude to the divinity, obeying His commandments and reciprocating His love (dispositions onto which divine grace can more easily be grafted).[26] For Spinoza, on the other hand, man is part of the *Deus sive natura*, but he does not belong to Him like property, nor does he owe gratitude or respect on the strength of an affinity or relationship that would have made him similar to God. Man devotes himself to God through a free and unilateral gesture, equivalent to the recognition of full participation in the life of the world (our love being just a part of the love that God, or all of nature, dedicates to itself for its own preservation). It is not a case of an *ex voto* dedicated to a superior being towards whom one intends to demonstrate servile obedience. In fact, "only free men are truly grateful to one another" (*E* 4.71). Note that Spinoza says "free men" and not simply "wise men," as in the case of the Stoics (see *SVF* III, 672).

Knowing the limits of our power more clearly, we can better concentrate on areas of effective action and thought. In this sense, it does not seem to me that Spinoza is, as Borges defined him, a "pathetic figure" who would seek compensation for individual weaknesses in fusion with the Whole of *amor Dei intellectualis*.[27] It is not a case of mystical union (however immanent), blessed contemplation, or annulment of the *I*, but rather of knowledge of the particularities, or articulation and delimitation of the parts. The *emendatio* of the passions occurs without sacrifice of one's own *utilitas*. Overturning Christian tradition, it is man – the wise and free man – who gives thanks for himself to God-nature, without asking for anything in exchange, *do ut non des*.[28] Man – not God – is "love,"

26 If for St John, "God is love" (1 John 4:8), it is also true that, for him, "in this is love: not that we loved God, but that he loved us" (I John 4:10).

27 See J.L. Borges, "Spinoza, une figure pathétique," *Europe* 637 (May 1962), 73–6. For Borges's interest in Spinoza – to whom he dedicated two noteworthy sonnets – see M. Abadi, "Spinoza in Borges's Looking Glass," *Studia Spinozana* 5 (1989), 29–42. Borges seems here to reprise the image of Spinoza presented by Unamuno (see, in the present volume, p. 313).

28 Thus, on this point, I do not share the thesis of the excellent study by S. Zac according to which *Deus sive natura* represents Spinoza's closest point of contact with the Christian idea of salvational love (Zac, *Spinoza et l'interprétation de l'Écriture* [Paris, 1965], 197). Neither salvation nor, conversely, sacrifice enter into Spinoza's system of values, of which these two assertions must be jointly taken into account: "The conatus to preserve oneself is the primary and sole basis of virtue" (*E* 4.22, cor.) and – with a Cartesian echo but in reference to *amor intellectualis* as the crowning achievement of reason – "Desire that arises from reason cannot be excessive" (*E* 4.61). From this point of view, his position moves far from the apologia for sacrifice made by Heidegger (and indirectly connected both to the analysis of fear in §30 of *Being and Time* and

the fulfilment of the desire that constitutes its essence. The wise man knows he is an active participant in the life of nature, tied to his fellow beings through the wisdom expressed by the necessity of all things. In thinking, he does not separate himself from other men, but unites with them, entering into harmony with what (though divided by the passions) they have in common: thought itself.[29]

Semper major

Philautia and *utilitas* end up being enhanced by insertion into the framework of the totality that encompasses knowledge and the individualizing love of every single thing. Spinoza does not demand any ascetic act, nor does he impose any duty of moral perfection – neither a *sacrificium imaginationis* nor a *sacrificium intellectus* and not even a superhuman effort of will and self-control.

Unlike the Stoics or Christian apologetics, the Spinozan *ordo amoris* does not have any objective character established or created by God. Order and disorder are not inherent in the inner structure of the universe. They depend only on human consideration and imagination (see *Ep.* 32), which does not exclude (as in the case of good and evil) that these may hold a positive or negative value for us. The same criterion is applied to beauty and ugliness. In one letter, Spinoza presents a sort of *aesthetica in nuce*, with which he not only inserts himself indirectly in

---

the rejection of security in favor of worry) when he asserts that "giving something up doesn't put up with any calculation by means of which it always just becomes resolved to a profit or loss, whether its aims are to be set high or low. Such calculation disfigures the essence of giving something up" (M. Heidegger, *Was ist Metaphysik?* [Frankfurt, 1960], 45, and *What Is Metaphysics,* trans. M. Groth). Spinoza denies any sort of intrinsic dignity to sacrifice and to "being-for-death."

29 Unlike Descartes, Spinoza is not so much the philosopher of the *ego*, of solitary individuality, but of the *nos*. I agree, in this sense and from another perspective, on the juxtaposition of the Cartesian search for simplicity and Spinozan knowledge of the *res singulares* carried out by P. Cristofolini, "Ipotesi sull'oggetto della scienza intuitiva," in *Studi sul Seicento e l'immaginazione* (Pisa, 1985), 95–111 (and see, by the same author, *Spinoza per tutti* [Milan, 1993]). It is necessary in this case, however, to understand "intuitive science," the getting closer to the things of the world, not in the framework of a plural and complex subject (of *nos* as the united power of men capable of enjoying their own activity), but of the wise man's disposition to not live in solitude, animated by selfish intentions. The only possible *nos*, though, that which depends on the greater "security" enjoyed in democracy, no longer has anything in common with the third type of knowledge.

the contemporaneous discussion of "taste" and objects to the age-old Platonic and Neo-Platonic tradition (that considered beauty as existing in itself and ugliness as a simple lack thereof), but also develops a proxemics of beauty, a knowledge of the distance at which things reveal themselves to be beautiful or ugly. "Beauty, most esteemed Sir," he writes to Boxel in *Ep.* 54.899, "is not so much a quality in the perceived object as an effect in him who perceives. If we were more long-sighted or more short-sighted, or if we were differently constituted, the things which we now think beautiful would appear ugly, and the ugly, beautiful. The most beautiful hand, seen through a microscope, would appear repulsive. Some things seen at a distance are beautiful, but when viewed at close range, ugly. So things regarded in themselves, or as related to God, are neither beautiful nor ugly ... Perfection and imperfection are designations not much different from beauty and ugliness."

In this sense, the myopia of the human mind denounced by Augustine (when he asserts that, within the great mosaic of the world, it succeeds in noticing only a few tiles at a time)[30] must not be confused with the Spinozan declaration of ignorance regarding how the individual elements are connected. When he states that "I do not know how each part of nature harmonizes with the whole, and how it coheres with other parts" (*Ep.* 30.844), Spinoza does not exclude the necessity for us of such links – the only ones that allow us access to knowledge at all levels. Rather, he affirms only that order is perspective – that is, it acquires meaning only from the human viewpoint and, furthermore, we possess a discontinuous and local awareness of it. The argument of the Stoics – that a single grain of fortuitousness, a single event without cause (*anaitios*) could destroy the rational harmony of the cosmos (see *SVF* II, 945) – is thus substantially supplemented by this conviction, which does not at all blunt the idea of a *per causas* knowability of the truth. As shown by science, which continues to accumulate undeniable successes, faith in the consistency of phenomena through which the perfect functioning of the *fabrica mundi* reveals itself is well placed. The presence of order can appear or can be discovered anywhere, in that which is most humble and in that which is most sublime: from the "stick of straw" admired – it is said – even on the bonfire by the pantheist Giulio Cesare Vanini to the "anatomy of a louse" extolled by Dutch microscopists; from the

30 August., *ord.* I, 2. The works of Augustine that Spinoza could have known are those contained in the *Epitome Augustini Operum omnium*, published in 1539, which appears among the volumes of his library. See J. Preposiet, *Bibliographie spinoziste*, 339, n. 17.

"meteorology" of the passions to the turbulence of the clouds; from the harmony of the rainbow to the attributes and modes of God. Spinoza no longer needs to support one of the classical *paradoxa stoicorum*, in which the greater the obedience to the laws of nature, the greater our liberty. In fact, it is not a case of simply knowing the course of things (trusting in it or, like Seneca, letting oneself be drawn by it) but also loving it, opening spaces of activity that are not incompatible with the superiority of the whole over the small part every being is.

Therefore, he does not go beyond reason and the law, because he rejects the rational dimension of knowledge, preferring to turn to the "black sun" of the mystical love of Meister Eckhart, Teresa of Ávila, or Juan de la Cruz. The basic motive is that reason and law are still connected secretly to the act of triggering, through conflict, a reduction of the power of existing, or *tristitia* (as an effect of residual fear and hope). Just as, in Paul, the "ancestral law" (Acts 22:3) is born together with sin, in Spinoza it is born as a restraint on human whims and passions incapable of self-control (but this "declining *conatus*" also produces sadness for Spinoza, and he does not at all distinguish, like Paul, between a "godly grief" that encourages penitence and salvation and one typical of the world, one that "produces death" [2 Cor. 7:10] – all *tristitia* is deadly, and God wants joy, not mourning). If men let themselves be themselves, guided spontaneously by healthy reason, laws would be useless (*TTP* 16.*531*, and in *OP* 129, 381). Constrictive universality, the leveller of the *res singulares*, is born in a reactive and oppositional form with respect to the unrestrained greed of men.

Reason and law guarantee some *securitas* indeed, but sometimes at the price of an endless struggle that divides and dissipates energies, obliging each person to live a relatively poor life, always conducted on the defensive.[31] On the other hand, love completes reason but does not annul it; it implements political and religious law but does not erase it. Intellectual love of God represents knowledge and happiness conjoined at the limit of the humanly desirable, the *cupiditas* that, through overabundance, spreads through everything. Paraphrasing Blake, we could say that reason, like the well, "holds" exact quantities of water, while love, like the fountain, "overflows." Although following the specific laws of fluid mechanics – which Pascal and Dutch hydraulic engineers, spread

31 Spinoza, a systematic philosopher, thus deals with moral law and reason in the sphere of "human bondage" (*Ethics*, book 4) and with *amor Dei intellectualis* or the *ordo amoris* in the sphere of "human freedom" (*Ethics*, book 5).

across Europe as experts on dykes and the channeling and draining of swamps, were beginning to codify in Spinoza's time – love was always excessive with respect to a fixed measure, which wants to collect the liquid once and for all.

Do Not Cry with Joy

Amor Dei intellectualis, like *ordo amoris,* is a further *transitio*: it takes its "sting" from the law and from death without the aid of grace. It offers *acquiescentia* in the place of transience, fullness of knowledge and feeling in the place of the substantially intellectualistic *ratio diligendi* of Aquinas[32] or the later concept of love as passion-torment (e.g., in the double root that is preserved in the German term for "passion," *Leidenschaft,* in its derivation from the root of *leiden,* "to suffer") or as love in the absence of knowledge, surrounded by gauzy veils of sentiment.

Thus, it does not seem to me that Unamuno or Horkheimer fully captured the sense of Spinozan *amor Dei intellectualis,* overestimating the permanence of intellectualistic remnants within it. With a grain (at most) of truth, Miguel de Unamuno speaks of the *formidable tragedia* of the *Ethics* of Spinoza, *pobre judio desesperado de Amsterdam* and *terrible intellectualista.* He adds that his love is a concept, his eternity a trick, and that "nothing could be more dreary, nothing more desolating, nothing more anti-vital than this happiness, this *beatitudo,* of Spinoza, that consists in the intellectual love of the mind towards God."[33]

For Horkheimer, on the other hand, intellectualism consists of the fact that individual things may not be loved for themselves:

> The unity of the universal and of the particular becomes evident in love. Loving a particular person, you love what is in all men. In fact, in all creatures, since one can love humanity – or better, life (loving humanity exclusively is a contradiction) – only in the concrete individual ... Spinoza ... is

32 The opposition is not between Aquinas's "moderate joy" and Spinoza's "radiant" one, which J. Kristeva refers to in *Histoires d'amour* (Paris, 1983); Engl. trans. *Tales of Love* (New York, 1987), 187. For Spinoza, what counts most is the intrinsic connection between feelings and knowledge.

33 M. de Unamuno, *Del sentimiento trágico de la vida* (Madrid, 1967), 78–9, and Engl. trans. by J.E. Crawford Flitch, 1921. See the former, p. 13, on *conatus* as desire for eternity conceived by this poor man immersed in the "Dutch fog." In reality, speaking of *conatus* as *nullum tempus finitum, sed indefinitum involvit* (*E* 3.8), Spinoza does not refer to eternity, but duration.

> not far from this awareness, but in his Stoicism, he wants to take into consideration the particular individual only *because* the whole is reflected in it, and this precisely *because* (so to speak, the reflection as condition or *a priori* justification of identification with the particular) it takes its weight from what is particular or transitory. Thus, love ends up being directed again toward the universal, which has lost its contents precisely with the intellectualization of the particular.[34]

It could be that with respect to our culture, Spinoza presents a concept of love that is less vital or passionate (in Hebrew, however, as Spinoza himself notes, *jadah* means both *science* and *love*), less concentrated on exclusive individuality, separated from the context of other beings. Of course, this love is not at all sad, desolate, or unhappy. To understand it – and evaluate the weight of Unamuno's and Horkheimer's objections – it is necessary to modify the perspective from which we look at it and to discover some of the reasons why it was assumed.

A sort of "romantic" prejudice leads to the assertion that love is spontaneity, that it is pure, involuntary, and arational immediacy of feeling. Its value should consist of the negation of every element of reflection and mediation: usefulness, calculation, premeditation, and knowledge. To some extent, it is precisely the generous violation of rules felt to be dry or rigid that legitimizes its value and justifies its occasional excesses. Rather than an ordered process, it is likened to disorderliness and "bolts of lightning." Rather than full and stable enjoyment, it is likened to an uncertain and transitory promise of happiness. Rather than calm security, it is likened to fortunate and unstable union, to a "double contingency." On the basis of the latter, not only is the object worthy of one's own affection discovered by chance among millions of beings, but this has also corresponded positively with the feeling directed towards it. In general terms, we could say that the presumed "intellectualism" of which Spinozan love is accused is merely the effect of a tendential reduction of love to the sphere of the imagination, typical of some of the exponents of contemporary sensibility.

34 M. Horkheimer, *Notizen 1950 bis 1969* (Frankfurt, 1974); Ital. trans. *Taccuini 1950–1969* (Genoa, 1988), 18–19.

Grammar of Love

According to the "Stendahlian" mentality with which the modern concept of love is tinged, it is not, therefore, tied to a progression of knowledge or to a growth of constancy, security, and joy. Rather, its distinctive traits are offered by the nebulousness of the emotions, by the unpredictability of events and their development (in logical terms, reciprocated love is highly improbable and its nature is characterized by fragility), by dangers that surround the life of each person at every moment, and by the undampened fluctuations of the soul. Taking Stendhal as the touchstone, synecdoche, or *pars pro toto* of widespread attitudes and the premise for the explanation of the ambiguities that Unamuno and Horkheimer encounter, we can observe that the structures of love and of the feelings in Spinoza are not only (and obviously) different, but they are also diametrically opposed. This asymmetry is noticeable point by point, at different levels. Thus, while in Spinoza love is expression and supreme specification of the known object and of knowledge itself, for Stendhal, a follower of the *ideologues*, it is an agglomeration, a partly unformed galaxy still to be analysed or whose components (largely destined to remain indistinguishable and unknown) remain to be resolved. It "resembles what we call the Milky Way in heaven, a gleaming mass formed by thousands of little stars, each of which may be a nebula."[35] The imagination and the emotions now perform an exclusive role. Admiration sets imagination in motion, which ends up adorning the loved being with all possible perfection: "Leave the mind of a lover to its natural movements for twenty-four hours, and this is what you will find. At the salt mines of Salzburg, a branch stripped of its leaves by winter is thrown into the abandoned depths of the mine. Taken out two or three months later, it is covered with brilliant crystals; the smallest twigs, those no stouter than the leg of a sparrow, are arrayed with an infinity of sparkling, dazzling diamonds; it is impossible to recognize the original branch."[36] This is the famous "first crystallization." It is not, however, sufficient to preserve love, because the soul tires of what is uniform and, therefore, tires even of happiness. At this point, doubt takes over, and with it hope and

35 Stendhal, *De l'amour*, ed. H. Martineau (Paris, 1947); Engl. trans. *On Love* (New York, 1916), 7.

36 Ibid., 22. The overestimation of the beloved object reduces love to a *consitutiva ficcíon*, such that, for Stendhal, it "is less than blind; it is visionary" (J. Ortega y Gasset, "Amor en Stendhal," in *Para la cultura de amor* [Madrid, n.d.], 261).

fear. This is the moment of the "second crystallization," when happiness emerges from temporary victory over uncertainties and from the realization of a hope. Because "love casts doubts upon things the best proved,"[37] its instability and inconstancy are and must be at maximum levels, so as to always be able to overtake and render love always equal and always different. Don't dare give up hope of the possible, but at the same time don't dare kill off fear, show excessive security, or give up danger. In fact, love is "a delicious flower, but one must have the courage to go and pick it on the edge of a frightful precipice."[38] From this perspective, according to Stendhal, love (like hope) could be defined in a Spinozan way – as an *inconstans laetitia* that, from time to time, searches and tries to find confirmation of the correspondence between one's own desire and that of the other. This symmetry of desire, however, rests precisely on doubt regarding possible reciprocal happiness.

Lovers must simultaneously feel full identity and full reciprocal otherness. If they were too similar, or if identity were to prevail, the reciprocal interest and attraction would end. Conversely, if they were too different – if their otherness were to become absolute – then every relationship would be blocked. This delicate equilibrium must be continually broken and reproduced, even artificially, and the presumed spontaneous feeling must be stirred so that the norm is transformed into surprise. Thus, when intimacy becomes excessive and habit risks overtaking and hardening the relationship, a change in mood, a greater closure of the range of opportunities for meeting (or of possibilities in general), an unexpected act, or even an argument create, along with increased difference, a sort of electric arc, a prerequisite for the striking of a new spark. If, however, the separation becomes excessive, a bold or rash act – like that of Julien Sorel, who climbs the window of Madame de Rênal – succeeds in getting the lovers back together. The important thing is that love not stagnate, that it does not advance customary rights of ownership, because "in love, possession is nothing, joy everything."[39]

Spinoza does not yet live, Stendhal-like, in a prosaic or post-heroic age where security has become a negative value, because the prevalence of the cold passions and interests risks making love disappear among some people, and the prevalence of other, "hot" passions encourages

37 Ibid., 33.
38 Ibid., 160.
39 Ibid., 124.

the vanity of possessing a "fashionable woman" who shines like a "fine horse."[40] For these (and other) reasons, it is difficult, then, to understand "intuitive science" as a surplus of knowledge and not a deficit, as a more suitable way for us to understand the *res particulares*. Further, contrary to Horkheimer's hypothesis, it is necessary to add that the latter are all "contingent and perishable" (*E* 2.31, cor.) and therefore "transitory." Knowledge of them *sub specie aeternitatis* does not at all imply a Medusa's gaze that petrifies them and makes them eternal in a static sense. It is not possible to remove them from time, because their "duration," the indeterminate extension of a time that had a beginning (ibid.), cannot be known. This type or species of knowledge concerns the eye of the mind, which has the capacity to feel and understand the eternal, that which does not change because it is removed from time and spatial extension (e.g., the idea of a triangle and its properties). But it is precisely through this vision *sub specie aeternitatis*, through the "filter" of a universal – that in incorporating itself in the concrete, it lost its generic nature – that I am familiar with the individual object or person in the richness of their definitions. In this sense, universality passes from its potentiality into intuitive science, and it is realized in the *res particulares*. It is no longer disinterested and coldly balanced knowledge but lucid, disproportionate interest in the many-sided "revealing" of the divine substance that appears even in those battles between spiders and flies that Spinoza (according to Colerus, the philosopher's first biographer) seemed to observe gladly and even provoke.

Love does not imply a negation of universality in favour of the blindness of the passions, the halo of indeterminacy of feeling, or the embellishments that desire (as evocation, in the present, of a future good) adds to the beloved thing. One knows satisfactorily only what one loves – that which creates an opening in the mind beyond the general patterns and routine of a sterile universal. Love is similar in this to a generative grammar in which *competence* in the use of universal rules permits *performances* – that is, the creation of infinite, well-formed phrases, unpredictable and innovative, that cannot be placed in advance into any particular pigeonhole. The linguistic code (like the logical one) is not violated, but is implemented and enriched. Necessity is not contradicted but articulated. From this standpoint, even the transformation of the passions into feelings, through the intermediate instrument of reason, is analogous to

40 Ibid., 20.

the setting of universal and abstract rules of a language. The functioning of these rules is completely unknown to a speaker who at first endures them and only later learns to use them not only passively, but to create new, infinite phrases whose fullness of meaning depends on his capabilities.[41] However, it is not a case either of simple application (*Anwendung*) of a general rule in a particular case,[42] nor "elastic" adaptation of the law of the variability of situations, nor, finally, of a supererogatory compensation with respect to incidental "sins" or a feeling of unworthiness. In the first place, it is because we are dealing with a product of the pure formalism of the law regarding intellectual and ethical invention without implying a retreat into the amorphous. Second, it is because in Spinoza, there is a separation between an epistemological wisdom and one that is exclusively "practical" (in the sense of the recent "rehabilitation of practical philosophy" that highlights, in the Aristotelian tradition, only the idea of "prudence" – applying rules case by case, as in *juris-prudentia* – and not that of "practical science").[43] Third, it is because the mere supererogatory compensations for violation of the law – or of love as pity, forgiveness, and benevolence – are not enough to strengthen themselves, because they do not push themselves beyond the logic (however symmetrically backwards) of reason and universality, re-establishing its power and restoring its rigidity after every deviation.

Thus, the "astonishment of reason" (as calculation and "number"), faced with the illogicality of two people in love becoming one (where reason "is wrong even having to be right"), here finds some if its most credible justifications. That "miracle" – sung by Shakespeare in the short

41 Spinoza, who had written a Hebrew grammar (*Compendium grammatices Linguae Hebreae*; see *Hebrew Grammar* in *CW*), did not think of the problem of grammar in the terms described above. See, however, *KV* 2.21.93: "For more power comes to us from the understanding of proportion itself, than from the understanding of the rule of proportion." On the *Compendium*, which has as its goal the structural study of the rules of Hebrew grammar – apart from its character as a "sacred language" (Augustine thought that in Paradise they spoke Hebrew) – see Z. Levy, "The Problem of Normativity in Spinoza's 'Hebrew Grammar,'" *Studia Spinozana* 3 (1987), 351–90.

42 In the sense in which K. Günther talks about it in *Der Sinn für Angemessenheit: Anwendungsdiskurse in Moral und Recht* (Frankfurt, 1988), responding to some difficulties posed by the theories of Habermas on the transcendental universality of the rules. More than an application of the universal to the particular, *scientia inuitiva* seems to have the nature of art when it is understood as knowledge of the particularity.

43 In this way, the *Etica more geometrico demonstrata* also avoids the Aristotelian duality of *espisteme* and *phronesis* – that is, a knowledge of the universal concepts (triangle, etc.) that cannot be different than they are and a knowledge of what, instead, "can be different" from what it is (see *Eth. Nic.* VI, 1 et seq.).

poem *The Phoenix and the Turtle* (symbols, respectively, of the rebirth and constancy of feelings) – is no longer completely incomprehensible: "That the self was not the same;/single nature's double name/neither two nor one was called. // Reason, in itself confounded,/saw division grow together,/to themselves yet either neither,/simple were so well compounded, // that it cried, 'How true a twain/seemeth this concordant one!/Love hath reason, reason none,/if what parts can so remain.'"[44] The inconsistency of the contradiction, deadlocked in love-passion, becomes creativity.

Incipit vita nova

The fresh and renewing character of *amor intellectualis* – where the mind is as if renewed, *tamquam jam inciperet esse* (*E* 5.31, schol.) – does not at all imply negation of the idea of necessity in favour of a sort of principle of indetermination. What's required is just greater acumen, an individualizing gaze (similar to that of the art of knowledge and feeling – an expression of protest against the absolute separation of universal and particular) that may have further developed the criterion (barely sketched by the Stoics) of distinguishing the specific ways in which a general law is expressed through an unlimited variety of evidence, with the weight of all the assessments that define the *res singulares*.

However, it is rare that men – although knowing good without loving it or loving it without knowing it – are disposed to abandon the satisfactions of that limited level of self-preservation with which they have become comfortable. Of course, no one can free himself from the *imbecillitas imaginandi* and from the rigid but consoling order of a reason that averts the chaos and disorder of the passions. In a seemingly strange and incongruous way, the ability of the highest forms of existence and knowledge to attract is lower than that of the levels that allow a lesser perfection, as if men recoiled from happiness. In fact, everyone is subject to the force of imagination, some to the force of reason, and relatively few reach intuitive science and the intellectual love of God and know, at the same time, how to use the *imaginandi potentia* (*E* 2.17, schol.) and all the force of *ratio* towards this end. The classical tradition had never fully investigated this "mystery" (which La Boétie treated with surprise and

44 W. Shakespeare, *The Phoenix and the Turtle* (1601), vv. 38–48. On the forms and consequences of the passion of love in Shakespeare, see, more generally, D.R.C. Marsh, *Passion Lends Them Power: A Study of Shakespeare's Love Tragedies* (Manchester, 1976).

consternation), often contenting itself with condemning men's vices and weakness with respect to the passions or glossing the Ovidian saying *video meliora, proboque, deteriora sequor.*[45] Although finding a way out in the ideal of the wise man, Spinoza had instead placed the problem at the centre of his own reflection, and he had searched for its reasons in the excessive power of all of nature and external causes over man, who cannot narcissistically profess to represent "an empire within an empire," in the insecurity of the conditions of existence and the incapacity of many individuals and communities to abandon the reduced life that they lead and that they largely desire. In this sense, it is not a case for him of getting out of the "minority state," Kant-like, through education or purely juridical guarantees,[46] but of increasing the power of existing, which already contains knowledge and education in itself, and which rights then accompany. It is passion itself, the suffering induced by passivity (i.e., the low level of activity and desire to live), that flushes out the latent possibilities of both a reason capable of expanding and further growth of the power of existing. And it is suffering that pushes towards that investigation and increases passion's level of activity, correcting its *diastrophe* (its perversion or, in this case, diffraction) and making previously dissipated or uncoordinated energies converge on the focal point of first reason and then intuitive science. It is a process of approaching the source of all activity, all light, and all *potentia*, which is God. The *Deus sive natura* towards which intellectual love is addressed is, in this sense, activity that is present and diffused in every individual thing. It does not correspond to the pure act and the immobility of the Aristotelian god, who acts through attraction and remains immobile and who is, therefore, compared to a lover who makes himself desire, to a magnet, or to the fulcrum of a lever that permits movement of an arm precisely because it stays still. From this point of view, at the highest level of intuitive science, the power of man cannot be limited, individually, to the active resistance or the "enlightened despotism" of the Stoics regarding the passions, nor politically, to the repressive absolutism that concentrates the rationality of the state and consciously abandons the masses to passions and illusions (and not even, conversely, to the impotence of utopias that exhaust the energies

45 See Ovid., *Met.* 7.20–1 and *E* 4.17, schol.

46 Religion preserves all of its power precisely because, having to address multitudes controlled by the passions, it must formulate commandments directed towards the salvation of peoples "in the form of law" (see *Ep.* 19.809).

of the passions with the mirage of a rationality completely independent of them).

In recognizing how few men there are who let themselves be guided normally by reason, and how rarer still are those moved by intellectual love without God's reciprocation, Spinoza certainly does not extract all the consequences from such observations. He is clear, however, in rejecting, on moral grounds, the palliatives of invective and melancholy, rigorism and opportunism, categorical certainties and "Pascalian" bets, and in rejecting, on political grounds, the perpetuation of control of the masses or their salvation through utopias. In principle, each of his efforts is directed towards increasing, among all men, the containment of causes and effects, of *tristitia*, and of coercion, promoting instead the *utilitas* of the individual and the collective.[47] With democracy, Spinoza intends to create a society in which each man – master of himself, free in that he is not tied to an oppressive, arbitrary power – can raise on this foundation a life that is happier or, at any rate, more secure.

Only in this way can the modern individual achieve real independence. With respect to the main road previously followed by religions and philosophies, the way that leads there would undergo a radical deviation. It would no longer pass, via a climb to heaven, through the tribulations of an existence consumed in the expectation of postponed happiness, nor in the hope of finally facing the God who concentrates all of our opaque desires. Rather, the ascents would be transformed in this world, into an

47 On piety in Spinoza, or the innate desire to do good in accordance with reason, see *E* 4.37, schol. 1, and L.C. Rice, "Pity and Philosophical Freedom in Spinoza," in *Spinoza in Political and Theological Thought*, ed. C. de Deugd (Amsterdam, 1984), 186. Spinoza's position differs from that of his admirer Nietzsche (who, however, criticized it) in the same way as it does in the case of Schopenhauer: in the inclination towards compassion. Nietzsche intended to develop the "will to power" of a few at the expense of the *tristitia* of the masses (which can be traced back to the conditions of life reached after that last "revolt of slaves" that was the French Revolution). The characteristic generosity of the Nietzschian virtues, however, does not pass through *amor* as an ascendant force, whereas the Spinozan *transitio* is bent in on itself by a new form of eternal Stoic return, by *amor fati* or (better) *ego fatum*. In Nietzsche it is the will, regaining strength, that tends to create its own artificial order through power, to the point of making it become nature. The plan is no longer that of La Boétie or Spinoza, of abandoning voluntary servitude or a democracy in which individuals may become collectively powerful through equitable redistribution of power and rights. It comes back to the big "fish" (see *TTP* 16.527), to Leviathans, "icy monsters," and their aristocratic representatives in the future (the *Übermenschen*) who will have the strength and license to devour the small.

ascension to the peak of oneself, to the truth, and to life in its fullness. In the Spinozan *ordo amoris*, each person would then experience *ex incrementum virium*, from the growth of his strength, the peaceful joy of finding himself at home in a universe enlightened by the omnipresence and omni-pervasiveness of God-nature. He would no longer need – like Petrarch ascending Mt. Ventoso – to find God, like Augustine, in the privacy of himself (*in interiore homine*). Nor would he need to devalue his being moved "to wonder by mountain peaks, by vast waves of the sea, by broad waterfalls on rivers, by the all-embracing extent of the ocean, by the revolutions of the stars" (*Conf.* x, 8.15). In Spinoza, *amor intellectualis* senses God everywhere and knows it "inhabits" not only the souls of the good and the virtuous, but all things – even those that seem most contemptible and wicked.

PART 4: THE GREAT HOPE

SECTION 1

Terror and Virtue

1. The Form of the Future

Expectations of Change

In the summer of 1789, Arthur Young, a noted English writer and agronomist, came across, between the fields at the side of a road, a peasant woman full of wrinkles who had aged prematurely. She was only twenty-eight but looked sixty or seventy. She had a small plot of land, a cow, and a skinny horse, but her family was so ruined by the exaction of duties imposed by feudal right (*car les tailles et les droits nous écrasent*) that all her hopes were centred on the expectation that the frightful misery would end and that the world would change.[1]

Her fate was not exceptional. A fourth or fifth of the harvest generally ended up in the hands of the feudal lord, and other forms of providing for oneself were punished severely. "Woe to the peasant" who might shoot "a partridge or a pigeon." The laws were "inviolable in the protection of beasts as if they were men and in persecuting men as if they were beasts."[2] Daily existence in the countryside was, in Spinozan terms, so dominated by *insecuritas* that it was often prevented from revealing itself not just to reason, but to humanity. The French peasants of this period were still as La Bruyère had described them a century before, in 1688: "wild animals, male and female, spread over the countryside … attached to the earth, that ransack and move about with an invincible obstinacy." They possess something similar to "an articulate voice, and when they rise to their feet they have a human face and, in effect, are men. At night,

1 A. Young, *Travels in France and Italy* (London, 1915 [1792]), 189. See also H. Taine, *AR* 255.

2 G. Salvemini, *La Rivoluzione francese* (Milan, 1972), 17.

they withdraw to their lairs, where they live on black bread, water, and roots." The only concession that La Bruyère acknowledged with respect to these animals was recognizing their right to subsistence: "They save other men the effort of sowing, plowing, and gathering in order to live, and they thus deserve not running out of the bread they have sown."[3]

The Revolution brought to the surface a suppressed story that expressed the faltering voice of those who did not have the right to speak about their own lives. It forced them to learn quickly, under the pressure of events. Used to living in holes and contenting themselves with black bread and wild greens, these dehumanized beings now began to feed themselves on aspirations that they expected to achieve. Their "power of existing" grew, and their gaze rose towards the future, above the daily horizon and beyond the perspective of a relatively sad and predictable passing of the years. The inclination to achieve happiness did not pass through knowledge, wisdom, or *amor Dei intellectualis,* but rather through a remixing of the passions and an overturning of the world as it had been until then.

The rapid succession of new and significant events mobilized long-repressed expectations in a big way, showing these people the path of possible satisfaction *per speculum et in aenigmate.* Beyond the wall of the present that separated the current world from its virtual image in the future and the enigma (or dark allegory) of its solution, there shone, in some indefinable space (atopian more than utopian), a reality more "real" than the existing one, which devalued everything as inessential and evil. The Revolution was intended to invert the current order; to reverse the primacy of what appears indisputable and true in favour of the possible and the "not yet"; and to give form to the promises of happiness.

Burdened with many meanings, every sign that might indicate that the old world was coming apart and every glimmer of possibility offered, from time to time, form, specificity, and direction to indeterminate expectations of the present and to desires imprisoned in the past's images of perfection. The widespread sense that things were moving rapidly, converging and conspiring towards an ending, radically changed the plot and direction of passions and feelings. The life plans of tens of millions of people changed irrevocably. Their destiny was separated by the course that they might have followed in other circumstances. There began for

3 La Bruyère, *Les caractères ou moeurs de ce siècle* (Paris, 1962 [1688]), 363.

them an uncertain and different journey in time, one that routed onto this path some of the aspirations previously placed in the afterlife.

One period of expectation preceded and accompanied the modern revolutions. The opening of the range of possibilities corresponded to the confused feeling that forbearance had gone too far. It was necessary at all costs to pass through narrow openings that could quickly close, a Red Sea that events had almost miraculously opened. Thus, there was a sort of insomnia, a revolutionary *agrypnia*, a watchfulness – similar to that of the Gospel's "wise virgins" awaiting their groom – so as not to be caught unprepared at the right moment. "*Estote parati*!" became a political imperative that required extreme attention to the smallest variations in the order of the world. The unsustainability of the situation suddenly seemed obvious, as soon as one could glimpse the real possibility of a decline in inequalities.

De Toqueville was the first to observe what is presented as a strange paradox. When the inequalities between men seem abysmally unbridgeable, almost no one who is "low" dares to imagine rising "high." He accepts the social ladder not only with resignation but with internal, unconscious consent, because it ends up seeming natural and unchangeable to him. On the other hand, when, for various reasons, the social filters become more porous, and it seems that each person "carries in his own backpack the marshal's baton," then every strong hierarchical structure of power seems intolerable and unjust. Far from being venerated, inequality and privilege become offensive and odious, causing envy and a push towards the unstoppable elimination of further inequalities.[4] Thus, the pyramid of power must be destroyed starting from the top, in order to create a "horizontal" community of free and equal men, politically orphaned "brothers" without a king to function as "father of the country."

The Hope and the Nightmare

The sudden expansion of the horizons of liberation reignited the hopes of change, polarizing the fantasy of images of a world supported by

4 See, for example, A. de Tocqueville, *DA* 629–30; Engl. trans., 138: "When inequality of conditions is the common law of society, the most marked inequalities do not strike the eye; when everything is nearly on the same level, the slightest are marked enough to hurt it. Hence the desire of equality always becomes more insatiable in proportion as equality is more complete."

greater justice and generating the inclination towards participating emotionally in common events and trying to understand them.[5] The local isolation of individuals and communities ended, and there began to be felt a sense of belonging not to a ruler, but to a social collective in motion, in which each person was called upon to fulfil his own role. The convocation of the Estates-General of France and the presentation, in the course of the spring of 1789, of countless *cahiers de doléance*[6] reawakened the hope (long timidly cultivated) that wrongs might be righted and evils, for the very fact of becoming public, might produce the remedy (in addition to scandal and malaise). The ideal of a more worthy life – different from the one known up to that point – no longer resembled a dream, even if it might sometimes have preserved the hallucinatory traits of a nightmare.

And in fact, the nightmare began immediately. As soon the great hope appeared, "great fear" appeared as well.[7] In the second half of July 1789 (a period critical for the harvest), the news coming from Paris of a presumed aristocratic plot against the Estates-General to starve the people was greeted with alarm in the provinces.[8] This immediately added to the already endemic terror of the bandits, such as the legendary Cartouche

5 For some aspects implicit in the rise of this new sensibility, see A. Vincent-Buffault, "Pleurer sous la Révolution (1789–1794)," in *Histoire des larmes,* XVIIe–XIXe *siècles.*

6 On the significance of mass expectations, see B. Baczko, *Les imaginaires sociaux: Mémoires et espoirs collectifs* (Paris, 1984). These were strengthened by images of a better future (proclaimed by Sebastien Mercier in the first great uchronic novel, *L'An 2440* – in which perfection moves from space, in general from remote islands, to time) confirmed by the realization of the age-old dream of flying (hot-air balloons), the defeat of mortal illnesses (smallpox), and by many other indications, including the lengthening of the average lifespan, which had drawn the attention even of Condorcet (and about which see I.F. Clarke, *The Patterns of Expectation, 1644–2001* [New York, 1979], particularly 1–61).

7 G. Lefebvre, *La Grande Peur de 1789* (Paris, 1931). I cite here from the edition edited by J. Revel (*La Grande Peur de 1789, suivi de Les foules révolutionnaires* [Paris, 1988]). In Lefebvre, "the contradictory double register of fear and hope, which places in the heart what can be called 'revolutionary mentality,' echoes that movement of 'conflict ... followed by expansion' that the author of the *Histoire socialiste* had already suggested" (Revel, 14).

8 On the rumors regarding the supposed plots to starve the people, see S. Kaplan, *Le complot de la famine: Histoire d'une rumeur au* XVIIIe *siècle* (Paris, 1982).

and Mandrin, who were rampant everywhere, extorting, killing, and mocking the authorities. Widespread in acute form since the end of the previous winter, this fear now reached fever pitch. The spectre of revenge by the nobles, threatened in their privileges, was accompanied by older ghosts of hunger and misery, triggering waves of panic, credulity, superstition, and violence: someone who is frightened creates fear. *Insecuritas* reached its maximum level.

In a society in which communication was predominantly oral, it was in this period that *errants* (peddlers, charlatans, *montreurs d'ours* and beggars whose number was multiplied by hunger) spread the news directly. The newspapers, for the few capable of reading or repeating them to others, arrived late with respect to the accelerated rhythm of events. The itinerant *errants* formed a fearsome army that, along with distorted information, also spread terror. Beyond being protagonists of small or great episodes of criminality, they often stoked the fire among harvesters or at the farms, if the welcome received by the peasants was not judged satisfactory.

The phenomenon of fear, which produces unease and bewilderment but also refocuses rebellion,[9] was the object of fundamental historiographical studies of the French Revolution, particularly in the 1930s. George Lefebvre's name is the most well known, but he is certainly not the only one to have outlined "a cartography and chronology of fear," indicating the lines of the panic's propagation along five currents and establishing their temporal articulation.[10] And even if sometimes his positions assume a dichotomous and "Manichean" nature,[11] his indisputable merit remains in having analysed the fear on a wide scale, establishing its origin, its correlations, and the zones of its diffusion, and simultaneously describing its structure and social metamorphoses in the framework of integrating its psychology with its history and politics. However, resting

9 Lefebvre, *La Grande Peur de 1789*, 56: "Thus, every revolution awakened in the peasant's soul the temptation to imitate it, and at the same time, it frightened it [the peasant's soul]. The people scared themselves."

10 See the studies of P. Conard, *La peur en Dauphiné (juliet–août 1789)* (Paris, 1904).

11 This is the thesis of M. Vovelle, *La mentalité révolutionnaire: Sociétés et mentalités sous la Révolution française* (Paris, 1985), 99.

on the shoulders of Lefebvre's thesis is the theoretical claim of representatives of the psychology of the masses, in particular Gustave Le Bon,[12] who had also applied his general hypotheses to the French Revolution.[13]

Although rejecting Le Bon's frameworks, which he considered rough, even Albert Mathiez, in the last great depiction of revolutionary fear, shows himself not to have escaped the viewpoint that considered fear as closely tied to the dimension of the masses' irrational panic. Anticipating the Sartrian categories of *Critique of Dialectical Reason*,[14] he sees in the crowd a heterogeneous and ephemeral aggregate of individuals, "as if it were formed on the sidewalks of the stations, at the moment of the passage of the trains or in the squares of a city, at the moment when the schools, offices, and factories poured out their populations, mixed with the charlatans and those who were walking by."[15] Among this crowd and the voluntary gathering there were the "*semi-voluntary* aggregates," particularly common in the *ancien régime*: peasants during the period of sowing and harvest, or residents of a village exiting Sunday mass.[16] It was a case of *rassemblements orientés vers l'action* which, because of the arrival of new facts (news, troubling events, etc.), entered into a "state of the crowd" in which the aggregate changed instantly into a *rassemblement révolutionnaire*, in what Sartre called a "group in fusion" when it reached "white heat."

---

12 For Le Bon, see in particular R.A. Nye, *The Origins of Crowd Psychology: Gustave Le Bon and the Crisis of Mass Democracy in the Third Republic* (London, 1975); S. Moscovici, *L'âge de foules: Un traite historique de psychologie des masses* (Paris, 1981); S. Barrow, *Distorting Mirrors: Visions of the Crowd in Late Nineteenth Century France* (New Haven, 1981); and A. Mucchi Faina, *L'abbraccio della folla: Cento anni di psicologia collettivo* (Bologna, 1982), 32 et seq. For the revolutionary crowds, see G. Rudé, *The Crowd in the French Revolution* (Oxford, 1959), and C. Lucas, "The Crowd and Politics," in *The French Revolution and the Creation of Modern Political Culture*, vol. 2: *The Political Culture of the French Revolution*, ed. C. Lucas (Oxford, 1987–9), 259–85.

13 See G. Le Bon, *La Révolution française et la psychologie des révolutions* (Paris, 1912).

14 See J.-P. Sartre, *Critique de la raison dialectique* (Paris, 1960).

15 A. Mathiez, *Les foules révolutionnaires* (Paris, 1934), 246.

16 Incidentally, Monday was feared. "On that day, they carried out the plans developed on Sunday" in the only moment when they had the time to meet each other (ibid., 248).

After the literarily memorable pages of Madame de Staël, Michelet, and Taine on the behaviour of the masses[17] – which lacked, however, an explicit thematization of the phenomenon and its dynamics – the contributions of Lefebvre and Mathiez were certainly fundamental. However, emphasizing the spontaneity or semi-spontaneity of behaviours of crowds, they underestimated the aspect of the institutionalization and the political and theoretical organization of fear (and hope) – particularly when, in the arc of a few years thick with changes, they passed from the "great fear" of 1789 and the "first terror" of the slaughter of September 1792 to the Jacobin Terror of 1793 and 1794.

---

17 See, for example, A.L.G. de Staël, *Principal Events of the French Revolution*, vol. 2 (London, 1818), 47: "These twenty thousand men made their way into the palace; their faces bore marks of that coarseness, both of feature and mind, of which the disgusting effect is not to be supported by the greatest philanthropist. Had they been animated by any true feeling, had they come to complain against injustice, against the dearness of corn ... in short, against any suffering which power and wealth can inflict on poverty, the rags which they wore, their hands blackened by labor, the premature old age of the women, the brutishness of the children, would all have excited pity. But their frightful oaths mingled with cries, their threatening gestures, their deadly instruments, exhibited a frightful spectacle, and one calculated to impair forever the respect that ought to be felt for our fellow creatures."

2. The Despotism of Liberty

Pleasure and Pain

From the point of view of political theories, the reversal of traditions brought to completion by the Jacobins through the Terror was radical. In Montesquieu, "fear" (*crainte*) is, in fact, typical of despotic governments, while "virtue" is characteristic of democratic, republican governments. *Crainte* implies the prevalence of pure will, the whim of a single man, the lack of laws or fixed rules that guarantee security of the lives and property of each person. What operates in despotism, however, is not simple *crainte* but the *corruption de la crainte*, of the very principle of its organization.[1] Such a regime is supported less by a positive foundation than by negative power – that is, by the disintegration of the *utilitas* that, from the Stoics to Spinoza, is the basis of individuals' self-preservation. In despotic regimes, men lose the reasons to live. They secretly prefer either the rule of the senses (which makes them forget the ills with which they are afflicted or that they inflict upon others) or death, for which they are already ready or resigned. From this point of view, according to Montesquieu, the Islamic religion is the most suited to despotism, since it represents *une crainte ajouté a la crainte*, both tempered by the promise of a final heavenly reward for obedience rendered on earth.

Unlike tyranny, which presumes an illegitimate origin of power, and unlike ancient dictatorship, which has an exceptional and strictly delimited character in time, despotism treats citizens as servants, applying to

1 *EdL* XXIV, III; V, XIV. The observations of A. Grosrichard on this point are interesting: *Structure du Sérail: La fiction du despotisme asiatique dans l'Occident classique* (Paris, 1979), 34 et seq., 49 et seq.

the political sphere the relationships of inequality that, in Greece and the philosophy of Aristotle, are characteristics of the domestic sphere in which a coupled relationship is naturally in force, one founded on "commanding and being commanded": wives, children, and slaves must simply obey their respective authority – the husband, father, and owner, strictly speaking, the master in a broad sense. Extending beyond its familial environment and applied to the "political" sphere – where equality among citizens should be in force – despotism becomes a form of degenerate power. In turn, the law (which must be, in an Aristotelian sense, "understanding without desire"; see *Pol.* III, 1287a and V, 1313b) ends up changing into its opposite, into reason subjected to desire.

Despotic regimes produce individuals completely separated from each other or (which is the same thing) held together by the repulsive force of the passions that isolate them, impeding every confidence and reciprocal solidarity and reducing citizens to subjects. This generates the most complete, fatalistic, and humble political passivity, barely interrupted by some angry and fleeting flame of rebellion (which – as Montesquieu would add later in the *Pensées*, in *OC*, vol. II, n. 998, p. 1268 – *le passions lentes ne raisonnent pas plus que les furieuses*, and the former may change into the latter).

In Montesquieu, despotism embodies all that an "enlightened" society abhors and considers diametrically opposed to it.[2] Paraphrasing Kant, we could say that it constitutes the most suitable response to the question, "What is *not* enlightenment?" Thinking of La Boétie, on the other hand, we could assert that despotism revives the dramatic question of why all men, even the sultan, may accept living in a state of substantial voluntary servitude like in an "animal park" (*TSV* 135).

Starting with the *Persian Letters*, the analysis of despotism in Montesquieu becomes deeper, enriched by two new elements: a criticism of absolutism (which, from Louis XIV onward, made the state the private property of the *moi* of a king who destroys intermediate bodies and dramatically diminishes the political weight of the nobility, a ruler who reigns through fear, a *prince* who places *une tête de Méduse dans sa poitrine* [*EdL* VIII, VI;

2 For a reconstruction of the history of the term "despotism," see A. Koebner, "Despot and Despotism: Vicissitudes of a Political Term," *Journal of the Warburg and Courtauld Institutes* 14 (1951), 275–302; F. Venturi, "Despotismo Orientale," *Rivista Storica Italiana* 72 (1960), 117–26; B. Kassem, *Décadence et absolutisme dans l'oeuvre de Montesquieu* (Geneva, 1960).

viii, vii]); and a description of the traits of voluptuousness and sensuality identified in the Ottoman Empire and Persia.

The despot is the first to be prisoner of lust, almost walled alive in the physical space of the harem or the seraglio. Ceding the reins of actual government to the grand vizier – through a delegation that produces a paradoxical void of power at its very centre – he commands by proxy in his own absence and from a distance, remote from his subjects. Every individual then wraps himself in the mantle of his specific passion, removing himself from the gaze of others, whom he basically avoids or ignores as possible sources of help, benefit, or advice. Everyone lives immersed in his own dominant passion: the subjects in *crainte* (a durable and paralysing state of the soul, leading to an almost animal-like obedience and distinguished from simple *peur*, which marks the immediate reaction to a danger); the despot in sensual pleasure; and the vizier in the drunkenness of a discretional and absolute power (but not devoid of fear, since he can be called to account for it at any moment, according to the master's unpredictable whims). Everyone places himself on this side of observance of laws dictated by reason, and everyone survives in the worst way – in stagnation and in the space of corruption of all civic and emotional ties.[3] And yet for centuries (the fact had not ceased to amaze foreign observers, particularly the Venetians), despite being subject to laws and habits so arbitrary and harmful to their own interests on the part of an intrinsically weak power, the subjects of these despotic regimes obey the authorities in a more ordered way than in any other political system.[4] The true danger lies in palace intrigues. But even here, we see the paradox in which despotisms, precisely because they refer

3 On the idea of Persia that was held in France during this period, see O.H. Bonnerot, *La Perse dans la littérature et la pensée françaises du* xviiie *siècle: De l'image au mythe* (Paris, 1988). Sade understood this aspect of Oriental despotism from a point of view that reverses the value normally attributed to it by Westerners: "Does not voluptuous Asia, keeping hidden the objects of its enjoyments, show us that lust wins by oppression and tyranny and that the passions are ignited much more strongly through all that is obtained by constraint than by what is given willingly?" (D.A.F de Sade, *Histoire de Juliette ou la prosperité du vice,* part 2). On the other hand, for Montesquieu, the Orient is "not so much a geographic area, as a worrisome place of the spirit in which all the worst inhuman impulses reign" (J.N. Shklar, *Montesquieu* [Oxford, 1987]; Ital. trans. *Montesquieu* [Bologna, 1990], 49–50).

4 See, for example, the text of the 1577 report of the Venetian ambassador Antoni Erizzo in L. Valensi, *Venise et la Sublime Porte: La naissance du despote* (Paris, 1989); Ital. trans. *Venezia e la Sublime Porta: La nascita del despota* (Bologna, 1989), 52.

to a constantly threatened individual, constitute the strongest and most durable regimes, capable of prospering even when their representatives are killed, one after another.[5]

According to Montesquieu, however, there is a crucial difference between the Asians and the French. The former "do not overcome the fear of death except by means of fear of punishment, which produces in the soul a new type of terror that makes it almost stupid," while the latter "banish fear through a satisfaction that is superior to it" (*LP* LXXXIX). It could be said that Europeans in general had conquered the *philautia* or love of self that the Easterners still did not know, except in the form of a mixture of *amor mortis* and sensuality (in pleasure, one escapes and is unaware of any superior *utilitas* with respect to that of the moment). Only by ignoring oneself – violating the Delphic principle of the *gnothi seauton* that constituted the patrimony of Western civilization from Socrates onward, along with the idea of self-control, continence, or *enkrateia* – does one succeed in making fear and oppression tolerable to the point of desiring and asking for "voluntary servitude."

Unlike *crainte*, republican *vertu politique* (as opposed to *morale* and *chrétienne*) requires compete transparency of the relationships between citizens, their tireless activity in the public sphere and, in particular, a marked love of equality of both rights and goods.[6] Reason, separated from the passions that lead to isolation, aims towards universality and organizes civil coexistence according to its own rules. Therefore, republics are constructed on the common participation of citizens in the government of society and on the consequent absence of each person's fear with respect to a power that emanates from everyone. Virtue, however (as love of laws and country, common goods produced endlessly by the activity of the citizens), demands the "renunciation of oneself," "sacrifice of one's dearest interests," and "continuous preference of the public

5 This was previously noted by Spinoza in *TTP* 17.*551*, but see also Montesquieu, *EdL* XIX, XXVII; *LP* CIII; and, for this last reference, A. Grosrichard, *Structure du Sérail*, 100.

6 See Montesquieu, *EdL* V, 6. For Montesquieu, however, who does not propose a model of ascetic republic, commerce does not constitute an obstacle to frugality. On the contrary, it develops sober and moderate habits (V, 3–6). The need for "frugality," which will become a central value in Jacobin thought, and in particular that of Saint-Just, depends on the principle of equality of goods. Montesquieu holds that commerce can be moralized through politics, maintaining the balance of powers, and avoiding monopolies. See V. Bertrand, "La conception du commerce dans l'Esprit des lois de Montesquieu," *Annales Historiques de la Révolution Française* 369–70 (1987), 266–90.

interest to one's own interests." He who submits to the laws must carry their weight himself.[7]

Monarchical states are ultimately governed by "honour," that is, by the power of another's opinion on an individual's self-esteem, as well as by respectful obedience to laws that permit and ensure hereditary inequalities of rank and fortune, but that also encourage an always-open competition (in which the ruler is the arbiter) to determine who has greater merit to compete in the redistribution of markers of prestige and rank.[8] This maintains the upward and downward movement of inequalities among subjects, without damaging – from Montesquieu's point of view – either the right of the individual to self-preservation or the system of social distinctions, the hierarchical ladder at whose summit sits the king. The limited change at the top is sufficient to keep alive psychological vigilance and faith in the crown on the part of the nobility of old-blood lineage (the class that demands, solely by right of birth, that it also be granted other fundamental goods, like political power), but it is not enough to prevent the monarchy from co-opting the middle and lower classes at higher social levels. This happens through the sale or granting of titles of nobility on the occasion of lending of money or following valuable acts that may demonstrate an individual's attachment (beyond himself) to his king and country. Such states supported by honour require only "a minimum of virtue" and reject, in particular, the primacy of the "heroic" virtues that were so admired by the ancients and so feared by Hobbes in the *Behemoth*. Not only is contribution by the majority of citizens to the governance of public things not requested, but it is actually considered damaging.

For Montesquieu, monarchical regimes are those in which movements and gears are reduced to a minimum, as in the "most beautiful machines."[9] In fact, the impulse comes to them from a single spring, and the balance wheel is represented by feedback automatisms of reciprocal

7 Montesquieu, *EdL* III, 5; IV, 5; III, 3. At least since the fifteenth century, the term "republic" has not indicated a specific type of state. On the contrary, with the rise of modern monarchical regimes, republics (Venice, Switzerland, the Dutch Republic) begin to assume a distinct physiognomy and are often presented as medieval fossils. See Y. Durand, *Les Républiques au temps des Monarchies* (Paris, 1973). For some aspects of republican regimes, see P. Riley, *The General Will before Rousseau* (Princeton, 1986).

8 Honour imposes "dying or being unworthy of living" (see Montesquieu, *LP* XC). On the pre-modern concept of honour, see P. Berger, "On the Obsolescence of the Concept of Honor," in *Revisions*, ed. A. McIntyre (London, 1983).

9 Montesquieu, *EdL* III, 5, and see II, 1 et seq.

hierarchical compensation. Each man has an opinion of himself that he tries to maintain, through constant adjustment, at the level of his own esteem and that of others, contributing to the continuous reformulation of social relationships. Because honour is ultimately based on the assignment to individuals of different values according to the will of public opinion and of the ruler, it represents the mirror opposite of virtue, as the consensual abolition of unjustifiable difference in the searching gaze of a public that possesses a sense of justice and a custom of rationality. This is why, although the symbol of monarchies is the "clock" (in which the vital impulse of a society's intermediate bodies derives from the energy supplied by the "spring" of the ruler), the allegory of democratic government in this case is offered by the "scale," by the balance of equality among the citizens, which tends to avoid imbalances and discrimination of power and goods. In both monarchies and republics, the political freedom of citizens rests on the "tranquility of spirit that comes from the opinion that each person has of his own safety." In order for this question to exist, however, it is necessary that "the government be such that one citizen need not be afraid of another citizen" (*EdL* XI, VI).

Crainte, vertu, and *honneur* constitute the operating patterns of states. These are political principles no longer founded on the number or quantity of those who command (one, a few, or many – both in the genuine and the corrupt form of government), nor even on their quality, but on the ways of exercising power. In each regime, there is always a unique passion at play – as a *hegemonikon* of the body politic, a heart that promotes the circulatory system of power – that establishes the rules governing the mutual relationship between individuals and classes. This can be presented, in positive terms, as love (modulated in variations of love of country in republics, sublimated love of self in monarchies, and self-esteem – as the lowest instinct of self-preservation – in despotism). In negative terms, it can be presented as fear (of laws in republics, opinion in monarchies, and death in despotism).[10] Every state presents a special tropism and "magnetic" orientation of the passions that must be adequately interpreted, because – human events not being controlled by chance (see, for example, *EdL* I, 1; *Cons.* XVIII) – it is possible to understand its meaning only if one knows its direction.

10 See Grosrichard, *Structure du Sérail*, 47.

Hybrids and Monsters

Although professing sincere admiration and almost veneration for the author of the *Esprit des lois*, the Jacobins (particularly Marat, who in 1785 had even written an elegy of Montesquieu for the Academy of Bordeaux) clearly distanced themselves from his positions.[11] The reason should not be sought, however, in Montesquieu's inclination to follow the English constitutional model or in his statements agreeing that democratic republics are impossible or undesirable in modern Europe.

The Jacobins had deeper reasons for reversing those political and sometimes age-old ideas that come together in this philosopher's work. They largely accepted entire blocks of it, but then they recombined them in forms that were new and "monstrous" (with the double meaning of "admirable" – because they were never seen before – and "repugnant" to the sensibility of men accustomed to classic systems of politics and consolidated, entrenched models of wisdom and humanity). Creating a type of new conceptual teratology and practice, they joined – with unheard-of boldness – something that had carefully been held separate from the political and philosophical tradition: fear and virtue, despotism and liberty, strength and reason, terror and philosophy, contempt for and promotion of the rights of man, death and regeneration. They thus introduced, under the pressure of events (sometimes through artificial and conscious selection of categories and political practices, sometimes in an almost spontaneous manner and through mere establishment of the facts) new hybrids of ideas, passions, and institutions.

Some conceptual "mutants" (like the "despotism of liberty") were born that would never disappear completely and would remain paradigmatic for revolutions to come. The consequences are disturbing: age-old political logic loses every fixed point of reference within these paradoxes and oxymora. Thought and practice must be reinvented day by day, integrated and strengthened with massive doses of rhetoric (directed towards both the actors and the spectators of revolutions). The risk appears – never defeated but always averted – of a collapse into the inestimable and incomprehensible. Opacity and blindness end up enveloping even the most lucid protagonists of revolutionary movements and constitute the repercussions of such logic.

---

11 Some notes on Montesquieu's impact on the Jacobins' thought can be found in N. Hampson, *Will & Circumstance: Montesquieu, Rousseau, and the French Revolution* (London, 1983), 3 et seq., 55 et seq.

The fatal implications of this catastrophe (I use the term with the value-free meaning of the sudden reversal of balanced situations) are not generally understood or measured. In fact, in a relatively brief span of time, new structures and architectures of ideas, passions, and institutions crystallized – assuming forms, combinations, and unexpected orientations. These were not mere reflection or mirroring of isolated events, with which it might be possible to establish a bijective mapping relationship. Rather, they constitute metamorphoses, more or less successful attempts to give order to "disorder." That is, they represent the result of successive and largely unintentional shocks with respect to those involved in the revolutionary process.

Because of these repercussions, the previous conceptual constellations that combined fear, hope, and reason in various ways changed their form, to the point of becoming almost unrecognizable and losing the points of reference to which political traditions and mentalities had accustomed individuals, groups, and peoples.

The first to be transformed was the role of fear and hope (with their retinue of passions cold and frigid or hot and burning, like panic or the desire for happiness that had largely been used by "theological-political" despotism, both Western and Eastern). Under the guidance of reason common to all men, the Jacobins now used these tools of emancipation not only for the French, but theoretically for all inhabitants of the planet. These passions (and in particular, fear and hope, which ancient and Spinozan wisdom had refused any sort of access to reason, considering them sources of superstition and uncontrollable explosive material that triggers imaginative processes) stopped being seen as harmful to reason itself or to public morals. Rather, they became its armed wing that routed enemies and heartened virtuous citizens. The line of separation no longer ran between the wise man and the common one, but between those who controlled the people through a partisan reason that presented itself as universal and those who were closed egoistically and fearfully in particular passions (especially in the fear experienced and not in the fear others are made to feel).

Immersed in the ideologies and mythologies that spontaneously or artificially flourished in this borderland, reason entered into a treaty of alliance (or at least a temporary armistice) between itself and the impulsive passions of movement and excess, attacking instead the cold passions of indifference to the common good, which were identified with rejecting or asserting the general interest against special privileges no longer acceptable in societies guided by the universality of laws and virtue. In the

Jacobins' ethics, the principle "he who is not with me is against me" possesses a serious and dangerous discriminating value.

The Colours of Reason

Although the actress who portrayed reason in the Parisian churches of Saint Sulpice and Notre Dame preserved its traditional cold colours (she was dressed in white with a blue cloak), reason itself – opposing its previous indifferent or asthenic forms – now also assumed the "color of living flame," to the point of representing the *pathos* and ardour of the "fire in the mind of men."[12]

The passions that had been previously weakened, blinded, and cut out of the sphere of rationality (absorbed almost entirely by interests made calculable by means of political economy) regain some of their distinct power of discernment, a "quotient of intelligence" that allows them to reopen themselves to a clear vision and comprehension of the world. In a manner that is seemingly paradoxical but actually complementary, they are thus rendered more "cold" and predictable, newly colonized or reclaimed by reason, which offers them a dam against instability and variability. This happens not through Spinozan *securitas*, but by means of institutions that organize, in a relatively lasting way, the security possible in the *insecuritas* that characterizes the state of exception, the uncertainty of the collective future.

The fall of the clear separation between reason and the passions (or, in Platonic terms, between *logistikon* and *epithymetikon*) entails the fall of the clear division between the wise man and the crowd and the consequent attempt, on one hand, to tear the wise man away from *ataraxy*, impartiality, irony, and detachment from the world (immersing him in the ferment of the passions, in the battle between the fronts, in engagement with events) and, on the other, of rationalizing the conduct and

12 Despite a widespread cliché, Robespierre was against the cult and idolatry of reason, which expresses only the mania of those who insist on wanting to achieve such abstractions. To combat this attitude, it was necessary for him to popularize *les principes métaphysiques de Locke et de Condillac*. See A. Aulard, *Le culte de la Raison et le culte de l'Être suprême, 1793–1794* (Paris, 1892; rpt., Aalen, 1974), 87. On the range of symbolic meanings attributed to reason, see E. Gombrich, "The Dream of Reason: Symbolism in the French Revolution," *British Journal for the 18th Century* 2, no. 3 (1979), 187–205.

impulses of the masses.[13] The political sphere is opened to this new type of "wise man" – provided, however, that he is transformed into a passionate partisan of universality. The Jacobins' desired plan thus aimed (more or less obscurely) at transforming passion into knowledge but also, with even greater force, at elaborating knowledge into passion and action. However, in making a "pedagogical" pact with the "despotism of liberty," in turning into an authoritarian tool, reason ends up backfiring on itself.

The Terror: Institutionalized Power

Revolutionary, institutionalized, bureaucratized, and nationalized fear metamorphosed into Terror, into a general principle of democracy applied to the "present needs of the country." Widespread in the capital and in the provinces, particularly after the laws of Prairial, it no longer had much in common with the relatively spontaneous *grande peur* of the summer of 1789.

Terror now became rational and reason terrible, and both declared themselves to be support for virtue: "What do they want," exclaimed Saint-Just, "those who now want neither virtue nor terror?"[14]

---

13 Voltaire – who discovered Spinoza's work at an advanced age and understood the *Ethics* better than all his contemporaries (see R. Pomeau, *Voltaire* [Paris, 1989], 42) – did not overlook the inherent danger in the will to give voice and authority back to the passions. This is why, against the apologia for the passions made by Diderot, who thought they were like the wind that moves the ship (*le vaisseau*), he adds: *et qui le submergent.*

14 L. de Saint-Just, *FIR* 506. Previously, in the youthful, erotic, and Voltaire-like poem "Organt" (the story of a paladin of Charlemagne who frees France from the kingdom of Mad Roland), Saint-Just had personified the Terror, who ruled in the bowels of the burning abyss of Etna. This volcano, once dear to Empedocles and Lucretius, would be to Hölderlin the symbol of purifying fire through which the wise man reunites with regenerative nature when all the attempts at political reform fail. In the poem of the future Jacobin leader, the *Terreur*, "surrounded by spirits, by ghosts," and by "fluttering dreams," seeks every night to *effrayer le sommeil des tyrans* (Saint-Just, *Organt: Poême in vingt chants* [Vatican, 1798], in *OC* 199–200; see also an indirect reference to this passage in A. Ollivier, *Saint-Just et la force des choses* [Paris, 1954], 55). In this case, the "fire in the mind of men" emerges directly from the volcanic abyss. Highlighted here is the centrality of the idea of nature in Saint-Just (*Je me détache de tout pour m'attacher à tout;* see *FIR*), connected to the conviction that human nature is good. (See M. Abensour, "La philosophie politique de Saint-Just," *Annales Historiques de la Révolution Française* 38 [1966], 1–32, and "La philosophie politique de Saint-Just: Problématique et cadres sociaux," in the same issue, 341–58.)

Until peace and victory, then, the "despotism of liberty" must inexorably strike its enemies and obligate them to obey what is right: "Strength does not make either reason or right. But it is perhaps impossible to do without it to enforce right and reason."[15] It was said that as long as the state of emergency lasted – owing to the difficulty of the struggles that France and the Revolution faced in order to survive – liberty and coercion, fear and hope would have to coexist (but the "Great Terror," as has been observed from Quinet forward, broke out precisely when the military situation of the republic had notably improved). The stated aim of these affirmations is that of breaking the (partly unconscious) conniving that ties the privileged to their selfishness and that ties all individuals to their sticky past, forcing each person to follow the urgent rhythm of events and changing himself along with it, associating his own will with the lot of an emerging collective identity.

Terror and virtue are indistinguishable; they must be mutually expressed and held back: "Virtue, without which terror is evil; terror, without which virtue is impotent."[16] The Jacobin plan expressed the voice of fear, previously mute or shouting, and supplied to reason (that was at first discursive or only verbally aggressive) the sharp and threatening tone of a real power that continued on to a rudimentary "scientific" organization of fear, using *rumores* and popular gossip to feed processes of change. Towards this end, reason used a new model of theological-political despotism that brought together state and church so that faith in the country, and in institutions, was joined with faith in the Supreme Being and in the immortality of the soul to generate obedience – discipline directed towards emancipation and not towards servitude.

However, while Spinoza attributed the highest *libertas humana* to the wise man, leaving mere *securitas* to the people, the Jacobins wanted instead to generalize and extend not only wisdom but collective liberty,

---

15 Saint-Just, *FIR* 506.

16 M. Robespierre, speech of 18 Pluvôse, Year II (5 February 1794), in *OC* X, 357. On the role of fear and political anxiety generally, see J. Palou, *La peur dans l'histoire* (Paris, 1958). A model for the revolutionaries of the relationship between despotism and terror had been the *Dialogue de Sylla et d'Eucrate* by Montesquieu (see, particularly, *OC* I, 501–7), which Saint-Just knew by heart. Its importance is emphasized by S. Luzzato, *Il Terrore ricordato: Memoria e tradizione dell'esperienza rivoluzionaria* (Genoa, 1988), 36–7. Not valid in the case of the Terror is the principle that Carl Schmitt asserts, in which, "when conflicts became irresolvable, thought tends to take refuge in a new 'neutral sphere'" (Schmitt, "Das Zeitalter der Neutralisierungen und Entpolitisierungen," in *Der Begriff des Politischen* [Berlin, 1963]).

without limitations or distinctions of class or knowledge. At least for the moment, however, they did not intend to renounce the rigours of law and repressive reason in favour of more tolerant political orders. Only friendship and brotherhood among citizens would produce gentler customs in the future, finally creating a hope detached from fear.

Fear, Degradation, and Servitude

The problem that bedeviled the Jacobins was that of separating reason from the servitude, cowardice, and degradation that until then had paralysed the consciences of the oppressed, blocking their redemption. It was a case of defeating their inertia, of tearing the network of acquiescence and complicity that still enveloped it and that – tightly woven over thousands of years and consecrated by habit and mentality – wound up being felt as a guarantee of self-preservation: "The masterpiece of the politics of despots is appropriating man's reason to make him an accomplice in servitude" (Robespierre, *OC* v, 208). The long custom of political nullity had so corrupted and numbed individuals as to show them to be incapable, in their own eyes, of achieving good.[17] In order for them to regain trust in their own strength, it was necessary to shake them. In fact, the use of powerful emotional charges, and the triggering of fear and of hope in reason, encouraged the rise of a more direct link between plans for individual life, modifications of the present, and expectations for the future.

In this swirling mixture of perspectives and values, however, it became difficult, for the most part, to know truly what was good and what the most suitable means might be for achieving it. Identifying the "thin line that separates guilt from innocence" required much acumen and "revolutionary" suspicion (which, according to the Incorruptible, is to liberty as jealousy is to love). In fact, all individuals, things, and events are subject to distorting evaluations and the sophistry of reason in search of excuses. Even the "blocks" of laws, concepts, and sentiments previously studied with the intent of raising a new dwelling for liberty could then be used – according to Saint-Just – without distinction either to build or bury it. "All the stones are cut for the structure of liberty: you can construct a temple or a tomb from the same stones."[18] Even in the awareness that "terror is a double-edged weapon that some use to avenge the

17 Saint-Just, *Discours sur la constitution à donnner à la France, OC* 419 (*OC2*, vol. 1, 424).
18 Ibid., *OC* 423 (*OC2*, vol. 1, 430).

people, and others use for tyranny,"[19] the Revolution found itself temporarily and paradoxically forced to use the tools of despotism to fight and destroy despotism itself.

Only "virtue" is a criterion suitable for recognizing the good, for distinguishing friends from enemies, for raising a temple to liberty, and for using terror in order to redeem a people. But how was this virtue to be understood and practised?

Virtue, Sentiment, and Interests

The Jacobin concept of "virtue" has often been seen as the unjust and backward reintroduction of morals into politics or, more recently, as a form of compensatory mobilization of a citizenry still in formation, *trop pauvrement conçue*. Within this, ethical legitimization would anticipate and contribute to producing formal and juridical legitimization, giving democracy its own dynamism, because it is the citizen himself who periodically modifies the political line.[20] The men of the Terror, however, tried to impose on the state and on society the rules of morals, returning to a pre-Machiavellian and pre-modern concept of politics, denying the autonomy of the individual and repressing the development of needs, desires, and consumption – in other words, of everything that characterizes modern democracy and economy.

Paraphrasing Alasdair McIntyre, it could be said that this idea was strengthened by the "post-virtue" represented by Thermidor, when everything that the Terror had banned reappeared triumphantly, and private vices returned to being vehicles of public virtues. Or it was strengthened by the subsequent phase when, in the first Restoration, even Quinet could think that if Robespierre and Saint-Just had brought their project to fruition, there would have remained nothing of France except "a Thebaid with about twenty political Trappists."[21]

The Jacobin position, however, was not as moralistic and private-enterprise as it might appear. Classically, *virtus* is power, the essential capacity to achieve good on the basis of canons of ethical excellence and within the social sphere. In Montesquieu's terms, the revolutionaries

19 Saint-Just, *Rapport au nom du Comité de salut public et du Comité de sûreté générale sur le personnes incarcérées, présenté à la Convention nationale dans la séance du 8 ventose an* II, in *OC* 706 (*OC2*, vol. 2, 239).

20 P. Jaume, *Le discours Jacobin et la démocatie* (Paris, 1989), 15.

21 E. Quinet, *La Révolution* (Paris, 1865), vol. 2, 304.

spoke of *vertu politique* more than *vertu morale*, even if they undoubtedly did not forget the Rousseauian regret for the loss of "virtue" in a modern world governed by interests, and even if they preserved (from Rousseau) those "Plutarchan" traits present in the nucleus of the original draft of *La prosopopée de Fabricius*. In that work, condemnation of the decline endured as a result of the "reign of virtue in Rome" (at the moment when the city changed from an austere and simple built-up area of brick into a magnificent capital of marble) is complete and final, since, in the place of the primitive frugality and industriousness of its citizens, luxury and indolence dominated (see *OC* III, 14 et seq.).

The revolutionaries adhered to an idea of virtue centred on devotion to the public good and the relationship of equality between citizens. Unlike the political logic of personalized obedience to what appeared to be the public good of a people embodied by an individual (according to the rule adopted by Eichmann: "Act in such a way that the Führer, if he knew your action, would approve it"), the Jacobins responded to the impersonal power of the "general will" (of which their liberty was part) with only their acts and their conscience. Further, they rejected extreme inequalities of wealth and misery. They attributed to virtue an element of more marked hostility towards "commerce," the predominance of exchanges promoted by utility and the search for maximum earnings (which introduced an inevitable contrast between those who sell and those who buy). However, they also rejected tones that were more sentimental than passionate (if we define sentiment as the impulse of the heart towards goodness, blocked by the harshness of selfish and individualistic interests). Therefore, it is significant that the accusation frequently raised against Robespierre during the Thermidor period was, on the one hand, that he ruined business by planning the destruction of Lyon and blocking the trading of Marseille and, on the other, that he effectively used the overheated passions of having the universal at "heart" as a tool to combat the "cold passions" of calculation and interest.[22]

22 Jacobin virtue risks, however, once again cancelling the *utilitas* of individuals, asking sacrifices of them not in the name of the monarch's "greater power of existing" but of their present and future emancipation. In the argument against selfishness and luxury, the Jacobins considered as incompatible both the classical and Machiavellian concept of virtue as the ability to deal with *fortuna* and (particularly) the link between *virtù* and values attributed to individuality and wealth. To use language drawn from another context, they had not passed "from the peasant-warrior" world that characterized the ancient citizenry, or from "Gothic *libertas*" to the "increasingly transactional

The warping and the sentimental and enthusiastic colouring that the concept of virtue acquired – diluting the classical connotations of strength and power, which had been preserved even in Rousseau (*E* 816–17) – depended in different ways on the type of virtue Rousseau himself declared he adhered to and on which he was "drunk": a virtue that is the fruit of a struggle with oneself in which the passions, originally directed towards self-preservation and then swollen beyond measure by the imagination and corruption, find their natural centre in *amour de soi*.[23] From this virtue comes an enjoyment that derives from contentment with oneself when one acts to promote self-preservation while remaining in harmony with others.

---

universe of 'commerce and the arts'" that had adopted good manners as a moral canon (see J.G.A. Pocock, *Virtue, Commerce, and History* [Cambridge, 1985], 48). For some traces of the tension just noted in Saint-Just, between the inclination to fix the Revolution "at the level of a stationary agrarian economy" and the uncertain perception of a request for greater social mobility on the part of the very classes that promoted the Revolution, see C.-H. Michalet, "Économie et politique chez Saint-Just: L'exemple de l'inflation," in *Annales Historique de la Révolution Française* 41 (1968), 60–110. During the debate on the constitution of 1791, the moderates had highlighted the role of "interests" in making the laws vital, while the Montagnards and Jacobins subsequently emphasized, instead, the function of "moral sovereignty" and "virtue" (see L. Jaume, "Il dibattito rivoluzionario su virtù e interessi," in *Filosofia politica* 3 [1989], 355–68). Often lamented is the fact that the political passions today may have disappeared. In reality, there has only been a modification of the relationships between passion and rationality set (particularly by the Jacobins) through the identification of a good part of politics with mass passionate mobilization, on the basis of stated rational or scientific principles (with the result that the passions must always be kept burning, perhaps at a low flame, to then make them occasionally reach white heat). It is not, then, the link between politics and passions that has been broken, but the link between passions and universality. Passion for the universal has diminished, but it is necessary to quickly add that we are talking about the universal as we have known it, embodied in particular macro-individuals who proclaim themselves bearers of long-range universality, rationality, and solidarity or of emancipation of the entire human race (state, class, or party). In modern times, it is these anonymous protagonists of politics that have assumed the Promethean task of building emotional consensus for projects for which only passionate support is asked. Fixed from above in this way, the "rational" end is only achieved through means provided from below, subsequently correcting course according to the circumstances. However, once automated and hypostatized, reason, as a monolithic block of ideas and principles, ends the passions by becoming simply friends or enemies, particularly when the common good or the general interest is declared to be simple and transparent.

23 "Drunk with virtue" is defined by Rousseau in *OC* I, 416. On virtue as a struggle and on the nature of the passions as connected to love of self and modified by the imagination, see *E* 490–1, 654, and E. Pulcini, *Amour-passion e amore coniugale: Rousseau e l'origine di un conflitto moderno* (Venice, 1990), 26–8, 40.

Wanting to identify themselves with their persecuted hero, the Jacobins welcomed this Rousseauian version of virtue, but departed from it on a fundamental point. They separated the concept of "virtue" from its Machiavellian link with "fortune," declaring it self-sufficient and even considering it compatible with the idea of "misfortune," but no longer limiting themselves to suffering and lamenting *le malheur*. Now that the historical perspectives had expanded towards a visible horizon of liberty, they fought to eliminate the obstacles that blocked the way to a life susceptible to greater fulfilment. They were convinced that the possibility of improving men and making them happy[24] was no longer a simple utopia.

This virtue is accessible to everyone and its practice does not imply an elevated social condition. In this sense, it is opposed to both the "monarchical virtue" theorized by Louis XIV (corresponding to the absolute and incomparable superiority of the king, with respect to whom any other rank was judged "impotent and sterile") and to aristocratic virtue (corresponding to blood and birth).[25] No longer able to rely on the spontaneity of custom corrupted by rampant egoism, this virtue rests on universal rules that must be rooted progressively in the existence of men and institutions so that one day – with the obstacles removed – the heart and reason may correspond. From this perspective, it is completely different from classical models. It is forced to assert itself, to reactivate and consume ancient yeasts – that is, to recover the remains of Greek and Roman ethical ideals. Paradoxically, it is a virtue after virtue.

24 C. Blum, *Rousseau and the Language of Virtue: The Language of Politics in the French Revolution* (Ithaca, 1986). Sentiment is passion sweetened by more tolerant reason. See R.F. Brissenden, *Virtue in Distress: Studies in the Novel of Sentiments from Richardson to Sade* (London, 1974), and N. Gilot and J. Sgard, *Le vocabulaire du sentiment dans l'œuvre de Jean-Jacques Rousseau* (Geneva, 1980). Behind the concept of human *perfectibilité* in Rousseau among the French revolutionaries, there was a long history of attempts aimed at redeeming man not only from the Pauline and Augustinian tradition – reinforced, in different ways, by Luther, Calvin, and Jansen, who wanted everyone indelibly marked with original sin and consequently needful of divine grace – but also from the naturalistic claim of his original wickedness. For some aspects of the problem, see R. Mercier, *La réhabilitation de la nature humaine* (Paris, 1960).

25 *Oeuvres de Louis XIV* (Paris, 1806), vol. 2, 67–8; see also C. Blum, *Rousseau and the Language of Virtue*, 23.

Man Enlightened by His Own Corruption

Although Robespierre may have conceived of virtue as "the soul of the Republic" (*OC* v, 17) and may have represented the struggle between virtue and vice as a gigantomachy that sees the entire human race engaged in the triumph of the common interest, the Jacobins did not connect "virtue" only with the anachronistic desire to make a monolithic concept of the public good prevail over the centrifugal tendencies of egoism. They were completely conscious of acting in extraordinary circumstances, in a state of exception triggered by a civil and international war with uncertain results. Therefore, it is not proper to generalize (and decontextualize) statements and attitudes assumed in specific situations, under the pressure and urgency of events (although, when the "revolutionary traditions" formed, what had often been a taking of position dictated by circumstances assumed the rigid character of exemplary doctrine). Violence and rebellions were declared legitimate only if they were reducible to the framework of collective events (as in the case of the September massacres)[26] or if placed under the patronage of the people, their representatives, or their vanguards.

Although they may have pointed directly to the liberating effects of *metus* and *spes*, the Jacobins – like Rousseau before them[27] – were, in other respects, close to the morals of the Stoics. Like the latter, they conceived of ethics in the horizon of public life and of service rendered to the state. A "holiday of Stoicism" was called for in the revolutionary calendar. Robespierre considered the Stoics, beyond being followers of "nature," to be "emulators of Brutus and Cato."[28] Saint-Just called Stoicism "virtue of the spirit and of the soul" and interpreted it as the

26 On the massacres and their modalities, see P. Caron, *Les massacres de septembre* (Paris, 1935), and F. Bluche, *Septembre 1792: Logiques d'un massacre* (Paris, 1986).

27 See L. Thomas, "Sénèque et Jean-Jacques Rousseau," *Bulletin de la Classe es Lettres et des Sciences Morales et Politiques et de la Classe des Beaux Arts, Académie Royale de Belgique* 2 (1900), 391–421, and L. Hermann, "Rousseau traducteur de Sénèque," *Annales de la Société Jean-Jacques Rousseau* 13 (1920–1), 215–24. Diderot's interest in Seneca cannot be forgotten: not only in the *Essai sur la vie de Sénèque le philosophe* (Paris, 1779) (where he states, incidentally, that he prefers Heraclitus, who wept for the madness of his brothers, to the Democritus that Burton had chosen as his model), but also in the *Essai sur le règnes de Claude et de Néron.*

28 See A. Mathiez, "Robespierre et le culte de l'Être suprême," in *Autour de Robespierre* (Paris, 1957), 115, and M. Robespierre, speech of 18 Floreal, Year II (7 May 1794), in *OC* x, 454.

"remedy in the evil," an antidote to the decadence of republics where the thirst for income and the consequent disintegration of moral norms were expressed. Therefore, it belongs to times of crisis, when for some it indicates the means of finding the path of goodness and leads man, "enlightened by his own corruption," to nature. It is a beacon that shines alone in the darkness of social life when – as happened in ancient Rome – laws, magistrates, and gods were laughed at.[29]

The Jacobins could not be indifferent to the values of consistency and self-control and the strict call to the ethics of duty taught by Stoicism. They aspired to spreading this doctrine, creating a type of mass Stoicism established through "spiritual exercises" to be completed largely in public view. Beyond republican virtues, they also needed to inherit from the Roman world the ideal of *auctoritas* – the prerogative of the state and its representatives. Great and virtuous is he who shows himself capable of tolerating any trial, in a disciplined manner and without complaint, in the name of obedience to the laws of the common good, embodied in institutions still *in fieri* that he commits himself to defend and promote.

Stoicism and Epicureanism once again appear to conflict as antecedents: the first with revolutionary ethics, the second with the aristocratic morals of Helvétius and D'Holbach. Although, according to Robespierre, Stoicism had in fact saved "the honor of human nature degraded by the vices of Caesar's successors," the "Epicurean sect undoubtedly claimed all of the villains who oppressed their country and all the cowards who let it be oppressed. Thus, although the philosopher whose name it bore was not personally a despicable man, the principles of his system, interpreted by corruption, led to consequences so disastrous that antiquity itself branded it with the title of the 'herd of Epicurus'" (*OC* x, 454).

Obviously, neither Saint-Just nor Robespierre took into account the tragic nature that served as a background for the thought of Epicurus, nor Montaigne's observation that "the corruption of the age is made up by the particular contribution of every individual man; some contribute treachery, others injustice, irreligion, tyranny, avarice, cruelty, according to their power. The weaker sort contribute folly, vanity, and idleness."[30]

D'Holbach's *Système de la nature* is entirely focused on the desire, both Epicurean and Lucretian, to liberate men from fear of the gods and of death. Every religion arises from fear, but also (and particularly) from

29 *FIR* 504. See also *OC* 281.

30 Montaigne, "Of Vanity," *ES* III, IX, 923 (*ESe* III, IX, 181).

the existence of evil. If evil did not exist, men would not have any need to fabricate "bizarre, unjust, bloodthirsty, and relentless" divinities (this is the new element of his theory).[31] Religion is therefore reduced to a theodicy held together by fear of invisible powers from which one can free himself (like Epicurus) through knowledge of everything – that is, through the negatory philosophy of every superstition and faith, Christianity included.[32] In D'Holbach and in *De l'esprit* by Helvétius (I, IV) (another reprobate from the Jacobins' point of view), praise of self-esteem as a sentiment capable of transforming every vice into virtue accompanies this struggle against fear and in favour of reason purified of waste.

While for Robespierre and Saint-Just the philosophy of the Epicureans came to designate the "system of egoism" (i.e., of luxury and dissipation), Stoic philosophy was consistently presented as a synonym for virtue, frugality, and obedience to duty. For revolutionary ethics, it thus assumed the nature of a distant model that projected its brilliance from Robespierre all the way to the young Gramsci, giving off a fascination that derived from the indissoluble interweaving of the ethics of duty and of political engagement.[33]

The Legacy of Brutus

Like Rousseau, the Jacobins believed that those who separated morals from politics were devoted to understanding nothing of either morals or politics. Moreover, like Montesquieu, they knew that in a republic, "private crimes are the most public," and the rejection of self-interest in favour of the common good constitutes the sum of all the specific virtues.[34] For the Jacobins, then, being virtuous did not mean looking after one's own moral perfection as a private matter but conforming strictly to the

31 See A. Minerbi Belgrado, *Paura e ignoranza: Studio sulla teoria della religione in D'Holbach* (Florence, 1983), 225 et seq. and 231 et seq. (for the frontal attack on Christianity).

32 In the words of Epicurus, it could be said that "it is not possible for one to rid himself of his fears about the most important things if he does not understand the nature of the universe but dreads some of the things he has learned in the myths. Therefore, it is not possible to gain unmixed happiness without natural science" (*Cap. Max.* XII; Engl. trans., 61).

33 On Gramsci as a reader of Marcus Aurelius, see R. Bodei, "Gramsci: Volontà, egemonia, razionalizzazione," in *Politica e Storia in Gramsci*, ed. F. Ferri (Rome, 1977), vol. 1, 97.

34 Montesquieu, *EdL* III, 5; IV, 5.

norms that produced good citizens. The attempt to generalize and assert the freedom from need and fear that the wise man enjoyed – through a phase of proclaimed, temporary abnegation – was accompanied by the search for the purity of the universality of law.

The fragility of good and happiness, put forth by Rousseau, was no longer perceived as a destiny. When individuals and institutions were modified by the *Grande Nation* (which assumed the task of instilling a new order and representing all of humanity), when the heavy boulder of oppression that weighed upon the shoulders of men was finally removed and shattered, then the rigid ethics of a virtue sanctioned by the state would truly be metabolized into working solidarity, and future generations would be able not only to return to the ancient virtues of uncorrupted republics, but to surpass them in splendour.

In eighteenth-century France, even before Montesquieu and Rousseau, this concept of virtue owed its fortune to Voltaire's "republican" tragedies, *Brutus* (1730) and *La mort de César* (1735). *Brutus* shows Brutus the Elder who, after having driven out Tarquinius Superbus and founded the republic, notices that his own son Titus is plotting a conspiracy with the monarchy in exile. He has no hesitation in condemning him to death, because for him, virtue means unconditionally sacrificing individual interest (love for one's own son) for the general interest (salvation of the country). In fact, it represents the necessary complement of the laws against the reign of whim, which characterizes the Romans from the first two lines of the tragedy: *Destructeurs des tyrans, vous n'avez pour rois/Que les dieux de Numa, vos vertus and nos lois.*[35] The fact that Titus is his son ensures that Brutus – consul of Rome, political embodiment of all the people – feels duty-bound to be even more severe with him than with a

---

35 "The scourge of tyrants, you who own no kings/but Numa's gods, your virtues, and your laws" (in *OC*, vol. 1, 315; *DW* 225). On Brutus as a model, see R.L. Herbert, *David, Voltaire, "Brutus" and the French Revolution* (London, 1972). Incidentally, the observation that Brutus the Younger was not a Stoic, but a pupil of the Skeptic Academy, was already old (see Sen., *Ad Helv. matr.* IX, 5–6). To measure the distance between the image of Brutus that Voltaire or Saint-Just had and what had existed in the previous period, one need only think of Machiavelli, who pointed out Brutus's pretending to be crazy in order to oppress kings and save the country (see *D* III, 2). Behind these heroic models traces can almost always be found – visible starting in the sixteenth century – of the Plutarchan *exempla* (for some aspects of the matter, see M.H. Horward, "The Influence of Plutarch in the Major European Literatures of the Eighteenth Century," diss., University of Maryland, 1967). Even before the Revolution, the *Parallel Lives* had so enflamed the young as to make them ready to pass, without excessive shock, from the scholastic and university classrooms to the fields of battle and to the assemblies:

stranger: *Lève-toi, cher appui qu'espérait ma veillesse:/Vien embrasser ton père: il t'a dû condamner;/Mais s'il n'était Brutus, il t'allait pardonner.*[36] Burke would later recall, with bitter irony, that during the Revolution there were "sons who called for the execution of their parents" and some "wretches, calling themselves fathers ... demand[ed] the murder of their sons, boasting that Rome had but one Brutus, but that they could show five hundred."[37] During the crucial period of the Revolution, Voltaire's *Brutus* (but not *La mort de César*, because of its description of the sudden change of the popular mood following Antony's funeral speech) was presented as often as three times per week,[38] to warm the patriotic climate and increase

---

"The oldest among us reported that on the eve of the new events, the prizes of rhetorical composition consisted of the debate between two orations, in the manner of Seneca the orator, in favor of Brutus the Elder and Brutus the Younger" (C. Nodier, *Souvenirs, épisodes et portraits pour servir à l'histoire de la Révolution et de l'Empire* [Paris, 1831], vol. 1, 82).

36 "Rise, wretched Titus, thou wert once the hope/of my old age, my best support; embrace/thy father who condemn'd thee: t'was his duty./Were he not Brutus, he had pardon'd thee" (act 5, scene 7, *OC* 384; *DW* 309).

37 E. Burke, *Letters on a Regicide Peace*, in *WB*, vol. 5, 209. Without adding to these extremes of "virtue," to someone who was (or wanted to seem) a perfect revolutionary it was enough to declare one had taken part in all the crucial events and holidays, to live with frugality and modesty, and to have read, every night, the "Declaration of the Rights of Man and of the Citizen" to his children. See R. Cobb, *The Police and the People: French Popular Protest 1789–1820* (Oxford, 1970); Ital. trans. *Polizia e popolo: La protesta popolare in Francia (1789–1820)* (Bologna, 1976), 85–6.

38 See R. Paulson, *Representations of Revolution (1789–1820)* (New Haven, 1983), 31. Robespierre, who highly venerated Brutus and Rousseau (the only ones who would have been worthy of presiding over the revolutionary assemblies; see *OC* VIII, 143–4), did not at all think highly of Voltaire from a moral point of view: "Caesar was a man of genius; Cato was a virtuous man, and certainly Cato was worth more than Caesar. Voltaire wrote *Brutus*; Voltaire was a man of genius; but the hero of the poem was worth more than the poet" (*OC* X, 158). Even more understandable is the fact that the Jacobins did not like the anti-heroic tone present in other works by Voltaire. They might have tolerated him if he had exclusively addressed (as he does on other occasions) the desire for glory by rulers, who sacrificed thousands of men to their passion. Regarding this proposition, see the insightful letter-poem of 22 May 1742 to Frederick II of Prussia, written immediately after the battle of Chotusitz (cited in E. Cassirer, *Die Philosophie der Aufklärung* [Tübingen, 1932]; Ital. trans. *La filosofia dell'illuminismo* [Florence, 1973], 304):

J'aime peu les héros, ils font trop de fracas
J'hais ces conquérant, fiers ennemis d'eux mêmes,
Qui dans les horreurs des combats
Ont placé leur bonheur suprême,

the feeling of solidarity among citizens, even in the case of a collision of duties and conflict between the imperatives of politics and the norms that regulated the most sacred familial ties (during this same period, the bust of Brutus was carried in procession beside that of Rousseau).

In *La mort de César* (*The Death of Caesar*), Voltaire shows another Brutus (Brutus the Younger, who plotted to kill Caesar, together with Cassius and the others) to be virtuous because, conquering filial affection for Caesar, he kills him as a tyrant (Saint-Just would say that Caesar was immolated in the full Senate "without other formalities than twenty-three blows of the dagger, and without other law than the liberty of Rome").[39] Voltaire's drama is centred on the conflict between the necessity (or not) of political forms to adapt themselves to changing customs and times, when virtue deteriorates into an excuse for permission or into sterile ethical nostalgia for a past that will not return, becoming an empty apologia for a general interest that is by now compromised, whose spoils are divided among everyone.[40]

In Voltaire's drama, a father condemns a son to death, and a son kills his father – this also requires the terrible production of good.[41] However, solution of the conflict through a choice in favour of obedience to the general interest, and in favour of empathy with the general will without a trace of the individual, breaks the "heart." That is, it damages virtue's

---

Cherchant partout la mort, et la faisant souffrir
A cent mille hommes leurs semblables.
Plus leur gloire a d'éclat, plus il sont haïssables.

It is certain, however, that the Jacobins would not generally have tolerated an attack on glory per se, since it is the complement of the virtue to which every good citizen must aspire.

39 Saint-Just, *Discours concernant le jugement de Louis* XVI, in *OC2*, vol. 1, 366.

40 According to Caesar: *Rome demande un maître,/Un jour a tes dépens tu l'apprendra peut-être, Tu vois nos citoyens plus puissants que des rois:/Nos mœurs changent, Brutus; il faut changer nos lois./La liberté n'est plus que le droit de se nuire./Rome, que détruit tout semble enfin se détruire … Dans nos temps corrompus, pleins de guerres civiles/Tu parles comme au temps de Dèces, des Emiles./Caton t'a trop séduit, mon cher fils, je prévois/Que sa triste vertu perdra l'État et toi* (*La mort de César*, act 2, scene 3, in *OC*, vol. 2, 347). Brutus, on the other hand, asserts that he detests Caesar only with the name of king, while *César citoyen sérait un dieu pour moi* (*OC*, vol. 2, 346). In the end, Caesar, almost aware of his destiny – *j'aime mieux mourir que de craindre la mort* (*OC*, vol. 2, act 3, scene 5, 351) – makes his way towards the Senate, inflexible in his decisions.

41 For the Jacobins, the image of Caesar's murderer, Brutus the Younger, is a double-edged sword in itself. In fact, Charlotte Corday also makes use of it to kill the "tyrant" Marat (see D. Arrasse, *La guillotine et l'imaginaire de la Terreur* [Paris, 1987], 105).

attempt to reconcile the reasons of the social heart and body with those of interest and individuality. Fear and terror constitute a further guarantee of virtue's effectiveness; they represent political sanctions that complement their otherwise predominantly moral character.

Terror must be unidirectional. It must emanate from below and radiate upward, because – according to Saint-Just – "We must scare those who govern. We must never scare the people."[42] The two thousand Jacobin sections scattered throughout France and the nearly one hundred thousand affiliates officially supported this credo and honoured those who sacrificed to make it triumph. They were the martyrs of the Revolution: Marat, Calier, and Lepeletier, to whom can be added the youths Barra and Viala, heroic victims of the cruel monarchy, and the entire crew of the *Vengeur du Peuple*, which sacrificed itself, it appears, singing the Marseillaise while the ship sank, struck by enemies. Along with its own calendar, the Revolution also created its own martyrology.[43] Everyone threw themselves courageously into it, facing death in order to defeat the representatives of an oppressive authority.

In a letter to his family, written shortly before being killed under the Directorate, Gracchus Babeuf would give one of the highest examples of republican virtue: "I hope that you will believe that I loved everyone very much. I cannot conceive of another way to make you happy if not through common happiness. I failed; I sacrificed myself; I also die for you ... You will like hearing all sensitive and honest hearts say, speaking of your husband, of your father, 'He was perfectly virtuous.'"[44] In tones that recall the argument against Pascal's *moi haïssable*, even Robespierre referred to the "baseness of the individual *I*" (*OC* x, 354 = *RG* 163) as

42 Saint-Just, *FIR* 530.

43 On the cult of the revolutionary martyrs, see A. de Baecque, "Le corps meurtri de la Révolution: Le discours politique et le blessures des martyres (1792–1794)," *Annales Historiques de la Révolution Française* 267 (1987), 17–41.

44 *Dernière lettre de Gracchus Babeuf, assassiné par la prétendue Haute Cour de Justice, à sa femme et à ses enfants* (Paris, n.d. – but composed on the night of 7–8 Priarial of Year IV – that is, the night of 26–7 May 1797), in F. Buonarroti, *Conspiration pour l'égalité dite de Babeuf, suivi du procès auquel donna lieu, et des pièces justificatives, etc.* [Brussels, 1828] (Paris, 1957). The missive concludes with the sentence: "I wrap myself in the bosom of a virtuous sleep." On the letters of those condemned to death during the Terror, when the executions took place in the Place de la Révolution, later significantly transformed into the Place de la Concorde and into the Place du Trône renversé, see O. Blanc, *La dernière lettre: Prisons et condamnés de la Révolutions* (Paris, 1984).

an antagonist of virtue. In periods of revolution, beyond being a luxury, "care of oneself" becomes a crime.

In fact, the virtuous citizen possesses a great mind, because he includes that of the people, and he lacks fear of his personal fate because, in pursuing the common good, his conscience is steady and satisfied.

Patriots and revolutionaries represent, at the same time, the modern version of the Aristotelian magnanimous man (see Saint-Just, *OC* 809, 818 = *TL* 191–2, 206) and the model of a sublime attitude. Unlike the magnanimous man, however, they do not feel superior to others for the simple fact that they give to the collective more than they eventually receive. They are limited to calmly fulfilling their own duty. And their nature is sublime in that they raise themselves above pettiness and exclusive attachment to their own interests and – conquering the natural impulse towards self-preservation – they expose themselves to mortal risks. In this sense, Robespierre calls the Parisian people "sublime" for the civic courage they demonstrated in confronting all their difficulties. In this sense, Robespierre himself will claim to have come to the world – implicitly as "the son of Mary" – to carry the sword for loving men. His is a love that is possible only after having eliminated, by means of necessary force, those who suffocate it: the modern Pharisees with their selfishness and hypocrisy.

The path is thus opened to the image of the "Sans-culotte Jesus," which then entered into the revolutionary martyrology.[45] Camille Desmoulins sarcastically ties it to the figure of the Terror itself, both in the sense of the biblical *Timor Domini initium sapientiae* and in the sense of the gospel episode of the bridegroom who, not seeing the guests, sends his servants to force passersby to enter – that *compelle eos intrare* that was used (from Augustine to Sepúlveda and beyond) to justify the forced conversion of entire populations to Christianity: "I think that it was good to make terror the order of the day, and make use of the formula of the Holy Spirit, according to which 'fear of the Lord is the beginning of wisdom'" and of the formula of the good Sans-culotte Jesus, who said, "Half will, half strength – always convert them, *compelle eos intrare*."[46]

Community, brotherhood, and horizontal relationships of *égalité* among citizens refer to a social pact that highlights the granitic and

45 On this phenomenon and its framing, see F.P. Bowman, *Le Christ romantique, 1789: Le sans-culotte de Nazareth* (Geneva, 1973), and D. Menozzi, *Letture politiche di Gesù: Dall'Antico Regime alla Rivoluzione* (Brescia, 1973).

46 C. Desmoulins, "Le Vieux Cordelier," *Journal Politique* 6 (rpt., Geneva, 1978), 120.

non-negotiable nature of the general will, the observance of which constitutes the essence of virtue. Even through this, the elementary foundations of individual and collective existence would be upset in a few years, and the same social hierarchy exemplarily (although momentarily) overturned. Then the social "dregs" would rise to the surface and the peaks would be submerged.

Fear and Guilt

Virtuous citizens, intrepid by character or by moral choice, are not afraid of confronting the "despotism of servitude," however it may present itself. They do not tolerate even the memory of it. They want the power of the republic to be universal and anonymous, whole and indivisible, continuously generated by all and everyone. The new collective sovereign that comes from their activity does not recognize any earthly power higher than itself and does not tolerate individuals who – through vanity or interest – may rise to become protagonists of a general process of revolutionary renewal, attributing special prerogatives to themselves. This is the meaning of the speech Robespierre gave on 11 Germinal of Year 2 (31 March 1794), the day after the arrest of Danton and Desmoulins. With rhetoric of great ability and effectiveness, which has nothing to do with the merit of the accusations against the accused, he presents his adversaries and former friends as individuals who professed to be "superior" to other citizens and passed themselves off as "idols," even if, as such, they had long since gone bad. They were very dangerous men, because they wanted to "destroy" equality. It does not matter – suggests the Incorruptible – whether France and the Revolution are owed to Danton and Desmoulins. They do not personify them and cannot represent them individually. No one can or must do that. The people and the Revolution are an absolute before which the individual loses importance. These men, instead, sacrificed the interest of the country "to personal ties, perhaps to fear." But, Robespierre moralizes, "whoever trembles at this moment is guilty." The innocent man does not fear the eye of public vigilance, the gaze of the citizens. And he adds: *mon cœur est exempt de crainte.*[47]

---

47 See M. Robespierre, speech of 11 Germinal, Year II, in *OC* X, 414, and C. Lefort, "La Terreur révolutionnaire," in *Essais sur le politique* (XIXe–XXe) (Paris, 1986), 75–109. Distancing himself from the "accusatory" model of Roman rights, in which an impartial judge imposed the burden of proof on the accuser, the Jacobins took, as their own,

Under this logic, the fear that is felt is a sign of guilt, which is rightly inflicted by virtue. And to show that he personally does not want to become an idol of the crowd and that he is not afraid, Robespierre recalls in the same speech that many friends of Danton had wanted to *inspirer des terreurs* in him. That is, they had explicitly pointed out that once the fuse of political violence had been lit, the fate of today's condemned could be his fate tomorrow. He does not exclude such an eventuality, but neither does he see "a public calamity" or a reason for fear: "What do the dangers matter to me! My life belongs to the country ... and if I die, it will be without reproach and without ignominy."[48]

Robespierre and Saint-Just preferred to be part of the exceptional organisms (like the Committee for Public Health) that did not seemingly permit their members to rise above the people. Moreover, in attributing to them the position of accusers over whom hangs the threat of changing into future accused, such emergency institutions established a temporary free zone between society and the state, a power parallel and more fluid that had its point of strength in the sections and in the public square. Through a sort of tragic irony, however, Robespierre and Saint-Just – wanting to respect revolutionary legality to the very end – fatally hesitated to resort to it at the moment of extreme need, before being condemned to death.

Robespierre, in particular, aspired to place himself as a hinge between the informal representation of the Jacobin clubs and the formal representation of the republic's institutions. In some respects, he too distrusted those who governed, but he knew that governing was necessary.[49]

---

the "inquisitory" model developed by the Catholic church, in which the penal action is promoted by the judge himself, on the basis of assumptions of guilt relative to the accused, which allows both a generalization of suspicion and little or almost no possibility for the accused to defend himself (on these two models, see I. Mereu, *Storia dell'intolleranza in Europa* [Milan, 1988]). In this context of asymmetry between someone who is afraid and guilty and someone who uses fear and remains innnocent, the observation of Engels should be reconsidered: "The *terreur* expressed cruelty that was largely useless, committed by people who were themselves fearful, in order to calm themselves" (letter to Marx of 4 September 1870. See *MEW* = K. Marx and F. Engels, *Werke* (Berlin, 1953), vol. 33, 53, and see I. Cappiello, "Il concetto di rivoluzione dei Giacobini e il ruolo del Terrore nelle riflessioni di Marx," *Discorsi* 7 (1987), 239–54.

48 Robespierre, speech of 11 Germinal, Year II, in *OC* X, 414.

49 On the Jacobin system of government, see some points in A.Z. Manfred, "La nature du pouvoir jacobin," *La pensée* 150 (1970), 62–83. On the functions of the Committee of Public Health see the book, whose tone is attributable to its date of publication, by H. Calvet, *Un instrument de la Terreur à Paris: Le Comité de Salut Publique et de surveillance du Département de Paris* (Paris, 1941).

To the degree it concerned his own life (as well as those of his enemies, of the innocent and the guilty, of Brutus and his sons), he belonged completely to the community.

However, it would be incorrect to think that primacy of politics represented the permanent ideal of all the Jacobins. Most, like Saint-Just, aspired – once their terrible public tasks had been discharged – to return to private life and solitude, according to the model offered by Cincinnatus and Rousseau, respectively. Politics was not everything. Rather, in normal times its exercise was drastically reduced, to the minimal intervention of the state into citizens' personal and social matters: "It is less about making people happy, than preventing them from being unhappy. Do not oppress – this is everything. And everyone will know how to find their own happiness. People in whom a preconception is established that they owe their own happiness to those who govern, would not preserve it for long … To be happy, it is necessary to isolate oneself as much as possible"[50]

Happiness – "a new thought in Europe," according to Saint-Just – was now accessible not only to wise men but to all men, even those destined, according to Burke, to "travel in the obscure walk of laborious life" (see *RRF* 43). Since, in Thomist terms, this hope of happiness *non potest frustrari*, the search for it became the object of a social plan and changed in some sense into a political obligation. Reason had the task of clearing the path of obstacles that placed themselves in the way of attainment of happiness itself, in a "race" that was no longer the Hobbesian one in which just one person wins, but where everyone should be able to arrive at the finish line (if urged on by virtue) more or less together.[51]

The general interest is produced, then, by combinations of virtue and fear, which generated the Terror like a sharp sword of justice capable of separating the good from the bad. In itself, the general interest is – like the republic – monolithic, non-negotiable, one, and indivisible. It is not born of improbable agreement between special interests, of stipulations between individuals, or of the free play of the (economic or political)

50 Saint-Just, *FIR* 507.

51 For an implicit divergence of perspectives among the Jacobins, keep in mind that Robespierre conceived of happiness only in the public sphere, as shown in his speech on peoples of colour on 24 September 1791, in which he says of himself: *Moi, qui ne connais ni bonheur, ni prospérité, ni moralité pour les hommes ni pour les nations sans liberté* (*OC* VII, 738). On this subject see F. Theriot, "La conception robespierriste du bonheur," *Annales Historique de la Révolution Française* 40 (1968), 207–26.

market of individual goods. If need be, it is necessary to force men to achieve the general will. But the common good cannot be delivered until men who think only of themselves have been eliminated. In fact, men will be able to be free and happy only if they are virtuous brothers, only if they are equals, capable of solidarity. But since the privileged are not at all disposed to let themselves be convinced by rational arguments, and egoism and indifference to the public good had, by then, set deep roots in the minds of individuals, the Terror became indispensable for achieving liberty, equality, and fraternity. The "tyranny" of the general will was thus presented as control of the best part of man – the rational and moral part – over himself, the triumph of virtue over vice, of the community over the elements of corruption. The solitary and melancholy tyrant of Baroque German dramas was no longer called upon to govern, but a collective tyrant, a strict and inflexible pedagogue.

To impose it, a complex system of persuasion must be set up by developing a revolutionary rhetoric that hinges, simultaneously or alternately, on arguments based both on necessity and the *force de choses* (when the revolution is considered an unavoidable event, an almost natural cataclysm) and on moral and juridical motivations requiring the active and conscious intervention of human will (when the emphasis falls on the complementary and equally felt need to affect events considered similarly automatic).[52] The simultaneous use of these two systems helps to understand the birth of the paradoxes and contradictions of revolution that come together in the concept of "despotism of liberty," in the oxymoronic choice – presented as necessary – that leads revolutionaries to feel called upon to achieve, in a short period of time, what is inevitable in the long term.

Such revolutionary rhetoric, which causes a profound modification of language and behaviour,[53] is not, however, limited to politics. It has

52 See R. Bodei, "Le dissonanze del mondo: La Rivoluzione francese e la filosofia tedesca tra Kant e Hegel," in *L'eredità della Rivoluzione francese*, ed. F. Furet (Rome, 1989), 109 et seq. On the use of means of mass communication, see P. Barbier and F. Vernillant, *L'histoire de France par les chanson* (Paris 1957); F. Moreau and E. Wahl, eds., *Chants de la Révolution française* (Paris, 1989); J.A. Leith, *Media and Revolution: Moulding a New Citizenry in France during the Terror* (Toronto, 1968); D. Hamiche, *Le Théâtre de la Révolution française* (Paris, 1973); M. Agulhon, *Marianne au combat: L'imagerie et le symbolisme républicain 1789 à 1880* (Paris, 1990).

53 On the rhetoric of the Revolution, see H.U. Gumbrecht, *Funktionen parlamentarischer Rhetorik in der Französishen Revolution* (Munich, 1978), and L. Hunt, *Politics, Culture and Class in the French Revolution* (Berkeley, 1984).

broader implications of a character that could almost be said to be metaphysical. It leads to a peculiar interweaving of objective automatisms and subjective intervention to guide its course – specifically, of *force des choses*[54] and voluntarism. The events possess an iron, cumulative, and inexorable logic of their own, but also a direction that can be encouraged or opposed, accelerated, or restrained. In the end, however, the comprehensive and powerful pressure of their moving mass prevails. If this is how things stand, politics must adapt to this logic, establishing new forms of participation in power and forging new actors who learn, in forced stages, the profession of *citoyen*. This requires an organized political pedagogy that quickly involves all ages and both sexes.[55]

Unlike Spinoza and the French materialists,[56] however, some Jacobins learned to be anti-determinists, glimpsing the possibility of emancipation not only from the chains of slavery, but from those of an iron and unchangeable destiny. They certainly sometimes had faith in an inevitable victory of the Revolution,[57] but the emphasis placed on the imponderable element of liberty and on the uncertainty of the times and results ended up modifying all fatalism. Without the active intervention of will and reason, without the decisive contribution of all virtuous citizens, the Revolution could also fail, falling prey to the inertia to which, for millennia, the majority of men had become accustomed.[58]

Form and Strength

Through the pictorial representation of exemplary acts of virtue, the art of this period gives credit to the idea that the tragic conflict between liberty and necessity, and between general will and special interests – all

54 On the *force des choses*, see Saint-Just, *Rapport au Comité de salut public et de sûreté générale sur les personnes incarcérées, presenté à la Convention nationale dans la séance du 8 ventose an* II [26 February 1794], in *OC* 705; Ital. trans. *TL* 149. Note that the expression *la force des chose peut nous entraîner à des résultats que nous n'avions pas prévus* refers more to the unexpected effects of the revolutionary process than to its necessity.

55 See M. Genty, *L'apprentissage de la citoyenneté 1789–1795* (Paris, 1987).

56 On the presence of Spinoza in French thought of the eighteenth century, see P. Vernière, *Spinoza et le pensé française avant la Révolution* (Paris, 1954).

57 See J.P. Marat, *L'Ami du peuple*, 18 November 1789: "The Revolution will be achieved unmistakably, without any human power being able to oppose it."

58 See Saint-Just, *Rapport au Comité de salut public et de sûreté générale sur les personnes incarcérées, presenté à la Convention nationale dans la séance du 8 ventose an* II [26 February 1794], in *OC* 701; Ital. trans. *TL* 142.

legitimate values at their respective levels – demands subordination of the second element of each pair to the first. We may consider the paintings of Jacques-Louis David, beginning with *The Lictors Bringing Brutus the Bodies of His Sons*, presented to the Salon in August 1789.[59] In a scene divided symmetrically into two sections, a conflict takes place between darkness and light. On the left, in the dark part of the painting, in the background are the lictors who enter carrying the bodies of the young sons of Brutus the Elder, the traitors of the country, while he – in the foreground, seated and bent over – bears a silent, wrenching pain. On the right, in the illuminated part of the painting, his wife and other women shout their suffering on a background of plain architecture of strictly geometric forms, which contrasts in its peaceful harmony with the stylized unseemliness of the scene.

David shows this same dramatization of the general will in *statu nascendi* at the moment when it is concentrated and constituted solemnly through an oath, in *Serment du Jeu de Paume* of 1791 – that is, in the foundational act of a new social pact, of a *union sacrée* between men in a nation "one and indivisible" that makes its citizens part of a larger and more powerful whole.[60] In this painting, the lightning and wind of the storm that swells the curtains of the high windows seems to allude to the presence of a lay Holy Spirit that has come to enrich the minds of the founders of the new France.[61] However, in the eyes of the Jacobins, the general will can be betrayed, as can be seen in the painting *La mort de Marat*, where Charlotte Corday d'Armont, in the guise of the "modern Judith," through a trick (a false request for help) takes

59 On David, see the observations of J. Starobinski, *178: Les emblèmes de la raison* (Paris, 1979), and A. Schnapper, *David: Témoin de son temps* (Fribourg, 1980). More generally, see F. Sprigarth, *Themen aus der Geschichte der römischen Republik in der französischen Malerie des 18. Jahrhunderts*, 2 vols. (Munich, 1968); J.J. Lévêque, *L'art et la Révolution française, 1789–1804* (Munich, 1986); and M. Stürmer, *Scherben des Glücks: Klassizismus und Revolution* (Berlin, 1987).

60 The subject of oath, the form of virtuous association for the achievement of an end of collective salvation, through the contracting parties' promise to confront both risk and death, had already been adopted in the *Serment des Horaces*. In this painting as well, the familial drama is interwoven with public events and is resolved in a dilemmatically neat way by Brutus, the same one that revolutionary thought intended to adopt. When the survivor, Horace, sees the crying of his sister, married to one of the three killed Curiatii, he kills her. In this case, even Machiavelli is against his absolution (see *D* 187–91).

61 On this painting, see, in a different context, P. Bordes, *Le Serment du Jeu de Paume de J.-L. David: Le peintre, son milieu et son temps de 1789 à 1792* (Paris, 1983).

advantage of Marat's "virtuous" generosity to have herself received and then to kill him. "N'ayant pu me corrompre, ils m'ont assassiné," David would write about the version of the painting that can now be found at the Museum of Reims. Virtue is contrasted with virtue. If, for the painter and his political friends, Marat is the very personification of virtue, for Andrea Chénier it is embodied, instead, by the avenging heroine: *Un scélérat de moins rampe dans cette fange./La vertu t'applaudit. De sa mâle louange/Entends, belle héroïne, entends l'auguste voix./O vertu, le poignard seule espoir de la terre,/est ton arme sacrée.*[62] The party organized by David the day after Marat's death is an indirect and massive response to the attempt to deny the possession of virtue to the "tribune of the people" and, at the same time, an epitome of all the revolutionary symbolism.[63]

The case of David shows, incidentally, the inadequacy of the image of calm composure that criticism still attributes to neoclassical art. It is true that both in painting and in architecture or sculpture – from Ledoux to Canova – the pure and genuine crystals of rationality seem to dominate, shining and smooth: cubes, spheres, cylinders, pyramids, circles, and squares. But these forms are marked as if by a wound, struck by an invisible hemorrhage of meaning. One thinks of the contrast between the white pyramids of Canova's funereal monuments (a pattern that recurs obsessively) and the door ajar at their base that opens onto the darkness of death and the afterlife of reason – a tragic tension analogous to the one we have just seen in David's canvas, *The Lictors Bringing Brutus the Bodies of His Sons.*

Thus, the meaning of the transmitted political message is not, generally, uninspired and self-satisfied serenity, a coldly academic reproduction of the ancient, but virile, dominant passions. The message is of conflicts

62 "A lowly villain crawls through the mud. Virtue applauds you. Listen, beautiful heroine, to the august voice of its manly praise. O virtue, the dagger – earth's only hope – is your sacred weapon" (A. Chénier, "À Charlotte de Corday," in *Oeuvres poétiques de André Chénier* [Paris, 1884], vol. 2, 295).

63 On this party of 14 July 1793 (which was supposed to commemorate the fourth anniversary of the taking of the Bastille, but which had greater emotional significance because Marat had been killed the day before) and its revolutionary symbolism – for example, flags depicting the *Oeil de la Sourveillance* – and on the subsequent opera of 5 April 1794 that it inspired, *La Réunion du 10 Août ou l'Inauguration de la République Française* by the "citizens" G. Bouquier and P. Moline (who show in the first act the fountain of the *Régénération* on the spot where the Bastille once stood), see R. Carnesecchi, "Una festa di David poco prima del Termidoro," *Eidos: Rivista di arti, lettere e musica* 3 (December, 1988), 48–57.

subject to reason's "virtuous symmetries," to the universality of the geometric form and an energy that can tame the rebellion and disorder of the amorphous, containing it within precise lines and volumes. It is not strange, then, that exactly where terrible events occurred, where life was more serious, art seemed (to paraphrase Schiller) even more serene. Reason, however, now conspired again with death. It knew how to inflict it and confront it according to procedures and rituals that were largely new.

The altars of reason and those of fear were erected beside one another. Celebrations of death and celebrations of life alternated, indirectly demonstrating how every sacrifice was inseparable from the birth and consolidation of new religions. The state of reason coexisted, in turn, with the reason of the state. In this way, the ethics of sacrifice tended once again to replace those of *utilitas*. And this happened to a degree more drastic and violent the more it was dimly perceived that fully restoring the system of the ancient virtues was impossible.

Even in the artistic field, the end of the neoclassical corresponded with the perception of the impossibility of being like the Spartans or Romans evoked by Robespierre and Saint-Just, those *exemplars humanae vitae* that were, by then, unattainable. At the conclusion of the Revolution's Jacobin phase, the "liberty of the moderns" finally abandoned its melancholy nostalgia for classical forms, which were felt as irretrievable, and stopped elaborating its mourning for values no longer consonant with (and often judged damaging to) the present and its horizons. From this viewpoint, the phenomenon of revolutionary neoclassicism represents the last grand attempt to prevent an exemplary past from passing away. From this point on, it would lose its normative character even in the political sphere. The revolutionary would abandon the vestments of Brutus, Agis, Gaius Gracchus, and other Plutarchan heroes to assume the more modern and inconspicuous ones of the conspirator or the intellectual agitator.

Collision of Principles

During the years of the French Revolution, however, the path of virtue remained harsh and difficult. The good citizen possessed no other guiding star than the static image of the primacy of the common good. He nevertheless knew well that it offered insufficient help to orient him in concrete situations, just as he dimly understood that pursuit of the general will brought to the fore dilemmas that were practically insolvable (which it was possible to get out of only through an act of authority) and contradictions that risked either paralysing thought or pushing him far towards the unknown.

With the Jacobin dictatorship, awareness grew of the irremovable presence of a field of contradictory tensions between principles at the moment they passed from theory to practice. A collision was felt between equally inalienable values that often showed a mutual incompatibility, collided, or imploded once they came into contact with reality.

The Jacobins' consistency – undeniable even in the opinion of their adversaries – made this conflict yet more acute and prevented it from being diluted over time, concentrating it in a brief period of months thick with pressing events and rapid choices, when thought and action were placed at the service of interests vital for those involved in the "storm of the Revolution." These men had to manoeuvre within an antagonistic and disjunctive logic founded on a strict rule of exclusion, on the forced choice in which every divergence becomes betrayal, an unbreakable enmity demanding decisions or immediate cuts. *Fraternité ou la Mort!* or *Vivre libre ou mourir*, or, as in 1793, *Liberté Egalité Unité Indivisibilité de la République ou la Mort* were its bywords. Solving the contradictions was postponed to the future, to the moment when final victory of the revolutionary cause could finally relax the unresolved tension between opposing concepts. With privilege and selfishness eliminated, with respect for the general interest transformed into widespread habit, liberty could do without the armour of despotism, the equality of the guillotine's "shortenings," and the fraternity of "fratricidal hate." Until then, however, the world of ethical and political values would remain divided.

Instead, the strengthening or the victory of one principle temporarily led to the weakening and defeat of the other. The world was again in turmoil. From the "chaos" into which it had plunged, the conditions of a new order could emerge. Now that "liberty passed its childhood," a "healthy anarchy" was capable of leading to the emancipation of individuals and peoples, while "absolute order" certainly led to despotism.[64] Precisely because liberty had not yet exited the stage in which it needed to live under protection, and because the "new world" was quickly taking shape, the Jacobins tended to defend fanatically all the *chances* of its process of development, establishing a rigid moral catechism in order to

64 Saint-Just, *Rapport fait au nom du Comité de salut public sur la nécessité de déclarer le gouvernement révolutionnaire jusqu'à la paix, présenté à la convention nationale dans la séance du 19 du Ier mois de l'an II,* in *OC* 528; Ital. trans. *Rapporto sulla necessità di dichiarare il governo rivoluzionario fino alla pace (10 ottobre 1793),* in *TL* 130.

avoid the rise of centrifugal forces in the interpretation and application of its values. They reproduced, on another level, the Spinozan distinction between the iron law of reason and the *res particulares* – transforming it, however, into conflict, into a relationship of mutual enmity. To find its own consistency and compactness, then, the torn reason of these conflicts had to trigger the Terror. Yet that way it could not avoid exposing itself to the risk of becoming a servant of the same tools that it had professed to use. The revolution that, in order to impose universal principles, had to rationalize the passions, experienced their essential insubordination and deaf resistance to all forms of definitive domestication.

This bifurcation of opposites (which had been initially joined within universal principles) was revealed every time that a principle was examined up close. It was then noted that, in order to achieve it, it was indispensable to pass to its opposite: liberty needed despotism, equality needed terror, and fraternity needed hate. Thus, the Revolution trained thought to confront the contradictions and accustomed it to considering, anew, the presence in daily life of tragic figures (like, for example, the "guilt of innocence" – that is, being objectively guilty for the birth and circumstances of a crime for which one is not subjectively responsible). Concentrating on more urgent problems, the Jacobins did not arrive at an explanation for the profound implications of these conflicts. The logic of exclusion did not offer answers.

In this context, greater liberty can mean (and often meant) less equality and less fraternity; more equality means less liberty and forced fraternity; and greater fraternity means less liberty and imposed equality (given that natural fraternity is a destiny, but ethical or political fraternity can, paradoxically, become an obligation). The transition from myriad partial liberties (which preserve the particularistic form of privilege) to a single liberty (which is jealous of its own universal character) is repaid with increased aversion to concreteness and greater suspicion towards determinations that are too precise and felt as dangerous, because it was feared that they could place conditions and limits on liberty, reducing its scope and importance. In this way, fear of marking boundaries (or conversely, the desire to keep the revolutionary process fluid) impeded the solution of the aporias.

Fraternité and Country

In the struggle to re-establish "warm" bonds in the environment of a society long dominated by inequality and the "coldness" of individual selfishness, the revolutionaries had not sought to institutionalize just the negative passions (those tied, Spinozanly, to *tristitia* or fear) but also the positive ones, like respect for reason and laws,[65] friendship and fraternity (even if the byword *fraternité* constituted the most neglected and most recent of the revolutionary triad).[66] In fact, it officially entered into the constellation of the "immortal principles" only in 1848, progressively acquiring two meanings that were barely alluded to originally: that of a body, at once political and emotional, that united the oppressed in the expectation of a more just world, and that of a concern of the entire society for its members who were less favoured by the "natural and social lottery" that had given birth to them and allowed them to grow, with or without special physical or intellectual gifts and more or less endowed with economic or cultural advantages.[67]

Even if its function was subsequently modified, *fraternité* was already an integral part of the theory and practice of the first French Revolution,

65 It seems to me that the circular sent to all bureaucrats of the republic in May 1794 is indicative of this new climate: "The essential quality of man in the order of nature is to stand upright. The nonsensical jargon of the old ministries must be replaced by a simple style, clear, and yet concise, free from expressions of servility, from obsequious formulae, stand-offishness, pedantry, or any suggestion that there is an authority superior to that of reason, or of the order established by law" (quoted by J.M. Thompson, *The French Revolution* [Oxford, 1945], 428).

66 In the language drawn from family relationships, all the republicans are brothers, but their true parent is the *patrie*. Regarding this, Victor Hugo would justify Rousseau's having abandoned his own children at an orphanage: "I admire that man. He denied his own children, that may be; but he adopted the people" (*Les Misérables*, IV.3 [Paris, 1938], vol. 2, 137).

67 In *fraternité*, Louis Blanc sees the culmination of a process that began in 1789 (the year of liberty, set under the sign of Voltaire), continued in 1793 (the year of equality, placed under the sign of Rousseau), and reaching all the way to 1848 (Year Zero of brotherhood, with which, revealingly, no philosopher's name is yet associated, perhaps because it seemed to represent the most utopian of all the values). More recent studies have been added to the few that existed previously on brotherhood (for example, J. Fitzjames Stephen, *Liberty, Equality, Fraternity* [1873; rpt., Cambridge, 1967]; and H. Krüger, "Brüderlichkeit, das dritte, fast vergessene Ideal der Demokratie," in *Festgabe für Theodor Maunz* [Munich, 1971], 249–65). See G. Antoine, *Liberté, égalité, fraternité ou les fluctuations d'une devise* (Paris, 1981); M. David, *Fraternité et Révolution française* (Paris, 1987); F. Rigotti, "Patriarcato e fratellanza: Immagini familiari nel discorso politico," *Teoria politica* 4, no. 2 (1988), 65–87; F. Furet and M. Ozouf, eds., "Fraternité" in *Dictionnaire critique de la Révolution française* (Paris, 1988); A. Martinelli, "I principi della Rivoluzione francese e la società moderna," in *Progetto 89: Tre saggi su libertà, eguaglianza e fraternità*, ed. A. Martinelli, M. Salvati, and S. Veca (Milan, 1989), 73 et seq.; G. Panella, "Fraternité: Semantica di un concetto," *Teoria politica* 5 (1989), 143–66.

from 1792 to Thermidor, when, in the course of a few years, it changed from an expression of visible unity among citizens into an anti-Jacobin value, since now it would no longer be based on suspicion but on mutual and unfailing trust. In any case, *fraternité* consistently indicated the horizontal solidarity that succeeded the official suppression of a society that had been expressed hierarchically in three states or orders and the voluntary cooperation among free and equal citizens. It was a complete manifestation of virtue as calm rejection of private interest; friendship among all citizens; affection that heals the wounds caused by social conflicts and civil war; an antidote to fear; and a pact (negatively) of reciprocal non-aggression and (positively) of mutual aid and advice aimed at a common betterment. Thus, "He who says that he does not believe in friendship," said Saint-Just, "is banished."[68]

With the term *fraternité*, there entered into political language a concept or metaphor that had previously circulated only within the family, the church, the Stoicism of Epictetus, and religious and Masonic sects, and that even now remained suspended between the ethical plane and the juridical-political one. But revolutionary brotherhood is antagonistic or "divided" brotherhood.[69] It is based on the separation of "we" from "others," on a cohesion cemented by exclusion. It should be spoken about, then, only in the plural,[70] thinking of the multiple spheres of different or opposing "we's." During the Revolution, however, *fraternité* was associated with a paradoxical form of discriminatory equality that professed to impose itself "in the singular," applying the same values that were declared common and universal to a society that was deeply divided. It was held that brotherhood that was full, total, and lacking in resentment could exist when – through a prior, contradictory restoration of the paternal principle of compulsion – the obstacles to liberty and equality were eliminated.

Even later, revolutionary ethics took as its own the connection between virtue as sacrifice of self and brotherhood as solidarity with one's group

68 Saint-Just, *FIR* 519. See also F. Fortunet, "L'amitié selon Saint-Just," in *Annales Historiques de la Révolution Française* 54 (1982), 181–95, which emphasized the paradoxical nature of the attempt to have friendship enter into the juridical sphere, to institutionalize it (and therefore, largely make it obligatory). More recently, R. Rolland, "La signification politique de l'amitié chez Saint-Just, " *Annales Historiques de la Révolution Française* 56 (1984), 324–38, identified instead a "political link without control" and an analog to the virtue.

69 See E. Bloch, *Naturrecht und menschliche Würde* (Frankfurt, 1977), 192 et seq.

70 See M. David, *Fraternité et Révolution française*, 83.

of reference – even when the party (with a revolutionary synecdoche, wanting to represent the *pars pro toto*) intended to be a nucleus that potentially contained the whole, the vehicle of the general interest and future conciliation. Virtue and brotherhood implied the rejection of possessive individualism and the mirror-like reversal of the tradition of classical political economy (in particular, the apologia of selfishness and "luxury"). In this latter tradition, at least from Mandeville onward, the general interest is conceived as the relatively harmonic reorganization of special interests, of individual egoisms that, in a type of social alchemy, produced the common good and public virtues. Private vices, selfishness, passions, and luxury are thus a propellant of associated life that it would not be wise to ban, because the driving forces of modern society would otherwise be bridled, individuals would lose their sense of responsibility, and stagnation would quickly be reached. Industry, "sweet" commerce, and the circulation of money produce happy vices that increase the general wealth.

Even subsequently (and up to the present) there remained the suspicion that *fraternité* (or even "solidarity") had a character that was pre-political or apolitical and, in any event, incompatible or difficult to reconcile with the market economy, a brake placed on efficiency that risked creating pockets of parasitism within society. Onto this was projected the shadow of the totalitarian or conventual community. This would have originally been an eminently Christian ideal, secularized by the despotic regimes that desperately sought perfection of the absolute in the defective relatively of the contingent, without realizing that the attempt to make the heavens fall to earth disturbs the natural order and produces enormous disasters. Therefore, the realm of brotherhood would not belong to this world or, at most, would extend to small groups.

If it might have been disposed to theoretical concessions, for the most part brotherhood could be realized only in the following ways: as a servomechanism that compensates for, in auxiliary and limited form, the biggest distortions in the social distribution of advantages and disadvantages; or (to a lesser degree) within a network of "partial solidarities"; or as the bond of a collective identity that is emerging or in crisis.[71] Modern democratic societies, lacking endemic poverty and anchored to an individualism and to a pluralism with a strong "anti-Jacobin" colouring

71 On this point, see A. Martinelli, "I principi della Rivoluzione francese e la società moderna," passim.

(where *pathos* for the indivisible totality of the social body has disappeared or been eased and where the memory of attacks on liberty perpetrated in our own time in the name of equality and fraternity remains burning), seem to tolerate only multiple and selective brotherhoods, not forced ones incapable of affecting the order of individual choices in a violent or manipulative way.

After the great waves of collective morality, brotherhood – or the excessive proximity of the "citizen," the "comrade," or the "companion" – appear too suffocating (despite the radical differences). In a world of multiple social belonging and divided loyalties (in which nation, state, or class do not absorb the interests of the individual more substantially), brotherhood emphasized the elective moment of individual choice, and it came ever closer to friendship or symbolic identification (more rarely practised) with some communities or causes. In these situations, the difficulties encountered by individuals in taking on ethical obligations of long duration led, on the one hand, to feeling more strongly the demands of broadening the spheres of solidarity and, on the other, to realizing the impervious nature of the passage from ethical terrain to the juridical-political realm of its realization. Within this framework, even the emphasis placed on altruism, as a surrogate of brotherhood, risks remaining a voice in the desert if it remains on ideological terrain characterized by refusal to place under discussion the conditions of individualism and pluralism (unquestionable up to this point) – as long as the fear is not abandoned of trying to determine (even in the events of the Revolution) the unsatisfied demands from which the need of solidarity and more fulfilling social ties might spring. Only this way, restrained within all its political limits, would brotherhood appear not only condemned to represent a simple tribal, gregarious relic or a distasteful obligation of excessive closeness with strangers, but also as a possible factor in enrichment of the individual, a moment of Spinozan sociality.

In the Jacobins, individualism and pluralism appear to be the principles responsible for society's disintegration, in the malign form of selfishness and the factions that corrode communal life. Luxury itself – far from seeming to them like an element of society's expression or an expression of the increased needs of the subject – is presented as the quintessence of the "Land of Cockaygne" that Danton had contrasted with the sad science of virtue and Jacobin frugality.

In fact, for Robespierre and Saint-Just, private vices are (and remain) public vices, and individualism and pluralism produce only misery, selfishness, and political corruption. Then, Marat, who in England had witnessed the perverse effects of the industrial revolution at its birth, had been convinced of the fact that the free "market" was just a further ring in the "chain of slavery." After all, several decades earlier, Rousseau had attacked the foundations of political economy not only in the prefatory note to *Narcisse* in 1759, but in more popular works like the *Nouvelle Héloïse* and *Émile.* In the *Nouvelle Héloïse* (volume 2, letter 14), Saint-Preux relates his Parisian experiences to Julie. Paris is the city of the world where the greatest inequalities reign, where the most sumptuous opulence is accompanied by the most deplorable misery. The selfishness is so great that "each person is mindful of his own interest, no one of the common good, and ... individual interests are always at odds with each other."[72] Every *côterie* has its rules, and what is true in one Parisian *salon* is false in the next. There is no need, like Pascal, to go too far from Paris, to go beyond the Pyrenees, or to move "three degrees of latitude" to find opposing truths. It is enough to travel the few hundred metres that separate one *salon* from another. There, "one learns to plead artfully the cause of the lie, to unsettle with much philosophy all the principles of virtue, to color one's passions and prejudices with subtle sophisms, and to lend to error a certain stylish turn in keeping with the maxims of the day."[73] In *Émile*'s famous *Profession of Faith of the Savoyard Vicar,* these criticisms become even broader and sharper. Neglecting the law of the heart and virtue, every philosophy will be nothing but the stylization of a particular form of selfishness, a great and elaborate sophism to justify privilege.

The Jacobins inherited from Rousseau an aversion both to everything that does not refer to the compact unity of the general interest – non-negotiable in itself – and to the violent rejection of the "sect" of the encylcopedists, those *philosophes* who tied the Enlightenment to despotic government, aristocracy, and the "system of selfishness." With their corrosive *esprit,* they were perhaps capable of triggering disruptive processes in the structures of existing powers but not of contributing to their reversal.

72 J.J. Rousseau, *Julie, ou La nouvelle Héloïse* (Amsterdam, 1761), vol. 2, letter 14; Engl. trans. *Julie, or The New Heloise,* trans. P. Stewart and J. Vaché (Lebanon, NH, 1997).
73 Ibid.

3. Between Hope and Fear

A Non-irresistible Destiny

In the period of enlightened despotism, the reason of the *philosophes*, and in particular of the "encyclopedists" (from Voltaire to Diderot to Maupertuis) had been placed in service of the authority of rulers like Frederick II or Catherine II. Philosophy had been supported by a power that at least appeared desirous of innovating; it had tried to give *auctoritas* to *veritas.* In one game of conditioning, suspicions, and reciprocal reservations, enlightened despots and *philosophes* had tried to make two long-hostile powers collaborate actively. Correcting Hobbes: now, together, and at least in its most generous intentions, *auctoritas et veritas faciunt legem.*

From the beginning and from his first journey to England, Marat had fought the alliance between enlightened despotism and philosophy, with both the novel *Les adventures du jeune comte Potowski* and the treatise *Les chaînes de l'esclavage.*[1] In the novel – written on the eve of the first partition of Poland – he accuses Catherine II, the presumed "Semiramis of the North," of governing her own subjects with "terror" (preventing

1 See Marat, *Les adventures du jeune comte Potowski: Un roman de cœur* (written between 1770 and 1772 and published posthumously, Paris, 1848) and *The Chains of Slavery* (London, 1774), a translation of the broader French, *Les chaînes de l'esclavage, ouvrage destiné à développer les noirs attentats des princes contre le peuple, les ressorts secrets, les ruses, les menées, les artifices, les coups d'État qu'ils emploient pour détruire la liberté et les scènes sanglantes que accompagnent le dispotisme* (Paris, Year I). There are three recent editions: Paris, 1972, ed. J.D. Selche; Paris, 1988, ed. M. Vovelle; and *Chaînes,* Paris, 1995, from which the quotes herein are taken. The title of Marat's work is so explicit and detailed as to not need any comment.

them from breathing freely and dangling a sword "over the head of the indiscreet") and suggests armed revenge of the "rights of the people" as the only remedy. The treatise *Les chaînes de l'esclavage* also reveals the plots and tools with which the oppressed are induced to obey oppressors and, in turn, oppress by proxy their fellow beings. In fact, despotism, if founded on the passivity of subjects and the prince, draws its "legions of salaried followers" (*légions de satellites stipendiés*) from the class of the indigent.[2]

For Marat, a reader and admirer of the *Traité sur la servitude volontaire,* there exists an answer to La Boétie's worried question about the reasons why men are so blinded by inventing their own masters and by delivering their lives into those masters' hands:

> But O good Lord! What strange phenomenon is this? What name shall we give it? What is the nature of this misfortune? What vice is it, or, rather, what degradation? To see an endless multitude of people not merely obeying, but driven to servility? Not ruled, but tyrannized over? These wretches have no wealth, no kin, nor wife nor children, not even life itself that they can call their own. They suffer plundering, wantonness, cruelty, not from an army, not from a barbarian horde, on account of whom they must shed their blood and sacrifice their lives, but from a single man; not from a Hercules nor from a Samson, but from a single little man. Too frequently this same little man is the most cowardly and effeminate in the nation, a stranger to the powder of battle and hesitant on the sands of the tournament; not only without energy to direct men by force, but with hardly enough virility to bed with a common woman![3]

There is, however, a fundamental difference between the positions of La Boétie and Marat. The first responds to this disturbing question in a sufficiently complex manner. He observes in men the simultaneous and dissenting presence of a dual desire to be free and to serve voluntarily. This fear of liberty cannot be attributed to the cowardice of a few individuals but to an attitude, even more monstrous, with no name (*Politics of Obedience,* 108) – that is, to the readiness on the part of millions of men and entire populations to tolerate pains and offences, spellbound "by the name of just one man," whom they should not fear (because there is

---

2 Marat, *Chaînes,* 80.

3 Boétie, *Politics of Obedience: The Discourse of Voluntary Servitude,* trans. H. Kurz (Auburn, 1975), 42; in the original text, *Discours de la servitude volontaire,* 106–7.

just one of him) and whom they should not regard highly (because he is cruel) (ibid., 175). They are, in a Spinozan sense, opaque to themselves, incapable of deciphering their own *utilitas* or capable of interpreting it only at the lowest level. Such individuals are unaware of the irresistible force that the coalition of their desires would assume and unaware of the complementary weakness of the individual who oppresses them, playing on their divisions and stirring up some against others: his guards, "archers," and "halberdiers" against the rest of the population. Voluntary servitude is thus capable of *dénaturer l'homme, seul né de vrai pour vivre franchement* (ibid., 122). For La Boétie, the paradox consists in the fact that the power of the multitude voluntarily founders upon impact with the impotence of an individual. Of this powerful impotence, the victims are not only the representatives of the common people or cowards, but the wise and courageous as well.

For Marat, on the other hand, the solution is much simpler and less enigmatic. The chains of slavery are unidirectional; they descend from above, as the fruit of an age-old conspiracy. The maximum abasement and objective moral degradation occurs when the oppressed person not only does not realize his own condition (thus rejecting himself and sacrificing his *utilitas*) but is changed into an accomplice and supporter of the power that perpetuates the misery, ignorance, and humiliation of all his fellow beings. He is a *homo patiens* in different senses. The first is that he endures and suffers from the bullying of one or more who depress, corrupt, and turn against him the *cupiditas* that – in other situations – would perhaps push him to increase his own power of existing and to be, in a Spinozan sense, *sui juris*. Second, he is a *homo patiens* because his activity is channelled, on one hand, to the benefit of people or institutions that have already accumulated a higher rate of *vis existendi* and, on the other, in the direction of a restlessness with no outlet that generally stops at the tolerance of suffering. We are in the state in which – given the length of the hierarchical scale – whoever is on the bottom often does not even dare to imagine a situation different from the one in which he has always lived and by which he was led to inhibit his desires, because he suspects or secretly knows the price of their remote achievement, however possible.

Revolution opens onto the future; it mobilizes existences and life plans; it lets openings of possibilities be glimpsed; it releases hopes and fears on a large scale. In Marat's terms, it breaks the "chains of slavery," it makes the *utilitas* of individuals be rediscovered in its "primitive" form of their link with "equals," with their brothers in suffering, connecting pain and the rejection of oneself to which they are accustomed to the promise of happiness through a collective *conatus* of liberation that demands unity. *Utilitas* and self-preservation still require abnegation, however, and in some cases, the halo of martyrdom.

The decisive political problem, which particularly marks this era, is whether even the abasement and degradation of the "humiliated and offended" – their point of view on the world – must be respected. They are not degraded or slaves by nature. There does not exist any inevitable moral destiny that made them be born or that had to make them become what they are. They are made the abject individuals of society by an induced "immoral fate" that, in principle, can destroy and change in the same way that it was created. (It could be added that for this reason, revolutions and modern "totalitarianisms" have proclaimed themselves representatives of the classes and ranks excluded from the process of identification with the state.) In the case in which all men unite their weak *conatus* to shake off oppression – and if they may come to understand that there is no natural hierarchy – then the "bad fate" becomes politically reversible. The despot traditionally governs with fear and will. Thus, he does not need to be careful in using his own weapons, in arousing fear in those he makes fearful. It is necessary to remove from one's eyes the bandage that prevents seeing beyond laws imposed in the exclusive interest of the person who commands. In enlightened despotism (whose principal representatives had, however, all disappeared when the Revolution began), reason was made to fall from above and its effects were measured out carefully so as not to disturb the existing hierarchical balance. Fear descended from the peaks to the base of society. With the Jacobins, however, reason was built up starting from the base of society and proceeded towards the creation of a new social order. It was accompanied by fear, the "rational violence" necessary to free men from their own chains.

The Terror cleared the way for reason. A widespread theory was inverted, one that would soon become a commonplace. According to this theory, philosophy had eroded the mentality, religion, and institutions of the old regime from within, opening the way for the Revolution. This theory is summarized well by Barnave: "Since the government did not permit itself to be talked about, philosophy during the *ancien régime* devoured superstition. When the moment to attack the government arrived, half of it was found to have been done, because (the altar having already been destroyed by opinion) philosophy was able to direct all its forces against the superstition of the throne."[4]

4 A.P.J.M. Barnave, fragment in *Oeuvres de Barnave* (Paris, 1843), vol. 2, 59.

For Marat, philosophy had certainly undermined, "in opinion," faith in the altar and in the throne, but it had not overturned them. It had functioned like a fuse that led to the explosion of a violence and desire for justice that was long suppressed and already overheated: "Philosophy prepared, began, and encouraged the current revolution; this is incontestable. But writings are not enough; actions are necessary. Now, to what do we owe our liberty if not to popular riots?"[5] And again: "It is these riots that have subjugated the aristocratic faction, against which the arms of philosophy had failed."[6]

Philosophy and reason are impotent and unarmed without revolution, but revolution is also blind and purely destructive without reason. Philosophy is the forerunner of revolution, because it erodes the foundations and undermines the grip of the existing conditions on the consciousness and customs of individuals. Revolution is the armed wing of philosophy, because it extends the theoretical plan into the actual reality of things. For the first time, violence was shown as a form of "reason of the people," instead of that of the state. And it was no longer a case, in a Machiavellian sense, of the people "seeming" good, like the Prince, but seeming and being terrible, a "Hercules" who arouses fear among the nation's enemies.

Philosophy certainly must not limit itself to interpreting the world, but change in the world does not take place exclusively through its weapons. For Marat, violence extends reason's intentions and causes a miracle that no one would have believed possible a short time before.[7] It maintains – in Robespierre's words – "the promises of philosophy."[8]

5 Marat, *L'Ami du peuple*, 10 November 1789. There exists a reprint of this newspaper (which officially began with that title in September 1789 and very soon reached almost a thousand issues, with a circulation of two thousand copies – not a modest figure at all, given the times and the custom of collective reading), in twenty volumes: *Marat dit l'Ami du peuple: Collection complète du journal* (Tokyo, 1967). On the influence of the revolutionary press, see J.R. Censer, *Prelude to Power: The Paris Radical Press* (Baltimore, 1976). On Marat's political thought, see, in particular, L.R. Gottschalk, *Jean-Paul Marat: A Study in Radicalisms* (London, 1967; 1st ed., New York, 1927); G. Walter, *Marat* (Paris, 1933); J. Massin, *Marat* (Paris, 1960); and M. Vovelle, introduction to Marat, *Écrits* (Paris, 1988).

6 Marat, *L'Ami du peuple*," 10 November 1789. Previously, in *Les chaînes de l'esclavage*, liberty was born, almost Machiavelli-like, from turmoil, from the *effervescence populaire*, from the *feu de la sédition*.

7 Marat, *Journal de la République*, 27 January 1793.

8 Robespierre, speech of 17 Pluviôse, Year II (5 February 1794), in *OC* X, 352 (*RG*, 161).

However much the myth of violence may be a "cultivated myth,"[9] a concept analogous to Marat's – that is, one that combines the effects of illumination of philosophy with the revolutionary activity of the people – ends up spreading even at the middle or "low" levels to become, literally, common.[10]

The Achievement of Philosophy

The idea of "popular movements" as the accomplishment of philosophy is presented by Marat as a clear antithesis to the hypothesis of a slow growth of civil progress. One cannot wait for reason to penetrate broadly into the social body according to the lazy automatisms of monarchical regimes and the slow evolution of customs shaped by centuries of inertia. It is necessary, first, to loosen its crippled mechanisms with a shock. And to do this, it is not even necessary to prod the uncertain inclinations of a long-suppressed human nature. Once freed from the weight of heavy institutions, it will find on its own – like a spring – the energy and direction to expand.

It is enough, says Marat, to *ne point s'opposer*, to act politically in negative form – that is, without intervening to restrain the power of such movements. At most, it is necessary to help them remove obstacles and impediments in order to "permit the indignation of the people to follow its natural course."[11] Marat, who was a doctor, followed the tradition of Hippocrates and Galen, where medicine must comply with nature's rhythms and not oppose them. Therefore, although not possessing the juridical training of Robespierre or Saint-Just (though he had read and meditated extensively on Montesquieu and Rousseau), he was not averse to finding an ethical-legal justification, of a contract-like stamp, for the most violent popular movements. Thus, he held that the poor had been driven back to the state of nature and had a right to violence as a new

9 See S. Romano, *Attualità di uno storico reazionario,* introduction to the collection of writings by A. Cochin, *L'esprit du jacobinisme* (Paris, 1979); Ital. trans. *Lo spirito del giacobinismo* (Milan, 1981), 15.

10 See, for example, the already cited opera, *La Réunion du 10 Août ou l'Inauguration de la République Française.* The first stanza of the final chorus says: *L'astre de la philosophie/ Vient d'éclairer le genre humain/Le peuple de la tyrannie a brisé/Le sceptre d'airan, je cède/Aux transports qui m'inspire/Sa sublime intrépidité./Et nous chantons dans nos délires/La Liberté, l'Egalité.* For the text of this *sans-culottide dramatique,* see R. Carnesecchi, "Una festa di David poco prima del Termidoro," 56.

11 Marat, *L'Ami du peuple,* 25 October 1790.

passport to the civil state from which they had been excluded: "For the honest citizen that society abandons to his misery and desperation returns to the state of nature and has the right to demand benefits with arms."[12] Since self-preservation is the "first duty of man," the person who is not guaranteed the possibility of living can well say: *Mais que dois-je à la société, moi qui ne la connais que par ses horreurs?*[13]

Previously a doctor to the poor among the miners of Newcastle's coal fields, Marat did not know the enlightened sides of England's political constitution, which had impressed both Montesquieu and Voltaire, with some reservations, as it would Hegel in 1831's *English Plan of Electoral Reform*, in which he also held it to be based on corruption. Marat's England is the country of injustice, according to what he had an opportunity to see, witnessing the devastating effects of the industrial revolution and the desperate misery into which it had led the majority of the people, whose frightful conditions were certainly not alleviated by the existence of establishments for the poor: "Dismal places! wherein the needy is kept alive by unwholesome food, lays in nastiness, breathes an infected air, and groans under the severe hand of a warden; wretched habitations! wherein abuses, diseases and hunger reign constantly."[14]

From this point of view, Marat's hate is love for *ces malheureux dévorés par la faim, sans foyers, sans asiles, et livrés au désespoir*,[15] affection focused on those who, condemned by an ultra-conservative society incapable of offering them a way out or to salvation,[16] were further denigrated and treated as beasts. The intent of the future "friend of the people" was to defend the 70 per cent of the population that consisted of the "mal nourris, mal vêtus, mal logés, mal couchés,"[17] and, particularly, the 30 per cent whose life was perpetual penitence, aggravated by fear of winter when – beyond overcoming seasonal hardships – even the possibility of finding

12 Marat, *La Constitution ou Projet de Déclaration des Droits de l'Homme et du Citoyen, suivi d'un Plan de Constitution juste, sage et libre* (Paris, 1789), 15. On this point, see H. Kessler, *Terreur: Ideologie und Nomenklatur der revolutionären Gewaltanwendungen in Frankreich von 1770 bis 1794* (Munich, 1973), 9 et seq.

13 Marat, *Plan de législation criminelle* [Neuchâtel, 1780] (Paris, 1790), 19.

14 Marat, *Discours aux Anglais le 15 avril 1774, sur les vices de leur Constitution, & les moyens d'y remédier*, in *Chaînes*, 285.

15 Marat, *Offrande à la Patrie ou discours au Tiers-État de France* (Paris, 1789), 57.

16 For this aspect, see F. Venturi, *Settecento riformatore*, vol. 4: *La caduta dell'Antico Regime: I grandi Stati riformatori* (Turin, 1984), 426 et seq.; F. Diaz, *Dal movimento dei lumi al movimento dei popoli* (Bologna, 1986), 544–5.

17 Marat, *L'Ami du peuple*, 30 July 1790.

work as day labourers in agricultural operations failed. In their struggle for survival, it was as if they realized each time – with amazement – that they existed.[18]

Faced with such conditions, reason is forced to express itself and silence its enemies (since there is "no liberty for the enemies of liberty"). It cannot remain indifferent. It must oppose those who prevent other men's access to a life that is more worthy. The "voice of reason" expresses itself in favour of the abolition of their ability to oppress. It pronounces a verdict that resounds and is terrible, since it imposes the "cruel necessity of slaughtering all of them."[19]

Therefore, terror is not only a duty dictated by intransigent justice, but also a right on the part of those who have been excluded from the advantages of society and those who stand beside them. Taking from reason and life the shackles that had imprisoned them, and allowing fuller satisfaction of each person's needs and desires, it achieves, in perspective, a leap forward in civilization because it spreads awareness of the fact that each person's existence is threatened by the social organization of the *ancien régime*, which was entirely based on privilege. The Terror strove to prevent the oppressed from remaining victims of the most refined and insidious trap that had ever held them, the trap of "superstitious respect for the laws."[20]

The people and the poor did not have to withstand such impotent desperation before avenging themselves, and they did not have to endure, before rebelling, such a host of criminal actions on the part of an overbearing minority that had always enjoyed the most complete impunity! And what did "the small number of victims that the people sacrificed on the altar of justice, in an insurrection" represent, compared to the "countless subjects that a despot reduced to misery, or sacrificed to his fury, to his greed, to his glory, to his whims?"[21]

18 See Marat, *L'Ami du peuple*, 10 July 1792: *Leur vie est une pénitence continuelle, ils redoutent l'hiver, ils appréhendent d'exister.* Similar statements were frequent and in those years were made even by the high clergy. For example, the day before the opening of the Estates-General, 4 May 1789, Monsignor de la Fare, archbishop of Nancy, addressed the king: "Sire, the people over which you reign is a people that has given unequivocal proof of its patience. It is a martyr people, to whom it seems that life has been left only to make it suffer longer" (quoted in F. Piro, *La festa della sfortuna* [Milan, 1989], 30).

19 Marat, *Journal de la République*, 20 November 1792, and *L'Ami du peuple*, 15 February 1791.

20 Marat, *L'Ami du peuple*, 25 April 1792.

21 Ibid., 10 November 1792.

Serial Death

At the beginning, Marat asked for six hundred heads, then twenty thousand, later one hundred thousand, and finally – on 24 October 1792 – two hundred seventy thousand. The penultimate request had been expressly motivated by the observation that if the initial six hundred heads had been cut off in due time (showing indulgence towards the people, instead of towards a few corrupt ones), there would not have been need later to require more of them. The political use of serial death was legitimized not so much by the obvious need to physically eliminate internal enemies of the Revolution, as by more complex ideological considerations. The cutting off of six hundred heads produced more freedom for Marat than all the philosophical treatises and any spread of the Enlightenment. The oppressed are not always capable of recognizing the friends of the people, and they unite with their oppressors, creating Vandeas and rebellions, making the application of force necessary. Later, in 1794, *sainte Guillotine est dans la plus brillante activité, et la bienfaisante terreur produit ici, d'une manière miraculeuse, ce que ne devait espérer d'un siècle au moins, par la raison et la philosophie.*[22] In the Jacobins, philosophy (in order to be effective) passed once again through death – not a *mortis meditatio* but a *mortis operatio*, so to speak.

The guillotine, a tool known and used since the fifteenth century (called *mannaia* in Italy) and then perfected by two physicians, Guillotin and Louis, now combined the efficiency of a machine that produced serial death with the function of a "sickle of equality." It thus united "cold technical modernity with the savage violence of physical mutilation," terror with velocity, because, as Cabanis observed, it *tranche les têtes avec la vitesse du regard.* It thus became a symbol and stereotype of the French Revolution, a real and symbolic means of government, an object that simultaneously generated real fears and imaginary frights and – in the words of Chaumette – threw up, between the men of the Terror and their enemies, "the barrier of eternity."[23] It was a tool that made people

22 These are the words of the citizen Gateau, administrator of military property, spoken on 27 Brumaio of Year II (quoted in Arrasse, *La guillotine et l'immaginaire de la Terreur,* 7). It should be noted how this idea of terror and popular executions as practical tools for carrying out ideals (otherwise ineffective and purely declamatory of reason and philosophy) had by now become common sense and had reached even to citizen Gateau.

23 Arrasse, *La guillotine et l'immaginaire de la Terreur,* 10, 49, 96. For Cabanis, see *Note sur le supplice de la guillotine,* in *Œuvres complètes* (Paris, 1823), vol. 2, 171. For Chaumette, see A. de Lamartine, *Histoire des Girondins* (Paris, 1884), vol. 3, 382.

forget the similarly brutal *noyades* (the drowning in the Loire of about two thousand prisoners loaded onto special barges), the shootings of Lyon and Toulon, and the "infernal columns" of Vandea.

Death in public changed its meaning. It was no longer a spectacle in which any sort of crime was substantively punished for its nature of direct or indirect, divine or human *lèse-majesté.*[24] It now represented a purifying ritual, the most immediate manifestation of the medical character of the Revolution, amputating the ill parts of society for the salvation of the whole. Previously, in Rousseau (who had been against terror-like laws),[25] radical upheavals could regenerate the social body. There were sometimes situations in the life of states "when revolutions cause, in peoples, what some crises cause in individuals; when the horror of the past takes the place of the void and when the state, enflamed by civil war, is reborn from its ashes, so to speak, and regains the vigor of youth in escaping the arms of death."[26]

Mass executions presented to the Jacobins such a means of "regenerating" the social body, one analogous to the mutilation of "octopi" – the hydras of water – that another great Genevan, Trembley, had carried out in famous experiments around the middle of the century, showing how one could reconstruct or *régénérer* a complete organism starting from its cut-off part.[27]

The moral the revolutionaries drew from this concept – which from an initial theological sense acquired a zoological meaning and was then drawn into the gravitational field of politics – was that peoples and individuals are reborn rejuvenated after the amputation of sick parts of the social body – even escaping the "arms of death," abandoning their previous organism to take on another.[28]

Since the beginning of the Revolution, Marat had theorized (a further tool of regeneration) a reversal of roles in which owners would need, in turn, to be tied to the glebes. In this way, princes, prelates, counts,

---

24 For a famous case of public execution during the *ancien régime,* see D. Van Kley, *The Damiens Affair and the Unraveling of the Ancien Regime* (Princeton, 1984).

25 Rousseau, *DL* 496.

26 Rousseau, *CS* II, 8.

27 See J.R. Baker, *Abraham Trembley of Geneva, Scientist and Philosopher (1710–1784)* (London, 1952).

28 For some historical testimony regarding this *pathos* for regeneration, see M. Ozouf, *La formation de l'homme nouveau,* in *L'homme régénéré: Essais sur la Révolution française* (Paris, 1989), 116–57.

marquises, and dukes would have been made subject to their lackeys or grooms.[29] A similar concept was expressed effectively by *Carmagnole*:

Il faut raccourcir le géants
Et rendre les petits plus grands
Tous à la même hauteur
Voilà le vrai bonheur …

The upside-down world of folkloric and utopian tradition was asking to be realized. In fact, "the class of the unfortunates, which insolent wealth designated with the name of 'villain,' is … the only one that, in this century of mud, still loves truth, justice, and liberty; the only one that – always consulting mere good sense and abandoning itself to the impulses of the heart – does not let itself be blinded by sophisms, nor seduced by compliments, nor corrupted by vanity; the only one that may be inviolably attached to the country."[30] For this, also according to Robespierre and Couthon, it was necessary to reverse the common way of thinking, establishing a "Festival of Misfortune": "Slaves adore fortune and power. We will honor misfortune, the misfortune that humanity cannot entirely banish from the earth, but which it consoles and relieves with respect."[31]

What is true is simple: according to Robespierre, good sans-culottes and the peasants can surpass, in knowledge of the truth and practice of virtue, philosophers like Condorcet, "that hired writer," or other great learned men. The defence of the "heart" is also the theoretical justification of the masses' possibility of conducting politics. Starting from Rousseau's distinction between general will and the will of all, it is true that a minority can present itself as interpreter of the general will without the need for immediate approval by the majority, but it is also true that, for the Jacobins, the revolutionary minorities expressed, gave voice to, and realized what the masses felt and wanted, without yet knowing how to sufficiently and articulately express it or bring it to conclusion. A minority ("three men would be enough to save the republic")

29 J.-P. Marat, *Offrande à la Patrie ou Discours au Tiers-État de France*, 33 n. The consistency of Marat's ideas throughout all phases of the Revolution should be noted. Also, for reasons of age and matured experience, his thought had already formed before 1789 (he was then forty-six years old, while Robespierre was thirty-one and Saint-Just, just twenty-two).

30 J.-P. Marat, *L'Ami du peuple*, 7 October 1790.

31 Robespierre (18 Floreal, Year II) in *OC* X, 461 (*RG*, 207). On this last point, see F. Piro, *La festa della sfortuna*, 7.

consolidated the general will and could therefore use violence in the name of the people. Marat, however, took an even more radical position. It was the majority of disinherited who, through rebellions, indicated to the popular representatives, the minority, the path to be followed. The poor were the Revolution's protagonists; their activity was the thermometer of the political situation. In their massacres lived virtue, love for the realization of the common good,[32] since they respected only those laws that increased equality.

Death for enemies without trial, summary executions (like the "slaughter of September") accelerated the journey towards the just society that rejected no one in the state of nature. The Terror's drama hides a remote truth: that of modern democracy's cruel origin, marked by conflict that certainly was not born – as per Benjamin Constant – only from the "pleasure of private life" and the relative lack of interest in politics as "participation," but from sussultatory movements of European and American society, which first saw great human masses mobilize and fight to achieve objectives of greater liberty and equality. Only afterward was it possible to delimit and carve out protected zones of private life within the institutions that emerged from that violent impact (and only with great effort are we trying today to ensure that the violence – born as a means and having become an end over time – may be reorganized politically and may lose the "therapeutic" character attributed to it).

Death in Public

With the Jacobins, what scandalized and indicated the newness of attitude was not so much terror itself (which had been practised since time immemorial), but the ways that terror was theorized and manifested. Unlike Machiavelli's suggestions, which aimed to obscure and disguise violence, it was exhibited and "staged in the public square." It presented itself, albeit with sometimes devious and indirect intentions, as what it wanted to be. Terror did not hide; it proclaimed itself. And even if the difference between political "being" and "appearing" was not suppressed but simply changed aspect, it is also true that the revolutionary "modern prince" did not strive in this case to appear to his fellow citizens to be different from what he was. On the contrary, he wanted to present himself as one of them, who shared universal and common values and who intended his actions to be visible and transparent. And if the distinction between politics and morals seemed gradually to disappear, that happened because he was trying to shorten the distance between the acts and ideas of those

32 Marat, *La Constitution ou Projet de Déclaration,* 7 et seq.; *L'Ami du peuple,* 2 January 1791.

who governed and those who were governed. The Jacobins reacted to the Machiavellian distinction between morals and politics – a sign of the objective contrast between the rules of politics and the rational norms of obedience – by using massive doses of the social bond represented by the pre-modern system, imitating the classical style of civic virtues.

The direct visibility of some events – for example, public debates or public executions – does not at all imply that the *arcana imperii* disappear. Nor does it imply that there might be abolished, through the press, preliminary control of what might otherwise have been destined to become a very visible event that, instead, took place without the majority of people noticing it. On the other hand, the political struggle by the tribunes of the Convention and in columns of the newspapers created a true theatre of collective visibility, even when most people ignored which machines might have been operating in the wings and even if the revolutionary "prince" presented his action to the people as if it were the work of the people themselves.

The exemplarity and immoral morality of the Terror consisted of its explicit link to reason, in having declared it practical for the success of the good life and supporting – in order to achieve justice and the "kingdom of God" on earth – the binding need for political violence exercised, with little clamour, by those who practised it without saying so. That is, it consisted of having carried "the sword" for fighting "egoism," rejecting indifference, and feeling solidarity with the painful events of those excluded from the privileges of a slim minority. With the goal of emancipation in sight, they theorized the necessity of performing acts similar to those perpetrated by the *ancien régime* to consolidate the authority of the existing conditions, except they were permitted the "metaphysical luxury" of pretending, which guided the necessary inflexibility of their conduct:

> In 1787, Louis XVI sacrificed eight thousand people of every age and sex in Paris, in the rue Mêlée, and on the Pont Neuf. The court renewed these acts in the Champ de Mars; the court hung [people] in the prisons; the drowned collected from the Seine were its victims. There were four hundred thousand prisoners. Each year, fifteen thousand smugglers were hung. Three thousand men were put to the wheel. In Paris there were more prisoners than today ... Fools that we are, we place metaphysical luxury into the display of our principles, and the kings, a thousand times more cruel that we, sleep in crime.[33]

33 Saint-Just, *Rapport au nom du Comité de salut public et du Comité de sûreté générale sur les personnes incarcérées, présenté à la Convention nationale dans la séance du 8 ventose an* II, in *OC2*, vol. 2, 231 (*TL* 140).

Without going on excessively about similar accounts, why do the thirty thousand victims of the Terror, most of whom were executed under the accusation of having participated in the civil war, arouse greater pity than the forty thousand who died before firing squads in France in 1944, after the liberation?[34] The attitude of the Jacobins, who transformed the Terror into an explicit political method, theorizing it as an indispensable remedy, was not only a way to make explicit how much political shame was previously hidden or veiled, but the beginning of a fundamental shift in political relations. In stating publicly the (albeit transitory) rationality of the violence, they set the conditions for its planning, in the form of the serialization of death.

The Altars of Fear

The Revolution had mowed down more victims among its supporters than among its enemies. The statement by the Girondist Vergniaud (reprised and made famous by, among others, Georg Büchner in *The Death of Danton*, in which the Revolution, like Chronos, devoured its children), is statistically true. It was calculated that of the sixteen thousand victims condemned by the Terror's tribunals (of which eleven thousand were in the provinces), aristocrats and "resistant priests" represented only 14 per cent. Another 14 per cent was from the *haute bourgeois*, while a full 72 per cent was made up of the same classes that had promoted the Revolution.[35] However, a history written from the point of view of the victims and not the executioners would show, through the wealth of biographical data, *the Terror per differentiam* – that is, the extreme lack of homogeneity among the different situations that characterized the condemned.[36]

34 See N. Hampson, *A Social History of the French Revolution* (London, 1963).

35 See D. Greer, *The Incidence of the Terror during the French Revolution: Statistical Interpretation* (Cambridge, MA, 1935), 25–37, 98 et seq., 196 (with variations in the figures, according to the parameters used). Among other things, Greer takes into account only the condemned, but not those summarily executed or assassinated, as in the case of those drowned in the Loire (which, because of these drownings, would become the "revolutionary river" and site of "vertical deportations") or of the civilian population killed in the zone of the so-called military Vandée. Greer's figures were corrected by Lefebvre, who raised to about forty thousand the number of those condemned to death. See Lefebvre, *Le gouvernement révolutionnaire, 2 juin–9 thermidore an* II (Paris, 1947).

36 See G. Armstrong Kelly, *Victims, Authority, and Terror: The Parallel Death of D'Orléans, Balley and Malesherbes* (Chapel Hill, 1982), 3 et seq.

Maximilien's cold, blue gaze did not just distinguish between the red heels of the aristocrats and the red berets of the sans-culottes, but also identified corruption among the most fervent republicans. Everyone was corruptible and, therefore, suspicious. For too long the chains of slavery had weighed on their minds and habits. Sophisms of selfishness and excess zeal are equally harmful. There is a revolutionary *mesotes* that it is necessary that one know how to recognize and practise at all times. The revolutionary government, according to Robespierre, "must row between two shoals, weakness and daring, moderatism and excess; the moderatism that is to moderation as impotence is to chastity; and the excesses that are to energy as dropsy is to health."[37] From this comes the paradoxical need, for whomever might govern a revolution in times of rapid change, to hold balance and imbalance together, in the continuous search for a "mobile centre" and a *plus ultra* in relation to the sequential playing out of uncertain and unexpected events.[38] However, in the case of revolutions, which may break out suddenly, perverse and undesirable effects cannot be avoided.[39]

By then, virtue consisted of knowing how to keep pace with the course of the world, with the universality that manifested itself in revolution. It was tied to the effort to interpret the most hidden sentiments of the people, translating them into explicit ideas and actions, killing all mediation, every theoretical and practical way that could hide the traps of the sophistry that justified privileges: "Identify yourselves with the thought for the secret movements of every heart. Overcome the intermediate ideas that separate you from the goal toward which you aim. It is better to hurry the march of the Revolution rather than follow it according to the whim of all the plots that encumber and obstruct it. It is up to you to determine the plan and hasten the results for the advantage of

37 Robespierre, 5 Nivôse, Year II, in *OC* X, 275 (*RG*, 148).

38 It is this search that distinguishes the cruelty of the Terror from the innumerable massacres perpetrated in the course of human history (on which see G. Ludwig, *Massenmord im Weltgeschehen: Bilanz zwei Jahrtausenden* [Stuttgart, 1951]).

39 See Saint-Just, *FIR2* 155 = 292: "There is no need to be frightened of changes; the danger lies only in the manner of carrying them out, all revolutions on earth are part of politics. This is why they have been full of crimes and catastrophes. Revolutions born of good laws and guided by able hands would change the face of the world without undermining it."

humanity. The rapid course of your politics will sweep away all the intrigues of the enemy."[40]

It requires the speed of lightning and an unprecedented concentration of force to overcome the static inertia of existing conditions, to lift the boulder of age-old oppression, guiding processes of change inclined to avoid all control and produce adverse effects. The most effective combination of weapons appears to be daring (which is the opposite of fear: not having it and, if necessary, inciting it in others)[41] and speed in thinking of solutions to pressing problems. These gifts end up being much more indispensable in conditions of accelerated change. What is required is wisdom that counts on the quick glance and swift consideration of the whole picture, rather than on the slow timing of common reflection (which involves an elevated propensity to risk on the part of political actors and progressive enclosure within ever smaller groups).

For Robespierre, this attitude corresponds to the imperative need to accelerate "the advances of human reason"[42] because, in the words of Saint-Just, it becomes evident that "slowness, delays," and "temporizing" are deadly, imprudent acts for those leading a revolution.[43] Vincenzio Russo, the "Neapolitan Jacobin" hung by Nelson on the mast of his flagship, effectively summarizes this inclination: "He who does not pursue the Revolution with speed betrays it. The Revolution cannot happen rapidly through opinions. But not much speed will occur by making revolution from facts that are opposed to the re-establishment of justice, nor will there ever be much of it in establishing the institutions capable of developing the seeds of opinions."[44] In this sense, "revolutionary" becomes

40 Saint-Just, *Rapport au nom du Comité de salut public sur le mode d'exécution du décret contre les ennemis de la Révolution de la Convention nationale dans la séance du 13 ventose an* II [3 March 1794], in *OC* 714.

41 For this example (which is not only the patrimony of the Jacobins, as shown in the famous conclusion of a speech by Danton: *De l'audace, encore de l'audace, toujours de l'audace, et la France est sauvée!*), see Saint-Just, *Rapport au nom du Comité de salut public et du Comité de sûreté générale sur les personnes incarcérées, présenté à la Convention nationale dans la séance du 8 ventose an* II [26 February 1794], in *OC* 707: "*Dare!* This word contains all the politics of our revolution."

42 See M. Robespierre, speech on the Constitution (10 May 1793), in *OC* IX, 495.

43 See Saint-Just, *Discours sur le jugement de Louis* XVI, in *OC* 376 = *TL* 54.

44 V. Russo, *Pensieri politici* [1798], in *Giacobini italiani*, ed. D. Cantimori (Bari, 1956), 315.

a neologism that comes to mean that which is capable *de maintenir cette révolution, et d'en accélérer ou régler la marche.*[45]

Terror, fear, betrayal, and suspicion lead minds to a political atmosphere similar to the one described by the "wise and virtuous Tacitus" regarding the Rome of Tiberius, Caligula, and Nero. The comparison between the times described by the ancient historian and the revolutionary period – when there was a constant risk of being accused of having committed *crimes de contre-révolution* – is fully and explicitly developed by Camille Desmoulins in the first issue of his newspaper *Le Vieux Cordelier.* In it, he notes how one can take refuge from individual and collective tyranny both by participating in public life and by living apart and acquiring a reputation for honesty (in which, in the sense of Tacitus, *quantu metu occultior, tanto famae adeptus*). This condition is alluded to in the exergue of the issue, which contains the words of *notre grand professeur Machiavel que je ne laisse point de citer* – that is: *Dès ceux qui gouvernent seront haïs leurs concurrens ne tarderont à être admirés.*[46]

In the capital of enlightened France (according to André Chénier's powerful image) there were now erected, to a greater degree than in Plutarch's Sparta, new and more imposing altars of fear: "Some ancient peoples had raised temples and altars to Fear ... We can say that Fear never had truer altars than those in Paris; that it was never honored by a cult more universal; that the entire city is its temple; that all good people have become its pontiffs, daily sacrificing their thought and their conscience to it."[47] Fear produced effects only seemingly paradoxical in revolutions: "Fear also gives courage. It ensures that it is placed solemnly on the side of the stronger man, who is wrong, to overpower the weaker

45 M.J.A.N. de Condorcet, *Sur le sens du mot "révolutionnaire,"* in *OE* XII, 615 et seq., where the nexus between revolution and acceleration of historical time is explicit.

46 C. Desmoulins, *Le Vieux Cordelier, journal politique,* no. 1, 48–50, 64, 29. Desmoulins, who would be guillotined on 5 April 1794 as "indulgent," would ultimately see in the Terror only *une égalité de la peur, le nivellement des courages, et les âmes les plus généreuses aussi basses que les plus vulgaires* (*Oeuvres complètes* [Paris, 1906], vol. 2, 262).

47 A. Chénier, *Les autels de la peur,* in *Œuvres en prose de André Chénier* (Paris, 1872), 69–70. Plutarch's passage on the sanctuaries of fear is of notable importance also for the Jacobins, admirers of Sparta, because it is found in one of the most widely read texts. In the *Lives of Agis and Cleomenes,* the king of Sparta who, with his colleague Agis – compared by Plutarch to Tiberius and Gaius Gracchus – represented to the Jacobins' eyes the martyrs to equality and agrarian reform, the victims of the aristocracy of the Spartans and of the Roman Senate, says: "Amongst the Lacedaemonians in the city of Sparta, there are not only temples of fear and death ... They do worship Fear, not as other spirits and devils that are hurtful, but because they are persuaded that nothing

man, who is also wrong."[48] It presents a contagious character. In fact, it propagates through mimicry, multiplying and specifying itself in a thousand different fears. Very few or none had the courage to oppose it, so as not to be silenced by the dangerous notoriety of "aristocrats" or "enemies of the country."

The Jacobins' implicit response is that a revolution cannot be made without being consistent in pursuit of its ends and without fighting its own enemies as a consequence, to the extent that those enemies are (differently fixed) obstacles to their realization. Robespierre stated this clearly in his speech to the Girondists on 5 November 1792: "Citizens, do you want a revolution without revolution? ... Who can, afterwards, mark the precise point when the waves of popular insurrection had to be broken up? At this price, what people will ever be able to break the yoke of despotism? ... Cry also for the guilty victims set aside for the vengeance of the laws, who fell under the sword of popular justice. But may your pain have an end, like all human things. Let us preserve some tears for the most moving calamities."[49] To the Incorruptible, the sensibility of someone who "moans almost exclusively about the enemies of liberty" ends up being "suspect."[50]

The Revolution could not stop, because to do so would expose it to failure. It was no different than a war, except that the enemies often spoke the same language and belonged to the same state as those who fought them. Once it was understood who the real adversaries were – *les hommes vicieux et les riches* – pity could not prevail. According to Saint-Just, it was necessary to govern "with iron" those who could not be governed "with justice."

Robespierre himself would end up a victim of the most incredible slander, fabricated specifically to destroy the people's image of him before his execution. For example, it was claimed that not only did he intend to make himself king, but that he was on the verge of marrying the daughter of Louis XVI.

---

preserves a commonwealth better than fear ... For men do use to reverence them whom they fear. And this was the cause why the chapel of Fear was by the hall of the Ephors, having in a manner a princely and absolute authority" (Plutarch, *Agis and Cleomenes*, 9). A cult of fear had also been instituted in Rome by Tullus Hostilius (see Min. Fel., *Oct.* xxv).

48 Chénier, *Les autels de la peur*, 75.

49 Robespierre, speech of 5 November 1792, in *OC* v, 89, 93–4.

50 Ibid., 94.

About twenty years after Robespierre's death, Vadier, one of the propagators of the rumours, would confess to Cambon from exile in Brussels, referring to himself, that *le danger de perdre la tête donna de l'imagination.*[51] It is not possible to be involuntarily more Spinozan: it is the fear of death that sets the imagination in motion. But the danger of losing one's head in this case also sharpens the mind, in one of the Latin senses of the term *ingenium*, understood as machination and shrewdness. Superstition, based *ex auditu et signis*, here finds voices and signs not produced spontaneously by nature or by the unconsidered behaviour of men, but consciously constructed and placed in circulation.

From the beginning of the Revolution to the end, the rumours, suspicions, and political naiveté (regarding the aristocratic plots of factions internal to the revolutionary process, with recurring accusations of planned or perpetrated massacres, betrayals completed or *in pectore*, and shortages threatened or provoked through the hoarding of goods) are some of the characteristic traits of the disastrous mental and social landscape of those difficult times.[52]

The rumours and gossip, the histories, the reconstructions of events *après coup*, the regrets, and the hatred subsequently had a *coda* even among the old Montagnards and Conventionalists forced into exile with the advent of the Restoration. Looking back, some identified the Terror with revolutionary government. Others (like Barère) felt *soumis à ces fatis victoribus auxquels l'antiquité éleva des autels.* Still others held that everything they had done several decades before carried the signs of failure. Like the death of Cassius, Brutus, and Cato the Younger, which did not serve to stop either the inevitable decline of the Roman republic nor the *despotisme épouvantable* of the first caesars, the French Revolution did not succeed in blocking the path to the despotism of Napoleon and the

51 See P.-J. Buchez and P.C. Roux, *Histoire parlementaire de la Révolution française* (Paris, 1837), vol. 34, 59.

52 Scattered indications for a history of the *rumores*, the logic of suspicion, or the apologetics of its spread during the revolutionary period can be found, beyond the classic and already noted text by Lefebvre, *La Grande Peur de 1789*, in L. Jacob, *Les suspects pendant la Révolution, 1789–1794* (Paris, 1952); R. Cobb, *Quelques aspects de la mentalité révolutionnaire (avril 1793–thermidore an* II) in *Terreur et subsistences, 1793–1795* (Paris, 1965), 11 et seq.; S. Kaplan, *Le complot de la famine: Histoire d'une rumeur au* XVIIIe *siècle* (Paris, 1982); M. Vovelle, *La mentalité révolutionnaire*, passim. For a comparison between the plague and the Terror, particularly with respect to the fear of the poor, see R. Baehrel, "Epidemie et Terreur: Histoire et sociologie," in *Annales Historiques de la Révolution Française* 23 (1951), 113–46.

other tyrants destined to follow him. The great hopes did not come true, even if these survivors' memories continued to arouse fear.[53]

Teratology of the Revolution

Conservative literature (from Burke to Taine) or Thermidorian and counter-revolutionary pamphleteering is full of descriptions of sinister faces: dirty, ragged, and toothless sans-culottes; brutal and savage peasants (similar to the floggers of Christ in Flemish paintings); bandits; the *dernière plèbe* of representatives of the "infamous professions"; cruel men; "furies of hell in the abased shape of the vilest of women"[54] (i.e., women who are quarrelsome, shameless, and thirsty for blood); and (conversely) aristocratic, virginal, and dignified youths led to prison or to the guillotine; calm men; and solemn, majestic old men insulted by the crowd during their final journey on the cart.[55] Taine, in particular, saw in the Revolution the annihilation – by means of assassins disguised by "philanthropy" – of that refined, aristocratic élite that had "worked for centuries to form itself" and whose disappearance he regretted, in comparison with the events of the Commune. These élites had created a masterpiece of worldly culture, "the distilled quintessence of all that is exquisitely elaborated by social art." But that was nothing compared to the court, to the *mince flacon d'or et de cristal* that contained *la substance d'une végétation humaine*, of a great aristocracy *transplantée en serre chaude et désormais stérile des fruits*, that only bore flowers and that was distilled *dans l'alambic royal* to extract a few drops of its aroma, whose price was *excessif*, but whose perfume was very fine.[56] These precious and insensitive human plants were capable of offering a spectacle of grace and dignity in the Terror's prisons – where they dressed carefully, held salons, composed madrigals, and practised gallantry – and in the cart that bore them to the scaffold, onto which they climbed with serenity and ease.[57]

---

53 The story of these emigrants, the painter David among them, was told by Luzzato, *Il Terrore ricordato*, particularly 32 et seq.

54 Burke, *RRF* 85.

55 See, among the many documents, the *Histoire de la Révolution de France de 1789, par Deux Amis de la liberté* (Paris, 1790–1803), vol. 13, and the *Mémoires du Comte Beugnot 1783–1815* (Paris, 1866). On these images of the revolutionary crowd, see G. Rudé, *The Crowd in the French Revolution*, 2 et seq., 232 et seq.

56 Taine, *AR* 81; Engl. trans., 103–4.

57 Taine, *AR* 128; Engl. trans., 169. On the French aristocracy, which produced a type of cultured, refined, and civil person and on the nobility of the provinces that imitated

The men of the Terror, on the other hand, were often depicted as bloodthirsty beasts in the framework of a teratology or a political pathology. Addressing the Jacobins, Vergniaud had previously asserted that "pursuing an ideal of perfection, a chimerical virtue, you behaved like beasts."[58] But it was starting from 9 Thermidor that these accusations grew in intensity and frequency. In proclamations by sections, popular societies, and armed revolutionaries, and in an avalanche of *pamphlets*, Couthon was labelled a "tiger altered by the blood of national representation" and Robespierre a "monster" or "reckless Pygmy."[59] The subsequent historiography abounds with such comparisons, speaking from time to time of "archangels of death" like Saint-Just (*corruptio optimi pessuma*) or icy "toads" like Marat, of "tigers" like Robespierre (also likened to "cats") and, en masse, of "hyenas," "wolves," and "serpents" – that is, beings characterized by subhuman or superhuman deformities, on a declining scale that, from Saint-Just's devilish beauty, descended all the way to Marat, portrayed even by Michelet as a "monster, a being beyond nature, beyond laws, beyond the sun." Their sexual identity was placed in doubt: Robespierre seemed to be of a "hermaphrodite race," Marat endowed with the nervous and fiery temperament of a "woman," Saint-Just an icy "virgin" of steel, whose skin was pure in a suspicious way: "With its singular character of luminosity and transparency, he seemed too beautiful."[60]

In general, according to Bonald, the French (or rather, European) revolution was *une appel fait à toutes les passions et à tous les erreurs; elle est, pour me servir de l'énergie d'une expression géométrique, le mal élevé a la plus haute puissance.*[61] On the other hand, Maistre describes the presumed "great men" of the Revolution (like Hannah Arendt would do later in

the court, see F. Bluche, *La vie quotidienne de la noblesse française* (Paris, 1973), 173 et seq., and P. Higonnet, *Class, Ideology and the Right of Nobles during the French Revolution* (Oxford, 1981).

58 See J. Jaurès, *Histoire socialiste de la Révolution française* (Paris, 1922–7), vol. 8, 125.

59 See B. Baczko, *Comment sortir de la Terreur: Thermidor et la Révolution* (Paris, 1989), 19, 64.

60 See ibid., 83, and J. Michelet, *Histoire de la Révolution française*, ed. G. Walter, (Pleïade edition, n.d.), vol. 1, 516 et seq.; vol. 2, 225 et seq. and passim. Saint-Just's beauty, which does not come through from his portraits, also seems to be the product more of legend than of truth. See A Philonenko, *Réflexions sur Saint-Just et l'existence légendaire*, in *Essais de philosophie de la guerre* (Paris, 1976), 69–71.

61 See *Pensées sur divers sujets* (1817), in *Œuvres complètes* (Paris, 1847–54), vol. 3, 328.

showing the "banality of evil" performed by Nazism) as bleak, banal, and petty beings, simple bureaucrats of death, whose thought came from "disgusting and fetid" roots. They were, however, capable of parading their own troops, "carrying newborns run through on their bayonets."[62] Taine, in turn, presents the revolutionaries as "buzzing insects … hatched on a sultry night"[63] and the French Revolution as a whole as one of those crocodiles placed behind a veil of gold and "on a carpet of crimson" that Egyptian priests showed to visitors within their temples. To this end, he considers himself as someone who sought for years to understand "the theology on which this cult was based."[64] For him, the revolutionaries were at once animals and handlers of the slaughterhouse (the *abattoir* and the *boucherie nationale*) that sent tens of thousands of French to their deaths. On the basis of their maxim of universal and perfect liberty, "they should have inaugurated a despotism worthy of Dahomey, a tribunal like that of the Inquisition, and raised human hecatombs similar to those of ancient Mexico."[65] After all – he continues – even today, "as formerly, students live in garrets, bohemians in lodgings, physicians without patients and lawyers without clients in lonely offices, so many Brissots, Dantons, Marats, Robespierres, and Saint-Justs in embryo; only, for lack of air and sunshine, they never come to maturity."[66]

The Revolution deeply stirred the water of the Acheron of the human mind and of society, mixing its good and its bad. Robespierre says: "In seeing the multitude of vices that the torrent of the Revolution rolled pell-mell with civic virtues, I sometimes feared being stained, in the eyes of posterity, by the impure proximity of those perverse men who mingled within the ranks of the sincere defenders of humanity."[67] He must almost admit defeat in his last speech: "I was made to fight crime, not govern it. The time has not yet come when good men may serve the country with impunity. The defenders of liberty will always be proscribed, until the band of scoundrels rules."[68] In the end, the Incorruptible, whose enemies tried to damage him by exacerbating the Terror and attributing responsibility for it to him, is almost resigned to losing his own life

62 See J. de Maistre, *Bienfaits de la Révolution française*, in *Œuvres complètes* (Lyon, 1884–6), vol. 3, 494.
63 Taine, *AN* 377; Engl. trans., 88.
64 Taine, *GR*, preface, 9.
65 Taine, *CJ* 571; Engl. trans., 6.
66 Ibid., 7.
67 Robespierre, speech of 8 Thermidor, Year II, in *OC* x, 567 (*RG* 215).
68 Ibid., 576 (*RG* 225).

so that the Revolution – that difficult "masterpiece of virtue and human reason" – could continue to unfold: "Oh, life! I will abandon it to them without regret! I have the experience of the past, and I see the future. What friend of the country could ever want to outlive the moment when he is no longer permitted either to serve it nor defend oppressed innocence?"[69] How (asks Saint-Just with famous images) can it be tolerated that in the spring of 1794, the Revolution was *glacée*, since "all the principles have weakened, there remain only some red hats worn in the affair. The exercise of terror has worn out crime, as strong liquors wear out the palate."[70] All that remains is to hope for the end of the experiment, consoling himself with the idea that, like the wicked, "great men do not die in their beds."[71] The hope that the Revolution revives is entrusted to the current sacrifice of its protagonists and, in the long term, to the work of their successors: to the faith in a future thawing of history.

Obsessive Familiarity with Death

The Jacobins were not only inspired to see fear of death as social medicine, but also to transform themselves into sacrificial victims offered to the country and to humanity. As Jaurès had already observed,[72] Robespierre was possessed by an "obsessive familiarity" with the idea of death (which, after all, was not infrequent in the Century of Light) and was fascinated by it – both his own death (*moi qui ne crois pas à la nécessité de vivre*) and that of others.[73] There was in him, in the manner of the Stoics, a constant anticipation, through thought, of the moment of his own death. It was, unlike Spinoza, a melancholy concept of philosophy more as *mortis* than as *vitae meditatio*, a rejection of the principle of self-preservation and

69 Ibid., 567 (*RG* 215). Shortly before dying, Robespierre wrote these verses: "The only just torment, in the final hour,/and the only one from which I will be torn,/is seeing, while dying, the pale and somber desire/distilling on my name, the shame and disgrace/of dying for the people and being loathed for it" (*Mémoires de Charlotte Robespierre sur ses deux frères*, with an introduction by A. Laponneraye [Paris, 1835], 121).

70 Saint-Just, *FIR* 508.

71 Ibid., 493.

72 See Jaurès, *Histoire socialiste de la Révolution française*, vol. 4, 396, and H. Guillemin, *Robespierre, politique et mystique* (Paris, 1987), 407. This statement, however, is different from those of many who see in Robespierre a dispenser of death, regarding which see J.-C. Frère, *La victoire de la mort: Robespierre et la révolution* (Paris, 1983).

73 For the seductiveness of death in the eighteenth century, see R. Favre, *La mort au siècle des Lumières* (Paris, 1970), and A. Farge, *La vie fragile: Violence, pouvoir et solidarités à Paris au* XVIIIe *siècle* (Paris, 1986), 211 et seq.

utilitas to the benefit not of a ruler, but of liberty. In fact, despite being against the death penalty in principle, he imposed it because *il faut que la Patrie vive.*[74] This is why, to the oppressor of the people, he left no legacy except *la vérité terrible et la mort* (*OC* x, 567 = *RG* 216).

It is significant, however, that this call to death sometimes assumed apologetic and pantoclastic tones. Restif de la Bretonne tells of having heard shouted, at one of the crucial moments of the Revolution, *Vive la mort!* (such an inscription can also be found in the room where Marat was killed): "But that was not all. Around two in the morning, I heard pass beneath my windows a group of cannibals ... one of them, whom I would have liked to see in order to read his hideous soul on his dreadful face, I would like to have seen, in order to understand how dirty his soul was, shouted furiously: '*Vive la mort!*' This was not second-hand; I heard it."[75] Taine, in turn, records this statement by Carrier: "We will make a cemetery of France, rather than regenerate in it in our own way."[76] The familiarity with death that can be found in revolutionary ethics and conduct comes not only from the disposition towards future sacrifices of self and others, but also from the decision to utilize, with a view to progress, those demonic, turbulent, and uncontrollable passions that traditional wisdom had always held at a distance.

Robespierre accepted death because he knew he was sick, probably with tuberculosis (like Spinoza), but particularly because he believed strongly that virtue be pursued in the world, as the destinies of Rousseau and Marat showed, and that a "premature death" might be reserved for great men. For him, then, it was completely likely that the "scoundrels" would attain victory, leveraging the passivity and corruptibility of men accustomed to servitude. This is also why vigilance must be sharp-eyed and diffident and "regeneration" radical. This was not triumphalism; the Revolution's victory was not at all guaranteed. Early on, by 1791, Robespierre stated that he knew the fate reserved for him. He added

74 See M. Robespierre, *Opinion de Maximilien Robespierre sur le jugement de Louis* XVI, in *OC* IX, 121, and J. Goulet, *Robespierre, la peine de mort et la Terreur* (Paris, 1983).

75 See R. de la Bretonne, *Nuits révolutionnaires* (which includes *La semaine nocturne* and *Nuits de Paris ou le spectateur nocturne* of 1790–4), ed. B. Didier (Paris, 1978). On this text, see B. Didier, *Écrire la Révolution 1789–1799* (Paris, 1989), 195–206, and, more generally, P. Testud, *Restif de la Bretonne et la création littéraire* (Geneva, 1977).

76 Taine, *GR* 53.

that he had never let into his calculations "the benefit of living long," because he believed that "death is the beginning of immortality."[77]

Obsessed in turn with the idea of the tomb and the communion of the living and the dead, Saint-Just stated that death would be little more than leaving "a life in which one is either the accomplice or the mute witness of evil … Fame is useless rumor. If we listen to past centuries, we will hear nothing further; those who walk among our own tombs will hear nothing more."[78] In *Fragments on Republican Institutions*, he refers to the "happiness" that he feels in sacrificing himself for the country and in not having "before his eyes" anything but the path that separates him from his "dead father and the steps of the Pantheon." He adds, "Circumstances are difficult only for those who draw back before the tomb. And I implore it, the tomb, as a grace granted me by Providence, to no longer be witness to the impunity of the betrayals committed against my country and humanity."[79] Saint-Just despises the dust he is made of, but he strongly believes (probably alluding to the destiny of someone who laboured well for the *respublica* in Cicero's *Somnium Scipionis*) that no one will succeed in tearing from him "the independent life" that is given in the "centuries and in the heavens." He similarly asserts that those who died for liberty and country must be honoured publicly. The subsequent idea of monuments to the fallen is already implicit here: "It is necessary that respect for the dead be a cult, and that it be believed that the martyrs of liberty are tutelary geniuses of the people and that immortality waits for those who imitate them."[80] Marat was also struck by a poorly identified illness (in 1782, after years of efforts dedicated to study, and coinciding with the death of his mother) that led him to bouts of serious depression for which only the Revolution would provide remedy.[81] Without resorting to forms of "wild psychoanalysis," we might think it is perhaps not by chance that many of the Terror's protagonists (including Couthon) had spent childhood afflicted by family misfortunes and had

77 Robespierre, *OC* x, 471, 475, 567. The position of Sieyès would be much different, as expressed in one of his famous jokes: "What did you do during the Terror?" "I lived."

78 Saint-Just, *Discours pour la défense de Robespierre*, in *OC2*, vol. 2, 479, 484.

79 Saint-Just, *FIR* 494.

80 Ibid., 527.

81 On "mourning and melancholy" in Marat, see G. Gaudenzi and R. Sartori, *Jean-Paul Marat: Scienziato e rivoluzionario* (Milan, 1989), 111–22. For an interesting picture of a melancholic adventurist of the Revolution, who had planned for an army of Amazons and whose case would be studied by Esquirol, see E. Roudinesco, *Théroigne de Méricourt: Une femme mélanconique sous la Révolution* (Paris, 1989), particularly 104 et seq.

to work through mourning at an early age, assuming, while very young, responsibilities bigger than they were. The "Festival of Misfortune" and that of virtue also partially find one of their distant origins here.

Barnave wrote that "fear is the dominant feeling in the better part of those who took active part in the Revolution."[82] The *fraternité* among the individuals and the erosion in each of love for life can be traced to fear's negative and destructive force. In the form of the Terror, it served to divide those who inspired it from those who potentially suffered from it; it ignited the imagination; it pushed *insecuritas* to extremes; and it caused an "inexplicable dizziness."[83] No one would call themselves safe from its omni-pervasive presence. The political wisdom of the revolutionary consists, then, in not being afraid and in accepting death without regrets, if it presents itself as useful to the cause. The Jacobins did not immediately aim towards *securitas*, towards the absence of fear and hope, but rather towards shaking consciousness so that it would change quickly. Reason must develop even more vigorously in the midst of dangers and passions.

---

82 A.P.J.M. Barnave, *Réflexions politiques sur la Révolution,* in *Œuvres de Barnave* (Paris, 1843), vol. 2, 21.

83 E. Quinet, *La Révolution*; Ital. trans. *La Rivoluzione* (Turin, 1953), vol. 2, 443 et seq.

SECTION 2

The Invisible Sovereign

1. *Homo ideologicus*

Vertical Solidarity

If the principle of brotherhood constitutes a type of horizontal solidarity among citizens, it also represents, from another point of view, the reverse of the vertical principle in which authority descends from above, from God himself.

The sovereign, as father and shepherd of peoples, was accustomed to govern his "children" or "flock" by means of indisputable *diktat* under the sign of divine sacredness, paternal benevolence, and protection of order. But now that the king was no longer there, he had been decapitated and his "throne was empty,"[1] sovereignty came directly from below, from the people, who ruled on their own as the legitimate, exclusive, and indivisible representatives of the general will.

As an analogue to the "fantastic" conjectures developed by Freud in *Totem and Taboo*, it could be said that during the French Revolution, brothers had come together to sacrifice the tyrannical father, transferring his prerogatives onto themselves, *collegialiter*. Paternal power – the Aristotelian supremacy of a father over his children "by nature" – seems to have deteriorated, as often happens in periods of crisis or ethical nostalgia, when the past or the future make many people more comfortable than the present.[2]

1 For this expression and some aspects of the transition, see P. Viola, *Il trono vuoto: La transizione della sovranità nella Rivoluzione francese* (Turin, 1988).

2 The weakening of the paternal figure and authority would later be observed by de Tocqueville in *Democracy in America*. In the same period, on the level of feelings, this phenomenon was accompanied by greater respect and attention to children and to childhood in general. See G. Snyders, *Die grosse Wende der Pädagogik: Die Entdeckung*

The deconsecration of the symbols of despotism, with the taking of the Bastille or the bursting of the people into the palace of Versailles, had been anonymous.[3] The new sovereignty must also be anonymous, the sovereignty that is no longer exercised in the name of an individual endowed with special powers and made taboo through anointment in the ceremony of Reims or institution of the highest crime of *lèse-majesté*, but in the name of a community that arose through an oath, defended from its internal enemies through codification of the crime of "*lèse-nation*."[4] Again in terms of the Freudian "historical novel," popular *fraternité* also seems to be generated thanks to a sort of a symbolic "totemic meal" in which all the participants are tied not only by a reciprocal charge of conspiracy (as protagonists or accomplices of regicide), but by the promise that no one would any longer be able to command independently from the common consensus of the group. Thus, the new fraternal sovereignty, obsessively suspicious of all forms of authority considered excessive (which recalls the ghost of the "father of the country") is determined to

---

des Kindes und die Revolution der Erziehung im 17. und 18. Jahrhundert in Frankreich (Paderborn, 1971), 194 et seq. For its artistic representation, see B. Algot Sorenson, *Herrschaft und Zärtlichkeit: Der Patriarchalismus und das Drama im 18. Jahrhundert* (Munich, 1984).

3 The attack on the Bastille had, after all, been an anonymous, collective, and not rationally premeditated act, as was observed first by Michelet and then by Sartre. In Michelet, it is even presented as an act of faith: *L'attaque de la Bastille ne fut nullement raisonnable. Ce fut un act de foi. Personne ne le proposa. Mais tous crûrent, et tous agirent* (*Histoire de la Révolution française*, vol. 1, 145). In Sartre, the attack on the Bastille – and the one on the Winter Palace in 1917 – were the most prominent examples of a philosophical concept that saw the "series": the diffuse and indifferent unity of a crowd (like one getting in line to wait for a bus) transforming suddenly into a "group," into an integral whole that, in exceptional moments like the ones noted, enters "into fusion" and passes "to white heat" (Jaurès spoke of historical "high temperature"), and then cools and disperses after such great collective actions, creators of history (see the references made in p. 332 of the present volume to the analogies with the proposals of Mathiez). Gradually, then, the movement becomes institutionalized and bureaucratized. Revolutions seek stability and normalcy, creating, again, relatively static societies (this is the "ultra-Bolshevik" aspect in favour of permanent revolution that Merleu-Ponty would blame on Sartre). See J.-P. Sartre, *Critique de la raison dialectique*, Italian trans. *Critica della ragione dialettica* (Milan, 1963), vol. 1, 386 et seq.; vol. 2, 17 et seq.

4 See G. Armstrong Kelly, "From Lèse-Majesté to Lèse-Nation: Treason in Eighteenth-Century France," *Journal of the History of Ideas* 42 (1981), 269–86. On the role of the Terror in the redefinition of the people, see B. Manin, "Saint-Just: La logique de la Terreur," *Libre* 6 (1973), 217. On national honour, see N. Hampson, "The French Revolution and the Nationalization of Honour," in *War and Society* (London, 1973).

fight those who might place themselves above the general principle of sovereignty shared among equals.

The figure of the monarch or the despot, unlike that of the people, is concretely individualized, visible, and can be shown – at least in its physical nature. According to English political theory of the Middle Ages (which also reverberated in France, in different form), there existed in the sovereign both a natural body, subject to all illnesses and eventually death, and a political body, invisible and intangible, removed from the passions and from corruption. The king never dies, but rather "deceases" – that is, he separates his immortal political body from his natural one.[5]

As early as Shakespeare's time, it was emphatically held that when a king died, the whole society and world risked ruin along with him: "The cesse of majesty/dies not alone, but like a gulf doth draw/what's near it with it. It is a massy wheel,/fix'd on the summit of the highest mount,/to whose huge spokes ten thousand lesser things/are mortis'd and adjoin'd; which when it falls,/each small annexment, petty consequence,/attends the boist'rous ruin. Never alone/did the king sigh, but with a general groan."[6]

The people do not enjoy the privilege of correspondence between the physical body and the political body, however temporary. Given the unstable multiplicity of human aggregations in space and time, the figure of the people is physically unimaginable. Authority, after all, is difficult to embody in deputies, in individuals who, by definition, are equal to others to whom they are obliged to express will and moods. To support it, a massive and repeated symbolic investment is necessary.

Politics now clashes with a difficult logic, with the paradox of having to represent the unrepresentable, with the constraint of making visible

---

5 On the sacred concept of the double body and the immortality of the king, see, for England, E.H. Kantorowicz, *The King's Two Bodies: A Study in Medieval Political Theology* (Princeton, 1957), particularly 7–10. On the king who, according to Bossuet, *comme image de Dieu,* can never die, and on the blood of Louis XVI collected by the crowd, see R. Giesey, *The Royal Funeral Ceremony in Renaissance France* (Geneva, 1960), French trans. *Le roi ne meurt jamais,* preface by F. Furet (Paris, 1987); and S. Bertelli, *Il corpo del re: Sacralità del potere nell'Europa medievale e moderna* (Florence, 1990). Some incidentally interesting observations can be found in F. Jesi, "L'accusa del sangue," *Comunità* 27 (October 1973), 295 et seq. This concept is accompanied by the idea of an extensive property of the state. See H.H. Rowen, *The King's State: Proprietary Dynasticism in Early Modern France* (New Brunswick, 1980). On the premises of the absolutism in the figure of the king during the French revolutionary period, see L. Marin, *Le portrait du roi* (Paris, 1981).

6 W. Shakespeare, *Hamlet,* act 3, scene 3.

the invisible superiority that comes "from below" by proxy.[7] If citizens are all equal – even in the utopian perspective of everyone ultimately being able to be different – how can someone who is equal to others also be superior to them unless, as in Orwell's *Animal Factory*, some are "more equal" than others? Or unless, being unable always and practically to deduce what is "high" from what is "low" and being unable to explain important and rapid decisions starting from the uncertain, divided, and slow opinion of the multitudes unaccustomed to complex choices, some individuals present themselves as supreme and unquestionable interpreters of the collective will, like those who know better than the people what is good for the people? But *quis iudicabit*? With the aim of being able to function, this system of power needs to strip citizens of their distinctiveness and dress them in the colours of a universal to which they are obliged to adapt themselves *a posteriori*.

To be acceptable, authority presupposes a "sublime verticality," the idea of a "height" that the imaginary monarch had wisely developed when creating "the majesty of the king." The project begun by the Jacobins aimed, instead, to legitimize the political sublime through the majesty of reason and its universal principles. Again using nuances (that Italian cannot express), it can be asserted that the *Vorstellung* (the perceptible representation of sovereignty embodied in the person of the monarch) ends, and the *Vertretung* (the representation, "standing in place of," or sovereignty that is not direct but deputized or abstracted) begins. The king, like the sun that shines its light on earth and is the direct source of authority that issues from the heavens, gives way to the delegate of the people, who shines with light reflected from below and receives his mandate from his fellow citizens. The hypothetically irreplaceable and self-referential uniqueness of the autocrat gives way to the interchangeable individuality of the citizen elected to public office. In the political sphere, the knot that ties the nature of the sovereign to his symbolic representation (*Vorstellung*) and his imperative language is loosened. In Kantian terms, the problem is now translated into the invention of new political ways to sensitively "display" an idea, to make perceptible

7 In an even more tragic way, this paradox will lead to the institutionalization and stabilization of rational forms of the principle of restlessness, inherent in the Revolution itself. This, in turn, will push towards a progressive separation of official ideology and practice, with the consequent need to maintain the illusion of consistency through the persistence, however disempowered, of the auxiliary tool of terror, which by nature is incapable of any crystallization.

popular sovereignty that is founded on universal, invisible, and abstract principles of reason.[8] The solution consists of alluding to an unimaginable totality, one shown exclusively through a political synecdoche, a *pars pro toto*. Through it, the revolutionary vanguard (individuals who are anonymous, replaceable, lacking natural charisma but capable of acquiring and losing it in the course of events) receive a revocable investiture from the political "body." They receive a type of sovereignty that must all the more theatrically overload its indescribability in a mask of power, the less it is known or consecrated by blood or traditional symbols of excellence. Only within this context does "virtue" become the new label of nobility.

The people are personified by individual "representatives" and magistrates, but they could be personified, at worst, by each citizen, by the "24 million kings" who lived in France.[9] This is the same as saying, "by no one in particular," since the people and the general will – like biological species – express the universality and continuity of the whole through the succession and disappearance of individuals. The people's delegates are at once within and above the individuals who make up the collective. Since they belong to it, they represent (in the form of *Vertretung*) the community, the brotherhood, the horizontal relationships of the citizens' equality and liberty. As the elected, above the citizens, they represent authority, the superiority of the general interest over special interests, the vertical relationships of submission and obedience of the citizens to the law and to the common good.

This unresolved ambiguity of Jacobinism produces dynamic effects in the development of modern democracy, because it generates conflict and encourages more rapid processes of change at the summits of power. Its essentially uncertain character shatters on impact with new situations, multiplying in a series of questions that serve as prompts for solution of the problems they pose. How can authority be produced when it is placed continually into discussion and made unstable by those who represent it and when, in the tribunal of reason, everyone is simultaneously judge and accused? What observance of the mandate does someone who is not considered better than his electors owe, personally, to those who delegate him as their representative? Who, and with what political

8 This aspect, translated by Burke in terms of "illusion," is taken up later in the present volume.

9 For this expression, see M. Mazzucchella, *24 milioni di re: Romanzo-diario (1791–1795) di un antiquario di Parigi* (Milan, 1968).

hermeneutics (in the presence of special laws) can judge the just and the unjust, the good and the bad? In a society of "brothers," what mechanisms are capable of preventing it from slipping back into other forms of personal power, like that of then-general Bonaparte, who vehemently rejected the idea of changing into a *cochon à l'engras de quelques millions* and who proposed throwing the "granite boulder" of his powerful will onto the "grains of sand" of a scattered multitude of individuals considered weak and powerless? Finally, how can the rise be avoided, to the place of the king (and for reasons of disciplining social unrest similar to those that historically led to the birth of absolutism), of someone who is not a Father of the people but a Big Brother, in some respects even more tyrannical than the overthrown parent, because he presumes to speak in the name of everyone and to give voice to their unconscious will, making everyone unanimously co-responsible for their own choices and transforming deviancy into betrayal of reason, equality, and humanity?

The new collective *hegemonikon* represented by the state and its *logos* tears the social fabric and the individual's mental structure from within. It imposes on all citizens (and not only on the wise man) the moral obligation to raise themselves "vertically" through "virtue," to the same universality that appears "horizontally" as collective will. Therefore, the Jacobins inserted themselves between the people and their representatives as a directly expressive part of the whole, exemplars of the *homo aequalis* that reproduces, at a different level, the *homo hierarchicus* (and because of this, they also did not aspire officially to public posts).[10] There is an anonymous etching, referring to crowns and tiaras, that bears the inscription *L'orgueil les forma, la raison les détruit.*[11] The Jacobins wanted to destroy, through reason, the pride of an *I*-ness (*egoità*) that raised itself above all others, wrapping itself in the guise of superiority. They could not, however, reject the pride of those who said – instead of "L'ètat, c'est moi" – "La volonté générale c'est nous." In this sense, despite some straining, Michelet is not completely wrong in asserting that they "raised pride to the second power," making frequent appeals to the

10 I use the terms in the meaning given to them by L. Dumont in *Homo aequalis* (Paris, 1976). See also Dumont's *Homo hierarchicus: Le système des castes et ses applications* (Paris, 1979). On the social hierarchies in France, see P. Mousnier, *Les hiérarchies sociales de 1450 à 1789* (Paris, 1969).

11 See *La Révolution française et l'Europe*, Catalog of the Exhibition of the Council of Europe (Paris, 1989), vol. 2, no. 549.

violence of the people, setting them against their enemies, but without consulting them.[12]

Sublime Illusions

The revolutionary principle of equality, then, threatens the *homo hierarchicus* to the point of undermining the very idea of an ordered scale of power. The elevated sense of "greatness" was not, in fact, placed by the Jacobins in the monarch's unreachable "height," but in the virtue accessible to everyone, in an attitude that rejected any sort of natural superiority of one individual over another. No longer able to credibly sustain an authority that drew its legitimate titles from divine right or simple tradition, partisans of the monarchy now had to occupy a more rearward line of defence, to save the essentials and prepare an eventual counteroffensive. The goal was reached through the development of a doctrine of illusions that – from Burke's *Reflections on the French Revolution* onward – tried to re-establish an authoritarian power that no longer rested either on faith or on religion.

For Burke, paradoxically, equality among men is a truth, while inequality is an illusion. And yet it is a beneficial illusion that cannot be rejected, a civilizing factor whose loss would plunge humanity back into the barbarity of its origins.

Queens and kings – deprived of the halo of superiority given by their subjects' imaginations and the "magnifying glass" of the passion that venerated them – appear as women and men like any others, or even worse than others: "On this scheme of things, a king is but a man; a queen is but a woman; a woman is but an animal; and an animal not of the highest order ... Regicide and parricide and sacrilege are but fictions of superstition, corrupting jurisprudence by destroying its simplicity" (*RRF* 90). An era of lofty sentiments, of honour and faithfulness, ended with this discovery, causing expulsion from the earthly paradise, accompanied by the loss of innocence and the consequent triggering of fratricidal struggles. It was the final sunset of an idealized Middle Ages of faith and healthy ignorance of the masses (as it would also be praised, a few years later, by Novalis in *Christianity or Europe*), and an enchanted universe of "chivalry"

12 Even before Cuoco and Michelet, the Jacobins' proceeding without consulting the people had already become a widespread *topos.*

and its values disappeared with it.[13] As testimony to the collapse of this world, Burke calls on his personal experience, recalling with sincere regret and emotion the magical moment when he ecstatically contemplated a sovereign, the young Marie Antoinette:

> It is now sixteen or seventeen years since I saw the queen of France, then the dauphiness, at Versailles; and surely never lighted this orb, which she hardly seemed to touch, a more delightful vision. I saw her just above the horizon, decorating and cheering the elevated sphere she just began to move in; glittering like the morning star, full of life, and splendor, and joy … I thought ten thousand swords must have leaped from their scabbards to avenge even a look that threatened her with insult.[14]

Once the Revolution had desecrated the delicate beauty of the queen and only a few had the courage to assume her defence, there was a radical reversal of the values that involved all of modern civilization:

> But the age of chivalry is gone. That of sophisters, economists, and calculators has succeeded, and the glory of Europe is extinguished forever. Never, never more, shall we behold that generous loyalty to rank and sex, that proud submission, that dignified obedience, that subordination of the heart, which kept alive, even in servitude itself, the spirit of an exalted freedom. The unbought grace of life, the cheap defense of nations, the nurse of manly sentiment and heroic enterprise is gone! It is gone, that sensibility of principle, that chastity of honour, which felt a stain like a wound, which inspired courage whilst it mitigated ferocity, which ennobled whatever it touched, and under which vice itself lost half its evil, by losing all its grossness.[15]

"Servitude" lost its own attractions when the monarchical virtue of "honour" gave way to the republican one of "equality."

When the illusions evaporated, everything rolled towards the abyss, attracted by the worst:

---

13 Burke, *RRF* 89. See also M. Girouard, *The Return to Camelot: Chivalry and the English Country Man* (New Haven, 1981), and W.C. Dowling, "Burke and the Age of Chivalry," *Yearbook of English Studies* 12 (1982), 109–24.

14 *RRF* 89.

15 Ibid.

> All the pleasing illusions, which made power gentle, and obedience liberal, which harmonized the different shades of life, and which, by a bland assimilation, incorporated into politics the sentiments which beautify and soften private society, are to be dissolved by this new conquering empire of light and reason. All the decent drapery of life is to be rudely torn off. All the super-added ideas, furnished from the wardrobe of a moral imagination, which the heart owns, and the understanding ratifies, as necessary to cover the defects of our naked shivering nature, and to raise it to dignity in our own estimation, are to be exploded as a ridiculous, absurd, and antiquated fashion.[16]

With the end of the illusions, however, no emancipation ensued, nor did they get nearer to the realm of the ultimately revealed truth. Behind the torn-away veil or drapery, there did not appear an image of wisdom, a statue of Isis, as in the myth, but the awful face of the Gorgon. Today's revolutionaries, heirs of the enlightened men of yesterday,[17] try desperately to control and rationalize this nameless horror. Instead of making men progress towards a higher level of civility and develop a higher

---

16 Ibid., 90. Illusion is a belief in which desire places a premium on a reality whose confirmation it does not seek. We know that, from Spinoza's point of view, the illusion is discovered (as in the case of the winged horse) only when some other antagonistic impression enters into conflict with it. In the present case, placing the idea of the queen's "winged feet" (which did not even seem to rest on humble earth) in contrast with the incompatible one of physical and moral equality among all men (whose feet rest firmly on earth), the revolutionaries showed the illusory character of the first image and all those derived from it. In the concept of illusion as something covering "naked and trembling" human nature and in the complementary one of unveiling (and because of this, a "metaphorical stripping" of sovereignty was spoken of – see R. Paulson, *Representations of Revolution (1789–1820)*, 21), an element of biblical tradition is discovered. This had already been placed in evidence by Torquato Accetto as the essential ingredient of "honest dissimulation," an attitude ennobled in Burke, transforming itself into a pillar of all of human civilization. See Accetto, *Della dissimulazione onesta*, ch. 1, 34: "Since man opened his eyes and knew that he was naked, this caused him to hide himself even from his Maker. And so the care of hiding was born nearly with the world itself, and at the first sight of defect. And for many, it passed into use by way of dissimulation."

17 On the relationship between Burke and the *philosophes*, see A. Cobban, *Edmund Burke and the Revolt against the Eighteenth Century: A Study of the Political and Social Thinking of Burke, Wordsworth, Coleridge and Southey* (London, 1960); and S.F. Deane, "Burke and the French 'philosophes,'" *Studies in Burke and His Time* 10, no. 2 (1968–9), 1113–37. For Burke's attitude towards political extremism, see M. Freeman, *Edmund Burke and the Critique of Political Radicalism* (Oxford, 1980).

form of knowledge (capable of recognizing the necessity of illusions), their "new empire of reason" brings men back to the state of nature. Its frigid, icy lights, which should dissipate the darkness of prejudices and the opacity of feelings, now illuminate individuals and peoples who have reverted to the violence of their beginnings, suffering from the fury of the elements, scattered on a desolate earth where the (sublime and terrible) elementary passions of selfish self-preservation and unarticulated fear dominate: "On the scheme of this barbarous philosophy, which is the offspring of cold hearts and muddy understandings, and which is as void of solid wisdom as it is destitute of all taste and elegance, laws are to be supported only by their own terrors, and by the concern which each individual may find in them from his own private speculations, or can spare to them from his own private interests."[18]

To these aspects of the French Revolution, Burke seems to apply categories he had introduced more than thirty years earlier in *A Philosophical Inquiry into the Origin of Our Ideas of the Sublime and Beautiful*, where he had placed the sublime under the sign of terror and death: "Whatever therefore is terrible … is sublime too."[19] And the most violent passions, those aroused by danger and the threat to the individual's self-preservation, are sublime indeed: "The ideas of pain, sickness, and death fill the mind with strong emotions of horror; but the ideas of life and health, though they put us in a capacity of being affected with pleasure, they make no such impression by the simple enjoyment. The passions therefore which are conversant about the preservation of the individual, turn chiefly on pain and danger, and they are the most powerful of all the passions." Death in particular is the "king of terrors."[20] Thus, considered from a safe distance, the French Revolution is implicitly more sublime spectacle than tragedy, as it not only shows terror in its pure state, in the naked threat of death to individuals' self-preservation, but also shows the reduction of civilization to its savage state, by stripping kings and powerful people of all superiority given to them by illusions.

The revolutionaries had the double shamelessness of denuding the truth of the illusions necessary for maintaining the social hierarchy (for

18 *RRF* 91.

19 Burke, *A Philosophical Inquiry into the Origins of Our Ideas of the Sublime and Beautiful* [1759] (London, 1959), part 2, section 2. From another perspective, on the "aesthetic" implications of the politics in Burke, see N. Wood, "The Aesthetic Dimension of Burke's Political Thought," *Journal of British Studies* 4 (1964), 41–64.

20 Burke, *A Philosophical Inquiry*, 1.6, 1.7.

Burke, as for Pascal, based not so much on divine right as on imagination – that is, on the parades of power and pomp destined to elicit obedience) and of displaying in public the miseries and the pudenda of politics. They were obsessed with the desire to "unveil" not only the conspiracies but the "demonic face of power" in all its aspects. Paradoxically, their fault was in telling the truth, because doing so caused men an unhappiness without illusions, by tearing away the garlands that covered the "chains of slavery" and robbing miseries of their only consolation. Equality is nature, but inequality is civilization.

Consequently, Burke proceeds to a conscious re-enchantment of the world, with the stated aim of re-establishing the old hierarchy of power via other means. However, once disenchantment had been produced and the truth, however terrible, had been glimpsed without the veil of illusions, it was difficult to confirm, at another level, how much reason had shown to be inconsistent. Would there still be men ready to kneel before the fetish of the sovereign, obeying a "naked king" who had lost the aura of his mystical power and had ceased to function as a living monstrance of God's authority on earth? The response is positive only on the condition of sacrificing the intellect and, with false conscience, introducing beliefs that are known to be rationally unjustifiable.

A process began of conscious fabrication of myths that would lead far, with disastrous effects in the twentieth century.

The Magician's Pot

Stripped of its illusions, feelings, and customs, and connected to terror and selfishness (which in turn are sublimated by the mask of the general will), reason, for Burke, withers. Owing to an excess of legitimate defence, it attacks what it does not immediately understand without striving to understand it, and it is therefore punished by its nemesis, impotence: "But that sort of reason which banishes the affections is incapable of filling their place."[21]

The too-prolonged wakefulness of reason – and not its sleep – generates monsters. Fortunately for them – adds Burke, follower of a philosophy of "prudence" that, against the Parisian "sophisters," rejects the universal and omnipresent nature of principles and laws that regulate

21 *RRF* 91.

the collective life of men[22] – the English were still exempt from a similarly lethal inclination towards intellectualistic abstraction:

> We preserve the whole of our feelings still native and entire, unsophisticated by pedantry and infidelity. We have real hearts of flesh and blood beating in our bosoms. We fear God; we look up with awe to kings; with affection to parliaments; with duty to magistrates; with reverence to priests; and with respect to nobility. Why? Because when such ideas are brought before our minds, it is *natural* to be so affected; because all other feelings are false and spurious, and tend to corrupt our minds, to vitiate our primary morals, to render us unfit for rational liberty; and by teaching us a servile, licentious, and abandoned insolence, to be our low sport for a few holidays, to make us perfectly fit for, and justly deserving of slavery, through the whole course of our lives.[23]

The English people were never seduced by general ideas and never rejected the patrimony of experience accumulated by tradition. They never rejected a wisdom that patiently connected the old to the new or, better still, that did not forget the prerequisites and constant structures of all forms of community. Precisely because it follows the rules and rhythms of nature, the English political order is the reflection of the wonderful cosmic one within whose cycles it is perfectly set: "Our political system is placed in a just correspondence and symmetry with the order of the world, and with the mode of existence decreed to a permanent body composed of transitory parts; wherein, by the disposition

22 Emphasizing the unrelated variety of situations at the expense of their moment of universality, and consequently absolutizing the empirical side of tradition, Burke offers a conservative version of Aristotelian *phronesis*. This had previously been noticed by André Chénier, according to whom Burke had never dissimulated in his speech and conduct "a profound disdain for all times of constant and immutable principles and all those philosophical examinations destined to lead men to notions that may be founded on nothing other than the truth and on the nature of things. It is there that he declares, in express terms, that he loves prejudices precisely because they are prejudices" (Chénier, *Réflexions sur l'esprit de parti*, in *Œuvres en prose de André Chénier* [Paris, 1872], 65). Even on a broader horizon, the insistence on "prudence" appears tied to defence of "prejudices" (see B. Constant, *Des réactions politiques* [1797] in *Cours de politique constitutionnelle* (rpt., Geneva, 1982), vol. 2, 117). In fact, as Madame de Staël would add, "Theory without experience is just a phrase; experience without theory is just a prejudice" (*Des circonstances actuelles qui peuvent terminer la Révolution et des Principes que doivent fonder la République en France* [1798] (Paris, 1906), 32).

23 *RRF* 101.

of a stupenduous [*sic*] wisdom, moulding together the great mysterious incorporation of the human race, the whole, at one time, is never old, or middle-aged, or young, but in a condition of unchangeable constancy, moves on through the varied tenour of perpetual decay, fall, renovation, and progression."[24] For Burke, in the succession of generations, tradition represents a type of "gyroscopic" and self-correcting coordination of thought and action that cannot be replaced by fully conscious planning. "When ancient opinions and rules of life are taken away, the loss cannot possibly be estimated. From that moment we have no compass to govern us, nor can we know distinctly to what port we steer."[25]

The Enlightenment and the French Revolution were based on *hybris*, on the presumption of a "knowledge" that wanted to make itself "master" of society, undermining the legitimate representatives of tradition, nobility, and clergy, whose success it had nonetheless generously promoted and protected.[26] But reason thus took on a weight that it was clearly incapable of carrying and unloaded it onto individuals in the form of a rigorous and fanatical morality and observance of universal principles and rhetoric that were empty, but no less dangerous because of the discretion introduced by their vagueness. It thus destroyed every trace of spontaneity in favour of rigid, punitive, and self-punitive norms, that sought in vain to replace the systems of self-regulation of customs offered by traditions. Thinking of the motto *sapere aude!* (which Kant placed under the Enlightenment's coat of arms, almost as a "heraldic" cartouche), it is evident that Burke was inclined to its exact opposite – that is, to keeping knowledge in a minority status.

Unlike the English, the French acted as if they did not have history at their backs, as if they were not the heirs of the generations of events that shaped them. Ignoring the conditioning of facts and healthy prejudices accumulated by the experience of centuries, they wanted to renew everything *ab imis fundamentis*. They pretended to be reborn from the ashes like the mythical Phoenix. In removing illusions and stripping men of their memories, however, they ended up cutting the roots that tied them to the *humus* of their past, transforming themselves into the stateless people of the time – monsters against nature who limited themselves to mechanically overturning what they found (the fruit of the effort and ingenuity of hundreds of generations) without being able to positively

24 Ibid., 39.
25 Ibid., 92.
26 Ibid.

suggest effective solutions to the problems they themselves had carelessly raised. This lack of concrete and verifiable proposals, covered by the fanfare of declamations on principles and morals, damaged the critical spirit.

Willingly deaf to the past's teaching, and not seriously worried about the future effects of changes introduced in a hurried manner, they proceeded along a road that they wanted to be straight, but they did not know where it led. Precisely because they moved haphazardly – in a direction contrary to history and experience, which had created traditions and illusions – the revolutionaries generally promoted an organized regression of humanity not only to the state of nature, but to the demonic and animal nature of the "swinish multitude," the legion of unclean spirits that emerge in the Gospel in the form of pigs from the body of the possessed.[27]

A new despotism developed from the lack of laws and traditions. It was a democratic sort of despotism that operated in the void left by hierarchical society and that was destined (despite its insistence on general will and virtue) to promote individualism. This was a concept that Burke introduced into European culture through scattered mentions and that was then diffused broadly, also as a term (in the 1820s, starting with different thinkers like Maistre, Saint-Simon, and de Tocqueville), to indicate how much it was opposed to ideals of compact community or socialism and how much it characterized the egalitarian democracy of the United States, which was destined to spread from America to all the continents.[28]

For Burke, under the principles of the Revolution, if established definitively, "the commonwealth itself would, in a few generations, crumble away, be disconnected into the dust and powder of individuality, and at length dispersed to all the winds of heaven."[29] The sanctification of the state through the creative fantasy of illusions is the indispensable tool for avoiding this falling apart and for fighting the inconstancy of men, since "individuals pass like shadows; but the commonwealth is fixed and stable."[30]

---

27 See, for example, Matt. 8:30–2. On this Burkian image, see D. Bindmann, *Sans-Culottes and Swinish-Multitude: The British Image of Revolutionary Crowd*, in *Kunst um 1800 und die Folgen: Werner Hoffman zu Ehren* (Munich, 1988), 87–94.

28 See S. Lukes, *Individualism* (Oxford, 1974).

29 *RRF* 113.

30 Burke, "Speech on the Economic Reform" [1780] in *Works* (The World's Classics) (London, 1906), vol. 2, 357. Quoted in Lukes, *Individualism.*

Illusions and prejudices carve out a zone of respect or a taboo area around authority, elevating what has value and is worth defending. They thus remove it from being profaned by criticism and, at the same time, place a limit on the destructiveness of those beings who are largely "naked [and] shivering"[31] but no less harmful because of that.

> To avoid therefore the evils of inconstancy and versatility, ten thousand times worse than those of obstinacy and the blindest prejudice, we have *consecrated* the state; that no man should approach to look into its defects or corruptions but with due caution; that he should never dream of beginning its reformation by its subversion; that he should approach to the faults of the state as to the wounds of a father, with pious awe and trembling solicitude. By this wise prejudice we are taught to look with horror on those children of their country who are prompt rashly to hack that aged parent in pieces, and put him into the kettle of magicians, in hopes that by their poisonous weeds, and wild incantations, they may regenerate the paternal constitution, and renovate their father's life.[32]

The wise man's constancy, which was legitimized among the Stoics by the consistency of reason, is now supported (positively) by prejudices and illusions and (negatively) by fear of social revolt. In the idea of *régénération,* Burke sees at work a sort of dark and superstitious attraction to political "black magic" on the part of those who otherwise defend pure rationality. Like the daughters of the King of Thessaly who, on the advice of Medea, tore their father to pieces criminally and uselessly, throwing

31 *RRF* 90.

32 *RRF* 113. Burke's *pietas* towards the state as a father is completely within the tradition of political thought. It is found, with other intents, even in Machiavelli, who calls patricide the enemy of country: "And truly he, who with his spirit and labor, makes himself an enemy of his native country, deservedly ought to be called a parricide; even though he may be acting out of some legitimate grievance. For if it is an evil deed to strike one's father or mother, whatever the reason, it follows out of necessity that striking one's country is a most infamous deed, because she is never the source of any persecution powerful enough to merit your insults. You must recognize that all good things come from her" (*A Discourse or Dialogue Concerning Our Language,* in W. Landon, *Politics, Patriotism and Language* [New York, 2005], 130). André Chénier, who had lived several years in England, attacks Burke because he defends the French monarchy and then, without any commiseration or human piety, rages with insulting expressions about his own king, George III, who had gone crazy in 1788, proposing in Parliament that the Prince of Wales become regent (see Chénier, *Réflexions sur l'esprit de parti,* 66).

him into a pot to have him be reborn rejuvenated, the revolutionaries deluded themselves that from the savage destruction of all that was more sacred, a new order would miraculously rise.

When Robespierre wrote that *cette glorieuse révolution … doit ébranler le monde pour le régénérer,*[33] he did not yet think that the regeneration of the world would have to pass through the "reducing to pieces," the decapitation of even the body of the state in the effigy of the sovereign.[34] Burke, however, had already arrived intuitively at this conclusion.

The lack of respect for the state as a living organism, even with all its defects, was also due to the French revolutionaries' theoretical training, which was imbued with (in particular, Rousseauian) doctrines of natural law. In interpreting the state as fruit of a "social contract," they thought that it would be lawful to dissolve it – tearing the whole thing to pieces – when the parties were no longer satisfied with its terms. They thus confused contracts of a private nature, which only bind those who stipulate to them, with those of a public nature: "Society is indeed a contract. Subordinate contracts, for objects of mere occasional interest, may be dissolved at pleasure; but the state ought not to be considered as nothing better than a partnership agreement in a trade of pepper and coffee, calico, or tobacco."[35] The difference of the contract instituted with a view towards maintenance of communal life consists in the fact that it "becomes a partnership not only between those who are living, but between the living, the dead, and those not yet born"[36] – that is, those who are joined by the temporal chain of the generations.

33 M. Robespierre, *Sur une lettre de l'abbé Raynal,* 31 May 1791, in *OC* VII, 449.

34 In the course of *cette glorieuse révolution,* however, some episodes would seem to confirm to the letter the inclination noted by Burke to materially dismember the body of those who embodied authority. See also what is probably the only case of "ritual" cannibalism recorded in Poleymieux, where, in 1791, a local lord who had committed a series of injustices was taken and cut to pieces by a local butcher. His head was raised on the point of a bayonet and his leg was carried over someone's shoulder. The rest of his body was burned on a pile of wood – not, however, before the tailor Bertier and the weaver Dru may have bit into some parts of the corpse. For these facts, see P. Viola, *Il trono vuoto,* 129–48, which attributes the fact to the "'great horror' that seized the people in France every time that its sovereignty, failing, left it ever more alone in the face of the unknown" (145).

35 *RRF* 113.

36 Ibid., 114.

Necessary Illusions

The French revolutionaries, however – and the Jacobins in particular – were not pure rationalists, contrary to exercising the power of the imagination, as Burke depicts them. Even Robespierre (although just within hypothetical reasoning) resorted to "creative fantasies" of God and the immortality of the soul as guarantees of virtue, stability of the social order, and the meaning of existence. Their task was in making private and public life consistent, both of them placed under the control of God's *oeil vivant* and the individual's conscience.[37]

Each person, then, cultivated his own myths; he reinforced his will to make others believe. Robespierre intended to consolidate equality, liberty, and justice through the double faith in God and the immortality of the soul (valid even if both beliefs were produced by a "creative fantasy" that agreed with reason thanks to a sort of pre-established harmony). Burke wanted, instead, to legitimize inequality, painting, in gloomy colours, the disastrous regression to which the return to equality would lead.

The entire post-revolutionary era had to deal with the simultaneous awareness of the loss of illusions (from the rational point of view) and the loss of their irreplaceable function (from the point of view of individual and social needs for meaning). At another, significant level of theoretical and poetic development, this conflict is also presented in the sphere of the Italian literature of the nineteenth century's first decades. Think of the Foscolo of the *Sepulchers*, in whose tomb "nuptials, courts, and altars" are presented as illusions necessary for communal life, or think of the veil of *The Graces*, a symbol of the beauty and of the civilization that ennobles, elevates, and rescues "nude and trembling human nature" from barbarism.

It is in Leopardi, however, that this problem assumes a strategic role (not without echoes of Burke, even if with opposite intentions). For young Leopardi, illusions are necessary to the human race and are a product of nature: "I consider illusions something that are real in some

37 On the basis of these premises, some quotidian attitudes and ideals of Maximilien Robespierre can be better explained. His sister recalled, "His private life is just a reflection of his public life. No intrigues, no complication in the details. Up close, he is no different from how he appears in the seats of the constituent assembly and of the convention. It is a scene that has neither curtain nor wings, and where the actors dress and undress in the presence of the audience" (C. Robespierre, *Mémoires de Charlotte Robespierre sur ses deux frères*, 74).

way, being that they are essential ingredients of the system of human nature and given by nature to all men, in such a way that it is not right to disdain them as dreams of just one man, but truly part of mankind and desired by nature, and without which our life would be the most miserable and barbaric thing, etc."[38] Nature, which manifests itself directly through illusions and passions, is superior to reason, which limits itself to fighting them with blind stubbornness without understanding the essence of the desire for happiness, the *cupiditas* that, almost in a Spinozan sense, constitutes the root of man as a natural being. Precisely because he ignores their deepest meaning at the very moment he believes he knows them and declares his own victory, not even the reason that he considers triumphant can eradicate the illusions and passions: "Illusions, to the extent that they may be enfeebled and exposed by reason, nevertheless still are part of the world, and they make up the greater part of our life. And knowing everything is not enough to lose them, even if they are known to be in vain. And once lost, they are not lost in such a way that a very vigorous root does not remain, and continuing to live, they return to re-emerge despite all the experience and certainty acquired."[39]

Once again in Spinozan terms, human reason cannot profess to raise itself proudly above nature and dominate it, although the latter was partly subdued by civilization, particularly in the most recent centuries: "Nature is thus immeasurably stronger than reason, such that even if depressed and weakened beyond all belief, there still remains enough to defeat its enemy, and this among its own followers, and in that very moment when they pray to it and spread it. In fact, with this praying and spreading of reason against nature, they give the victory to nature over reason."[40] Illusions last despite reason, and the very vehemence with which the advocates of reason attack it reveals a side of them that is passionate about naturalness. If the modern trend of spreading philosophy, encountering the "positive lack of nearly all the objects of illusion,"

38 G. Leopardi, *Zibaldone di pensieri*, ed. A.M. Moroni (Milan, 1988), vol. 1, 52.

39 Ibid., vol. 1, 167.

40 Ibid., vol. 1, 169. If he does not want to be a "halved philosopher," the thinker must experience passions and illusions, "not because the heart and fantasy may often tell more truth than cold reason, but because the same very cold reason needs to be familiar with all of these things, if it wants to penetrate into the system of nature, and develop it ... Reason needs the imagination and the illusions that it destroys; the true of the false; the substantive of the seeming; the insensitivity more perfect than the deepest sensitivity; the ice of the fire; the patience of the impatience; the powerlessness of the highest power; geometry and algebra, poetry, etc." (ibid., vol. 2, 663, 665).

would necessarily prevail and lead to wild and radical destruction of illusions, humanity would extinguish itself like those great animals whose fossils were studied in the previous century and continued to be actively studied in the time of the poet, with Lamarck and Cuvier. If men can truly become accustomed to "having before their eyes continually and without pause the pure and naked truth, there would be nothing left of this human race than the bones, like those of other animals spoken of in the last century. It is no more possible for man to live wholly detached from nature, from which we are distancing ourselves ever more, than it is that a tree cut from its root may flower and bear fruit."[41]

The French revolutionaries were the first victims of their fatal illusion. They wanted "to extinguish passion with reason" instead of "converting reason into passion."[42] They intended to "geometrize" life, superimposing reason over it:

> The French Revolution, given that it was prepared by philosophy, was not carried out by it, because philosophy, especially modern [philosophy], is not capable in itself of doing anything. And even if philosophy were good at carrying out a revolution itself, it could not maintain it. It is truly pitiful to see how those French republican legislators believed they were preserving and ensuring its duration, and following the course, nature, and aim of the Revolution, by reducing everything to pure reason and pretending for the first time, *ab orbe condito*, to geometrize life.[43]

These legislators (continues Leopardi with Burkian expressions) "do not see that the rule of reason is that of despotism with a thousand ends, but briefly, here is one of them: Pure reason dissipates illusions and leads selfishness by the hand."[44] That is, they fought selfishness and set virtue against it as an antidote, but they did not realize the existence of a close complicity between reason reduced to calculation (once deprived of illusions, that is) and the "cold passion" of selfishness. They did not see that once the illusions were extinguished, virtue – as availability to elevate oneself to the common good, even through sacrifice – wanes. They did not notice that liberty and equality thus disappear, and that there

41 Ibid., vol. 1, 169.
42 Ibid., vol. 1, 206.
43 Ibid., vol. 1, 130.
44 Ibid., vol. 1, 131.

remains only the instinct for self-preservation at the lowest level, one very compatible with servitude. Brutus, then, is truly dead.[45]

The error of all the French revolutionaries (not only the "fanatics" but the persecuted wise men like Condorcet) was "to make a people exactly philosophic and reasonable" through the cults of Goddess Reason, the new republican calendar, and Robespierre's Festival of the Supreme Being. In this way, they reversed the order of things, which wanted human reason (that "little reason") to be founded on life and nature, considering themselves, instead, the silent model of the "great reason" to which thought must give voice: "Such that I do not wonder and do not pity them principally for having believed in the mirage of being able to achieve a dream and a utopia, but for not having seen that reason and life are two incompatible things – in fact, to have considered that the entire, exact, and universal use of reason and philosophy would be the foundation and reason and source of the life and strength and happiness of a people."[46]

45 See ibid., vol. 1, 206: "But when the only passion in the world is selfishness, then there is good reason to rail against passion. But how do we extinguish selfishness with the reason as its nursemaid, dissipating the illusions?"; ibid., vol. 1, 324: "With natural beliefs and illusions removed, there is no reason, it is neither possible nor human, that another may sacrifice his possible advantage to the good of others – something essentially contrary to self-esteem, essential to all animals"; ibid., vol. 1, 303–4: "Those whom selfishness dominates can only serve or rule. It is the same with our princes. They rule and should know how to serve ... Liberty requires *homines non mancipia, andras kai ouk andrapoda*, and he who is a slave of selfishness, either serving masters or himself, and ruling with low inclinations, cannot involve the free or equal condition. Love of self is inseparable from man. This leads him to elevate himself. With the elevation, etc., the total satisfaction of self-esteem is impossible; thus man cannot live. Now, in the state of perfect liberty and equality, the individual does not make progress without virtue or true merits, because his virtue, honors, riches, advantages, etc. depend on the multitude, which cannot judge according to particular emotions and inclinations, because these are various and infinite and do not agree with each other. It is necessary for one to judge according to universal rules and opinions – that is, true ones." These passages, noted at length, show the use – with intentions often diametrically opposed to those of Burke – that Leopardi makes of illusions, even in the moment when he discovers the fact of its vanity (see, for example, the poem "Brutus the Younger," on a virtue that is just an empty word). They serve to keep alive the inclination towards the general interest, liberty, and equality. The thought that included the nature of illusions, however, reasons according to a *de jure* pattern of how things should be and not a *de facto* one of how they actually are, because of the general weakening of nature.

46 Ibid., vol. 1, 233–4.

The Body of the Monarch

In his own way, Hegel also understood the problem of the crisis of sovereignty and tried to find a solution that, even in its modern parts, preserves archaic elements from which it did not succeed in freeing itself. In fact, he tried to attribute to the state an intrinsically rational nature, purified of all will, and he transformed the function of the king into that of a "dot on the *i*," of a pure, anonymous terminus of decision-making processes. The king assumes a verticality that no longer seems to have anything intrinsically lofty but that is not reduced to pure formal functionality, because the monarch embodies and visibly represents the state and the unity of the collective (something that the Directorate, for example – a pure "moral body" torn by internal conflicts – was incapable of doing).

In his effort to "deduce" sovereignty rationally – apart from divine right and legitimacy attributed to the traditions of the *altes Recht*, of the old customary right – Hegel was driven back, beyond Hobbes, to the mystical body of the king. It is true that it was a case of a single "King's body," the mortal one, and that his "mysticism" of sovereignty now appeared completely profane, precisely because it was a naturalistic-biological fact of being sons or relatives of the king, which legitimized sovereignty (paraphrasing Aristotle, it could be said that there now existed kings "by nature," just as it was once held that there were free men and slaves by nature). However, it is also true that this single body added and reconciled the two natures of sovereignty, the physical and the political.

Hegel had to anchor what remained of the *homo hierarchicus* in a society largely composed of *hominess aequales*, to a hierarchy established at its summits by chance, to a "naked nature" not cloaked in illusions. According to the famous so-called servant/master dialectic of *Phenomenology of the Spirit*, the men of civil society are emancipated from servitude through work and the fear of death, and they enter into a network of reciprocal and simultaneous autonomy and dependence. Now, however, at the apex of the state, there again appears the Lord, whom provident nature exempted from the hard practice of worry and trouble.

The dialectic, also evoked by the contradictions triggered by the revolutionary experience, stops at the threshold of the throne and a monarch who no longer intrinsically incites fear and respect, who limits himself to being the first functionary of the state, the depository of the most important decision-making processes. The reason, bound politically to the presumption of naturalness that is not further justifiable, is found in embarrassment – all the more so since it is incapable of guaranteeing either happiness or the "satisfaction" of men within the sphere of the state.[47]

An anachronistic remnant is inserted into the concept of rationality, one that acts as a gauge for understanding the difficulties of the problem. Hegel also intends to save the natural and hereditary character of sovereignty for reasons tied specifically to German history, since the elective monarchy, typical of the Holy Roman Empire – lasting until 1806 and studded with "electoral capitulations" – had led to the ruin and impotence of the central power. But his core worry is guaranteeing the rights of the individual – of the immense (*masslose*) modern subjectivity that the Jacobins had denied – in the framework of an order not subject to perpetual political instability, to which the spread of individualism and organized economic and political groups could lead.

This is why he persists in seeking a reconciliation of liberty and authority and in anchoring civil society to a state that is no longer either patriarchal or absolutist but guided by a hereditary constitutional monarch, in which public opinion has minimal weight and the class of functionaries, instead, represents the true framework of political rationality. This is why, ultimately, he seeks (Hobbes-like) *die letzte entscheidende Subjektivität* – the subjectivity that decides in the final instance, even if it knows well that its figure is tied to *die höchste Zufälligkeit*, the supreme fortuitousness of nature.[48] And although its sovereignty may not be born in the shadow of illusions, the executioner, or the force that would empower the vulture to devour the innocent lamb (as asserted, respectively, by Burke, Maistre, and Von Haller), it is still true that the state that arose from the French Revolution as a structure of reason, in contrast to the will of the *ancien régime*, cannot in any way be deduced from similar assumptions.

What Foucault called "obsession of sovereignty" was shown paradoxically in a macroscopic way right after the decapitation and death of the sovereign, when it passed from morals and politics based on prohibitions and punishments (on saying "no") to the prevalence of weapons of seduction and widespread desire interwoven with power, of politics carried out not only in the agora or the prince's cabinet, but also in the bedroom

---

47 I have dealt with this last point in R. Bodei, *Sistema ed epoca in Hegel* (Bologna, 1975), 170 et seq.

48 See Hegel, *Vorlesungen über Naturrecht und Staatswissenschaft, Heidelberg 1817/18, mit Nachträgen aus den Vorlesungen 1818/19: Nachgeschrieben von P. Wannenman* (Hamburg, 1983), §139, 204.

or in the schools (by saying "yes").[49] When the "who" commands or when the Kelsenian "totemic mask" of sovereignty seems to disappear behind the image of a turbulent micro-physical power (or assumes an aspect smoothed by the norm, by negotiation to produce laws endowed with impersonal rationality), that is the time when the need for corroborating reason, for assigning a supplemental authority to it, is made more acute. The norm and reason are thus called upon to forge new chains of command, to develop forms of rights and morals more consonant with the situations, but also (and particularly) to legitimize obedience starting from the fragile basis of seduction or pure universality. In the latter case, the action of endorsing the universal, of decreeing its validity, can again be ascribed to a sovereign gesture, one that does not reason only on the free play of opinions.

The problem of the crumbling of power in a series of centrifugal forces of an individualistic sort is posed as much in post-revolutionary thought as it is in Jacobin thought. The former is forced to resort to the mysterious help of nature or the fabrication of illusions to find a substitute for the lost charisma of the sovereign. The latter is forced to place the general will under the patronage of the Supreme Being and practise terror to re-establish the majesty and credibility of power, thus triggering a circular process in which he who commands – no longer distinguishing himself in principle from he who obeys – is pushed to tear and split himself, to be simultaneously sovereign and subject. From this point of view, Benjamin Constant's accusation in *De l'esprit de conquête,* in which, with the Revolution and with the Empire, *l'on immole à l'être abstrait les êtres réels: et l'on offre au people en masse l'holocauste du peuple en détail,*[50] contains a truth that surpasses its intentions.

49 See M. Foucault, *Microfisica del potere* (Turin, 1977), 15 et seq., and G. Marramao, "L'ossessione della sovranità," in *Effetto Foucault* (Milan, 1986), 171–83.

50 Significantly, this statement was chosen as the exergue of the book by Isaiah Berlin, *Four Essays on Liberty* (Oxford, 1969). More balanced is Hegel's comment on the real power of revolutionary "abstractions": "Hence, when these abstractions attained to power, there was enacted the most tremendous spectacle which the human race has ever witnessed. All the usages and institutions of a great state were swept away. It was then proposed to begin over again starting from the thought, and as the basis of the state to will only what was judged to be rational. But as the undertaking was begun with abstractions void of all ideas, it ended in scenes of tragic cruelty and horror" (*Philosophie des Rechts* [1821]; Engl. trans. *Hegel's Philosophy of Right* (London, 1896), 242 [§258 A]).

The Victory of Opinion?

Some interpretations of the effects produced by the fall of the monarchy are not completely convincing – interpretations originating at the beginning of the twentieth century that have been more recently re-proposed in even more elaborate form. In them, the sphere of power, "having become vacant," would simply be invaded by politics understood as "ideology" – that is, by the power of public opinion, whose spokespeople exercise power in the name of the people.

A "reactionary historian" of great insight like Cochin, in his time, held the Enlightenment responsible for having prepared the Revolution through the spread of nihilistic talk and the systematic defamation of adversaries: "Since another practice characteristic of the sect is that of persecution. Before the bloody Terror of 1793 there was, from 1765 to 1780, in the republic of letters, a bloodless Terror, of which the *Encyclopédie* was its Committee of Public Health and D'Alembert, its Robespierre. The first cut reputations like the second did with heads. Its guillotine was defamation – infamy, as it was called then."[51]

For Furet, who refers in an innovative way to some of his theses (interweaving them with those of the de Tocqueville of *L'Ancien régime et la Révolution*), public opinion had to rapidly fill a void of power, replacing, in the course of the last decades of the eighteenth century, the prerogatives of the throne, already placed under discussion by the aristocratic revolution: "Real society rebuilt another world of political society, outside and far from the monarchy: a new world structured on the individual and no longer on its institutional groups, a world founded on that vague thing called 'opinion' that is created in the cafés, the salons, the theatre boxes, and the 'societies.'"[52] The "word" thus seems to become sovereign in a political space that is presented (to someone who was always excluded from power) as free, no longer encumbered by the crumbling structure of monarchical institutions, flattened, and ready to receive new structures planned according to the most daring architectonic experiments. According to Furet, with the monarchy destroyed, the way would open to new absolutisms that threaten the individual rights just proclaimed.

Now, even if the fall of the monarchy certainly constituted a traumatic event for a society with a prevalent peasant majority (accustomed

51 Augustin Cochin, *L'esprit du jacobinisme* (Paris, 1979), 35.
52 F. Furet, *Penser la Révolution française* (Paris, 1978), 67–8.

to considering the sovereign as protector of the overbearing manner of the nobles, a being so distant as to seem close to God), there is no need to overestimate its symbolic impact.[53] The idea that public opinion and democratic ideology might monopolize this sphere of power, previously empty, itself seems an ideological statement, one that recalls the Freudian theory of the child who talks in the dark since that way "the dark becomes clear" and because he thus succeeds in warding off a worrisome void.

The trend (observed by de Tocqueville and emphasized by Furet) of seeing the Revolution as bringing to completion a process of state and administrative centralization, begun with the absolutism of Louis XIII and Louis XIV, contains many aspects of truth. It would be inaccurate, however, to collapse the entire phenomenon into this trend, excessively emphasizing the element of historical continuity and considering as mere epiphenomenon the awareness of the protagonists. There certainly exists a gap between "the intentions of the actors and the historical role that they take on."[54] To "think of the French Revolution" one cannot, however, reduce what the Revolution's protagonists and contemporaries said or carried out to mere ideology or to pure "experience." This overlooks the element (itself objective, because it produces some effects) of awareness of inaugurating a new era and triggering a series of new processes within history. After all, can the Revolution and the fear of conspiracy be reduced to a "delirium of power" that – along with the "will of the people" – might constitute "the democratic imagination of

---

53 The episode of the peasants' trust in the king (reported by Michelet) is revealing: "A peasant, speaking with a lord, had not uncovered; the noble knocked his hat to the ground: 'If you do not pick it up,' said the peasant, 'the *Grands Jours* are coming, and the king will cut your head off.' The noble was afraid, and picked it up" (J. Michelet, *Histoire de la Révolution française*, vol. 1, 314). It is also true, however, that very soon, with the acquisition of national goods from the lands expropriated from the church and from *emigrés,* in exchange for *assignats* (paper that was worth ever less), their attitude changed, at least temporarily: "Never did an army in battle, never did a soldier ready to fire march with a more eager heart. For them, it was the conquest, the revenge on the old regime, doubly happy – happy of winning and of winning at the expense of their enemies" (Michelet, quoted by F. Piro, *La festa della sfortuna*, 49).

54 See Furet, *Penser la Révolution française*, 35. From this perspective, Furet's attempt to reflect upon contemporaneous events from a distance, according to the model of "cold-history" of Lévi-Strauss, is significant: "The day will come when the political convictions that have fed the debates of our societies for the past two centuries will seem as surprising to humanity as the inexhaustible variety and ferocity of the religious conflicts of Europe between the fifteenth and seventeenth centuries seem to us" (27).

power"?[55] The objection that the Jacobins did not believe in the value of opinions but in a single truth – logically and morally clear to those who were liberated from the selfishness and privileges that dulled judgment – evidently does not constitute an irresistible argument. If anything, it would serve to indicate (if there were still a need) the presence of a "delirium of truth" manifested through the premise of always being right and the desire to annul the past and the plurality of the voices of the present. The response must be sought elsewhere.

Hybridizations

The response can be found in the rise of a new "species" that asserted itself in these years: the *homo ideologicus* that now began to spread, revealing itself at a distance as the result of a cross between the Spinozan "wise man" and the traditional demagogue. In joining philosophy and politics, thought and transformative practice, the French Revolution generated that hybrid figure of "intellectual," agitator, and journalist (like Marat) who sought legitimization through the connection of current events. He interpreted events that were changing rapidly, inserting them into the channel flowing towards an ending to which history extended and to whose real achievement all good citizens should contribute.

According to a pattern that would become typical in all the great projects of revolutionary transformation in the last two centuries (and which, from France, would extend to various continents, passing in a different way from Robespierre, Marat, or Saint-Just to Blanqui, to Marx, to Lenin, or to Mao), this new modern species of politician-intellectual sought a consensus founded on "scientific" or universal principles of reason. In place of the rising *transitio* that Spinoza offered individually to the wise man, the Revolution itself is presented as a collective *transitio* towards another earthly reality to construct in common.

It was no longer a case of placing philosophers under the guidance of the *polis* or of the empire – according to the proposals of Plato or the experience of Marcus Aurelius – but rather of inventing a new figure who, through knowledge and the hold on processes underway, is capable of interpreting the world while it is changing, of joining the hyper-realism of the astute politician with the candour of the utopian. He should be endowed with the stubborn determination to modify the course of events

55 Ibid., 35.

while standing within them, temporarily accepting their tough rules in order to then change them. He should be capable of transcending existing conditions without considering the future as a path of escape, of passing through the disorder and the will to create a "new order."

The revolutionary *homo ideologicus* asserts himself in the moment when he claims to apply to politics not wisdom, but rigorous – or even scientific – philosophical reason. As he appeals to reason (and not merely to passions and myths), he distinguishes himself from previous and subsequent demagogues, since he refers to a plan of progressive rationalization of the socially harmful passions (once their causes have been eliminated, Spinozanly), and appears, instead, different from traditional wise men.

He thus represents the link between the *homo hierarchicus* of the aristocratic societies of the *ancien régime* – whose privileges even the wise man and the scholar had enjoyed – and the *homo aequalis* of future societies, whose advent was only proclaimed but not realized, because the obstacles existing at the beginning of inequality among men still, in large part, remained to be removed. The old Christian idea of equality of men before God[56] also awaited its achievement on earth. Men of this type were its promoters, the priests who indicated the inferno of this world in the present, the paradise in the future, and the purgatory in the phase of transition.

Compared to the Epicurean wise man, who retreated into the *templa serena* of wisdom, or the Stoic wise man who sought to conform himself (and, as much as possible, the state) to the eternal order of the cosmos, the ideological man – the intellectual-leader, the politician-revolutionary – did not withdraw from the world; he did not seek refuge in inwardness. He knew how to make inevitable sacrifices on the altars of a reason that unfolded in reality according to its own laws, but also according to the laws of fear. Revolution is a demanding divinity who dispenses the collective good only by passing often through the suffering of individuals. This is the price of knocking down the barriers that separated philosophy from "popular movements," reason from the heart, and wisdom as the possession of a few from virtue as potential common good.

Marat, Robespierre, and Saint-Just (although having had intellectual ambitions and ideas that changed the world), certainly did not correspond to the model of the wise man who isolated reason from the

56 On the history of this ideal, see G. Kerr, *"Vor Gott sind wir alle gleiche": Soziale Gleichheit, soziale Ungleichheit und Religion* (Dusseldorf, 1983).

passions. The ideology was born precisely from this cross between them, from the instrumental use that reason – even with the goal of emancipation – made of the "hot" passions of fear and hope.

The exponents of Jacobinism were not philosophers. They were, however, inspired by philosophy. They wanted to make it real in the world, have it descend not just Socratically "into the houses of men" but also into public life, into constitutions, and into ideals of individuals' conduct. At the same time, however, they were not simply people destined to serve and repress their own power of existing, yielding to the fates of their peers. And yet they no longer were similar to the old demagogues, since they no longer explicitly appealed to just the elementary passions or to myths, considering reason and the reason of the state merely as a tool. Yes, they used myths, but they placed them under the aegis of reason. They were "journalists" like Marat, lawyers or agitators like Robespierre and Saint-Just. They used persuasion, but they were persuaded to use it for the benefit of the people. They believed that they were avoiding every manipulation precisely because they appealed simultaneously to the public dimension of truth supported by reason and to the private dimension of the voice of a heart not completely corrupted by selfishness and sophisms. They used the universal to raise the dictates of the "heart" to the level of truth, a means of realizing the "dream of a thing," to fulfil the hopes of the oppressed. But in all of their projects, there remains a more general question, one posed by Georg Büchner in his drama *The Death of Danton*: Is it men who make revolutions or is it revolutions that make men?[57]

57 See G. Büchner, *Dantons Tod*, in *Sämtliche Werke*, ed. W.R. Lehmann (Hamburg, 1967), vol. 1, 32: "We did not make the Revolution, but the Revolution made us."

SECTION 3

Heaven on Earth

1. Reason in Myth

The Celestial Tyrant

In *The Gods Are Athirst* of 1912, Anatole France effectively presents the collision of two mentalities and two worlds. During the Terror, the young Jacobin Evariste Gamelin debates animatedly with the impoverished former noble Brotteaux des Islettes. Both are in line to buy bread:

> "Virtue," said he [Gamelin], "is natural to mankind; God has planted the seed of it in the heart of mortals."
>
> Old Brotteaux was a sceptic and found in his atheism an abundant source of self-satisfaction. "I see this much, *citoyen* Gamelin, that, while a Revolutionary for what is of this world, you are, where Heaven is concerned, of a conservative, or even a reactionary temper. Robespierre and Marat are the same to you. For me, I find it strange that Frenchmen, who will not put up with a mortal king any longer, insist on retaining an immortal tyrant, far more despotic and ferocious. For what is the Bastille, or even the *Chambre Ardente* beside Hellfire? Humanity models its gods on its tyrants, and you, who reject the original, preserve the copy!"
>
> "Oh! *citoyen!*" protested Gamelin, "are you not ashamed to hold such language? How can you confound the dark divinities born of ignorance and fear with the Author of Nature? Belief in a benevolent God is necessary for morality. The Supreme Being is the source of all the virtues and a man cannot be a Republican if he does not believe in God. Robespierre knew this, who, as we all remember, had the bust of the philosopher Helvétius removed from the Hall of the Jacobins, because he had taught Frenchmen the lessons of slavery by preaching atheism ... I hope, at least, *citoyen* Brotteaux, that, as soon as the Republic has established the worship of Reason, you will not refuse your adhesion to so wise a religion!"

> "I love reason, but I am no fanatic in my love," was Brotteaux's answer. "Reason is our guide and beacon-light; but when you have made a divinity of it, it will blind you and instigate you to crime," – and he proceeded to develop his thesis, standing both feet in the kennel, as he had once been used to perorate, seated in one of Baron d'Holbach's gilt armchairs, which, as he was fond of saying, formed the basis of natural philosophy.
>
> "Jean Jacques Rousseau," he proceeded, "who was not without talents, particularly in music, was a scampish fellow who professed to derive his morality from Nature while all the time he got it from the dogmas of Calvin. Nature teaches us to devour each other and gives us the example of all the crimes and all the vices; but it is well to know that this is simply and solely a convenient expedient invented by men in order to lie comfortably together. What we call morality is merely a desperate enterprise, a forlorn hope, on the part of our fellow creatures to reverse the order of the universe, which is strife and murder, the blind interplay of hostile forces."[1]

This page by Anatole France is interesting not only because it shows, in artistically stylized form, real historical trends (France, a friend of Jean Jaurès, had a first-rate knowledge of the events and protagonists of the French Revolution), but also because he accurately understood an element of difference of Jacobin thought with respect to more recent revolutionary ideologies or to those of the past.

By now, we are used to associating materialism and revolution, but Brotteaux, who went around with a copy of Lucretius's *De rerum natura* in the "pocket of his puce-colored jacket," though politically conservative and a representative of the *ancien régime*, was materialistic and atheist.

1 A. France, *Les dieux ont soif* (Paris, 1912); Engl. trans. *The Gods are Athirst* (London, 1913), 68. For an evaluation of this text in the framework of the literary interpretations of the French Revolution, see L. Bozan, *L'alchimia del Terrore* (Naples, 1989). France paraphrases here both the statements of D'Holbach (see, for example, *Politique naturelle*, Discours III, §§12 et seq., and *Système de la nature*, I XIX, according to which religion, making men accustomed to fearing an invisible sovereign and adoring *des dieux bizarres, injustes, sanguinaires, implacables*, makes them cowardly even towards the visible ones) and the texts of the Jacobins. For the aversion towards Helvétius on the part of Robespierre, who considered him "one of the most cruel persecutors of Rousseau," see *OC*, vol. 9, 144, and on the lack of correspondence between philosophical radicalism and political radicalism, see D. Roche, *Salons, lumières, engagement politique: La côterie d'Holbach dévoilée*, in *Les Républicain des lettres: Gens de culture et Lumières au XVIIIe siècle* (Paris, 1988), 242–53. On D'Holbach, see A. Minerbi Belgrado, *Paura e ignoranza: Studio sulla teoria della religione in D'Holbach*, particularly 103 et seq.

Atheism is, in fact, for Robespierre and most of the Jacobins (as it had been for Rousseau) "aristocratic," while the belief in God was *toute populaire* (see Rousseau, *NH* v, letter iv, and Robespierre, *OC* x, 197). In fact, it suppresses in tyrants, egoists, and evil-doers the fear of an otherworldly *rex tremendae maiestatis*; it takes away from the people the faith in divine punishment of the wicked and hope in the reward of virtue.

Virtue needs God. Otherwise, it would not be able to establish either a just politics or a tolerable morals. The gloomy vision of nature espoused by Brotteaux (whose eighteenth-century materialism, not unmindful of Sade, is reinforced in France by late-positivistic colouring) could encourage only egoism and tyranny. The Jacobin position, however, is different also with respect to other revolutionary ideologies with a religious base, in which the Bible or the Koran, heresies and mythologems, orient reality. L'*Être infini, que l'homme adore*,[2] the heavenly tyrant, is an entity conceivable by the heart and by reason, author of nature, guarantee of virtue. It does not hide impenetrable mysteries and does not possess any positive, historical characterization, according to the teachings of traditional religions.

But achieving virtue also requires a personal and direct commitment, which implies risk of destruction and self-destruction. The Lucretian wise man – in this case, the materialist Brotteaux – can certainly sympathize with men, both standing "with his feet in the mud" and seated comfortably on the "gilded armchairs" of Baron D'Holbach. He can look at the "shipwreck" of society from the solid "shore" of his science – lacking fears, but also hopes – and contemplate spectacles of death without becoming involved in the events or in the dangers run by other men (*tui sine parte pericli*), without being infected by the passions of the masses who, similar to crazy ants, do not seem to know what they are doing:

> It is sweet, when on the great sea the winds trouble its water, to behold from land another's deep distress; not that it is a pleasure and delight that any should be afflicted, but because it is sweet to see from what evils you are yourself exempt. It is sweet also to look upon the mighty struggles of war arrayed along the plains without sharing yourself in the danger. But nothing is more welcome than to hold the lofty and serene positions well

2 The feast of the Supreme Being, 20 Prairial of Year ii (8 June 1794), opened with these words, sung in chorus. For an interesting testimony, see A.G.F. Rebmann, *Ludwig Wagehals* (Leipzig, 1795), 174 et seq., also in V. Hermand, ed., *Von Deutschen Republik, 1775–1795: Texte radikaler Demokraten* (Frankfurt, 1975), 155 et seq.

fortified by the learning of the wise, from which you may look down upon others and see them wandering all abroad and going astray in their search for the path of life.[3]

The French revolutionary (the Jacobin in particular) had, instead, inaugurated a new wisdom: that of those who throw themselves into the "waves," of those who confront the "storm" of the Revolution, determined to remain firm with the unfolding of events and to share a collective destiny. He accepts calmly being subject to fear without succumbing, and subject to hope without losing sight of the harshness of the times, striving along with the others so that in the future, a world may form without fear and without a desperate need for hope. It is this new way of creating – in Spinozan language – a *nos*, a collective dimension, however lacking in joy in the short term, tied to an ascetic perspective of rejection of self and of death, if necessary, for the victory of the cause. In its way, however, it is full of an *amor* that asserts itself, at first, in the form of conflict with a part of humanity, displaying a sprit of division and enmity that should ultimately lead to a new social pact among all men.

A History of Humiliations

Let's take another look at the novel of Anatole France. Gamelin sees Robespierre, troubled, walking in a public garden. His "blue and cold" gaze (which by now also replaces that of Marat, "bird of Minerva, whose eye discovered the conspirators in the darkness in which they hid" – note the echo of Hegelian expressions, which will later return) knows how to discern the subtle line that separates guilt from innocence.[4] Gamelin addresses him mentally:

I saw your sadness, Maximilien; I understood your thought. Your melancholy, your weariness and even that expression of fear in your eyes, everything in you says, 'Stop the Terror and let brotherhood begin. Frenchmen, be united, be virtuous, be good. Love one another …' And yet, I will make use of your designs so that you may, with your wisdom and your goodwill, place an end to civil discord, extinguish fratricidal hate, turn the executioner into a gardener

3 See Lucr., II, 1–10. On this subject and its framing, see H. Blumenberg, *Schiffbruch mit Zuschauer: Paradigma einer Daseinsmetapher* (Frankfurt, 1979); Ital. trans. *Naufragio con spettatore: Paradigma di una metafora dell'esistenza* (Bologna, 1985), with an introduction by R. Bodei, "Distanza di sicurezza," 7–23.

4 France, *Les dieux on soif*, 286.

> who will sever heads of cabbage and lettuce. I will prepare, with my colleagues of the Tribunal, the paths to clemency, exterminating the conspirators and traitors.[5]

For Robespierre, men live in a half-reality that needs to be led to completion by integrating the work of God with the reversal of the dynamic of human events as they had unfolded to that point: "The moral world, much more than the physical world, appears full of contrasts and enigmas. Nature tells us that man is born for liberty, while the experience of centuries shows man as a slave. His rights are written in his heart, and his humiliation is written in history ... The centuries and the earth are the legacy of crime and of tyranny; liberty and virtue have barely rested an instant on some points of the globe: Sparta shines as a light in endless darkness."[6] History, up to this point, had been the theatre of oppression and enslavement of men, of abuse and chance. In it, "the despots took control of human reason to make it an accomplice of servitude." Detached from the "heart," as happened in the "sect" of the encyclopedists, from the immediacy of the sentiment in which human dignity took refuge, reason is just a sophism in the service of selfishness. But it could be said that from this perspective, even the heart is just the voice – plain, simple, humiliated, and lacking articulate arguments, of pure and uncorrupted reason. If this reason could speak without enticements and without obstacles, it would speak in the same way as the heart. The immediacy of feeling would thus succeed, finally, in translating itself into clear and distinct language. History had been the history of conditionings of reason, of its corruption, or of its silencing. It had been the history, up to that point, of abuses and unpredictability. If, however, the obstacles to development of reason were to be removed, if the roots of oppression and selfishness could be eradicated, then reason would express nature in its possibilities for unimpeded development. Nature and history would no longer be in opposition, and reason would achieve, within history, the flowering of the human faculties. And yet, how can the obstacles

---

5 Ibid., 330. Cf. G.W.F. Hegel, *Phänomenologie des Geistes*, in *Gesammelte Werke*, vol. 9 (Hamburg, 1968), 320; Engl. trans. *The Phenomenology of Mind*, vol. 2 (New York, 1910), 599: "The sole and only work and deed accomplished by universal freedom is therefore *death* – a death that achieves nothing, embraces nothing within its grasp; for what is negated is the unachieved, unfulfilled punctual entity of the absolutely free self. It is thus the most cold-blooded, mean, and meaningless death of all, with no more significance than cleaving a head of cabbage or swallowing a draught of water."

6 M. Robespierre, speech of 18 Floreal, Year II (7 May 1794), in *OC* X, 443–4.

be effectively removed? Can reason free itself on its own, with its own strengths, and change the meaning of history?

The Supreme Being is not responsible for the misery of man. Revolution is a theodicy of the *Deus sive natura*, since it places an end to the scandal and humiliation of history, and it rescues, at the same time, human nature from the slavery in which it was constrained. Evil does not come mythically from original sin or the arrogance of Adam, but from the power of the tyranny of the few and from the complementary tolerance of the many who – in Spinozan terms – were not yet supplied (either individually or *collegialiter*) with the *conatus* sufficient to resist oppression or to govern themselves.

Calming Worry

The general interest does not possess, in itself, sufficient strength of persuasion and mobilization of minds to be imposed by terror alone or just by earthly hope. In their turn, the conflicts caused by the collision between the principles of *liberté, égalité,* and *fraternité* – at the moment of their political application – could not be justified by simple reason if there were not a greater penalty in making tolerable the contradictions and suffering that flow from it. Religion and revolutionary myths offer the horizon of meaning to frame them and not surrender to them.

But how? At first glance, Robespierre's Supreme Being could seem like just the invisible guarantor of the general will, the spiritual bond of a struggling nation, the political protagonist of a deism of the state, or the cult object of a nationalized religion. The divine "living eye" would then limit itself to distributing rewards and punishments, scrutinizing consciences, penetrating them to the point that Maximilien's "blue" eye would never succeed in reaching and establishing the presence of evil where not even the most suspicious member of the Committee of Public Health would be able to spot it.

When we speak of revolutionary cults, we think generally of the famous parade of the allegorical cart on which were enthroned the effigies of the Supreme Being and of Robespierre who, in a sky-blue suit and yellow pants, moves forward with a bundle of wheat. Few will perhaps think of the moving figure of the gentle old man – nicknamed *Système* and described by Renan in *Memories of Childhood and Youth*[7] – who, when

7 See E. Renan, *Souvenirs d'enfance et de jeunesse* (Paris, 1883), 109 (and see the entire fifth chapter of book 3).

he died, at the height of the Restoration and persecuted by the priests, left among his "subversive" books and his meagre things a pathetic relic of his own youth as a Jacobin and a man of the Terror: some dried flowers, tied by a tricolour ribbon, that he had carried to the ceremonies in honour of the Supreme Being.

Is it proper, however, to reduce the revolutionary cults to the single dimension of a "feast day" directed towards consolidation of civil ties – that is, to an *instrumentum regni* – forgetting that every feast day is always secretly connected to the complementary logic of sacrifice? Or is it more proper to say, as de Toqueville had already asserted, that the political revolution intrinsically assumed the aspect of a "religious revolution?"[8]

On this point, the interpretations diverge in opposite directions. Mathiez traced the idea of God in Robespierre back to that of a "social utility,"[9] without accepting the glaringly obvious fact that for Robespierre and Saint-Just, faith and politics, the spiritual dimension and the temporal one, were inseparable, just as their reference to God and the immorality of the soul was sincere and fervent. He did not realize that in abolishing the throne, the Jacobins had maintained the altar, decapitating only one of the two heads of theological-political despotism.

If Robespierre cannot be considered the astute *meneur de foules* who used the religious faith of the lower classes to consolidate the Revolution, neither is he the *mystique assassin* of whom Aulard spoke.[10] As Jaurès (and in Italy, Manzoni) had previously glimpsed, he possessed a deep religious sense of life that could not find complete satisfaction in the earthly, historical, and practical achievements – however grandiose – of the Revolution.[11]

His plan aimed at creating a religion without mysteries, without priests, without miracles, without the need and presence of the extra-ordinary, capable, above all, of reconciling men with the highest goals, showing them the injustice of the world in its current state. Atheism destroys this perspective, applying itself to sophistic reasonings. To oppose it, his effigy was solemnly burned during the feast of the Supreme Being, and from its ashes there then arose a figure, a symbol of philosophy that paid homage to the divinity and recognized its existence. In a curious but not

8 de Tocqueville, *AR* 618.

9 See A. Mathiez, *La Révolution et l'Église* (Paris, 1910), 70, and "Robespierre et le culte de l'Être suprême," in *Autour de Robespierre*, 93–128.

10 See A. Aulard, *Le Culte de la Raison et le culte de l'Être suprême.*

11 J. Jaurès, *Histoire socialiste de la Révolution française*, vol. 6, 43–5.

completely singular way, Joseph Maistre accuses the Incorruptible of collusion with Protestantism, as his religiosity is founded on the free examination of "individual reason" and reconciles faith and knowledge. This is why, for the admirer of the Calvinist Rousseau, "The Gospel taught by the Protestant church never frightened Robespierre."[12]

Jacobinism strove, however, to bring to fruition a more complex operation, to make the figure of the political revolutionary coincide with that of the religious reformer, according to the model traditionally offered by Moses. The aim is that of connecting external observance of the laws with their internal credibility and thereby develop a feeling of belonging to a Providentially ordered whole.

Robespierre felt the need to preserve and transplant into another area the sense of the sacred, to *replacer le sacré au cœur de la cité.*[13] He also felt the more incidental (but no less significant) need of calming the worry over the apparent absurdity of many events and the ubiquity of death in such tormented times. Christian hope, as theological virtue, splits in him, harmonically, into lay hope in the future society that will have to rise as a consequence of the Revolution and religious hope in the recompense owed to the virtuous and the good. Faith in the hereafter must not divert men from active attention to this life or dissuade them from working towards the betterment of life in this world. The messianic utopia rests on a plan that continues to draw strength from heaven but that does not repudiate earth or the fate of future generations. Now that history had ceased, in perspective, to be only the scenario for the humiliation and suffering for the many, now that the Supreme Being had finally pushed men to rebel, the Kingdom of God was truly present on earth, even if it would never be complete in this world. With the words of Thomas Münzer, the Jacobins felt they had arrived at a turning point in the age-old course of events: *Es ist Zeit,*[14] the time to radically change the face of history has arrived, is mature, at the cost of sacrificing, with opposing destinies, the wicked and the virtuous on the altar of the public good.

12 J. de Maistre, *Réflexions sur le Protestantisme,* in *Oeuvres complètes,* vol. 8, 87.

13 See J.P. Domecq, *Robespierre, dernier temps* (Paris, 1984), 200; and H. Guillemin, *Robespierre, politique et mystique,* 347 et seq. A similar formula, the *transfert de sacralité,* can also be found in M. Ozouf, *La fête révolutionnaire 1789–1799* (Paris, 1976).

14 See T. Münzer, "Briefwechsel," in *Schriften und Briefe* (Gütersloh, 1968), 381, and T. La Rocca, *Es ist Zeit: Apocalisse e storia: Studio su Thomas Münzer (1490–1525)* (Bologna, 1988), 17 et seq.

No *contemptus mundi* can be found among the greatest exponents of Jacobinism, even if there begins to be alive in them the awareness of an inevitable vocation for death, to which anyone who takes the Revolution seriously exposes himself. But the *meditatio mortis* of the wise man changes into real and imminent danger that no longer comes – as it did for Seneca – from a tyrannical emperor, but rather from friends or from yesterday's allies. The Revolution begins a potentially endless process of self-purgation by those who appear (sometimes to their own victims) like the waste that accumulates along the way that must be disposed of.

"The Memory of Our Life That Has Passed"

In their defence of the sacred, Robespierre, Saint-Just, and Couthon rejected the "De-Christianization of France"[15] and had the Convention approve, on 18 Floréal of Year II, an article by which "the French people recognize the existence of the Supreme Being and the immortality of the soul."[16] The state rejects its prerogative of *superiorem non recognoscens*: above its own existence, it now once again places metaphysical entities who protect existence and development.

The choice of the term "Supreme Being" must not raise thoughts of a deism of a Spinozan or Voltairian sort, accompanied by the rejection of or contempt for historical religions. Actually, it is a typical expression of

15 See M. Vovelle, *Religion et Révolution: La déchristianisation de l'an* II (Paris, 1976). For a synoptic vision of the change of the tables of the values introduced by de-Christianization, see 232–5. On the de-Christianization of Year II, see also the issue dedicated to that topic by the *Annales Historiques de la Révolution Française* 233 (July–September 1978); O. Hufton, "The Reconstruction of the Church," in *Beyond the Terror: Essays in French Regional and Social History*, ed. G. Lewis and C. Lucas (Cambridge, 1983); and S. Bianchi, "Les curés rouges dans la Révolution française," in *Annales Historiques de la Révolution Française* 57 (1985), 447–9. Interesting as a document is F. Lebrun, *Dieu et Révolution: Les sermons d'un curé angevin avant et pendant la Révolution*, with a preface by J. Delumeau (Paris, 1988).

16 See the etching preserved in the Bibliothèque Nationale of Paris that bears, in block letters, the words *Le peuple français reconnaît l'Être suprême et l'immortalité de l'âme* and depicts a shining sun, a peasant sowing seeds, a beehive, some flowers, wheat, and a woman who is showing the words to a young boy. The Supreme Being, the Sun, enriches nature (archaically seen under the sign, it could be said, of Virgil's *Georgics*), that is perpetuated through the seed and spontaneous generation – this should be the traditional meaning of the presence of the bees, already in Virgil held to be born by the corruption of living bodies – and whose cult is passed down among men through education.

Rousseau[17] that Robespierre takes up and elaborates without implying a decreased admiration for Christianity. In fact, he considers the Gospel a "holy book" and "the son of Mary" a just and virtuous man because he had wanted to present himself to the world as a poor man, attacking the opulence of the rich and powerful (see *OC* v, 117 et seq.), declaring blessed, in the Sermon on the Mount, those who thirsted for justice and were persecuted because of this. Jesus's struggle had been that of bringing "the kingdom of God" to earth, to establish a republic of "pure hearts"[18] and to "inspire man to a religious respect for man."[19]

Hope for the next life is necessary for the achievement of justice in this world.

In the brief period of six months (from Brumaire to Germinal of Year II), however, there was triggered in France a violent campaign of de-Christianization. The churches changed into Temples of Truth or of Reason; the sacred furnishings and the silverware were sold; thousands of priests abandoned the tunic and often married, provoking *les larmes de Saint Pierre.*[20] According to the promoters of this campaign, there was thus finally given back to the Eternal the only non-superstitious cult worthy of Him, since only the heart of man became the altar, taking the place of the precious ornaments (whose sole function was that of elevating the pride of the priests and making an impression on the peoples' imagination in order to better subjugate them).

The events and indications of this process of de-Christianization are many: the revolutionary calendar, beyond replacing Christian historical-liturgical time with a cosmic-natural one, was introduced by some with the not-so-hidden intention of abolishing Sunday and getting rid of people's habit of going to mass.[21] Hébert, in the columns of the newspaper *Le Père*

---

17 In this, Robespierre faithfully follows Rousseau. See *CS* IV, 3: *L'existence de la divinité, puissante, intelligente, bienfaisante, prévoyante, et pourvoyante, la vie à venir, le bonheur des justes, le châtiment des méchants, la sainteté du contrat social, voilà les dogmes positifs.*

18 Robespierre, speech of 8 Thermidor, Year II, in *OC* X.

19 Robespierre, 18 Floreal, Year II, in *OC* X, 197, and see Guillemin, *Robespierre, politique et mystique*, 382.

20 See Vovelle, *Religion et Révolution: La déchristianisation de l'an* II, 19–144. Previously, the decree of 26 August 1792 had given resistant priests fifteen days to leave France. Forty thousand emigrated.

21 On the ideas of Romme, who made the biggest contribution to the birth of the revolutionary calendar, and on its meaning, see A. Galante Garrone, *Gilbert Romme: Story of a Revolutionary* (Turin, 1959), 401 et seq.; and B. Baczko, *Le calendrier républicain* (Paris, 1984).

Duchesne, derides how many still believed in the existence of the afterlife. In the provinces, the cross was defined as "a counter-revolutionary symbol."[22] The deputy Lequinio, addressing the people of Rochefort in the "Temple of Truth" (the former cathedral), after having declared that there existed no future and that the heavenly call of Christian paradise was just the seductive song of a deceitful siren, asserted that "nothing will remain of us except the divided molecules that formed us and the memory of our life that has passed."[23]

Only Robespierre rejected attacking the Catholic doctrine and cult decisively, and he was therefore accused by some adversaries of *caresser les préjugés du peuple.* He immediately replied that he did "not want to eliminate the kingdom of superstition in order to establish the kingdom of atheism"[24] – that is, to have egoism and immorality triumph in its place.

Like Marat[25] and unlike Helvétius or Cloots, he does not at all claim that the soul is a mirage as ridiculous as that "phantom called God." And moreover, unlike Collot d'Herbois and Fouché (a former priest who considered Christianity a servile religion, friend of despotism), he did not think that the Revolution marked, in this sense, the triumph of the enlightened. When, on 19 September 1793, Chaumette and Fouché had decreed at Nevers that there be placed, on the doors of the cemeteries of the department of Nièvre, the inscription *La mort est un sommeil éternel,* and Fouché proposed replacing the crosses on the tombs with the

22 See J. Gallerand, *Les cultes sous la Terreur en Loire-et-Cher* (Blois, 1928), 377 et seq.

23 See M. Vovelle, *La mentalité révolutionnaire: Sociétés et mentalités souls la Révolution française,* 220.

24 See F. Bluche, *Danton* (Paris, 1984), 404.

25 Previously, in 1772, Marat had defended, against the materialists, the duality of heart and body and the non-derivability of the passions (significantly, glory is noted) from the body, citing among other things the desire for death that every man gets, balanced only by love of self. See J.-P. Marat, *Essay on the Human Soul* (issued anonymously, London, 1772); French trans. *De l'homme, ou des principes et des lois de l'influence de l'âme sur le corps et du corps sur l'âme,* 3 vols. (Amsterdam, 1775–6). Marat would hold that this work had been boycotted by the *philosophes,* because it opposed the materialistic theses that denied the existence of the soul. See *La correspondence de Marat* (Paris, 1908), letter 22. For some theoretical aspects, see S. Moravia, *Scienza e filosofia in Francia (1780–1815)* (Florence, 1974), 152–4. On Marat's scientific knowledge, on his desperate efforts to achieve glory, on some acute scientific intuitions, and on his final resentment of cultural institutions, see G. Gaudenzi and R. Sartori, *Jean-Paul Marat: Scienziato e rivoluzionario,* particularly 33 et seq.

statue of sleep,[26] Robespierre reacted with his final, inspired speech to the Convention.

It was 8 Thermidor of Year II (26 July 1794), and he did not yet know that just two days separated him from crossing that threshold beyond which he would be able to investigate (or not) the possible existence of God and the immortality of the soul. Nor could he imagine that one week later, in a provincial village, thanks would be given to the Supreme Being – with a sort of Thermidorian *Te Deum* – for having saved France from this monster that had created it.

But here are his own words: "No, Chaumette, no Fouché, death is not an eternal sleep. Citizens, erase from the tombs that maxim, carved by sacrilegious hands, that casts a funereal veil on nature, that discourages oppressed innocence, and that insults death. Rather, carve there this one: 'Death is the beginning of immortality.'"[27] Irreligiousness is a false objective that dissipates the revolutionary energy of the people, as happened at the moment when (as he says in another speech, not given, against Fabre d'Eglantine) "a philosophy, venal and prostituted to tyranny, forgot thrones in order to overturn altars, placed religion in opposition to patriotism, put morality in contradiction with itself, confused the cause of the church with that of despotism, the Catholics with the conspirators, and wanted to force the people to see, in the Revolution, the triumph not of virtue, but of atheism, not the source of its happiness, but the destruction of all moral and religious ideals" (*OC* x, 333).

Raison publique cannot be founded on the egoism preached by the atheists. It needs a moral basis that distinguishes between the bad people and the good (see *OC* x, 456). They must be able to count on a fitting compensation for the injustice suffered and fought in the world, for misfortune and suffering (even Robespierre – with reasoning that is often found in the religious sphere, and so that everything might make complete sense – transforms a demand into a demonstration, an unsatisfied need into the necessity for its fulfilment). To acclimate the cult of the Supreme Being, therefore, he and his followers placed in operation one of the most incisive campaigns (or counter-campaigns) of political mobilization that history had ever known, actively supported in

26 It has been asked whether the responsibility for these acts really dates to Fouché and Chaumette or to the local Jacobins. See N. Bossut, "Aux origines de la déchristianisation dans la Nièvre: Fouché, Chaumette, ou les jacobins nivernais?" *Annales Historique de la Révolution Française* 284 (1986), 181–202.

27 Robespierre, Speech of 8 Thermidor, Year II, in *OC* x, 575.

this undertaking by "constitutional priests," worried about showing the reciprocal reconcilability of religion and revolution.[28]

The Wounds of Life

Promoting the political disenchantment of the monarchy, but restraining the cosmic-religious one, the Jacobins tried to prevent a hemorrhage of feeling from the body of events and of the world, in the same period when the principles of equality and of the impersonality of popular rule – making individuals interchangeable – risked overwhelming any hierarchy. The parallel fears of death and of the divinity – rejected by Spinoza and by the Lucretius whom Brotteaux des Islettes kept in his "puce-colored jacket pocket" – were now re-evaluated in the conviction that it was necessary to terrorize the bad so that the good and the innocent would be safe. The making sacred of death in public, an act of expiation owed to all citizens as perverse compensation for trampled and ignored virtue, also belongs to this same logic.

Despite the inversion of sign, the step from here to the exaltation of the executioner would not, historically, be very long. It would be completed by Joseph Maistre in pages that are famous, but often poorly understood, of the *Soirées de Saint-Pétersbourg*, when he would spin an elegy for that "abject being, capable of domestic feelings, instrument of expiation and divine justice."[29] The *exécuteur* returns once again to

28 See M. Vovelle, *La Révolution contre la Raison: De la Révolution à l'Être suprême* (Paris, 1988), 47 et seq., 130, 160 et seq.

29 See G. Lenotre, *La Guillotine et les exécuteurs des arrêts criminels pendant la Révolution* (Paris, 1920); J. Delarue, *Le métier de bourreau* (Paris, 1979), 19; D. Arrasse, *La guillotine et l'immaginaire de la Terreur*, 72, 149 et seq.; and C.-H. Sanson, *La Révolution française vue par son bourreau*, ed. M. Lebailly (Paris, 1988) (where Sanson, a cultured man in his own way, whose family had carried out the profession of execution for centuries, shows himself to be an acute observer of events and people, such as when he shows the nonchalance of Adrien Lamourette, who said in prison, "Faut-il s'étonner de mourir? La mort n'est qu'un accident de l'existence," or when he tells how the threat of ending up under the guillotine was directed towards him; see 128, 329 et seq.). On the executioner as creator of civilization (and indirectly, on the role of fear), see J. de Maistre, *Les soirées de Saint-Pétersbourg*, in *Oeuvres complètes*, vol. 4, 31–4. Regarding this passage, cf. S. Ruffino-E. Randone, "L'orrido fiore del bene," in *Arte pietà e morte nella confraternita della Misericordia a Torino* (Turin, 1978), 107–43, and M. Ravera, *Joseph de Maistre pensatore dell'origine*, 105 et seq. For the idea of "salvation through blood," the role of sacrifices and, more generally, for the intrinsic interest with which the new

carry out a "civilizing" function, guiding man towards earthly and otherworldly good.

The exponents of the Restoration now rejected with disdain the ideas put forth by Brotteaux des Islettes and by his beloved Latin poet – namely, that many vices, many "wounds of life" (from avarice to blind desire for honours) are fed, in no small part, precisely by the fear of death aroused by religions:

> haec vulnera vitae
> non minimam partem mortis formidine aluntur.[30]

With Robespierre, along with the return of fear, there was also a re-emergence of hope in a possible defeat of corruption and the consequent salvation of individuals and peoples. Precisely because they were associated with a sacred dimension, fear and hope assumed a new and strong political connotation: against the materialism and philosophy of many Enlightenment figures, they became a supplementary guarantee of the sensible nature of this world and of the high destination of rational beings in the universe. In the new theological-political Jacobin despotism, religion represented a shield not only against political chaos, but against the recurring suspicion that the entire universe could be ruled by an absurd violence.

The Jacobins reintroduced those heavenly rewards and punishments that Spinoza had condemned but that Voltaire himself had defended as a restraint on the delights and consolation of virtue. However, virtue not being the actual result of happiness and the increase in individuals' power of existing, but rather the premise of a future happiness to which, in a Spinozan sense, *tristitia* for present sacrifices is connected, it also needs, like religion, to appeal to fear and to hope, to establish a new Trinitarian cult in which fear, hope, and reason are sublimated in an *amor Dei* that is not just intellectual.

To institute new, unifying values capable of opposing the feared disintegration of social ties,[31] the men of the Terror needed to rest politics

---

themes of the Revolution were reprised, deformed, and transliterated according to old canons, see J. de Maistre, *Les soirées de Saint-Pétersbourg*, vol. 5, 126, and *Éclaircissements sur les Sacrifices*, in *Œuvres complètes*, vol. 5, 360.

30 Lucretius, *De rer. nat.* III, 63–4.

31 In Paretian terms, they used to this end old "remnants" of communitarian feelings and values (expression of attitudes and interests that cannot be rationalized further, largely drawn from the Greek and Roman world) and mixed them with the new.

on a new national theocracy. The laws, the holidays, and the revolutionary cults elicited new forms of donation and organization of meaning, forcefully offering again the question – previously raised by Machiavelli in his *Discourses* – of whether the earthly, "lay," disenchanted dimension of political life is really sufficient to preserve, by itself, the life of states.

Creative Fantasies

Beyond aiming at the communitarian and patriotic value of the holidays and making up the first official civic religion in Europe after the triumph of Christianity, the religiosity promoted by the Jacobins made use of the cult of Reason or of the Supreme Being (which is also the celebration of the victory of men over *natura lapsa* and the promise of their resurrection and redemption) to unite myth and reason – that is, to give strength and imaginative visibility to the new principles.

Arguing in a way that was counterfactual for him, Robespierre, after having declared that there did not exist any advantage in persuading man *qu'une force aveugle présede à ses destinées et frappe au hasard le crime et la vertu,* comes to state that if even the ideas of God and the immortality of the soul were not necessarily true, they would nonetheless be useful as a product of an *instinct sacré* that "compensates for the insufficiency of human authority." It is necessary to beware of undermining this *soutien pour la vertu* that supports the weak temper of men: "How could these ideas not be true? At least, I cannot imagine how nature could have suggested to man fictions more useful than any reality. And if the existence of God, if the immortality of the soul were only dreams, they would still be the most beautiful concepts of the human mind."[32]

Note that these creative fantasies are "more useful than any reality." Religion and myth – although they may not reduce themselves to a political tool – consolidate revolutionary authority and help general will and virtue to triumph. And this happens both for their intrinsic content of truth (because they inscribe the Revolution in a cosmic context of salvation) and as fantasies that (unlike the superstitions of despotism) extol reason instead of depressing it. In one sense, to paraphrase Dostoevsky:

That is, they made use of a particular "instinct of combinations" typical of revolutionary thought, they applied it to these arational elements, and they then made it valid against the conservative propensity to maintain the "permanence of the aggregates," of the previous conglomerations of betrayed ideas and passions.

32 Robespierre, 18 Floreal, Year II, in *OC* X, 452.

if there were no God and the soul did not enjoy immortality, everything would be lawful for the egoists and the enemies of the Revolution. Each person would feel authorized to claim the subjective right of behaving like characters in the novels of the Marquis de Sade. Moreover, an immediate danger would be created for institutions, since atheism, according to Robespierre, is an integral part of "a system of conspiracy against the republic."[33]

Reason is no longer presented as a faculty neatly opposed to this sacred instinct or to fantasy. From this perspective, even the myths and holidays become "symbols of reason." Placing itself in the service of reason, the imagination no longer risks being considered an inferior faculty of which knowledge and *raison d'état* would have to be ashamed to the point of expelling it from their control or secretly making use of it. Myth, the fruit of the "creative fantasies" (allowed by Robespierre, however, only in a hypothetical way), becomes the forerunner of reason, and this in turn becomes interpretation of the myth, the *fabula docet* of the story of the heart. In political terms, this means erecting a bridge between the masses, governed by myth and by "virtuous" passions, and the *élites*, largely guided by reason (that, in itself, is exposed to sophisms and corrects itself precisely by leaning on these "creative fantasies").

An indivisible binomial is formed: without Maximilien's far-seeing blue eye, the masses are a force that is just, but blind, while the leaders of the Revolution – without the energy supplied by the masses and without their infallible instinct – are impotent and corruptible.

Robespierre does not contest the philosophers' having different opinions on religion and perhaps not even being atheists. In this sense, Michelet is right only in part when he speaks of the "papacy" of Robespierre, because his was more a moral-religious teaching, aimed at establishing the new laws of the republic.[34] The Incorruptible thought and acted by placing himself in the extremely political perspective of the Rousseauian "legislator," the demiurge who orders political chaos and who knows that he is unable to "nationalize atheism," because such a decision, raising egoism to a rule of life, would lead every society to certain ruin. Consequently, "in the eyes of the legislator, everything that is useful to the world, and good in practice, is the truth."[35] That it may be good in practice does

33 Ibid.
34 See J. Michelet, *Histoire de la Révolution française*, vol. 2, 819–29.
35 Ibid.

not mean that it is not true in itself, valid for reason as well as for the heart (Robespierre was not a pragmatist in the manner of James). This is why, he adds, preaching atheism is a way to fight philosophy and absolve superstition. This does not take away, however, that the Revolution may need myth as its locomotive energy, as the wind that fills "the sails of reason" and permits politicians to direct its course.

Robespierre cannot be judged as a simple irrational bigot, limiting himself to emphasizing his "passion for conformity," typical of a man raised and spoiled by the small attentions of the women of the family, even considering him a hypocrite, a *libertin par imagination*,[36] a despot surrounded by a potential harem of fanatics in perpetual adoration of his figure. Moreover, he is neither an enemy of the enlightened as such, a fanatic of the sentimental immediatism attributed to Rousseau, nor just a petty bureaucrat of the Revolution, proud and vain. And this is not even from a sociological point of view, as an individual who would reflect the mentality and traditional values of the *petit bourgeoisie* or the popular classes which – apparently – did not at all share positions that could be assimilated to those of the Incorruptible.[37]

Despite some appearances and a strong historiographic tradition that depicts him with these traits, Robespierre was, in reality, a follower of

---

36 See F. Furet, *Penser la Révolution française,* 70, and C. Robespierre, *Mémoires de Charlotte Robespierre sur ses deux frères,* 85: "My aunts and I spoiled him with lots of the small attentions of which only women are capable." This statement, however, cannot be extrapolated from a context in which – even for reasons of familial *pietas* – there are emphasized, instead, Maximilien's desire for justice and his dedication to his relatives (having become, morally, "head of the family" after the early death of both his parents, guiding and loving Augustin and Charlotte). He distanced himself from Arras at the age of eleven to study in Paris, and after graduating in law and choosing the profession of lawyer, he constantly defended the poor (just like Couthon). Further, he was opposed to the "fervid imagination" and the "fiery temperament" of Marat, who had complained about his excessive indulgence. He had once said to Marat: "In making heads fall, you compromise the Revolution, you make it detestable. The scaffold is always fatal; it must be used rarely and only in serious cases in which the country is heading toward catastrophe" (ibid.). In an anonymous pamphlet (attributed to J.-J. Dussaulx, *Portrait exécrable du traître Robespierre* [1794] (Paris, n.d.)), this portrait is offered instead: "Low and vindictive, chaste by temperament, and libertine by imagination, the look of women was not the last of the charms of his supreme power: he placed *cocquetterie* in his ambition ... In particular, he exercised his prestige over tender imaginations."

37 As A. Soboul asserts in "Jean-Jacques Rousseau et le jacobinisme," *Studi Storici* 4 (1963), 3–22 et seq.

the Enlightenment and a fervid supporter of the progresses of reason. But he sees the Enlightenment movement – particularly in the speech of 18 Floréal of Year II – through a deep fracture, divided into two divergent and antithetical pieces. On one side, there were the "encyclopedists" (a group made up of some estimable persons and many "charlatans") and, on the other, the one and true *philosophe* of the Enlightenment, Rousseau.[38] The confraternity of encyclopedists, "in political matters, remained above the rights of the people. In moral matters, it went far beyond the destruction of religious prejudices ... This sect spread with much zeal the opinion of materialism that prevailed among the greats and among the beautiful spirits. This is largely due to that species of practical philosophy that, reducing egoism to a system, sees human society as a war of trickery, success as regulation of the just and the unjust, probity as an affair of taste or of decency, the world as the patrimony of clever scoundrels"[39] If in Robespierre – as in Marat or in Saint-Just, all of them men endowed with intellectual ambitions – there is not lacking a sort of Nietzschian *ressentiment* against the academies and *la république des lettres*, there is nonetheless also present, perhaps for the first time, an explicit condemnation of the *trahison des clercs*, of intellectuals' lack of interest in, and hostility towards, defence and practical promotion of the values they themselves had contributed to spreading.[40] That is, the accused were precisely those who had normally been attacked by opponents of the Revolution for having fomented and promoted it. According to Robespierre, they did not show themselves to be up to the situation and, with their hypocrisies, they remained behind compared to

38 See M. Robespierre, *OC* X, 454 et seq. and *OC* IV, 68. Anna Maria Battista had the merit of reconsidering a problem that had seemed settled, that of the relationship between the Jacobins and Rousseau, and of highlighting the fracture identified by Robespierre in the Enlightenment's internal development (see A.M. Battista, "Il 'Rousseau' dei giacobini," in Battista et al., *Il "Rousseau" dei giacobini* [Urbino, 1988], 29–76). For other aspects of the problem, see F.A. Kafker, "Les Encyclopédistes et la Terreur," in *Revue d'histoire moderne et contemporaine* 14 (1967), 284–95; R. Barny, *Jean-Jacques Rousseau dans la Révolution française, 1787–91: Contribution à l'analyse de l'idéologie révolutionnaire bourgeoise* (Paris, 1977); and the collection of rare texts on Rousseau edited by Barny: *Jean-Jacques Rousseau dans la Révolution française (1789–1801)* (Paris, 1977).

39 Robespierre, 18 Floreal, Year II, in *OC* X.

40 On the moderatism of the Enlightenment *salons* and on the discontinuity that thus existed between philosophical radicalism and political commitment, see D. Roche, *Les Républicains des Lettres: Gens de culture et Lumières au* XVIIIe *siècle* (Paris, 1988).

common people guided by virtue and love for country. It is true that they did not enjoy enough "light" to be enlightened on the path to knowledge (as the greatest representatives of this sect thought that the task of educating men was not up to them, but to their apostles). As compensation, however, the last were, evangelically, the first. Further, the success of preserving their own faith intact was up to them, since the impious opinions of the encyclopedists had not touched it.

D'Holbach, however, so hated by Robespierre, is categorical in his proposal to spread atheism only among the "great and beautiful spirits" – excluding the masses, which would not have understood it: "Atheism, as well as philosophy and all profound and abstract sciences, then, is not calculated for the uninformed, neither is it suitable for the majority of mankind."[41] He would probably even have agreed with Robespierre in restraining or blocking propaganda for it at the popular level (certainly not by drastic means). This does not, however, prevent him from observing that it may not be true that religion always represents a support for morals and politics. In fact, it contains a permanent threat to social order and to virtue: "Religion itself destroys the effect of those terrors. The remission of sin emboldens the wicked man to his last moment."[42]

D'Holbach states further that such elite philosophical doctrines are not at all harmful to society: "The peaceable Epicurus never disturbed Greece; the poem of Lucretius caused no civil wars in Rome; Bodin was not the author of the league; the writings of Spinoza have not excited the same troubles in Holland as the disputes of Gomar and d'Arminius. Hobbes did not cause blood to flow in England, although, in his time, religious fanaticism made a king perish on the scaffold."[43] D'Holbach agrees with the ancient theory of Xenophanes in which men shape the gods in their image and likeness (and they depict them as such with red hair, like the Thracians, or with a snub nose, like the Ethiopians), and he would certainly have approved of Montaigne's assertion that "Man is certainly stark mad; he cannot make a flea, and yet he will be making gods by dozens."[44]

Although not distinguishing between common people and "great and beautiful spirits," Robespierre does not deny anyone the right to state

41 D'Holbach, *The System of Nature*, 324.

42 Ibid., 348.

43 Ibid., 311.

44 Montaigne, "Apology for Raimond de Sebonde," *ES* II, XIII, 511 (*ESe* II, XII, 229).

their own philosophical theories. What matters to him is that atheism not be transformed into a principle of political morals, into anti-religion of the state, and that philosophers not basely place their wisdom in the service of the mighty, degrading themselves to the position of postulants lining up in the antechambers of the powerful.

The Other Half of the Globe

In any case, all the ideas of the French Revolution cannot be reduced to myth, transforming them into chapters of that great *meta-récits* of emancipation and liberation of man from the chains of slavery of which Lyotard spoke – that is, into a fable for adults that tells of the unavoidable triumph of good over evil, of the oppressed over the oppressors, of the virtuous over the corrupt.[45]

The French Revolution certainly created a new form of civil religion and political mythology, one that also had the task of hiding the paradoxes caused by the new course of events. But it did not exclusively generate some myths that were noble in their intentions and disastrous in their results. It set forth a number of real problems, in theory and in politics, that largely still remain to be sorted out.

For example, it identified the question of a "crippled" development of rationality, an incomplete Enlightenment. Although casting light on other areas of knowledge, this leaves politics and ethics completely in the dark, implicitly evoking the surrogate of the myth – the integrator of the meaning of things, the hypothesis raised to certainty – about their still-invisible side: "Man's reason still resembles the globe that he inhabits: half is immersed in darkness, while the other is illuminated. The people of Europe made amazing progress in what is called the arts and sciences, and they seem ignorant of the first notions of public morals."[46] In this respect, Robespierre does not accept Voltaire's resignation, his half-enlightenment. To Voltaire's fable of Reason and Truth (where they once again take refuge in the well from which they had emerged, tricked

45 It is a case of foundation myths of the legislator, in which *auctoritas* is placed as the basis of *veritas*, in the same way power is placed in Foucault. Not every story is, however, self-legitimizing because, for example, the whole history of philosophy, from Socrates to Kant and beyond, testifies to the constant effort of philosophy to place itself under discussion to found its own statements on critical bases.

46 Robespierre, 18 Floreal, Year II, in *OC* x, 444.

by false hopes),[47] he could have opposed these same two figures while they continued to fight intrepidly in the sun to assert themselves against the evils of the worlds and despots partially responsible for it. The price paid by Robespierre to modify Voltaire's scepticism about the possibility of changing the world, however, is that of intolerance, of the institution of a public monopoly of reason and truth.

Jacobin reason not only emerged from the "well" but decisively spilled into reality, rejecting the very idea of hiding. In fact, it became so visible and omnipresent as to penetrate institutions and consciences to fulfil the Promethean plan of emancipation that had previously led human societies to make a bid for heaven and to control the power of lightning through science[48] but had not yet been able to extend itself to political and social relationships: "Half of the revolution of the world has already been completed; the other half must be completed."[49] Reason and religion, together, must contribute to illuminating the hemisphere, still dark for many, of civil virtue and good, transforming the Revolution into theophany, into the appearance of a God who finally promises to alleviate the suffering of men, even on earth.

So that the Enlightenment would not remain half-completed, Robespierre asserts the necessity of exploring the human "heart of darkness," to uncover and illuminate it through the light that comes from the universal.[50] This leads him to a type of supremacy of practical reason that does not exclude – but rather demands – rigorous use of theoretical and scientific reason, with the aim of helping the other, un-enlightened part

47 The fable (noted in M. Vovelle, *La Révolution contre la Raison*, 7–8) shows Reason and Virtue, after having always lived hidden in a well, deciding finally to emerge, attracted by the spectacle of Europe's renewal thanks to Enlightenment principles. But then, seeing that massacres and the wickedness of man had not at all ceased, they return to their hiding places, disappointed.

48 One of the most brilliant cases won by the young lawyer Robespierre at Arras, in 1783, had as its object precisely the claim of the utility of lightning rods, which were spreading – not without objections – through the 1780s. See H. Meidinger, *Geschichte des Blitzableiters* (Karlsruhe, 1888), 25 et seq.

49 Robespierre, 18 Floreal, Year II, in *OC* X.

50 Even for Kant, the French Revolution had the great merit of showing, through signs that were memorable, demonstrative, and prognostic (that is, with respect to the past that is not forgotten, the present currently underway, and the expectations for the future), that progress of the human race is possible, that the passage to a better age of men is not blocked, that the other half of the globe is not destined to remain forever in darkness.

of the intellectual and moral globe to emerge progressively from obscurity and show its hidden face.

These are, in fact, the premises of the vast ethical-political program announced at the Convention: "We want to substitute … principles for practices, duties for good manners, the dominion of reason for the tyranny of fashion."[51] – that is, to establish universal and public norms in the place of the seeming spontaneity of custom and the unquestionable authority of tradition. Natural right had begun to codify such principles in written, juridical formulas. As universals, they eradicate abuses, privileges, and discrimination, acclimating equality and virtue. Robespierre realized that their hold is intrinsically weak, that they require both initial violence (or heroic virtue) to transplant and consolidate them, and time to take possession of them, to "somatize" them. After being broken away from old habits contaminated by despotism (thanks to the principles), the citizen would eventually be able to return to the respect of customs as a habit, to a squared automatism or, better still, to a reconstructed spontaneity – that is, to an spontaneity of conduct mediated by the absorption and metabolism within its rational laws: "The masterpiece of society would be creating in him [the citizen] a quick instinct for moral things that, without the slow help of reason, would lead him to do the good and avoid the bad, since the individual reason of each man led astray by his passions, is often just a sophist arguing his case."[52]

The Voice of Isis

However much the general will might at first manifest itself through universal principles, it survives only if it succeeds in expressing itself in customs, institutions, and juridical systems. The process of developing norms is thus presented in a backwards way compared to previous methods. It no longer passes from a body of values that are shared – albeit in an unthinking way – to their conscious codification. On the contrary, it starts from criteria that are pre-established rationally and proceeds to their (planned and artificial) grafting onto the habits, sentiments, and passions of the people.

On one hand, reason strives to become fixed in habit, to establish a "revolutionary tradition," theoretically capable of renewing itself. On

51 Robespierre, 18 Pluviôse, Year II, in *OC* X, 352.
52 Robespierre, 18 Floreal, Year II, in *OC* X, 452.

the other, since revolution cannot appeal to the recent past that it contributed to erasing, it is paradoxically forced to extend its own roots into the future in search of nourishment and legitimization. Indicating goals to reach, formulating predictions, and raising hopes, it secularizes the Pascalian *pari*, ultimately raising its level of uncertainty and risk. If, in fact, its promises are not fulfilled in socially acceptable time, the responsibilities for failure will not be able to be unloaded endlessly on plots of internal and external enemies or on the "harsh replies of history." The revolution itself will sooner or later have to recognize that it triggered, from the beginning, an internal mechanism of self-destruction. Given the conditions, however, there remains just one alternative, one that itself includes – even if positively – a clause of self-dissolution. On the basis of this latter, as soon as the *régénération* has run its course and the proper moral "instinct" has replaced the current corrupt customs, the revolution will solemnly abdicate its prerogatives and will declare finished the temporary period of joint cooperation of reason and terror.[53]

Revolutionary education was offered to reform both reason and sentiment, to connect universalism and the community, rules and the impulses of the heart, the temporarily unavoidable laws of politics and the promotion of lasting ties of solidarity. In diluting across the generations the glacial rigidity of principles, leaving them time and suitable paths to channel themselves into an "instinct" that had become vigorous and clear, Jacobin thought tried to avoid early the "abstractly rationalistic conception of rationality" for which it would be blamed.

After all, solving this contradiction (on the basis of which individuals came to follow their own autonomy through largely heteronymous means) was not something for the short term. Each person would simultaneously remain protagonist and antagonist of himself. For an indefinite period, "that which produces the common good" would remain "terrible," in the sense of Saint-Just. However, at the moment when worry about the general interest is imposed on consciences, even virtue would cease to be too demanding. It would stop configuring itself as a series of isolated acts that require forms of heroism and unilateral sacrifice, and it

53 This does not mean, however, that the Jacobins aimed at a sort of "mimetic sovereignty" in which the person who commands is forced, in a society of equals, to validate his own behaviour to the average level of the prevailing morality among the citizens, imitating their ideas, tastes, and even the most tolerable and widespread defects, to present himself as one of them.

would better respect the natural desire for self-preservation and development of individuals' "power of existing."

Once this goal was reached, the despotism of liberty, with its connected fear of death, would finally be extinguished. The Revolution would then be presented as a painful but indispensable rite of passage to a better age of the human race. From the perspective of Rousseau and of Kant, it would appear as a severe collective pedagogy oriented towards the abandonment, at first painful, of the state of minority to which men – satisfied with collateral benefits – usually become attached. At least implicitly, even the Jacobins attributed to moral law and to reason the nature of "Isis." That is, they invested it with the character of sacredness and "respect" (*Achtung*) that, according to Kant, is reserved for a divinity whose face must always remain partially hidden, removed from the irreverently inquiring and direct gaze of those who do not recognize its majesty: "The veiled goddess before whom we of both parties bend our knees is the moral law in us, in its inviolable majesty. We do indeed perceive her voice and also understand very well her command. But when we are listening, we are in doubt whether it comes from man, from the perfected power of his own reason, or whether it comes from an other, whose essence is unknown to us and speaks to man through this, his own reason."[54] Moral law constitutes a bridge between the divine and the human. In fact, one could assert with similar validity that it is – at the same time – "in us" and "above us" (or at least, that its nature leaves us a healthy uncertainty about its own provenance).

Yet for Kant, as for the Jacobins, fear and trembling are justified even before the sublime majesty of reason, before that which is so elevated in man that it leads him to the unknown limit of his powers. If this reverence were lacking, the worst appetites and desires would prevail, introducing anarchy: "Now, every human being finds in reason the idea of duty, and trembles as he listens to its adamant voice when inclinations, which try to make him deaf and disobedient to this voice, arise within him."[55]

54 Kant, "Von einem neuerdings erhobenen vornehmen Ton der Philosophie," in *Gesammelte Schriften*, vol. 8, 405; Engl. trans. "On a Newly Arisen Superior Tone in Philosophy," in *Raising the Tone of Philosophy: Late Essays by Immanuel Kant, Transformative Critique by Jacques Derrida*, ed. and trans. P. Fenves (Baltimore, 1993), 71.

55 Ibid., 402; Engl. trans., 68. The "living eye" of the divinity continues to keep watch over Jacobin reason, weakening the attempts of modern political philosophy (from Machiavelli to Hobbes and Spinoza) to deduce sovereignty only from human origins.

Fear, however, does not exclude hope. It provides to will the supplementary energy to better concentrate itself on the achievement of its own ends. It is the premise of liberty, understood as testing of the new, the search for an "absolute future." Hope is not reduced, therefore, to simple consolation, to a surrogate of vain or unfulfilled promises, to a "bread of the poor." Even if it may seem today to have lost part of its meaning and its *pathos*,[56] it historically carried out both an essential role of support of revolutionary planning, and the function of excitement or amazement that underestimated the obstacles that every plan meets because of complexity and the relative unpredictability of events.

Only after the collective release from the "chains of slavery" – imposed on each person both by others and by one's own passions – will oppression endured and voluntarily tolerated appear inconceivable. The reversal of the viewpoint employed by Rousseau in the *Social Contract*, where he rejects the idea of a natural inequality among men in which some are destined to command and others to obey, would become almost obvious. Rousseau says that Aristotle was correct; he was wrong only in mistaking a factual situation for an immutable condition: "Aristotle was right, but he mistook the effect for the cause. Every man born in slavery is born because of slavery; nothing is more certain. Slaves lose everything in their chains, even the desire to escape them. They love their servitude like the companions of Ulysses loved their animalization. Therefore, if there are some slaves by nature, it is because there had been slaves against nature. Strength made the first slaves; their cowardice perpetuated them."[57]

The means of reversing oppression and weaning juvenile humanity from its inclination to servitude, indispensable up to this point, would no longer be necessary. The monstrous union of liberty and despotism, virtue and terror, reason and violence, happiness and death would, prospectively, be able to be dissolved. In fact, it would be time itself, the acceleration of the historical movement imprinted by the Revolution, that illuminates the other half of the moral world, that completes the half-enlightenment at which the representatives of the "sect" of encyclopedists had stopped. In fact, future history would split the compounds by force, dividing the conceptual and political "centaurs" who combined, in one body, despotism and liberty, virtue and sacrifice, hate and brotherhood, fear and hope. In both individual and collective life, the human

56 For some more specific considerations about its current state, see R. Bodei, "La speranza dopo il crollo delle speranze," *Il Mulino* 40, no. 1 (1991), 5–13.

57 Rousseau, *CS* I, II.

side could thus separate itself from the feral side. Violence, rigidity of reason and will, obsession with death, and cults of regeneration would seem like levers to raise human nature from the humiliation suffered in history, to re-establish, at a higher level, the interrupted relationships between "reason" (which had become sophistry) and the "heart" (degraded into an inarticulate or mute sentiment).

At the time, it was held that it was necessary to be cruel so that those who followed would be happy. The Revolution removed the causes that made men wicked and corrupt, to this end using, for the last time, the means of the oppressors. Only at this price would reason be able to put down its armour, breaking itself away from fear and hope, and understanding how both egoism and sacrifice of self are complementary attitudes that can be abolished together, as sides of the same socially conditioned attitude.

The Jacobin Revolution – examined here in its "grammar" – leaves as a legacy to philosophical theory and subsequent political practice a crucial dilemma. Even if declared temporary, does not the use of terror, tyranny, and violent passions, instead of leading to liberty and equality, risk, by its "abstractness," triggering counterproductive effects, achieving the opposite of what it proposed? But conversely, by presenting the revolutionaries as inexperienced sorcerer's apprentices, incapable of keeping under control the destructive forces they evoked, do we not incur the opposite risk, of pre-constructing a convenient alibi for the benefit of inaction or the risk of a lazy notion of social metabolism?

It would be necessary to have the strength to direct one's gaze, theoretically and historically, towards these idols (reason, terror, and morals) whose image it would not be lawful or wise to gaze at directly. Perhaps Gorgon and Isis would then reveal a common element, a blinding opacity to which it would be impossible to become accustomed or to "mithridatize." Perhaps the gaze directed downward, "stirring the Acheron," and that upward, partially raising the veil of a glorious mystery, would show a secret complicity.

Without forgetting the tragic advancement achieved by the world and the consciousness of billions of people even through such traumatic events, this will to understand could contribute, on the one hand, to limiting the residual damage caused by the persistence of the conglomeration of reason-fear-hope in institutions and in mentality. On the other, it could contribute to avoiding any plan of wide-ranging change being condemned in advance as a forerunner of perverse effects, almost as if the latter constituted a fatal result of the Promethean arrogance of the human race. So that the problems are not removed and forgotten with a bad conscience, it is necessary to better practise intellectual courage, ignoring Kant's advice (completely sensible in other circumstances) regarding the "Isis" of reason and moral law or the advice of Dante's Virgil towards the Gorgon:

> Volgiti 'n dietro e tien lo viso chiuso;
> ché se 'l Gorgon si mostra e tu 'l vedessi,
> nulla sarebbe del tornar mai suso.[58]

Ruminating about History

Untying the knots that bind reason to the passions, and liberty to terror, also means not yielding today to the desire to imitate the symmetrically antagonistic solutions developed initially by the French revolutionaries and by Burke. Modern democracy is born from the encounter, still *in itinere*, of a radical Jacobin tradition with a grassroots and centralist stamp, and a liberal-conservative tradition of fence-sitting tied to hyper-realistic criteria of concreteness. The first, overwhelmed by Thermidor or by the Napoleonic empire, did not leave merely ashes, however, but the "fire" of the ideas in the minds of men and drifting sparks of hope in their expectations. The second, at the time victorious, produced a "praise of slowness" of empirics and history.

Since Burke's *Reflections on the French Revolution*, a defamatory accusation of "abstractness" has weighed on the Jacobins, an abstractness synonymous with cold rationality, lacking passions, incapable of getting a grip on reality, becoming more merciless and inhumane the more the world resisted its rough and inadequate intervention. Guided by an ethics of intention and a fanatically inflexible will, the revolutionaries expected to renew society and accelerate the dynamics of events, without realizing that their ideas and "immortal principles" rested on a static concept of "human nature," invariable in time and space (on a "lost paradigm," in Edgar Morin's expression.)[59]

---

58 Dante, *Inferno* 9:55–7. "Turn your back and keep your eyes shut,/for if the Gorgon head appears and should you see it,/all chance for your return above is lost" (trans. R. Hollander and J. Hollander [New York, 2000]).

59 Taine developed one of the harshest and most cutting formulations of this polemical argument, which has become a commonplace: "There is nothing more dangerous than a general idea in narrow and empty minds. Since they are empty, it [the idea] does not encounter any knowledge that presents itself as an obstacle; since they are

The opposition to the "abstractions," having interpreted these intellectualistic and *a priori* visions of the processes of transformation, had its positive side in the creation and development of a new concept of history, of that "historicism" of which Burke offered the first, model version.[60] In this case, the term must be understood as synonymous with increased attention not only to the perverse effects but to the barriers, the local inequalities, the stickiness, and the tortuousness of historical journeys.

Burke does not simply reject reason in favour of illusions. Rather, he tends to consider it an internal requirement of the course of history, making it integral with the slow maturation of customs and interweaving it with the idea of an irremovable and fruitful complexity (see *RRF* 72). Disturbing such a slow rhythm of growth, breaking its temporal continuity, erasing the memory of the path, cutting the strings of tradition, modifying the still-precarious equilibriums of the existing state of things in an irreversible and irreparable way, was the equivalent of committing a crime for which there existed no adequate penalty. Fortunately, this plan appeared destined to fail. If, in fact, the past were truly forgotten and "no one generation could link with the other,"[61] men would advance gropingly, as if they were blind.

For Burke, however, recovering memory and tradition means preventing its direct impact on all the expectations and hopes for public happiness that – having arisen in the past – were projected onto a future radically different from the present. With this, the cult of history and tradition aimed at transforming itself into an antidote to the Revolution, classically defined as *rerum novarum cupiditas*, a permanent threat to the duration of any society: "A spirit of innovation is generally the result of a selfish temper and confined views. People will not look forward to posterity, who never look backward to their ancestors."[62]

---

narrow; it does not delay in occupying them completely. From that moment, they no longer belong to themselves, they are controlled by it. It acts in them, and through them. Man is possessed, in the proper sense of the term. Something that is not him, a monstrous parasite, a strange and disproportionate thought, lives within him, develops there, and generates the evil will with which he is full" (*GR* 47–8).

60 Among the few studies on Burke's historicism are the chapter in the classic book by F. Meinecke ("Die Entstehung des Historismus," in *Werke*, vol. 3 [Munich, 1959]) and W. Rodney Kilcup, "Burke's Historicism," *Journal of Modern History* 59 (1977), 394–410.

61 *RRF* 112.

62 Ibid., 39.

If, against the break with the past perpetrated by the revolutionaries, one claims historical continuity, then conversely, against the reason of natural law, the need is stressed for humanity's clean break from the natural dimension. In particular, contrary to Rousseau, it is not true that man emerges good from the hands of the Creator and that civilization then corrupts him. Outside civil life, he is a "naked and trembling" being who needs illusions in order to survive. With the age of Enlightenment closed, the logic of creative fantasy once again replaced that of reason. It was no longer a case – as in Robespierre – of promoting myths of reason, but of regressing to myths of the imagination. These were indispensable for abandoning men who "travel in the obscure walk of laborious life" to their immutable "destiny," without deluding them with vain promises of happiness and universal equality.[63] And although Burke may have been convinced that "in England we have not yet been completely embowelled of ... those inbred sentiments [of] which we are the faithful guardians ... in order that we may be filled, like stuffed birds in a museum, with chaff and rags, and paltry blurred shreds of paper about the rights of man,"[64] it was implicitly a case by then, even for him, of an artificially manipulated imagination, programmed to fabricate (i.e., to reproduce sequentially) sentiments and emotions. This raises the suspicion that he may have been speaking all the more of spontaneity and sense of history, the more he feared that they were disappearing (something similar seems to happen to the Jacobins in their insistence on "virtue").

Nothing, however, could better illustrate Burke's idea of the calm, long-lived, laconic, and "bovine" robustness of traditions and feelings of the English than this idyllic image – worthy of a painting by Constable – used for the purpose of making stand out, by contrast, the violent, fleeting, noisy, and bothersome restlessness of the talking crickets of the French Revolution: "Because half a dozen grasshoppers under a fern make the field ring with their importunate chink, whilst thousands of great cattle, reposed beneath the shadow of the British oak, chew the cud and are silent, pray do not imagine that those who make the noise

---

63 Ibid., 43. This is language that would be reprised by the Thermidorians, at the moment when they promised to place an end to the fear and violence of the sans-culottes. This was thus expressed, in fact, on the first of Prairial in Year III by a judge in Dieppe regarding men of low extraction who had assumed the role of protagonists during the Terror: "Oppression and tyranny had pulled them from their social nothingness. Justice and humanity had plunged them back, probably forever" (see R. Cobb, *The Police and the People: French Popular Protest 1789–1820* [Oxford, 1970], 173).

64 Ibid., 101.

are the only inhabitants of the field; that of course, they are many in number; or that, after all, they are other than the little, shriveled, meagre, hopping, though loud and troublesome insects of the hour."[65] The silent rumination of history and customs creates the "influential metaphysics" on which the principal convictions of conservative historicism are founded. History identifies rhythms that cannot be forced with impunity. Liberty, not meted out over time and ignorant of its conditionings, is as explosive as the power of "wild gas … plainly broke loose."[66]

A Chiasmus

While Burke is for maintaining faiths and ideas considered as partially random conglomerations or as alluvial lands resulting from accumulated deposits and made fertile over time, the Jacobins showed themselves, instead, to be clearly on the side of the disaggregation and deep excavation of these historical-geological formations, in order to examine their components and create structures of meaning and power less accidental and less stratified in hierarchical forms. For this reason, they wanted to delegitimize and abolish privileges derived from tradition and history, replacing will and discrimination with reason and equity.

Why should they, after all, consider history and tradition as a metric of judgment, when the two always meant oppression and slavery for most men? Is not Jacobin "abstractness" – its virtual rejection of history – perhaps the clearest manifestation of the will not to be discouraged or intimidated by the accumulation of debris that needs to be removed or by the number of bonds to be broken in order to introduce the order and consistency of reason? Precisely because the distance between what we are and what we could be appears enormous, it is necessary to rush to fill the gap between the too-solid concreteness attributed to the existing state and the possibility of the gradual maturation of the abstractly possible, making the seeds of universal principles – scattered and suffocated up to this point – bear fruit. Rejecting the fetishism of the real and the

65 Ibid., 100.

66 Ibid., 9. Burke reprises this image from great countryman Jonathan Swift, who, in *A Tale of a Tub* (1704) alludes to liberty as a "wild gas" that "brookes loose" (see *Tale of a Tub*, ed. A.C. Guthkelch and D. Nicol Smith [Oxford, 1958], 215–16). On this and other metaphors by Burke, see P.E. Ray, "The Metaphors of Edmund Burke: Figurative Patterns and Meanings in His Political Prose," diss., Yale University, 1973; I. Kramnick, *The Rage of Edmund Burke* (New York, 1977); and R. Paulson, *Representations of Revolution (1789–1820)*, 58–9.

pursuit of chimerical aims, one will perhaps succeed in offering to human nature, renewed by the unimpeded development of its potentialities, a future from the "ancient heart."[67]

In some respects, then, the revolutionaries end up less abstract and naturalistic than they think. Rather, they are "naturalistic" in that they regard reason and virtue, which had always existed potentially, as compressed springs or laws carved in the hearts of men. In their own way, however, they are "historicist," since they consider history as the sum total of the real conditionings to be recognized and removed. Their adversaries, on the other hand, are historicist because they resort to history and tradition to explain the differences in the development of peoples and individuals and to warn against the temptation to force the inertial rhythms of growth on the part of those who overestimate the synoptic and long-range gaze of men (and, particularly, those who proclaim themselves their vanguards), but they are "naturalistic" in that they refer to the presumed inalterability of some aspects of the existing state, given that they regard as eternal both egoism and the destiny of the oppressed classes, and the (what had become) natural supremacy of the bloodline aristocracy and the monarchy.

The result of this is a sort of chiasmus, in the form of an *X*, and a special, criss-crossed, double blindness, a double scotoma. For the revolutionaries, there is nature in advancement and history in the obstacles to it. For the historicists, there is history in the difficulties of development and nature in the resistances that oppose them. Further, for the former, reality must adapt to truth; for the latter, truth must adapt to reality. That is, for the revolutionaries, politics results from a universal plan, "abstract" in the best sense, because it represents a struggle to dissolve all the arbitrary concretions that historical reality has solidified. For the historicists, on the other hand, politics is a wise prolongation of natural history by other means.

Both positions develop on the basis of assumptions, often unconscious and never sufficiently analysed, that attribute a new role to the passions in the formation of politics and individuality. Thus, it is presumed that the social body, in itself, is inert. When it is too lazy in its movements, it must consequently be pushed forward through massive doses of passionate energy – capable, however, of activating reason and virtue. Conversely, if its

67 See the report presented in January 1794 by the deputy H. Grégoire, *Rapport sur l'ouverture d'un concours pour les livres élémentaires de la première education, part Grégoire (Séance du 3 pluviose)*, in L. Hunt, *Politics, Culture & Classes in the French Revolution*, 10.

acceleration ends up being too rapid, it is thought that its pace must be slowed according to the Burkian model of "prudence." Another pre-analytic assumption consists of belief that the moral heredity of the past and the power of traditions' attraction are greatly weakened or exhausted, at least at the level of the consciousness of the subjects. Even in this case, the perspectives diverge, although they remain complementary. In fact, for the Jacobins it is necessary to complete society's destruction and reconstruct its edifice on new foundations designed by "impassioned reason." Alternately, for the historicists, it is necessary to readapt old convictions and old customs to the demands that are changing gradually and locally.

The Amnesty of Memory

The period immediately following the fall of Jacobin power did not, however, encourage either the permanence of the revolutionary ideal of historical discontinuity or the full victory of the Burkian model of continuity as recovery of the past. At least for the short term, the course of events showed itself to be more inventive and unpredictable than the models developed to simulate its direction.

Rather, the representatives of the Thermidor regime realized the impracticability of the plan for a complete *régénération* of the social body, even if they returned gradually to consider the different forms of inequality and lack of liberty, of egoism and corruption, not only constitutive of human nature but even useful to the collective goodwill. The subsequent abolition of the revolutionary calendar, decreed by Napoleon, "moralized" and reintegrated into the temporal continuum the traumatic event *par excellence*, symbolically eliminating its exceptional nature (i.e., simultaneously, the character of a break with the past, the conviction that every moment begins or develops the process of change in the sphere of current events, the opening up to a wide range of collective expectations for an "absolute future"). There was not a new beginning, a Year Zero from which history and humanity would have to begin again (even if this did not prevent some from fearing and others from hoping that, since the Revolution "burst open" once, it could always decide to complete its interrupted journey). If looked at from this perspective, historicism appears, in more general terms, as the effort to reabsorb the discontinuous into the continuous, to reduce it to a simple ill-omened parenthesis of disorder, one that was certainly painful but that could be closed after every crisis had been overcome, like a fever.

But the Thermidorians did not limit themselves to healing the wound caused to society by the period of Jacobin Terror, nor did they reconstruct historical continuity with the help of memory. They made use of another technique: a sort of amnesia-amnesty of memory, a collective and self-inflicted *damnatio memoriae*. That is, they forgot or distorted facts and episodes that appeared compromising or too painful to be remembered. They thus proclaimed wounds remaining to be healed as definitively closed, or they annulled the event retroactively. The process that placed an end to the Revolution saw, as protagonists, many of those who had drawn legitimacy from it and who had been directly involved in what now appears as a "system" of crimes. But it also saw a small number of men who rejected the new course of events and remained attached to the immobile image of a recent past from which shone the hope of a remote future that would redeem their expectations. Because of this, on the one hand, one could see the casual, nonchalant, and shameless "opportunism" of many and, on the other, the long fidelity given by some to the theory and practice of the Jacobin tradition even when it long since seemed to have failed.

The case of the leading Thermidorians – themselves, in large part, regicides and terrorists – is not isolated. Rather, it seems typical of all the terminal phases of modern revolutions. It now represents their "ghost," the proof that they had grown old, that they had lost the "eternal youth" that they attributed to themselves, demonstrating *l'usure et la décrépitude qui tuent les rêves.*[68] It was the end of fears, but also the end of hopes.

Besides the most conspicuous phenomena of fashion and a renewed joy of life among the classes that had endured the Revolution, there triumphed the new realism and the explicit passage to a politics of power and military expansion of the republic that – having become compact and "regenerated" in its mobilizing strength – "forgot" and repaid the defeated classes with the dividends of the *esprit de conquête*, thus atoning for what was inexpiable.

With the usual evocative dramatic nature of the historian who does not accept the law of oblivion and the *damnatio memoriae* of traumatic episodes of the past, one who speaks with the dead in order to understand the actions of the living,[69] Michelet describes the scene of Robespierre being led to the scaffold, at the moment when the passions and the interests of individuals, even as they had once supported and idolized him,

68 See B. Baczko, *Comment sortir de la Terreur: Thermidor et la Révolution*, 56 et seq., 92 et seq., 351–3.

69 To use an expression of Mona Ouzouf, Michelet did not want to employ *le travail de l'oubli*. See Ozouf, "Thermidor et le travail de l'oubli," in *L'École de France: Essais sur la Révolution, l'utopie et l'enseignement* (Paris, 1984), 91–108.

changed direction, and his enemies, remaining in the shadows, could finally take their revenge:

> Robespierre, his head wrapped in a dirty rag stained with black blood and supporting his dislocated jaw, in that horrible situation that had never happened to a defeated man, bearing the dreadful weight of the curse of a people, preserved his stiff attitude, his steady bearing, his dry and fixed eye. His intellect was full, floating over his situation, undoubtedly untangling what was true and what was false in the rage directed toward him. The windows were horrible, rented out no matter what the cost. Unknown figures had come to light that had hidden for a long time. A world of rich men, of whores, strutted on those balconies. Thanks to that violent reaction of public sensibility, their savage fury dared to show itself. The women in particular offered an intolerable spectacle. Shameless, semi-nude with the excuse that it was July, their breasts loaded with flowers, resting their elbows on velvet, leaning out halfway into rue Saint-Honoré, with the men behind them, shouting in a high-pitched voice: 'To death! To the guillotine!' Boldly, that day they pulled out their large *toilettes*, and that night they had a gala dinner. No one held back any longer. De Sade left prison on the 10th of Thermidor ... Robespierre had drunk all the venom in the world. He finally arrived at port, in Place de la Révolution. He climbed the steps of the scaffold with a firm step ... He died nobly, seriously, and simply ... A few days after Thermidor, a man, who is still living and who then was ten years old, was taken by his parents to the theatre, and upon leaving admired the long line of shiny carriages that, for the first time, struck his eyes. Men in jackets, their hats off, said to the spectators who were exiting, 'Do you need a carriage, *my lord*?' The child did not understand these new terms too well. He made them explain, and he was told only that there had been a great change, with the death of Robespierre.[70]

70 J. Michelet, *Histoire de la Révolution française,* vol. 2, 1146–7, 1148, and R. Barthes, *Michelet par lui-même* (Paris, 1969); Ital. trans. *Michelet* (Naples, 1989), 76–9. On the mentality of this period, see F. Gendron, *La jeunesse dorée: Épisodes de la Révolution française* (Quebec City, 1979). Barthes himself also emphasizes Michelet's attraction to death and to that "gift of tears," that must be characteristic of the historian: "I had a beautiful illness that darkened my youth but was just right for a historian. I loved death. I lived for nine years at the gates of Père-Lachaise, my only walk at the time. Then I lived near Bièvre, amid the large gardens of convents and other tombs. I lived a life that people could have called buried, having no other company than that of the past and, as friends, those who were buried" (Michelet, *Histoire de France,* preface of 1869 [Paris, 1871], xv, and Barthes, Ital. trans., 133).

With Thermidor, in addition to the most abject fear, the "great hope" also ended. All the "citizens" were put back in their places at least temporarily. Social hierarchies restructured themselves; expectations and desires were restored. Nothing, however – whether good or bad – could ever return to what it had been.

Abbreviations

The following lists abbreviations of the authors and texts principally used. For other authors or collections of work, standard abbreviations are used. The particular editions cited here were not necessarily those used in the original development of this book. English translations listed are those used in preparation of this edition and cited throughout the text. Sources listed below without corresponding English translations either are not quoted directly in the text (in which case, citations to sources and pages listed in the original Italian edition have been retained) or, in the case of several quotations from Italian, French, and Spanish sources, have been newly translated for this edition.

Arist.	**Aristotle:**
AO	*Aristotelis Opera*, ed. I. Bekker (Berlin, 1831; rpt., Berlin, 1960–3)
O	*Opere*, Italian trans. by various authors, ed. G. Giannantoni (Rome-Bari, 1973)
De me. et rem.	*De memoria et reminiscentia*
Eth. Eud.	*The Eudemian Ethics*, trans. H. Rackham (London, 1935)
Eth. Nic.	*The Nichomachean Ethics*, trans. David Ross (Oxford, 1998)
Magna Mor.	*Magna Moralia*, in *W*
Met.	*Metaphysica*
Pol.	*Politics*, trans. C.D.C. Reeve (Indianapolis, 1998)
Rhet.	*On Rhetoric*, trans. George Kennedy (New York, 2007)
W	*The Works of Aristotle*, trans. and ed. W.D. Ross (Oxford, 1915)

August. **Augustine of Hippo:**

NBA *Nuova Biblioteca Agostiniana: Opere di Sant'Agostino,* Italian-Latin edition, edited by the Cattedra Agostiniana of the "Augustinianum" of Rome, directed by P.A. Trapè, Italian trans. by various authors (Rome, 1969)

PL *Opera,* in *Patrologiae Cursus Completus,* Latin Series, ed. J. Migne, 217 vols. (*PL,* vols. 32–45) (Paris, 1861–2)

civ. *De civitate Dei,* in *PL,* vol. 41; *City of God,* vol. 1, ed. M. Dods (Edinburgh, 1888)

conf. *Confessiones,* in *PL,* vol. 32; *Confessions,* trans. Henry Chadwick (Oxford, 1998)

ep. *Epistulae,* in *PL,* vol. 33–4

ord. *De ordine,* in *PL,* vol. 32

trin. *De Trinitate,* in *PL,* vol. 42

Boétie, Étienne de la:

DSV *Discours de la servitude volontaire,* according to the text established by P. Léonard (Paris, 1976); *The Politics of Obedience: The Discourse of Voluntary Servitude,* trans. Harry Kurz (Auburn, AL, 2008).

Burke, Edmund:

WB *Works,* Bohn's British Classics, 8 vols. (London, 1854–89; rpt. 1893)

RRF *Reflections on the Revolution in France,* in *Burke: Select Works,* ed. E.J. Payne, vol. 2 (Oxford, 1881)

Burton, Robert:

AM *The Anatomy of Melancholy* [1621] (New York, 1871)

AMi *Anatomia della malinconia,* Italian trans., ed. J. Starobinski (Padua, 1983)

Condorcet, Marie-Jean Antoine Nicolas de:

OE *Oeuvres de Condorcet,* ed. A. Condorcet O'Connor and M.F. Arago (Paris, 1847–9)

Descartes, René:

AT *Oeuvres de Descartes,* ed. C. Adam and P. Tannery (Paris, 1897–1913; rpt. Paris, 1964)

Op. *The Philosophical Writings of Descartes*, ed. John Cottingham, R. Stoothoff, D. Murdoch, 2 vols. (Cambridge, 1984)

CE *The Correspondence between Princess Elisabeth of Bohemia and René Descartes*, trans. and ed. Lisa Shapiro (Chicago, 2007)

DM *Discourse on the Method* (*Discours de la méthode*), in *Op.*, vol. 1.

H *Treatise on Man* (*L'homme*), in *Op.*, vol. 1; *Treatise of Man*, trans. Thomas Steele (Cambridge, MA, 1972)

M *Meditations on First Philosophy, with Selections from the Objections and Replies*, trans. Michael Moriarty (Oxford, 2008)

O *Olympica*, in *AT*, vol. 10

P *Principles of Philosophy* (*Principia*), in *Op.*, vol. 1

PA *Les passions de l'âme*, in *AT*, vol. 10; English trans. *The Passions of the Soul* (*Les passions de l'âme*), in *Op.*, vol. 1; and *The Philosophy of Descartes*, trans. and ed. Henry Torrey (New York, 1892)

PL *Philosophical Letters*, trans. and ed. Anthony Kenny (Minneapolis, 1981)

PP *The Princess and the Philosopher: Letters of Elisabeth of the Palatine to René Descartes*, by Andrea Nye (Lanham, 1999)

R *Rules for the Direction of the Mind* (*Regulae ad directionem ingenii*), in *Op.*, vol. 1

Diogenes Laertius:

Diog. Laert. *De vitis et placitis philosophorum*

D'Holbach, Paul Heinrich Dietrich:

Syst. *Système de la nature ou des lois du monde physique et du monde moral*, edited by D. Diderot (Paris, 1821); *The System of Nature, or Laws of The Moral and Physical World*, trans. H.D. Robinson (Boston, 1889)

Epict. **Epictetus:**

D *Discourses*, in *Discourses and Selected Writings*, trans. Robert Dobbin (London, 2008)

Ench. *Enchiridion*, in *Discourses and Selected Writings*, trans. Robert Dobbin (London, 2008)

Epic. **Epicurus**

O *Opere*, ed. G. Arrighetti (Torino, 1967)

Max. cap. *Principal Doctrines,* in *W*; *Massime capitali,* in *W*

Sent. Vat. *Vatican Sayings* (*Sententiae Vaticanae*), in *W*

W *Letters, Principal Doctrines, and Vatican Sayings,* trans. and ed. Russel Geer (New York, 1964)

Freud, Sigmund:

GW *Gesammelte Werke* (Frankfurt, 1969)

OSF *Opere di Sigmund Freud* (Turin, 1966–80)

Gracián, Baltasar:

Ob. *Obras completas,* ed. A. del Hoyo (Madrid, 1960)

Or. *Oráculo manual y arte de prudencia,* in *Ob.*; *The Art of Worldly Wisdom,* trans. Joseph Jacobs (London, 1904)

Hobbes, Thomas:

OL *Opera philosophica, quae latine scripsit, omnia,* ed. G. Molesworth, 5 vols. (London, 1839–45)

EW *The English Works,* ed. G. Molesworth, 11 vols. (London, 1829–45; rpt., Aalen, 1961–2)

B *Behemoth,* ed. F. Tönnies [1889], with a new introduction by M.M. Goldsmith (London, 1969)

DC *De Cive,* in *OL,* vol. 2; *Citizen,* in *MC*

De corp. *De corpore,* in *OL,* vol. 1; *Concerning Body,* in *EW,* vol. 1

DH *De homine,* in *OL,* vol. 1; English translation, *Man,* in *MC*

El. *Elements of Law and Politics,* ed. F. Tönnies [Cambridge, 1929] (London, 1889)

L *Leviathan,* in *EW,* vol. 3

MC *Man and Citizen (De Homine and De Cive),* trans. C. Wood, T.S.K. Scott-Craig, B. Gert, and T. Hobbes, ed. B. Gert (Indianapolis, 1991)

Quest. *Questions Concerning Liberty, Necessity and Change,* in *EW,* vol. 4

Leibniz, Gottfried Wilhelm:

PhS *Philosophische Schriften,* ed. C.I. Gebhardt (Berlin, 1875–90; rpt., Hildesheim, 1965); *The Monadology and Other Philosophical Writings,* trans. and ed. Roberta Latta (Oxford, 1898)

Lipsius, Justus:

OO *Opera omnia, postremo ab ipso aucta et recensita* (Antwerp, 1637)

De const. *De Constantia libri* IV [1584], in *OO*, vol. 4; *Two Books of Constancie* (London, 1595)

Manud. *Manuductio ad Stoicam philosophiam* [1604], in *OO*, vol. 4

Phys. Stoic. *Physiologia Stoicorum* [1604], in *OO*, vol. 4

Pol. *Politicorum libri* VI [1586], in *OO*, vol. 4; *Politica*, trans. and ed. Jan Waszink (Assen, 2004)

Machiavelli, Niccolò:

OC *Opere complete*, with an introduction by G. Procacci (Milan, 1960–2)

Cl. *Clizia*, in *Il teatro e gli scritti letteraria*, in *OC*, vol. 8; English translation, *Clizia*, trans. and ed. Daniel Gallagher (Long Grove, IL, 1996)

CW *Machiavelli: The Chief Works and Others*, trans. Allan Gilbert (Durham, NC, 1965)

D *Discorsi sopra la prima deca di Tito Livio*, in *OC*, vol. 1; *The Discourses*, trans. L. Ricci and C.E. Detmold, ed. M. Lerner (New York, 1950)

L *The Private Letters*, in *The Portable Machiavelli*, trans. and ed. Peter Bondanella and Mark Musa (New York, 1979); *Lettere*, in *OC*, vol. 6

P *The Prince*, trans. George Bull (London, 1999)

SF *Storie fiorentine*, in *OC*, vol. 7; *The History of Florence*, in *CW*, vol. 3

Marat, Jean-Paul:

TC *Textes choisis*, ed. M. Vovelle (Paris, 1963)

Chaînes *Les Chaînes de l'Esclavage*, in *Oeuvres Politiques: 1789–1793*, ed. J. de Cock and C. Goëtz, vol. 7 (April–August 1792) (Brussels, 1995)

LDP *L'Ami du peuple*, in *TC*

Marcus Aurelius:

Marc. Aur. *Tas eis eauton*, in *Pensées*, trans. A.I. Trannoy (Paris, 1983); *The Meditations of Marcus Aurelius Antoninus*, trans. John Jackson (Oxford, 1906)

Montaigne, Michel de:

OC *Oeuvres complètes,* ed. A. Thibaudet and M. Rat (Paris, 1962)

ES *Essais,* in *OC*

ESe *Essays: The Essays of Michel de Montaigne,* trans. Charles Cotton, 3 vols. (London, 1905–8)

Montesquieu (Charles-Louis de Secondat):

OC *Oeuvres complètes,* ed. R. Caillois, 2 vols. (Paris, 1949–51)

Cons. *Considérations sur les causes de la grandeur des Romains et de leur décadence,* in *OC,* vol. 2

Dial. *Dialogue de Sylla ed d'Eurcrate,* in *OC,* vol. 1

EdL *Esprit des lois,* in *OC,* vol. 2

LP *Lettres persanes,* in *OC,* vol. 1

Pascal, Blaise:

OC *Oeuvres complètes,* ed. J. Chevalier (Paris, 1954)

D *Discours sur le passions de l'amour,* in *OC*

Entr. *Entretien avec M. de Saci,* in *OC*

P *Pensées,* in *OC.* The number given in citations is the number of the fragment in the Chevalier edition.

Pe *Pensées,* English trans. W.F. Trotter (New York, 1958)

PG:

PG *Patrologiae Cursus Completus,* Series Graeca, ed. J. Migne, 161 vols. (Paris 1857–66)

Plat. **Plato:**

Op. *Platonis opera,* ed. J. Burnet, 5 vols. (Oxford, 1899–1907)

OC *Opere complete,* 8 vols., plus one of indices, Italian trans. by various authors (Rome-Bari, 1982)

Conv. *Convivium,* Italian trans. *Simposio,* in *OC,* vol. 3

Eut. *Eutiphrones,* Italian trans. *Eutifrone,* in *DC,* vol. 1

Gorg. *Gorgias,* in *The Dialogues of Plato,* vol. 3 (New York, 1871)

Lach. *Lachetes,* Italian trans. *Lachete,* in *OC,* vol. 4

Leg. *The Laws* (*Leges*), in *The Works of Plato,* trans. George Burges, vol. 5 (London, 1852)

Men.	*Meno,* Italian trans. *Menone,* in *OC,* vol. 5
Phaedo	*Phaedo,* trans. H.N. Fowler (London, 1913)
Phaedr.	*Phaedrus,* Italian trans. *Fedro,* in *OC,* vol. 3
Resp.	*Republic* (*Respublica*), in *The Dialogues of Plato,* trans. R. Jowett, vol. 3 (New York, 1892)
Tim.	*The Timaeus of Plato,* trans. R.D. Archer-Hind (New York, 1888)
Plut.	**Plutarch:**
An. an corp.	*Animine an corporis affectiones sint peiores,* in *Mor.*, vol. 6
Cleo.	*The Lives of Agis and Cleomenes,* in *Plutarch's Lives,* trans. Thomas North, vol. 8 (London, 1899)
De prof.	*Quomodo quis suos in virtute sentiat profecto,* in *Mor.*, vol. 1
De plac. philos.	*De placitis philosophorum,* in *Mor.*, vol. 11
De sup.	*De superstitione,* in *Mor.*, vol. 2
De tranq.	*On Tranquility of Mind* (*De tranquillitate animi*), in *Mor.*, vol. 6, trans. W.C. Helmbold (Cambridge, 1939)
M-I	*Moralia I: "La serenità interiore" e altri scritti sulla terapia dell'anima,* ed. G. Pisani (Pordendone, 1989)
Mor.	*Moralia,* 15 vols. (Cambridge, MA, 1927–2004)
Non posse suav.	*Non posse suaviter vivere secundum Epicuri praecepta,* in *Mor.*, vol. 14
Whether	*Whether Affections of the Soul Are Worse than Those of the Body,* in *Plutarch's Moralia,* trans. S. White (Boston, 1878)

Robespierre, Maximilien:

OC	*Oeuvres complètes,* 10 vols. (Paris, 1912–67) (*Discours,* vols. 7–10)
RG	*La rivoluzione giacobina,* writings and speeches edited by U. Cerroni (Rome, 1975)
SC	*La scalata al cielo: Discorsi,* ed. M.A. Cattaneo (Verona, 1989)

Rousseau, Jean-Jacques:

OEC	*Oeuvres complètes,* ed. B. Gagnebin and M. Raymond (Paris, 1969)

CS	*Contrat social,* in *OEC,* vol. 3
DL	*Des lois,* in *OEC,* vol. 3
E	*Émile,* in *OEC,* vol. 4
NH	*Nouvelle Héloïse,* in *OEC,* vol. 2

Saint-Just, Louis de:

OC	*Oeuvres complètes,* ed. M. Duval (Paris, 1984)
OC2	*Oeuvres complètes de Saint-Just,* 2 vols. (Paris, 1908)
FIR	*Fragments d'institutions républicaines,* in *OC2*
TL	*Discours et rapports* (Paris, 1957)

Schopenhauer, Arthur:

SW	*Werke,* ed. J. Frauenstadt (Leipzig, 1874)
W	*Die Welt als Wille und Vorstellung,* in *SW,* vols. 2–3; Italian trans. *Il mondo come volontà e rappresentazione,* 2 vols. (Bari, 1968)
WiN	*Über den Willen in der Natur,* in *SW,* vol. 4, *On the Will in Nature,* trans. E.F.J. Payne (New York, 1992)

Sen.	**Seneca, Lucius Annaeus:**
D	*Dialogorum libri XII,* ed. L.D. Reynolds (Oxford, 1977)
Dial.	*Dialoghi,* ed. A. Marastoni (Milan, 1979)
ME	*Moral Essays,* trans. J.W. Basore, 3 vols. (London, 1928–35)
ST	*Seneca's Tragedies,* trans. F.J. Miller, 2 vols. (London, 1957–60)
Ad Helv. matr.	*Ad Helviam matrem de consolatione,* in *D*
Ad Marc.	*De consolatione ad marciam,* in *ME,* vol. 2
Ad Pol.	*Ad Polibium de consolatione,* in *D*
De ben.	*De beneficiis, ad Helvium Liberalem, libri* VII, ed. C. Hosius (Lipsiae, 1915)
De brev. vit.	*De brevitate vitae,* in *ME,* vol. 2
De clem.	*De clementia,* in *ME,* vol. 1
De const. sap.	*De constantia sapientis,* in *ME,* vol. 1
De ira	*De ira,* in *ME,* vol. 1
De prov.	*De providentia,* in *ME,* vol. 1

De tranq. an.	*On Tranquility of Mind* (*De tranquillitate animi*), in *ME*, vol. 2
De vit. beat.	*De vita beata*, in *ME*, vol. 2
Herc. Oet.	*Hercules Oetaeus*, in *ST*, vol. 2
Letters	*Letters* (*Ep. ad Lucilium epistulae morales*), trans. Richard Gummere, 3 vols. (Cambridge, MA, 1917–25); Italian trans. G. Monti, ed. A. Beltrami (Rome, 1931). See also *Lettere a Lucilio* with facing text, ed. C. Barone, 2 vols. (Milan, 1989)
Med.	*Medea*, in *ST*, vol. 1
Mor.	*Seneca's Morals*, trans. Roger L'Estrange (Chicago, 1888)
Nat. quaest.	*Naturalium quaestionum ad Lucilium, libri* VII, ed. A. Gercke (Lipsiae, 1907; rpt., Stuttgart, 1970); *Natural Questions*, trans. Harry Hine (Chicago, 1998)
Oed.	*Oedipus*, in *ST*, vol. 1
Phaedr.	*Hippolytus* (*Phaedra*), in *ST*, vol. 1
Thyest.	*Thyestes*, in *ST*, vol. 2
Troades	*Troades*, in *ST*, vol. 1

Spinoza, Baruch:

CW	*Complete Works*, trans. Samuel Shirley, ed. Michael Morgan (Indianapolis, 2002)
OS	*Opera*, Im Auftrag der Heidelberger Akademie der Wissenschaften, ed. C. Gebhardt, 4 vols. (Heidelberg, n.d.; [1924; rpt., 1972]). See also a fifth volume, *Supplementa* (Heidelberg, 1987), which contains Gebhardt's comments on *TP* and *TTP* and an appendix by C. Altwicker on subsequent studies related to the two works.
E	*Etica more geometrico demonstrata*, in *OS*, vol. 2; *Ethics*, in *CW* (indicated with the part [book], followed by the proposition and, depending on the case, by the following abbreviations: aff. def. = definition of the affections; app. = appendix; ax. = axiom; ch. = chapter; cor. = corollary; dem. = demonstration/proof; expl. = explanation; praef. = prefaces; prop. = proposition; schol. = scholium)

Ep. *Epistulae*, in *OS*, vol. 4; *Letters*, in *CW*. The numerals indicate the letter, followed by the pages in the English translation.

KV *Korte Verhandeling: Breve trattato*, bilingual critical edition, ed. F. Mignini (L'Aquila, 1986) (all in *OS*, vol. 1); *Short Treatise on God, Man, and His Well-Being*, in *CW*. References indicate the part and chapter.

TIE *Tractatus de intellectus emendatione*, in *OS*, vol. 2; *Treatise on the Emendation of the Intellect*, in *CW*. References indicate the section.

TP *Tractatus politicus*, in *OS*, vol. 3; *Political Treatise*, in *CW*. References indicate the chapter and paragraph.

TTP *Tractatus theologico-politicus*, in *OS*, vol. 3; *Theological-Political Treatise*, in *CW*. References indicate the chapter and, in italics, the page number of the English translation.

SVF:

SVF *Storicorum Veterum Fragmenta*, ed. A. von Arnim, 3 vols. (Leipzig, 1903–5). In 1924 a fourth volume of *Indices* was added, edited by M. Adler, reproduced (Stuttgart, 1964). The Italian translation, largely based on this edition, is *Stoici antichi*, ed. M. Isnarde Parente, 2 vols. (Turin, 1989)

Taine, Hyppolite:

OFC *Les origines de la France contemporaine* [1876–93], 2 vols. (Paris, 1986)

AN *La Révolution: L'Anarchie*, in *OFC*, vol. 1; *Spontaneous Anarchy*, in *R*, vol. 2

AR *L'Ancien Régime*, in *OFC*, vol. 1; *The Ancient Régime*, trans. John Durand, rev. ed. (New York, 1896)

CJ *La Révolution: La conquête jacobine*, in *OFC*, vol. 1; in *R*, vol. 2

GR *La Révolution: Le gouvernement révolutionnaire*, in *OFC*, vol. 2

R *The Revolution*, trans. John Durand, 2 vols. (London, 1878–81)

Tocqueville, Alexis de:

OE *Oeuvres complètes*, under the direction of J.P. Mayer (Paris, 1951)

ARR *L'Ancien Régime et la Révolution*, in *OE*, vol. 2; *The Old Regime and the Revolution*, trans. John Bonner (New York, 1856)

DA *De la démocratie en Amérique*, in *OE*, vol. 1; *Democracy in America*, trans. and ed. Phillips Bradley (New York, 1945)

Voltaire (François-Marie Arouet):

OC	*Oeuvres complètes* (Paris, 1784)
DW	*The Works of M. Voltaire*, vol. 1 (London, 1761)

Index

THE LORENZO DA PONTE ITALIAN LIBRARY

General Editors: Luigi Ballerini and Massimo Ciavolella

Pellegrino Artusi, *Science in the Kitchen and the Art of Eating Well* (2003). Translated by Murtha Baca and Stephen Sartarelli. Introduction by Luigi Ballerini. Foreword by Michele Scicolone.

Lauro Martines, *An Italian Renaissance Sextet: Six Tales in Historical Context* (2004). Translated by Murtha Baca.

Aretino's Dialogues (2005). Translated by Raymond Rosenthal. Introduction by Margaret Rosenthal.

Aldo Palazzeschi, *A Tournament of Misfits: Tall Tales and Short* (2005). Translated by Nicolas J. Perella.

Carlo Cattaneo, *Civilization and Democracy: The Salvemini Anthology of Cattaneo's Writings* (2006). Edited and introduced by Carlo G. Lacaita and Filippo Sabetti. Translated by David Gibbons.

Benedetto Croce, *Breviary of Aesthetics: Four Lectures* (2007). Translated by Hiroko Fudemoto. Introduction by Remo Bodei.

Antonio Pigafetta, *The First Voyage around the World (1519–1522): An Account of Magellan's Expedition* (2007). Edited and introduced by Theodore J. Cachey Jr.

Raffaello Borghini, *Il Riposo* (2008). Edited and translated by Lloyd H. Ellis Jr.

Paolo Mantegazza, *The Physiology of Love and Other Writings* (2008). Edited with an introduction and notes by Nicoletta Pireddu. Translated by David Jacobson.

Renaissance Comedy: The Italian Masters, Volume 2 (2008). Edited with an introduction by Donald Beecher.

Renaissance Comedy: The Italian Masters, Volume 1 (2008). Edited with an introduction by Donald Beecher.

Cesare Beccaria, *On Crimes and Punishments and Other Writings* (2008). Edited by Aaron Thomas. Translated by Aaron Thomas and Jeremy Parzen. Foreword by Bryan Stevenson. Introduction by Alberto Burgio.

Leone Ebreo, *Dialogues of Love* (2009). Edited by Rossella Pescatori. Translated by Cosmos Damian Bacich and Rossella Pescatori.

Boccaccio's Expositions on Dante's Comedy (2009). Translated by Michael Papio.

My Muse Will Have a Story to Paint: Selected Prose of Ludovico Ariosto (2010). Translated with an introduction by Dennis Looney.

The Opera of Bartolomeo Scappi (1570): L'arte et prudenza d'un maestro cuoco (The Art and Craft of a Master Cook) (2011). Translated with commentary by Terence Scully.

Pirandello's Theatre of Living Masks: New Translations of Six Major Plays (2011). Translated by Umberto Mariani and Alice Gladstone Mariani.

From Kant to Croce: Modern Philosophy in Italy, 1800–1950 (2012). Edited and translated with an introduction by Brian Copenhaver and Rebecca Copenhaver.

Giovan Francesco Straparola, *The Pleasant Nights,* Volume 2 (2012). Edited with an introduction by Donald Beecher.

Giovan Francesco Straparola, *The Pleasant Nights,* Volume 1 (2012). Edited with an introduction by Donald Beecher.

Giovanni Botero, *On the Causes of the Greatness and Magnificence of Cities* (2012). Translated with an introduction by Geoffrey Symcox.

John Florio, *A Worlde of Wordes* (2013). A critical edition with an introduction by Hermann W. Haller.

Giordano Bruno, *On the Heroic Frenzies* (2013). A translation of *De gli eroici furori* by Ingrid D. Rowland. Edited by Eugenio Canone.

Alvise Cornaro, *Writings on the Sober Life: The Art and Grace of Living Long* (2014). Translated by Hiroko Fudemoto. Introduction by Marisa Milani. Foreword by Greg Critser.

Dante Alighieri, *Dante's Lyric Poetry: Poems of Youth and of the* Vita Nuova *(1283–1292)* (2014). Edited with a general introduction and introductory essays by Teodolinda Barolini. With new verse translations by Richard Lansing. Commentary translated into English by Andrew Frisardi.

Vincenzo Cuoco, *Historical Essay on the Neapolitan Revolution of 1799* (2014). Edited and introduced by Bruce Haddock and Filippo Sabetti. Translated by David Gibbons.

Vittore Branca, *Merchant Writers: Florentine Memoirs from the Middle Ages and Renaissance* (2015). Translated by Murtha Baca.

Carlo Goldoni, *Five Comedies* (2016). Edited by Gianluca Rizzo and Michael Hackett, with Brittany Asaro. With an introduction by Michael Hackett and an essay by Cesare de Michelis.

Those Who from Afar Look like Flies: An Anthology of Italian Poetry from Pasolini to the Present (2016). Edited by Luigi Ballerini and Beppe Cavatorta. Foreword by Marjorie Perloff.

Guittone d'Arezzo, *Selected Poems and Prose* (2017). Selected and translated with an introduction by Antonello Borra.

Giordano Bruno, *The Ash Wednesday Supper* (2018). A new translation of *La cena de le ceneri* with the Italian text annotated and introduced by Hilary Gatti.

Giacomo da Lentini, *The Complete Poetry* (2018). Translated and annotated by Richard Lansing. Introduction by Akash Kumar.

Remo Bodei, *Geometry of the Passions: Fear, Hope, Happiness: Philosophy and Political Use* (2018). Translated by Gianpiero W. Doebler.

Scipio Sighele, *The Criminal Crowd and Other Writings on Mass Society* (2018). Edited with an introduction and notes by Nicoletta Pireddu. Translated by Nicoletta Pireddu and Andrew Robbins. With a foreword by Tom Huhn.